FREEDOM AND EQUALITY

Civil Liberties and the Supreme Court

GILBERT L. ODDO

Goodyear Publishing Company
Santa Monica, California

Library of Congress Cataloging in Publication Data

Oddo, Gilbert Lawrence.
    Freedom and equality.

    Includes indexes.
    1. Civil rights — United States — Cases. 2. United
States. Supreme Court. I. Title.
KF4748.03   342'.73'085   78-27592
ISBN   0-87620-330-6
ISBN   0-87620-329-2 pbk.

For SAL

Y-3306-1 (c)
Y-3292-3 (p)

ISBN: 0-87620-330-6 (c)
ISBN: 0-87620-329-2 (p)

Current Printing (last number)

10   9   8   7   6   5   4   3   2   1

Production Editor: Pam Tully
Copyeditor: Derek Gallagher
Compositor: Composition Type

Printed in the United States of America

FREEDOM AND EQUALITY
Civil Liberties and the Supreme Court

PREFACE

The often decisive role the Supreme Court plays in American politics makes it *the* unique judicial body in the world. From the Marshall era during the early years of the Republic to the years when it was known as the Warren Court, the Supreme Court has many times been the major influence, the sharp cutting edge determining the course of virtually every aspect of American political, economic, and social life. All this makes the Supreme Court a fascinating study and I have been drawn to it since graduate school days at Georgetown University, days which also afforded an "on the spot" look at the Court and its work.

Because its theoretical and (hopefully) its practical dedication to human rights is a distinguishing feature of American constitutional government, the work of the Supreme Court as the final arbiter on many of these matters takes on added significance. This then becomes the rationale for what follows: to give the student of American politics insight into the role the Supreme Court plays in delineating, interpreting, and reinterpreting, here widening the scope, here narrowing it, that vast panorama of legal disputes coming before it under the constitutional umbrella of "freedom and equality."

Over the years I have been particularly grateful to Professor C. Herman Pritchett now of the University of California at Santa Barbara who, again since graduate days, has been my unseen mentor. Reading Pritchett's books and journal articles on the Supreme Court and particularly on the Roosevelt Court of the late 1930's and 1940's originally sparked my interest in the Court. As the many citations from his works indicate, his scholarship has been invaluable in the preparation of this book and I sincerely acknowledge his influence on my work.

My colleagues Ernest Morin and John Chambers have been helpful and enthusiastic during our many conversations while I was preparing the manuscript.

My research assistant Ingrid Nunez and the staff of the Law Library at the University of San Diego, particularly Marguerite Most, did yeoman work sorting out the major decisions along with the written opinions of the justices, upon which the book is based. They made the tasks pleasant and orderly, and once again I am in their debt.

Kathy Conant did the meticulous typing and also prepared the table of cases, the index of cases, and the general index. To say that she was indispensable is to belabor the obvious.

Jim Boyd, Derek Gallagher, Pam Tully, and the other editorial staff at Goodyear also contributed their many talents without which the book would not have been completed.

Finally, the traditional disclaimer, I alone am responsible for any errors of fact or interpretation.

G. L. Oddo
San Diego
January 1979

CONTENTS

TABLE OF CASES

FREEDOM AND EQUALITY

Civil Liberties and the Supreme Court

I

THE FIRST
AMENDMENT

First Amendment guarantees, considered by most students of the American political system to be the greatest bulwark of individual freedom in the Constitution, involve five basic concepts. The Amendment protects, against infringement by Congress (the states were not brought under its umbrella until well into this century), the rights of freedom of religion, of speech, of the press, to assemble peaceably and to petition the government for a redress of grievances. Adopted in December 1791, the First Amendment is part of the Bill of Rights (the first ten amendments). Much of its language and context was taken from a similar amendment to the Virginia Constitution, itself largely the work of James Madison and Thomas Jefferson.

During the ratification debate on the original Constitution that came out of the Philadelphia Convention, several key states objected to the absence of specific provisions guaranteeing human freedoms. Madison pledged to add a Bill of Rights to the Constitution as soon as the First Congress convened in 1789. Himself elected to the first Congress, Madison was the key figure during the Congressional deliberations. Accordingly, two years later, after ratification by the states, the first ten amendments became part of the Constitution.

What follows here in Part I are among the more important recent Supreme Court decisions that have touched upon these First Amendment freedoms. Involved are such controversial subjects as the meaning and application of "the free exercise of religion," "establishment of religion," separation of church and state, religion in the public schools, aid to private schools, "the child-benefit" theory, "excessive entanglement," prior restraint, freedom of the press, assembly rights, preferred treatment, freedom of speech, clear and present danger, obscenity, pornography, and censorship. That these topics have occasioned a myriad of fascinating and significant Supreme Court decisions, many of which deal with the most sensitive questions in the life of a political democracy, should be clear from what follows.

1

FREE EXERCISE OF RELIGION

The First Amendment contains two clauses that touch upon religious freedoms, one that states that Congress can make no law respecting an establishment of religion (the no-establishment clause) and the other that Congress cannot prohibit the free exercise of religion (the free exercise clause). Most constitutional scholars agree that, in recent years, the Supreme Court's interpretation of these two clauses has varied largely because the history of each has been different. For example, in 1791 when the Bill of Rights was adopted there already was in the United States a firmly established principle of religious freedom and (to a lesser extent) of religious toleration. Long, often tragic, experience in England, and on the new continent as well, with religious persecution and intolerance had developed in the new nation, at the very least, a theoretical consensus on the meaning of the term "free exercise of religion." The First Amendment no-establishment clause, however, was at odds with prevailing conditions in England and with experience in several of the colonies where there had been officially "established" churches. For this reason, as Pritchett suggests, the principle of church and state separation, that is, no-establishment, has been a uniquely American phenomenon that has had to be defined and redefined by the Supreme Court in accord with practical experience wrought over the years in case by case analysis. As a result the Court has developed a set of principles upholding the general position that government must remain "neutral" in its dealings with the churches, that it cannot give preferential treatment to one church over another or favor one set of religious beliefs over another. As noted by Pritchett, one of these important principles is called the "secular regulation rule." As it has been interpreted by the Supreme Court, this rule means that a citizen has no constitutional right to be exempt "on free exercise of religious grounds, from the compulsion of general regulations dealing with non-religious matters." The secular regulation suggests, therefore, that a distinction must be made between belief and action. It has meant that while religious *beliefs* must have "absolute protection," actions, although they are often related to religious beliefs or observances, and this, of course, has presented problems, "must conform with the regulations established by the community to protect public order, health, welfare, and morals."[1]

1. Charles H. Pritchett, *The American Constitution* (New York: McGraw-Hill, 1977), p. 392.

3

Reynolds v. United States, 98 U.S. 145 (1879)

Secular regulation of religiously inspired "actions" to conform with "public order and morals" was first developed by the Court in the last years of the nineteenth century in cases dealing with the Mormon practice of polygamy. The controlling decision was *Reynolds* v. *United States*. There the Supreme Court upheld the constitutionality of a Congressional Statute that made polygamy illegal. Mormons, in defense, argued that polygamy was an integral part of their religious *beliefs* and, therefore, that Congress had denied them the First Amendment guarantee of "free exercise" of religion. Thus the apparent dichotomy between "actions" subject to regulation and "beliefs" immune from "public scrutiny."

In *Reynolds* the Supreme Court decided against the Mormons. It ruled that religious "beliefs" cannot be used as justification for overt actions (polygamy) that Congress had made illegal. The Court therefore upheld the right of Congress to regulate religiously inspired action (polygamy) that in its judgment was contrary to the public welfare. *Reynolds* marks the first application of the "secular regulation" rule the Supreme Court has redefined in more recent cases.

Mr. Chief Justice Waite delivered the opinion of the (unanimous) Court, saying in part:

[T]his inquiry is not as to the power of Congress to prescribe criminal laws for the Territories, but as to the guilt of one who knowingly violates a law which has been properly enacted, if he entertains a religious belief that the law is wrong.

Congress cannot pass a law for the government of the Territories which shall prohibit the free exercise of religion. The first amendment to the Constitution expressly forbids such legislation. Religious freedom is guaranteed everywhere throughout the United States, so far as congressional interference is concerned. The question to be determined is, whether the law now under consideration comes within this prohibition.

The word "religion" is not defined in the Constitution. We must go elsewhere, therefore, to ascertain its meaning, and nowhere more appropriately, we think, than to the history of the times in the midst of which the provision was adopted. The precise point of the inquiry is, what is the religious freedom which has been guaranteed.

Before the adoption of the Constitution, attempts were made in some of the colonies and States to legislate not only in respect to the establishment of religion, but in respect to its doctrines and precepts as well. The people were taxed, against their will, for the support of religion, and sometimes for the support of particular sects to whose tenets they could not and did not subscribe. Punishments were prescribed for a failure to attend upon public worship, and sometimes for entertaining heretical opinions. The controversy upon this general subject was animated in many of the States, but seemed at last to culminate in Virginia. In 1784, the House of Delegates of that State having under consideration "a bill establishing provision for teachers of the Christian religion," postponed it until the next session, and directed that the bill should be published and distributed, and that the people be requested "to signify their opinion respecting the adoption of such a bill at the next session of assembly."

This brought out a determined opposition. Amongst others, Mr. Madison prepared a "Memorial and Remonstrance," which was widely circulated and signed, and in which he demonstrated "that religion, or the duty we owe the

Creator," was not within the cognizance of civil government. Semple's Virginia Baptists, Appendix. At the next session the proposed bill was not only defeated, but another, "for establishing religious freedom," drafted by Mr. Jefferson, was passed.

. . . In the preamble of this act (12 Hening's Stat. 84) religious freedom is defined; and after a recital "that to suffer the civil magistrate to intrude his powers into the field of opinion, and to restrain the profession or propagation of principles on supposition of their ill tendency, is a dangerous fallacy which at once destroys all religious liberty," it is declared "that it is time enough for the rightful purposes of civil government for its officers to interfere when principles break out into overt acts against peace and good order." In these two sentences is found the two distinctions between what properly belongs to the church and what to the State.

In a little more than a year after the passage of this statute the convention met which prepared the Constitution of the United States. Of this convention Mr. Jefferson was not a member, he being then absent as minister to France. As soon as he saw the draft of the Constitution proposed for adoption, he, in a letter to a friend, expressed his disappointment at the absence of an express declaration insuring the freedom of religion, . . . but was willing to accept it as it was, trusting that the good sense and honest intentions of the people would bring about the necessary alterations.

. . . Five of the States, while adopting the Constitution, proposed amendments. Three — New Hampshire, New York, and Virginia — included in one form or another a declaration of religious freedom in the changes they desired to have made, as did also North Carolina, where the convention at first declined to ratify the Constitution until the proposed amendments were acted upon. Accordingly, at the first session of the first Congress the amendment now under consideration was proposed with others by Mr. Madison. It met the views of the advocates of religious freedom, and was adopted. Mr. Jefferson afterwards, in reply to an address to him by a committee of the Danbury Baptist Association, . . . took occasion to say: "Believing with you that religion is a matter which lies solely between man and his God; that he owes account to none other for his faith or his worship; that the legislative powers of the government reach actions only, and not opinions, — I contemplate with sovereign reverence that act of the whole American people which declared that their legislature should 'make no law respecting an establishment of religion or prohibiting the free exercise thereof,' thus building a wall of separation between church and State. Adhering to this expression of the supreme will of the nation in behalf of the rights of conscience, I shall see with sincere satisfaction the progress of those sentiments which tend to restore man to all his natural rights, convinced he has no natural right in opposition to his social duties." Coming as this does from an acknowledged leader of the advocates of the measure, it may be accepted almost as an authoritative declaration of the scope and effect of the amendment thus secured. Congress was deprived of all legislative power over mere opinion, but was left free to reach actions which were in violation of social duties or subversive of good order.

Polygamy has always been odious among the northern and western nations of Europe, and, until the establishment of the Mormon Church, was almost exclusively a feature of the life of Asiatic and of African people. At common law, the second marriage was always void, . . . and from the earliest history of England polygamy has been treated as an offence against society. . . .

. . . In the face of all this evidence, it is impossible to believe that the constitutional guaranty of religious freedom was intended to prohibit legislation in respect to this most important feature of social life. Marriage, while from its very nature a sacred obligation, is nevertheless, in most civilized nations, a civil contract, and usually regulated by law. Upon it society may be said to be built, and out of its times spring social relations and social obligations and duties, with which government is necessarily required to deal. In fact, according as monogamous or polygamous marriages are allowed, do we find the principles on which the government of the people, to a greater or less extent, rests. Professor Lieber says, polygamy leads to the patriarchal principle, and which, when applied to large communities, fetters the people in stationary despotism, while that principle cannot long exist in connection with monogamy. . . . there cannot be a doubt that, unless restricted by some form of constitution, it is within the legitimate scope of the power of every civil government to determine whether polygamy or monogamy shall be the law of social life under its dominion.

In our opinion, the statute immediately under consideration is within the legislative power of Congress. It is constitutional and valid as prescribing a rule of action for all those residing in the Territories, and in places over which the United States have exclusive control. This being so, the only question which remains is, whether those who make polygamy a part of their religion are excepted from the operation of the statute. If they are, then those who do not make polygamy a part of their religious belief may be found guilty and punished, while those who do, must be acquitted and go free. This would be introducing a new element into criminal law. Laws are made for the government of actions, and while they cannot interfere with mere religious belief and opinions, they may with practices. Suppose one believed that human sacrifices were a necessary part of religious worship, would it be seriously contended that the civil government under which he lived could not interfere to prevent a sacrifice? Or if a wife religiously believed it was her duty to burn herself upon the funeral pile of her dead husband, would it be beyond the power of the civil government to prevent her carrying her belief into practice?

So here, as a law of the organization of society under the exclusive dominion of the United States, it is provided that plural marriages shall not be allowed. Can a man excuse his practices to the contrary because of his religious belief? To permit this would be to make the professed doctrines of religious belief superior to the law of the land, and in effect to permit every citizen to become a law unto himself. Government could exist only in name under such circumstances.

Hamilton v. Regents of the University of California, 293 U.S. 215 (1934)

In *Reynolds* an act of Congress was challenged by Mormons as violating their free exercise of religious beliefs. The Supreme Court upheld Congress. Some forty-five years later, in *Hamilton* v. *Regents of the University of California* the issue turned on whether a *state* statute infringed upon the free exercise clause. Once again the Court used the secular regulation principle as the basis for its decision.

Involved in *Hamilton* was a California law requiring "every able-bodied male student" enrolled in the state university to complete a course in military science and tactics. The law was challenged by a group of religiously motivated conscientious objectors who by conviction were not only opposed to wars but also to any form of military training. They charged that by compelling them to participate in a military science course, the California statute had violated their religious beliefs. Once again the Supreme Court upheld the statutory power and opposed the claim that it infringed upon religious freedom. In dismissing the argument that compulsory military training violated the First Amendment, the Court held that every citizen has the duty and obligation "to support and defend government against all enemies."

Mr. Justice Butler delivered the opinion of the (unanimous) court, saying in part:

> Appellants assert — unquestionably in good faith — that all war, preparation for war, and the training required by the university, are repugnant to the tenets and discipline of their church, to their religion and to their consciences. The "privilege" of attending the university as a student comes not from federal sources but is given by the State. It is not within the asserted protection. The only "immunity" claimed by these students is freedom from obligation to comply with the rule prescribing military training. But that "immunity" cannot be regarded as not within, or as distinguishable from, the "liberty" of which they claim to have been deprived by the enforcement of the regents' order. If the regents' order is not repugnant to the due process clause, then it does not violate the privileges and immunities clause. Therefore we need only decide whether by state action the "liberty" of these students has been infringed. . . .
>
> . . . California has not drafted or called them to attend the university. They are seeking education offered by the State and at the same time insisting that they be excluded from the prescribed course solely upon grounds of their religious beliefs and conscientious objections to war, preparation for war and military education. Taken on the basis of the facts alleged in the petition, appellants' contentions amount to no more than an assertion that the due process clause of the Fourteenth Amendment as a safeguard of "liberty" confers the right to be students in the state university free from obligation to take military training as one of the conditions of attendance.
>
> Viewed in the light of our decisions that proposition must at once be put aside as untenable.
>
> Government, federal and state, each in its own sphere owes a duty to the people within its jurisdiction to preserve itself in adequate strength to maintain peace and order and to assure the just enforcement of law. And every citizen owes the reciprocal duty, according to his capacity, to support and defend government against all enemies. . . .
>
> . . . The privilege of the native-born conscientious objector to avoid bearing arms comes not from the Constitution but from the acts of Congress. That body may grant or withhold the exemption as in its wisdom it sees fit; and if it be withheld, the native-born conscientious objector cannot successfully assert the privilege. No other conclusion is compatible with the well-nigh limitless extent of the war powers as above illustrated, which include, by necessary implication, the power, in the last extremity, to compel the armed service of any citizen in the land, without regard to his objections or his views in respect of the justice or morality of the particular war or of war in general. . . .
>
> Plainly there is no ground for the contention that the regents' order, requiring able-bodied male students under the age of twenty-four as a condition of their enrollment to take the prescribed instruction in military science and tactics, transgresses any constitutional right asserted by these appellants.

Pierce v. Society of Sisters, 268 U.S. 510 (1925)

In 1922 the State of Oregon passed a Compulsory Education Act requiring every parent or guardian to send his or her children to a public school. Heavily supported by well established anti-Catholic elements in the state, the Oregon law was widely interpreted as being directed at the state's Catholic parochial school system. Three years later it occasioned a Supreme Court decision, *Pierce* v. *Society of Sisters,* that for the first time applied the First Amendment guarantee of religious freedom to the states through the Fourteenth Amendment. *Pierce* thus paved the way for a series of religious freedom decisions that would cement into constitutional law the principle that the First Amendment guarantee was protected against *state* as well as against congressional action. *Pierce* is also significant for having formed the legal and constitutional basis for the nation's private as well as parochial schools. In *Pierce,* the Supreme Court ruled the Oregon law invalid as an unreasonable interference with the liberty of parents "to direct the upbringing of [their] children." The Court also ruled the Oregon law invalid on grounds that it destroyed the property rights of the Society of Sisters who owned the religious schools.

Mr. Justice McReynolds delivered the opinion of the (unanimous) Court, saying in part:

> No question is raised concerning the power of the State reasonably to regulate all schools, to inspect, supervise and examine them, their teachers and pupils; to require that all children of proper age attend some school, that teachers shall be of good moral character and patriotic disposition, that certain studies plainly essential to good citizenship must be taught, and that nothing be taught which is manifestly inimical to the public welfare.
>
> The inevitable practical result of enforcing the Act under consideration would be destruction of appellees' primary schools, and perhaps all other private primary schools for normal children within the State of Oregon. These parties are engaged in a kind of undertaking not inherently harmful, but long regarded as useful and meritorious. Certainly there is nothing in the present records to indicate that they have failed to discharge their obligations to patrons, students or the State. And there are no peculiar circumstances or present emergencies which demand extraordinary measures relative to primary education.
>
> Under the doctrine of *Meyer* v. *Nebraska,* 262 U.S. 390, we think it entirely plain that the Act of 1922 unreasonably interferes with the liberty of parents and guardians to direct the upbringing and education of children under their control. As often heretofore pointed out, rights guaranteed by the Constitution may not be abridged by legislation which has no reasonable relation to some purpose within the competency of the State. The fundamental theory of liberty upon which all governments in this Union repose excludes any general power of the State to standardize its children by forcing them to accept instruction from public teachers only. The child is not the mere creature of the State; those who nurture him and direct his destiny have the right, coupled with the high duty, to recognize and prepare him for additional obligations.

With *Pierce* establishing the applicability of the First Amendment's guarantees to the States, two decades later the Supreme Court was able to tackle a number of difficult cases involving religious freedom claims of Jehovah's Witnesses.

West Virginia State Board of Education v. Barnette, 319 U.S. 624 (1943)

In the 1940s the constitutionality of two state compulsory flag saluting laws came before the Supreme Court. Involved in both cases were Jehovah's Witnesses and their claims of religious freedom under the First Amendment. That the Court seemed unsure and hesitant is evidenced by the fact that within three years the Court did a complete flip-flop on the issue, approving compulsory flag saluting in one case *(Gobitis)* and declaring it unconstitutional in the other *(Barnette)*.

In *Minersville School District* (Pennsylvania) v. *Gobitis*,[1] the Supreme Court ruled against a claim by Jehovah's Witnesses that by compelling their children to salute the American flag under threat of expulsion from the public school system, the school district was infringing upon their religious freedom. Jehovah's Witnesses insist that flag saluting is "idol worship" or worshipping a "graven image" and they instruct their children that it is contrary to their interpretation of the Bible. Speaking for the majority of eight (with only Justice Stone in dissent) Justice Frankfurter argued that the First Amendment's free exercise of religion clause did *not* relieve the political obligation of Jehovah's Witnesses to obey a general law that was not specifically aimed at restricting freedom of religious belief. According to Justice Frankfurter, the only substantive question was whether a school board was justified in requiring flag saluting on the assumption that it would help further "legitimate educational ends." In *Gobitis* the majority concluded that the school board had acted within its power under the constitution.

Three years later in *Barnette* the Court reversed itself. The issue was similar. Does the action of a state (West Virginia) making it compulsory for children in public schools to salute the flag by "extending the right arm: palm upward," and reciting the pledge of allegiance, violate the First Amendment? In a 6–3 decision, the Supreme Court struck down the West Virginia statute as a violation of religious freedom. Justices Roberts and Reed, in opposition, merely noted that in their judgment the Court should have abided by the *Gobitis* precedent. Justice Frankfurter, on the other hand, wrote a long dissenting opinion chastising the majority for its willingness to use judicial review in such cases. He urged the Court as he was to do on many such occasions, to exercise "judicial self restraint" and what he called "judicial humility" in determining the constitutionality of such state laws. Frankfurter chided the majority for confining "the political power of the Congress of the United States and the legislatures of forty-eight states." To strike down a law like this, Justice Frankfurter said, "is to deny a power to all government."

The majority, however, took a less restrictive, more activist view of judicial review, restraint, and humility. Justice Jackson argued that to sustain a compulsory flag salute law would require the Court to say "that a Bill of Rights which guards the individual's right to speak his own mind, left it open to public authorities to compel him to utter what is *not* in his mind." The *Gobitis* decision, Jackson said, assumed that power exists in the states to impose "flag salute discipline upon school children. . ." In *Barnette* the Court now decided that the states had no such power because it infringed upon the free exercise

1. 310 U.S. 586 (1940).

clause of the First Amendment.

Mr. Justice Jackson delivered the opinion of the Court, saying in part:

The very purpose of a Bill of Rights was to withdraw certain subjects from the
vicissitudes of political controversy, to place them beyond the reach of majorities
and officials and to establish them as legal principles to be applied by the courts.
One's right to life, liberty, and property, to free speech, a free press, freedom of
worship and assembly, and other fundamental rights may not be submitted to
vote; they depend on the outcome of no elections. . . .

In weighing arguments of the parties it is important to distinguish between
the due process clause of the Fourteenth Amendment as an instrument for
transmitting the principles of the First Amendment and those cases in which it is
applied for its own sake. The test of legislation which collides with the Fourteenth Amendment, because it also collides with the principles of the First, is
much more definite than the test when only the Fourteenth is involved. Much of
the vagueness of the due process clause disappears when the specific prohibitions of the First become its standard. The right of a State to regulate, for
example, a public utility may well include, so far as the due process test is
concerned, power to impose all of the restrictions which a legislature may have a
"rational basis" for adopting. But freedoms of speech and of press, of assembly,
and of worship may not be infringed on such slender grounds. They are susceptible of restriction only to prevent grave and immediate danger to interests
which the State may lawfully protect. It is important to note that while it is the
Fourteenth Amendment which bears directly upon the State it is the more specific limiting principles of the First Amendment that finally govern this case.

Nor does our duty to apply the Bill of Rights to assertions of official authority
depend upon our possession of marked competence in the field where the invasion of rights occurs. True, the task of translating the majestic generalities of the
Bill of Rights, conceived as part of the pattern of liberal government in the
eighteenth century, into concrete restraints on officials dealing with the problems of the twentieth century, is one to disturb self-confidence. These principles
grew in soil which also produced a philosophy that the individual was the center
of society, that his liberty was attainable through mere absence of governmental
restraints, and that government should be entrusted with few controls and only
the mildest supervision over men's affairs. We must transplant these rights to a
soil in which the *laissez-faire* concept or principle of non-interference has with-
ered at least as to economic affairs, and social advancements are increasingly
sought through closer integration of society and through expanded and
strengthened governmental controls. These changed conditions often deprive
precedents of reliability and cast us more than we would choose upon our own
judgment. But we act in these matters not by authority of our competence but by
force of our commissions. We cannot, because of modest estimates of our competence in such specialties as public education, withhold the judgment that history
authenticates as the function of this Court when liberty is infringed.

4. Lastly, and this is the very heart of the *Gobitis* opinion, it reasons that
"National unity is the basis of national security," that the authorities have "the
right to select appropriate means for its attainment," and hence reaches the
conclusion that such compulsory measures toward "national unity" are constitutional. *Id.* at 595. Upon the verity of this assumption depends our answer in this
case.

National unity as an end which officials may foster by persuasion and example is not in question. The problem is whether under our Constitution compulsion as here employed is a permissible means for its achievement.

Struggles to coerce uniformity of sentiment in support of some end thought essential to their time and country have been waged by many good as well as by evil men. Nationalism is a relatively recent phenomenon but at other times and places the ends have been racial or territorial security, support of a dynasty or regime, and particular plans for saving souls. As first and moderate methods to attain unity have failed, those bent on its accomplishment must resort to an ever-increasing severity. As governmental pressure toward unity becomes greater, so strife becomes more bitter as to whose unity it shall be. Probably no deeper division of our people could proceed from any provocation than from finding it necessary to choose what doctrine and whose program public educational officials shall compel youth to unite in embracing. Ultimate futility of such attempts to compel coherence is the lesson of every such effort from the Roman drive to stamp out Christianity as a disturber of its pagan unity, the Inquisition, as a means to religious and dynastic unity, the Siberian exiles as a means to Russian unity, down to the fast failing efforts of our present totalitarian enemies. Those who begin coercive elimination of dissent soon find themselves exterminating dissenters. Compulsory unification of opinion achieves only the unanimity of the graveyard.

It seems trite but necessary to say that the First Amendment to our Constitution was designed to avoid these ends by avoiding these beginnings. There is no mysticism in the American concept of the State or of the nature or origin of its authority. We set up government by consent of the governed, and the Bill of Rights denies those in power any legal opportunity to coerce that consent. Authority here is to be controlled by public opinion, not public opinion by authority.

The case is made difficult not because the principles of its decision are obscure but because the flag involved is our own. Nevertheless, we apply the limitations of the Constitution with no fear that freedom to be intellectually and spiritually diverse or even contrary will disintegrate the social organization. To believe that patriotism will not flourish if patriotic ceremonies are voluntary and spontaneous instead of a compulsory routine is to make an unflattering estimate of the appeal of our institutions to free minds. We can have intellectual individualism and the rich cultural diversities that we owe to exceptional minds only at the price of occasional eccentricity and abnormal attitudes. When they are so harmless to others or to the State as those we deal with here, the price is not too great. But freedom to differ is not limited to things that do not matter much. That would be a mere shadow of freedom. The test of its substance is the right to differ as to things that touch the heart of the existing order.

If there is any fixed star in our constitutional constellation, it is that no official, high or petty, can prescribe what shall be orthodox in politics, nationalism, religion, or other matters of opinion or force citizens to confess by word or act their faith therein. If there are any circumstances which permit an exception, they do not now occur to us.

We think the action of the local authorities in compelling the flag salute and pledge transcends constitutional limitations on their power and invades the sphere of intellect and spirit which it is the purpose of the First Amendment to our Constitution to reserve from all official control.

2

SEPARATION OF CHURCH AND STATE

Everson v. Board of Education, 330 U.S. 1 (1947)

A suit to determine whether a state could reimburse parents whose children attended parochial schools for the bus fares those children paid on public buses in order to get to their schools, gave the Supreme Court its first opportunity to interpret the First Amendment's establishment of religion clause. The case was *Everson* v. *Board of Education of Ewing Township* (New Jersey) and it became the occasion for the Court to announce, in Justice Black's words, its "high wall" of separation dictum.

A district taxpayer (Everson) filed suit in a New Jersey state court challenging the right of a school board to reimburse parents of parochial school children for public bus fares. He contended that by using tax money in this manner the State was satisfying the personal desires of parents to choose a Catholic education for their children "rather than the public's interest in the general education of all children." This, Everson argued, violated the due process clause of the Fourteenth Amendment. Speaking for a badly split Court, Justice Black quickly dismissed Everson's due process position. The fact that a state law, passed to satisfy a public need, happens to coincide with the personal desires of Catholic parents, Justice Black said, "is certainly an inadequate reason for us to say that a legislature has erroneously appraised the public need." *Everson* also challenged the New Jersey Statute as a "law respecting an establishment of religion" and therefore a violation of the First Amendment's no-establishment clause.

It was this aspect of the *Everson* dispute that occasioned the most serious controversy and accounted for the Court's 5–4 split. Justice Rutledge, with whom Justices Jackson, Frankfurter, and Burton joined, wrote a long dissenting opinion bitterly criticizing the majority for breaching the "high wall" separating church and state. "Neither so high nor so impregnable today as yesterday," Rutledge wrote, "is the First Amendment's wall of separation." This breach will lead to others, Rutledge said, "others will be tempted we may be sure." For Rutledge and the other dissenters, *Everson* was not "just a little case over bus fares." For them the integrity of the First Amendment was involved. In Rutledge's words:

12

Two great drives are constantly in motion to abridge in the name of education, the complete division of religion and civil authority which our forefathers made. One is to introduce religious education and observances into the public schools. The other, to obtain public funds for the aid and support of various private religious schools. In my opinion both avenues were closed by the Constitution. Neither should be opened by this Court. The matter is not one of quantity, to be measured by the amount of money expended. Now, as in Madison's day, it is one of principle, to keep separate the separate sphere as the First Amendment drew them; to prevent the first experiment upon our liberties; and to keep the question from becoming entangled in corrosive precedents. We should not be less strict to keep strong and untarnished the one side of the shield of religious freedom than we have been of the other.

The majority, however, saw the *Everson* issues differently. For Justice Black, New Jersey's law reimbursing parents was a valid policy of giving benefits to all children and their parents for bus rides. It was not, Black insisted, a matter of state aid to religious schools. Black's reasoning led to the "child-benefit" theory of state aid, which the Supreme Court would encounter and use later in a series of related cases. New Jersey's legislation, Black wrote, contributed no money to parochial schools. New Jersey did "no more than provide a general program to help parents get their children, regardless of their religion, safely and expeditiously to and from accredited schools."

Accordingly, the Court ruled that New Jersey's reimbursement plan did not violate the First Amendment's no-establishment clause. The state, Justice Black said, must *not* exclude some of its citizens from receiving the benefits of public welfare legislation "because of their faith or lack of it." He argued that the First Amendment requires the State to be "neutral" in its dealings with believers and nonbelievers. By espousing this "neutrality" and "child-benefit" position the majority argued that New Jersey's action was not "the slightest breach" in the "high wall" separating church and state as Rutledge and the dissenters feared.

Mr. Justice Black delivered the opinion of the Court, saying in part:

> The meaning and scope of the First Amendment, preventing establishment of religion or prohibiting the free exercise thereof, in the light of its history and the evils it was designed forever to suppress, have been several times elaborated by the decisions of this Court prior to the application of the First Amendment to the states by the Fourteenth. The broad meaning given the Amendment by these earlier cases has been accepted by this Court in its decisions concerning an individual's religious freedom rendered since the Fourteenth Amendment was interpreted to make the prohibitions of the First applicable to state action abridging religious freedom. There is every reason to give the same application and broad interpretation to the "establishment of religion" clause. The interrelation of these complementary clauses was well summarized in a statement of the Court of Appeals of South Carolina, quoted with approval by this Court in *Watson* v. *Jones,* 13 Wall. 679, 730: "The structure of our government has, for the preservation of civil liberty, rescued the temporal institutions from religious interference. On the other hand, it has secured religious liberty from the invasion of the civil authority."
>
> The "establishment of religion" clause of the First Amendment means at least this: Neither a state nor the Federal Government can set up a church. Neither can pass laws which aid one religion, aid all religions, or prefer one religion over

another. Neither can force nor influence a person to go to or to remain away from church against his will or force him to profess a belief or disbelief in any religion. No person can be punished for entertaining or professing religious beliefs or disbeliefs, for church attendance or non-attendance. No tax in any amount, large or small, can be levied to support any religious activities or institutions, whatever they may be called, or whatever form they may adopt to teach or practice religion. Neither a state nor the Federal Government can, openly or secretly, participate in the affairs of any religious organizations or groups and *vice versa*. In the words of Jefferson, the clause against establishment of religion by law was intended to erect "a wall of separation between church and State." *Reynolds* v. *United States, supra* at 164.

We must consider the New Jersey statute in accordance with the foregoing limitations imposed by the First Amendment. But we must not strike that state statute down if it is within the State's constitutional power even though it approaches the verge of that power. See *Interstate Ry.* v. *Massachusetts,* Holmes, J., *supra* at 85, 88. New Jersey cannot consistently with the "establishment of religion" clause of the First Amendment contribute tax-raised funds to the support of an institution which teaches the tenets and faith of any church. On the other hand, other language of the amendment commands that New Jersey cannot hamper its citizens in the free exercise of their own religion. Consequently, it cannot exclude individual Catholics, Lutherans, Mohammedans, Baptists, Jews, Methodists, Non-believers, Presbyterians, or the members of any other faith, *because of their faith, or lack of it,* from receiving the benefits of public welfare legislation. While we do not mean to intimate that a state could not provide transportation only to children attending public schools, we must be careful, in protecting the citizens of New Jersey against state-established churches, to be sure that we do not inadvertently prohibit New Jersey from extending its general state law benefits to all its citizens without regard to their religious belief.

Measured by these standards, we cannot say that the First Amendment prohibits New Jersey from spending tax-raised funds to pay the bus fares of parochial school pupils as a part of a general program under which it pays the fares of pupils attending public and other schools. It is undoubtedly true that children are helped to get to church schools. There is even a possibility that some of the children might not be sent to the church schools if the parents were compelled to pay their children's bus fares out of their own pockets when transportation to a public school would have been paid for by the State. The same possibility exists where the state requires a local transit company to provide reduced fares to school children including those attending parochial schools, or where a municipally owned transportation system undertakes to carry all school children free of charge. Moreover, state-paid policemen, detailed to protect children going to and from church schools from the very real hazards of traffic, would serve much the same purpose and accomplish much the same result as state provisions intended to guarantee free transportation of a kind which the state deems to be best for the school children's welfare. And parents might refuse to risk their children to the serious danger of traffic accidents going to and from parochial schools, the approaches to which were not protected by policemen. Similarly, parents might be reluctant to permit their children to attend schools which the state had cut off from such general government services as ordinary police and fire protection, connections for sewage disposal, public highways and sidewalks. Of course, cutting off church schools from these services, so separate and so indisputably marked off from the religious function, would make it far more difficult for the schools to operate. But such is obviously not the purpose of the First Amendment. That Amendment requires the state to be a neutral in its relations with groups of religious believers and non-believers; it does not require the state to be their adversary. State power is no more to be used so as to handicap religions than it is to favor them.

This Court has said that parents may, in the discharge of their duty under state compulsory education laws, send their children to a religious rather than a public school if the school meets the secular educational requirements which the state has power to impose. See *Pierce v. Society of Sisters*, 268 U.S. 510. It appears that these parochial schools meet New Jersey's requirements. The State contributes no money to the schools. It does not support them. Its legislation, as applied, does no more than provide a general program to help parents get their children, regardless of their religion, safely and expeditiously to and from accredited schools.

The First Amendment has erected a wall between church and state. That wall must be kept high and impregnable. We could not approve the slightest breach. New Jersey has not breached it here.

McCollum v. Board of Education, 333 U.S. 203 (1948)

Released-time programs, devised by many school boards throughout the country in the 1940s in an effort to give public school children opportunity for some religious education, came before the Supreme Court twice within four years, 1948 and 1952. As it was in the flag saluting cases, the Court's record was inconsistent. It invalidated one released-time program (Champaign, Illinois) as an unconstitutional mix of church and state, and approved the other (New York City).

McCollum v. Board of Education was the first of two released-time cases. The Champaign, Illinois school board had established a program allowing public school children, with the consent of their parents, to attend classes given by Protestant ministers, Catholic priests, and Jewish rabbis. Classes were conducted one hour per week during regular school hours and in the school building. Although the religious teachers were not paid by the School District, they were supervised by the District School superintendent and attendance was mandatory for the volunteers who chose to participate in the program. As the parent of a child enrolled in Champaign schools, the appellant, Mrs. Vashti McCollum, brought suit against the School Board charging that its "joint-public school-religious group" released-time program violated the no-establishment of religion clause of the First Amendment. With only Justice Reed in dissent the Supreme Court ruled in favor of Mrs. McCollum.

Justice Black wrote for the majority (Justice Frankfurter wrote a long concurring opinion joined by Justices Jackson, Rutledge and Burton) that utilization of a state tax-supported public school system "and its machinery for compulsory public schools attendance" for "sectarian groups" to give religious instructions to public school children on public school property was a violation of the First Amendment's "no-establishment" clause.

In dissent Justice Reed disagreed with this conclusion. He noted that the phrase "an establishment of religion" in the First Amendment "may have been intended by Congress to be aimed only at a state church." Reviewing the pertinent history of the First Amendment during the 1789 Congressional debates, Justice Reed quoted the words of James Madison, perhaps more than anyone else said to be "the father of the Bill of Rights." On the floor of the

House of Representatives during the debate over adoption of the Bill of Rights, Madison indicated that the no-establishment clause meant "that Congress should not establish a religion and enforce the legal observation of it by law, nor compel men to worship God in any manner contrary to their conscience." Never, until its decision in *McCollum,* Justice Reed concluded, "has this Court so widened its interpretation" of no-establishment to do what clearly was not intended by the original meaning of the First Amendment. He argued that by not recognizing "the interest of our nation in religion" and by refusing to grant school boards the opportunity to "present religion as an optional extra-curricular subject" in a voluntary released-time program, the majority was misreading and misapplying the intent of the "establishment of religion" clause.

On the other hand, as the majority read the *McCollum* facts, use of tax-supported property for religious instruction coupled with the "close cooperation" between the Champaign School Board and the city's Religious Council in promoting religious education added up to an unconstitutional breach of the "high wall" of separation between church and state that Justices Rutledge and Black had erected in the *Everson* case.

Mr. Justice Black delivered the opinion of the Court, saying in part:

The operation of the State's compulsory education system thus assists and is integrated with the program of religious instruction carried on by separate religious sects. Pupils compelled by law to go to school for secular education are released in part from their legal duty upon the condition that they attend the religious classes. This is beyond all question a utilization of the tax-established and tax-supported public school system to aid religious groups to spread their faith. And it falls squarely under the ban of the First Amendment (made applicable to the States by the Fourteenth) as we interpreted it in *Everson v. Board of Education,* 330 U.S. 1.

Recognizing that the Illinois program is barred by the First and Fourteenth Amendments if we adhere to the views expressed both by the majority and the minority in the *Everson* case, counsel for the respondents challenge those views as dicta and urge that we reconsider and repudiate them. They argue that historically the First Amendment was intended to forbid only government preference of one religion over another, not an impartial governmental assistance of all religions. In addition they ask that we distinguish or overrule our holding in the *Everson* case that the Fourteenth Amendment made the "establishment of religion" clause of the First Amendment applicable as a prohibition against the States. After giving full consideration to the arguments presented we are unable to accept either of these contentions.

To hold that a state cannot consistently with the First and Fourteenth Amendments utilize its public school system to aid any or all religious faiths or sects in the dissemination of their doctrines and ideals does not, as counsel urge, manifest a governmental hostility to religion or religious teachings. A manifestation of such hostility would be at war with our national tradition as embodied in the First Amendment's guaranty of the free exercise of religion. For the First Amendment rests upon the premise that both religion and government can best work to achieve their lofty aims if each is left free from the other within its respective sphere. Or, as we said in the *Everson* case, the First Amendment has erected a wall between Church and State which must be kept high and impregnable.

Here not only are the State's tax-supported public school buildings used for the dissemination of religious doctrines. The State also affords sectarian groups an invaluable aid in that it helps to provide pupils for their religious classes through use of the State's compulsory public school machinery. This is not separation of Church and State.

Zorach v. Clauson, 343 U.S. 306 (1952)

Four years after *McCollum,* in *Zorach* v. *Clauson,* a slightly reconstructed Supreme Court (Justices Clark and Minton had replaced Justices Murphy and Rutledge) gave its stamp of approval to New York City's released-time program. In *Zorach* the Court seemed to be responding to the widespread public furor its *McCollum* ruling had occasioned in church circles all over the country. In part to compensate for the Court's decision in *McCollum,* New York City's released-time program differed in some details from Champaign's. In New York the released-time religious classes were held off public school property. Those children who chose not to be participants remained in their classrooms. There was no expenditure of public funds involved in the program. For these reasons, a new majority of six, with Justice Douglas as its spokesman, decided that the *McCollum* rule was not controlling.

Justices Black, Frankfurter, and Jackson each wrote separate dissents. Justice Black noted that for him the *McCollum* "high wall" of separation still prevailed. "Government should not be allowed," he said, "under cover of the soft euphemism of 'cooperation' to steal into the sacred area of religious choice." For Justice Frankfurter, as well, the *McCollum* precedent should have been followed in *Zorach.* "Happily," he said, its high wall principles were not specifically disavowed by the Court. "From this I draw the hope that in future variations [of released-time programs] which are bound to come here, these principles may again be honored . . ." For Justice Jackson, the majority had "cynically magnified the distinctions between *McCollum* and *Zorach* he said were "trivial." The wall of separation between church and state that *McCollum* attempted to erect, Jackson said, "has become even more warped and twisted than I expected. . . . It takes more subtlety of mind than I possess to deny that [New York's released-time program] is governmental constraint in support of religion."

For the majority, however, several factors controlled. There was no element of coercion, there was no use of public property, no discontinuation of public education as there had been in *McCollum,* no expenditure of public funds, and therefore, the Court concluded, there was no breach in the wall of separation. New York had neither prohibited the free exercise of religion nor made a law respecting an establishment of religion within the meanings of the First Amendment.

Mr. Justice Douglas delivered the opinion of the Court, saying in part:

[W]e do not see how New York by this type of "released time" program has made a law respecting an establishment of religion within the meaning of the First Amendment. There is much talk of the separation of Church and State in the history of the Bill of Rights and in the decisions clustering around the First

Amendment. . . . There cannot be the slightest doubt that the First Amendment reflects the philosophy that Church and State should be separated. And so far as interference with the "free exercise" of religion and an "establishment" of religion are concerned, the separation must be complete and unequivocal. The First Amendment within the scope of its coverage permits no exception; the prohibition is absolute. The First Amendment, however, does not say that in every and all respects there shall be a separation of Church and State. Rather, it studiously defines the manner, the specific ways, in which there shall be no concert or union or dependency one on the other. That is the common sense of the matter. Otherwise the state and religion would be aliens to each other — hostile, suspicious, and even unfriendly. Churches could not be required to pay even property taxes. Municipalities would not be permitted to render police or fire protection to religious groups. Policemen who helped parishioners into their places of worship would violate the Constitution. Prayers in our legislative halls; the appeals to the Almighty in the messages of the Chief Executive; the proclamations making Thanksgiving Day a holiday; "so help me God" in our courtroom oaths — these and all other references to the Almighty that run through our laws, our public rituals, our ceremonies would be flouting the First Amendment. A fastidious atheist or agnostic could even object to the supplication with which the Court opens each session: "God save the United States and this Honorable Court."

We would have to press the concept of separation of Church and State to these extremes to condemn the present law on constitutional grounds. The nullification of this law would have wide and profound effects. A Catholic student applies to his teacher for permission to leave the school during hours on a Holy Day of Obligation to attend a mass. A Jewish student asks his teacher for permission to be excused for Yom Kippur. A Protestant wants the afternoon off for a family baptismal ceremony. In each case the teacher requires parental consent in writing. In each case the teacher, in order to make sure the student is not a truant, goes further and requires a report from the priest, the rabbi, or the minister. The teacher in other words cooperates in a religious program to the extent of making it possible for her students to participate in it. Whether she does it occasionally for a few students, regularly for one, or pursuant to a systematized program designed to further the religious needs of all the students does not alter the character of the act.

We are a religious people whose institutions presuppose a Supreme Being. We guarantee the freedom to worship as one chooses. We make room for as wide a variety of beliefs and creeds as the spiritual needs of man deem necessary. We sponsor an attitude on the part of government that shows no partiality to any one group and that lets each flourish according to the zeal of its adherents and the appeal of its dogma. When the state encourages religious instruction or cooperates with religious authorities by adjusting the schedule of public events to sectarian needs, it follows the best of our traditions. For it then respects the religious nature of our people and accommodates the public service to their spiritual needs. To hold that it may not would be to find in the Constitution a requirement that the government show a callous indifference to religious groups. That would be preferring those who believe in no religion over those who do believe. Government may not finance religious groups nor undertake religious instruction nor blend secular and sectarian education nor use secular institutions to force one or some religion on any person. But we find no constitutional requirement which makes it necessary for government to be hostile to religion and to throw its weight against efforts to widen the effective scope of religious influence. The government must be neutral when it comes to competition between sects. It may not thrust any sect on any person. It may not make a religious observance compulsory. It may not coerce anyone to attend church, to observe a religious holiday, or to take religious instruction. But it can close its doors or suspend its operations as to those who want to repair to their religious sanctuary for worship or instruction. No more than that is undertaken here.

This program may be unwise and improvident from an educational or a community viewpoint. That appeal is made to us on a theory, previously advanced, that each case must be decided on the basis of "our own prepossessions." . . . Our individual preferences, however, are not the constitutional standard. The constitutional standard is the separation of Church and State. The problem, like many problems in constitutional law, is one of degree.

In the *McCollum* case the classrooms were used for religious instruction and the force of the public school was used to promote that instruction. Here, as we have said, the public schools do no more than accommodate their schedules to a program of outside religious instruction. We follow the *McCollum* case. But we cannot expand it to cover the present released-time program unless separation of Church and State means that public institutions can make no adjustments of their schedules to accommodate the religious needs of the people. We cannot read into the Bill of Rights such a philosophy of hostility to religion.

3

RELIGION IN THE SCHOOLS

Engel v. Vitale, 370 U.S. 421 (1962)

Ten years after *Zorach* two additional "high wall" rulings were handed down, these regarding the widespread practice of requiring prayers in the public schools. Each, in particular the first, *Engel* v. *Vitale,* occasioned great outbursts of indignation at what critics called the Court's inflexible, secularizing "wall of separation" position. *Engel* dealt with a rather innocuous twenty-two word "nonsectarian" prayer adopted by the New York State Board of Regents for use in the state's public schools. The Regents' prayer read: "Almighty God, we acknowledge our dependence upon thee, and we beg thy blessings upon us, our parents, our teachers, and our Country." Parents of ten New York school children brought suit against the state, insisting that use of an "official prayer" in the public schools was contrary to the religious beliefs of them and their children. They argued further that state authorization of the school prayer violated that part of the First Amendment that affirms that "Congress shall make no law respecting an establishment of religion."

In a 6–1 decision (Justices Frankfurter and White did not participate and Justice Stewart was in dissent) the Supreme Court agreed with the ten parents and struck down the New York schools prayer as a constitutionally unallowable "establishment of religion." Justice Black wrote for the majority.

In his dissent, as Justice Reed had done in *McCollum,* Justice Stewart accused the Court of misapplying "a great constitutional principle." He could not understand "how an 'official religion' is established by letting those who want to say a prayer say it." On the contrary, Justice Stewart concluded, "I think that to deny the wish of these school children to join in reciting this prayer is to deny them the opportunity of sharing in the spiritual heritage of our Nation."

As might be expected Justice Black saw the issue differently. The Court ruled that a prayer (although compliance was voluntary) "composed by governmental officials as part of a governmental program to further religious beliefs was a breach of the high wall of separation between Church and State."

Mr. Justice Black delivered the opinion of the Court, saying in part:

20

We think that by using its public school system to encourage recitation of the Regents' prayer, the State of New York has adopted a practice wholly inconsistent with the Establishment Clause. There can, of course, be no doubt that New York's program of daily classroom invocation of God's blessings as prescribed in the Regents' prayer is a religious activity. It is a solemn avowal of divine faith and supplication for the blessings of the Almighty. The nature of such a prayer has always been religious, none of the respondents has denied this and the trial court expressly so found:

> "The religious nature of prayer was recognized by Jefferson and has been concurred in by theological writers, the United States Supreme Court and State courts and administrative officials, including New York's Commissioner of Education. A committee of the New York Legislature has agreed.
>
> "The Board of Regents as *amicus curiae,* the respondents and intervenors all concede the religious nature of prayer, but seek to distinguish this prayer because it is based on our spiritual heritage. . . ."

By the time of the adoption of the Constitution, our history shows that there was a widespread awareness among many Americans of the dangers of a union of Church and State. These people knew, some of them from bitter personal experience, that one of the greatest dangers to the freedom of the individual to worship in his own way lay in the Government's placing its official stamp of approval upon one particular kind of prayer or one particular form of religious services. They knew the anguish, hardship and bitter strife that could come when zealous religious groups struggled with one another to obtain the Government's stamp of approval from each King, Queen, or Protector that came to temporary power. The Constitution was intended to avert a part of this danger by leaving the government of this country in the hands of the people rather than in the hands of any monarch. But this safeguard was not enough. Our Founders were no more willing to let the content of their prayers and their privilege of praying whenever they pleased be influenced by the ballot box than they were to let these vital matters of personal conscience depend upon the succession of monarchs. The First Amendment was added to the Constitution to stand as a guarantee that neither the power nor the prestige of the Federal Government would be used to control, support or influence the kinds of prayer the American people can say — that the people's religions must not be subjected to the pressures of government for change each time a new political administration is elected to office. Under that Amendment's prohibition against governmental establishment of religion, as reinforced by the provisions of the Fourteenth Amendment, government in this country, be it state or federal, is without power to prescribe by law any particular form of prayer which is to be used as an official prayer in carrying on any program of governmentally sponsored religious activity.

There can be no doubt that New York's state prayer program officially establishes the religious beliefs embodied in the Regents' prayer. The respondents' argument to the contrary, which is largely based upon the contention that the Regents' prayer is "non-denominational" and the fact that the program, as modified and approved by state courts, does not require all pupils to recite the prayer but permits those who wish to do so to remain silent or be excused from the room, ignores the essential nature of the program's constitutional defects. Neither the fact that the prayer may be denominationally neutral nor the fact that its observance on the part of the students is voluntary can serve to free it from the limitations of the Establishment Clause, as it might from the Free Exercise Clause, of the First Amendment, both of which are operative against the States by virtue of the Fourteenth Amendment. Although these two clauses may in certain instances overlap, they forbid two quite different kinds of governmental encroachment upon religious freedom. The Establishment Clause, unlike the Free Exercise Clause, does not depend upon any showing of direct governmental compulsion and is violated by the enactment of laws which establish an official religion whether those laws operate directly to coerce nonobserving individuals or not.

. . . The New York laws officially prescribing the Regents' prayer are inconsistent both with the purposes of the Establishment Clause and with the Establishment Clause itself.

It has been argued that to apply the Constitution in such a way as to prohibit state laws respecting an establishment of religious services in public schools is to indicate a hostility toward religion or toward prayer. Nothing, of course, could be more wrong. The history of man is inseparable from the history of religion. And perhaps it is not too much to say that since the beginning of that history many people have devoutly believed that "More things are wrought by prayer than this world dreams of." It was doubtless largely due to men who believed this that there grew up a sentiment that caused men to leave the cross-currents of officially established state religions and religious persecution in Europe and come to this country filled with the hope that they could find a place in which they could pray when they pleased to the God of their faith in the language they chose. And there were men of this same faith in the power of prayer who led the fight for adoption of our Constitution and also for our Bill of Rights with the very guarantees of religious freedom that forbid the sort of governmental activity which New York has attempted here. These men knew that the First Amendment, which tried to put an end to governmental control of religion and of prayer, was not written to destroy either. They knew rather that it was written to quiet well-justified fears which nearly all of them felt arising out of an awareness that governments of the past had shackled men's tongues to make them speak only the religious thoughts that government wanted them to speak and to pray only to the God that government wanted them to pray to. It is neither sacrilegious nor antireligious to say that each separate government in this country should stay out of the business of writing or sanctioning official prayers and leave that purely religious function to the people themselves and to those the people choose to look to for religious guidance.

It is true that New York's establishment of its Regents' prayer as an officially approved religious doctrine of that State does not amount to a total establishment of one particular religious sect to the exclusion of all others — that, indeed, the governmental endorsement of that prayer seems relatively insignificant when compared to the governmental encroachments upon religion which were commonplace 200 years ago. To those who may subscribe to the view that because the Regents' official prayer is so brief and general there can be no danger to religious freedom in its governmental establishment, however, it may be appropriate to say in the words of James Madison, the author of the First Amendment:

"[I]t is proper to take alarm at the first experiment on our liberties. . . . Who does not see that the same authority which can establish Christianity, in exclusion of all other Religions, may establish with the same ease any particular sect of Christians, in exclusion of all other Sects? That the same authority which can force a citizen to contribute three pence only of his property for the support of any one establishment, may force him to conform to any other establishment in all cases whatsoever?"

School District of Abington Township v. Schempp, 374 U.S. 203 (1963)

Public outcry, and it exceeded in intensity what followed *McCollum,* at what opponents of the Supreme Court's *Engel* ruling called the creeping secularization of American life, was given additional fuel a year later in *School District of Abington Township* (Pennsylvania) v. *Schempp.* There the Court reaffirmed its "no prayers" in the public schools position outlined by Justice Black in *Engel.* At issue in *Schempp* were state laws in Maryland and Pennsylvania that allowed local school boards to require daily readings from the Bible and recitation of the Lord's Prayer at the beginning of each school day. Although the laws in both states permitted school children to be excused from attending or participating in the prayers upon written request of their parents, the Supreme Court found, nevertheless, that the State laws establishing these prayers violated the "no-establishment" clause of the First Amendment. Once again the public outburst occasioned by *Engel* was repeated. Here and there a few "sensible voices" were heard including that of President Kennedy who urged that the public make an effort to understand the Court's interpretation of the Constitution. By and large, however, the opposition was loud and vituperative. The Court was severely criticized as "Godless," as being opposed to prayer, and worse, as "un-American." In Congress a number of constitutional amendments were, and have been continually, introduced ever since (most notably by Senator Everett Dirksen of Illinois in 1966), that would authorize prayers in the public schools. Up to this point none has passed. Congressional sentiment seemed to reflect the public mood. There is substantial evidence that the Supreme Court's "no-prayer" dictums are being ignored, evaded, or winked at in many school districts. The lesson seems inescapably clear: Court rulings that run counter to what the public perceives as proper policy are often impossible to uphold or enforce.

Schempp was an 8–1 decision with Justice Clark speaking for the majority and Justice Stewart the lone dissenter. Once again as he had in *Engel* Stewart accused the majority of "fallaciously oversimplifying" church and state separation. The majority's high wall view, Stewart said, might one day lead the Court to outlaw spending federal funds to employ chaplains for the Armed Services as a violation of the no-establishment clause. However, in a long concurring opinion, Justice Brennan took particular pains to note that the Court had no intention of going that far. Brennan's opinion chronicled, as did Black's for the majority in *Engel,* the long history of evils caused by "established" religions in Europe and in the American colonies. Brennan also noted in detail the evolution in the United States away from established churches through the First and Fourteenth Amendments. He concluded that "no establishment" was a uniquely American phenomenon that had developed as a result of peculiar American circumstances.

Mr. Justice Clark delivered the opinion of the Court, saying in part:

> The wholesome "neutrality" of which this Court's cases speak thus stems from a recognition of the teachings of history that powerful sects or groups might bring about a fusion of governmental and religious functions or a concert or dependency of one upon the other to the end that official support of the State or

Federal Government would be placed behind the tenets of one or of all or-thodoxies. This the Establishment Clause prohibits. And a further reason for neutrality is found in the Free Exercise Clause, which recognizes the value of religious training, teaching and observance and, more particularly, the right of every person to freely choose his own course with reference thereto, free of any compulsion from the state. This the Free Exercise Clause guarantees. Thus, as we have seen, the two clauses may overlap. As we have indicated, the Establish-ment Clause has been directly considered by this Court eight times in the past score of years and, with only one Justice dissenting on the point, it has consis-tently held that the clause withdrew all legislative power respecting religious belief or the expression thereof. The test may be stated as follows: What are the purpose and the primary effect of the enactment? If either is the advancement or inhibition of religion then the enactment exceeds the scope of legislative power as circumscribed by the Constitution. That is to say that to withstand the strictures of the Establishment Clause there must be a secular legislative purpose and a primary effect that neither advances nor inhibits religion. *Everson* v. *Board of Education, supra.* . . . The Free Exercise Clause, likewise considered many times here, withdraws from legislative power, state and federal, the exertion of any restraint on the free exercise of religion. Its purpose is to secure religious liberty in the individual by prohibiting any invasions thereof by civil authority. Hence it is necessary in a free exercise case for one to show the coercive effect of the enactment as it operates against him in the practice of his religion. The distinc-tion between the two clauses is apparent — a violation of the Free Exercise Clause is predicated on coercion while the Establishment Clause violation need not be so attended.

Applying the Establishment Clause principles to the cases at bar we find that the States are requiring the selection and reading at the opening of the school day of verses from the Holy Bible and the recitation of the Lord's Prayer by the students in unison. These exercises are prescribed as part of the curricular activities of students who are required by law to attend school. They are held in the school buildings under the supervision and with the participation of teachers employed in those schools. None of these factors, other than compulsory school attendance, was present in the program upheld in *Zorach* v. *Clauson.* The trial court . . . has found that such an opening exercise is a religious ceremony and was intended by the State to be so. We agree with the trial court's finding as to the religious character of the exercises. Given that finding, the exercises and the law requiring them are in violation of the Establishment Clause. . . .

It is insisted that unless these religious exercises are permitted a "religion of secularism" is established in the schools. We agree of course that the State may not establish a "religion of secularism" in the sense of affirmatively op-posing or showing hostility to religion, thus "preferring those who believe in no religion over those who do believe." *Zorach* v. *Clauson, supra,* at 314. We do not agree, however, that this decision in any sense has that effect. In ad-dition, it might well be said that one's education is not complete without a study of comparative religion or the history of religion and its relationship to the advancement of civilization. It certainly may be said that the Bible is worthy of study for its literary and historic qualities. Nothing we have said here indicates that such study of the Bible or of religion, when presented objectively as part of a secular program of education, may not be effected consistently with the First Amendment. But the exercises here do not fall into those categories. They are religious exercises, required by the States in violation of the command of the First Amendment that the Government maintain strict neutrality, neither aiding nor opposing religion.

Finally, we cannot accept that the concept of neutrality, which does not permit a State to require a religious exercise even with the consent of the majority of those affected, collides with the majority's right to free exercise of religion. While the Free Exercise Clause clearly prohibits the use of state action to deny the rights of free exercise to *anyone*, it has never meant that a majority could use the machinery of the State to practice its beliefs. Such a contention was effectively answered by Mr. Justice Jackson for the Court in *West Virginia Board of Education* v. *Barnette*, 319 U.S. 624, 638 (1943):

> "The very purpose of a Bill of Rights was to withdraw certain sub-jects from the vicissitudes of political controversy, to place them be-yond the reach of majorities and officials and to establish them as legal principles to be applied by the courts. One's right to ... freedom of worship .... and other fundamental rights may not be submitted to vote; they depend on the outcome of no elections."

The place of religion in our society is an exalted one, achieved through a long tradition of reliance on the home, the church and the inviolable citadel of the individual heart and mind. We have come to recognize through bitter experience that it is not within the power of government to invade that citadel, whether its purpose or effect be to aid or oppose, to advance or re-tard. In the relationship between man and religion, the State is firmly com-mitted to a position of neutrality. Though the application of that rule re-quires interpretation of a delicate sort, the rule itself is clearly and concisely stated in the words of the First Amendment.

4

AID TO PRIVATE SCHOOLS

Board of Education v. Allen, 392 U.S. 236 (1968)

Does a New York statute requiring school districts to buy and then loan textbooks to children in parochial (and other private) schools come under the "child-benefit" theory that the Court began developing in its *Everson* bus fare ruling? Or does the state practice of free textbooks breach the wall of separation between church and state that the Supreme Court had alluded to in *Everson* and had built in the two prayer cases, *Engel* and *Schempp,* as well as in its *McCollum* (but not *Zorach*) released-time decisions? These were the issues in *Board of Education* v. *Allen.*

By upholding the constitutionality of the New York statute, the Supreme Court majority of six applied the child-benefit principle of the *Everson* case that permits religiously oriented schools "to share in the social gains from government programs that are [themselves] religiously neutral." As in *Everson,* the Court ruled that New York's "benefits" accrued to children and their parents — not to the religious schools the children attended. Speaking for the majority, Justice White noted that New York was making available "to all children the benefits of a general program to lend school books free of charge."

The Court's ruling drew three separate, angry dissents, from Justices Black, Douglas, and Fortas. Justice Black argued that New York's free textbook statute was a "flat, flagrant, open violation" of the First Amendment's no-establishment clause. "In saying this," Black noted, "I am not unmindful of the fact that New York purported to follow the *Everson* rule in which this Court in an opinion written by me" upheld a New Jersey law authorizing reimbursement of bus fares to parents whose children attended parochial schools. Justice Black insisted that the Court should have distinguished between books "which are the heart of any school" and bus fares "which provide a convenient and helpful public transportation service." For Black it was clear that a state could provide one (bus fares) without violating the First Amendment, but not the other (books).

In his dissent, Justice Douglas was equally caustic about what he considered a serious breach of the wall of separation between church and state. "Whatever may be said of *Everson,*" Douglas argued, "there is nothing ideological about a bus, . . . a school lunch, . . . a public nurse, or a scholarship." The constitutionality of such aid to parochial school children is one thing, Douglas wrote, but "the textbook goes to the very heart of education in a parochial school. It is the chief, although not solitary, instrumentality for propagating a particular religious creed or faith." As Justice Douglas read the New York Statute, it gave parochial school authorities the right to ask for whatever books they wanted to use. "Can there be the slightest doubt," Douglas asked, "that the head of the parochial school will select the book or books that best promote its sectarian creed?"

Justice Fortas used similar arguments in his dissent. New York's law, Fortas said, calls for providing "special, separate, and particular books" for use in parochial schools. "This is the feature that makes it impossible . . . to reach any conclusion other than that this statute is an unconstitutional use of public funds to support an establishment of religion."

The majority was certainly aware of these objections to its position. Justice White based the Court's conclusion upholding the New York statute on the assumption that the law "merely makes available to all children" the advantages of a general aid program, the financial benefits of which are to "parents and children, not to schools." To meet Douglas' point that the state was "propagating a particular creed or faith," the Court maintained "it cannot be assumed that [New York] school authorities are unable to distinguish between secular and religious books or that they will not honestly discharge their duties to approve only secular books."

Mr. Justice White delivered the opinion of the Court, saying in part:

> *Everson* v. *Board of Education,* 330 U.S. 1 (1947), is the case decided by this Court that is most nearly in point for today's problem. New Jersey reimbursed parents for expenses incurred in busing their children to parochial schools. The Court stated that the Establishment Clause bars a State from passing "laws which aid one religion, aid all religions, or prefer one religion over another," and bars too any "tax in any amount, large or small . . . levied to support any religious activities or institutions, whatever they may be called, or whatever form they may adopt to teach or practice religion." 330 U.S., at 15–16. Nevertheless, said the Court, the Establishment Clause does not prevent a State from extending the benefits of state laws to all citizens without regard for their religious affiliation and does not prohibit "New Jersey from spending tax-raised funds to pay the bus fares of parochial school pupils as a part of a general program under which it pays the fares of pupils attending public and other schools." The statute was held to be valid even though one of its results was that "children are helped to get to church schools" and "some of the children might not be sent to the church schools if the parents were compelled to pay their children's bus fares out of their own pockets." 330 U.S., at 17. As with public provision of police and fire protection, sewage facilities, and streets and sidewalks, payment of bus fares was of some value to the religious school, but was nevertheless not such support of a religious institution as to be a prohibited establishment of religion within the meaning of the First Amendment. . . .
>
> . . . The express purpose of §701 was stated by the New York Legislature to be furtherance of the educational opportunities available to the young. Appellants have shown us nothing about the necessary effects of the statute that is contrary to its stated purpose. The law merely makes available to all children the benefits of a general program to lend school books free of charge. Books are furnished at

the request of the pupil and ownership remains, at least technically, in the State. Thus no funds or books are furnished to parochial schools, and the financial benefit is to parents and children, not to schools. Perhaps free books make it more likely that some children choose to attend a sectarian school, but that was true of the state-paid bus fares in *Everson* and does not alone demonstrate an unconstitutional degree of support for a religious institution.

Of course books are different from buses. Most bus rides have no inherent religious significance, while religious books are common. However, the language of §701 does not authorize the loan of religious books, and the State claims no right to distribute religious literature. Although the books loaned are those required by the parochial school for use in specific courses, each book loaned must be approved by the public school authorities; only secular books may receive approval. The law was construed by the Court of Appeals of New York as "merely making available secular textbooks at the request of the individual student," *supra,* and the record contains no suggestion that religious books have been loaned. Absent evidence, we cannot assume that school authorities, who constantly face the same problem in selecting textbooks for use in the public schools, are unable to distinguish between secular and religious books or that they will not honestly discharge their duties under the law. In judging the validity of the statute on this record we must proceed on the assumption that books loaned to students are books that are not unsuitable for use in the public schools because of religious content. . . .

Underlying these cases, and underlying also the legislative judgments that have preceded the court decisions, has been a recognition that private education has played and is playing a significant and valuable role in raising national levels of knowledge, competence, and experience. Americans care about the quality of the secular education available to their children. They have considered high-quality education to be an indispensable ingredient for achieving the kind of nation, and the kind of citizenry, that they have desired to create. Considering this attitude, the continued willingness to rely on private school systems, including parochial systems, strongly suggests that a wide segment of informed opinion, legislative and otherwise, has found that those schools do an acceptable job of providing secular education to their students. This judgment is further evidence that parochial schools are performing, in addition to their sectarian function, the task of secular education.

Against this background of judgment and experience, unchallenged in the meager record before us in this case, we cannot agree with appellants either that all teaching in a sectarian school is religious or that the processes of secular and religious training are so intertwined that secular textbooks furnished to students by the public are in fact instrumental in the teaching of religion. This case comes to us after summary judgment entered on the pleadings. Nothing in this record supports the proposition that all textbooks, whether they deal with mathematics, physics, foreign languages, history, or literature, are used by the parochial schools to teach religion. No evidence has been offered about particular schools, particular courses, particular teachers, or particular books. We are unable to hold, based solely on judicial notice, that this statute results in unconstitutional involvement of the State with religious instruction or that §701, for this or the other reasons urged, is a law respecting the establishment of religion within the meaning of the First Amendment.

Lemon v. Kurtzman, 403 U.S. 602 (1971)

Having decided in *Allen* that textbooks could be loaned to parochial school children without violating the First Amendment's no-establishment of religion clause, in *Walz v. Tax Commission*[1] the Court was asked to rule on the question of tax exemption for church property. Speaking for the majority of eight (only Justice Douglas dissented), Chief Justice Burger interpreted the two religion clauses in the traditional manner, loosely and leniently. The Court therefore continued the established practice of granting tax exemptions to churches. Justice Douglas alone argued that tax exemptions were a form of direct subsidy to the churches, which violated the First Amendment. The Chief Justice noted, however, that the two religion clauses were intended "to insure that no religion be sponsored or favored, none commanded, and none inhibited."

Walz is also significant because the Burger Court announced new guidelines to govern the relationship between states and religion. States must be neutral and impartial, the Chief Justice said, they could *not* become "excessively entangled" with religion or the churches. That excessive entanglement, whatever its meaning or application, would violate the First Amendment was clearly the Court's intent.

The meaning and application of the *Walz* term "excessive entanglement" was quickly tested a year later in *Lemon v. Kurtzman*. This case involved somewhat similar aid to private schools programs in two states, Rhode Island and Pennsylvania. Rhode Island had adopted a program that paid salary supplements to teachers who taught secular subjects in parochial schools. Pennsylvania's program reimbursed the state's private (parochial) schools for teachers' salaries, textbooks, and other classroom materials that were used to teach secular subjects. In *Lemon,* the Supreme Court declared both statutes unconstitutional under the two freedom of religion clauses of the First Amendment. Once again Chief Justice Burger was the Court's spokesman. He found that "the cumulative impact of the entire relationship . . . involves excessive entanglement between government and religion." For this reason, the Court ruled the Rhode Island and Pennsylvania schemes invalid.

Mr. Chief Justice Burger delivered the opinion of the Court, saying in part:

> The language of the Religion Clauses of the First Amendment is at best opaque, particularly when compared with other portions of the Amendment. Its authors did not simply prohibit the establishment of a state church or a state religion, an area history shows they regarded as very important and fraught with great dangers. Instead they commanded that there should be "no law *respecting* an establishment of religion." A law may be one "respecting" the forbidden objective while falling short of its total realization. A law "respecting" the proscribed result, that is, the establishment of religion, is not always easily identifiable as one violative of the Clause. A given law might not *establish* a state religion but nevertheless be one "respecting" that end in the sense of being a step that could lead to such establishment and hence offend the First Amendment.
>
> In the absence of precisely stated constitutional prohibitions, we must draw lines with reference to the three main evils against which the Establishment Clause was intended to afford protection: "sponsorship, financial support, and active involvement of the sovereign in religious activity." *Walz v. Tax Commission,* 397 U.S. 664, 668 (1970).

1. 397 U.S. 664 (1970).

Every analysis in this area must begin with consideration of the cumulative criteria developed by the Court over many years. Three such tests may be gleaned from our cases. First, the statute must have a secular legislative purpose; second, its principal or primary effect must be one that neither advances nor inhibits religion, *Board of Education* v. *Allen,* 392 U.S. 236, 243 (1968); finally, the statute must not foster "an excessive government entanglement with religion." *Walz, supra,* at 674.

Inquiry into the legislative purposes of the Pennsylvania and Rhode Island statutes affords no basis for a conclusion that the legislative intent was to advance religion. On the contrary, the statutes themselves clearly state that they are intended to enhance the quality of the secular education in all schools covered by the compulsory attendance laws. There is no reason to believe the legislatures meant anything else. A State always has a legitimate concern for maintaining minimum standards in all schools it allows to operate. As in *Allen,* we find nothing here that undermines the stated legislative intent; it must therefore be accorded appropriate deference.

In *Allen* the Court acknowledged that secular and religious teachings were not necessarily so intertwined that secular textbooks furnished to students by the State were in fact instrumental in the teaching of religion. 392 U.S., at 248. The legislatures of Rhode Island and Pennsylvania have concluded that secular and religious education are identifiable and separable. In the abstract we have no quarrel with this conclusion.

The two legislatures, however, have also recognized that church-related elementary and secondary schools have a significant religious mission and that a substantial portion of their activities is religiously oriented. They have therefore sought to create statutory restrictions designed to guarantee the separation between secular and religious educational functions and to ensure that State financial aid supports only the former. All these provisions are precautions taken in candid recognition that these programs approached, even if they did not intrude upon, the forbidden areas under the Religion Clauses. We need not decide whether these legislative precautions restrict the principal or primary effect of the programs to the point where they do not offend the Religion Clauses, for we conclude that the cumulative impact of the entire relationship arising under the statutes in each State involves excessive entanglement between government and religion.

In *Walz* v. *Tax Commission, supra,* the Court upheld state tax exemptions for real property owned by religious organizations and used for religious worship. That holding, however, tended to confine rather than enlarge the area of permissible state involvement with religious institutions by calling for close scrutiny of the degree of entanglement involved in the relationship. The objective is to prevent, as far as possible, the intrusion of either into the precincts of the other.

Our prior holdings do not call for total separation between church and state; total separation is not possible in an absolute sense. Some relationship between government and religious organizations is inevitable. *Zorach* v. *Clauson,* 343 U.S. 306, 312 (1952); *Sherbert* v. *Verner,* 374 U.S. 398, 422 (1963) (HARLAN, J., dissenting). Fire inspections, building and zoning regulations, and state requirements under compulsory school-attendance laws are examples of necessary and permissible contacts. Indeed, under the statutory exemption before us in *Walz,* the State had a continuing burden to ascertain that the exempt property was in fact being used for religious worship. Judicial caveats against entanglement must recognize that the line of separation, far from being a "wall," is a blurred, indistinct, and variable barrier depending on all the circumstances of a particular relationship.

This is not to suggest, however, that we are to engage in a legalistic minuet in which precise rules and forms must govern. A true minuet is a matter of pure form and style, the observance of which is itself the substantive end. Here we examine the form of the relationship for the light that it casts on the substance.

In order to determine whether the government entanglement with religion is excessive, we must examine the character and purposes of the institutions that are benefited, the nature of the aid that the State provides, and the resulting relationship between the government and the religious authority. MR. JUSTICE HARLAN, in a separate opinion in *Walz, supra,* echoed the classic warning as to "programs, whose very nature is apt to entangle the state in details of administration. ..." *Id.,* at 695. Here we find that both statutes foster an impermissible degree of entanglement.

Tilton v. Richardson, 403 U.S. 672 (1971)

On the same day the Supreme Court handed down its *Lemon* ruling, striking down attempts by two states to grant aid to parochial schools. It also decided that federal construction grants for private church-related colleges and universities were permissible under the constitution. The case was *Tilton* v. *Richardson,* and it involved the Higher Education Facilities Act that Congress had passed in 1963 providing construction grants for the nation's colleges and universities.

Speaking for a badly split (5–4) Court, Chief Justice Burger said that the purpose of the 1963 law was to aid education, not religion. Accordingly, the majority ruled that because the Court could and did separate the secular from the religious activities of the church-related schools, federal construction grants for "secular buildings" passed the constitutional test under the First Amendment.

Justice Douglas joined by Justices Black and Marshall dissented and Justice Brennan filed another dissenting opinion. Justice White wrote a concurring opinion, thus making the majority of five (with Chief Justice Burger and Justices Harlan, Stewart, and Blackmun) arguing that because the essential purpose of the federal aid was secular in nature, the fact that some of the recipients were church-related schools did not make the aid or the Act unconstitutional. In his dissent, Justice Douglas agreed with only one aspect of the Court's ruling. The majority had found, and Douglas agreed, that one portion of the 1963 Act, which allowed the buildings built under the federal grants to revert after twenty years to ownership by the church-related universities, was plainly an unconstitutional gift of taxpayer funds. But for Douglas the Court's ruling had other infirmities. He was not impressed with the majority's decision that what Douglas called "small violations" of the First Amendment over a period of years are unconstitutional (*Lemon*), "while a huge violation (a federal construction grant) occurring only once is de minimis. I cannot agree with such sophistry." Justice Douglas also took issue with the Chief Justice's contention that surveillance to ensure compliance with the secular nature of the grants would not pose serious problems. "If surveillance is not searching and continuous," Douglas wrote, "this federal financing is obnoxious" under the establishment clause of the First Amendment. For Douglas, surveillance created "an (excessive) entanglement of government and religion which the First Amendment was designed to avoid." He cited *Lemon* to support his position.

The majority distinguished *Tilton* from *Lemon* v. *Kurtzman* on grounds that in *Lemon* state aid was given to church-related primary and secondary schools dealing with "impressionable children." In *Tilton,* the majority said, there was "less danger . . . that religion will permeate the area of secular education since religious indoctrination is not a substantial purpose or activity of these church-related colleges." For this reason the Court concluded that the Higher Education Facilities Act of 1963 was constitutional because it had "neither the purpose nor the effect of promoting religion."

Mr. Chief Justice Burger announced the judgment of the Court, saying in part:

> We . . . turn to the question of whether excessive entanglements characterize the relationship between government and church under the Act. *Walz* v. *Tax Comm'n, supra,* at 674–676. Our decision today in *Lemon* v. *Kurtzman* and *Robinson* v. *DiCenso* has discussed and applied this independent measure of constitutionality under the Religion Clauses. There we concluded that excessive entanglements between government and religion were fostered by Pennsylvania and · Rhode Island statutory programs under which state aid was provided to parochial elementary and secondary schools. Here, however, three factors substantially diminish the extent and the potential danger of the entanglement.
>
> In *DiCenso* the District Court found that the parochial schools in Rhode Island were "an integral part of the religious mission of the Catholic Church." There, the record fully supported the conclusion that the inculcation of religious values was a substantial if not the dominant purpose of the institutions. The Pennsylvania case was decided on the pleadings, and hence we accepted as true the allegations that the parochial schools in that State shared the same characteristics.
>
> Appellants' complaint here contains similar allegations. But they were denied by the answers, and there was extensive evidence introduced on the subject. Although the District Court made no findings with respect to the religious character of the four institutions of higher learning, we are not required to accept the allegations as true under these circumstances, particularly where, as here, appellants themselves do not contend that these four institutions are "sectarian."
>
> There are generally significant differences between the religious aspects of church-related institutions of higher learning and parochial elementary and secondary schools. The "affirmative if not dominant policy" of the instruction in pre-college church schools is "to assure future adherents to a particular faith by having control of their total education at an early age." *Walz* v. *Tax Comm'n, supra,* at 671. There is substance to the contention that college students are less impressionable and less susceptible to religious indoctrination. Common observation would seem to support that view, and Congress may well have entertained it. The skepticism of the college student is not an inconsiderable barrier to any attempt or tendency to subvert the congressional objectives and limitations. Furthermore, by their very nature, college and postgraduate courses tend to limit the opportunities for sectarian influence by virtue of their own internal disciplines. Many church-related colleges and universities are characterized by a high degree of academic freedom and seek to evoke free and critical responses from their students.
>
> The record here would not support a conclusion that any of these four institutions departed from this general pattern. All four schools are governed by Catholic religious organizations, and the faculties and student bodies at each are

predominantly Catholic. Nevertheless, the evidence shows that non-Catholics were admitted as students and given faculty appointments. Not one of these four institutions requires its students to attend religious services. Although all four schools require their students to take theology courses, the parties stipulated that these courses are taught according to the academic requirements of the subject matter and the teacher's concept of professional standards. The parties also stipulated that the courses covered a range of human religious experiences and are not limited to courses about the Roman Catholic religion. The schools introduced evidence that they made no attempt to indoctrinate students or to proselytize. Indeed, some of the required theology courses at Albertus Magnus and Sacred Heart are taught by rabbis. Finally, as we have noted, these four schools subscribe to a well-established set of principles of academic freedom, and nothing in this record shows that these principles are not in fact followed. In short, the evidence shows institutions with admittedly religious functions but whose predominant higher education mission is to provide their students with a secular education.

Since religious indoctrination is not a substantial purpose or activity of these church-related colleges and universities, there is less likelihood than in primary and secondary schools that religion will permeate the area of secular education. This reduces the risk that government aid will in fact serve to support religious activities. Correspondingly, the necessity for intensive government surveillance is diminished and the resulting entanglements between government and religion lessened. Such inspection as may be necessary to ascertain that the facilities are devoted to secular education is minimal and indeed hardly more than the inspections that States impose over all private schools within the reach of compulsory education laws.

The entanglement between church and state is also lessened here by the nonideological character of the aid that the Government provides. Our cases from *Everson* to *Allen* have permitted church-related schools to receive government aid in the form of secular, neutral, or nonideological services, facilities, or materials that are supplied to all students regardless of the affiliation of the school that they attend. In *Lemon* and *DiCenso*, however, the state programs subsidized teachers, either directly or indirectly. Since teachers are not necessarily religiously neutral, greater governmental surveillance would be required to guarantee that state salary aid would not in fact subsidize religious instruction. There we found the resulting entanglement excessive. Here, on the other hand, the Government provides facilities that are themselves religiously neutral. The risks of Government aid to religion and the corresponding need for surveillance are therefore reduced.

Finally, government entanglements with religion are reduced by the circumstance that, unlike the direct and continuing payments under the Pennsylvania program, and all the incidents of regulation and surveillance, the Government aid here is a one-time, single-purpose construction grant. There are no continuing financial relationships or dependencies, no annual audits, and no government analysis of an institution's expenditures on secular as distinguished from religious activities. Inspection as to use is a minimal contact.

No one of these three factors standing alone is necessarily controlling; cumulatively all of them shape a narrow and limited relationship with government which involves fewer and less significant contacts than the two state schemes before us in *Lemon* and *DiCenso*. The relationship therefore has less potential for realizing the substantive evils against which the Religion Clauses were intended to protect.

We think that cumulatively these three factors also substantially lessen the potential for divisive religious fragmentation in the political arena. This conclusion is admittedly difficult to document, but neither have appellants pointed to any continuing religious aggravation on this matter in the political processes. Possibly this can be explained by the character and diversity of the recipient colleges and universities and the absence of any intimate continuing relationship or dependency between government and religiously affiliated institutions. The potential for divisiveness inherent in the essentially local problems of primary and secondary schools is significantly less with respect to a college or university whose student constituency is not local but diverse and widely dispersed.

Meek v. Pittenger, 421 U.S. 349 (1975)

Shortly after *Tilton*, two similar cases came before the Court; one involved *state*-funded (as opposed to federally funded) building construction grants to private church-related colleges (*Hunt* v. *McNair*)[1] and the second involved an annual financial grant program to church-related colleges (*Roemer* v. *Board of Public Works of Maryland*)[2]. Using the *Tilton* precedent that such aid at the college and university level did not violate the no-establishment clause of the First Amendment, the Court upheld both state programs. In *Hunt* the Court ruled in favor of a South Carolina construction grant program and in *Roemer* it approved, albeit narrowly (5–4) a Maryland program of annual financial grants to private church-related colleges.

Similarly, the Supreme Court had several opportunities to restate and re-enforce its 1971 "excessive entanglement" ruling. In both, the *Lemon* precedent was sustained.

In *Committee for Public Education and Religious Liberty* v. *Nyquest*[3], for example, the Court struck down three aid plans that the New York state legislature had devised to assist private elementary and secondary schools; direct money grants for building maintenance and repair, tuition reimbursements for parents whose children attended private schools, and tax relief for parents who did not qualify for reimbursements. The Court ruled against all three New York aid programs because, as Justice Powell noted, they clearly had the "impermissible effect of advancing religion," and thus "entangled" church and state in violation of *Lemon* and the First Amendment's no-establishment clause.

In *Sloan* v. *Lemon*[4] the Supreme Court invalidated a Pennsylvania plan to reimburse parents of private school children, once again because it "advanced religion." During the same year the Court struck down still another New York plan to reimburse private schools for the costs involved in administering examinations and maintaining school records. The case was *Levitt* v. *Committee for Public Education and Religious Liberty*.[5] Chief Justice Burger wrote for the Court that such state services provided for private schools were constitution-ally different from the permissible bus rides (*Everson*) and state-loaned textbooks *(Allen)*.

Then two years later the Supreme Court was confronted with yet another ingenious Pennsylvania effort to channel state aid to private schools. The case

1. 413 U.S. 734 (1973).   4. 413 U.S. 825 (1973).
2. 96 S. Ct. 2337 (1976).   5. 413 U.S. 472 (1973).
3. 413 U.S. 756 (1973).

was *Meek* v. *Pittenger* and involved a state proposal to finance such auxiliary services as counseling, testing, speech, and hearing therapy for children in private schools as well as lending equipment, other materials, and textbooks to the schools. The Court approved only the textbook loan aspect of Pennsylvania's aid packages and declared the other parts unconstitutional as violating the no-establishment clause. In *Meek* the Court was badly divided. Justice Stewart wrote for the Court and was joined by Justices Douglas, Brennan, and Marshall in all but that part of the Court's judgment that upheld the textbook loan program. In addition and to further complicate matters, three separate dissenting opinions were filed. Justice Rehnquist (joined by Justice White) noted that he was "disturbed" by the Court's ruling against the Pennsylvania aid package. He was convinced, as Stewart was earlier in *Engel,* that the Court was misapplying the no-establishment clause and thereby "throw[ing] its weight on the side of those who believe that our society should be a purely secular one . . ." Chief Justice Burger dissented, arguing that he could not accept "the Court's extravagant suggestion of potential entanglement" that it found in Pennsylvania's program of auxiliary services to private schools. In the Chief Justice's view the entanglement was not "excessive," as it had been in *Lemon.* Justice Brennan, joined by Justices Douglas and Marshall, also wrote a separate opinion, dissenting in part and concurring in part with the Court's judgment. Brennan's dissent focused upon the textbook loan part of Pennsylvania's program. He and his colleagues thought it to be unconstitutional along with the other auxiliary services the Court had invalidated.

Rehnquist's dissent contained the following paragraph quoted from Justice White's dissenting opinion in *Nyquist.* It is reproduced here because it sums up succinctly the opposition viewpoint to what seems clear has been the Court's general position in cases dealing with state financial aid packages, of one sort or another (apart from textbooks), to private schools.

> Positing an obligation on the State to educate its children, which every State acknowledges, it should be wholly acceptable for the States to contribute to the secular education of children going to sectarian schools rather than to insist that if parents want to provide their children with religious as well as secular education, the state will refuse to contribute anything to their secular training.

In *Meek* the Court invalidated all but the textbook loan part of the Pennsylvania program, ruling that, as in *Allen,* the state was "merely mak[ing] available to all children the benefits of a general aid program to lend school books free of charge . . ." However, the other aspects of the Pennsylvania package did not meet with the Supreme Court's approval.

Mr. Justice Stewart delivered the opinion of the badly fragmented Court, saying in part:

> It is, of course, true that as part of general legislation made available to all students, a State may include church-related schools in programs providing bus transportation, school lunches, and public health facilities — secular and nonideological services unrelated to the primary, religious-oriented educational function of the sectarian school. The indirect and incidental benefits to church-related schools from those programs do not offend the constitutional prohibition against establishment of religion. . . . But the massive aid provided the church-

related nonpublic schools of Pennsylvania by Act 195 is neither indirect nor incidental.

For the 1972–1973 school year the Commonwealth authorized just under $12 million of direct aid to the predominantly church-related nonpublic schools of Pennsylvania through the loan of instructional material and equipment pursuant to Act 195. To be sure, the material and equipment that are the subjects of the loan — maps, charts, and laboratory equipment, for example — are "self-polic[ing], in that starting as secular, nonideological and neutral, they will not change in use." 374 F. Supp. 639, 660. But faced with the substantial amounts of direct support authorized by Act 195, it would simply ignore reality to attempt to separate secular educational functions from the predominantly religious role performed by many of Pennsylvania's church-related elementary and secondary schools and to then characterize Act 195 as channeling aid to the secular without providing direct aid to the sectarian. Even though earmarked for secular purposes, "when it flows to an institution in which religion is so pervasive that a substantial portion of its functions are subsumed in the religious mission," state aid has the impermissible primary effect of advancing religion.

The church-related elementary and secondary schools that are the primary beneficiaries of Act 195's instructional material and equipment loans typify such religion-pervasive institutions. The very purpose of many of those schools is to provide an integrated secular and religious education; the teaching process is, to a large extent, devoted to the inculcation of religious values and belief. . . . Substantial aid to the educational function of such schools, accordingly, necessarily results in aid to the sectarian school enterprise as a whole. "[T]he secular education those schools provide goes hand in hand with the religious mission that is the only reason for the schools' existence. Within the institution, the two are inextricably intertwined." . . .

. . . For this reason, Act 195's direct aid to Pennsylvania's predominantly church-related, nonpublic elementary and secondary schools, even though ostensibly limited to wholly neutral, secular instructional material and equipment, inescapably results in the direct and substantial advancement of religious activity, . . . and thus constitutes an impermissible establishment of religion.

5

CENSORSHIP (OBSCENITY)

Obscenity, what it is, and what it is *not,* along with the permissible legal restraints on the obscene, have a long, checkered history both in England and the United States. In England, first attempts to define obscenity date back to the 1868 case, *Regina* v. *Hicklin.*[1] There Justice Cockburn wrote the following definition, since known as the "effects" test or the *Hicklin* rule. "I think the test of obscenity is this," Judge Cockburn said, "whether the tendency of the matter charged as obscenity is to deprave and corrupt those whose minds are open to such immoral influences, and into whose hands a publication of this sort may fall."[2]

In the United States the long prevailing puritanical attitude on matters concerning sexual mores greatly influenced early attempts by Congress, State legislatures, and the Courts to define the obscene. At least two key questions need to be asked concerning obscenity and its various early brushes with the law. Why did Congress and the State legislatures enact laws against obscenity during the late years of the nineteenth century? And why did the Courts for so long uphold the constitutionality of this obscenity legislation? Pritchett provides reasonable answers. "First," he says, "obscenity has long been regarded as bad in and of itself. It is indecent. It is a violation of good moral standards. It appeals to 'prurient interest' and stimulates impure sexual thoughts." He goes on to note that obscenity "arouses feelings of disgust and revulsion . . . it induces unhealthy psychological excitement." As to why American courts consistently ruled on behalf of early obscenity laws, Pritchett has this comment: ". . . obscenity (was) regarded as criminally punishable because of its evil effects on individuals and society . . . it leads to immoral or anti-social conduct. It [results] in the advocacy of improper sexual values."[3]

Whatever shortcomings the *Hicklin* rule and the definition of obscenity it, and the American experience, may have had, and perhaps Judge Learned Hand's opinion in the 1913 Kennerly decision forms the most eloquent critique of them,[4] the *Hicklin* rule prevailed in American jurisprudence until 1934. Then in the famous *Ulysses* (book) case Judge Augustus Hand of the Circuit Court specifically rejected Justice Cockburn's standard and replaced it

1. Law Reports, 3 Queen's Bench 360 (1868).

2. As quoted in Pritchett, op. cit., at 352.

3. Ibid.

4. As quoted by Pritchett, Judge Hand wrote, ". . . I question whether in the end man will regard that as obscene which is honestly relevant to the adequate expression of innocent ideas, and whether they will not believe that truth and beauty are too precious to society at large to be mutilated in the interests of those most likely to pervert them to base uses."

with a more enlightened one of his own. In *United States* v. *One Book Entitled "Ulysses"*[5] Hand said that the "proper test" of an obscene book is its "dominant effect." Applying this test ". . . the established reputation of the work in the estimation of approved critics . . . [is] persuasive . . . evidence, for works of art are not likely to sustain a high position with no better warrant for their existence than their obscene content." Despite the flowery eloquence of both Judge Learned Hand and Judge Augustus Hand, which doubtless was a vast improvement over *Hicklin*'s more provincial, restrictive view of obscenity, the constitutional test for obscenity remained illusive and vague. In 1957 the Supreme Court finally undertook the task of clearing up this matter or at least attempting to do so in *Roth* v. *United States* and its companion case *Alberts* v. *California*. *Roth* dealt with federal obscenity laws and *Alberts* with state obscenity laws.

Roth v. United States, 354 U.S. 476 (1957)

In *Roth* the Supreme Court upheld the validity of federal obscenity laws by deciding very simply that obscenity is not within the area of constitutionally protected freedom of speech. Similarly, *Alberts* upheld state obscenity laws.

Roth had been convicted of violating Federal postal laws by mailing an obscene book, circulars, and advertising. The Supreme Court sustained the conviction. Speaking for the majority of six (Justice Harlan wrote a dissent as did Justice Douglas joined by Justice Black), Justice Brennan took pains to note that "sexual matters and obscenity are not synonymous terms." Obscenity deals with sexual matters in a way appealing to "prurient interest," and has a tendency "to excite lustful thoughts." In his dissent, Justice Douglas argued that the majority had made legality of a publication depend upon "the purity of thought which a book . . . instills in the mind of the reader." Douglas doubted that this standard is "faithful to the command of the First Amendment." In his dissent, Justice Harlan found problems beneath the majority's "disarming generalizations" that left him with "serious misgivings" about the Court's decision. Because of the significance of the ruling we reproduce here portions of the majority opinion and portions of the Harlan and Douglas dissents.

Mr. Justice Brennan delivered the opinion of the Court, saying in part:

We hold that obscenity is not within the area of constitutionally protected speech or press.

It is strenuously urged that these obscenity statutes offend the constitutional guaranties because they punish incitation to impure sexual *thoughts,* not shown to be related to any overt antisocial conduct which is or may be incited in the persons stimulated to such *thoughts.* In *Roth,* the trial judge instructed the jury: "The words 'obscene, lewd and lascivious' as used in the law, signify that form of immorality which has relation to sexual impurity and has a tendency to excite lustful *thoughts.*" (Emphasis added.) In *Alberts,* the trial judge applied the test laid down in *People* v. *Wepplo,* 78 Cal. App. 2d Supp. 959, 178 P. 2d 853, namely, whether the material has "a substantial tendency to deprave or corrupt its readers by inciting lascivious *thoughts* or arousing lustful desires." (Emphasis

5. 72 F. 2d 705 (1934).

added.) It is insisted that the constitutional guaranties are violated because convictions may be had without proof either that obscene material will perceptibly create a clear and present danger of antisocial conduct, or will probably induce its recipients to such conduct. But, in light of our holding that obscenity is not protected speech, the complete answer to this argument is in the holding of this Court in *Beauharnais* v. *Illinois, supra,* at 266:

> "Libelous utterances not being within the area of constitutionally protected speech, it is unnecessary, either for us or for the State courts, to consider the issues behind the phrase 'clear and present danger.' Certainly no one would contend that obscene speech, for example, may be punished only upon a showing of such circumstances. Libel, as we have seen, is in the same class."

However, sex and obscenity are not synonymous. Obscene material is material which deals with sex in a manner appealing to a prurient interest. The portrayal of sex, *e.g.,* in art, literature and scientific works, is not itself sufficient reason to deny material the constitutional protection of freedom of speech and press. Sex, a great and mysterious motive force in human life, has indisputably been a subject of absorbing interest to mankind through the ages; it is one of the vital problems of human interest and public concern.

The early leading standard of obscenity allowed material to be judged merely by the effect of an isolated excerpt upon particularly susceptible persons. . . . Some American courts adopted this standard but later decisions have rejected it and substituted this test: whether to the average person, applying contemporary community standards, the dominant theme of the material taken as a whole appeals to prurient interest. The *Hicklin* test, judging obscenity by the effect of isolated passages upon the most susceptible persons, might well encompass material legitimately treating with sex, and so it must be rejected as unconstitutionally restrictive of the freedoms of speech and press. On the other hand, the substituted standard provides safeguards adequate to withstand the charge of constitutional infirmity.

. . . In summary, then, we hold that these statutes, applied according to the proper standard for judging obscenity, do not offend constitutional safeguards against convictions based upon protected material, or fail to give men in acting adequate notice of what is prohibited.

Mr. Justice Harlan dissented, saying in part:

My basic difficulties with the Court's opinion are threefold. First, the opinion paints with such a broad brush that I fear it may result in a loosening of the tight reins which state and federal courts should hold upon the enforcement of obscenity statutes. Second, the Court fails to discriminate between the different factors which, in my opinion, are involved in the constitutional adjudication of state and federal obscenity cases. Third, relevant distinctions between the two obscenity statutes here involved, and the Court's own definition of "obscenity," are ignored.

In final analysis, the problem presented by these cases is how far, and on what terms, the state and federal governments have power to punish individuals for disseminating books considered to be undesirable because of their nature or supposed deleterious effect upon human conduct. Proceeding from the premise that "no issue is presented in either case, concerning the obscenity of the material involved," the Court finds the "dispositive question" to be "whether obscenity is utterance within the area of protected speech and press," and then holds that "obscenity" is not so protected because it is "utterly without redeeming social importance." This sweeping formula appears to me to beg the very question before us. The Court seems to assume that "obscenity" is a peculiar *genus* of "speech and press," which is as distinct, recognizable, and classifiable as poison ivy is among other plants. On this basis the *constitutional* question before us simply becomes, as the Court says, whether "obscenity," as an abstraction, is protected by the First and Fourteenth Amendments, and the question whether a *particular* book may be suppressed becomes a mere matter of classification, of "fact," to be entrusted to a factfinder and insulated from independent constitutional judgment. But surely the problem cannot be solved in such a generalized fashion. Every communication has an individuality and "value" of its own. The suppression of a particular writing or other tangible form of expression is, therefore, an *individual* matter, and in the nature of things every such suppression raises an individual constitutional problem, in which a reviewing court must determine for *itself* whether the attacked expression is suppressable within constitutional standards. Since those standards do not readily lend themselves to generalized definitions, the constitutional problem in the last analysis becomes one of particularized judgments which appellate courts must make for themselves.

I do not think that reviewing courts can escape this responsibility by saying that the trier of the facts, be it a jury or a judge, has labeled the questioned matter as "obscene," for, if "obscenity" is to be suppressed, the question whether a particular work is of that character involves not really an issue of fact but a question of constitutional *judgment* of the most sensitive and delicate kind. Many juries might find that Joyce's "Ulysses" or Boccaccio's "Decameron" was obscene, and yet the conviction of a defendant for selling either book would raise, for me, the gravest constitutional problems, for no such verdict could convince me, without more, that these books are "utterly without redeeming social importance." In short, I do not understand how the Court can resolve the constitutional problems now before it without making its own independent judgment upon the character of the material upon which these convictions were based. I am very much afraid that the broad manner in which the Court has decided these cases will tend to obscure the peculiar responsibilities resting on state and federal courts in this field and encourage them to rely on easy labeling and jury verdicts as a substitute for facing up to the tough individual problems of constitutional judgment involved in every obscenity case.

Mr. Justice Douglas dissented, saying in part:

Any test that turns on what is offensive to the community's standards is too loose, too capricious, too destructive of freedom of expression to be squared with the First Amendment. Under that test, juries can censor, suppress, and punish what they don't like, provided the matter relates to "sexual impurity" or has a tendency "to excite lustful thoughts." This is community censorship in one of its worst forms. It creates a regime where in the battle between the literati and the Philistines, the Philistines are certain to win. If experience in this field teaches anything, it is that "censorship of obscenity has almost always been both irrational and indiscriminate." . . . The test adopted here accentuates that trend.

Kingsley Books v. Brown, 354 U.S. 436 (1957)

Within a short time after *Roth* had upheld the constitutionality of obscenity laws by insisting that obscenity was not protected by the First Amendment, the Supreme Court had other opportunities to rule on similar pornography and obscenity cases. That the Court continued to have difficulty defining terms, and problems in its attempt to reconcile changing and differing attitudes about sexual mores with the allowable limits of constitutional freedoms, is painfully apparent in these rulings.

Kingsley Books v. *Brown* is a case in point. A slim majority of five, led by Justice Frankfurter, ruled that because booklets and pamphlets displayed for sale by the appellants "were clearly obscene," the State of New York under Section 22 of its criminal code did not violate freedom of the press and speech when it ordered them destroyed. The Court's decision brought forth three separate dissenting opinions, by Chief Justice Warren, Justice Douglas joined by Justice Black, and Justice Brennan. All three dissents found serious constitutional infirmities with the New York law that the majority upheld. For the Chief Justice, in the absence of prior judicial determination, books and "other objects of expression [simply] should not be destroyed." "It savors too much of book burning," Warren said. Justice Douglas objected on similar grounds. Nothing is more devastating to First Amendment guarantees, Douglas argued, "than the power to restrain publication before even a hearing is held. This is prior restraint and censorship at its worst." To Justice Brennan the "fatal defect" in the New York obscenity statute was the absence of the right to a jury trial. Jury trials in obscenity cases, Brennan said, "provide a peculiarly competent application of the standard for judging obscenity which, by its definition, calls for an appraisal of material according to the average person's application of contemporary community standards." Brennan's short dissent did not attempt to define "average person" or "contemporary community standards." But difficult, if not impossible to define as these terms may be, they nevertheless are the core of the problem the Court must grapple with in obscenity or pornography cases.

In upholding the New York statute as a proper mechanism for dealing with obscenity, the Supreme Court concluded the state had acted within its powers to safeguard the public interest "in effectuating judicial condemnation of obscene matter."

Mr. Justice Frankfurter delivered the opinion of the Court, saying in part:

New York enacted this procedure on the basis of study by a joint legislative committee. Resort to this injunctive remedy, it is claimed, is beyond the constitutional power of New York in that it amounts to a prior censorship of literary product and as such is violative of that "freedom of thought, and speech" which has been "withdrawn by the Fourteenth Amendment from encroachment by the states."

In an unbroken series of cases extending over a long stretch of this Court's history, it has been accepted as a postulate that "the primary requirements of decency may be enforced against obscene publications." . . . And so our starting point is that New York can constitutionally convict appellants of keeping for sale the booklets incontestably found to be obscene. . . . The immediate problem then is whether New York can adopt as an auxiliary means of dealing with such obscene merchandising the procedure of §22–a.

We need not linger over the suggestion that something can be drawn out of the Due Process Clause of the Fourteenth Amendment that restricts New York to the criminal process in seeking to protect its people against the dissemination of pornography. It is not for this Court thus to limit the State in resorting to various weapons in the armory of the law. Whether proscribed conduct is to be visited by a criminal prosecution or by a *qui tam* action or by an injunction or by some or all of these remedies in combination, is a matter within the legislature's range of choice. . . . If New York chooses to subject persons who disseminate obscene "literature" to criminal prosecution and also to deal with such books as deodands of old, or both, with due regard, of course, to appropriate opportunities for the trial of the underlying issue, it is not for us to gainsay its selection of remedies. Just as *Near* v. *Minnesota, supra,* one of the landmark opinions in shaping the constitutional protection of freedom of speech and of the press, left no doubts that "Liberty of speech, and of the press, is also not an absolute right," . . . it likewise made clear that "the protection even as to previous restraint is not absolutely unlimited." *Id.,* at 716. To be sure, the limitation is the exception; it is to be closely confined so as to preclude what may fairly be deemed licensing or censorship.

The method devised by New York in §22–a for determining whether a publication is obscene does not differ in essential procedural safeguards from that provided under many state statutes making the distribution of obscene publications a misdemeanor. For example, while the New York criminal provision brings the State's criminal procedure into operation, a defendant is not thereby entitled to a jury trial. In each case a judge is the conventional trier of fact; in each, a jury may as a matter of discretion be summoned. . . . (Appellants, as a matter of fact, did not request a jury trial, they did not attack the statute in the courts below for failure to require a jury, and they did not bring that issue to this Court.) Of course, the Due Process Clause does not subject the States to the necessity of having trial by jury in misdemeanor prosecutions. . . .

It only remains to say that the difference between *Near* v. *Minnesota, supra,* and this case is glaring in fact. The two cases are no less glaringly different when judged by the appropriate criteria of constitutional law. Minnesota empowered its courts to enjoin the dissemination of future issues of a publication because its past issues had been found offensive. In the language of Mr. Chief Justice Hughes, "This is of the essence of censorship." . . . As such, it was found unconstitutional. This was enough to condemn the statute wholly apart from the fact that the proceeding in *Near* involved not obscenity but matters deemed to be derogatory to a public officer. Unlike *Near,* §22–a is concerned solely with obscenity and, as authoritatively construed, it studiously withholds restraint upon matters not already published and not yet found to be offensive.

A Book Named "John Cleland's Memoirs of a Woman of Pleasure" v. Attorney General of Massachusetts, 383 U.S. 413 (1966)

Two famous and controversial cases dealing with obscenity and pornography were decided by the Supreme Court on the same day, March 31, 1966. One dealt with Ralph Ginzburg and his magazine *Eros,* the other with *John Cleland's Memoirs of a Woman of Pleasure,* a book popularly called *Fanny Hill.* In *Ginzburg* v. *United States*[1] a slim majority of five, led by Justice Brennan, af-

1. 383 U.S. 463 (1966).

firmed Ginzburg's conviction under the Federal obscenity statute. The Court agreed that Ginzburg was guilty of pandering, of purveying publications openly advertised to appeal to prurient and erotic interest. The Court found that Ginzburg had even sought mailing privileges from "places with salaciously suggestive names;" Intercourse, Pennsylvania and Middlesex, New Jersey. Justice Brennan concluded that Ginzburg had exploited his erotica for the sake of its prurient appeal. The Court ruled that his conviction for mailing obscene material should stand under the standards set forth in the *Roth* case.

In *A Book Named "John Cleland's Memoirs of a Woman of Pleasure"* v. *Attorney General of Massachusetts* the Supreme Court reversed a judgment of a Massachusetts Court that had found *Fanny Hill* obscene and therefore not entitled to First and Fourteenth Amendment protection. In a 6–3 ruling, with Justice Brennan again writing for the majority (Justices Clark, Harlan, and White wrote separate dissents), the Supreme Court once again attempted to clarify its definition of the obscene. Brennan, who did the Court's yeoman work in this field, now summarized the three elements that, he argued, must independently be satisfied before a book can be held obscene: (a) the dominant theme of the material taken as a whole appeals to prurient interest in sex; (b) the material is patently offensive because it affronts contemporary community standards relating to the description of representation of sexual matters; and (c) the material is utterly without redeeming social value. Making up the majority were Justice Brennan joined by Chief Justice Warren and Justice Fortas. Justice Douglas wrote a separate concurring opinion and Justices Black and Stewart also concurred for the reasons they expressed in their respective dissents in *Ginzburg*.

In a footnote to the Court's opinion, Justice Brennan quoted what he termed the expert judgment of four professors of literature at four Massachusetts universities. They characterized *Fanny Hill* as a "minor 'work of art' having 'literary merit' and 'historical value' and containing a good deal of 'deliberate calculated comedy'. It is a piece of 'social history of interest to anyone who is interested in fiction as a way of understanding society in the past'." It was this testimony that apparently helped convince the majority that *Fanny Hill* had some socially redeeming value and was, therefore, not obscene.

Mr. Justice Brennan announced the judgment of the Court, saying in part:

> We defined obscenity in *Roth* in the following terms: "[W]hether to the average person, applying contemporary community standards, the dominant theme of the material taken as a whole appeals to prurient interest." 354 U.S., at 489. Under this definition, as elaborated in subsequent cases, three elements must coalesce: it must be established that (a) the dominant theme of the material taken as a whole appeals to a prurient interest in sex; (b) the material is patently offensive because it affronts contemporary community standards relating to the description or representation of sexual matters; and (c) the material is utterly without redeeming social value.
>
> The Supreme Judicial Court erred in holding that a book need not be "unqualifiedly worthless before it can be deemed obscene." A book cannot be proscribed unless it is found to be *utterly* without redeeming social value. This is so even though the book is found to possess the requisite prurient appeal and to be patently offensive. Each of the three federal constitutional criteria is to be applied independently; the social value of the book can neither be weighed against nor canceled by its prurient appeal or patent offensiveness. Hence, even

on the view of the court below that *Memoirs* possessed only a modicum of social value, its judgment must be reversed as being founded on an erroneous interpretation of a federal constitutional standard.

Miller v. California, 413 U.S. 15 (1973)

Is possession of obscene or pornographic material in the privacy of one's home constitutionally protected? A unanimous Court ruled, in *Stanley* v. *Georgia*[1], that it was. But two years later in *United States* v. *Reidel*[2] the Supreme Court ruled that, despite *Stanley,* pornography destined for private ownership *could* be barred from the mails. Then in the same year a 6–3 decision (Justices Black, Douglas, and Marshall in dissent), *United States* v. *Thirty Seven Photographs,*[3] upheld the seizure by custom officials of obscene photographs taken from the luggage of a traveller returning from abroad. Thus, the Supreme Court seemed to be saying in these three cases, that private possession of obscene materials could *not* be enjoined but attempts to use the mails (and luggage) to gain possession of such materials was *not* constitutionally privileged.

These three decisions further muddied the waters. Then in 1973 the Burger Court considered two other significant obscenity cases. In both the Chief Justice attempted once again to redefine in "more concrete" fashion the constitutional meaning of obscenity and pornography, a matter that had plagued and confused the Court and the public since the *Roth* decision some sixteen years earlier. In so doing Chief Justice Burger signalled that the Court (albeit by a narrow majority of five) had abandoned the "redeeming social value" standard set forth by Justice Brennan in *Roth* and other cases, and had substituted still another clarification, "whether the work, taken as a whole, lacks serious literary, artistic, political, or scientific value."

In *Paris Adult Theatre I* v. *Slaton*[4] the Court decided 5–4 (Justice Douglas wrote a dissent, and Justice Brennan joined by Justices Stewart and Marshall wrote another) that "adult theaters" showing obscene or pornographic films were *not* protected by the First Amendment. But it was in *Miller* v. *California,* decided on the same day, where the Chief Justice attempted to clarify and redefine the Supreme Court's obscenity position.

In *Miller,* the appellant was convicted of violating a California statute by mailing "unsolicited sexually explicit material." The California law had been written to comply with the Supreme Court's 1966 *Fanny Hill* ruling. A trial court judge had instructed a jury to evaluate the material by "contemporary [California] community standards." A badly split (5–4) Supreme Court upheld Miller's conviction.

Brennan's dissent reaffirmed the opposition he had expressed in *Paris Adult Theatre.* He opposed the Court's ruling for upholding a statute that was "unconstitutionally overboard and therefore invalid on its face." Brennan, the author of most of the Court's obscenity rulings now, dramatically changed his mind, arguing that, however they try, no single formula enunciated by the Supreme Court, the Congress, or the state legislatures can adequately distin-

1. 394 U.S. 557 (1969).   3. 402 U.S. 363 (1971).
2. 402 U.S. 351 (1971).   4. 413 U.S. 49 (1973).

guish "unprotected obscenity" from expression protected by the First Amendment. And why, Brennan asked, should the First Amendment protect only those expressions that had "serious literary or political value," as the majority position reasoned in *Miller?* Who decides what is "serious" or what has "literary or political value?"

Justice Douglas' dissenting opinion expressed again his long-standing views opposing all forms of censorship. He concluded with the following characteristically liberal words:

> "We deal with highly emotional, not rational questions. To many the Song of Solomon is obscene. I do not think we, the judges, were given the constitutional power to make definitions of obscenity. If it is to be defined let the people debate and decide by a constitutional amendment what they want to ban as obscene and what standards they want the legislatures and the Courts to apply. Perhaps the people will decide that the path towards a mature, integrated society requires that all ideas competing for acceptance must have no censor. Perhaps they will decide otherwise. Whatever the choice, the Courts will have some guidelines. Now we have none except our own predilections."

For his part, the Chief Justice reviewed the long history of Court obscenity decisions and tried mightily to bring them all together into an understandable and logical whole. If the fact that there were four dissenters, including Justice Brennan's "agonizing re-appraisal," is an indication of continuing judicial misgivings and ambivalence, and very likely it is, it would seem that as yet the Supreme Court has not come up with the "final" word on obscenity and pornography issues.

Mr. Chief Justice Burger delivered the opinion of the Court, saying in part:

> The dissent of MR. JUSTICE BRENNAN reviews the background of the obscenity problem, but since the Court now undertakes to formulate standards more concrete than those in the past, it is useful for us to focus on two of the landmark cases in the somewhat tortured history of the Court's obscenity decisions. In *Roth v. United States,* 354 U.S. 476 (1957), the Court sustained a conviction under a federal statute punishing the mailing of "obscene, lewd, lascivious or filthy . . ." materials. The key to that holding was the Court's rejection of the claim that obscene materials were protected by the First Amendment. Five Justices joined in the opinion stating:
>
> > "All ideas having even the slightest redeeming social importance — unorthodox ideas, controversial ideas, even ideas hateful to the prevailing climate of opinion — have the full protection of the [First Amendment] guaranties, unless excludable because they encroach upon the limited area of more important interests. But implicit in the history of the First Amendment is the rejection of obscenity as utterly without redeeming social importance. . . . This is the same judgment expressed by this Court in *Chaplinsky v. New Hampshire,* 315 U.S. 568, 571–572:
> >
> > > "'. . . There are certain well-defined and narrowly limited classes of speech, the prevention and punishment of which have never been thought to raise any Constitutional problem. *These include the lewd and obscene. . . . It has been well observed that such utterances are no essential part of any exposition of ideas, and are of such slight social value as a step to truth that any benefit that may be derived from them is clearly outweighed by the social interest in order and morality.'* . . . "We hold that obscenity is not within the area of constitutionally protected speech or press."

Nine years later, in *Memoirs v. Massachusetts,* 383 U.S. 413 (1966), the Court veered sharply away from the *Roth* concept and, with only three Justices in the plurality opinion, articulated a new test of obscenity. The plurality held that under the *Roth* definition

"as elaborated in subsequent cases, three elements must coalesce: it must be established that (a) the dominant theme of the material taken as a whole appeals to a prurient interest in sex; (b) the material is patently offensive because it affronts contemporary community standards relating to the description or representation of sexual matters; and (c) the material is utterly without redeeming social value." . . .

The sharpness of the break with *Roth,* represented by the third element of the *Memoirs* test and emphasized by MR. JUSTICE WHITE's dissent, *id.,* at 460–462, was further underscored when the *Memoirs* plurality went on to state:

"The Supreme Judicial Court erred in holding that a book need not be 'unqualifiedly worthless before it can be deemed obscene.' A book cannot be proscribed unless it is found to be *utterly* without redeeming social value." . . .

While *Roth* presumed "obscenity" to be "utterly without redeeming social importance," *Memoirs* required that to prove obscenity it must be affirmatively established that the material is *"utterly* without redeeming social value." Thus, even as they repeated the words of *Roth,* the *Memoirs* plurality produced a drastically altered test that called on the prosecution to prove a negative, *i.e.,* that the material was *"utterly* without redeeming social value"—a burden virtually impossible to discharge under our criminal standards of proof. Such considerations caused Mr. Justice Harlan to wonder if the *"utterly* without redeeming social value" test had any meaning at all.

Apart from the initial formulation in the *Roth* case, no majority of the Court has at any given time been able to agree on a standard to determine what constitutes obscene, pornographic material subject to regulation under the States' police power. . . . We have seen "a variety of views among the members of the Court unmatched in any other course of constitutional adjudication." . . . This is not remarkable, for in the area of freedom of speech and press the courts must always remain sensitive to any infringement on genuinely serious literary, artistic, political, or scientific expression. This is an area in which there are few eternal verities.

The case we now review was tried on the theory that the California Penal Code §311 approximately incorporates the three-stage *Memoirs* test, *supra.* But now the *Memoirs* test has been abandoned as unworkable by its author, and no Member of the Court today supports the *Memoirs* formulation.

This much has been categorically settled by the Court, that obscene material is unprotected by the First Amendment. . . . "The First and Fourteenth Amendments have never been treated as absolutes [footnote omitted]." . . . We acknowledge, however, the inherent dangers of undertaking to regulate any form of expression. State statutes designed to regulate obscene materials must be carefully limited. . . . As a result, we now confine the permissible scope of such regulation to works which depict or describe sexual conduct. That conduct must be specifically defined by the applicable state law, as written or authoritatively construed. A state offense must also be limited to works which, taken as a whole, appeal to the prurient interest in sex, which portray sexual conduct in a patently offensive way, and which, taken as a whole, do not have serious literary, artistic, political, or scientific value.

The basic guidelines for the trier of fact must be: (a) whether "the average person, applying contemporary community standards" would find that the work, taken as a whole, appeals to the prurient interest, *Kois* v. *Wisconsin, supra,* at 230, quoting *Roth* v. *United States, supra,* at 489; (b) whether the work depicts or describes, in a patently offensive way, sexual conduct specifically defined by the applicable state law; and (c) whether the work, taken as a whole, lacks serious literary, artistic, political, or scientific value. We do not adopt as a constitutional standard the "*utterly* without redeeming social value" test of *Memoirs* v. *Massachusetts,* 383 U.S., at 419; that concept has never commanded the adherence of more than three Justices at one time. See *supra,* at 21. If a state law that regulates obscene material is thus limited, as written or construed, the First Amendment values applicable to the States through the Fourteenth Amendment are adequately protected by the ultimate power of appellate courts to conduct an independent review of constitutional claims when necessary.

We emphasize that it is not our function to propose regulatory schemes for the States. That must await their concrete legislative efforts. It is possible, however, to give a few plain examples of what a state statute could define for regulation under part (b) of the standard announced in this opinion, *supra:*

(a) Patently offensive representations or descriptions of ultimate sexual acts, normal or perverted, actual or simulated.

(b) Patently offensive representations or descriptions of masturbation, excretory functions, and lewd exhibition of the genitals.

Sex and nudity may not be exploited without limit by films or pictures exhibited or sold in places of public accommodation any more than live sex and nudity can be exhibited or sold without limit in such public places. At a minimum, prurient, patently offensive depiction or description of sexual conduct must have serious literary, artistic, political, or scientific value to merit First Amendment protection. . . . For example, medical books for the education of physicians and related personnel necessarily use graphic illustrations and descriptions of human anatomy. In resolving the inevitably sensitive questions of fact and law, we must continue to rely on the jury system, accompanied by the safeguards that judges, rules of evidence, presumption of innocence, and other protective features provide, as we do with rape, murder, and a host of other offenses against society and its individual members.

The dissenting Justices sound the alarm of repression. But, in our view, to equate the free and robust exchange of ideas and political debate with commercial exploitation of obscene material demeans the grand conception of the First Amendment and its high purposes in the historic struggle for freedom. It is a "misuse of the great guarantees of free speech and free press. . . ." . . . The First Amendment protects works which, taken as a whole, have serious literary, artistic, political, or scientific value, regardless of whether the government or a majority of the people approve of the ideas these works represent. "The protection given speech and press was fashioned to assure unfettered interchange of *ideas* for the bringing about of political and social changes desired by the people." . . . But the public portrayal of hard-core sexual conduct for its own sake, and for the ensuing commercial gain, is a different matter.

There is no evidence, empirical or historical, that the stern 19th century American censorship of public distribution and display of material relating to sex, . . . in any way limited or affected expression of serious literary, artistic, political, or scientific ideas. On the contrary, it is beyond any question that the era following Thomas Jefferson to Theodore Roosevelt was an "extraordinarily vigorous period," not just in economics and politics, but in *belles lettres* and in "the outlying fields of social and political philosophies." We do not see the harsh hand of censorship of ideas — good or bad, sound or unsound — and "repression" of political liberty lurking in every state regulation of commercial exploitation of human interest in sex.

6

CENSORSHIP (MOTION PICTURES)

Censorship of obscene and/or pornographic materials whether they are motion pictures, books, magazines, or photographs has always posed particularly difficult questions for the Supreme Court to decide. As we have seen, in recent years a score or more "obscenity" cases have come before it. The Court's rulings have varied in their rhetorical flourish, in their legal and constitutional terminology, and in their attempts to reconcile censorship with First Amendment freedoms and "acceptable community standards." The Court has not been, and because of the nature of the subject, perhaps *cannot* be, precise on these matters. In the absence of generally accepted definitions of such "slippery," difficult terms as obscenity, pornography, and even (in a highly pluralistic society) of what "acceptable community standards" means, the Court has had to tread softly, break new ground cautiously, and backtrack here and there. The results have been largely confusing, contradictory, and often unsatisfactory. This much should be apparent from the obscenity rulings and from the following censorship cases. Let us consider the Court's dilemma in the matter of motion pictures.

Burstyn v. Wilson, 343 U.S. 495 (1952)

The first case, decided in a more simple, "less sophisticated" era, when motion pictures were considered "escape entertainment" and not vehicles for the dissemination of controversial ideas, was *Mutual Film Corp. v. Industrial Commission of Ohio.*[1] There the Supreme Court approved state censorship of motion pictures on the assumption that films, like the burlesque and vaudeville of the time, could be subject to state regulation and control on moral grounds. *Mutual Film* went undisturbed until 1952. Then in *Burstyn v. Wilson* the Supreme Court began the new censorship, or no-censorship era that still largely prevails and that, because of the often ambiguous language in some of the Court's decisions, accounts for much of the confusion on the subject. Involved in *Burstyn* was the film *The Miracle,* which religious groups in New York felt portrayed the birth of Christ in a sacrilegious manner.

1. 236 U.S. 230 (1915).

The Court ruled that provisions of the New York Education Law that forbid the commercial showing of a motion picture without a license was invalid as a "prior restraint" upon the exercise of First Amendment freedoms. *Burstyn* therefore specifically reversed *Mutual Film* and brought motion pictures under the (partial) protection of the First Amendment's freedom of speech clause. In *Burstyn*, the Court acknowledged for the first time that films were a "form of expression" entitled to protection under the First Amendment. As subsequent cases indicated, however, motion pictures did not receive absolute protection. But in *Burstyn* a unanimous Court went just far enough to decide that a state may *not* place prior restraint on the showing of a motion picture on the basis of a censor's conclusion that the film was "sacrilegious."

Mr. Justice Clark delivered the opinion of the Court, saying in part:

> It cannot be doubted that motion pictures are a significant medium for the communication of ideas. They may affect public attitudes and behavior in a variety of ways, ranging from direct espousal of a political or social doctrine to the subtle shaping of thought which characterizes all artistic expression. The importance of motion pictures as an organ of public opinion is not lessened by the fact that they are designed to entertain as well as to inform. As was said in *Winters v. New York,* 333 U.S. 507, 510 (1948):
>
> > "The line between the informing and the entertaining is too elusive for the protection of that basic right [a free press]. Everyone is familiar with instances of propaganda through fiction. What is one man's amusement, teaches another's doctrine."
>
> It is urged that motion pictures do not fall within the First Amendment's aegis because their production, distribution, and exhibition is a large-scale business conducted for private profit. We cannot agree. That books, newspapers, and magazines are published and sold for profit does not prevent them from being a form of expression whose liberty is safeguarded by the First Amendment. We fail to see why operation for profit should have any different effect in the case of motion pictures.
>
> It is further urged that motion pictures possess a greater capacity for evil, particularly among the youth of a community, than other modes of expression. Even if one were to accept this hypothesis, it does not follow that motion pictures should be disqualified from First Amendment protection. If there be capacity for evil it may be relevant in determining the permissible scope of community control, but it does not authorize substantially unbridled censorship such as we have here.
>
> For the foregoing reasons, we conclude that expression by means of motion pictures is included within the free speech and free press guaranty of the First and Fourteenth Amendments. To the extent that language in the opinion in *Mutual Film Corp. v. Industrial Comm'n, supra,* is out of harmony with the views here set forth, we no longer adhere to it.
>
> To hold that liberty of expression by means of motion pictures is guaranteed by the First and Fourteenth Amendments, however, is not the end of our problem. It does not follow that the Constitution requires absolute freedom to exhibit every motion picture of every kind at all times and all places. That much is evident from the series of decisions of this Court with respect to other media of communication of ideas. Nor does it follow that motion pictures are necessarily subject to the precise rules governing any other particular method of expression. Each method tends to present its own peculiar problems. But the basic principles

of freedom of speech and the press, like the First Amendment's command, do not vary. Those principles, as they have frequently been enunciated by this Court, make freedom of expression the rule. There is no justification in this case for making an exception to that rule.

Times Film Corp. v. Chicago, 365 U.S. 43 (1961)

Because *Burstyn* did not ban all censorship or prior restraint of motion pictures, the Court has proceeded case by case judging each dispute on its merits, assuming, as it stated in *Burstyn,* that while films are constitutionally protected as freedom of expression, movie censorship is not of itself unconstitutional. In 1959, for example, the Court overturned a ban imposed by New York on the film *Lady Chatterly's Lover.* The case was *Kingsley International Pictures Corp. v. Regents.*[1] New York had banned the film because it portrayed adultery in an approving manner. Speaking for a unanimous Court, Justice Stewart noted that the Constitution does not only protect those ideas shared by a majority of the people. It also must protect advocacy of unpopular or "improper" ideas and themes. Ideas cannot be prosecuted, Justice Stewart said, because ideas cannot be obscene.

Movie censorship arose again in *Times Film Corp. v. Chicago.* There the film involved was *Don Juan.* Strangely, as the majority opinion made clear, there was nothing in the record to indicate the nature or content of the film. The petitioner, Times Film Corporation, claimed that the nature of *Don Juan* was irrelevant, arguing that even if the film contained the "basest type of pornography" or incited to riot, or advocated the violent overthrow of orderly government, it was nonetheless free to be shown without prior submission to a censor for examination. The petitioner challenged the very concept of prior restraint. The Court, however, was unwilling to go that far. Although it was badly split (5–4), it ruled that freedom of expression is not absolutely guaranteed under the First Amendment and therefore that, although motion pictures are protected by the free speech guarantee, "there is no absolute freedom to exhibit publicly, at least once, every kind of motion picture."

Justice Clark, the author of the *Burstyn* ruling, again spoke for the majority in *Times.* Here, however, the Warren Court fragmented. Chief Justice Warren, joined by Justices Black, Brennan, and Douglas, wrote one dissent and Justice Douglas, joined by the Chief Justice and Justice Black, wrote another.

Douglas took the absolutist view that all censorship of motion pictures was prior restraint and therefore an unconstitutional violation of the First Amendment. Chief Justice Warren's dissent charged the Court with having approved "unlimited censorship of motion pictures" through a restrictive licensing procedure. The Court's decision, the Chief Justice insisted, "presents a real danger of eventual censorship for every form of communication, be it newspapers, journals, books, magazines, television, radio, or public speeches." "I submit," the Chief Justice said, "that in arriving at its decision the Court has interpreted our cases contrary to their intention . . . and in exalting the censor of motion pictures has endangered the First and Fourteenth Amendment rights of all others engaged in the dissemination of ideas."

1. 360 U.S. 684 (1959).

The majority took a more cautious approach to "prior restraint." It held that the petitioner's claim, supported by the four dissenters, "is founded upon the claim of absolute privilege against prior restraint under the First Amendment — a claim without sanction in our cases . . ."

Mr. Justice Clark delivered the opinion of the Court, saying in part:

> Chicago emphasizes here its duty to protect its people against the dangers of obscenity in the public exhibition of motion pictures. To this argument petitioner's only answer is that regardless of the capacity for, or extent of, such an evil, previous restraint cannot be justified. With this we cannot agree. We recognized in *Burstyn, supra,* that "capacity for evil . . . may be relevant in determining the permissible scope of community control," at p. 502, and that motion pictures were not "necessarily subject to the precise rules governing any other particular method of expression. Each method," we said, "tends to present its own peculiar problems." . . . Certainly petitioner's broadside attack does not warrant, nor could it justify on the record here, our saying that — aside from any consideration of the other "exceptional cases" mentioned in our decision — the State is stripped of all constitutional power to prevent, in the most effective fashion, the utterance of this class of speech. It is not for this Court to limit the State in its selection of the remedy it deems most effective to cope with such a problem, absent, of course, a showing of unreasonable strictures on individual liberty resulting from its application in particular circumstances. . . . We, of course, are not holding that city officials may be granted the power to prevent the showing of any motion picture they deem unworthy of a license. . . .
>
> As to what may be decided when a concrete case involving a specific standard provided by this ordinance is presented, we intimate no opinion. The petitioner has not challenged all — or for that matter any — of the ordinance's standards. Naturally we could not say that every one of the standards, including those which Illinois' highest court has found sufficient, is so vague on its face that the entire ordinance is void. At this time we say no more than this — that we are dealing only with motion pictures and, even as to them, only in the context of the broadside attack presented on this record.

Freedman v. Maryland, 380 U.S. 51 (1965)

Four years after *Times,* the Warren Court moved a bit closer to abolishing all movie censorship. In *Freedman* v. *Maryland* a unanimous Court, while still not declaring censorship of films unconstitutional per se, did impose such strict procedural limits on state and local censorship boards that for all practical purposes their authority has been emasculated. In fact, since *Freedman* many states and communities have disbanded their movie censorship boards. As we shall see, however, the issue of film censorship did not die. It arose again after the Supreme Court had lost its Warren flavor, when the more conservative Burger (Nixon) Court took over in the 1970s. Yet even the Burger Court's record, surprisingly, is mixed. It has had four opportunities to rule on "prior restraint" cases involving films or theatrical productions. It ruled against "prior restraint" in three of the four.

In *Jenkins* v. *Georgia*[1] for example, the Court actually viewed the film *Carnal Knowledge* and decided it was not obscene. Therefore, it concluded that its public showing could not be prohibited by a local community's narrow in-

1. 418 U.S. 153 (1974).

terpretation of the Court's *Miller* ruling (above). Similarly, the rock musical *Hair* came under scrutiny in *Southeastern Promotions Ltd.* v. *Conrad.*[2] There the Supreme Court ruled that Chattanooga, Tennessee's refusal to rent a city auditorium for the performance of *Hair* was "prior restraint" that could only be imposed if the safeguards laid down in *Freedman* had been followed. The Court decided they had not. In *Roaden* v. *Kentucky*[3] the Burger Court decided that seizure of a film (by a local sheriff) without a constitutionally valid warrant was "unreasonable prior restraint." However, in *Heller* v. *New York*[4] the Court upheld seizing a film (by a judge) in an instance where the judge who issued the warrant viewed the film before signing the seizure warrant.

In *Freedman* the Supreme Court laid down three procedural safeguards a censor must follow to avoid constitutionally invalid censorship of films: (1) the burden rests on the censor to prove that the film is obscene or pornographic and therefore outside First Amendment protection; (2) the censor must pass judgment on the film "in the shortest period [of time] compatible with sound judicial procedure"; and (3) the censorship procedure must assure "prompt" judicial review of the censor's decision. In the years since *Freedman*, by and large, these safeguards continue to prevail.

Mr. Justice Brennan delivered the opinion of the Court, saying in part:

> The administration of a censorship system for motion pictures presents peculiar dangers to constitutionally protected speech. Unlike a prosecution for obscenity, a censorship proceeding puts the initial burden on the exhibitor or distributor. Because the censor's business is to censor, there inheres the danger that he may well be less responsive than a court — part of an independent branch of government — to the constitutionally protected interests in free expression. And if it is made unduly onerous, by reason of delay or otherwise, to seek judicial review, the censor's determination may in practice be final.
>
> Applying the settled rule of our cases, we hold that a noncriminal process which requires the prior submission of a film to a censor avoids constitutional infirmity only if it takes place under procedural safeguards designed to obviate the dangers of a censorship system. First, the burden of proving that the film is unprotected expression must rest on the censor. As we said in *Speiser* v. *Randall,* 357 U.S. 513, 526, "Where the transcendent value of speech is involved, due process certainly requires . . . that the State bear the burden of persuasion to show that the appellants engaged in criminal speech." Second, while the State may require advance submission of all films, in order to proceed effectively to bar all showings of unprotected films, the requirement cannot be administered in a manner which would lend an effect of finality to the censor's determination whether a film constitutes protected expression. The teaching of our cases is that, because only a judicial determination in an adversary proceeding ensures the necessary sensitivity to freedom of expression, only a procedure requiring a judicial determination suffices to impose a valid final restraint. . . . To this end, the exhibitor must be assured, by statute or authoritative judicial construction, that the censor will, within a specified brief period, either issue a license or go to court to restrain showing the film. Any restraint imposed in advance of a final judicial determination on the merits must similarly be limited to preservation of

2. 420 U.S. 546 (1975).

3. 413 U.S. 496 (1973).

4. 413 U.S. 483 (1973).

the status quo for the shortest fixed period compatible with sound judicial resolution. Moreover, we are well aware that, even after expiration of a temporary restraint, an administrative refusal to license, signifying the censor's view that the film is unprotected, may have a discouraging effect on the exhibitor. . . . Therefore, the procedure must also assure a prompt final judicial decision, to minimize the deterrent effect of an interim and possibly erroneous denial of a license.

Without these safeguards, it may prove too burdensome to seek review of the censor's determination. Particularly in the case of motion pictures, it may take very little to deter exhibition in a given locality. The exhibitor's stake in any one picture may be insufficient to warrant a protracted and onerous course of litigation. The distributor, on the other hand, may be equally unwilling to accept the burdens and delays of litigation in a particular area when, without such difficulties, he can freely exhibit his film in most of the rest of the country; for we are told that only four States and a handful of municipalities have active censorship laws.

It is readily apparent that the Maryland procedural scheme does not satisfy these criteria. First, once the censor disapproves the film, the exhibitor must assume the burden of instituting judicial proceedings and of persuading the courts that the film is protected expression. Second, once the Board has acted against a film, exhibition is prohibited pending judicial review, however protracted. Under the statute, appellant could have been convicted if he had shown the film after unsuccessfully seeking a license, even though no court had ever ruled on the obscenity of the film. Third, it is abundantly clear that the Maryland statute provides no assurance of prompt judicial determination. We hold, therefore, that appellant's conviction must be reversed. The Maryland scheme fails to provide adequate safeguards against undue inhibition of protected expression, and this renders the §2 requirement of prior submission of films to the Board an invalid previous restraint.

7

FREEDOM OF SPEECH

Despite the views of a relatively few "absolutists," including at least one recent Justice of the Supreme Court, under the Constitution of the United States no one has an unqualified right to free speech. It is an accepted fact that not all speech is protected absolutely by the free speech clause of the First Amendment. By its nature freedom of speech is not, has never been, and cannot be an absolute right. Libel and slander laws bear witness to this truism. Nor was free speech ever intended to be so by Madison, Jefferson, and the other framers of the Bill of Rights. There *are* limits to free speech; that much is generally acknowledged by constitutional lawyers. The problem, of course, is to determine precisely (if possible) what those limits are and who sets them.

In recent years the leading exponent of the view that freedom of speech is an unqualified, absolute right, at least until his last years on the Supreme Court, was Justice Black. In *Smith* v. *California*[1] for example, Black interpreted the First Amendment's "Congress shall make no law" to mean precisely that, *no* law infringing on freedom of speech. For civil libertarian Black, First Amendment freedoms were "wholly beyond the reach" of the federal government to regulate and presumably safe from state regulation as well. However, most students of the Supreme Court and the Constitution do not accept Black's "absolutist" position. They would subscribe to the words of Justice Murphy (himself a leading advocate of civil liberties) in the *Chaplinsky* case (below) where he noted: "It is well understood that the right of free speech is not absolute at all times and under all circumstances."

Therefore, as we noted, the questions become, if there are limits, what are those limits and who sets them? And further, do they change as the political climate of the country may change? Do war, peace, or domestic turmoil make a difference? In conflicts between individual freedom and the rights of society (government), which prevails? Under what rules or guidelines? These are among the many vexing problems the Supreme Court has grappled with since 1919 in a myriad of free speech cases.

Perhaps the most flagrant federal violation of free speech in American history was the Adams inspired Sedition Act of 1798. It provided for the severe punishment of "false, scandalous, and malicious writings against the government, either house of Congress, or the President, if published with

1. 361 U.S. 147 (1959).

intent to defame any of them or to excite against them the hatred of the people, or to stir up sedition." Although many persons were indicted and convicted under the 1798 Sedition law, its provisions were never tested before the Supreme Court. For this reason the Court did not have its first opportunity to rule on the First Amendment's free speech guarantee until 1919. Then, a series of cases arose from World War I's Espionage and Sedition laws.

Schenck v. United States, 240 U.S. 147 (1919)

The Espionage Act of 1917 made it illegal to make or circulate "false statements" with the intent of disrupting "military success" or to obstruct recruiting for the services. Its companion piece, the 1918 Sedition Act, made it a crime to obstruct in any way the sale of government bonds or to say or publish anything intended to breed contempt for the law. It also made it illegal to incite "resistance to the government or promote the cause of its enemies."

The test case was *Schenck* v. *United States.* There, Justice Holmes's now famous "clear and present danger" rule made its first appearance in American jurisprudence. It has since formed the basis for many subsequent free speech decisions, some of which, as we shall see, twisted and turned Holmes's words in ways never intended. Schenck was convicted under the Espionage Act of circulating literature urging young men to resist World War I draft laws, which he characterized as "unconstitutional despotism." Speaking for a unanimous Court, Justice Holmes wrote that, ". . . the question in every case is whether the words used are used in such circumstances and are of such a nature as to create a clear and present danger that they will bring about the substantive evils that Congress has a right to prevent . . ."

Shortly after *Schenck* the Supreme Court decided two more cases dealing with the Espionage and Sedition laws. Once again Justice Holmes wrote the opinion of the Court in both *Frohwerk* v. *United States*[2] and *Debs* v. *United States.*[3] *Frohwerk* dealt with the writings of a pro-German newspaperman who was sharply critical of the United States war effort against Germany. *Debs* dealt with speeches the famous Socialist labor leader had made against the war. The Supreme Court upheld the conviction of both men, because, as Holmes noted, their writing and speeches were an immediate "clear and present danger" to American society.

A short time later Justice Holmes and his liberal colleague, Justice Brandeis, split off from the majority of seven and dissented in a case, *Abrams* v. *United States,*[4] where Holmes insisted the Court had misapplied the clear and present danger rule. Abrams had been convicted of circulating pamphlets attacking the United States for sending American troops to fight with remnants of the Russian White Army in Siberia and in the Murmansk area against the Red Army of the Bolsheviks, who in November 1917 had seized power in Russia. Abrams called for a general strike among American workers in munitions factories to protest their government's intervention in the Russian Civil War. Justice Holmes insisted that the majority had interpreted *Schenck's* clear

2. 249 U.S. 204 (1919).

3. Ibid., at 211.

4. 250 U.S. 616 (1919).

and present danger rule much too narrowly. He and Brandeis did not feel that Abrams posed the immediate threat to "the lawful and pressing purposes" of the Espionage Act to warrant suppressing his free speech rights.

In the controlling *Schenck* case, the circular in question used "impassioned language" quoting the Thirteenth Amendment's abolition of involuntary servitude and likening the draft to slavery and the draftee to a convict. Schenck argued that conscription was "despotism in its worst form" and a "monstrous wrong against humanity in the interest of Wall Street's chosen few." The circular went on to deny the power of the American government to send its citizens "away to foreign shores to shoot up the people of other lands." Justice Holmes acknowledged that at another time Schenck's circular might have passed constitutional muster. But not in time of war.

Mr. Justice Holmes delivered the opinion of the Court, saying in part:

> We admit that in many places and in ordinary times the defendants in saying all that was said in the circular would have been within their constitutional rights. But the character of every act depends upon the circumstances in which it is done. The most stringent protection of free speech would not protect a man in falsely shouting fire in a theatre and causing a panic. It does not even protect a man from an injunction against uttering words that may have all the effect of force. The question in every case is whether the words used are used in such circumstances and are of such a nature as to create a clear and present danger that they will bring about the substantive evils that Congress has a right to prevent. It is a question of proximity and degree. When a nation is at war many things that might be said in time of peace are such a hindrance to its effort that their utterance will not be endured so long as men fight and that no Court could regard them as protected by any constitutional right. It seems to be admitted that if an actual obstruction of the recruiting service were proved, liability for words that produced that effect might be enforced. The statute of 1917 in §4 punishes conspiracies to obstruct as well as actual obstruction. If the act, (speaking, or circulating a paper,) its tendency and the intent with which it is done are the same, we perceive no ground for saying that success alone warrants making the act a crime.

Gitlow v. New York, 268 U.S. 652 (1925)

Just as he had in *Abrams,* once again in *Gitlow* v. *New York* Justice Holmes chided the Court for too narrowly construing *Schenck*'s clear and present danger rule. Admittedly Justice Holmes's rule is not easy to apply, particularly so, as was the case in *Gitlow,* when the New York statute in question made only certain specific kinds of speech illegal. For this reason if someone makes a speech of the type "forbidden" by law, the Supreme Court's options are narrowed. The Court may declare the statute unconstitutional as a violation of the First or Fourteenth Amendment or both. But, properly interpreted, and this of course is the key, *Schenck*'s clear and present danger rule does limit the Court. According to Holmes, the Supreme Court can rule only that the statute in question *has* in fact been violated. If there has been no active statutory violation, Holmes insists, free speech must be upheld. This was the substance of the disagreement between Holmes and the majority in the *Gitlow* controversy, Holmes's argument that no statutory violation had taken place. *Gitlow* is also the first application of the First Amendment's free speech clause to the states.

Gitlow was convicted for violating New York's Criminal Anarchy Act of 1902 which made it a felony to advocate "by word of mouth or writing" overthrowing organized government "by force or violence." Passed after the assassination of President McKinley in the state by an avowed anarchist, New York's law also made it a felony to print, publish, or circulate "any book . . . or [other] printed matter" advocating the overthrow of the government. Gitlow, a militant Marxist (never quite identified in the record as a member of the Communist Party), had distributed a document similar in content to the Communist Manifesto through the aegis of a New York City based organization called "Revolutionary Age." According to Justice Sanford's majority opinion, "there was no evidence of any effect resulting from the publication and circulation" of Gitlow's manifesto.

It was this point that occasioned the Holmes and Brandeis dissent, which charged the Court with misapplying the reasoning of *Schenck*'s clear and present danger rule. "Whatever may be said of (Gitlow's) redundant discourse," Justice Holmes wrote, "it had no chance of starting a present conflagration." Holmes then went on to express the traditional libertarian position on freedom of speech. "If in the long run," Holmes said, "the beliefs expressed in proletarian dictatorship are destined to be accepted by the dominant forces of the community, the only meaning of free speech is that they should be given their chance and have their way."

In *Gitlow,* the Court fashioned what can only be called a more conservative interpretation of the First Amendment than clear and present danger. To determine the allowable limits of free expression it devised the so-called "bad tendency test." As noted in *Gitlow* this makes a speech illegal if it has a tendency, "however remote," to encourage or bring about acts that violate the law. Under Holmes's clear and present danger rule, speech is punishable only when there is an immediate danger that it may cause an illegal action to take place. Clear and present danger, Holmes argues, was not intended to test the constitutionality of a statute like New York's criminal anarchy law. Holmes reasoned that its function was simply to determine if a speech did lead to action. If it did not this would enable the Court to declare that the statute forbidding the action had *not* been violated. According to Holmes, this was the crucial infirmity of the majority's reasoning in *Gitlow.* No action had resulted from Gitlow's activities. Therefore, Holmes insisted, New York's statute had not been violated. But in *Gitlow* the more conservative interpretation of free speech prevailed. Thus in the two pivotal cases, *Schenck* and *Gitlow,* two opposing views concerning the allowable limits of free speech emerge, clear and present danger, generally held by the more liberal jurists and the bad tendency test, more often than not relied upon by conservative jurists. The two positions have been at odds since the 1919 and 1925 decisions. As noted, *Gitlow* has the additional distinction of being the first case in which the Supreme Court incorporated the free speech provisions of the First Amendment to the states via the Fourteenth Amendment. Subsequent decisions would use this precedent in many diverse cases.

Mr. Justice Sanford delivered the opinion of the Court, saying in part:

The sole contention here is, essentially, that as there was no evidence of any concrete result flowing from the publication of the Manifesto or of circumstances showing the likelihood of such result, the statute as construed and applied by the trial court penalizes the mere utterance, as such, of "doctrine" having no quality of incitement, without regard either to the circumstances of its utterance or to the likelihood of unlawful sequences; and that, as the exercise of the right of free expression with relation to government is only punishable "in circumstances involving likelihood of substantive evil," the statute contravenes the due process clause of the Fourteenth Amendment. The argument in support of this contention rests primarily upon the following propositions: 1st, That the "liberty" protected by the Fourteenth Amendment includes the liberty of speech and of the press; and 2nd, That while liberty of expression "is not absolute," it may be restrained "only in circumstances where its exercise bears a causal relation with some substantive evil, consummated, attempted or likely," and as the statute "takes no account of circumstances," it unduly restrains this liberty and is therefore unconstitutional.

The precise question presented, and the only question which we can consider under this writ of error, then is, whether the statute, as construed and applied in this case by the state courts, deprived the defendant of his liberty of expression in violation of the due process clause of the Fourteenth Amendment.

The statute does not penalize the utterance or publication of abstract "doctrine" or academic discussion having no quality of incitement to any concrete action. It is not aimed against mere historical or philosophical essays. It does not restrain the advocacy of changes in the form of government by constitutional and lawful means. What it prohibits is language advocating, advising or teaching the overthrow of organized government by unlawful means . . .

The Manifesto, plainly, is neither the statement of abstract doctrine nor, as suggested by counsel, mere prediction that industrial disturbances and revolutionary mass strikes will result spontaneously in an inevitable process of evolution in the economic system. It advocates and urges in fervent language mass action which shall progressively foment industrial disturbances and through political mass strikes and revolutionary mass action overthrow and destroy organized parliamentary government. It concludes with a call to action in these words: "The proletariat revolution and the Communist reconstruction of society — *the struggle for these* — is now indispensable. . . . The Communist International calls the proletariat of the world to the final struggle!" This is not the expression of philosophical abstraction, the mere prediction of future events; it is the language of direct incitement.

The means advocated for bringing about the destruction of organized parliamentary government, namely, mass industrial revolts usurping the functions of municipal government, political mass strikes directed against the parliamentary state, and revolutionary mass action for its final destruction, necessarily imply the use of force and violence, and in their essential nature are inherently unlawful in a constitutional government of law and order. That the jury were warranted in finding that the Manifesto advocated not merely the abstract doctrine of overthrowing organized government by force, violence and unlawful means, but action to that end, is clear.

For present purposes we may and do assume that freedom of speech and of the press — which are protected by the First Amendment from abridgment by Congress — are among the fundamental personal rights and "liberties" protected by the due process clause of the Fourteenth Amendment from impairment by the States. . . .

It is a fundamental principle, long established, that the freedom of speech and of the press which is secured by the Constitution, does not confer an absolute right to speak or publish, without responsibility, whatever one may choose, or an unrestricted and unbridled license that gives immunity for every possible use of language and prevents the punishment of those who abuse this freedom. . . .

By enacting the present statute the State has determined, through its legislative body, that utterances advocating the overthrow of organized government by force, violence and unlawful means, are so inimical to the general welfare and involve such danger of substantive evil that they may be penalized in the exercise of its police power. That determination must be given great weight. Every presumption is to be indulged in favor of the validity of the statute. And the case is to be considered "in the light of the principle that the State is primarily the judge of regulations required in the interest of public safety and welfare;" and that its police "statutes may only be declared unconstitutional where they are arbitrary or unreasonable attempts to exercise authority vested in the state in the public interest." . . .

That a State in the exercise of its police power may punish those who abuse this freedom by utterances inimical to the public welfare, tending to corrupt public morals, incite to crime, or disturb the public peace, is not open to question....

We cannot hold that the present statute is an arbitrary or unreasonable exercise of the police power of the State unwarrantably infringing the freedom of speech or press; and we must and do sustain its constitutionality.

This being so it may be applied to every utterance — not too trivial to be beneath the notice of the law — which is of such a character and used with such intent and purpose as to bring it within the prohibition of the statute. This principle is illustrated in *Fox* v. *Washington, supra,* p. 277; . . . . In other words, when the legislative body has determined generally, in the constitutional exercise of its discretion, that utterances of a certain kind involve such danger of substantive evil that they may be punished, the question whether any specific utterance coming within the prohibited class is likely, in and of itself, to bring about the substantive evil, is not open to consideration. It is sufficient that the statute itself be constitutional and that the use of the language comes within its prohibition.

It is clear that the question in such cases is entirely different from that involved in those cases where the statute merely prohibits certain acts involving the danger of substantive evil, without any reference to language itself, and it is sought to apply its provisions to language used by the defendant for the purpose of bringing about the prohibited results. There, if it be contended that the statute cannot be applied to the language used by the defendant because of its protection by the freedom of speech or press, it must necessarily be found, as an original question, without any previous determination by the legislative body, whether the specific language used involved such likelihood of bringing about the substantive evil as to deprive it of the constitutional protection. In such cases it has been held that the general provisions of the statute may be constitutionally applied to the specific utterance of the defendant if its natural tendency and probable effect was to bring about the substantive evil which the legislative body might prevent.

. . . And the general statement in the *Schenck Case* (p. 52) that the "question in every case is whether the words are used in such circumstances and are of such a nature as to create a clear and present danger that they will bring about the substantive evils," — upon which great reliance is placed in the defendant's argument — was manifestly intended, as shown by the context, to apply only in cases of this class, and has no application to those like the present, where the legislative body itself has previously determined the danger of substantive evil arising from utterances of a specified character. . . .

And finding, for the reasons stated, that the statute is not in itself unconstitutional, and that it has not been applied in the present case in derogation of any constitutional right, the judgment of the Court of Appeals is *Affirmed.*

8

PICKETING

An Alabama statute passed during the industrial turmoil of the 1930s made it unlawful "to loiter" or "to picket" near a place of business for the purpose of influencing or inducing persons to boycott or for the purpose of "interfering or impeding" the business. Did Alabama's anti-picketing law violate the First Amendment's free speech guarantee or was picketing a form of constitutionally privileged, protected speech?

Thornhill v. Alabama, 310 U.S. 88 (1940)

These were the crucial questions in *Thornhill* v. *Alabama*.

The petitioner was convicted in Tuscaloosa County for having been "on the picket line" at the plant of the Wood Preserving Company, which was in the midst of an organizing dispute with a local union. In a historic 8–1 decision (only Justice McReynolds of "nine old men" fame dissented) the Supreme Court reversed Thornhill's conviction and for the first time brought peaceful picketing under the umbrella of the First Amendment. The Court had taken its first cautious step to give picketing some constitutional protection in 1921 when it ruled, in *American Steel Foundries* v. *Tri City Central Trades Council*,[1] that strikers could maintain one picket at a factory "for each point of ingress and egress." In *Thornhill*, however, the Court gave full approval to peaceful picketing as a form of constitutionally protected expression.

However, no sooner had the ink dried on *Thornhill* than the Court began to have second thoughts. It continued to acknowledge that picketing was a form of speech and therefore privileged, but the Court adopted the position that picketing was something besides mere speech. It was also a form of coercion and therefore subject to regulation if that element of coercion should lead to a breach of the peace. Since 1942 the Supreme Court has held fast to this position.[2] Yet *Thornhill* remains the pivotal decision. Its protection of picketing as a form of free speech has never been rescinded.

Mr. Justice Murphy delivered the opinion of the Court, saying in part:

1. 257 U.S. 184 (1921).

2. See *Milk Wagon Drivers Union* v. *Meadowmoor Dairies*, 312 U.S. 287 (1941) and *Carpenters and Joiners Union* v. *Ritter's Cafe*, 315 U.S. 722 (1942).

The freedom of speech and of the press, which are secured by the First Amendment against abridgment by the United States, are among the fundamental personal rights and liberties which are secured to all persons by the Fourteenth Amendment against abridgment by a State.

The safeguarding of these rights to the ends that men may speak as they think on matters vital to them and that falsehoods may be exposed through the processes of education and discussion is essential to free government. Those who won our independence had confidence in the power of free and fearless reasoning and communication of ideas to discover and spread political and economic truth. Noxious doctrines in those fields may be refuted and their evil averted by the courageous exercise of the right of free discussion. Abridgment of freedom of speech and of the press, however, impairs those opportunities for public education that are essential to effective exercise of the power of correcting error through the processes of popular government. . . .

It is recognized now that satisfactory hours and wages and working conditions in industry and a bargaining position which makes these possible have an importance which is not less than the interests of those in the business or industry directly concerned. The health of the present generation and of those as yet unborn may depend on these matters, and the practices in a single factory may have economic repercussions upon a whole region and affect widespread systems of marketing. The merest glance at state and federal legislation on the subject demonstrates the force of the argument that labor relations are not matters of mere local or private concern. Free discussion concerning the conditions in industry and the causes of labor disputes appears to us indispensable to the effective and intelligent use of the processes of popular government to shape the destiny of modern industrial society. The issues raised by regulations, such as are challenged here, infringing upon the right of employees effectively to inform the public of the facts of a labor dispute are part of this larger problem. We concur in the observation of Mr. Justice Brandeis, speaking for the Court in *Senn's* case (301 U.S. at 478): "Members of a union might, without special statutory authorization by a State, make known the facts of a labor dispute, for freedom of speech is guaranteed by the Federal Constitution." . . . We hold that the danger of injury to an industrial concern is neither so serious nor so imminent as to justify the sweeping proscription of freedom of discussion embodied in §3448.

The State urges that the purpose of the challenged statute is the protection of the community from the violence and breaches of the peace, which, it asserts, are the concomitants of picketing. The power and the duty of the State to take adequate steps to preserve the peace and to protect the privacy, the lives, and the property of its residents cannot be doubted. But no clear and present danger of destruction of life or property, or invasion of the right of privacy, or breach of the peace can be thought to be inherent in the activities of every person who approaches the premises of an employer and publicizes the facts of a labor dispute involving the latter. We are not now concerned with picketing *en masse* or otherwise conducted which might occasion such imminent and aggravated danger to these interests as to justify a statute narrowly drawn to cover the precise situation giving rise to the danger. . . . Section 3448 in question here does not aim specifically at serious encroachments on these interests and does not evidence any such care in balancing these interests against the interest of the community and that of the individual in freedom of discussion on matters of public concern.

9

BREACH OF THE PEACE

Under their general police power to preserve law and order, all states have statutes defining and punishing such offenses as a "breach of the peace." Some are more narrowly drawn than others. Some, liberally drawn, are often interpreted narrowly by law enforcement officials and judges who seek to strike a balance between the legitimate claims of free speech and the necessities of preserving an orderly society.

Cantwell v. Connecticut, 310 U.S. 296 (1940)

Three Supreme Court decisions that follow illustrate the dimensions of the problem. The first is *Cantwell* v. *Connecticut.* There Newton Cantwell and his two sons, all Jehovah's Witnesses, were convicted in New Haven for the common law offense of breaching the peace. The record showed that Cantwell had stopped two men on the street and asked for permission to play a phonograph record for them. The two men agreed. But when the record, entitled "Enemies," attacked the Catholic Church scurrilously, both men, who were Catholics, became angry, and as the record notes, "were tempted to strike Cantwell unless he went away." Told to leave, Cantwell did so. No argument or violence ensued. A Connecticut court convicted Cantwell, ruling that the charge against him was not assault or breach of the peace, but "invoking or inciting others" to a breach of the peace. A unanimous Supreme Court reversed Cantwell's conviction and ruled the Connecticut statute was a violation of the free speech guarantee of the First Amendment made applicable to the states by the Fourteenth. Thus *Cantwell* continued the process begun in *Gitlow* and *Thornhill,* nationalizing the Bill of Rights and applying its provision to the states.

Mr. Justice Roberts delivered the opinion of the Court, saying in part:

We hold that the statute, as construed and applied to the appellants, deprives them of their liberty without due process of law in contravention of the Fourteenth Amendment. The fundamental concept of liberty embodied in that Amendment embraces the liberties guaranteed by the First Amendment. The

First Amendment declares that Congress shall make no law respecting an establishment of religion or prohibiting the free exercise thereof. The Fourteenth
Amendment has rendered the legislatures of the states as incompetent as Congress to enact such laws. The constitutional inhibition of legislation on the subject
of religion has a double aspect. On the one hand, it forestalls compulsion by law
of the acceptance of any creed or the practice of any form of worship. Freedom
of conscience and freedom to adhere to such religious organization or form of
worship as the individual may choose cannot be restricted by law. . . .

The record played by Cantwell embodies a general attack on all organized
religious systems as instruments of Satan and injurious to man; it then singles
out the Roman Catholic Church for strictures couched in terms which naturally
would offend not only persons of that persuasion, but all others who respect the
honestly held religious faith of their fellows. The hearers were in fact highly
offended. One of them said he felt like hitting Cantwell and the other that he was
tempted to throw Cantwell off the street. The one who testified he felt like
hitting Cantwell said, in answer to the question "Did you do anything else or
have any other reaction?" "No, sir, because he said he would take the victrola and
he went." The other witness testified that he told Cantwell he had better get off
the street before something happened to him and that was the end of the matter
as Cantwell picked up his books and walked up the street.

Cantwell's conduct, in the view of the court below, considered apart from the
effect of his communication upon his hearers, did not amount to a breach of the
peace. One may, however, be guilty of the offense if he commit acts or make
statements likely to provoke violence and disturbance of good order, even
though no such eventuality be intended. Decisions to this effect are many, but
examination discloses that, in practically all, the provocative language which
was held to amount to a breach of the peace consisted of profane, indecent,
or abusive remarks directed to the person of the hearer. Resort to epithets or
personal abuse is not in any proper sense communication of information or
opinion safeguarded by the Constitution, and its punishment as a criminal act
would raise no question under that instrument.

We find in the instant case no assault or threatening of bodily harm, no
truculent bearing, no intentional discourtesy, no personal abuse. On the contrary, we find only an effort to persuade a willing listener to buy a book or to
contribute money in the interest of what Cantwell, however misguided others
may think him, conceived to be true religion.

In the realm of religious faith, and in that of political belief, sharp differences
arise. In both fields the tenets of one man may seem the rankest error to his
neighbor. To persuade others to his own point of view, the pleader, as we know, at
times, resorts to exaggeration, to vilification of men who have been, or are,
prominent in church or state, and even to false statement. But the people of this
nation have ordained in the light of history, that, in spite of the probability of
excesses and abuses, these liberties are, in the long view, essential to enlightened
opinion and right conduct on the part of the citizens of a democracy.

The essential characteristic of these liberties is, that under their shield many
types of life, character, opinion and belief can develop unmolested and un-
obstructed. Nowhere is this shield more necessary than in our own country for a
people composed of many races and of many creeds. There are limits to the
exercise of these liberties. The danger in these times from the coercive activities
of those who in the delusion of racial or religious conceit would incite violence
and breaches of the peace in order to deprive others of their equal right to the
exercise of their liberties, is emphasized by events familiar to all. These and
other transgressions of those limits the States appropriately may punish.

Although the contents of the record not unnaturally aroused animosity, we think that, in the absence of a statute narrowly drawn to define and punish specific conduct as constituting a clear and present danger to a substantial interest of the State, the petitioner's communication, considered in the light of the constitutional guarantees, raised no such clear and present menace to public peace and order as to render him liable to conviction of the common law offense in question.

Chaplinsky v. New Hampshire, 315 U.S. 568 (1942)

It happens rarely, but in *Chaplinsky* v. *New Hampshire* the Supreme Court had an opportunity to rule on a First Amendment free speech, breach of the peace dispute that was at once significant and yet comparatively uncluttered and simple. Chaplinsky was convicted in the Municipal Court of Rochester, New Hampshire for violating a statute that specified that "no person shall address any offensive or derisive word to any other person who is lawfully in any street or place nor call him by any name or exclamation in his presence and hearing with intent to deride, offend or annoy him or to prevent him from pursuing his lawful business or occupation."

Chaplinsky, a member of Jehovah's Witnesses, was distributing Witness literature on the streets of Rochester. A group of local citizens complained to the City Marshal that Chaplinsky was denouncing all religion as a "racket." The marshal informed them that Chaplinsky was acting within his protected right of freedom of speech. A short time later a disturbance occurred. A traffic officer then proceeded with Chaplinsky to the police station without informing him that he was under arrest. En route, the two encountered the marshal who warned Chaplinsky that the crowd was getting "restless" and there was danger of a riot. Chaplinsky thereupon cursed the marshal with the following words: "You are a God-damned racketeer" and "a damned Fascist and the whole government of Rochester are Fascists or agents of Fascists." Subsequently Chaplinsky argued that the New Hampshire statute under which he was convicted violated the First Amendment guarantees of freedom of speech, press, and worship. A unanimous Supreme Court disagreed.

For Justice Murphy, no argument was necessary to demonstrate that such words as "damned racketeer" and "damned Fascist" are unprotected by the First Amendment. Murphy said that the "epithets" Chaplinsky used are likely to provoke the "average person" to retaliate and cause a breach of the peace, and are therefore not constitutionally privileged.

Mr. Justice Murphy delivered the opinion of the Court, saying in part:

On the authority of its earlier decisions, the state court declared that the statute's purpose was to preserve the public peace, no words being "forbidden except such as have a direct tendency to cause acts of violence by the persons to whom, individually, the remark is addressed." It was further said: "The word 'offensive' is not to be defined in terms of what a particular addressee thinks. . . . The test is what men of common intelligence would understand would be words likely to cause an average addressee to fight. . . . The English language has a number of words and expressions which by general consent are 'fighting words' when said without a disarming smile. . . . Such words, as ordinary men know, are likely to cause a fight. So are threatening, profane or obscene revilings. Derisive and annoying words can be taken as coming within the purview of the statute as heretofore interpreted only when they have this characteristic of plainly tending to excite the addressee to a breach of the peace. . . . The statute, as construed, does no more than prohibit the face-to-face words plainly likely to cause a breach of the peace by the addressee, words whose speaking constitutes a breach of the peace by the speaker — including 'classical fighting words', words in current use less 'classical' but equally likely to cause violence, and other disorderly words, including profanity, obscenity and threats."

We are unable to say that the limited scope of the statute as thus construed contravenes the Constitutional right of free expression. It is a statute narrowly drawn and limited to define and punish specific conduct lying within the domain of state power, the use in a public place of words likely to cause a breach of the peace. . . . This conclusion necessarily disposes of appellant's contention that the statute is so vague and indefinite as to render a conviction thereunder a violation of due process. A statute punishing verbal acts, carefully drawn so as not unduly to impair liberty of expression, is not too vague for a criminal law. . . . Our function is fulfilled by a determination that the challenged statute, on its face and as applied, does not contravene the Fourteenth Amendment.

Terminiello v. Chicago, 337 U.S. 1 (1949)

Justice Holmes's "clear and present danger rule" was perhaps applied most nearly as it was originally intended in *Terminiello* v. *Chicago*. There a narrow majority of five, led by Justice Douglas, reversed a state court ruling and found that a Chicago ordinance forbidding any "breach of the peace" was too narrowly drawn and therefore violated the First and Fourteenth Amendments. Three separate dissents were filed, by Chief Justice Vinson, Justice Frankfurter, and Justice Jackson joined by Justice Burton. The Chief Justice charged the majority with having based its decision on "one offending sentence" in the trial judge's statement to the jury. The trial judge had interpreted the Chicago ordinance to the jury by noting that *any* speech "which stirs the public to anger, invites dispute, brings about a condition of unrest, or creates a disturbance" was breach of the peace and thus a violation of the City ordinance. Chief Justice Vinson argued "that a reversal on such a basis does not accord with any principle governing review of state court decisions heretofore announced by this Court."[1] Justice Frankfurter acknowledged in his dissent that freedom of speech "undoubtedly means freedom to express views . . . that may provide resentment." But he doubted that "indulging in such stuff" as Terminiello had used in his speech is "hardly so deserving as to lead this Court to single them out as beneficiaries of the first departure from the restrictions that bind this Court in reviewing judgments of State courts."[2] In his long dissent Justice Jackson reproduced Terminiello's scurrilous rabble-rousing speech. A somewhat edited (by Jackson) version follows below because it does indicate the broad umbrella of latitude and protection the slim liberal majority was willing to give a speech that however hateful and incitive, did not, in Justice Douglas's judgment, present a clear and immediate danger to society. To sustain that view Douglas's opinion turned on the narrow charge to the jury that gave the majority its opportunity to invalidate the Chicago ordinance.

1. 337 U.S. at 7.
2. Ibid., at 11–12.

From Justice Jackson's dissent:

"Father Terminiello: Now, I am going to whisper my greetings to you, Fellow Christians. I will interpret it. I said, 'Fellow *Christians,*' and I suppose there are *some of the scum got in by mistake,* so I want to tell a story about *the scum:*

". . . And nothing I could say tonight could begin to express the contempt I have for the *slimy scum* that got in by mistake.

". . . The subject I want to talk to you tonight about is the attempt *that is going on right outside this hall tonight,* the attempt that is going on to *destroy America by revolution. . . .*

"My friends, it is no longer true that it can't happen here. It is happening here, and it only depends upon you, good people, who are here tonight, depends upon all of us together, as Mr. Smith said. The tide is changing, and if you and I turn and run from that tide, we will all be drowned in this tidal wave of Communism which is going over the world.

". . . I am not going to talk to you about the menace of Communism, which is already accomplished, in Russia, where from eight to fifteen million people were murdered in cold blood by their own countrymen, and millions more through Eastern Europe at the close of the war are being murdered by these murderous Russians, hurt, being raped and sent into slavery. *That is what they want for you, that howling mob outside.*

"I know I was told one time that my winter quarters were ready for me in Siberia. I was told that. Now, I am talking about the fifty-seven varieties that we have in America, and we have fifty-seven varieties of pinks and reds and pastel shades in this country; and all of it can be traced back to the twelve years we spent under the New Deal, because that was the build-up for what is going on in the world today.

"Now, Russia promised us we would ga [*sic*] back to the official newspaper of Russia. Primarily, it was back about 1929. They quoted the words of George E. Dimitroff, who at that time was the Executive Secretary of the Communist International. I only quote you this one passage. I could quote thousands of paragraphs for you. Let me quote you: 'The worldwide nature of our program is not mere talk, but an all embracing *blood-soaked reality.*' *That is what they want for us, a blood-soaked reality but it was promised to us by the crystal gazers in Washington;* and you know what I mean by the 'crystal gazers', I presume.

"First of all, we had Queen Eleanor. Mr. Smith said, 'Queen Eleanor is now one of the world's communists. She is one who said this — imagine, coming from the spouse of the former President of the United States for twelve long years — this is what she said: 'The war is but a step in the revolution. The war is but one step in the revolution, and we know who started the war.'

"Then we have Henry Adolph Wallace, the sixty million job magician. You know we only need fifty-four million jobs in America and everybody would be working. He wants sixty million jobs, because some of the bureaucrats want two jobs apiece. Here he is, what he says about revolution: 'We are in for a profound revolution. Those of us who realize the inevitableness of the revolution, and are anxious that it be *gradual and bloodless* instead of *somewhat bloody. Of course, if necessary, we will have it more bloody.*'

"And then Chief Justice Stone had this to say: 'A way has been found for the effective suppression of speeches and press and religion, despite constitutional guarantee,' — from the Chief Justice, from the Chief Justice of the United States.

"Now, my friends, they are planning another ruse; and if it ever happens to this cou-try [*sic*], God help America. They are going to try to put into Mr. Edgar Hoover's position a man by the name of *George Swarzwald.* I think even those who were uneducated on so-called sedition charges, that the majority of the individuals in this department, that Christ-like men and women who realize today what is going on in this country, men who are in this audience today, who want *to know the names of those people, before they are outside, they want to know the names if any. Did you hear any tonight that you recognize? Most of them probably are imported. They are imported from Russia, certainly. If you know the names, please send them to me immediately. . . .*

". . . Didn't you ever read the Morgenthau plan for the starvation of little babies and pregnant women in Germany? Whatever could a child that is born have to do with Hitler or anyone else at the beginning of the war? Why should every child in Germany today not live to be more than two or three months of age? Because Morgenthau wants it that way, and so did F.D.R. . . . *You will know who is behind it when I tell you the story* of a doctor in Akron, Ohio. He boasted to a friend of mine within the last few days, while he was in the service of this country as a doctor, he and others of his kind made it a practice — now, this was not only one man — made it a practice to amputate the limbs of every German they came in contact with whenever they could get away with it; so, that they could never carry a gun. Imagine men of that caliber, sworn to serve this beautiful country of ours, *why should we tolerate them?*

"My friends, this moment someone reminded me of the plan to sterilize them. The nurses, they tell me are going to inject diseases in them, syphilis and other diseases in *every one that came there all of one race, all non-Christians. . . .*

"Now, we are going to get the threats of the people of Argentine, the people of Spain. We have now declared, according to our officials, to have declared Franco to have taken the place of Hitler. *Franco was the savior of what was left of Europe.*

"Now, let me say, I am going to talk about — I almost said, about the Jews. Of course, I would not want to say that. However, I am going to talk about some Jews. I hope that — I am a Christian minister. We must take a Christian attitude. I don't want you to go from this hall with hatred in your heart for any person, for no person. . . .

"Now, this danger which we face — let us call them Zionist Jews if you will, let's call them atheistic, communistic Jewish or Zionist Jews, then let us not fear to condemn them. You remember the Apostles when they went into the upper room after the death of the Master, they went in there, after locking the doors; they closed the windows. (At this time there was a very loud noise as if something was being thrown into the building.)

"Don't be disturbed. That happened, by the way, while Mr. Gerald Smith was saying 'Our Father who art in heaven;' (just then a rock went through the window.) *Do you wonder they were persecuted in other countries in the world? . . .*

"You know I have always made a study of the psychology, sociology of mob reaction. It is exemplified out there. Remember there has to be a leader to that mob. He is not out there. He is probably across the street, looking out the window. There must be certain things, money, other things, in order to have successful mob action; there must be rhythm. There must be some to beat a cadence. Those mobs are chanting; that is the caveman's chant. They were trained to do it. They were trained this afternoon. They are being led; *there will be violence.*

"That is why I say to you, men, don't you do it. Walk out of here dignified. The police will protect you. Put the women on the inside, where there will be no hurt to them. Just walk; don't stop and argue. . . . They want to picket our meetings. They don't want us to picket their meetings. It is the same kind of tolerance, if we said there was a bedbug in bed, 'We don't care for you,' or if we looked under the bed and found a snake and said, 'I am going to be tolerant and leave the snake there.' We will not be tolerant of that mob out there. We are not going to be tolerant any longer.

"We are strong enough. We are not going to be tolerant of their smears any longer. We are going to *stand up and dare them to smear us.* . . .

"So, my friends, since we spent much time tonight trying to quiet the howling mob, I am going to bring my thoughts to a conclusion, and the conclusion is this. We must all be like the Apostles before the coming of the Holy Ghost. We must not lock ourselves in an upper room for fear of the Jews. I speak of the Communistic Zionistic Jew, and those are not American Jews. We don't want them here; we want them to go back where they came from."

For the slim majority of five, Justice Douglas acknowledged that Terminiello, a Catholic priest, had filled his speech with "provocative, challenging" words; that an ugly, riotous turmoil had taken place in and outside the auditorium where he spoke. But in a democracy, Douglas said, "a function of free speech . . . is to invite dispute." To accomplish its purpose the majority used the trial Judge's words to the jury (*any* speech that stirs the public to anger) as the critical point in concluding that the Chicago ordinance, as interpreted by the local court and as applied against Terminiello, was an unconstitutional violation of freedom of speech.

Mr. Justice Douglas delivered the opinion of the Court, saying in part:

> As we have noted, the statutory words "breach of the peace" were defined in instructions to the jury to include speech which "stirs the public to anger, invites dispute, brings about a condition of unrest, or creates a disturbance. . . ." That construction of the ordinance is a ruling on a question of state law that is as binding on us as though the precise words had been written into the ordinance. . . .
>
> The vitality of civil and political institutions in our society depends on free discussion. As Chief Justice Hughes wrote in *De Jonge* v. *Oregon*, 299 U.S. 353, 365, it is only through free debate and free exchange of ideas that government remains responsive to the will of the people and peaceful change is effected. The right to speak freely and to promote diversity of ideas and programs is therefore one of the chief distinctions that sets us apart from totalitarian regimes.
>
> Accordingly a function of free speech under our system of government is to invite dispute. It may indeed best serve its high purpose when it induces a condition of unrest, creates dissatisfaction with conditions as they are, or even stirs people to anger. Speech is often provocative and challenging. It may strike at prejudices and preconceptions and have profound unsettling effects as it presses for acceptance of an idea. That is why freedom of speech, though not absolute, . . . is nevertheless protected against censorship or punishment, unless shown likely to produce a clear and present danger of a serious substantive evil that rises far above public inconvenience, annoyance, or unrest.
>
> . . . There is no room under our Constitution for a more restrictive view. For the alternative would lead to standardization of ideas either by legislatures, courts, or dominant political or community groups.
>
> The ordinance as construed by the trial court seriously invaded this province. It permitted conviction of petitioner if his speech stirred people to anger, invited public dispute, or brought about a condition of unrest. A conviction resting on any of those grounds may not stand.

Feiner v. New York, 340 U.S. 315 (1951)

Two years later, in sharp contrast with its *Terminiello* ruling in which the liberal majority of five went (perhaps) to great lengths to uphold Terminiello's right to make a highly inflammatory speech, the Supreme Court upheld a breach of the peace conviction involving a somewhat similar type of speech. On this occasion Chief Justice Vinson spoke for the majority of six while Justice Black and Justice Douglas (joined by Justice Minton) wrote separate dissents.

Feiner made a provocative, name-calling speech to approximately eighty, mostly black, listeners on a street corner in Syracuse, New York.

Justice Douglas's dissent notes from the record a part of what Feiner, a young college student, said.

"Mayor Costello (of Syracuse) is a champagne-sipping bum; he does not speak for the Negro people."

"The Fifteenth Ward is run by corrupt politicians, and there are horse rooms operating there."

"President Truman is a bum."

"Mayor O'Dwyer [of New York City] is a bum."

"The American Legion is a Nazi Gestapo."

"The Negroes don't have equal rights: they should rise up in arms and fight for their rights."[1]

As Feiner was speaking the crowd blocked the sidewalks and became noisy and restless. One man in the audience threatened Feiner with bodily harm. Two police officers present, sensing that violence was likely, asked Feiner to stop speaking. Three times he refused. Finally, Feiner was arrested and later convicted of violating a New York statute forbidding incitement to breach of the peace.

In the majority opinion, Chief Justice Vinson acknowledged that police officers cannot be used as "an instrument for the suppression of unpopular views." But, he said, "When a speaker passes the bounds of argument or persuasion and undertakes incitement to riot, the police are not powerless to prevent a breach of the peace." Justice Douglas took sharp issue with this use of police power. The record shows, Douglas wrote in dissent, that Feiner faced an unsympathetic audience and "the threat of one man to haul [him] from the stage." Douglas insisted it was precisely "against that kind of threat that speakers need police protection. If they do not receive it and instead the police throw their weight on the side of those who would break up the meeting, the police become the new censors of speech. Police censorship has all the vices of the censorship from city halls which we have repeatedly struck down."[2]

The Court decided, however, that in accord with rulings in three state courts that had found Feiner guilty of inciting breach of the peace, it should not reverse Feiner's conviction "in the name of free speech." It found no conflict between the New York statute and the First Amendment.

Mr. Chief Justice Vinson delivered the opinion of the Court, saying in part:

The findings of the New York courts as to the condition of the crowd and the refusal of petitioner to obey the police requests, supported as they are by the

1. 340 U.S. at 330.
2. Ibid., at 331.

record of this case, are persuasive that the conviction of petitioner for violation of public peace, order and authority does not exceed the bounds of proper state police action. This Court respects, as it must, the interest of the community in maintaining peace and order on its streets. . . . We cannot say that the preservation of that interest here encroaches on the consitutional rights of this petitioner.

We are well aware that the ordinary murmurings and objections of a hostile audience cannot be allowed to silence a speaker, and are also mindful of the possible danger of giving overzealous police officials complete discretion to break up otherwise lawful public meetings. "A State may not unduly suppress free communication of views, religious or other, under the guise of conserving desirable conditions." . . . But we are not faced here with such a situation. It is one thing to say that the police cannot be used as an instrument for the suppression of unpopular views, and another to say that, when as here the speaker passes the bounds of argument or persuasion and undertakes incitement to riot, they are powerless to prevent a breach of the peace. Nor in this case can we condemn the considered judgment of three New York courts approving the means which the police, faced with a crisis, used in the exercise of their power and duty to preserve peace and order. The findings of the state courts as to the existing situation and the imminence of greater disorder coupled with petitioner's deliberate defiance of the police officers convince us that we should not reverse this conviction in the name of free speech.

Edwards v. South Carolina, 372 U.S. 229 (1963)

In another "breach of the peace" dispute, this one decided during the early 1960s in the midst of the civil rights movement in the South, the Supreme Court upheld the right to demonstrate by peaceable assembly on public property. The case was *Edwards* v. *South Carolina*. It involved a group of black college students who had gathered on South Carolina's State House lawn to protest the state's segregation policies. Police ordered them to disperse. When they refused they were arrested and subsequently convicted in a state court for breach of the peace. With only Justice Clark in dissent, the Supreme Court reversed the conviction ruling that the South Carolina statute in question infringed upon free speech and free assembly rights in violation of the First and Fourteenth Amendments. In contrast to the *Feiner* decision (above) where the Court seemed to sanction a relatively simple formula for police suppression of free speech (i.e., rowdies who wish to silence a speaker deliberately create a disturbance; police are called and move in requesting the speaker to stop; if he or she refuses, the speaker, not the rowdies, is charged with disturbing the peace), in *Edwards* the majority looked carefully at the record and ruled there was no justification for the police dispersal order. The Court found no evidence of violence but only "peaceable assembly and a peaceable expression of grievances." Both, the majority of eight decided, are constitutionally protected.

Mr. Justice Stewart delivered the opinion of the Court, saying in part:

The circumstances in this case reflect an exercise of . . . basic constitutional rights in their most pristine and classic form. The petitioners felt aggrieved by laws of South Carolina which allegedly "prohibited Negro privileges in this State." They peaceably assembled at the site of the State Government and there peaceably expressed their grievances "to the citizens of South Carolina, along with the Legislative Bodies of South Carolina." Not until they were told by police officials that they must disperse on pain of arrest did they do more. Even then, they but sang patriotic and religious songs after one of their leaders had delivered a "religious harangue." There was no violence or threat of violence on their part, or on the part of any member of the crowd watching them. Police protection was "ample." . . .

We do not review in this case criminal convictions resulting from the evenhanded application of a precise and narrowly drawn regulatory statute evincing a legislative judgment that certain specific conduct be limited or proscribed. If, for example, the petitioners had been convicted upon evidence that they had violated a law regulating traffic, or had disobeyed a law reasonably limiting the periods during which the State House grounds were open to the public, this would be a different case.

The Fourteenth Amendment does not permit a State to make criminal the peaceful expression of unpopular views. "[A] function of free speech under our system of government is to invite dispute. It may indeed best serve its high purpose when it induces a condition of unrest, creates dissatisfaction with conditions as they are, or even stirs people to anger. Speech is often provocative and challenging. It may strike at prejudices and preconceptions and have profound unsettling effects as it presses for acceptance of an idea. That is why freedom of speech . . . is . . . protected against censorship or punishment, unless shown likely to produce a clear and present danger of a serious substantive evil that rises far above public inconvenience, annoyance, or unrest. . . . There is no room under our Constitution for a more restrictive view.

Cox v. Louisiana, 379 U.S. 536 (1965)

Two years after *Edwards* the Supreme Court was faced with another dispute involving the Southern black civil rights movement. This pertained to a Louisiana breach of the peace law, as well as a state statute that attempted to limit meetings and demonstrations in the area around a courthouse. In *Cox* v. *Louisiana* the state's anti-demonstration statute was modelled after a 1949 law passed by Congress during the trials of Communist Party leaders.[1] The federal statute, which has not been tested in the Courts, made it illegal to picket, demonstrate, or parade near a federal court building as a way of "interfering with the administration of Justice."

In *Cox,* the appellant, who was a minister and a field secretary of CORE (the Congress of Racial Equality), had led some 2,000 black college students in a march protesting the state's racial segregation policies. Cox was convicted in a Louisiana court for violating both the anti-demonstration law and the breach of the peace statute.

With Justice Goldberg speaking for the majority, a badly fragmented Supreme Court reversed both convictions. In the ruling (No. 24) dealing with the Louisiana law, the Court decided that it deprived Cox of free speech and free assembly rights guaranteed by the First Amendment. Justice Goldberg acknowledged that a state has the right to impose nondiscriminatory restrictions on the use of its streets and other public places and further that free

---

1. See *Dennis* v. *United States* (below).

speech and assembly do not mean that everyone may address a group any place at any time. Nevertheless, the Court ruled that by giving such broad discretion (to public officers) to decide such delicate constitutional questions, Louisiana had "sanction [ed] suppression of free expression and [had] facilitat[ed] denial of equal protection."

In addition to the majority opinion, Justices Black, Clark, and White (joined by Harlan) wrote separate opinions concurring in part and dissenting in part from the Court's judgment. Each of the separate opinions agreed with the majority's view reversing Cox's breach of the peace conviction (No. 24), on grounds that *Edwards* v. *South Carolina* (above) controlled the issue. While concurring on number 24, they disagreed with the Court's overturn of Cox's conviction on the Courthouse picketing issue (No. 49). Each of the four dissenters would have sustained the constitutionality of Louisiana's anti-demonstration law as a valid expression of state or city authority to regulate passage on streets and buildings.

The slim majority thought otherwise. Cox had been told by Baton Rouge's highest police officials that the scheduled location for the demonstration, 101 feet from the Courthouse steps, was not "near" the Courthouse within the meaning of Louisiana's anti-demonstration law. Justice Goldberg reasoned that to allow Cox's conviction to stand for "exercising a privilege" to demonstrate, which police had told him was legal, "would be to allow a type of entrapment" that violates the due process clause of the Fourteenth Amendment. The majority had no apparent quarrel with the constitutionality of the Louisiana statute. They disagreed only with the manner in which it was applied to Cox. "There can be no question," Justice Goldberg wrote, "that a state has a legitimate interest in protecting its judicial system from the pressures picketing near a courthouse might create." But, the Court went on, local officials cannot grant permission to demonstrate and then arrest those who demonstrate where they were told they could.

Mr. Justice Goldberg delivered the opinion of the Court, saying in part (in No. 49):

> The record shows that at no time did the police recommend, or even suggest, that the demonstration be held further from the courthouse than it actually was. The police admittedly had prior notice that the demonstration was planned to be held in the vicinity of the courthouse. They were prepared for it at that point and so stationed themselves and their equipment as to keep the demonstrators on the far side of the street. As Cox approached the vicinity of the courthouse, he was met by the Chief of Police and other officials. At this point not only was it not suggested that they hold their assembly elsewhere, or disband, but they were affirmatively told that they could hold the demonstration on the sidewalk of the far side of the street, 101 feet from the courthouse steps. This area was effectively blocked off by the police and traffic rerouted.
>
> Thus, the highest police officials of the city, in the presence of the Sheriff and Mayor, in effect told the demonstrators that they could meet where they did, 101 feet from the courthouse steps, but could not meet closer to the courthouse. In effect, appellant was advised that a demonstration at the place it was held would not be one "near" the courthouse within the terms of the statute.
>
> In *Raley* v. *Ohio,* 360 U.S. 423, this Court held that the Due Process Clause prevented conviction of persons for refusing to answer questions of a state investigating commission when they relied upon assurances of the commission,

either express or implied, that they had a privilege under state law to refuse to answer, though in fact this privilege was not available to them. The situation presented here is analogous to that in *Raley*, which we deem to be controlling. As in *Raley*, under all the circumstances of this case, after the public officials acted as they did, to sustain appellant's later conviction for demonstrating where they told him he could "would be to sanction an indefensible sort of entrapment by the State — convicting a citizen for exercising a privilege which the State had clearly told him was available to him." . . . The Due Process Clause does not permit convictions to be obtained under such circumstances.

This is not to say that had the appellant, entirely on his own, held the demonstration across the street from the courthouse within the sight and hearing of those inside, or *a fortiori*, had he defied an order of the police requiring him to hold this demonstration at some point further away out of the sight and hearing of those inside the courthouse, we would reverse the conviction as in this case. In such cases a state interpretation of the statute to apply to the demonstration as being "near" the courthouse would be subject to quite different considerations. . . .

There remains just one final point: the effect of the Sheriff's order to disperse. The State in effect argues that this order somehow removed the prior grant of permission and reliance on the officials' construction that the demonstration on the far side of the street was not illegal as being "near" the courthouse. This, however, we cannot accept. Appellant was led to believe that his demonstration on the far side of the street violated no statute. He was expressly ordered to leave, not because he was peacefully demonstrating too near the courthouse, nor because a time limit originally set had expired, but because officials erroneously concluded that what he said threatened a breach of the peace. This is apparent from the face of the Sheriff's statement when he ordered the meeting dispersed: "Now, you have been allowed to demonstrate. Up until now your demonstration has been more or less peaceful, but what you are doing now is a direct violation of the law, a disturbance of the peace, and it has got to be broken up immediately." . . . Appellant correctly conceived, as we have held in No. 24, *ante,* that this was not a valid reason for the dispersal order. He therefore was still justified in his continued belief that because of the original official grant of permission he had a right to stay where he was for the few additional minutes required to conclude the meeting. In addition, even if we were to accept the State's version that the sole reason for terminating the demonstration was that appellant exceeded the narrow time limits set by the police, his conviction could not be sustained. Assuming the place of the meeting was appropriate — as appellant justifiably concluded from the official grant of permission — nothing in this courthouse statute, nor in the breach of the peace or obstruction of public passages statutes with their broad sweep and application that we have condemned in No. 24, . . . authorizes the police to draw the narrow time line, unrelated to any policy of these statutes, that would be approved if we were to sustain appellant's conviction on this ground. Indeed, the allowance of such unfettered discretion in the police would itself constitute a procedure such as that condemned in No. 24. . . . In any event, as we have stated, it is our conclusion from the record that the dispersal order had nothing to do with any time or place limitation, and thus, on this ground alone, it is clear that the dispersal order did not remove the protection accorded appellant by the original grant of permission.

Of course this does not mean that the police cannot call a halt to a meeting which though originally peaceful, becomes violent. Nor does it mean that, under properly drafted and administered statutes and ordinances, the authorities cannot set reasonable time limits for assemblies related to the policies of such laws and then order them dispersed when these time limits are exceeded. . . . We merely hold that, under circumstances such as those present in this case, appellant's conviction cannot be sustained on the basis of the dispersal order.

Nothing we have said here or in No. 24, *ante,* is to be interpreted as sanctioning riotous conduct in any form or demonstrations, however peaceful their conduct or commendable their motives which conflict with properly drawn statutes and ordinances designed to promote law and order, protect the community against disorder, regulate traffic, safeguard legitimate interests in private and public property, or protect the administration of justice and other essential governmental functions.

Liberty can only be exercised in a system of law which safeguards order. We reaffirm the repeated holdings of this Court that our constitutional command of free speech and assembly is basic and fundamental and encompasses peaceful social protest, so important to the preservation of the freedoms treasured in a democratic society. We also reaffirm the repeated decisions of this Court that there is no place for violence in a democratic society dedicated to liberty under law, and that the right of peaceful protest does not mean that everyone with opinions or beliefs to express may do so at any time and at any place. There is a proper time and place for even the most peaceful protest and a plain duty and responsibility on the part of all citizens to obey all valid laws and regulations. There is an equally plain requirement for laws and regulations to be drawn so as to give citizens fair warning as to what is illegal; for regulation of conduct that involves freedom of speech and assembly not to be so broad in scope as to stifle First Amendment freedoms, which "need breathing space to survive," . . . for appropriate limitations on the discretion of public officials where speech and assembly are intertwined with regulated conduct; and for all such laws and regulations to be applied with an equal hand. We believe that all of these requirements can be met in an ordered society dedicated to liberty. We reaffirm our conviction that "[f]reedom and viable government are . . . indivisible concepts." . . .

The application of these principles requires us to reverse the judgment of the Supreme Court of Louisiana.

10

SYMBOLIC SPEECH

"Symbolic speech," as Pritchett defines the term, at times has involved communicating ideas or protests by such unusual means "as burning a draft card, pouring blood over draft files" in order to express opposition to American involvement in Vietnam.[1] At times it has seemed that certain forms of symbolic speech of this nature may be more effective in making a point of protest than conventional speaking. Is such "symbolic speech" constitutionally privileged under the free speech guarantee of the First Amendment? The Supreme Court has answered yes and no to that question.

Perhaps the widest variety of symbolic speech cases to reach the Supreme Court dealt with disputes related to the civil rights movement and to protests occasioned by the war in Vietnam. In *Garner* v. *Louisiana*[2] for example, the Court had to decide if trespassing on private property that is clearly illegal, becomes legal when it is used as "a form of expression" or as "social protest." Speaking for the Court, Justice Harlan acknowledged that a sit-in "was a form of expression" that was constitutionally privileged but he denied that the Fourteenth Amendment protected demonstrations on private property if the owner objected.

In *Bell* v. *Maryland*,[3] decided three years later, Justice Black made much the same point for the Court. Demonstrators or participants in a sit-in, Black said, had no legal right to be in a restaurant against the owner's wishes. Ultimately the sit-in matter was settled by Congress in the 1964 Civil Rights Act, which made it illegal to discriminate along racial lines in places of "public accommodation." In this instance Congress was "ahead" of the Supreme Court. That was usually not the case in civil rights matters.

Tinker v. Des Moines School District, 393 U.S. 503 (1969)

Symbolic speech problems also arose during the Vietnam protest movement. Once again the Supreme Court's record was mixed. In *United States* v. *O'Brien*[4] the Court ruled that draft card burning was *not* a form of constitutionally protected free speech.

1. Pritchett, op. cit., at 323.
2. 368 U.S. 157 (1961).
3. 378 U.S. 226 (1964).
4. 391 U.S. 367 (1968).

However, a year later in *Tinker* v. *Des Moines School District* the Supreme Court upheld the right of students to wear black armbands to protest the Vietnamese War. In *Tinker,* Justices Black (now more conservative than earlier) and Harlan wrote separate dissents upholding the School Board's decision forbidding the armbands.

The petitioners were three students aged 13, 15, and 16, two of whom, John and Mary Beth Tinker, were brother and sister. To protest the war they decided to wear black armbands. Thereupon the School Board adopted a policy suspending students who refused to remove the armbands. The petitioners were suspended. However, this form of "symbolic speech" was upheld by the Supreme Court.

Mr. Justice Fortas delivered the opinion of the Court, saying in part:

> Under our Constitution, free speech is not a right that is given only to be so circumscribed that it exists in principle but not in fact. Freedom of expression would not truly exist if the right could be exercised only in an area that a benevolent government has provided as a safe haven for crackpots. The Constitution says that Congress (and the States) may not abridge the right to free speech. This provision means what it says. We properly read it to permit reasonable regulation of speech-connected activities in carefully restricted circumstances. But we do not confine the permissible exercise of First Amendment rights to a telephone booth or the four corners of a pamphlet, or to supervised and ordained discussion in a school classroom.

> If a regulation were adopted by school officials forbidding discussion of the Vietnam conflict, or the expression by any student of opposition to it anywhere on school property except as part of a prescribed classroom exercise, it would be obvious that the regulation would violate the constitutional rights of students, at least if it could not be justified by a showing that the students' activities would materially and substantially disrupt the work and discipline of the school. . . . In the circumstances of the present case, the prohibition of the silent, passive "witness of the armbands," as one of the children called it, is no less offensive to the Constitution's guarantees.

> As we have discussed, the record does not demonstrate any facts which might reasonably have led school authorities to forecast substantial disruption of or material interference with school activities, and no disturbances or disorders on the school premises in fact occurred. These petitioners merely went about their ordained rounds in school. Their deviation consisted only in wearing on their sleeve a band of black cloth, not more than two inches wide. They wore it to exhibit their disapproval of the Vietnam hostilities and their advocacy of a truce, to make their views known, and, by their example, to influence others to adopt them. They neither interrupted school activities nor sought to intrude in the school affairs or the lives of others. They caused discussion outside of the classrooms, but no interference with work and no disorder. In the circumstances, our Constitution does not permit officials of the State to deny their form of expression.

11

FREEDOM OF THE PRESS

The First Amendment also guarantees freedom of the press, and a 1925 Minnesota statute that provided for abatement as a public nuisance any "malicious, scandalous and defamatory newspaper, magazine or other periodical," gave the Supreme Court opportunity for its first significant anticensorship, free press decision.

Near v. Minnesota, 283 U.S. 697 (1931)

Near v. *Minnesota* involved what has been called "Minnesota's gag law." The Minnesota statute established an injunction process, enforceable by contempt of court charges, that could shut down a newspaper for printing malicious, scandalous, obscene or otherwise defamatory material. According to the statute, the injunction could be lifted only by convincing the court that issued the injunction that in the future the publication would refrain from printing such objectionable material. Thus the question arose, did the Minnesota statute sanction "prior restraint" or "previous censorship," both of which violate traditional free press constitutional principles? The newspaper involved in *Near* was a Minnesota weekly that consistently attacked local law enforcement authorities charging them with tolerating "gangsters" and accepting graft from the illegal operators they were supposed to police. A badly split (5–4) Supreme Court declared the Minnesota statute unconstitutional and for the first time, therefore, applied the First Amendment's freedom of the press guarantee to the states via the due process clause of the Fourteenth Amendment. In this sense, *Near* was another highly significant step in the long process by which the Supreme Court has "nationalized" First Amendment freedoms and protected them from state as well as federal impairment.

Led by Justice Butler, four dissenters (Justices Van Devanter, McReynolds, and Sutherland) sharply criticized the majority viewpoint. Butler argued that because the Minnesota statute did not "authorize administrative control" in advance of publication it should not be stricken down as "prior restraint." Similarly, Justice Butler noted, because a court injunction could be issued only *after* a publication had violated the statute, what took place was not "previous restraint" but "abating a nuisance already committed." He went on to say: "It is of importance that the States shall be untrammeled and free to employ all just and appropriate measures to prevent abuses of the liberty of the press."

Clearly the slim majority did not look upon the Minnesota statute as a "just and appropriate measure." Calling the state law the "essence of censorship" the Supreme Court ruled it an unconstitutional violation of freedom of the press.

Mr. Chief Justice Hughes delivered the opinion of the Court, saying in part:

The object of the statute is not punishment, in the ordinary sense, but suppression of the offending newspaper or periodical. The reason for the enactment, as the state court has said, is that prosecutions to enforce penal statutes for libel do not result in "efficient repression or suppression of the evils of scandal." Describing the business of publication as a public nuisance, does not obscure the substance of the proceeding which the statute authorizes. It is the continued publication of scandalous and defamatory matter that constitutes the business and the declared nuisance. In the case of public officers, it is the reiteration of charges of official misconduct, and the fact that the newspaper or periodical is principally devoted to that purpose, that exposes it to suppression. In the present instance, the proof was that nine editions of the newspaper or periodical in question were published on successive dates, and that they were chiefly devoted to charges against public officers and in relation to the prevalence and protection of crime. In such a case, these officers are not left to their ordinary remedy in a suit for libel, or the authorities to a prosecution for criminal libel. Under this statute, a publisher of a newspaper or periodical, undertaking to conduct a campaign to expose and to censure official derelictions, and devoting his publication principally to that purpose, must face not simply the possibility of a verdict against him in a suit or prosecution for libel, but a determination that his newspaper or periodical is a public nuisance to be abated, and that this abatement and suppression will follow unless he is prepared with legal evidence to prove the truth of the charges and also to satisfy the court that, in addition to being true, the matter was published with good motives and for justifiable ends.

This suppression is accomplished by enjoining publication and that restraint is the object and effect of the statute.

. . . The statute not only operates to suppress the offending newspaper or periodical but to put the publisher under an effective censorship. When a newspaper or periodical is found to be "malicious, scandalous and defamatory," and is suppressed as such, resumption of publication is punishable as a contempt of court by fine or imprisonment. Thus, where a newspaper or periodical has been suppressed because of the circulation of charges against public officers of official misconduct, it would seem to be clear that the renewal of the publication of such charges would constitute a contempt and that the judgment would lay a permanent restraint upon the publisher, to escape which he must satisfy the court as to the character of a new publication. Whether he would be permitted again to publish matter deemed to be derogatory to the same or other public officers would depend upon the court's ruling. In the present instance the judgment restrained the defendants from "publishing, circulating, having in their possession, selling or giving away any publication whatsoever which is a malicious, scandalous or defamatory newspaper, as defined by law." The law gives no definition except that covered by the words "scandalous and defamatory," and publications charging official misconduct are of that class. While the court, answering the objection that the judgment was too broad, saw no reason for construing it as restraining the defendants "from operating a newspaper in harmony with the public welfare to which all must yield," and said that the defendants had not indicated "any desire to conduct their business in the usual and legitimate manner," the manifest inference is that, at least with respect to a new publication directed against official misconduct, the defendant would be held, under penalty of punishment for contempt as provided in the statute, to a manner of publication which the court considered to be "usual and legitimate" and consistent with the public welfare.

If we cut through mere details of procedure, the operation and effect of the statute in substance is that public authorities may bring the owner or publisher of a newspaper or periodical before a judge upon a charge of conducting a business of publishing scandalous and defamatory matter — in particular that the matter consists of charges against public officers of official dereliction — and unless the owner or publisher is able and disposed to bring competent evidence to satisfy the judge that the charges are true and are published with good motives and for justifiable ends, his newspaper or periodical is suppressed and further publication is made punishable as a contempt. This is of the essence of censorship.

The question is whether a statute authorizing such proceedings in restraint of publication is consistent with the conception of the liberty of the press as historically conceived and guaranteed. In determining the extent of the constitutional protection, it has been generally, if not universally, considered that it is the chief purpose of the guaranty to prevent previous restraints upon publication.

The fact that for approximately one hundred and fifty years there has been almost an entire absence of attempts to impose previous restraints upon publications relating to the malfeasance of public officers is significant of the deep-seated conviction that such restraints would violate constitutional right. Public officers, whose character and conduct remain open to debate and free discussion in the press, find their remedies for false accusations in actions under libel laws providing for redress and punishment, and not in proceedings to restrain the publication of newspapers and periodicals. The general principle that the constitutional guaranty of the liberty of the press gives immunity from previous restraints has been approved in many decisions under the provisions of state constitutions.

Nor can it be said that the constitutional freedom from previous restraint is lost because charges are made of derelictions which constitute crimes. With the multiplying provisions of penal codes, and of municipal charters and ordinances carrying penal sanctions, the conduct of public officers is very largely within the purview of criminal statutes. The freedom of the press from previous restraint has never been regarded as limited to such animadversions as lay outside the range of penal enactments. Historically, there is no such limitation; it is inconsistent with the reason which underlies the privilege, as the privilege so limited would be of slight value for the purposes for which it came to be established.

The statute in question cannot be justified by reason of the fact that the publisher is permitted to show, before injunction issues, that the matter published is true and is published with good motives and for justifiable ends. If such a statute, authorizing suppression and injunction on such a basis, is constitutionally valid, it would be equally permissible for the legislature to provide that at any time the publisher of any newspaper could be brought before a court, or even an administrative officer (as the constitutional protection may not be regarded as resting on mere procedural details) and required to produce proof of the truth of his publication, or of what he intended to publish, and of his motives, or stand enjoined. If this can be done, the legislature may provide machinery for determining in the complete exercise of its discretion what are justifiable ends and restrain publication accordingly. And it would be but a step to a complete system of censorship. The recognition of authority to impose previous restraint upon publication in order to protect the community against the circulation of charges of misconduct, and especially of official misconduct, necessarily would carry with it the admission of the authority of the censor against which the constitutional barrier was erected. The preliminary freedom, by virtue of the very reason for its existence, does not depend, as this Court has said, on proof of truth.

For these reasons we hold the statute, so far as it authorized the proceedings in this action under clause (b) of section one, to be an infringement of the liberty of the press guaranteed by the Fourteenth Amendment.

Lovell v. Griffin, 303 U.S. 444 (1938)

Is the distribution of religious (or any other) handbills protected under the freedom of the press provision of the First Amendment? Is a municipal ordinance that requires official permission from a municipal administrator before handbills can be distributed a valid use of local "police power"? These were the questions the Supreme Court had to answer in *Lovell* v. *Griffin*. Involved was a city ordinance in Griffin, Georgia that "in its broad sweep" prohibited the distribution of "circulars, handbooks, or literature of any kind" without a license from the city manager. The appellant, Alma Lovell, a member of the Jehovah's Witnesses, was convicted of violating the ordinance for having distributed without a license a pamphlet and a magazine called *Golden Age*. Counsel for the city argued that the ordinance was necessary because, without it, the city would have "sanitary problems" keeping the streets clear of discarded pamphlets and circulars.

Speaking for a unanimous Court (Justice Cardozo did not participate in the case) Chief Justice Hughes declared that the Griffin ordinance was "invalid on its face." A free press, the Court ruled, is not confined to newspapers and periodicals, it applies also to pamphlets and leaflets. Subjecting the distribution of such forms of literature to prior licensing, the Court said, "strikes at the very foundation of freedom of the press" and is an unconstitutional form of censorship.

Mr. Chief Justice Hughes delivered the opinion of the Court, saying in part:

We think that the ordinance is invalid on its face. Whatever the motive which induced its adoption, its character is such that it strikes at the very foundation of the freedom of the press by subjecting it to license and censorship. The struggle for the freedom of the press was primarily directed against the power of the licensor. It was against that power that John Milton directed his assault by his "Appeal for the Liberty of Unlicensed Printing." And the liberty of the press became initially a right to publish *"without* a license what formerly could be published only *with* one." While this freedom from previous restraint upon publication cannot be regarded as exhausting the guaranty of liberty, the prevention of that restraint was a leading purpose in the adoption of the constitutional provision. . . . Legislation of the type of the ordinance in question would restore the system of license and censorship in its baldest form.

The liberty of the press is not confined to newspapers and periodicals. It necessarily embraces pamphlets and leaflets. These indeed have been historic weapons in the defense of liberty, as the pamphlets of Thomas Paine and others in our own history abundantly attest. The press in its historic connotation comprehends every sort of publication which affords a vehicle of information and opinion.

New York Times v. United States, 403 U.S. 713 (1971)

In a "less spectacular" prior restraint, freedom of the press case decided just weeks before the controversy concerning publication of the Pentagon papers burst on the scene, the Supreme Court voided an injunction against publication and distribution of leaflets by irate homeowners against an Illinois realtor accused of "blockbusting" tactics. The leaflets were designed to inform the realtor's home neighborhood of his practice of "busting" previously all white housing areas. The case was *Organization for a Better Austin* v. *Keefe*.[1]

There the Court rejected arguments by Keefe (the realtor) who maintained that the injunction enjoining distribution of the leaflet was necessary to protect his privacy. The Court ruled the injunction void as a prior restraint on speech and publication and therefore a violation of the First Amendment's free press guarantee.

Shortly thereafter the Supreme Court decided the most far-reaching and controversial freedom of the press case in its history, the Pentagon papers dispute involving President Nixon and two of his long term journalistic adversaries, the *New York Times* and the *Washington Post. New York Times Co.* v. *United States* had all the makings of high drama. Although what Justice Holmes wrote about "great cases" making "bad law" may certainly apply here, it would be difficult to overstate the significance of the Court's ruling in this classic confrontation between "national security" and "freedom of the press."

It began unobtrusively enough. On Sunday, June 13, 1971 the *New York Times* printed a story on its front pages with the following headline: "Vietnam Archive: Pentagon Study Traces 3 Decades of Growing U.S. Involvement." The *Times* also included three pages of documentary materials based upon a 7,000-page top-secret study conducted by Pentagon Intelligence personnel tracing United States involvement in Vietnam during the presidencies of Eisenhower, Kennedy, Johnson, and Nixon. The study had been turned over to the *Times* by Daniel Ellsberg, a one-time Pentagon employee and a former Marine officer with service in Vietnam, who had access to the study while working in California for the Rand Corporation, a private research organization with close Pentagon ties.

The *Times* printed a second installment on Monday, June 14, and that night, just as the Tuesday edition was about to appear, the Justice Department called and asked the newspaper to stop further publication, charging it was violating Federal espionage laws. When the *Times* refused, Attorney General Mitchell sought and was granted an injunction by New York District Court Judge Gurfein, the first such against a newspaper in the nation's history. Three days later a District Court in Washington, D.C. refused to grant the Justice Department an injunction to stop the Washington *Post* from publishing the Pentagon papers. The next day, Judge Gurfein, who had granted the New York injunc-

1. 402 U.S. 415 (1971).

tion during his first day on the federal bench, rescinded it. Within hours
Judge Gurfein was overruled by a Circuit Court of Appeal in New York, but
the Washington Circuit Court upheld the Washington District Court.

Judicial action had proceeded with amazing swiftness. The Justice Department received its New York injunction on June 15. On the 18th it was in court
again, this time in Washington, D.C. The Circuit Court of Appeal acted on
June 19. The Supreme Court agreed to hear the cases on June 25, actually
heard arguments on June 26, and four days later handed down its historic
decision voiding the injunctions.

A badly divided (6–3) Court announced its ruling in a three paragraph per
curiam opinion noting that the Justice Department had not met the "heavy
burden" necessary to justify prior restraint on freedom of the press. All nine
justices then wrote separate opinions. The majority was made up of Justices
Black, Douglas, Brennan, Marshall, Stewart, and White. The dissenters were
Chief Justice Burger, who angrily blasted the newspapers for accepting and
printing "stolen property," and Justices Harlan and Blackmun. All three dissenters protested the uncommon haste of the Court's action. Blackmun was
particularly bitter, warning that if publication of the Pentagon papers pro-
longed the war in Vietnam or delayed the freeing of American POWs, "then
the Nation's people will know where the responsibility for these sad consequences rests." Despite the general view at the time that the decision was a
major victory for freedom of the press, Pritchett's assessment of the Court's
decision seems accurate and reasonable. He writes that "while the result in
New York Times was clear enough, the Court's opinions do not add up to a
sound defense of freedom of the press. It would appear that at least four
members of the Court (Burger, Harlan, Blackmun, and White) and possibly
five (add Stewart) believed that the newspapers could be criminally punished
for their action."[2] Thus the decision was not the ringing endorsement of an
untrammeled press. National security, tenuous and specious as the Nixon
arguments were in this case, continued to have its judicial adherents.

Reproduced here is part of the Court's per curiam opinion and the relevant
portions of the concurring opinions of Justices Black, Brennan, Stewart and
White, and of the dissenting opinions of Chief Justice Burger and Justices
Harlan and Blackmun.

Per Curiam.
We granted certiorari in these cases in which the United States seeks to enjoin
the New York Times and the Washington Post from publishing the contents of a
classified study entitled "History of U.S. Decision-Making Process on Viet Nam
Policy." *Post,* pp. 942, 943.

"Any system of prior restraints of expression comes to this Court bearing a
heavy presumption against its constitutional validity." *Bantam Books, Inc. v. Sullivan,* 372 U.S. 58, 70 (1963); see also *Near v. Minnesota,* 283 U.S. 697 (1931). The
Government "thus carries a heavy burden of showing justification for the imposition of such a restraint." *Organization for a Better Austin v. Keefe,* 402 U.S. 415, 419
(1971). The District Court for the Southern District of New York in the *New York
Times* case and the District Court for the District of Columbia and the Court of
Appeals for the District of Columbia Circuit in the *Washington Post* case held that
the Government had not met that burden. We agree.

2. Pritchett, op. cit., at 338.

The judgment of the Court of Appeals for the District of Columbia Circuit is therefore affirmed. The order of the Court of Appeals for the Second Circuit is reversed and the case is remanded with directions to enter a judgment affirming the judgment of the District Court for the Southern District of New York. The stays entered June 25, 1971, by the Court are vacated. The judgments shall issue forthwith.

So ordered.

MR. JUSTICE BLACK, with whom MR. JUSTICE DOUGLAS joins, concurring.

I adhere to the view that the Government's case against the Washington Post should have been dismissed and that the injunction against the New York Times should have been vacated without oral argument when the cases were first presented to this Court. I believe that every moment's continuance of the injunctions against these newspapers amounts to a flagrant, indefensible, and continuing violation of the First Amendment. Furthermore, after oral argument, I agree completely that we must affirm the judgment of the Court of Appeals for the District of Columbia Circuit and reverse the judgment of the Court of Appeals for the Second Circuit for the reasons stated by my Brothers DOUGLAS and BRENNAN. In my view it is unfortunate that some of my Brethren are apparently willing to hold that the publication of news may sometimes be enjoined. Such a holding would make a shambles of the First Amendment.

Our Government was launched in 1789 with the adoption of the Constitution. The Bill of Rights, including the First Amendment, followed in 1791. Now, for the first time in the 182 years since the founding of the Republic, the federal courts are asked to hold that the First Amendment does not mean what it says, but rather means that the Government can halt the publication of current news of vital importance to the people of this country.

In seeking injunctions against these newspapers and in its presentation to the Court, the Executive Branch seems to have forgotten the essential purpose and history of the First Amendment. When the Constitution was adopted, many people strongly opposed it because the document contained no Bill of Rights to safeguard certain basic freedoms. They especially feared that the new powers granted to a central government might be interpreted to permit the government to curtail freedom of religion, press, assembly, and speech. In response to an overwhelming public clamor, James Madison offered a series of amendments to satisfy citizens that these great liberties would remain safe and beyond the power of government to abridge. Madison proposed what later became the First Amendment in three parts, two of which are set out below, and one of which proclaimed: "The people shall not be deprived or abridged of their right to speak, to write, or to publish their sentiments; *and the freedom of the press, as one of the great bulwarks of liberty, shall be inviolable.*" (Emphasis added.) The amendments were offered to *curtail* and *restrict* the general powers granted to the Executive, Legislative, and Judicial Branches two years before in the original Constitution. The Bill of Rights changed the original Constitution into a new charter under which no branch of government could abridge the people's freedoms of press, speech, religion, and assembly. Yet the Solicitor General argues and some members of the Court appear to agree that the general powers of the Government adopted in the original Constitution should be interpreted to limit and restrict the specific and emphatic guarantees of the Bill of Rights adopted later. I can imagine no greater perversion of history. Madison and the other Framers of the First Amendment, able men that they were, wrote in language they earnestly believed could never be misunderstood: "Congress shall make no law . . . abridging the freedom . . . of the press. . . ." Both the history and language of the First

Amendment support the view that the press must be left free to publish news, whatever the source, without censorship, injunctions, or prior restraints.

MR. JUSTICE BRENNAN, concurring.

The error that has pervaded these cases from the outset was the granting of any injunctive relief whatsoever, interim or otherwise. The entire thrust of the Government's claim throughout these cases has been that publication of the material sought to be enjoined "could," or "might," or "may" prejudice the national interest in various ways. But the First Amendment tolerates absolutely no prior judicial restraints of the press predicated upon surmise or conjecture that untoward consequences may result. Our cases, it is true, have indicated that there is a single, extremely narrow class of cases in which the First Amendment's ban on prior judicial restraint may be overridden. Our cases have thus far indicated that such cases may arise only when the Nation "is at war," *Schenck* v. *United States,* 249 U.S. 47, 52 (1919), during which times "[n]o one would question but that a government might prevent actual obstruction to its recruiting service or the publication of the sailing dates of transports or the number and location of troops." *Near* v. *Minnesota,* 283 U.S. 697, 716 (1931). Even if the present world situation were assumed to be tantamount to a time of war, or if the power of presently available armaments would justify even in peacetime the suppression of information that would set in motion a nuclear holocaust, in neither of these actions has the Government presented or even alleged that publication of items from or based upon the material at issue would cause the happening of an event of that nature. "[T]he chief purpose of [the First Amendment's] guaranty [is] to prevent previous restraints upon publication." *Near* v. *Minnesota, supra,* at 713. Thus, only governmental allegation and proof that publication must inevitably, directly, and immediately cause the occurrence of an event kindred to imperiling the safety of a transport already at sea can support even the issuance of an interim restraining order. In no event may mere conclusions be sufficient: for if the Executive Branch seeks judicial aid in preventing publication, it must inevitably submit the basis upon which that aid is sought to scrutiny by the judiciary. And therefore, every restraint issued in this case, whatever its form, has violated the First Amendment — and not less so because that restraint was justified as necessary to afford the courts an opportunity to examine the claim more thoroughly. Unless and until the Government has clearly made out its case, the First Amendment commands that no injunction may issue.

MR. JUSTICE WHITE, with whom MR. JUSTICE STEWART joins, concurring.

I concur in today's judgments, but only because of the concededly extraordinary protection against prior restraints enjoyed by the press under our constitutional system. I do not say that in no circumstances would the First Amendment permit an injunction against publishing information about government plans or operations. Nor, after examining the materials the Government characterizes as the most sensitive and destructive, can I deny that revelation of these documents will do substantial damage to public interests. Indeed, I am confident that their disclosure will have that result. But I nevertheless agree that the United States has not satisfied the very heavy burden that it must meet to warrant an injunction against publication in these cases, at least in the absence of express and appropriately limited congressional authorization for prior restraints in circumstances such as these.

MR. CHIEF JUSTICE BURGER, dissenting.

So clear are the constitutional limitations on prior restraint against expression, that from the time of *Near* v. *Minnesota,* 283 U.S. 697 (1931), until recently in *Organization for a Better Austin* v. *Keefe,* 402 U.S. 415 (1971), we have had little occasion to be concerned with cases involving prior restraints against news reporting on matters of public interest. There is, therefore, little variation among the members of the Court in terms of resistance to prior restraints against publication. Adherence to this basic constitutional principle, however, does not make these cases simple. In these cases, the imperative of a free and unfettered press comes into collision with another imperative, the effective functioning of a complex modern government and specifically the effective exercise of certain constitutional powers of the Executive. Only those who view the First Amendment as an absolute in all circumstances — a view I respect, but reject — can find such cases as these to be simple or easy.

These cases are not simple for another and more immediate reason. We do not know the facts of the cases. No District Judge knew all the facts. No Court of Appeals judge knew all the facts. No member of this Court knows all the facts.

Why are we in this posture, in which only those judges to whom the First Amendment is absolute and permits of no restraint in any circumstances or for any reason, are really in a position to act?

I suggest we are in this posture because these cases have been conducted in unseemly haste. MR. JUSTICE HARLAN covers the chronology of events demonstrating the hectic pressures under which these cases have been processed and I need not restate them. The prompt setting of these cases reflects our universal abhorrence of prior restraint. But prompt judicial action does not mean unjudicial haste.

Here, moreover, the frenetic haste is due in large part to the manner in which the Times proceeded from the date it obtained the purloined documents. It seems reasonably clear now that the haste precluded reasonable and deliberate judicial treatment of these cases and was not warranted. The precipitate action of this Court aborting trials not yet completed is not the kind of judicial conduct that ought to attend the disposition of a great issue.

The newspapers make a derivative claim under the First Amendment; they denominate this right as the public "right to know"; by implication, the Times asserts a sole trusteeship of that right by virtue of its journalistic "scoop." The right is asserted as an absolute. Of course, the First Amendment right itself is not an absolute, as Justice Holmes so long ago pointed out in his aphorism concerning the right to shout "fire" in a crowded theater if there was no fire. There are other exceptions, some of which Chief Justice Hughes mentioned by way of example in *Near* v. *Minnesota.* There are no doubt other exceptions no one has had occasion to describe or discuss. Conceivably such exceptions may be lurking in these cases and would have been flushed had they been properly considered in the trial courts, free from unwarranted deadlines and frenetic pressures. An issue of this importance should be tried and heard in a judicial atmosphere conducive to thoughtful, reflective deliberation, especially when haste, in terms of hours, is unwarranted in light of the long period the Times, by its own choice, deferred publication.

It is not disputed that the Times has had unauthorized possession of the documents for three to four months, during which it has had its expert analysts studying them, presumably digesting them and preparing the material for publication. During all of this time, the Times, presumably in its capacity as trustee of the public's "right to know," has held up publication for purposes it considered proper and thus public knowledge was delayed. No doubt this was for a good reason; the analysis of 7,000 pages of complex material drawn from a vastly greater volume of material would inevitably take time and the writing of good news stories takes time. But why should the United States Government, from whom this information was illegally acquired by someone, along with all the counsel, trial judges, and appellate judges be placed under needless pressure? After these months of deferral, the alleged "right to know" has somehow and suddenly become a right that must be vindicated instanter.

Would it have been unreasonable, since the newspaper could anticipate the Government's objections to release of secret material, to give the Government an opportunity to review the entire collection and determine whether agreement could be reached on publication? Stolen or not, if security was not in fact jeopardized, much of the material could no doubt have been declassified, since it spans a period ending in 1968. With such an approach — one that great newspapers have in the past practiced and stated editorially to be the duty of an honorable press — the newspapers and Government might well have narrowed the area of disagreement as to what was and was not publishable, leaving the remainder to be resolved in orderly litigation, if necessary. To me it is hardly believable that a newspaper long regarded as a great institution in American life would fail to perform one of the basic and simple duties of every citizen with respect to the discovery or possession of stolen property or secret government documents. That duty, I had thought — perhaps naively — was to report forthwith, to responsible public officers. This duty rests on taxi drivers, Justices, and the New York Times. The course followed by the Times, whether so calculated or not, removed any possibility of orderly litigation of the issues. If the action of the judges up to now has been correct, that result is sheer happenstance.

Our grant of the writ of certiorari before final judgment in the *Times* case aborted the trial in the District Court before it had made a complete record pursuant to the mandate of the Court of Appeals for the Second Circuit.

The consequence of all this melancholy series of events is that we literally do not know what we are acting on. As I see it, we have been forced to deal with litigation concerning rights of great magnitude without an adequate record, and surely without time for adequate treatment either in the prior proceedings or in this Court. It is interesting to note that counsel on both sides, in oral argument before this Court, were frequently unable to respond to questions on factual points. Not surprisingly they pointed out that they had been working literally "around the clock" and simply were unable to review the documents that give rise to these cases and were not familiar with them. This Court is in no better posture. I agree generally with MR. JUSTICE HARLAN and MR. JUSTICE BLACKMUN but I am not prepared to reach the merits.

MR. JUSTICE HARLAN, dissenting.

With all respect, I consider that the Court has been almost irresponsibly feverish in dealing with these cases.

Both the Court of Appeals for the Second Circuit and the Court of Appeals for the District of Columbia Circuit rendered judgment on June 23. The New York Times' petition for certiorari, its motion for accelerated consideration thereof, and its application for interim relief were filed in this Court on June 24 at about 11 a.m. The application of the United States for interim relief in the *Post* case was also filed here on June 24 at about 7:15 p.m. This Court's order setting a hearing before us on June 26 at 11 a.m., a course which I joined only to avoid the possibility of even more peremptory action by the Court, was issued less than 24 hours before. The record in the *Post* case was filed with the Clerk shortly before 1 p.m. on June 25; the record in the *Times* case did not arrive until 7 or 8 o'clock that same night. The briefs of the parties were received less than two hours before argument on June 26.

The frenzied train of events took place in the name of the presumption against prior restraints created by the First Amendment. Due regard for the extraordinarily important and difficult questions involved in these litigations should have led the Court to shun such a precipitate timetable. In order to decide the merits of these cases properly, some or all of the following questions should have been faced:

1. Whether the Attorney General is authorized to bring these suits in the name of the United States. Compare *In re Debs,* 158 U.S. 564 (1895), with *Youngstown Sheet & Tube Co. v. Sawyer,* 343 U.S. 579 (1952). This question involves as well the construction and validity of a singularly opaque statute — the Espionage Act, 18 U.S.C. §793(e).

2. Whether the First Amendment permits the federal courts to enjoin publication of stories which would present a serious threat to national security. See *Near v. Minnesota,* 283 U.S. 697, 716 (1931) (dictum).

3. Whether the threat to publish highly secret documents is of itself a sufficient implication of national security to justify an injunction on the theory that regardless of the contents of the documents harm enough results simply from the demonstration of such a breach of secrecy.

4. Whether the unauthorized disclosure of any of these particular documents would seriously impair the national security.

5. What weight should be given to the opinion of high officers in the Executive Branch of the Government with respect to questions 3 and 4.

6. Whether the newspapers are entitled to retain and use the documents notwithstanding the seemingly uncontested facts that the documents, or the originals of which they are duplicates, were purloined from the Government's possession and that the newspapers received them with knowledge that they had been feloniously acquired. Cf. *Liberty Lobby, Inc. v. Pearson,* 129 U.S. App. D.C. 74, 390 F. 2d 489 (1967, amended 1968).

7. Whether the threatened harm to the national security or the Government's possessory interest in the documents justifies the issuance of an injunction against publication in light of —

a. The strong First Amendment policy against prior restraints on publication;

b. The doctrine against enjoining conduct in violation of criminal statutes; and

c. The extent to which the materials at issue have apparently already been otherwise disseminated.

These are difficult questions of fact, of law, and of judgment; the potential consequences of erroneous decision are enormous. The time which has been available to us, to the lower courts, and to the parties has been wholly inadequate for giving these cases the kind of consideration they deserve. It is a reflection on the stability of the judicial process that these great issues — as important as any that have arisen during my time on the Court — should have been decided under the pressures engendered by the torrent of publicity that has attended these litigations from their inception.

MR. JUSTICE BLACKMUN, dissenting.

I strongly urge, and sincerely hope, that these two newspapers will be fully aware of their ultimate responsibilities to the United States of America. Judge Wilkey, dissenting in the District of Columbia case, after a review of only the affidavits before his court (the basic papers had not then been made available by either party), concluded that there were a number of examples of documents that, if in the possession of the Post, and if published, "could clearly result in great harm to the nation," and he defined "harm" to mean "the death of soldiers, the destruction of alliances, the greatly increased difficulty of negotiation with our enemies, the inability of our diplomats to negotiate. . . ." I, for one, have now been able to give at least some cursory study not only to the affidavits, but to the material itself. I regret to say that from this examination I fear that Judge Wilkey's statements have possible foundation. I therefore share his concern. I hope that damage has not already been done. If, however, damage has been done, and if, with the Court's action today, these newspapers proceed to publish the critical documents and there results therefrom "the death of soldiers, the destruction of alliances, the greatly increased difficulty of negotiation with our enemies, the inability of our diplomats to negotiate," to which list I might add the factors of prolongation of the war and of further delay in the freeing of United States prisoners, then the Nation's people will know where the responsibility for these sad consequences rests.

Branzburg v. Hayes, 408 U.S. 665 (1972)

How "privileged and confidential" are a newspaper reporter's sources of information? Should a reporter be compelled to answer grand jury questions concerning information received in confidence? Reporters claim they must guarantee complete confidentiality to their informants, arguing that many times critical information about an important story or investigation will be given only if the informant can be certain his identity will not be revealed. Many states have protected this special informant-reporter relationship by adopting so-called "shield laws" that guarantee the confidentiality of a reporter's sources of information. There is no Federal shield law.

In *Branzburg* v. *Hayes* a badly split (5–4) Supreme Court dealt with the subject for the first time and rejected a reporter's claim of confidentiality. It ruled instead that reporters have the same obligation "as other citizens" to answer questions before a grand jury "relevant to an investigation into the commission of crime." Justice White wrote a long, detailed opinion for the majority that made essentially one point, that reporters are as accountable to grand jury investigations as any private citizen would be. He argued that if grand juries began abusing their powers the Courts would then intervene to restrain them.

The Court's decision drew separate dissents from Justice Douglas and Justice Stewart with whom Justices Brennan and Marshall joined. Douglas insisted that the Court had impeded the "wide open and robust dissemination" of ideas which are essential to both a free press and "intelligent self-government." In his dissent Justice Stewart took pointed issue with what he called the Court's "crabbed view" of freedom of the press under the First Amendment, which he noted caustically, "reflects a disturbing insensitivity to the crucial role of an independent press in our society." Stewart charged that the majority had invited "state and federal authorities to undermine the independence of the press by attempting to annex the journalistic profession as an investigative arm of government." Stewart was convinced that the Court's decision would impair the "constitutionally protected functions" of the press and would "in the long run harm rather than help the administration of justice."

The majority, with its spokesman insisting over and again that reporters, as everyone else, have all the obligations of citizenship to give testimony to a grand jury, thought otherwise.

Mr. Justice White delivered the opinion of the Court, saying in part:

The issue in these cases is whether requiring newsmen to appear and testify before state or federal grand juries abridges the freedom of speech and press guaranteed by the First Amendment. We hold that it does not.

Petitioners . . . press First Amendment claims that may be simply put: that to gather news it is often necessary to agree either not to identify the source of information published or to publish only part of the facts revealed, or both; that if the reporter is nevertheless forced to reveal these confidences to a grand jury, the source so identified and other confidential sources of other reporters will be measurably deterred from furnishing publishable information, all to the detriment of the free flow of information protected by the First Amendment. Although the newsmen in these cases do not claim an absolute privilege against official interrogation in all circumstances, they assert that the reporter should not be forced either to appear or to testify before a grand jury or at trial until and unless sufficient grounds are shown for believing that the reporter possesses information relevant to a crime the grand jury is investigating, that the information the reporter has is unavailable from other sources, and that the need for the information is sufficiently compelling to override the claimed invasion of First Amendment interests occasioned by the disclosure. Principally relied upon are prior cases emphasizing the importance of the First Amendment guarantees to individual development and to our system of representative government, decisions requiring that official action with adverse impact on First Amendment rights be justified by a public interest that is "compelling" or "paramount," and those precedents establishing the principle that justifiable governmental goals may not be achieved by unduly broad means having an unnecessary impact on protected rights of speech, press, or association. The heart of the claim is that the burden on news gathering resulting from compelling reporters to disclose confidential information outweighs any public interest in obtaining the information.

We do not question the significance of free speech, press, or assembly to the country's welfare. Nor is it suggested that news gathering does not qualify for First Amendment protection; without some protection for seeking out the news, freedom of the press could be eviscerated. But these cases involve no intrusions upon speech or assembly, no prior restraint or restriction on what the press may publish, and no express or implied command that the press publish what it prefers to withhold. No exaction or tax for the privilege of publishing, and no penalty, civil or criminal, related to the content of published material is at issue here. The use of confidential sources by the press is not forbidden or restricted; reporters remain free to seek news from any source by means within the law. No attempt is made to require the press to publish its sources of information or indiscriminately to disclose them on request.

The sole issue before us is the obligation of reporters to respond to grand jury subpoenas as other citizens do and to answer questions relevant to an investigation into the commission of crime. Citizens generally are not constitutionally immune from grand jury subpoenas; and neither the First Amendment nor any other constitutional provision protects the average citizen from disclosing to a grand jury information that he has received in confidence. The claim is, however, that reporters are exempt from these obligations because if forced to respond to subpoenas and identify their sources or disclose other confidences, their informants will refuse or be reluctant to furnish newsworthy information in the future. This asserted burden on news gathering is said to make compelled testimony from newsmen constitutionally suspect and to require a privileged position for them.

... as we have earlier indicated, news gathering is not without its First Amendment protections, and grand jury investigations if instituted or conducted other than in good faith, would pose wholly different issues for resolution under the First Amendment. Official harassment of the press undertaken not for purposes of law enforcement but to disrupt a reporter's relationship with his news sources would have no justification. Grand juries are subject to judicial control and subpoenas to motions to quash. We do not expect courts will forget that grand juries must operate within the limits of the First Amendment as well as the Fifth.

Landmark Communications v. Virginia, 98 S. Ct. 1535 (1978)

The most recent free press Court decision was *Landmark Communications* v. *Virginia,* decided in 1978. There a unanimous Supreme Court overturned a state court conviction of a Virginia newspaper, *The Virginian Pilot,* that had been found guilty of a confidentiality provision of a Virginia statute. The statute in question created a Judicial Inquiry and Review Commission to consider complaints against judges thought to be senile or otherwise unfit to continue on the bench. The law required commissioners, staff, and witnesses to keep proceedings confidential. The law also went a step further and made it a crime for a third party, not in any way connected with the commission or its work, to divulge confidential information related to commission hearings.

After the *Virginian Pilot* reported that the commission had studied complaints against a local domestic relations court judge, the newspaper was indicted and ultimately convicted for having violated the statute in question. The Supreme Court of Virginia termed the newspaper report a "clear and present danger" to the proper administration of justice.

Disagreeing with the Virginia court's narrow interpretation of the "Holmes dictum," the Supreme Court ruled that Virginia had invalidly asserted its power to impose prior censorship on the newspaper. Speaking for the Court, Chief Justice Burger noted that the *Virginian Pilot* had "served those interests in public scrutiny and discussion of public affairs which the First Amendment was adopted to protect."

12

FREEDOM OF ASSEMBLY

Does a state statute making "criminal syndicalism" illegal violate the First Amendment's "freedom of assembly" guarantee when it is applied for participation in a public meeting of an organization that is believed to advocate "violence, revolution or other unlawful acts?" Or is the First Amendment right to peaceable assembly safeguarded against state interference of this sort by the due process clause of the Fourteenth Amendment? Specifically, can a state (Oregon) punish one of its citizens (DeJonge) for assisting in the conduct of a peaceful public meeting called under the auspices of the local Communist Party?

DeJonge v. Oregon, 299 U.S. 353 (1937)

These were the questions decided by the Supreme Court in 1937, in its first ruling concerning the First Amendment's freedom of assembly clause. The record showed that DeJonge had taken part in a meeting on July 27, 1934 sponsored by the Communist Party in Portland, Oregon. Attended by some 150–300 people, the meeting had been called to protest what the Portland Communist Party called "illegal raids on workers' hall and homes" and against the shooting of striking longshoremen by Portland police. DeJonge, himself a member of the Communist Party, spoke at the meeting protesting conditions in the city jail, and the actions of the police in the maritime strike. He urged people to purchase Communist Party literature in order to help the Party carry on its revolutionary activities. The meeting was orderly and peaceful. While it was in progress it was raided by police officers and DeJonge and others were arrested. Ultimately DeJonge was convicted of violating Oregon's criminal syndicalism law. Communist literature seized at the meeting was used by the state as evidence to indicate that the Party advocated criminal syndicalism which was illegal in Oregon.

In a pivotal decision the Supreme Court overturned DeJonge's conviction and declared Oregon's statute a violation of the First Amendment's freedom of assembly clause made applicable to the states by the Due Process Clause of the Fourteenth Amendment. Once again, as it did in *Gitlow*, the Court nationalized a portion of the Bill of Rights and incorporated its provisions under the umbrella of the Fourteenth Amendment. While acknowledging that states are entitled to protect themselves from those who would use force or violence to affect political change, the Court ruled nevertheless that Oregon's law went far beyond what is permissible under the First and Fourteenth Amendments. Accordingly it struck down the Oregon statute as a violation of protected rights to free speech and peaceful assembly.

Mr. Chief Justice Hughes delivered the opinion of the Court, saying in part:

> It thus appears that, while defendant was a member of the Communist Party, he was not indicted for participating in its organization, or for joining it, or for soliciting members or for distributing its literature. He was not charged with teaching or advocating criminal syndicalism or sabotage or any unlawful acts, either at the meeting or elsewhere. He was accordingly deprived of the benefit of evidence as to the orderly and lawful conduct of the meeting and that it was not called or used for the advocacy of criminal syndicalism or sabotage or any unlawful action. His sole offense as charged, and for which he was convicted and sentenced to imprisonment for seven years, was that he had assisted in the conduct of a public meeting, albeit otherwise lawful, which was held under the auspices of the Communist Party.
>
> The broad reach of the statute as thus applied is plain. While defendant was a member of the Communist Party, that membership was not necessary to conviction on such a charge. A like fate might have attended any speaker, although not a member, who "assisted in the conduct" of the meeting. However innocuous the object of the meeting, however lawful the subjects and tenor of the addresses, however reasonable and timely the discussion, all those assisting in the conduct of the meeting would be subject to imprisonment as felons if the meeting were held by the Communist Party. This manifest result was brought out sharply at this bar by the concessions which the Attorney General made, and could not avoid, in the light of the decision of the state court. Thus if the Communist Party had called a public meeting in Portland to discuss the tariff, or the foreign policy of the Government, or taxation, or relief, or candidacies for the offices of President, members of Congress, Governor, or state legislators, every speaker who assisted in the conduct of the meeting would be equally guilty with the defendant in this case, upon the charge as here defined and sustained. The list of illustrations might be indefinitely extended to every variety of meetings under the auspices of the Communist Party although held for the discussion of political issues or to adopt protests and pass resolutions of an entirely innocent and proper character.
>
> ... First Amendment rights may be abused by using speech or press or assembly in order to incite to violence and crime. The people through their legislatures may protect themselves against that abuse. But the legislative intervention can find constitutional justification only by dealing with the abuse. The rights themselves must not be curtailed. The greater the importance of safeguarding the community from incitements to the overthrow of our institutions by force and violence, the more imperative is the need to preserve inviolate the constitutional rights of free speech, free press and free assembly in order to maintain the opportunity for free political discussion, to the end that government may be responsive to the will of the people and that changes, if desired, may be obtained by peaceful means. Therein lies the security of the Republic, the very foundation of constitutional government.

It follows from these considerations that, consistently with the Federal Constitution, peaceable assembly for lawful discussion cannot be made a crime. The
holding of meetings for peaceable political action cannot be proscribed. Those
who assist in the conduct of such meetings cannot be branded as criminals on
that score. The question, if the rights of free speech and peaceable assembly are
to be preserved, is not as to the auspices under which the meeting is held but as
to its purpose; not as to the relations of the speakers, but whether their utterances transcend the bounds of the freedom of speech which the Constitution
protects. If the persons assembling have committed crimes elsewhere, if they
have formed or are engaged in a conspiracy against the public peace and order,
they may be prosecuted for their conspiracy or other violation of valid laws. But
it is a different matter when the State, instead of prosecuting them for such
offenses, seizes upon mere participation in a peaceable assembly and a lawful
public discussion as the basis for a criminal charge.

We are not called upon to review the findings of the state court as to the
objectives of the Communist Party. Notwithstanding those objectives, the defendant still enjoyed his personal right of free speech and to take part in a peaceable
assembly having a lawful purpose, although called by that Party. The defendant
was none the less entitled to discuss the public issues of the day and thus in a
lawful manner, without incitement to violence or crime, to seek redress of alleged grievances. That was of the essence of his guaranteed personal liberty.

We hold that the Oregon statute as applied to the particular charge as defined
by the state court is repugnant to the due process clause of the Fourteenth
Amendment.

Cox v. New Hampshire, 312 U.S. 569 (1941)

Over the years many local communities have adopted ordinances that require granting a permit before a parade, a public meeting or, in some instances, picketing, may take place. The rationale of these ordinances is decep-
tively simple. Local governmental authorities have the responsibility to keep
their city streets and sidewalks usable, safe, and open to the general public.
True enough; yet many times the permit process places so much discretionary
authority in a local official that he or she may grant or deny groups the right
to march or hold protest meetings for capricious and often discriminatory
reasons. The Supreme Court has had several opportunities to wrestle with the
validity of the permit process, having to decide if and when it has been used to
deny legitimate rights under the First Amendment's freedom of assembly
clause.

One such instance occurred in *Cox* v. *New Hampshire*. In *Cox* the appellants
were five Jehovah's Witnesses who, along with sixty-three other Witnesses,
were convicted in a Manchester, New Hampshire municipal court of "parading" on a public street without the special license that a state statute required.
The Witnesses had marched peaceably, single file along a downtown street
carrying picket signs advertising a religious rally. The sole charge against Cox
and the others was that they were "taking part in a parade or procession" on
the streets of Manchester *without* the required permit. The state maintained,
and the Supreme Court agreed, that there was no evidence Cox had been
prosecuted for distributing leaflets, for issuing invitations to a public meeting,

or for maintaining or expressing religious beliefs. For this reason a unanimous Court ruled that the local ordinance did not contravene First Amendment freedoms. The Court ruled that the statute had been administered fairly and in a nondiscriminatory manner. It decided, therefore, that if a municipality has authority to control use of its public streets, "as it undoubtedly has, it cannot be denied authority to give consideration without unfair discrimination to the time, place and manner" that its streets may be used.

Mr. Chief Justice Hughes delivered the opinion of the Court, saying in part:

> Civil liberties, as guaranteed by the Constitution, imply the existence of an organized society maintaining public order without which liberty itself would be lost in the excesses of unrestrained abuses. The authority of a municipality to impose regulations in order to assure the safety and convenience of the people in the use of public highways has never been regarded as inconsistent with civil liberties but rather as one of the means of safeguarding the good order upon which they ultimately depend. The control of travel on the streets of cities is the most familiar illustration of this recognition of social need. Where a restriction of the use of highways in that relation is designed to promote the public convenience in the interest of all, it cannot be disregarded by the attempted exercise of some civil right which in other circumstances would be entitled to protection. One would not be justified in ignoring the familiar red traffic light because he thought it his religious duty to disobey the municipal command or sought by that means to direct public attention to an announcement of his opinions. As regulation of the use of the streets for parades and processions is a traditional exercise of control by local government, the question in a particular case is whether that control is exerted so as not to deny or unwarrantedly abridge the right of assembly and the opportunities for the communication of thought and the discussion of public questions immemorially associated with resort to public places.

Walker v. Birmingham, 388 U.S. 307 (1967)

Ten years after the *Cox* decision the Supreme Court *did* invalidate local ordinances in two cases where it found that the permit process *had* been used to deny, in a capricious manner, the exercise of valid First Amendment freedoms. In *Kunz v. New York,*[1] for example, with Chief Justice Vinson writing for the majority of eight (Jackson was the lone dissenter), the Court struck down a New York City ordinance that gave an administrative official excessive "discretionary power to control in advance the right of citizens to speak on religious matters on the city streets."

And in *Niemotko v. Maryland*[2] the Court also struck down a local ordinance that had been used by a city council to deny a group of Jehovah's Witnesses use of a city park to conduct religious services. There the Court concluded that the permit process was used to deny use of the park because the city council objected to the religious beliefs of the Witnesses. In a unanimous decision the Supreme Court ruled that the city council had infringed upon First Amendment freedoms of speech and religion and therefore that the ordinance in question was unconstitutional.

1. 340 U.S. 290 (1951).
2. 340 U.S. 268 (1951).

Then some sixteen years later the Supreme Court decided its most controversial "permit" case, *Walker* v. *City of Birmingham*. And it did still another "about face" on the issue. The setting for this dispute was the highly volatile set of circumstances created by the black civil rights movement and its assault on the bastions of southern segregation and racial discrimination.

In *Walker* petitioners were eight black ministers who had been convicted of criminal contempt for violating an *ex parte* injunction issued by a Jefferson County, Alabama court. They had engaged in street parades without a Birmingham municipal permit on Good Friday and Easter Sunday 1963, days when the City of Birmingham and its Police Chief Eugene "Bull" O'Connor had become symbols of vehement official hostility to the civil rights movement. Birmingham's permit ordinance made it unlawful "to organize or hold ... or to take part or participate in any parade procession or other public demonstration" without a permit. The ordinance provided that a permit might be granted by the city commission "unless in its judgment the public welfare, peace, safety, health, decency, good order, morals or convenience require that it be refused."

The petitioners attempted to obtain a permit but were unsuccessful. There was evidence that they were treated "harshly and rudely" by city officials. One of the petitioners, Reverend Shuttlesworth, testified at the trial that he had asked Police Chief O'Connor for a permit and was told, "No, you will not get a permit in Birmingham, Alabama to picket. I will picket you over to the City Jail."

In *Walker* the Supreme Court was badly split (5–4). Justice Stewart wrote for the majority. Three separate dissents were filed, by Chief Justice Warren and Justices Brennan and Douglas. The majority of five upheld the petitioners' conviction on the grounds that the Birmingham injunction was "consistent with the strong interest of the city government in regulating the use of its streets and other public places." Justice Stewart admitted that "the generality of language" in Birmingham's permit ordinance raised "substantial constitutional issues." But he went on to say that the ordinance was not void on its face.

In a subsequent decision involving many of the same participants decided two years after *Walker, Shuttlesworth* v. *Birmingham*,[3] the Court did another 180-degree turn and ruled a similar local ordinance unconstitutional. In *Walker*, however, the majority concluded that the petitioners should not have disobeyed the ordinance without first having tested its constitutionality in the courts. Each of the three dissenting opinions took serious exception to the majority's position.

The four excerpts that follow illustrate the deep division on the Supreme Court; Justice Stewart for the Court, Chief Justice Warren and Justices Douglas and Brennan in dissent.

Mr. Justice Stewart said in part:

> This case would arise in quite a different constitutional posture if the petitioners, before disobeying the injunction, had challenged it in the Alabama courts, and had been met with delay or frustration of their constitutional claims. But there is no showing that such would have been the fate of a timely motion to modify or dissolve the injunction. There was an interim of two days between the

3. 394 U.S. 147 (1969).

issuance of the injunction and the Good Friday march. The petitioners give absolutely no explanation of why they did not make some application to the state court during that period. The injunction had issued *ex parte;* if the court had been presented with the petitioners' contentions, it might well have dissolved or at least modified its order in some respects. If it had not done so, Alabama procedure would have provided for an expedited process of appellate review. It cannot be presumed that the Alabama courts would have ignored the petitioners' constitutional claims. Indeed, these contentions were accepted in another case by an Alabama appellate court that struck down on direct review the conviction under this very ordinance of one of these same petitioners.

The rule of law upon which the Alabama courts relied in this case was one firmly established by previous precedents. We do not deal here, therefore, with a situation where a state court has followed a regular past practice of entertaining claims in a given procedural mode, and without notice has abandoned that practice to the detriment of a litigant who finds his claim foreclosed by a novel procedural bar. . . . This is not a case where a procedural requirement has been sprung upon an unwary litigant when prior practice did not give him fair notice of its existence. . . .

The Alabama Supreme Court has apparently never in any criminal contempt case entertained a claim of nonjurisdictional error. In *Fields* v. *City of Fairfield,* 273 Ala. 588, 143 So. 2d 177, decided just three years before the present case, the defendants, members of a "White Supremacy" organization who had disobeyed an injunction, sought to challenge the constitutional validity of a permit ordinance upon which the injunction was based. The Supreme Court of Alabama, finding that the trial court had jurisdiction, applied the same rule of law which was followed here:

> "As a general rule, an unconstitutional statute is an absolute nullity and may not form the basis of any legal right or legal proceedings, yet until its unconstitutionality has been judicially declared in appropriate proceedings, no person charged with its observance under an order or decree may disregard or violate the order or the decree with immunity from a charge of contempt of court; and he may not raise the question of its unconstitutionality in collateral proceedings on appeal from a judgment of conviction for contempt of the order or decree. . . ."

These precedents clearly put the petitioners on notice that they could not bypass orderly judicial review of the injunction before disobeying it. Any claim that they were entrapped or misled is wholly unfounded, a conclusion confirmed by evidence in the record showing that when the petitioners deliberately violated the injunction they expected to go to jail.

The rule of law that Alabama followed in this case reflects a belief that in the fair administration of justice no man can be judge in his own case, however exalted his station, however righteous his motives, and irrespective of his race, color, politics, or religion. This Court cannot hold that the petitioners were constitutionally free to ignore all the procedures of the law and carry their battle to the streets. One may sympathize with the petitioners' impatient commitment to their cause. But respect for judicial process is a small price to pay for the civilizing hand of law, which alone can give abiding meaning to constitutional freedom.

Mr. Chief Justice Warren dissented (in part):

I do not believe that giving this Court's seal of approval to such a gross misuse of the judicial process is likely to lead to greater respect for the law any more than it is likely to lead to greater protection for First Amendment freedoms. The *ex parte* temporary injunction has a long and odious history in this country, and its susceptibility to misuse is all too apparent from the facts of the case. As a weapon against strikes, it proved so effective in the hands of judges friendly to employers that Congress was forced to take the drastic step of removing from federal district courts the jurisdiction to issue injunctions in labor disputes. The labor injunction fell into disrepute largely because it was abused in precisely the same way that the injunctive power was abused in this case. Judges who were not sympathetic to the union cause commonly issued, without notice or hearing, broad restraining orders addressed to large numbers of persons and forbidding them to engage in acts that were either legally permissible or, if illegal, that could better have been left to the regular course of criminal prosecution. The injunctions might later be dissolved, but in the meantime strikes would be crippled because the occasion on which concerted activity might have been effective had passed. Such injunctions, so long discredited as weapons against concerted labor activities, have now been given new life by this Court as weapons against the exercise of First Amendment freedoms. Respect for the courts and for judicial process was not increased by the history of the labor injunction.

Mr. Justice Douglas (joined by Chief Justice Warren and Justices Brennan and Fortas) dissented (in part):

The evidence shows that a permit was applied for. Mrs. Lola Hendricks, a member of the Alabama Christian Movement for Human Rights, authorized by its president, Reverend Shuttlesworth, on April 3, went to the police department and asked to see the person in charge of issuing permits. She then went to the office of Commissioner Eugene "Bull" Connor and told him that "we came up to apply or see about getting a permit for picketing, parading, demonstrating." She asked Connor for the permit, "asked if he could issue the permit, or other persons who would refer me to, persons who would issue a permit." Commissioner Connor replied, "No, you will not get a permit in Birmingham, Alabama to picket. I will picket you over to the City Jail." On April 5, petitioner Shuttlesworth sent a telegram to Commissioner Connor requesting a permit to picket on designated sidewalks on April 5 and 6. The message stated that "the normal rules of picketing" would be observed. The same day, Connor wired back a reply stating that he could not individually grant a permit, that it was the responsibility of the entire Commission and that he "insist[ed] that you and your people do not start any picketing on the streets in Birmingham, Alabama." Petitioners' efforts to show that the City Commission did not grant permits, but that they were granted by the city clerk at the request of the traffic division were cut off.

The record shows that petitioners did not deliberately attempt to circumvent the permit requirement. Rather they diligently attempted to obtain a permit and were rudely rebuffed and then reasonably concluded that any further attempts would be fruitless.

The right to defy an unconstitutional statute is basic in our scheme. Even when an ordinance requires a permit to make a speech, to deliver a sermon, to picket, to parade, or to assemble, it need not be honored when it is invalid on its face. *Lovell v. Griffin,* 303 U.S. 444, 452, 453; *Thornhill v. Alabama,* 310 U.S. 88, 97; *Jones v. Opelika,* 316 U.S. 584, 602, adopted per curiam on rehearing, 319 U.S. 103, 104; *Cantwell v. Connecticut,* 310 U.S. 296, 305–306; *Thomas v. Collins,* 323 U.S. 516, *Staub v. City of Baxley,* 355 U.S. 313, 319.

By like reason, where a permit has been arbitrarily denied, one need not pursue the long and expensive route to this Court to obtain a remedy. The reason is the same in both cases. For if a person must pursue his judicial remedy

before he may speak, parade, or assemble, the occasion when protest is desired
or needed will have become history and any later speech, parade, or assembly
will be futile or pointless.

Mr. Justice Brennan (joined by Chief Justice Warren and Justices Douglas
and Fortas) dissented (in part):

The Court today lets loose a devastatingly destructive weapon for infringement of freedoms jealously safeguarded not so much for the benefit of any given
group of any given persuasion as for the benefit of all of us. We cannot permit
fears of "riots" and "civil disobedience" generated by slogans like "Black Power"
to divert our attention from what is here at stake — not violence or the right of
the State to control its streets and sidewalks, but the insulation from attack of *ex
parte* orders and legislation upon which they are based even when patently impermissible prior restraints on the exercise of First Amendment rights, thus
arming the state courts with the power to punish as a "contempt" what they
otherwise could not punish at all. Constitutional restrictions against abridgments
of First Amendment freedoms limit judicial equally with legislative and executive power. Convictions for contempt of court orders which invalidly abridge
First Amendment freedoms must be condemned equally with convictions for
violation of statutes which do the same thing. I respectfully dissent.

13

THE COMMUNIST PARTY

When the Supreme Court decided in *Gitlow* v. *New York* (above) that the guarantees of the First Amendment applied to the states via the due process clause of the Fourteenth, it paved the way for review of a long series of state laws that dealt with political radicalism, in particular with membership in the Communist Party and its implications. Such issues as the free advocacy of political ideas, guilt by association, and their clash with First Amendment freedoms as they applied to members of the Communist Party were involved.

Whitney v. California, 274 U.S. 357 (1927)

The problem first arose in *Whitney* v. *California*. The appellant was convicted of the felony of helping to organize in 1919 the Communist Labor Party of California. California's "criminal syndicalism" law made it a crime to assist in forming a society for teaching syndicalism, for becoming a member of such a society, or for assembling with others for that purpose. California's law was similar to New York's statute under which Gitlow was convicted and was one of many such state laws spawned by the 1901 assassination of President McKinley by an avowed "anarchist."

Commenting in a concurring opinion in *Whitney,* Justice Brandeis (joined by Justice Holmes) made the following observation concerning California's law: "There is guilt although the society may not contemplate immediate promulgation of the doctrine (criminal syndicalism). Thus the accused is to be punished, not for contempt, incitement or conspiracy, but for a step in preparation, which, if it threatens the public order at all, does so only remotely. The novelty in the prohibition introduced is that the statute aims, not at the practice of criminal syndicalism, nor even directly at the preaching of it, but at association with those who propose to teach it."[1]

If the Brandeis assessment of the California statute is accurate, and that seems to be a reasonable conclusion, by affirming Whitney's conviction the Supreme Court had sanctioned the "pernicious doctrine" of guilt by association. Why then did that Court's two outstanding civil libertarians, Holmes and Brandeis, go along with the majority? Brandeis explains:

---

1. 274 U.S. at 373.

I am unable to assent to the suggestion in the opinion of the Court that assembling with a political party formed to advocate the desirability of a proletarian revolution by mass action at some date necessarily far in the future, is not a right within the protection of the Fourteenth Amendment. In the present case, however, there was other testimony which tended to establish the existence of a conspiracy, on the part of members of the International Workers of the World,[2] to commit present serious crimes; and likewise to show that such a conspiracy would be furthered by the activity of the society of which Miss Whitney was a member. Under these circumstances the judgment of the state court cannot be disturbed.[3]

In the record there was testimony that Whitney had *not* joined the Communist Labor Party because she believed or understood it to be an instrument of terror or violence. Yet because the Court concluded that the intent of the Party was to teach criminal syndicalism, which *was* a crime in California, it sustained Whitney's conviction. Therefore, Whitney was not found guilty of a specific illegal act but instead was found guilty of associating with a party that was presumed to advocate an illegal doctrine, criminal syndicalism. This view hardly seems in accord with the best of the American civil liberties tradition.

Mr. Justice Sanford delivered the opinion of the Court, saying in part:

That the freedom of speech which is secured by the Constitution does not confer an absolute right to speak, without responsibility, whatever one may choose, or an unrestricted and unbridled license giving immunity for every possible use of language and preventing the punishment of those who abuse this freedom; and that a State in the exercise of its police power may punish those who abuse this freedom by utterances inimical to the public welfare, tending to incite to crime, disturb the public peace, or endanger the foundations of organized government and threaten its overthrow by unlawful means, is not open to question. . . .

By enacting the provisions of the Syndicalism Act the State has declared, through its legislative body, that to knowingly be or become a member of or assist in organizing an association to advocate, teach or aid and abet the commission of crimes or unlawful acts of force, violence or terrorism as a means of accomplishing industrial or political changes, involves such danger to the public peace and the security of the State, that these acts should be penalized in the exercise of its police power. That determination must be given great weight. Every presumption is to be indulged in favor of the validity of the statute, . . . and it may not be declared unconstitutional unless it is an arbitrary or unreasonable attempt to exercise the authority vested in the State in the public interest. . . .

The essence of the offense denounced by the Act is the combining with others in an association for the accomplishment of the desired ends through the advocacy and use of criminal and unlawful methods. It partakes of the nature of a criminal conspiracy. . . . That such united and joint action involves even greater danger to the public peace and security than the isolated utterances and acts of individuals, is clear. We cannot hold that, as here applied, the Act is an unreasonable or arbitrary exercise of the police power of the State, unwarrantably infringing any right of free speech, assembly or association, or that those persons are protected from punishment by the due process clause who abuse such rights by joining and furthering an organization thus menacing the peace and welfare of the State.

2. The IWW or Wobblies of the Post World War I era.
3. 274 U.S. at 379.

We find no repugnancy in the Syndicalism Act as applied in this case to either the due process or equal protection clauses of the Fourteenth Amendment on any of the grounds upon which its validity has been here challenged.

Stromberg v. California, 283 U.S. 359 (1931)

Four years after its ruling in *Whitney* had given support to the constitutionally unsupportable concept of "guilt by association," the Supreme Court sensed what it had done and began the intricate process of reversing itself. The first step was *Stromberg* v. *California*. There with Chief Justice Hughes speaking for the majority of seven (Justices McReynolds and Butler wrote separate dissents) the Court struck down a section of the California Penal Code that made it illegal to display a red (communist) flag "in a public place or in a meeting place." In *Stromberg*, as it did later in *DeJonge* v. *Oregon* (see above) the Court reversed a state court conviction because it concluded that because the accused in each case had not personally violated any criminal law they could not be found guilty by association.

The record showed that Stromberg, a nineteen-year-old member of the Young Communist League, was a supervisor at a summer camp for children. She testified that she taught the children history and economics, and tried to teach them such esoteric topics as "class consciousness" and the "solidarity of the working class." The specific charge against her concerned a daily ceremony at the camp during which Stromberg supervised the children in raising a homemade replica of the Soviet Union's red flag. In connection with the daily flag raising, Stromberg also led the children to recite a pledge of allegiance "to the worker's red flag, and to the cause for which it stands; one aim throughout our lives, freedom for the working class."[1] There was further evidence that the camp's library was stacked with a varied assortment of Communist literature. Stromberg testified, however, that none of the literature was ever brought to the attention of the children and that she had never taught "anarchism, sedition, or violence" to the children. In her trial there was no evidence to the contrary. As the Supreme Court saw the issue, it narrowed to whether one clause of California's penal code making display of the red flag illegal, under which Stromberg had been convicted in State Court, violated the due process clause of the Fourteenth Amendment. The Court ruled that it did.

Mr. Chief Justice Hughes delivered the opinion of the Court, saying in part:

> We are thus brought to the question whether any one of the three clauses, as construed by the state court, is upon its face repugnant to the Federal Constitution so that it could not constitute a lawful foundation for a criminal prosecution. The principles to be applied have been clearly set forth in our former decisions. It has been determined that the conception of liberty under the due process clause of the Fourteenth Amendment embraces the right of free speech. . . . The right is not an absolute one, and the State in the exercise of its police power may punish the abuse of this freedom. There is no question but that the State may

1. 283 U.S. at 362.

thus provide for the punishment of those who indulge in utterances which incite to violence and crime and threaten the overthrow of organized government by unlawful means. There is no constitutional immunity for such conduct abhorrent to our institutions. . . . We have no reason to doubt the validity of the second and third clauses of the statute as construed by the state court to relate to such incitements to violence.

The question is thus narrowed to that of the validity of the first clause, that is, with respect to the display of the flag "as a sign, symbol or emblem of opposition to organized government," and the construction which the state court has placed upon this clause removes every element of doubt. The state court recognized the indefiniteness and ambiguity of the clause. The court considered that it might be construed as embracing conduct which the State could not constitutionally prohibit. Thus it was said that the clause "might be construed to include the peaceful and orderly opposition to a government as organized and controlled by one political party by those of another political party equally high minded and patriotic, which did not agree with the one in power. It might also be construed to include peaceful and orderly opposition to government by legal means and within constitutional limitations." The maintenance of the opportunity for free political discussion to the end that government may be responsive to the will of the people and that changes may be obtained by lawful means, an opportunity essential to the security of the Republic, is a fundamental principle of our constitutional system. A statute which upon its face, and as authoritatively construed, is so vague and indefinite as to permit the punishment of the fair use of this opportunity is repugnant to the guaranty of liberty contained in the Fourteenth Amendment. The first clause of the statute being invalid upon its face, the conviction of the appellant, which so far as the record discloses may have rested upon that clause exclusively, must be set aside.

Dennis v. United States, 341 U.S. 404 (1951)

By far the most controversial Communist Party dispute to come before the Supreme Court was *Dennis* v. *United States.* Involved was the Smith Act, an anti-subversion law passed by Congress just prior to World War II, and the eleven top leaders of the American Communist Party. The Smith Act attempted to meet the problem of subversion in five ways. It made punishable (1) knowing or willing advocacy or teaching the overthrow of the American government, (2) dissemination of literature advocating the overthrow; (3) organizing into groups to advocate the overthrow; (4) anyone, knowing the purpose of such a group, who joins: and (5) a conspiracy to do any of the above.

Dennis tested the constitutionality of the Smith Act. The Supreme Court had to decide if the law violated the free speech, press, and assembly rights of the First Amendment. Begun in the cold war-charged atmosphere of 1948, the trial in New York City of the top Communist leaders lasted nine sensational months. Unfortunately, because of the notoriety the trial received in the media, it is likely that here again Justice Holmes' little dictum "great cases make bad law" applies. Certainly in "cooler" times the results may well have been different. Justice Black suggested this possibility in his dissenting opinion.

The major problem confronting the Supreme Court was how to reconcile the free speech guarantee of the First Amendment with the Smith Act and Dennis's conviction by a lower court, both of which made advocacy of ideas and speech a violation of criminal law. Five separate opinions were written in *Dennis.* Four of them, including Chief Justice Vinson's majority opinion, attempted to interpret and reapply Holmes' clear and present danger rule to the facts of the case.

As Justice Frankfurter noted in his long concurring opinion, ". . . few questions of comparable importance have come before this Court in recent years."[1] Frankfurter, who was never an advocate of the generally more liberal "preferred position" for First Amendment freedoms that Black and Douglas upheld, and who was also never a devotee of Holmes's clear and present danger rule, concluded that in striking a balance between free speech and what he perceived to be a real Communist threat to national security, the Smith Act must prevail.

Dennis and the other ten top leaders of the American Communist Party maintained they had a right under the Constitution to advocate a political theory (their interpretation of Marxism-Leninism) as long as their advocacy did not create an immediate danger to the continued existence of American government. On the other hand, the government asserted its right to protect the national security against possible subversion.

In his concurring opinion Justice Jackson called *Dennis* the "latest of [a] neverending, because never successful, quest for some legal formula that will secure an existing order against revolutionary radicalism."[2] Jackson doubted that the clear and present danger rule was such a formula. When faced with "the problem of a well-organized, nationwide conspiracy," Jackson concluded, the Supreme Court cannot "hold our government captive in a judge-made verbal trap."[3]

For the two dissenters, Justices Black and Douglas, the issues in *Dennis* took different dimensions. Black indicated quite clearly his feeling that the nation-wide anti-communist hysteria prompted by the cold war had motivated the Court's majority. Black insisted that the Smith Act that authorized "this prior restraint" on advocacy, free speech, and free press was an unconstitutional violation of the First Amendment. Public opinion, "being what it now is," Black wrote, "hardly anyone will protest the conviction of the Communist leaders. There is hope, however, that in calmer times, when present pressures, passions and fears subside, this, or some later, Court will restore the First Amendment liberties to the high preferred place where they belong in a free society."[4]

In his long dissent, Justice Douglas eloquently defended free speech and the "noble place" it has in a free society. He cited the First Amendment's clause, "Congress shall make no law . . . abridging the freedom of speech," and ended by comparing the repressive Soviet system of government with the American heritage of political freedom. Douglas quoted from former Soviet Foreign Minister Andre Vishinsky, who in 1938 wrote the following in his book, *The Law of the Soviet State:* "In our state, naturally, there is and can be no

1. 341 U.S. at 518.   3. Ibid., at 568.
2. Ibid., at 561.   4. Ibid., at 581.

place for freedom of speech, press and so on for the foes of socialism."
Douglas added these words: "Our concern should be that we accept no such
standard for the United States. Our faith should be that our people will never
give support to these advocates of revolution, so long as we remain loyal to the
purposes for which our nation was founded."[5]

Chief Justice Vinson spoke for Justices Reed, Burton, and Minton, and
along with the concurring opinions of Justices Frankfurter and Jackson, they
made up the majority of six (Justice Clark did not participate). In his opinion
the Chief Justice reviewed the long history of free speech cases from *Schenck*
and *Gitlow.* He too paid verbal homage to the clear and present danger rule.
But in essence the application by the majority of Holmes's view of the allowable limits of First Amendment freedoms to *Dennis* seems the product of
rather tortured reasoning. At the very least its interpretation of a rule that was
originally designed to determine what constitutes an immediate threat to
society that might warrant suppressing free speech and press, greatly exag-
gerated the power and influence of Communist Party leadership. Dennis and
his few friends were speaking and writing largely to and for themselves. Not
many Americans were paying heed.

The Supreme Court affirmed Dennis's conviction. Rather than Holmes'
clear and present danger rule, the Court seemed to rely more heavily on
"clear and *probable* danger" or even clear and "possible" danger as the appropriate test in this confrontation between "national security" and free speech.
It seems reasonable to conclude that clear and *probable* or *possible* danger sets
more narrow and restrictive limits on free speech than "clear and present
danger," as interpreted by its adherents, would.

Mr. Chief Justice Vinson announced the judgment of the Court, saying in
part:

> The obvious purpose of the statute is to protect existing Government, not
> from change by peaceable, lawful and constitutional means, but from change by
> violence, revolution and terrorism. That it is within the *power* of the Congress to
> protect the Government of the United States from armed rebellion is a proposi-
> tion which requires little discussion. Whatever theoretical merit there may be to
> the argument that there is a "right" to rebellion against dictatorial governments
> is without force where the existing structure of the government provides for
> peaceful and orderly change. We reject any principle of governmental helpless-
> ness in the face of preparation for revolution, which principle, carried to its
> logical conclusion, must lead to anarchy. No one could conceive that it is not
> within the power of Congress to prohibit acts intended to overthrow the Gov-
> ernment by force and violence. The question with which we are concerned here
> is not whether Congress has such *power,* but whether the *means* which it has
> employed conflict with the First and Fifth Amendments to the Constitution.
>
> One of the bases for the contention that the means which Congress has
> employed are invalid takes the form of an attack on the face of the statute on the
> grounds that by its terms it prohibits academic discussion of the merits of
> Marxism-Leninism, that it stifles ideas and is contrary to all concepts of a free
> speech and a free press. Although we do not agree that the language itself has
> that significance, we must bear in mind that it is the duty of the federal courts to
> interpret federal legislation in a manner not inconsistent with the demands of
> the Constitution.

5. Ibid., at 591.

The very language of the Smith Act negates the interpretation which petitioners would have us impose on that Act. It is directed at advocacy, not discussion. Thus, the trial judge properly charged the jury that they could not convict if they found that petitioners did "no more than pursue peaceful studies and discussions or teaching and advocacy in the realm of ideas." He further charged that it was not unlawful "to conduct in an American college or university a course explaining the philosophical theories set forth in the books which have been placed in evidence." Such a charge is in strict accord with the statutory language, and illustrates the meaning to be placed on those words. Congress did not intend to eradicate the free discussion of political theories, to destroy the traditional rights of Americans to discuss and evaluate ideas without fear of governmental sanction. Rather Congress was concerned with the very kind of activity in which the evidence showed these petitioners engaged.

But although the statute is not directed at the hypothetical cases which petitioners have conjured, its application in this case has resulted in convictions for the teaching and advocacy of the overthrow of the Government by force and violence, which, even though coupled with the intent to accomplish that overthrow, contains an element of speech. For this reason, we must pay special heed to the demands of the First Amendment marking out the boundaries of speech.

We pointed out in *Douds, supra,* that the basis of the First Amendment is the hypothesis that speech can rebut speech, propaganda will answer propaganda, free debate of ideas will result in the wisest governmental policies. It is for this reason that this Court has recognized the inherent value of free discourse. An analysis of the leading cases in this Court which have involved direct limitations on speech, however, will demonstrate that both the majority of the Court and the dissenters in particular cases have recognized that this is not an unlimited, unqualified right, but that the societal value of speech must, on occasion, be subordinated to other values and considerations.

. . . Overthrow of the Government by force and violence is certainly a substantial enough interest for the Government to limit speech. Indeed, this is the ultimate value of any society, for if a society cannot protect its very structure from armed internal attack, it must follow that no subordinate value can be protected. If, then, this interest may be protected, the literal problem which is presented is what has been meant by the use of the phrase "clear and present danger" of the utterances bringing about the evil within the power of Congress to punish.

Obviously, the words cannot mean that before the Government may act, it must wait until the *putsch* is about to be executed, the plans have been laid and the signal is awaited. If Government is aware that a group aiming at its overthrow is attempting to indoctrinate its members and to commit them to a course whereby they will strike when the leaders feel the circumstances permit, action by the Government is required. The argument that there is no need for Government to concern itself, for Government is strong, it possesses ample powers to put down a rebellion, it may defeat the revolution with ease needs no answer. For that is not the question. Certainly an attempt to overthrow the Government by force, even though doomed from the outset because of inadequate numbers or power of the revolutionists, is a sufficient evil for Congress to prevent. The damage which such attempts create both physically and politically to a nation makes it impossible to measure the validity in terms of the probability of success, or the immediacy of a successful attempt. In the instant case the trial judge charged the jury that they could not convict unless they found that petitioners intended to overthrow the Government "as speedily as circumstances would permit." This does not mean, and could not properly mean, that they would not strike until there was certainty of success. What was meant was that the revolutionists. would strike when they thought the time was ripe. We must therefore reject the contention that success or probability of success is the criterion. . . .

The question in this case is whether the statute which the legislature has enacted may be constitutionally applied. In other words, the Court must examine judicially the application of the statute to the particular situation, to ascertain if the Constitution prohibits the conviction. We hold that the statute may be applied where there is a "clear and present danger" of the substantive evil which the legislature had the right to prevent. Bearing, as it does, the marks of a "question of law," the issue is properly one for the judge to decide.

There remains to be discussed the question of vagueness — whether the statute as we have interpreted it is too vague, not sufficiently advising those who would speak of the limitations upon their activity. It is urged that such vagueness contravenes the First and Fifth Amendments. This argument is particularly nonpersuasive when presented by petitioners, who, the jury found, intended to overthrow the Government as speedily as circumstances would permit. . . .

We agree that the standard as defined is not a neat, mathematical formulary. Like all verbalizations it is subject to criticism on the score of indefiniteness. But petitioners themselves contend that the verbalization "clear and present danger" is the proper standard. We see no difference, from the standpoint of vagueness, whether the standard of "clear and present danger" is one contained *in haec verba* within the statute, or whether it is the judicial measure of constitutional applicability. We have shown the indeterminate standard the phrase necessarily connotes. We do not think we have rendered that standard any more indefinite by our attempt to sum up the factors which are included within its scope. We think it well serves to indicate to those who would advocate constitutionally prohibited conduct that there is a line beyond which they may not go — a line which they, in full knowledge of what they intend and the circumstances in which their activity takes place, will well appreciate and understand. . . .

We hold that §§2(a) (1), 2(a) (3) and 3 of the Smith Act do not inherently, or as construed or applied in the instant case, violate the First Amendment and other provisions of the Bill of Rights, or the First and Fifth Amendments because of indefiniteness. Petitioners intended to overthrow the Government of the United States as speedily as the circumstances would permit. Their conspiracy to organize the Communist Party and to teach and advocate the overthrow of the Government of the United States by force and violence created a "clear and present danger" of an attempt to overthrow the Government by force and violence. They were properly and constitutionally convicted for violation of the Smith Act.

Yates v. United States, 354 U.S. 298 (1957)

The Supreme Court's reasoning in *Dennis* gave substance and constitutional validity to the idea that the Communist Party was "a criminal conspiracy dedicated to overthrowing the government of the United States by force and violence."[1] If that was the case, then were the lesser functionaries of the

1. Robert Cushman, *Leading Constitutional Decisions* (Englewood Cliffs, N.J.: Prentice-Hall, 1977), p. 252.

Communist Party also subject to prosecution under the Smith Act? After *Dennis,* acting upon this belief, the government moved against fourteen "second-string" Communists, all of whom were leaders of the Party in California. The key ruling was *Yates* v. *United States.* There, in a decision that found the nine jurists divided in an unusual fashion, the Court reversed the convictions of five of the fourteen and sent the case of the other nine back for reconsideration. Justice Harlan spoke for the majority of six. Or was it a majority? Justices Brennan and Whittaker did not participate and Justice Burton in his cryptic two sentence concurring opinion agreed with the Court except on one minor point, the meaning of the word "organize" as used in the Smith Act. Justice Black, joined by Justice Douglas, concurred in part and dissented in part. Black and Douglas would have reversed all fourteen convictions because "the statutory provisions (of the Smith Act) on which these prosecutions are based abridge freedom of speech, press, and assembly in violation of the First Amendment . . ."[2] And finally, there was Justice Clark who, dissenting, asserted that he would affirm the lower court convictions of all fourteen defendants.

Justice Harlan's long majority opinion strove mightily to cope with the issues. Harlan noted that, in his judgment, the Smith Act, as interpreted by the Court in *Dennis,* did *not* prohibit advocacy and teaching the forcible overthrow of the government "as an abstract principle." He read *Dennis* to mean that advocacy had to be accompanied by the presence of a group of sufficient size and cohesion directed toward action to accomplish the overthrow. Harlan was satisfied that this condition *had* been met in *Dennis,* but not in *Yates.* In essence then, harking back once again to the clear and present danger rule which the majority supposedly discarded in *Dennis,* what the Court seemed to be saying in *Yates* was: The eleven top leaders of the Communist Party, because of their position of leadership, *did* present an immediate threat to society and therefore the decision in *Dennis* was justified. But the fourteen second-stringers did not and therefore their convictions could not stand.

Mr. Justice Harlan delivered the opinion of the Court, saying in part:

> Petitioners contend that the instructions to the jury were fatally defective in that the trial court refused to charge that, in order to convict, the jury must find that the advocacy which the defendants conspired to promote was of a kind calculated to "incite" persons to action for the forcible overthrow of the Government. It is argued that advocacy of forcible overthrow as mere *abstract doctrine* is within the free speech protection of the First Amendment; that the Smith Act, consistently with that constitutional provision, must be taken as proscribing only the sort of advocacy which incites to illegal *action;* and that the trial court's charge, by permitting conviction for mere advocacy, unrelated to its tendency to produce forcible action, resulted in an unconstitutional application of the Smith Act. The Government, which at the trial also requested the court to charge in terms of "incitement," now takes the position, however, that the true constitutional dividing line is not between inciting and abstract advocacy of forcible overthrow, but rather between advocacy as such, irrespective of its inciting qualities, and the mere discussion or exposition of violent overthrow as an abstract theory. . . .

2. 354 U.S. at 339.

There can be no doubt from the record that in so instructing the jury the court regarded as immaterial, and intended to withdraw from the jury's consideration, any issue as to the character of the advocacy in terms of its capacity to stir listeners to forcible action. Both the petitioners and the Government submitted proposed instructions which would have required the jury to find that the proscribed advocacy was not of a mere abstract doctrine of forcible overthrow, but of action to that end, by the use of language reasonably and ordinarily calculated to incite persons to such action. The trial court rejected these proposed instructions on the ground that any necessity for giving them which may have existed at the time the *Dennis* case was tried was removed by this Court's subsequent decision in that case. . . .

We are thus faced with the question whether the Smith Act prohibits advocacy and teaching of forcible overthrow as an abstract principle, divorced from any effort to instigate action to that end, so long as such advocacy or teaching is engaged in with evil intent. We hold that it does not.

The distinction between advocacy of abstract doctrine and advocacy directed at promoting unlawful action is one that has been consistently recognized in the opinions of this Court, beginning with *Fox* v. *Washington,* 236 U.S. 273, and *Schenck* v. *United States,* 249 U.S. 47. This distinction was heavily underscored in *Gitlow* v. *New York,* 268 U.S. 652, in which the statute involved was nearly identical with the one now before us, and where the Court, despite the narrow view there taken of the First Amendment, said:

> "The statute does not penalize the utterance or publication of abstract 'doctrine' or academic discussion having no quality of incitement to any concrete action. . . . It is not the abstract 'doctrine' of overthrowing organized government by unlawful means which is denounced by the statute, but the advocacy of action for the accomplishment of that purpose. . . . This [Manifesto] . . . is [in] the language of direct incitement. . . . That the jury were warranted in finding that the Manifesto advocated not merely the abstract doctrine of overthrowing organized government by force, violence and unlawful means, but action to that end, is clear. . . . That utterances inciting to the overthrow of organized government by unlawful means, present a sufficient danger of substantive evil to bring their punishment within the range of legislative discretion, is clear.". . .

We need not, however, decide the issue before us in terms of constitutional compulsion, for our first duty is to construe this statute. In doing so we should not assume that Congress chose to disregard a constitutional danger zone so clearly marked, or that it used the words "advocate" and "teach" in their ordinary dictionary meanings when they had already been construed as terms of art carrying a special and limited connotation. . . . The *Gitlow* case and the New York Criminal Anarchy Act there involved, which furnished the prototype for the Smith Act, were both known and adverted to by Congress in the course of the legislative proceedings. . . . The legislative history of the Smith Act and related bills shows beyond all question that Congress was aware of the distinction between the advocacy or teaching of abstract doctrine and the advocacy or teaching of action, and that it did not intend to disregard it. The statute was aimed at the advocacy and teaching of concrete action for the forcible overthrow of the Government and not of principles divorced from action.

The Government's reliance on this Court's decision in *Dennis* is misplaced. The jury instructions which were refused here were given there, and were referred to by this Court as requiring "the jury to find the facts *essential* to establish the substantive crime." . . . It is true that at one point in the late Chief Justice's opinion it is stated that the Smith Act "is directed at advocacy, not discussion," . . .

but it is clear that the reference was to advocacy of action, not ideas, for in the very next sentence the opinion emphasizes that the jury was properly instructed that there could be no conviction for "advocacy in the realm of ideas." The two concurring opinions in that case likewise emphasize the distinction with which we are concerned. . . .

In failing to distinguish between advocacy of forcible overthrow as an abstract doctrine and advocacy of action to that end, the District Court appears to have been led astray by the holding in *Dennis* that advocacy of violent action to be taken at some future time was enough. It seems to have considered that, since "inciting" speech is usually thought of as something calculated to induce immediate action, and since *Dennis* held advocacy of action for future overthrow sufficient, this meant that advocacy, irrespective of its tendency to generate action, is punishable, provided only that it is uttered with a specific intent to accomplish overthrow. In other words, the District Court apparently thought that *Dennis* obliterated the traditional dividing line between advocacy of abstract doctrine and advocacy of action.

This misconceives the situation confronting the Court in *Dennis* and what was held there.

At the outset, in view of the conclusions reached in Part I of this opinion, we must put aside as against all petitioners the evidence relating to the "organizing" aspect of the alleged conspiracy, except insofar as it bears upon the "advocacy" charge. That, indeed, dilutes in a substantial way a large part of the evidence, for the record unmistakably indicates that the Government relied heavily on its "organizing" charge. Two further general observations should also be made about the evidence as to the "advocacy" charge. The first is that both the Government and the trial court evidently proceeded on the theory that advocacy of abstract doctrine was enough to offend the Smith Act, whereas, as we have held, it is only advocacy of forcible action that is proscribed. The second observation is that both the record and the Government's brief in this Court make it clear that the Government's thesis was that the Communist Party, or at least the Communist Party of California, constituted the conspiratorial group, and that membership in the conspiracy could therefore be proved by showing that the individual petitioners were actively identified with the Party's affairs and thus inferentially parties to its tenets. This might have been well enough towards making out the Government's case if advocacy of the abstract doctrine of forcible overthrow satisfied the Smith Act, for we would at least have little difficulty in saying on this record that a jury could justifiably conclude that such was one of the tenets of the Communist Party; and there was no dispute as to petitioners' active identification with Party affairs. But when it comes to Party advocacy or teaching in the sense of a call to forcible action at some future time we cannot but regard this record as strikingly deficient. At best this voluminous record shows but a half dozen or so scattered incidents which, even under the loosest standards, could be deemed to show such advocacy. Most of these were not connected with any of the petitioners, or occurred many years before the period covered by the indictment. We are unable to regard this sporadic showing as sufficient to justify viewing the Communist Party as the nexus between these petitioners and the conspiracy charged. We need scarcely say that however much one may abhor even the abstract preaching of forcible overthrow of government, or believe that forcible overthrow is the ultimate purpose to which the Communist Party is dedicated, it is upon the evidence in the record that the petitioners must be judged in this case.

We must, then, look elsewhere than to the evidence concerning the Communist Party as such for the existence of the conspiracy to advocate charged in the indictment. As to the petitioners Connelly, Kusnitz, Richmond, Spector, and

Steinberg we find no adequate evidence in the record which would permit a jury to find that they were members of such a conspiracy. For all purposes relevant here, the sole evidence as to them was that they had long been members, officers or functionaries of the Communist Party of California; and that standing alone, as Congress has enacted in §4 (f) of the Internal Security Act of 1950, makes out no case against them. So far as this record shows, none of them has engaged in or been associated with any but what appear to have been wholly lawful activities, or has ever made a single remark or been present when someone else made a remark, which would tend to prove the charges against them. Connelly and Richmond were, to be sure, the Los Angeles and Executive Editors, respectively, of the Daily People's World, the West Coast Party organ, but we can find nothing in the material introduced into evidence from that newspaper which advances the Government's case.

Moreover, apart from the inadequacy of the evidence to show, at best, more than the abstract advocacy and teaching of forcible overthrow by the Party, it is difficult to perceive how the requisite specific intent to accomplish such overthrow could be deemed proved by a showing of mere membership or the holding of office in the Communist Party. We therefore think that as to these petitioners the evidence was entirely too meagre to justify putting them to a new trial, and that their acquittal should be ordered.

As to the nine remaining petitioners, we consider that a different conclusion should be reached. There was testimony from the witness Foard, and other evidence, tying Fox, Healey, Lambert, Lima, Schneiderman, Stack, and Yates to Party classes conducted in the San Francisco area during the year 1946, where there occurred what might be considered to be the systematic teaching and advocacy of illegal action which is condemned by the statute. It might be found that one of the purposes of such classes was to develop in the members of the group a readiness to engage at the crucial time, perhaps during war or during attack upon the United States from without, in such activities as sabotage and street fighting, in order to divert and diffuse the resistance of the authorities and if possible to seize local vantage points. There was also testimony as to activities in the Los Angeles area, during the period covered by the indictment, which might be considered to amount to "advocacy of action," and with which petitioners Carlson and Dobbs were linked. From the testimony of the witness Scarletto, it might be found that individuals considered to be particularly trustworthy were taken into an "underground" apparatus and there instructed in tasks which would be useful when the time for violent action arrived. Scarletto was surreptitiously indoctrinated in methods, as he said, of moving "masses of people in time of crisis." It might be found, under all the circumstances, that the purpose of this teaching was to prepare the members of the underground apparatus to engage in, to facilitate, and to cooperate with violent action directed against government when the time was ripe. In short, while the record contains evidence of little more than a general program of educational activity by the Communist Party which included advocacy of violence as a theoretical matter, we are not prepared to say, at this stage of the case, that it would be impossible for a jury, resolving all conflicts in favor of the Government and giving the evidence as to these San Francisco and Los Angeles episodes its utmost sweep, to find that advocacy of action was also engaged in when the group involved was thought particularly trustworthy, dedicated, and suited for violent tasks.

Nor can we say that the evidence linking these nine petitioners to that sort of advocacy, with the requisite specific intent, is so tenuous as not to justify their retrial under proper legal standards. Fox, Healey, Lambert, Lima, Schneiderman, Stack, and Yates, as members of the State and San Francisco County

Boards, were shown to have been closely associated with Ida Rothstein, the principal teacher of the San Francisco classes, who also during this same period arranged in a devious and conspiratorial manner for the holding of Board meetings at the home of the witness Honig, which were attended by these petitioners. It was also shown that from time to time instructions emanated from the Boards or their members to instructors of groups at lower levels. And while none of the written instructions produced at the trial were invidious in themselves, it might be inferred that additional instructions were given which were not reduced to writing. Similarly, there was evidence of close association between petitioners Carlson and Dobbs and associates or superiors of the witness Scarletto, which might be taken as indicating that these two petitioners had knowledge of the apparatus in which Scarletto was active. And finally, all of these nine petitioners were shown either to have made statements themselves, or apparently approved statements made in their presence, which a jury might take as some evidence of their participation with the requisite intent in a conspiracy to advocate illegal action.

As to these nine petitioners, then, we shall not order an acquittal.

Scales v. United States, 367 U.S. 203 (1961)

In *Yates,* Justice Harlan had noted that the required "specific intent" to overthrow the government could *not* "be deemed proved by a showing of mere membership or the holding of office in the Communist Party." Four years after *Yates,* the Supreme Court specifically passed judgment for the first time on the validity of the "membership clause" of the Smith Act. How was membership in the Communist Party to be dealt with? Was mere membership in the Party punishable under the Act? Or did the Smith Act in this instance violate the First Amendment's freedom of assembly clause? A badly split (5–4) Supreme Court answered these questions in *Scales* v. *United States.*

Scales argued that Section 2 of the Smith Act, the membership clause, had been superseded in 1950 by the Subversive Activities Control Act. This law, enacted by Congress during the height of the post World War II McCarran-McCarthy-Mundt-Nixon anti-communist fervor, required registration of all Communist Party members. It also provided that "neither the holding of office nor membership in any Communist organization" was itself a violation of the law. Scales used this provision as the basis for his defense.

Writing for the majority, Justice Harlan concluded that the 1950 Act merely clarified the Smith Act's membership clause; it did not repeal it. Harlan went on to conclude that Section 2 did not make membership illegal per se. Only "active" membership, he said, that knowingly and with specific intent is used to help bring about the overthrow of government is illegal. As it read the evidence, the Supreme Court concluded that Scales's membership in the Communist Party was of the "active," "knowing" variety. Accordingly the Supreme Court affirmed his conviction under Section 2. Not however without drawing three sharp dissenting opinions by Justices Black, Douglas, and Brennan (joined by Chief Justice Warren and Douglas). Black argued that Scales had been convicted "under a law that is at best, unconstitutionally vague and, at worst, ex post facto . . . I think his conviction should be reversed on that ground."[1] Justice Douglas wrote that "even the Alien and Sedition laws, shameful reminders of an early chapter in intolerance, never went so far as we go today." Douglas insisted that the Court had legalized guilt by association, which up to this time had been considered abhorrent and outside the American tradition. "Sending a man to prison when he committed no unlawful act," Douglas noted, ". . . borrows from . . . totalitarian philosophy."[2] For his part Justice Brennan felt that the 1950 Act made illegal something other than mere membership in the Communist Party. "Something more," according to Brennan, *had* to be some kind of unlawful activity. After the 1950 Act was passed, Brennan said, membership without other activity "was no longer sufficient for Smith Act prosecutions." Brennan argued that the Court should have reversed Scales's conviction because "that seems to me to be the only fair way" to reconcile Section 2 of the Smith Act with the 1950 Act.[3] But the majority thought otherwise.

Mr. Justice Harlan delivered the opinion of the Court, saying in part:

> Petitioner's constitutional attack goes both to the statute on its face and as applied. At this point we deal with the first aspect of the challenge and with one part of its second aspect. The balance of the latter, which essentially concerns the sufficiency of the evidence, is discussed in the next section of this opinion.
>
> It will bring the constitutional issues into clearer focus to notice first the premises on which the case was submitted to the jury. The jury was instructed that in order to convict it must find that within the three-year limitations period (1) the Communist Party advocated the violent overthrow of the Government, in the sense of present "advocacy of action" to accomplish that end as soon as circumstances were propitious; and (2) petitioner was an "active" member of the Party, and not merely "a nominal, passive, inactive or purely technical" member, with knowledge of the Party's illegal advocacy and a specific intent to bring about violent overthrow "as speedily as circumstances would permit."
>
> The constitutional attack upon the membership clause, as thus construed, is that the statute offends (1) the Fifth Amendment, in that it impermissibly imputes guilt to an individual merely on the basis of his associations and sympathies, rather than because of some concrete personal involvement in criminal conduct; and (2) the First Amendment, in that it infringes on free political expression and association. Subsidiarily, it is argued that the statute cannot be interpreted as including a requirement of a specific intent to accomplish violent overthrow, or as requiring that membership in a proscribed organization must be "active" membership, in the absence of both or either of which it is said the statute becomes *a fortiori* unconstitutional. It is further contended that even if the adjective "active" may properly be implied as a qualification upon the term "member," petitioner's conviction would nonetheless be unconstitutional, because so construed the statute would be impermissibly vague under the Fifth and Sixth Amendments, and so applied would in any event infringe the Sixth Amendment, in that the indictment charged only that Scales was a "member," not an "active" member, of the Communist Party.
>
> Before reaching petitioner's constitutional claims, we should first ascertain whether the membership clause permissibly bears the construction put upon it below. We think it does.
>
> The trial court's definition of the kind of organizational advocacy that is proscribed was fully in accord with what was held in *Yates v. United States*, 354 U.S. 298. And the statute itself requires that a defendant must have knowledge of the organization's illegal advocacy.

1. 367 U.S. 260–61.   3. Ibid., at 289.
2. Ibid., at 263.

The only two elements of the crime, as defined below, about which there is controversy are therefore "specific intent" and "active" membership. As to the former, this Court held in *Dennis* v. *United States,* 341 U.S. 494, 499–500, that even though the "advocacy" and "organizing" provisions of the Smith Act, unlike the "literature" section (note 1, *supra),* did not expressly contain such a specific intent element, such a requirement was fairly to be implied. We think that the reasoning of *Dennis.* . . . [p]etitioner's particular constitutional objections to this construction are misconceived. The indictment was not defective in failing to charge that Scales was an "active" member of the Party, for that factor was not in itself a discrete element of the crime, but an inherent quality of the membership element. As such it was a matter not for the indictment, but for elucidating instructions to the jury on what the term "member" in the statute meant. Nor do we think that the objection on the score of vagueness is a tenable one. The distinction between "active" and "nominal" membership is well understood in common parlance . . . , and the point at which one shades into the other is something that goes not to the sufficiency of the statute, but to the adequacy of the trial court's guidance to the jury by way of instructions in a particular case. . . . Moreover, whatever abstract doubts might exist on the matter, this case presents no such problem. For petitioner's actions on behalf of the Communist Party most certainly amounted to active membership by whatever standards one could reasonably anticipate, and he can therefore hardly be considered to have acted unadvisedly on this score.

We find no substance in the further suggestion that petitioner could not be expected to anticipate a construction of the statute that included within its elements activity and specific intent, and hence that he was not duly warned of what the statute made criminal. It is, of course, clear that the lower courts' construction was narrower, not broader, than the one for which petitioner argues in defining the character of the forbidden conduct and that therefore, according to petitioner's own construction, his actions were forbidden by the statute. The contention must then be that petitioner had a right to rely on the statute's, as *he* construed it, being held unconstitutional. Assuming, *arguendo,* that petitioner's construction was not unreasonable, no more can be said than that — in light of the courts' traditional avoidance of constructions of dubious constitutionality and in light of their role in construing the purpose of a statute — there were two ways one could reasonably anticipate this statute's being construed, and that petitioner had clear warning that his actions were in violation of both constructions. There is no additional constitutional requirement that petitioner should be entitled to rely upon the statute's being construed in such a way as possibly to render it unconstitutional. In sum, this argument of a "right" to a literal construction simply boils down to a claim that the view of the statute taken below did violence to the congressional purpose. Of course a litigant is always prejudiced when a court errs, but whether or not the lower courts erred in their construction is an issue which can only be met on its merits, and not by reference to a "right" to a particular interpretation.

We hold that the statute was correctly interpreted by the two lower courts, and now turn to petitioner's basic constitutional challenge.

In our jurisprudence guilt is personal, and when the imposition of punishment on a status or on conduct can only be justified by reference to the relationship of that status or conduct to other concededly criminal activity (here advocacy of violent overthrow), that relationship must be sufficiently substantial to satisfy the concept of personal guilt in order to withstand attack under the Due Process Clause of the Fifth Amendment. Membership, without more, in an organization engaged in illegal advocacy, it is now said, has not heretofore been recognized by this Court to be such a relationship. This claim stands, and we shall examine it, independently of the claim made under the First Amendment.

Any thought that due process puts beyond the reach of the criminal law all individual associational relationships, unless accompanied by the commission of specific acts of criminality, is dispelled by familiar concepts of the law of conspiracy and complicity. While both are commonplace in the landscape of the criminal law, they are not natural features. Rather they are particular legal concepts manifesting the more general principle that society, having the power to punish dangerous behavior, cannot be powerless against those who work to bring about that behavior. . . . The fact that Congress has not resorted to either of these familiar concepts means only that the enquiry here must direct itself to an analysis of the relationship between the fact of membership and the underlying substantive illegal conduct, in order to determine whether that relationship is indeed too tenuous to permit its use as the basis of criminal liability. In this instance it is an organization which engages in criminal activity, and we can perceive no reason why one who actively and knowingly works in the ranks of that organization, intending to contribute to the success of those specifically illegal activities, should be any more immune from prosecution than he to whom the organization has assigned the task of carrying out the substantive criminal act. Nor should the fact that Congress has focussed here on "membership," the characteristic relationship between an individual and the type of conspiratorial quasi-political associations with the criminal aspect of whose activities Congress was concerned, of itself require the conclusion that the legislature has traveled outside the familiar and permissible bounds of criminal imputability. In truth, the specificity of the proscribed relationship is not necessarily a vice; it provides instruction and warning.

What must be met, then, is the argument that membership, even when accompanied by the elements of knowledge and specific intent, affords an insufficient quantum of participation in the organization's alleged criminal activity, that is, an insufficiently significant form of aid and encouragement to permit the imposition of criminal sanctions on that basis. It must indeed be recognized that a person who merely becomes a member of an illegal organization, by that "act" alone need be doing nothing more than signifying his assent to its purposes and activities on one hand, and providing, on the other, only the sort of moral encouragement which comes from the knowledge that others believe in what the organization is doing. It may indeed be argued that such assent and encouragement do fall short of the concrete, practical impetus given to a criminal enterprise which is lent for instance by a commitment on the part of a conspirator to act in furtherance of that enterprise. A member, as distinguished from a conspirator, may indicate his approval of a criminal enterprise by the very fact of his membership without thereby necessarily committing himself to further it by any act or course of conduct whatever.

In an area of the criminal law which this Court has indicated more than once demands its watchful scrutiny . . . , these factors have weight and must be found to be overborne in a total constitutional assessment of the statute. We think, however, they are duly met when the statute is found to reach only "active" members having also a guilty knowledge and intent, and which therefore prevents a conviction on what otherwise might be regarded as merely an expression of sympathy with the alleged criminal enterprise, unaccompanied by any significant action in its support or any commitment to undertake such action.

Thus, given the construction of the membership clause already discussed, we think the factors called for in rendering members criminally responsible for the illegal advocacy of the organization fall within established, and therefore presumably constitutional, standards of criminal imputability.

Noto v. United States, 367 U.S. 290 (1961)

On the same day that *Scales* was decided, a unanimous Supreme Court reversed a conviction for membership in the Communist Party. Involved in *Noto,* as it had been in *Scales,* was the Court's interpretation of the Smith Act's membership clause. The Court's reversal of Noto's conviction rested on its findings that the Communist Party group to which he belonged (Noto had been Chairman of the Erie County, New York Communist Party) had not advocated violence or the forceful overthrow of the government but had merely been involved in the teaching of abstract Communist theory. It was this point which distinguished *Noto* from *Scales.* The Court decided that Scales was an advocate, Noto was not.

Mr. Justice Harlan delivered the opinion of the Court, saying in part:

... The great bulk of the evidence in this record seems to us to come within the purview of the first of the contrasted alternatives elaborated in the concurring opinion in *Dennis* v. *United States,* 341 U.S. 494, 545, and referred to in the passage just quoted. We held in *Yates,* and we reiterate now, that the mere abstract teaching of Communist theory, including the teaching of the moral propriety or even moral necessity for a resort to force and violence, is not the same as preparing a group for violent action and steeling it to such action. There must be some substantial direct or circumstantial evidence of a call to violence now or in the future which is both sufficiently strong and sufficiently pervasive to lend color to the otherwise ambiguous theoretical material regarding Communist Party teaching, and to justify the inference that such a call to violence may fairly be imputed to the Party as a whole, and not merely to some narrow segment of it.

Surely the offhand remarks that certain individuals hostile to the Party would one day be shot cannot demonstrate more than the venomous or spiteful attitude of the Party towards its enemies, and might indicate what could be expected from the Party if it should ever succeed to power. The "industrial concentration" program, as to which the witness Regan testified in some detail, does indeed come closer to the kind of concrete and particular program on which a criminal conviction in this sort of case must be based. But in examining that evidence it appears to us that, in the context of this record, this too fails to establish that the Communist Party was an organization which presently advocated violent overthrow of the Government now or in the future, for that is what must be proven. The most that can be said is that the evidence as to that program might justify an inference that the leadership of the Party was preparing the way for a situation in which future acts of sabotage might be facilitated, but there is no evidence that such acts of sabotage were presently advocated; and it is *present* advocacy, and not an intent to advocate in the future or a conspiracy to advocate in the future once a groundwork has been laid, which is an element of the crime under the membership clause. To permit an inference of present advocacy from evidence showing at best only a purpose or conspiracy to advocate in the future would be to allow the jury to blur the lines of distinction between the various offenses punishable under the Smith Act.

The kind of evidence which we found in *Scales* sufficient to support the jury's verdict of present illegal Party advocacy is lacking here in any adequately substantial degree. It need hardly be said that it is upon the particular evidence in a particular record that a particular defendant must be judged, and not upon the evidence in some other record or upon what may be supposed to be the tenets of the Communist Party.

United States v. Robel, 389 U.S. 258 (1967)

During the "Red Scare" fervor of the immediate post World War II era, in addition to the Smith Act, the government also had the McCarran Act of 1950 in its anti-communist, anti-subversion arsenal. Passed over President Truman's veto during the most troublesome times of the cold war, the law started its legislative history as the Mundt-Nixon bill of 1948. Its supporters felt that Communist activity could be crippled in the United States if Party members were forced to register as such. The law demanded name, address, sources of funds and expenditures and, among other provisions, severely limited the right of Communist Party members to work in defense plants.

The mandatory registration features of the law were upheld in *Communist Party* v. *Subversive Activities Control Board.*[1] The Supreme Court refused to consider the possibility that the McCarran Act, with its multiple requirements, had been enacted as a way of making it impossible for the Communist Party to function and had, therefore, in effect "outlawed" the Party![2] Instead, the Court treated the law as a "simple" registration vehicle and accepted it as constitutionally valid on those grounds.

Some three years later, however, in *Aptheker* v. *Secretary of State,*[3] the Supreme Court ruled that the passport provisions of the McCarran Act, which had been used by the State Department to deny a passport to a known Communist Party official, were an unconstitutional restriction of a citizen's right to travel. In 1967, the more liberal Warren Court continued to chip away at the McCarran Act by striking down its provision restricting defense plant employment. Thus in *United States* v. *Robel,* with Chief Justice Warren writing for the majority of six (Justice White joined by Justice Harlan dissented and Justice Marshall did not participate), the Court ruled that the statute established "guilt by association" without any need to show that a threat of sabotage or espionage actually existed. For this reason, the Chief Justice wrote, Congress had exceeded its "ample power to safeguard national defense" when it wrote provisions into the McCarran Act specifying that members of the Communist Party would not be employed in defense plants.

In his dissent, the "less activist" Justice White argued that the Court should have left it to Congress to decide the requirements of national security. Acknowledging that the majority had worthy motives, "the widest bounds for the exercise of individual liberty consistent with the security of the country," Justice White insisted nevertheless that the Court had overstepped its bounds. Requirements of national security are a concern of Congress, he said. "These are matters about which judges should be wary . . ."[4]

Mr. Chief Justice Warren delivered the opinion of the Court, saying in part:

> The Government seeks to defend the statute on the ground that it was passed pursuant to Congress' war power. The Government argues that this Court has given broad deference to the exercise of that constitutional power by the national legislature. That argument finds support in a number of decisions of this Court. However, the phrase "war power" cannot be invoked as a talismanic incantation to support any exercise of congressional power which can be brought within its ambit. "[E]ven the war power does not remove constitutional limitations

---

1. 367 U.S. 1 (1961).

2. Pritchett makes this point. op. cit., at 379.

3. 378 U.S. 500 (1964).

4. 389 U.S. at 289.

safeguarding essential liberties." . . . More specifically in this case, the Government asserts that §5 (a) (1) (D) is an expression "of the growing concern shown by the executive and legislative branches of government over the risks of internal subversion in plants on which the national defense depend[s]." Yet, this concept of "national defense" cannot be deemed an end in itself, justifying any exercise of legislative power designed to promote such a goal. Implicit in the term "national defense" is the notion of defending those values and ideals which set this Nation apart. For almost two centuries, our country has taken singular pride in the democratic ideals enshrined in its Constitution, and the most cherished of those ideals have found expression in the First Amendment. It would indeed be ironic if, in the name of national defense, we would sanction the subversion of one of those liberties — the freedom of association — which makes the defense of the Nation worthwhile.

When Congress' exercise of one of its enumerated powers clashes with those individual liberties protected by the Bill of Rights, it is our "delicate and difficult task" to determine whether the resulting restriction on freedom can be tolerated. . . . The Government emphasizes that the purpose of §5 (a) (1) (D) is to reduce the threat of sabotage and espionage in the Nation's defense plants. The Government's interest in such a prophylactic measure is not insubstantial. But it cannot be doubted that the means chosen to implement that governmental purpose in this instance cut deeply into the right of association. Section 5 (a) (1) (D) put appellee to the choice of surrendering his organizational affiliation, regardless of whether his membership threatened the security of a defense facility, or giving up his job. When appellee refused to make that choice, he became subject to a possible criminal penalty of five years' imprisonment and a $10,000 fine. The statute quite literally establishes guilt by association alone, without any need to establish that an individual's association poses the threat feared by the Government in proscribing it. The inhibiting effect on the exercise of First Amendment rights is clear.

It has become axiomatic that "[p]recision of regulation must be the touchstone in an area so closely touching our most precious freedoms." . . . Such precision is notably lacking in §5 (a) (1) (D). That statute casts its net across a broad range of associational activities, indiscriminately trapping membership which can be constitutionally punished and membership which cannot be so proscribed. It is made irrelevant to the statute's operation that an individual may be a passive or inactive member of a designated organization, that he may be unaware of the organization's unlawful aims, or that he may disagree with those unlawful aims. It is also made irrelevant that an individual who is subject to the penalties of §5 (a) (1) (D) may occupy a nonsensitive position in a defense facility. Thus, §5 (a) (1) (D) contains the fatal defect of overbreadth because it seeks to bar employment both for association which may be proscribed and for association which may not be proscribed consistently with First Amendment rights. . . . This the Constitution will not tolerate.

We are not unmindful of the congressional concern over the danger of sabotage and espionage in national defense industries, and nothing we hold today should be read to deny Congress the power under narrowly drawn legislation to keep from sensitive positions in defense facilities those who would use their positions to disrupt the Nation's production facilities. We have recognized that, while the Constitution protects against invasions of individual rights, it does not withdraw from the Government the power to safeguard its vital interests. . . . Spies and saboteurs do exist, and Congress can, of course, prescribe criminal penalties for those who engage in espionage and sabotage. The Government can deny access to its secrets to those who would use such information to harm the

Nation. And Congress can declare sensitive positions in national defense industries off limits to those who would use such positions to disrupt the production of defense materials. The Government has told us that Congress, in passing §5 (a) (1) (D), made a considered judgment that one possible alternative to that statute — an industrial security screening program — would be inadequate and ineffective to protect against sabotage in defense facilities. It is not our function to examine the validity of that congressional judgment. Neither is it our function to determine whether an industrial security screening program exhausts the possible alternatives to the statute under review. We are concerned solely with determining whether the statute before us has exceeded the bounds imposed by the Constitution when First Amendment rights are at stake. The task of writing legislation which will stay within those bounds has been committed to Congress. Our decision today simply recognizes that, when legitimate legislative concerns are expressed in a statute which imposes a substantial burden on protected First Amendment activities, Congress must achieve its goal by means which have a "less drastic" impact on the continued vitality of First Amendment freedoms.... The Constitution and the basic position of First Amendment rights in our democratic fabric demand nothing less.

Brandenburg v. Ohio, 395 U.S. 444 (1969)

What the Supreme Court began in *Whitney* v. *California* (above) came full circle forty two years later in *Brandenburg* v. *Ohio*. In *Whitney*, despite the objections of its outspoken civil libertarians, Justices Brandeis and Holmes, the Court upheld California's criminal syndicalism law. It thereby sanctioned the idea of "collective guilt," presumption of guilt, or guilt by association that, as Justice Douglas would note later, "had been considered abhorrent and outside the American tradition." Guilt by association makes it unnecessary to commit an unlawful act in order to be found guilty in a court of law. Merely associating with persons or organizations (i.e., the Communist Party), even if for perfectly legal purposes, is itself proof of guilt. This "pernicious view" prevailed throughout many of the cases considered above dealing with communists and First Amendment freedoms. It came to an end, in *Brandenburg* v. *Ohio*, a case, interestingly enough, dealing not with membership in the Communist Party but in the Ku Klux Klan. Involved was Ohio's criminal syndicalism law, which made it unlawful to "voluntarily assemble with any group or assemblage of persons formed to reach or advocate the doctrines of criminal syndicalism."

In a brief, unsigned, unanimous per curiam opinion the Supreme Court struck down the Ohio statute and specifically overruled *Whitney* v. *California*. In the process it (apparently) formally ended a unique, often irrational, era in American jurisprudence that in many instances seemed squarely at odds with all that is best in the nation's constitutional traditions.

Accordingly, we are here confronted with a statute which, by its own words and as applied, purports to punish mere advocacy and to forbid, on pain of criminal punishment, assembly with others merely to advocate the described type of action. Such a statute falls within the condemnation of the First and Fourteenth Amendments. The contrary teaching of *Whitney* v. *California, supra,* cannot be supported, and that decision is therefore overruled.

Garner v. Board of Public Works, 341 U.S. 716 (1951)

Loyalty oaths, those peculiarly American answers to the anti-communist paranoia of the 1940s, have come before the Supreme Court on several occasions. During the cold war hysteria there surfaced a myriad of loyalty oaths prescribed by federal, state and local law, the simplistic notion being that mere recitation by rote of a few words or phrases would insure loyalty to American institutions. Various oaths were required by law of government employees, teachers, professors, labor union officials, and others. The purpose seemed always to be the same; to keep Communists and their sympathizers out of so-called "sensitive" positions; to ensure that only those "loyal" to American institutions, and swearing an oath was considered prima facie evidence of such loyalty, held those positions. In the fifteen-year period from 1951 to 1966, the Supreme Court had numerous opportunities to pass judgment on a wide assortment of loyalty oath statutes. The Court's record is mixed. As in many civil liberty disputes, the results seem to hinge upon whether the Court's liberals or conservatives were temporarily in the ascendancy. Liberals usually ruled against loyalty oaths, finding them abhorrent to the constitutional guarantees of personal freedom, while conservatives generally ruled in their favor, approving them in the name of national security.

Garner v. *Board of Public Works* is the first case in point. Involved was a Los Angeles City Charter that provided that no one who "advises, advocates or teaches" the overthrow of the government by force, was eligible for either public office or public employment. The charter also required each city officer and employee to take an oath professing loyalty to American institutions and affirming that they had not within the past five years belonged to any organization whose purpose was the forceful overthrow of government. Five separate opinions were written in *Garner.* Justice Clark spoke for the majority, Justices Frankfurter and Burton concurred in part and dissented in part while Justices Black and Douglas each wrote separate dissents. Douglas's opinion was the more significant of the two dissents. He argued that petitioners were disqualified for public office or employment "not for what they are today, not because of any program they currently espouse, not because of standards relating to fitness for the office, but for what they once advocated."[1] As Douglas read the record there was nothing to indicate any of the (seventeen)[2] petitioners had actually ever advocated the violent overthrow of the government. The vice in such instances, Douglas argued, is the "presumption of guilt which can only be removed by the expurgatory oath. That punishment . . . violates . . . the constitutional prohibition against bills of attainder . . ."[3]

However the majority did not believe the oath was a violation of either the bill of attainder provision or the ex post facto provision of Article I, Section 9 of the Constitution. As Justice Frankfurter said in his concurring opinion, "the Constitution does not guarantee public employment." Frankfurter and

1. 341 U.S. at 735–36.

2. Two employees were dismissed because they refused to disclose if they had been members of the Communist Party, fifteen for refusing to take the oath.

3. Ibid., at 736.

the majority felt that "no unit of government can be denied the right to keep out of its employ those who seek to overthrow the government by force or violence or are knowingly members of an organization engaged in such endeavor . . ."[4] The Douglas and Frankfurter views offer an example of the classic dichotomy between liberal and conservative on civil liberty questions.

Mr. Justice Clark delivered the opinion of the Court, saying in part:

> We think that a municipal employer is not disabled because it is an agency of the State from inquiring of its employees as to matters that may prove relevant to their fitness and suitability for the public service. Past conduct may well relate to present fitness; past loyalty may have a reasonable relationship to present and future trust. Both are commonly inquired into in determining fitness for both high and low positions in private industry and are not less relevant in public employment. The affidavit requirement is valid. . . .
>
> The Charter amendment defined standards of eligibility for employees and specifically denied city employment to those persons who thereafter should not comply with these standards. While the amendment deprived no one of employment with or without trial, yet from its effective date it terminated any privilege to work for the city in the case of persons who thereafter engaged in the activity proscribed.
>
> The ordinance provided for administrative implementation of the provisions of the Charter amendment. The oath imposed by the ordinance proscribed to employees activity which had been denied them in identical terms and with identical sanctions in the Charter provision effective in 1941. The five-year period provided by the oath extended back only to 1943.
>
> The ordinance would be *ex post facto* if it imposed punishment for past conduct lawful at the time it was engaged in. Passing for the moment the question whether separation of petitioners from their employment must be considered as punishment, the ordinance clearly is not *ex post facto*. The activity covered by the oath had been proscribed by the Charter in the same terms, for the same purpose, and to the same effect over seven years before, and two years prior to the period embraced in the oath. Not the law but the fact was posterior.
>
> Nor are we impressed by the contention that the oath denies due process because its negation is not limited to affiliations with organizations known to the employee to be in the proscribed class. We have no reason to suppose that the oath is or will be construed by the City of Los Angeles or by California courts as affecting adversely those persons who during their affiliation with a proscribed organization were innocent of its purpose, or those who severed their relations with any such organization when its character became apparent, or those who were affiliated with organizations which at one time or another during the period covered by the ordinance were engaged in proscribed activity but not at the time of affiant's affiliation. We assume that scienter is implicit in each clause of the oath. As the city has done nothing to negative this interpretation, we take for granted that the ordinance will be so read to avoid raising difficult constitutional problems which any other application would present. . . . It appears from correspondence of record between the city and petitioners that although the city welcomed inquiry as to its construction of the oath, the interpretation upon which we have proceeded may not have been explicitly called to the attention of petitioners before their refusal. We assume that, if our interpretation of the oath is correct, the City of Los Angeles will give those petitioners who heretofore refused to take the oath an opportunity to take it as interpreted and resume their employment.

4. Ibid., at 725.

Elfbrandt v. Russell, 384 U.S. 11 (1966)

Fifteen years passed between *Garner,* which upheld loyalty oaths, and *Elfbrandt* v. *Russell,* where the Supreme Court by a narrow 5–4 margin (almost but not quite) declared them unconstitutional per se. In the interim between the two cases, the Supreme Court had several other opportunities to pass judgment on loyalty oath statutes. For example, in *Cramp* v. *Board of Public Instruction*[1] the Court invalidated a Florida loyalty oath statute as too broadly drawn. Similarly in *Baggett* v. *Bullitt*[2] the Court voided two State of Washington statutory provisions requiring teachers to swear they were not "subversives" on grounds that the language was "vague, uncertain, and broad."

Perhaps the most (in)famous and controversial anti-Communist loyalty oath appeared in Section 9 (h) of the 1947 Taft-Hartley Labor-Management Relations Act, itself in this respect a victim of cold war paranoia. Section (h) applied to labor union officials, who were required to deny membership in the Communist Party as a condition for holding their positions in the Union. The Supreme Court upheld Section 9 (h) and its loyalty oath provision in *American Communications Association* v. *Douds.*[3] When Congress discovered that the oath was ineffective, because avowed Communists in the labor movement were quite willing to take the oath and lie about their political affiliations, it was repealed in 1959. In its place Congress substituted a provision making it a crime for a member of the Communist Party to be an *officer* of a labor union. In 1965 the Supreme Court narrowly (5–4) voided that provision in *United States* v. *Brown*[4] as an unconstitutional bill of attainder.

But the key loyalty oath decision was *Elfbrandt* v. *Russell.* There a split (5–4) Supreme Court, with Justice Douglas writing for the majority, struck down an Arizona loyalty oath law because it was not narrowly enough drawn to punish *specific* conduct. As such the Court ruled that the Arizona statute infringed upon freedom of political association guaranteed by the First Amendment.

The petitioner, a teacher, filed suit against the state, arguing she could not in good conscience take the oath not knowing what it meant. Unable to determine the oath's precise scope or essential meaning, the Supreme Court reversed Elfbrandt's conviction. Not, however, without a vigorous dissent written by Justice White (joined by Justices Clark, Harlan, and Stewart). White insisted that a state acts within its powers by disqualifying from public employment employees whose membership in the Communist Party is concurrent with public employment. In White's view the Court erred "in holding that the Act is overbroad because it includes state employees who are knowing members [of the Communist Party] but who may not be active and who may lack the specific intent to further the illegal aims of the Party."[5] According to White, membership in the Communist Party was enough to disqualify a person from public employment. No specific illegal act was necessary. But in *Elfbrandt* the five more liberal members of the Warren Court prevailed and

1. 368 U.S. 278 (1961). See also Whitehill v. Elkins, 389 U.S. (1967), where a Maryland loyalty oath statute was invalidated.

2. 377 U.S. 360 (1964).

3. 339 U.S. 382 (1950).

4. 381 U.S. 437 (1965).

5. 384 U.S. at 22–23.

the majority came as close as the Court has come in declaring all loyalty oaths unconstitutional.

Mr. Justice Douglas delivered the opinion of the Court, saying in part:

Any lingering doubt that proscription of mere knowing membership, without any showing of "specific intent," would run afoul of the Constitution was set at rest by our decision in *Aptheker v. Secretary of State,* 378 U.S. 500. We dealt there with a statute which provided that no member of a Communist organization ordered by the Subversive Activities Control Board to register shall apply for or use a passport. We concluded that the statute would not permit a narrow reading of the sort we gave §2385 in *Scales.* . . . The statute, as we read it, covered membership which was not accompanied by a specific intent to further the unlawful aims of the organization, and we held it unconstitutional.

The oath and accompanying statutory gloss challenged here suffer from an identical constitutional infirmity. One who subscribes to this Arizona oath and who is, or thereafter becomes, a knowing member of an organization which has as "one of its purposes" the violent overthrow of the government, is subject to immediate discharge and criminal penalties. Nothing in the oath, the statutory gloss, or the construction of the oath and statutes given by the Arizona Supreme Court, purports to exclude association by one who does not subscribe to the organization's unlawful ends. Here as in *Baggett v. Bullitt, supra,* the "hazard of being prosecuted for knowing but guiltless behavior" . . . is a reality. People often label as "communist" ideas which they oppose; and they often make up our juries. "[P]rosecutors too are human." . . . Would it be legal to join a seminar group predominantly Communist and therefore subject to control by those who are said to believe in the overthrow of the Government by force and violence? Juries might convict though the teacher did not subscribe to the wrongful aims of the organization. And there is apparently no machinery provided for getting clearance in advance.

Those who join an organization but do not share its unlawful purposes and who do not participate in its unlawful activities surely pose no threat, either as citizens or as public employees. Laws such as this which are not restricted in scope to those who join with the "specific intent" to further illegal action impose, in effect, a conclusive presumption that the member shares the unlawful aims of the organization. . . . The unconstitutionality of this Act follows *a fortiori* from *Speiser v. Randall,* 357 U.S. 513, where we held that a State may not even place on an applicant for a tax exemption the burden of proving that he has not engaged in criminal advocacy.

This Act threatens the cherished freedom of association protected by the First Amendment, made applicable to the States through the Fourteenth Amendment. . . . A statute touching those protected rights must be "narrowly drawn to define and punish specific conduct constituting a clear and present danger to a substantial interest of the State. . . . Legitimate legislative goals "cannot be pursued by means that broadly stifle fundamental personal liberties when the end can be more narrowly achieved." . . . A law which applies to membership without the "specific intent" to further the illegal aims of the organization infringes unnecessarily on protected freedoms. It rests on the doctrine of "guilt by association" which has no place here. . . . Such a law cannot stand.

II

THE FOURTH AMENDMENT

"The right of the people to be secure in their persons, houses, papers and effects, against unreasonable searches and seizures, shall not be violated, and no warrants shall issue, but upon probable cause, supported by oath or affirmation, and particularly describing the place to be searched, and the persons or things to be seized." The Fourth Amendment, guarantor of personal privacy, became part of the Constitution largely because of resentment among many American colonists, especially in New England, concerning the British Army practice of search and seizure to enforce Parliament's tax laws.

With one major exception, the *Boyd* case, the Fourth Amendment was largely dormant until the twentieth century. In recent years, however, it has occasioned a growing body of constitutional law. Involved in most disputes has been the incorporation issue, whether Fourth Amendment guarantees apply to the states under the Fourteenth Amendment. Recent Fourth Amendment disputes have focused on such uniquely modern-day problems as the permissible limits in criminal proceedings of evidence procured by electronic surveillance (wiretapping), the necessity for search warrants, and perhaps most controversial, contraceptive and abortion issues. The Supreme Court has also attempted to define precisely how to apply the constitutional term "unreasonable search and seizure."

1

SEARCH AND SEIZURE

Boyd v. United States, 116 U.S. 616 (1886)

The Court's first major Fourth Amendment decision was *Boyd* v. *United States*. Involved in *Boyd* was an 1874 law, amending Federal customs revenue regulations, that authorized Federal courts to require defendants to produce in court their "private books, invoices and papers." Speaking for a unanimous Court, Justice Bradley wrote that the Fourth Amendment's protection against unreasonable search and seizure extends beyond actual entry, search, or seizure.[1] Making it compulsory for a man to produce his private papers, Bradley said, was contrary to the Constitution. For this reason the Court ruled the 1874 law unconstitutional on grounds that simply forcing a defendant to produce his private papers, even when there was no specific search and seizure involved, violated the search and seizure provisions of the Fourth Amendment.

Boyd, which gave both Fourth and Fifth Amendment protection to private papers, was valid in its entirety for ninety years. Then in 1976 the Burger Court withdrew Fifth Amendment protection of private papers. That case was *Andresen* v. *Maryland*.[2] Once this was done the same Court went on to uphold the government's right to demand from banks microfilmed copies of checks and deposit slips on grounds that a customer's dealings with his bank are not to be considered "private" within the meaning of the Fourth Amendment. More recently the Burger Court has sanctioned police searches of newspaper offices. And in the process it has caused an uproar in printed media circles.

Boyd is a landmark decision. For the first time the Supreme Court delineated the meaning and application of an important constitutional provision that because of advances in technology has since become much more deeply embroiled in legal disputes.

Mr. Justice Bradley delivered the opinion of the Court, saying in part:

1. In a concurring opinion Justice Miller, joined by Chief Justice White, agreed with the Court's position but on Fifth Amendment "self incrimination" grounds. 116 U.S. at 639.

2. 96 S. Ct. 2737 (1976).

But, in regard to the Fourth Amendment, it is contended that, whatever might have been alleged against the constitutionality of the acts of 1863 and 1867, that of 1874, under which the order in the present case was made, is free from constitutional objection, because it does not authorize the search and seizure of books and papers, but only requires the defendant or claimant to produce them. That is so; but it declares that if he does not produce them, the allegations which it is affirmed they will prove shall be taken as confessed. This is tantamount to compelling their production; for the prosecuting attorney will always be sure to state the evidence expected to be derived from them as strongly as the case will admit of. It is true that certain aggravating incidents of actual search and seizure, such as forcible entry into a man's house and searching amongst his papers, are wanting, and to this extent the proceeding under the act of 1874 is a mitigation of that which was authorized by the former acts; but it accomplishes the substantial object of those acts in forcing from a party evidence against himself. It is our opinion, therefore, that a compulsory production of a man's private papers to establish a criminal charge against him, or to forfeit his property, is within the scope of the Fourth Amendment to the Constitution, in all cases in which a search and seizure would be; because it is a material ingredient, and effects the sole object and purpose of search and seizure.

The principal question, however, remains to be considered. Is a search and seizure, or, what is equivalent thereto, a compulsory production of a man's private papers, to be used in evidence against him in a proceeding to forfeit his property for alleged fraud against the revenue laws — is such a proceeding for such a purpose an "*unreasonable* search and seizure" within the meaning of the Fourth Amendment of the Constitution? or, is it a legitimate proceeding? . . .

We think that the notice to produce the invoice in this case, the order by virtue of which it was issued, and the law which authorized the order, were unconstitutional and void, and that the inspection by the district attorney of said invoice, when produced in obedience to said notice, and its admission in evidence by the court, were erroneous and unconstitutional proceedings.

Weeks v. United States, 232 U.S. 383 (1914)

Among the more controversial aspects of recent Fourth Amendment disputes has been the development by the Supreme Court of an "exclusionary rule" as protection against unconstitutional search and seizure. The rule, which states that illegally obtained evidence *must* be excluded from federal court proceedings, has occasioned intense debate with both sides disagreeing as to its wisdom and application. Pritchett explains the controversy in this way: "one theory is that (the exclusionary rule) is intended to act as a deterrent to police misconduct." On the other hand law enforcement officials call the rule an impediment to their necessary surveillance work. "A second argument is that it preserves the integrity of the courts, for accepting unconstitutionally secured evidence would make them partners in the illegality. Still a third position is that the rule gives effect to a personal constitutional right the government cannot infringe upon and that [therefore] the [exclusionary] rule needs no other justification."[1] There is no unanimity in legal circles on this matter. Obviously law enforcement officials are generally opposed. But as Pritchett points out, several leading American authorities on the rule of evi-

1. Pritchett, op. cit., at 435.

dence are also opposed. Justice Cardoza, an outstanding legal scholar in his own right, was one such authority who thought it intolerable that "the criminal should go free because the constable has blundered."[2]

The exclusionary rule made its first appearance in *Weeks* v. *United States*. The record in *Weeks* indicates the following: Weeks was arrested without a warrant at the Union Station in Kansas City where he was employed. Other officers had gone to Weeks's home, obtained a key from a neighbor, entered, searched, and seized papers and other personal articles that were then turned over to the United States Marshal. Later the same day, officers returned to Weeks's home with the Marshal, searched again and found other letters in a dresser drawer. Neither the Marshal nor the police officers had a search warrant.

In applying the guarantees of the Fourth Amendment in *Weeks,* Justice Day, speaking for a unanimous Court, made the following point: If letters and private documents can be seized by police officers without a warrant and used as evidence to obtain a conviction "the protection of the Fourth Amendment . . . might as well be stricken from the Constitution."[3] The Court rejected such practices and reversed the conviction. In the process it developed for the first time an "exclusionary rule" to establish the constitutionally admissable limits of evidence in a Federal Court.

Mr. Justice Day delivered the opinion of the Court, saying in part:

> We therefore reach the conclusion that the letters in question were taken from the house of the accused by an official of the United States acting under color of his office in direct violation of the constitutional rights of the defendant; that having made a reasonable application for their return, which was heard and passed upon by the court, there was involved in the order refusing the application a denial of the constitutional rights of the accused, and that the court should have restored these letters to the accused. In holding them and permitting their use upon the trial, we think prejudicial error was committed. As to the papers and property seized by the policemen, it does not appear that they acted under any claim of Federal authority such as would make the Amendment applicable to such unauthorized seizures. The record shows that what they did by way of arrest and search and seizure was done before the finding of the indictment in the Federal court, under what supposed right or authority does not appear. What remedies the defendant may have against them we need not inquire, as the Fourth Amendment is not directed to individual misconduct of such officials. Its limitations reach the Federal Government and its agencies.

Wolf v. Colorado, 338 U.S. 25 (1949)

Do the search and seizure guarantees of the Fourth Amendment apply to the states, as First Amendment rights do, through the due process clause of the Fourteenth? Or to put it another way, are Bill of Rights guarantees "incorporated" under the Fourteenth Amendment's due process clause? In a confusing 1949 decision the Supreme Court appeared to have answered both yes and no to that question. In the same case, in answer to still another Fourth

2. Ibid.
3. 232 U.S. at 343.

Amendment question, is illegally obtained evidence excluded from a state court, a majority of six said emphatically not.

The case was *Wolf v. Colorado.* Its difficult and inconsistent ruling would stand for twelve years. On the one hand, in the majority opinion Justice Frankfurter, who was never an advocate of incorporation, even in First Amendment disputes, agreed with Justice Cardozo's view that the due process clause of the Fourteenth Amendment did *not* incorporate the guarantees of the original Bill of Rights.[1] At the same time he maintained that the security of privacy against arbitrary intrusion by police "which is at the core of the Fourth Amendment — is basic to a free society."[2] Frankfurter concluded, "it is therefore implicit in the 'concept of ordered liberty' and as such enforceable against the states through the Due Process Clause."[3]

In 1949 even the usually liberal Roosevelt Court was not yet ready to accept full incorporation. That would come later with the Warren Court. Concerning the applicability of evidence secured in violation of the Fourth Amendment (the exclusionary rule of the *Weeks* case) the Supreme Court ruled in *Wolf* that it could *not* be imposed upon the states by the Fourteenth Amendment.

Three sharply critical, dissenting opinions were written in *Wolf*: by Justice Douglas, by Justice Murphy joined by Justice Rutledge, and by Justice Rutledge. Murphy and Rutledge took particular issue with the Court's reasoning. Murphy argued that the Court's decision "will do inestimable harm to the cause of fair police methods in our cities and states. Even more important, perhaps, it must have tragic effect upon public respect for our judiciary. For the Court now allows what is indeed shabby business; lawlessness by officers of the law."[4] Justice Rutledge summarily rejected the Court's "simultaneous conclusion that the mandate embodied in the Fourth Amendment, although binding on the states, does not carry with it the one sanction — exclusion of evidence taken in violation of the Amendment's terms." Failure to observe this, Rutledge said, "means that the protection of the Fourth Amendment . . . might as well be stricken from the Constitution."[5]

For the majority, Justice Frankfurter relied heavily on the fact that since the 1914 *Weeks* decision, thirty-one states had specifically rejected its exclusionary rule while sixteen states had accepted it. This position, and the *Palko* decision (below), which rejected incorporation of Fifth Amendment rights to the states through the due process clause of the Fourteenth, formed the basis for the Court's vacillating ruling in *Wolf*.

Mr. Justice Frankfurter delivered the opinion of the Court, saying in part:

> For purposes of ascertaining the restrictions which the Due Process Clause imposed upon the States in the enforcement of their criminal law, we adhere to the views expressed in *Palko v. Connecticut, supra,* 302 U.S. 319. That decision speaks to us with the great weight of the authority, particularly in matters of civil liberty, of a court that included Mr. Chief Justice Hughes, Mr. Justice Brandeis, Mr. Justice Stone and Mr. Justice Cardozo, to name only the dead. In rejecting the suggestion that the Due Process Clause incorporated the original Bill of Rights, Mr. Justice Cardozo reaffirmed on behalf of that Court a different but deeper and more pervasive conception of the Due Process Clause. This Clause

1. As expressed in Palko v. Connecticut, 302 U.S. at 325 (below).   4. Ibid., at 46.

2. 338 U.S. at 26–27.   5. Ibid., at 47.

3. Ibid., at 27–28.

exacts from the States for the lowliest and the most outcast all that is "implicit in the concept of ordered liberty." . . .

Due process of law thus conveys neither formal nor fixed nor narrow requirements. It is the compendious expression for all those rights which the courts must enforce because they are basic to our free society. But basic rights do not become petrified as of any one time, even though, as a matter of human experience, some may not too rhetorically be called eternal verities. It is of the very nature of a free society to advance in its standards of what is deemed reasonable and right. Representing as it does a living principle, due process is not confined within a permanent catalogue of what may at a given time be deemed the limits or the essentials of fundamental rights.

To rely on a tidy formula for the easy determination of what is a fundamental right for purposes of legal enforcement may satisfy a longing for certainty but ignores the movements of a free society. It belittles the scale of the conception of due process. The real clue to the problem confronting the judiciary in the application of the Due Process Clause is not to ask where the line is once and for all to be drawn but to recognize that it is for the Court to draw it by the gradual and empiric process of "inclusion and exclusion." . . . This was the Court's insight when first called upon to consider the problem; to this insight the Court has on the whole been faithful as case after case has come before it since *Davidson* v. *New Orleans* was decided.

The security of one's privacy against arbitrary intrusion by the police — which is at the core of the Fourth Amendment — is basic to a free society. It is therefore implicit in "the concept of ordered liberty" and as such enforceable against the States through the Due Process Clause. The knock at the door, whether by day or by night, as a prelude to a search, without authority of law but solely on the authority of the police, did not need the commentary of recent history to be condemned as inconsistent with the conception of human rights enshrined in the history and the basic constitutional documents of English-speaking peoples.

Accordingly, we have no hesitation in saying that were a State affirmatively to sanction such police incursion into privacy it would run counter to the guaranty of the Fourteenth Amendment. But the ways of enforcing such a basic right raise questions of a different order. How such arbitrary conduct should be checked, what remedies against it should be afforded, the means by which the right should be made effective, are all questions that are not to be so dogmatically answered as to preclude the varying solutions which spring from an allowable range of judgment on issues not susceptible of quantitative solution. . . .

The jurisdictions which have rejected the *Weeks* doctrine have not left the right to privacy without other means of protection. Indeed, the exclusion of evidence is a remedy which directly serves only to protect those upon whose person or premises something incriminating has been found. We cannot, therefore, regard it as a departure from basic standards to remand such persons, together with those who emerge scatheless from a search, to the remedies of private action and such protection as the internal discipline of the police, under the eyes of an alert public opinion, may afford. Granting that in practice the exclusion of evidence may be an effective way of deterring unreasonable searches, it is not for this Court to condemn as falling below the minimal standards assured by the Due Process Clause a State's reliance upon other methods which, if consistently enforced, would be equally effective. Weighty testimony against such an insistence on our own view is furnished by the opinion of Mr. Justice (then Judge) Cardozo in *People* v. *Defore,* 242 N.Y. 13, 150 N.E. 585. We cannot brush aside the experience of States which deem the incidence of such conduct by the police too slight to call for a deterrent remedy not by way of

disciplinary measures but by overriding the relevant rules of evidence. There
are, moreover, reasons for excluding evidence unreasonably obtained by the
federal police which are less compelling in the case of police under State or local
authority. The public opinion of a community can far more effectively be
exerted against oppressive conduct on the part of police directly responsible to
the community itself than can local opinion, sporadically aroused, be brought to
bear upon remote authority pervasively exerted throughout the country.

We hold, therefore, that in a prosecution in a State court for a State crime the
Fourteenth Amendment does not forbid the admission of evidence obtained by
an unreasonable search and seizure. And though we have interpreted the
Fourth Amendment to forbid the admission of such evidence, a different question would be presented if Congress under its legislative powers were to pass a
statute purporting to negate the *Weeks* doctrine. We would then be faced with the
problem of the respect to be accorded the legislative judgment on an issue as to
which, in default of that judgment, we have been forced to depend upon our
own. Problems of a converse character, also not before us, would be presented
should Congress under §5 of the Fourteenth Amendment undertake to enforce
the rights there guaranteed by attempting to make the *Weeks* doctrine binding
upon the States.

Mapp v. Ohio, 367 U.S. 643 (1961)

That the Court would have problems applying the tortured reasoning of
Justice Frankfurter's majority opinion in the *Wolf* case became readily apparent in subsequent disputes. *Rochin* v. *California*[1] is one such instance. *Rochin*
was a narcotics case. Sheriff's deputies illegally entered Rochin's home, forced
open the bedroom door and found him seated on the bed. Rochin immediately gulped down two capsules that were on the nightstand. After failing to pry open his mouth, deputies immediately rushed Rochin to a hospital,
handcuffed, where at the direction of the deputies, doctors pumped Rochin's
stomach and recovered the two capsules of morphine. Rochin was subsequently convicted with the morphine capsules as the principal evidence
against him. Speaking for a unanimous Court, Justice Frankfurter, himself
the author of the *Wolf* rule, which sanctioned the admission in a state court of
evidence illegally secured, reversed Rochin's conviction. Frankfurter argued
that in this instance the conduct of law enforcement officials was "too close to
the rack and screw to permit constitutional differentiation."

Two years later in *Irvine* v. *California*,[2] more "incredible" police activity won
the approval of the Supreme Court, albeit narrowly 5–4, with Frankfurter
one of the dissenters. In *Irvine,* California police had illegally broken into the
home of a suspected bookmaker. They planted microphones throughout the
house. On the basis of a month or more of electronic snooping, Irvine was
arrested, tried, and convicted. Justice Jackson wrote for the majority of five
(Justice Black with Justice Douglas concurring wrote one dissent and Justice
Frankfurter joined by Justice Burton wrote another). Jackson admitted that
police had illegally trespassed, and possibly had also committed burglary.
Nevertheless the majority refused to rule the inadmissibility of evidence se-

1. 342 U.S. 165 (1952).
2. 347 U.S. 128 (1954).

cured in this manner. Jackson insisted that the Court should continue to "adhere to *Wolf* as stating the law [in] search and seizure cases." Understandably, Frankfurter found the Court's reasoning difficult to fathom. "Surely," he said, "the Court does not propose to announce a new absolute, namely, that even the most reprehensible means for securing a conviction will not taint a verdict so long as the body of the accused was not touched by state officials."

Finally, in *Mapp* v. *Ohio* the *Wolf* rule was irrevocably overruled. In a 6–3 decision (Justice Harlan joined by Justices Frankfurter and Whittaker dissented) the Warren Court ruled that all evidence obtained by searches and seizures in violation of the Fourth Amendment is inadmissible in state criminal trials. Thus was the Fourth Amendment incorporated.

Mapp was convicted for having violated an Ohio statute that made possession or "control [of] an obscene, lewd or lascivious book or picture" illegal. Evidence indicated that police officers had broken into Mapp's home without a warrant, and, as the Court's majority opinion described it, "ran roughshod over [the] appellant" grabbing her and twisting her arm. The search turned up obscene materials in a basement trunk. In his dissent, Justice Harlan chided the majority for having "forgotten the sense of judicial restraint which, with due regard for stare decisis, is one element that should enter into deciding whether a past decision of this Court should be overruled."[3] This was Harlan's way of telling the Court it should have upheld the *Wolf* ruling. But the majority would have none of it.

Mr. Justice Clark delivered the opinion of the Court, saying in part:

> Since the Fourth Amendment's right of privacy has been declared enforceable against the States through the Due Process Clause of the Fourteenth, it is enforceable against them by the same sanction of exclusion as is used against the Federal Government. Were it otherwise, then just as without the *Weeks* rule the assurance against unreasonable federal searches and seizures would be "a form of words," valueless and undeserving of mention in a perpetual charter of inestimable human liberties, so too, without that rule the freedom from state invasions of privacy would be so ephemeral and so neatly severed from its conceptual nexus with the freedom from all brutish means of coercing evidence as not to merit this Court's high regard as a freedom "implicit in the concept of ordered liberty." At the time that the Court held in *Wolf* that the Amendment was applicable to the States through the Due Process Clause, the cases of this Court, as we have seen, had steadfastly held that as to federal officers the Fourth Amendment included the exclusion of the evidence seized in violation of its provisions. Even *Wolf* "stoutly adhered" to that proposition. The right to privacy, when conceded operatively enforceable against the States, was not susceptible of destruction by avulsion of the sanction upon which its protection and enjoyment had always been deemed dependent under the *Boyd*, *Weeks* and *Silverthorne* cases. Therefore, in extending the substantive protections of due process to all constitutionally unreasonable searches — state or federal — it was logically and constitutionally necessary that the exclusion doctrine — an essential part of the right to privacy — be also insisted upon as an essential ingredient of the right newly recognized by the *Wolf* case. In short, the admission of the new constitutional right by *Wolf* could not consistently tolerate denial of its most important constitutional privilege, namely, the exclusion of the evidence which an accused had been forced to give by reason of the unlawful seizure. To hold otherwise is to grant the right but in reality to withhold its privilege and enjoyment. Only last year the

3. 367 U.S. at 672.

court itself recognized that the purpose of the exclusionary rule "is to deter — to compel respect for the constitutional guaranty in the only effectively available way — by removing the incentive to disregard it." . . .

Indeed, we are aware of no restraint, similar to that rejected today, conditioning the enforcement of any other basic constitutional right. The right to privacy, no less important than any other right carefully and particularly reserved to the people, would stand in marked contrast to all other rights declared as "basic to a free society." . . . This Court has not hesitated to enforce as strictly against the States as it does against the Federal Government the rights of free speech and of a free press, the rights to notice and to a fair, public trial, including, as it does, the right not to be convicted by use of a coerced confession, however logically relevant it be, and without regard to its reliability. . . . And nothing could be more certain than that when a coerced confession is involved, "the relevant rules of evidence" are overridden without regard to "the incidence of such conduct by the police," slight or frequent. Why should not the same rule apply to what is tantamount to coerced testimony by way of unconstitutional seizure of goods, papers, effects, documents, etc.? We find that, as to the Federal Government, the Fourth and Fifth Amendments and, as to the States, the freedom from unconscionable invasions of privacy and the freedom from convictions based upon coerced confessions do enjoy an "intimate relation" in their perpetuation of "principles of humanity and civil liberty [secured] . . . only after years of struggle," . . . .

Moreover, our holding that the exclusionary rule is an essential part of both the Fourth and Fourteenth Amendments is not only the logical dictate of prior cases, but it also makes very good sense. There is no war between the Constitution and common sense. Presently, a federal prosecutor may make no use of evidence illegally seized, but a State's attorney across the street may, although he supposedly is operating under the enforceable prohibitions of the same Amendment. Thus the State, by admitting evidence unlawfully seized, serves to encourage disobedience to the Federal Constitution which it is bound to uphold. Moreover, as was said in *Elkins*, "[t]he very essence of a healthy federalism depends upon the avoidance of needless conflict between state and federal courts." . . .

The ignoble shortcut to conviction left open to the State tends to destroy the entire system of constitutional restraints on which the liberties of the people rest. Having once recognized that the right to privacy embodied in the Fourth Amendment is enforceable against the States, and that the right to be secure against rude invasions of privacy by state officers is, therefore, constitutional in origin, we can no longer permit that right to remain an empty promise. Because it is enforceable in the same manner and to like effect as other basic rights secured by the Due Process Clause, we can no longer permit it to be revocable at the whim of any police officer who, in the name of law enforcement itself, chooses to suspend its enjoyment. Our decision, founded on reason and truth, gives to the individual no more than that which the Constitution guarantees him, to the police officer no less than that to which honest law enforcement is entitled, and, to the courts, that judicial integrity so necessary in the true administration of justice.

Ker v. California, 374 U.S. (1963)

Despite the *Mapp* ruling, which specifically overruled *Wolf* and brought the Fourth Amendment's illegal search and seizure provisions to bear on the states, the Supreme Court remained divided and confused on the admissibility of search and seizure evidence in a state court. *Ker v. California,* decided two years after *Mapp,* exemplifies that division and confusion. In *Ker,* the Court was split 5–4 with Justice Clark, the author of *Mapp,* again speaking for the majority and Justice Brennan leading Chief Justice Warren and Justices Douglas and Brennan in dissent. The central question in *Ker* was whether a search conducted by police officers without a warrant, which turned up marijuana, was a legal incident to an arrest that the majority felt was legal and the dissenters argued was illegal.

After considerable surveillance of both Mr. and Mrs. Ker and their associates, police concluded that illegal marijuana traffic was taking place in their apartment. Accordingly, police believed they had "probable cause" to arrest the Kers. They proceeded to do so, entering the apartment unannounced. In the process they searched it without a warrant and found marijuana. The Kers were subsequently convicted for illegal possession of marijuana. Did this search and seizure violate the *Mapp* rule? A slim majority of the Court thought not. Justice Brennan disagreed, arguing that the "unannounced intrusion of the arresting officers into the apartment violated the Fourth Amendment." Because the arrests were illegal, Brennan said, the *Mapp* rule requires excluding "evidence which was the product of the search incident to those arrests . . ."[1]

The Court's examination of the facts led it to a different conclusion. Although the majority expressed its fidelity to the Fourth Amendment and to the *Mapp* exclusionary rule, it concluded that the facts, as it read them in *Ker,* did not violate either. Accordingly, it affirmed the California court's conviction.

Mr. Justice Clark delivered the opinion of the Court, saying in part:

> This Court's long-established recognition that standards of reasonableness under the Fourth Amendment are not susceptible of Procrustean application is carried forward when that Amendment's proscriptions are enforced against the States through the Fourteenth Amendment. And, although the standard of reasonableness is the same under the Fourth and Fourteenth Amendments, the demands of our federal system compel us to distinguish between evidence held inadmissible because of our supervisory powers over federal courts and that held inadmissible because prohibited by the United States Constitution. We reiterate that the reasonableness of a search is in the first instance a substantive determination to be made by the trial court from the facts and circumstances of the case and in the light of the "fundamental criteria" laid down by the Fourth Amendment and in opinions of this Court applying that Amendment. Findings of reasonableness, of course, are respected only insofar as consistent with federal constitutional guarantees. . . .
>
> Applying this federal constitutional standard we proceed to examine the entire record including the findings of California's courts to determine whether the evidence seized from petitioners was constitutionally admissible under the circumstances of this case. . . .
>
> The evidence at issue, in order to be admissible, must be the product of a search incident to a lawful arrest, since the officers had no search warrant. The lawfulness of the arrest without warrant, in turn, must be based upon probable cause, which exists "where 'the facts and circumstances within their [the officers']

1. 374 U.S. at 46–47.

knowledge and of which they had reasonably trustworthy information [are] sufficient in themselves to warrant a man of reasonable caution in the belief that' an offense has been or is being committed." . . .

It is contended that the lawfulness of the petitioners' arrests, even if they were based upon probable cause, was vitiated by the method of entry. This Court, in cases under the Fourth Amendment, has long recognized that the lawfulness of arrests for federal offenses is to be determined by reference to state law insofar as it is not violative of the Federal Constitution. . . . A fortiori, the lawfulness of these arrests by state officers for state offenses is to be determined by California law. California Penal Code, §844, permits peace officers to break into a dwelling place for the purpose of arrest after demanding admittance and explaining their purpose. Admittedly the officers did not comply with the terms of this statute since they entered quietly and without announcement, in order to prevent the destruction of contraband. The California District Court of Appeal, however, held that the circumstances here came within a judicial exception which had been engrafted upon the statute by a series of decisions . . . and that the non-compliance was therefore lawful.

Since the petitioners' federal constitutional protection from unreasonable searches and seizures by police officers is here to be determined by whether the search was incident to a lawful arrest, we are warranted in examining that arrest to determine whether, notwithstanding its legality under state law, the method of entering the home may offend federal constitutional standards of reasonableness and therefore vitiate the legality of an accompanying search. We find no such offensiveness on the facts here.

Having held the petitioners' arrests lawful, it remains only to consider whether the search which produced the evidence leading to their convictions was lawful as incident to those arrests. The doctrine that a search without warrant may be lawfully conducted if incident to a lawful arrest has long been recognized as consistent with the Fourth Amendment's protection against unreasonable searches and seizures. . . .

Petitioners contend that the search was unreasonable in that the officers could practicably have obtained a search warrant. The practicability of obtaining a warrant is not the controlling factor when a search is sought to be justified as incident to arrest . . . ; but we need not rest the validity of the search here on *Rabinowitz,* since we agree with the California court that time clearly was of the essence. The officers' observations and their corroboration, which furnished probable cause for George Ker's arrest, occurred at about 9 p.m., approximately one hour before the time of arrest. The officers had reason to act quickly because of Ker's furtive conduct and the likelihood that the marijuana would be distributed or hidden before a warrant could be obtained at that time of night. Thus the facts bear no resemblance to those in *Trupiano* v. *United States,* 334 U.S. 699 (1948), where federal agents for three weeks had been in possession of knowledge sufficient to secure a search warrant.

The search of the petitioners' apartment was well within the limits upheld in *Harris* v. *United States, supra,* which also concerned a private apartment dwelling. The evidence here, unlike that in *Harris,* was the instrumentality of the very crime for which petitioners were arrested, and the record does not indicate that the search here was as extensive in time or in area as that upheld in *Harris.*

The petitioners' only remaining contention is that the discovery of the brick of marijuana cannot be justified as incidental to arrest since it preceded the arrest. This contention is of course contrary to George Ker's testimony, but we reject it in any event. While an arrest may not be used merely as the pretext for a search without warrant, the California court specifically found and the record supports both that the officers entered the apartment for the purpose of arresting George Ker and that they had probable cause to make that arrest prior to the entry.

Terry v. Ohio, 392 U.S. 1 (1968)

"Stop and frisk," which is closely related to search and seizure, is common police procedure when interrogating suspicious persons without a warrant. The practice was upheld by the Warren Court in *Terry* v. *Ohio*. Fourth Amendment problems arise in stop and frisk cases because many times what arouses an officer's suspicions and leads to a stop and frisk may be short of probable cause for arrest. In *Terry*, for example, a Cleveland police officer in plain clothes, who had been patrolling the same beat for many years, observed two and then three men walking up and down a downtown street suspiciously peering into store windows. The officer suspected they were "casing" a potential robbery victim. He approached the three, identified himself as a police officer and asked their names. When he received a vague response, the officer spun the petitioner (Terry) around and frisked him. He ordered the three into a store, frisked them again and came up with two revolvers. The two with the revolvers were arrested and charged with carrying concealed weapons. Thus the Court had to decide whether Terry's Fourth Amendment rights had been violated.

In this instance, the Warren Court, with its largely unwarranted reputation for being unreasonably tough on police officers and "soft" on criminals, upheld the stop and frisk procedure and refused to overturn Terry's conviction. The Chief Justice's long majority opinion, quoted at some length here, admirably sums up the delicate problem the Court faces in attempting to balance "proper police procedure" with basic constitutional guarantees.

Mr. Chief Justice Warren delivered the opinion of the Court, saying in part:

> This case presents serious questions concerning the role of the Fourth Amendment in the confrontation on the street between the citizen and the policeman investigating suspicious circumstances. . . .
>
> . . . The question is whether in all the circumstances of this on-the-street encounter, his right to personal security was violated by an unreasonable search and seizure.
>
> We would be less than candid if we did not acknowledge that this question thrusts to the fore difficult and troublesome issues regarding a sensitive area of police activity — issues which have never before been squarely presented to this Court. Reflective of the tensions involved are the practical and constitutional arguments pressed with great vigor on both sides of the public debate over the power of the police to "stop and frisk" — as it is sometimes euphemistically termed — suspicious persons.
>
> On the one hand, it is frequently argued that in dealing with the rapidly unfolding and often dangerous situations on city streets the police are in need of an escalating set of flexible responses, graduated in relation to the amount of information they possess. For this purpose it is urged that distinctions should be made between a "stop" and an "arrest" (or a "seizure" of a person), and between a "frisk" and a "search." Thus, it is argued, the police should be allowed to "stop"

a person and detain him briefly for questioning upon suspicion that he may be connected with criminal activity. Upon suspicion that the person may be armed, the police should have the power to "frisk" him for weapons. If the "stop" and the "frisk" give rise to probable cause to believe that the suspect has committed a crime, then the police should be empowered to make a formal "arrest," and a full incident "search" of the person. This scheme is justified in part upon the notion that a "stop" and a "frisk" amount to a mere "minor inconvenience and petty indignity," which can properly be imposed upon the citizen in the interest of effective law enforcement on the basis of a police officer's suspicion.

On the other side the argument is made that the authority of the police must be strictly circumscribed by the law of arrest and search as it has developed to date in the traditional jurisprudence of the Fourth Amendment. It is contended with some force that there is not — and cannot be — a variety of police activity which does not depend solely upon the voluntary cooperation of the citizen and yet which stops short of an arrest based upon probable cause to make such an arrest. The heart of the Fourth Amendment, the argument runs, is a severe requirement of specific justification for any intrusion upon protected personal security, coupled with a highly developed system of judicial controls to enforce upon the agents of the State the commands of the Constitution. Acquiescence by the courts in the compulsion inherent in the field interrogation practices at issue here, it is urged, would constitute an abdication of judicial control over, and indeed an encouragement of, substantial interference with liberty and personal security by police officers whose judgment is necessarily colored by their primary involvement in "the often competitive enterprise of ferreting out crime." . . . This, it is argued, can only serve to exacerbate police-community tensions in the crowded centers of our Nation's cities. . . .

The exclusionary rule has its limitations, however, as a tool of judicial control. It cannot properly be invoked to exclude the products of legitimate police investigative techniques on the ground that much conduct which is closely similar involves unwarranted intrusions upon constitutional protections. Moreover, in some contexts the rule is ineffective as a deterrent. Street encounters between citizens and police officers are incredibly rich in diversity. They range from wholly friendly exchanges of pleasantries or mutually useful information to hostile confrontations of armed men involving arrests, or injuries, or loss of life. Moreover, hostile confrontations are not all of a piece. Some of them begin in a friendly enough manner, only to take a different turn upon the injection of some unexpected element into the conversation. Encounters are initiated by the police for a wide variety of purposes, some of which are wholly unrelated to a desire to prosecute for crime. Doubtless some police "field interrogation" conduct violates the Fourth Amendment. But a stern refusal by this Court to condone such activity does not necessarily render it responsive to the exclusionary rule. Regardless of how effective the rule may be where obtaining convictions is an important objective of the police, it is powerless to deter invasions of constitutionally guaranteed rights where the police either have no interest in prosecuting or are willing to forgo successful prosecution in the interest of serving some other goal.

Proper adjudication of cases in which the exclusionary rule is invoked demands a constant awareness of these limitations. The wholesale harassment by certain elements of the police community, of which minority groups, particularly Negroes, frequently complain, will not be stopped by the exclusion of any evidence from any criminal trial. Yet a rigid and unthinking application of the exclusionary rule, in futile protest against practices which it can never be used effectively to control, may exact a high toll in human injury and frustration of efforts to prevent crime. No judicial opinion can comprehend the protean variety of the street encounter, and we can only judge the facts of the case before us. Nothing we say today is to be taken as indicating approval of police conduct outside the legitimate investigative sphere. Under our decision, courts still retain their traditional responsibility to guard against police conduct which is overbearing or harassing, or which trenches upon personal security without the objective evidentiary justification which the Constitution requires. When such conduct is identified, it must be condemned by the judiciary and its fruits must be excluded from evidence in criminal trials. And, of course, our approval of legitimate and restrained investigative conduct undertaken on the basis of ample factual justification should in no way discourage the employment of other remedies than the exclusionary rule to curtail abuses for which that sanction may prove inappropriate.

Having thus roughly sketched the perimeters of the constitutional debate over the limits on police investigative conduct in general and the background against which this case presents itself, we turn our attention to the quite narrow question posed by the facts before us: whether it is always unreasonable for a policeman to seize a person and subject him to a limited search for weapons unless there is probable cause for an arrest. Given the narrowness of this question, we have no occasion to canvass in detail the constitutional limitations upon the scope of a policeman's power when he confronts a citizen without probable cause to arrest him. . . .

Our first task is to establish at what point in this encounter the Fourth Amendment becomes relevant. That is, we must decide whether and when Officer McFadden "seized" Terry and whether and when he conducted a "search." There is some suggestion in the use of such terms as "stop" and "frisk" that such police conduct is outside the purview of the Fourth Amendment because neither action rises to the level of a "search" or "seizure" within the meaning of the Constitution. We emphatically reject this notion. It is quite plain that the Fourth Amendment governs "seizures" of the person which do not eventuate in a trip to the station house and prosecution for crime — "arrests" in traditional terminology. It must be recognized that whenever a police officer accosts an individual and restrains his freedom to walk away, he has "seized" that person. And it is nothing less than sheer torture of the English language to suggest that a careful exploration of the outer surfaces of a person's clothing all over his or her body in an attempt to find weapons is not a "search." Moreover, it is simply fantastic to urge that such a procedure performed in public by a policeman while the citizen stands helpless, perhaps facing a wall with his hands raised, is a "petty indignity." It is a serious intrusion upon the sanctity of the person, which may inflict great indignity and arouse strong resentment, and it is not to be undertaken lightly. . . .

The distinctions of classical "stop-and-frisk" theory thus serve to divert attention from the central inquiry under the Fourth Amendment — the reasonableness in all the circumstances of the particular governmental invasion of a citizen's personal security. "Search" and "seizure" are not talismans. We therefore reject the notions that the Fourth Amendment does not come into play at all as a limitation upon police conduct if the officers stop short of something called a "technical arrest" or a "full-blown search."

In this case there can be no question, then, that Officer McFadden "seized" petitioner and subjected him to a "search" when he took hold of him and patted down the outer surfaces of his clothing. We must decide whether at that point it was reasonable for Officer McFadden to have interfered with petitioner's personal security as he did. And in determining whether the seizure and search were "unreasonable" our inquiry is a dual one — whether the officer's action was justified at its inception, and whether it was reasonably related in scope to the circumstances which justified the interference in the first place. . . .

If this case involved police conduct subject to the Warrant Clause of the Fourth Amendment, we would have to ascertain whether "probable cause" existed to justify the search and seizure which took place. However, that is not the case. We do not retreat from our holdings that the police must, whenever practicable, obtain advance judicial approval of searches and seizures through the warrant procedure. . . . But we deal here with an entire rubric of police conduct — necessarily swift action predicated upon the on-the-spot observations of the officer on the beat — which historically has not been, and as a practical matter could not be, subjected to the warrant procedure. Instead, the conduct involved in this case must be tested by the Fourth Amendment's general proscription against unreasonable searches and seizures.

Nonetheless, the notions which underlie both the warrant procedure and the requirement of probable cause remain fully relevant in this context. In order to assess the reasonableness of Officer McFadden's conduct as a general proposition, it is necessary "first to focus upon the governmental interest which allegedly justifies official intrusion upon the constitutionally protected interests of the private citizen," for there is "no ready test for determining reasonableness other than by balancing the need to search [or seize] against the invasion which the search [or seizure] entails." . . . And in justifying the particular intrusion the police officer must be able to point to specific and articulable facts which, taken together with rational inferences from those facts, reasonably warrant that intrusion. The scheme of the Fourth Amendment becomes meaningful only when it is assured that at some point the conduct of those charged with enforcing the laws can be subjected to the more detached, neutral scrutiny of a judge who must evaluate the reasonableness of a particular search or seizure in light of the particular circumstances. And in making that assessment it is imperative that the facts be judged against an objective standard: would the facts available to the officer at the moment of the seizure or the search "warrant a man of reasonable caution in the belief" that the action taken was appropriate? . . . Anything less would invite intrusions upon constitutionally guaranteed rights based on nothing more substantial than inarticulate hunches, a result this Court has consistently refused to sanction. . . . And simple "'good faith on the part of the arresting officer is not enough.' . . . If subjective good faith alone were the test, the protections of the Fourth Amendment would evaporate, and the people would be 'secure in their persons, houses, papers, and effects,' only in the discretion of the police." . . .

Applying these principles to this case, we consider first the nature and extent of the governmental interests involved. One general interest is of course that of effective crime prevention and detection; it is this interest which underlies the recognition that a police officer may in appropriate circumstances and in an appropriate manner approach a person for purposes of investigating possibly criminal behavior even though there is no probable cause to make an arrest. It was this legitimate investigative function Officer McFadden was discharging when he decided to approach petitioner and his companions. He had observed Terry, Chilton, and Katz go through a series of acts, each of them perhaps innocent in itself, but which taken together warranted further investigation. There is nothing unusual in two men standing together on a street corner, perhaps waiting for someone. Nor is there anything suspicious about people in such circumstances strolling up and down the street, singly or in pairs. Store windows, moreover, are made to be looked in. But the story is quite different where, as here, two men hover about a street corner for an extended period of time, at the end of which it becomes apparent that they are not waiting for anyone or anything; where these men pace alternately along an identical route, pausing to stare in the same store window roughly 24 times; where each completion of this route is followed immediately by a conference between the two men on the corner; where they are joined in one of these conferences by a third man who leaves swiftly; and where the two men finally follow the third and rejoin him a couple of blocks away. It would have been poor police work indeed for an officer of 30 years' experience in the detection of thievery from stores in this same neighborhood to have failed to investigate this behavior further.

The crux of this case, however, is not the propriety of Officer McFadden's taking steps to investigate petitioner's suspicious behavior, but rather, whether there was justification for McFadden's invasion of Terry's personal security by searching him for weapons in the course of that investigation. We are now concerned with more than the governmental interest in investigating crime; in addition, there is the more immediate interest of the police officer in taking steps to assure himself that the person with whom he is dealing is not armed with a weapon that could unexpectedly and fatally be used against him. Certainly it would be unreasonable to require that police officers take unnecessary risks in the performance of their duties. American criminals have a long tradition of armed violence, and every year in this country many law enforcement officers are killed in the line of duty, and thousands more are wounded. Virtually all of these deaths and a substantial portion of the injuries are inflicted with guns and knives.

In view of these facts, we cannot blind ourselves to the need for law enforcement officers to protect themselves and other prospective victims of violence in situations where they may lack probable cause for an arrest. When an officer is justified in believing that the individual whose suspicious behavior he is investigating at close range is armed and presently dangerous to the officer or to others, it would appear to be clearly unreasonable to deny the officer the power to take necessary measures to determine whether the person is in fact carrying a weapon and to neutralize the threat of physical harm.

We must still consider, however, the nature and quality of the intrusion on individual rights which must be accepted if police officers are to be conceded the right to search for weapons in situations where probable cause to arrest for crime is lacking. Even a limited search of the outer clothing for weapons constitutes a severe, though brief, intrusion upon cherished personal security, and it must surely be an annoying, frightening, and perhaps humiliating experience. Petitioner contends that such an intrusion is permissible only incident to a lawful arrest, either for a crime involving the possession of weapons or for a crime the commission of which led the officer to investigate in the first place. However, this argument must be closely examined.

Petitioner does not argue that a police officer should refrain from making any investigation of suspicious circumstances until such time as he has probable cause to make an arrest; nor does he deny that police officers in properly discharging their investigative function may find themselves confronting persons who might well be armed and dangerous. Moreover, he does not say that an officer is always unjustified in searching a suspect to discover weapons. Rather, he says it is unreasonable for the policeman to take that step until such time as the situation evolves to a point where there is probable cause to make an arrest. When that point has been reached, petitioner would concede the officer's right to conduct a search of the suspect for weapons, fruits or instrumentalities of the crime, or "mere" evidence, incident to the arrest.

There are two weaknesses in this line of reasoning, however. First, it fails to take account of traditional limitations upon the scope of searches, and thus recognizes no distinction in purpose, character, and extent between a search incident to an arrest and a limited search for weapons. The former, although justified in part by the acknowledged necessity to protect the arresting officer from assault with a concealed weapon, . . . is also justified on other grounds, . . . and can therefore involve a relatively extensive exploration of the person. A search for weapons in the absence of probable cause to arrest, however, must, like any other search, be strictly circumscribed by the exigencies which justify its initiation. . . . Thus it must be limited to that which is necessary for the discovery of weapons which might be used to harm the officer or others nearby, and may realistically be characterized as something less than a "full" search, even though it remains a serious intrusion.

A second, and related, objection to petitioner's argument is that it assumes that the law of arrest has already worked out the balance between the particular interests involved here—the neutralization of danger to the policeman in the investigative circumstance and the sanctity of the individual. But this is not so. An arrest is a wholly different kind of intrusion upon individual freedom from a limited search for weapons, and the interests each is designed to serve are likewise quite different. An arrest is the initial stage of a criminal prosecution. It is intended to vindicate society's interest in having its laws obeyed, and it is inevitably accompanied by future interference with the individual's freedom of movement, whether or not trial or conviction ultimately follows. The protective search for weapons, on the other hand, constitutes a brief, though far from inconsiderable, intrusion upon the sanctity of the person. It does not follow that because an officer may lawfully arrest a person only when he is apprised of facts sufficient to warrant a belief that the person has committed or is committing a crime, the officer is equally unjustified, absent that kind of evidence, in making any intrusions short of an arrest. Moreover, a perfectly reasonable apprehension of danger may arise long before the officer is possessed of adequate information to justify taking a person into custody for the purpose of prosecuting him for a crime. Petitioner's reliance on cases which have worked out standards of reasonableness with regard to "seizures" constituting arrests and searches incident thereto is thus misplaced. It assumes that the interests sought to be vindicated and the invasions of personal security may be equated in the two cases, and thereby ignores a vital aspect of the analysis of the reasonableness of particular types of conduct under the Fourth Amendment. . . .

Our evaluation of the proper balance that has to be struck in this type of case leads us to conclude that there must be a narrowly drawn authority to permit a reasonable search for weapons for the protection of the police officer, where he has reason to believe that he is dealing with an armed and dangerous individual, regardless of whether he has probable cause to arrest the individual for a crime. The officer need not be absolutely certain that the individual is armed; the issue is whether a reasonably prudent man in the circumstances would be warranted in the belief that his safety or that of others was in danger. . . . And in determining whether the officer acted reasonably in such circumstances, due weight must be given, not to his inchoate and unparticularized suspicion or "hunch," but to the specific reasonable inferences which he is entitled to draw from the facts in light of his experience. . . . The sole justification of the search in the present situation is the protection of the police officer and others nearby, and it must therefore be confined in scope to an intrusion reasonably designed to discover guns, knives, clubs, or other hidden instruments for the assault of the police officer.

The scope of the search in this case presents no serious problem in light of these standards. Officer McFadden patted down the outer clothing of petitioner and his two companions. He did not place his hands in their pockets or under the outer surface of their garments until he had felt weapons, and then he merely reached for and removed the guns. He never did invade Katz' person beyond the outer surfaces of his clothes, since he discovered nothing in his pat-down which might have been a weapon. Officer McFadden confined his search strictly to what was minimally necessary to learn whether the men were armed and to disarm them once he discovered the weapons. He did not conduct a general exploratory search for whatever evidence of criminal activity he might find.

We conclude that the revolver seized from Terry was properly admitted in evidence against him. At the time he seized petitioner and searched him for weapons, Officer McFadden had reasonable grounds to believe that petitioner was armed and dangerous, and it was necessary for the protection of himself and others to take swift measures to discover the true facts and neutralize the threat of harm if it materialized. The policeman carefully restricted his search to what was appropriate to the discovery of the particular items which he sought. Each case of this sort will, of course, have to be decided on its own facts. We merely hold today that where a police officer observes unusual conduct which leads him reasonably to conclude in light of his experience that criminal activity may be afoot and that the persons with whom he is dealing may be armed and presently dangerous, where in the course of investigating this behavior he identifies himself as a policeman and makes reasonable inquiries, and where nothing in the initial stages of the encounter serves to dispel his reasonable fear for his own or others' safety, he is entitled for the protection of himself and others in the area to conduct a carefully limited search of the outer clothing of such persons in an attempt to discover weapons which might be used to assault him. Such a search is a reasonable search under the Fourth Amendment, and any weapons seized may properly be introduced in evidence against the person from whom they were taken.

Chimel v. California, 395 U.S. 752 (1969)

It is basic to the privacy guarantee of the Fourth Amendment that a judge, not law enforcement officials, must issue a search warrant after determining when and if a citizen's privacy may be invaded. Courts have ruled that a search without a warrant is "unreasonable" unless it can be justified by "extraordinary circumstances." And, in fact, most of the cases that have come before the Supreme Court involving search and seizure disputes arose when there had been failure to secure a warrant. For this reason the Court has had to devise the "special circumstances" that could permit warrantless searches. Two examples, as Cushman notes, are the warrantless search of an automobile before it can escape, and the search without a warrant of a person by a law enforcement officer when it is necessary to protect both the arresting officer and evidence of the crime.[1] In both instances, stopping to procure a search warrant would hardly be practical. However, because "probable cause" is necessary in order to get a search warrant, the arresting officer must satisfy a judge that probable cause existed to search *without* a warrant. An officer making a legal arrest, with sufficient cause, may also, with or without a search

1. Cushman, op. cit., at 338.

warrant, seize evidence within "plain sight" and within the "immediate area." These difficult to interpret rules have been the cause of intense debate in search and seizure cases.

In *Harris* v. *United States*,[2] for example, the Supreme Court upheld (5–4) a warrantless search of Harris's four room apartment although everything found was certainly not in "plain sight" and only within a loosely "elastic" definition of the "immediate area" rule. A year later in *Trupiano* v. *United States*,[3] again by a 5–4 vote, the Court invalidated a warrantless search and seizure of a New Jersey man's illegal still on grounds that the arresting officers had had enough time to secure a warrant but neglected to do so. Then in 1950, in *United States* v. *Rabinowitz*,[4] the Court overruled *Trupiano* and upheld a widespread warrantless search of *Rabinowitz*'s property solely on the basis of a lawful arrest warrant.

After going back and forth on this matter for more than twenty years the Court took what appeared to be a definitive step away from the loose "plain sight" and "immediate area" rationale of *Harris* and *Rabinowitz*. In *Chimel* v. *California*, the Warren Court specifically overruled both cases. Yet within five years, two Burger Court decisions, *United States* v. *Edwards*[5] and *Cardwell* v. *Lewis*,[6] seemed to take the Court back to the older view on warrantless searches.

In *Edwards*, for example, the Court, again 5–4, upheld a police warrantless search of an arrestee's clothes the morning after he had been arrested. Similarly in *Cardwell*, the Court upheld the warrantless search and seizure of the defendant's car to compare tire marks and paint scrapings at the scene of a murder. The "law and order" Burger Court rationalized its decision on grounds that cars were not entitled to the same "stringent warrant requirements" as other private property.[7]

In *Chimel*, the Supreme Court reversed a conviction in a California court on grounds that police officers had violated the petitioner's Fourth Amendment rights by seizing evidence in his home without a search warrant. The facts showed that police had searched Chimel's three-bedroom house, garage, and attic, opening desk drawers and the like. They had a valid arrest warrant for Chimel on a charge that he had burglarized a coin shop. The warrantless search turned up coins that were then used as evidence in Chimel's trial. In a 7 – 2 decision (Justice White joined by Justice Black dissented), the Warren Court reversed the petitioner's conviction. In the process the Court reviewed warrantless search cases from *Harris* onward. We reproduce substantial portions of that review for it illuminated this often vexing constitutional tangle.

Mr. Justice Stewart delivered the opinion of the Court, saying in part:

> In that case [*Harris*], officers had obtained a warrant for Harris' arrest on the basis of his alleged involvement with the cashing and interstate transportation of a forged check. He was arrested in the living room of his four-room apartment, and in an attempt to recover two canceled checks thought to have been used in effecting the forgery, the officers undertook a thorough search of the entire apartment. Inside a desk drawer they found a sealed envelope marked "George

2. 331 U.S. 145 (1947).   5. 415 U.S. 800 (1974).
3. 334 U.S. 699 (1948).   6. 417 U.S. 583 (1974).
4. 339 U.S. 56 (1950).   7. Cushman, op. cit., at 342.

Harris, personal papers." The envelope, which was then torn open, was found to contain altered Selective Service documents, and those documents were used to secure Harris' conviction for violating the Selective Training and Service Act of 1940. The Court rejected Harris' Fourth Amendment claim, sustaining the search as "incident to arrest."

Only a year after *Harris,* however, the pendulum swung again. In *Trupiano* v. *United States,* 334 U.S. 699, agents raided the site of an illicit distillery, saw one of several conspirators operating the still, and arrested him, contemporaneously "seiz[ing] the illicit distillery.". . . The Court held that the arrest and others made subsequently had been valid, but that the unexplained failure of the agents to procure a search warrant — in spite of the fact that they had had more than enough time before the raid to do so — rendered the search unlawful. The opinion stated:

> "It is a cardinal rule that, in seizing goods and articles, law enforcement agents must secure and use search warrants wherever reasonably practicable. . . . This rule rests upon the desirability of having magistrates rather than police officers determine when searches and seizures are permissible and what limitations should be placed upon such activities. . . . To provide the necessary security against unreasonable intrusions upon the private lives of individuals, the framers of the Fourth Amendment required adherence to judicial processes wherever possible. And subsequent history has confirmed the wisdom of that requirement."

> "A search or seizure without a warrant as an incident to a lawful arrest has always been considered to be a strictly limited right. It grows out of the inherent necessities of the situation at the time of the arrest. But there must be something more in the way of necessity than merely a lawful arrest." . . .

In 1950, two years after *Trupiano,* came *United States* v. *Rabinowitz,* 339 U.S. 56, the decision upon which California primarily relies in the case now before us. In *Rabinowitz,* federal authorities had been informed that the defendant was dealing in stamps bearing forged overprints. On the basis of that information they secured a warrant for his arrest, which they executed at his one-room business office. At the time of the arrest, the officers "searched the desk, safe, and file cabinets in the office for about an hour and a half," . . . and seized 573 stamps with forged overprints. The stamps were admitted into evidence at the defendant's trial, and this Court affirmed his conviction, rejecting the contention that the warrantless search had been unlawful. The Court held that the search in its entirety fell within the principle giving law enforcement authorities "[t]he right 'to search the place where the arrest is made in order to find and seize things connected with the crime. . . .'" . . . *Harris* was regarded as "ample authority" for that conclusion. . . . The opinion rejected the rule of *Trupiano* that "in seizing goods and articles, law enforcement agents must secure and use search warrants wherever reasonably practicable." The test, said the Court, "is not whether it is reasonable to procure a search warrant, but whether the search was reasonable."

Rabinowitz has come to stand for the proposition, *inter alia,* that a warrantless search "incident to a lawful arrest" may generally extend to the area that is considered to be in the "possession" or under the "control" of the person arrested. And it was on the basis of that proposition that the California courts upheld the search of the petitioner's entire house in this case. That doctrine, however, at least in the broad sense in which it was applied by the California courts in this case, can withstand neither historical nor rational analysis.

Even limited to its own facts, the *Rabinowitz* decision was, as we have seen, hardly founded on an unimpeachable line of authority. As Mr. Justice Frankfurter commented in dissent in that case, the "hint" contained in *Weeks* was, without persuasive justification, "loosely turned into dictum and finally elevated to a decision." . . . And the approach taken in cases such as *Go-Bart, Lefkowitz,* and *Trupiano* was essentially disregarded by the *Rabinowitz* Court.

Nor is the rationale by which the State seeks here to sustain the search of the petitioner's house supported by a reasoned view of the background and purpose of the Fourth Amendment. Mr. Justice Frankfurter wisely pointed out in his *Rabinowitz* dissent that the Amendment's proscription of "unreasonable searches and seizures" must be read in light of "the history that gave rise to the words" — a history of "abuses so deeply felt by the Colonies as to be one of the potent causes of the Revolution. . . ." . . . The Amendment was in large part a reaction to the general warrants and warrantless searches that had so alienated the colonists and had helped speed the movement for independence. In the scheme of the Amendment, therefore, the requirement that "no Warrants shall issue, but upon probable cause," plays a crucial part. As the Court put it in *McDonald* v. *United States,* 335 U.S. 451:

> "We are not dealing with formalities. The presence of a search warrant serves a high function. Absent some grave emergency, the Fourth Amendment has interposed a magistrate between the citizen and the police. This was done not to shield criminals nor to make the home a safe haven for illegal activities. It was done so that an objective mind might weigh the need to invade that privacy in order to enforce the law. The right of privacy was deemed too precious to entrust to the discretion of those whose job is the detection of crime and the arrest of criminals. . . . And so the Constitution requires a magistrate to pass on the desires of the police before they violate the privacy of the home. We cannot be true to that constitutional requirement and excuse the absence of a search warrant without a showing by those who seek exemption from the constitutional mandate that the exigencies of the situation made that course imperative." . . .

Rabinowitz and *Harris* have been the subject of critical commentary for many years, and have been relied upon less and less in our own decisions. It is time, for the reasons we have stated, to hold that on their own facts, and insofar as the principles they stand for are inconsistent with those that we have endorsed today, they are no longer to be followed.

Application of sound Fourth Amendment principles to the facts of this case produces a clear result. The search here went far beyond the petitioner's person and the area from within which he might have obtained either a weapon or something that could have been used as evidence against him. There was no constitutional justification, in the absence of a search warrant, for extending the search beyond that area. The scope of the search was, therefore, "unreasonable" under the Fourth and Fourteenth Amendments, and the petitioner's conviction cannot stand.

Stone v. Powell, 96 S. Ct. 3037 (1976)

As we have noted before, the Burger Court slowly but inexorably has chipped away at the major Warren Court rulings in criminal justice disputes. The Miranda rule, modified and weakened, has withstood the assault fairly well, as has the exclusionary rule fashioned in the Mapp decision. Perhaps the most significant erosion of Warren Court guidelines took place in 1976 in *Stone* v. *Powell.* There the Court ruled, through Justice Powell, that convictions in state courts could not be challenged on federal habeas corpus grounds. In a 6 — 3 decision, Powell wrote that where a state had provided an opportunity for full and fair litigation of a Fourth Amendment illegal search and seizure claim, a state prisoner could not be granted habeas corpus relief on grounds that evidence introduced at his trial had been obtained in violation of Fourth Amendment rights. Powell concluded in the context of this case "contribution of the exclusionary rule . . . was minimal as compared to the substantial societal costs of applying the rule." Powell did stress that state courts would continue to be obligated to enforce *Mapp* v. *Ohio,* where the Warren Court had fashioned the exclusionary rule, and he expressed confidence that state court judges would uphold federal constitutional rights, including habeas corpus. In effect, however, the Burger Court suggested that it preferred to leave enforcement of constitutional guarantees to the state courts. And this was a significant step away (backward) from the principles expressed over and again in Warren Court criminal justice decisions.

2

ELECTRONIC SURVEILLANCE

Wiretapping, hidden microphones, and other types of electronic surveillance, what is their relation to the unreasonable search and seizure and privacy provisions of the Fourth Amendment? The Supreme Court has had several significant opportunities to express itself on this issue and its record is mixed. It upheld wiretapping in its early rulings and moved away from such support in subsequent cases. The Court was almost always split on the issue.

Olmstead v. United States, 277 U.S. 438 (1928)

The first time the Supreme Court confronted wiretapping was in *Olmstead* v. *United States*. There, in what would become a typical (5–4) split on wiretap issues, the Court affirmed a Washington state court decision against a group of bootleggers who had been found guilty of violating the Prohibition laws with evidence obtained by wiretaps on their telephones. Speaking for the slim majority, Chief Justice Taft concluded that the Fourth Amendment had not been violated since, in the majority's judgment, no actual "trespass" had been committed on the defendant's property. Phone lines had been tapped in the basement of an office building and therefore, the Court reasoned, they were technically not on Olmstead's property. Four separate dissents were written, by Justices Holmes, Brandeis, Stone, and Butler, with Brandeis' dissent being the most comprehensive. "Decency, security and liberty alike," Brandeis wrote, "demand that government officials shall be subjected to the same rules of conduct that are commands to the citizen."[1]

In 1909, the State of Washington had made the interception of telephone messages illegal. However in *Olmstead* Chief Justice Taft argued that Washington's law did *not* affect the rules of evidence applicable in federal court criminal cases. He insisted that federal law had not been violated. Brandeis disagreed. "For good or for ill," he said, "[government] teaches the whole people by its examples. Crime is contagious. If the government becomes a lawbreaker, it breeds contempt for law, it invites every man to become a law unto himself . . . it invites anarchy." Brandeis insisted that the Court should "reso-

---

1. 277 U.S. at 485.

lutely set its face" against the "pernicious doctrine" that agents of the federal government "may commit crimes in order to secure the conviction of a private criminal."[2]

In his dissent, Justice Butler thought the central consideration was whether the government, consistent with the Fourth Amendment, "[may] have its officers whenever they see fit, tap wires, listen to, take down and report, the private messages and conversations transmitted by telephones." Butler thought not.

The majority concluded, however, that Fourth Amendment rights of privacy did *not* apply because there had not been, in the narrow, literal sense, a search and seizure of Olmstead's property.

Mr. Chief Justice Taft delivered the opinion of the Court, saying in part:

> Nor can we, without the sanction of congressional enactment, subscribe to the suggestion that the courts have a discretion to exclude evidence, the admission of which is not unconstitutional, because unethically secured. This would be at variance with the common law doctrine generally supported by authority. There is no case that sustains, nor any recognized text book that gives color to such a view. Our general experience shows that much evidence has always been receivable although not obtained by conformity to the highest ethics. The history of criminal trials shows numerous cases of prosecutions of oath-bound conspiracies for murder, robbery, and other crimes, where officers of the law have disguised themselves and joined the organizations, taken the oaths and given themselves every appearance of active members engaged in the promotion of crime, for the purpose of securing evidence. Evidence secured by such means has always been received.
>
> A standard which would forbid the reception of evidence if obtained by other than nice ethical conduct by government officials would make society suffer and give criminals greater immunity than has been known heretofore. In the absence of controlling legislation by Congress, those who realize the difficulties in bringing offenders to justice may well deem it wise that the exclusion of evidence should be confined to cases where rights under the Constitution would be violated by admitting it.
>
> The statute of Washington, adopted in 1909, provides (Remington Compiled Statutes, 1922, §2656–18) that:
>
> "Every person . . . who shall intercept, read or in any manner interrupt or delay the sending of a message over any telegraph or telephone line . . . shall be guilty of a misdemeanor."
>
> This statute does not declare that evidence obtained by such interception shall be inadmissible, and by the common law, already referred to, it would not be. . . . Whether the State of Washington may prosecute and punish federal officers violating this law and those whose messages were intercepted may sue them civilly is not before us. But clearly a statute, passed twenty years after the admission of the State into the Union can not affect the rules of evidence applicable in courts of the United States in criminal cases.

Goldman v. United States, 316 U.S. 129 (1942)

In another case, differing from *Olmstead* only in that a hidden microphone instead of a telephone was the instrument for eavesdropping, the Supreme

2. Ibid.

Court once again ruled that electronic surveillance did not violate the Fourth Amendment. And once again the Court was divided; here 5–3, with Justice Roberts writing for the majority and Chief Justice Stone and Justices Murphy and Frankfurter in dissent. The Chief Justice and Justice Frankfurter, in a brief statement, declared their agreement with the Brandeis dissent in *Olmstead.* Justice Murphy's dissent picked up the Brandeis mantle in much more detail. "The right to privacy," Murphy wrote, is "as dear as any to free men, little can or need be added to what was said . . . [in Brandeis'] memorable dissent [in *Olmstead*]. . . .Suffice it to say that the spiritual freedom of the individual depends in no small measure upon the preservation of that right."[1] Murphy insisted that the "bug" in *Goldman* "was an unreasonable search and seizure within the clear intendment of the Fourth Amendment." A majority of the Roosevelt Court, interestingly enough with the usually liberal Justices Black and Douglas included in its numbers, thought otherwise.

Mr. Justice Roberts delivered the opinion of the Court, saying in part:

We hold that what was heard by the use of the detectaphone was not made illegal by trespass or unlawful entry.

The petitioners contend that the trespass committed in Shulman's office when the listening apparatus was there installed, and what was learned as the result of that trespass, was of some assistance on the following day in locating the receiver of the detectaphone in the adjoining office, and this connection between the trespass and the listening resulted in a violation of the Fourth Amendment. Whatever trespass was committed was connected with the installation of the listening apparatus. As respects it, the trespass might be said to be continuing and, if the apparatus had been used it might, with reason, be claimed that the continuing trespass was the concomitant of its use. On the other hand, the relation between the trespass and the use of the detectaphone was that of antecedent and consequent. Both courts below have found that the trespass did not aid materially in the use of the detectaphone. Since we accept these concurrent findings, we need not consider a contention based on a denial of their verity.

. . . We hold that the use of the detectaphone by Government agents was not a violation of the Fourth Amendment.

In asking us to hold that the information obtained was obtained in violation of the Fourth Amendment, and that its use at the trial was, therefore, banned by the Amendment, the petitioners recognize that they must reckon with our decision in *Olmstead* v. *United States,* 227 U.S. 438. They argue that the case may be distinguished. The suggested ground of distinction is that the *Olmstead* case dealt with the tapping of telephone wires, and the court adverted to the fact that, in using a telephone, the speaker projects his voice beyond the confines of his home or office and, therefore, assumes the risk that his message may be intercepted. It is urged that where, as in the present case, one talks in his own office, and intends his conversation to be confined within the four walls of the room, he does not intend his voice shall go beyond those walls and it is not to be assumed he takes the risk of someone's use of a delicate detector in the next room. We think, however, the distinction is too nice for practical application of the Constitutional guarantee, and no reasonable or logical distinction can be drawn between what federal agents did in the present case and state officers did in the *Olmstead* case.

The petitioners ask us, if we are unable to distinguish *Olmstead* v. *United States,* to overrule it. This we are unwilling to do. That case was the subject of pro-

1. 316 U.S. at 137.

longed consideration by this court. The views of the court, and of the dissenting justices, were expressed clearly and at length. To rehearse and reappraise the arguments pro and con, and the conflicting views exhibited in the opinions, would serve no good purpose. Nothing now can be profitably added to what was there said. It suffices to say that we adhere to the opinion there expressed.

Berger v. New York, 388 U.S. 41 (1967)

As we have seen in both *Olmstead* and *Goldman,* the Supreme Court ruled that wiretaps and hidden microphones did *not* violate the Fourth Amendment. However, numerous efforts in Congress to legalize electronic surveillance across the board have failed. Several states did pass wiretapping legislation, authorizing the practice only if it had been approved beforehand by a judge. New York was one such state and in 1967 the Warren Court declared New York's statute unconstitutional.

The case was *Berger v. New York.* Once again the Court was badly divided, either 6–3 or 5–4, depending on whether Justice Stewart is counted with the majority. Stewart wrote a concurring opinion stating that while he agreed "fully" with the dissenters (Justices Black, Harlan, and White) he felt that New York's law was "unconstitutionally insufficient to constitute probable cause to justify an intrusion of the scope and duration that was permitted in this case."[1]

On the other hand, disagreeing with the dissenters, Justice Clark wrote for the majority that Fourth Amendment protection must include "words" or "conversation" and therefore the use of electronic devices to "capture" them was an unreasonable search and seizure within the meaning of the Constitution.

New York's statute authorized a wiretap for a period of sixty days. The Supreme Court decided that this extended time was constitutionally excessive. This seemed to be the point of Stewart's confusing concurring opinion.

Berger was convicted on two counts of conspiracy to bribe the chairman of the New York State liquor authority. All the evidence against Berger came from a two-month wiretap that indicated that he acted as a go-between in the attempted bribery. In his dissent, Justice Black drew a distinction between the Fourth Amendment's ban on "unreasonable searches and seizures" and the term "invasions of privacy," which he said, "like a chameleon has a different color for every turning," and which, he insisted, was outside the scope of the Constitution. Black accused the Court of "sleight of hand tricks" in transforming the meaning of the Fourth Amendment to include a right to privacy. "In fact, use of 'privacy' as the key word in the Fourth Amendment," Black said, "simply gives this Court a useful new tool, as I see it, both to usurp the policy making power of the Congress and to hold more state and federal laws unconstitutional when the Court entertains a sufficient hostility to them."[2] Black could not agree that New York's law was unconstitutional, arguing against the majority's premise, that all laws that "unreasonably" invade privacy violate the Fourth Amendment.

1. 388 U.S. at 70.
2. Ibid., at 77.

For the majority, Justice Clark reviewed the "ancient practice" of eavesdropping and the evolution of scientific detection techniques. He concluded that the law, "though jealous of individual privacy," has not kept pace with the development of the sophisticated listening devices now available to the eavesdropper. In particular, the Court ruled that the New York statute in question authorized "indiscriminate uses" of electronic devices and gave "broadside authorization" rather than the "carefully circumscribed" guidelines needed to prevent invasions of privacy.

Mr. Justice Clark delivered the opinion of the Court, saying in part:

> We believe the statute here is equally offensive. First, as we have mentioned, eavesdropping is authorized without requiring belief that any particular offense has been or is being committed; nor that the "property" sought, the conversations, be particularly described. The purpose of the probable-cause requirement of the Fourth Amendment, to keep the state out of constitutionally protected areas until it has reason to believe that a specific crime has been or is being committed, is thereby wholly aborted. Likewise the statute's failure to describe with particularity the conversations sought gives the officer a roving commission to "seize" any and all conversations. It is true that the statute requires the naming of "the person or persons whose communications, conversations or discussions are to be overheard or recorded. . . ." But this does no more than identify the person whose constitutionally protected area is to be invaded rather than "particularly describing" the communications, conversations, or discussions to be seized. As with general warrants this leaves too much to the discretion of the officer executing the order. Secondly, authorization of eavesdropping for a two-month period is the equivalent of a series of intrusions, searches, and seizures pursuant to a single showing of probable cause. Prompt execution is also avoided. During such a long and continuous (24 hours a day) period the conversations of any and all persons coming into the area covered by the device will be seized indiscriminately and without regard to their connection with the crime under investigation. Moreover, the statute permits, and there were authorized here, extensions of the original two-month period — presumably for two months each — on a mere showing that such extension is "in the public interest." Apparently the original grounds on which the eavesdrop order was initially issued also form the basis of the renewal. This we believe insufficient without a showing of present probable cause for the continuance of the eavesdrop. Third, the statute places no termination date on the eavesdrop once the conversation sought is seized. This is left entirely in the discretion of the officer. Finally, the statute's procedure, necessarily because its success depends on secrecy, has no requirement for notice as do conventional warrants, nor does it overcome this defect by requiring some showing of special facts. On the contrary, it permits unconsented entry without any showing of exigent circumstances. Such a showing of exigency, in order to avoid notice, would appear more important in eavesdropping, with its inherent dangers, than that required when conventional procedures of search and seizure are utilized. Nor does the statute provide for a return on the warrant thereby leaving full discretion in the officer as to the use of seized conversations of innocent as well as guilty parties. In short, the statute's blanket grant of permission to eavesdrop is without adequate judicial supervision or protective procedures. . . .
>
> . . . Our concern with the statute here is whether its language permits a trespassory invasion of the home or office, by general warrant, contrary to the command of the Fourth Amendment. As it is written, we believe that it does.

Katz v. United States, 389 U.S. 347 (1967)

Immediately after apparently ruling in *Berger* that almost any wiretap law would be struck down as an invasion of privacy, the Supreme Court backtracked a bit. In *Katz v. United States* the Court began spelling out the necessary steps and procedures that would enable it to declare wiretap laws constitutionally valid. In *Katz* three such steps emerged: one, prior authorization by a judge; two, a showing of probable cause and three, the tap must be strictly for law enforcement purposes only. *Katz,* a 7–1 decision (with only Justice Black in dissent), also specifically overruled both *Olmstead* and *Goldman.*

Speaking for the majority, Justice Stewart emphasized that the Fourth Amendment was designed to protect "people not places." In *Katz,* government agents had bugged a public telephone booth, which the petitioner, a gambler, used to place bets. The Court ruled that the government's eavesdropping violated the privacy upon which Katz had "justifiably relied" when using the telephone booth. The tap was, therefore, illegal "search and seizure" within the meaning of the Fourth Amendment.

Mr. Justice Stewart delivered the opinion of the Court, saying in part:

The Government stresses the fact that the telephone booth from which the petitioner made his calls was constructed partly of glass, so that he was as visible after he entered it as he would have been if he had remained outside. But what he sought to exclude when he entered the booth was not the intruding eye — it was the uninvited ear. He did not shed his right to do so simply because he made his calls from a place where he might be seen. No less than an individual in a business office, in a friend's apartment, or in a taxicab, a person in a telephone booth may rely upon the protection of the Fourth Amendment. One who occupies it, shuts the door behind him, and pays the toll that permits him to place a call is surely entitled to assume that the words he utters into the mouthpiece will not be broadcast to the world. To read the Constitution more narrowly is to ignore the vital role that the public telephone has come to play in private communication. . . .

We conclude that the underpinnings of *Olmstead* and *Goldman* have been so eroded by our subsequent decisions that the "trespass" doctrine there enunciated can no longer be regarded as controlling. The Government's activities in electronically listening to and recording the petitioner's words violated the privacy upon which he justifiably relied while using the telephone booth and thus constituted a "search and seizure" within the meaning of the Fourth Amendment. The fact that the electronic device employed to achieve that end did not happen to penetrate the wall of the booth can have no constitutional significance.

The question remaining for decision, then, is whether the search and seizure conducted in this case complied with constitutional standards. In that regard, the Government's position is that its agents acted in an entirely defensible manner: They did not begin their electronic surveillance until investigation of the petitioner's activities had established a strong probability that he was using the telephone in question to transmit gambling information to persons in other States, in violation of federal law. Moreover, the surveillance was limited, both in scope and in duration, to the specific purpose of establishing the contents of the petitioner's unlawful telephonic communications. The agents confined their surveillance to the brief periods during which he used the telephone booth, and they took great care to overhear only the conversations of the petitioner himself.

Accepting this account of the Government's actions as accurate, it is clear that this surveillance was so narrowly circumscribed that a duly authorized magistrate, properly notified of the need for such investigation, specifically informed of the basis on which it was to proceed, and clearly apprised of the precise intrusion it would entail, could constitutionally have authorized, with appropriate safeguards, the very limited search and seizure that the Government asserts in fact took place. Only last Term we sustained the validity of such an authorization, holding that, under sufficiently "precise and discriminate circumstances," a federal court may empower government agents to employ a concealed electronic device "for the narrow and particularized purpose of ascertaining the truth of the . . . allegations" of a "detailed factual affidavit alleging the commission of a specific criminal offense." . . . Discussing that holding, the Court in *Berger* v. *New York,* 388 U.S. 41, said that "the order authorizing the use of the electronic device" in *Osborn* "afforded similar protections to those . . . of conventional warrants authorizing the seizure of tangible evidence." Through those protections, "no greater invasion of privacy was permitted than was necessary under the circumstances.". . . Here, too, a similar judicial order could have accommodated "the legitimate needs of law enforcement" by authorizing the carefully limited use of electronic surveillance.

The Government urges that, because its agents relied upon the decisions in *Olmstead* and *Goldman,* and because they did no more here than they might properly have done with prior judicial sanction, we should retroactively validate their conduct. That we cannot do. It is apparent that the agents in this case acted with restraint. Yet the inescapable fact is that this restraint was imposed by the agents themselves, not by a judicial officer. They were not required, before commencing the search, to present their estimate of probable cause for detached scrutiny by a neutral magistrate. They were not compelled, during the conduct of the search itself, to observe precise limits established in advance by a specific court order. Nor were they directed, after the search had been completed, to notify the authorizing magistrate in detail of all that had been seized. In the absence of such safeguards, this Court has never sustained a search upon the sole ground that officers reasonably expected to find evidence of a particular crime and voluntarily confined their activities to the least intrusive means consistent with that end. Searches conducted without warrants have been held unlawful "notwithstanding facts unquestionably showing probable cause,". . . for the Constitution requires "that the deliberate, impartial judgment of a judicial officer . . . be interposed between the citizen and the police. . . ." . . . . "Over and again this Court has emphasized that the mandate of the [Fourth] Amendment requires adherence to judicial processes," . . . and that searches conducted outside the judicial process, without prior approval by judge or magistrate, are *per se* unreasonable under the Fourth Amendment — subject only to a few specifically established and well-delineated exceptions.

It is difficult to imagine how any of those exceptions could ever apply to the sort of search and seizure involved in this case. Even electronic surveillance substantially contemporaneous with an individual's arrest could hardly be deemed an "incident" of that arrest. Nor could the use of electronic surveillance without prior authorization be justified on grounds of "hot pursuit." And, of course, the very nature of electronic surveillance precludes its use pursuant to the suspect's consent.

The Government does not question these basic principles. Rather, it urges the creation of a new exception to cover this case. It argues that surveillance of a telephone booth should be exempted from the usual requirement of advance authorization by a magistrate upon a showing of probable cause. We cannot agree. . . .

These considerations do not vanish when the search in question is transferred from the setting of a home, an office, or a hotel room to that of a telephone booth. Wherever a man may be, he is entitled to know that he will remain free from unreasonable searches and seizures. The government agents here ignored "the procedure of antecedent justification . . . that is central to the Fourth Amendment," a procedure that we hold to be a constitutional precondition of the kind of electronic surveillance involved in this case. Because the surveillance here failed to meet that condition, and because it led to the petitioner's conviction, the judgment must be reversed.

United States v. White, 401 U.S. 745 (1971)

Some years before the Supreme Court's decisions in *Berger* and *Katz*, both of which seemed to give added constitutional protection to individual privacy by invalidating wiretap laws, the Court had decided an important "third party bugging" dispute. The case was *On Lee* v. *United States.*[1] In *On Lee* the Court, divided (5–4) as it always seemed to be in Fourth Amendment cases, upheld a conviction secured by evidence obtained through "third party bugging." The record showed that On Lee had talked to a friend who was, in fact, an undercover agent with a concealed microphone. The friend was transmitting conversation to a federal agent outside On Lee's home. The Supreme Court, over Justice Frankfurter's objection (he called such eavesdropping a "dirty business"), affirmed On Lee's conviction. Although neither *Berger* nor *Katz* had specifically overturned *On Lee,* it seemed certain that given those Fourth Amendment rulings of the Warren Court concerning the allowable invasions of privacy, that *On Lee* and its "third party bugging" sanction would soon be a dead letter. But in *United States* v. *White* the Burger Court rescued *On Lee* and once again upheld evidence obtained through a "third party bugging." Again the Court was badly divided.

In *White,* a Court of Appeals had assumed that *Katz* had overruled *On Lee* and had decided, therefore, that the third party informant's (agent) testimony was inadmissible under the Fourth Amendment. But the slim majority of five, led by Justice White, decided otherwise. Not however without vigorous dissents by Justices Douglas, Harlan, and Marshall. Justice Brennan wrote a concurring opinion in which he stated agreement with Douglas and Harlan who would have overturned *On Lee.* Therefore, in *White,* four Justices stood against "third party bugging." In his dissent, Douglas argued that "wholly pre-arranged" episodes of third party surveillance of the type that occurred in *White,* and there were eight such episodes, "reaffirm the need for judicial supervision," the absence of which "promises to lead us into a police state."[2] Harlan's dissent condemned surveillance of this sort as undermining "that confidence and sense of security in dealing with one another that is characteristic of individual relationships between citizens in a free society."[3]

1. 343 U.S. 747 (1952).

2. 401 U.S. at 760.

3. Ibid., at 787.

White was convicted on a narcotics charge as a result of evidence introduced at his trial by government agents who in turn had received the information from a third party informant carrying a transmitter during a series of
conversations with White. The issue was whether the Fourth Amendment, as
interpreted by the Warren Court in *Berger* and *Katz*, barred from evidence
testimony received in this manner by government narcotics agents. A slim
majority of the Supreme Court ruled the testimony admissible. Concurring
opinions by Justices Black, who the record indicates was an avid defender of
First Amendment freedoms but who, surprisingly, was hardly ever an advocate of Fourth Amendment guarantees, and the usually liberal Brennan made
possible the majority.

Mr. Justice White announced the judgment of the Court and an opinion in
which Chief Justice Burger and Justices Stewart and Blackmun joined, saying
in part:

> Our problem is not what the privacy expectations of particular defendants in
> particular situations may be or the extent to which they may in fact have relied
> on the discretion of their companions. Very probably, individual defendants
> neither know nor suspect that their colleagues have gone or will go to the police
> or are carrying recorders or transmitters. Otherwise, conversation would cease
> and our problem with these encounters would be nonexistent or far different
> from those now before us. Our problem, in terms of the principles announced in
> *Katz*, is what expectations of privacy are constitutionally "justifiable" — what ex-
> pectations the Fourth Amendment will protect in the absence of a warrant. So
> far, the law permits the frustration of actual expectations of privacy by permit-
> ting authorities to use the testimony of those associates who for one reason or
> another have determined to turn to the police, as well as by authorizing the use
> of informants in the manner exemplified by *Hoffa* and *Lewis*. If the law gives no
> protection to the wrongdoer whose trusted accomplice is or becomes a police
> agent, neither should it protect him when that same agent has recorded or
> transmitted the conversations which are later offered in evidence to prove the
> State's case.
>
> Inescapably, one contemplating illegal activities must realize and risk that his
> companions may be reporting to the police. If he sufficiently doubts their
> trustworthiness, the association will very probably end or never materialize. But
> if he has no doubts, or allays them, or risks what doubt he has, the risk is his. In
> terms of what his course will be, what he will or will not do or say, we are
> unpersuaded that he would distinguish between probable informers on the one
> hand and probable informers with transmitters on the other. Given the possibil-
> ity or probability that one of his colleagues is cooperating with the police, it is
> only speculation to assert that the defendant's utterances would be substantially
> different or his sense of security any less if he also thought it possible that the
> suspected colleague is wired for sound. At least there is no persuasive evidence
> that the difference in this respect between the electronically equipped and the
> unequipped agent is substantial enough to require discrete constitutional recog-
> nition, particularly under the Fourth Amendment which is ruled by fluid con-
> cepts of "reasonableness."
>
> Nor should we be too ready to erect constitutional barriers to relevant and
> probative evidence which is also accurate and reliable. An electronic recording
> will many times produce a more reliable rendition of what a defendant has said
> than will the unaided memory of a police agent. It may also be that with the

recording in existence it is less likely that the informant will change his mind, less chance that threat or injury will suppress unfavorable evidence and less chance that cross-examination will confound the testimony. Considerations like these obviously do not favor the defendant, but we are not prepared to hold that a defendant who has no constitutional right to exclude the informer's unaided testimony nevertheless has a Fourth Amendment privilege against a more accurate version of the events in question.

It is thus untenable to consider the activities and reports of the police agent himself, though acting without a warrant, to be a "reasonable" investigative effort and lawful under the Fourth Amendment but to view the same agent with a recorder or transmitter as conducting an "unreasonable" and unconstitutional search and seizure. . . .

3

CONTRACEPTION AND ABORTION

Three extremely sensitive and controversial cases touching upon a delicate area of personal privacy rights under the Fourth Amendment have been decided by the Supreme Court in recent years. Two dealt with the dissemination of contraceptive advice, the other, by far the most emotional, dealt with abortion.

Griswold v. Connecticut, 381 U.S. 479 (1965)

The first case was *Griswold* v. *Connecticut* and concerned a Connecticut statute making it a crime for any one to use any drug or article to prevent conception. Speaking for the Court's majority of seven (Justices Black and Stewart wrote separate dissents), Justice Douglas wrote that the state law forbidding use of contraceptives violated the right of marital privacy "which is within the penumbra of specific guarantees of the Bill of Rights." Pritchett has called the Court's reasoning in *Griswold* "the foremost example of the new substantive due process of law" with which, in recent years, the Court "has been challenging old inequalities."[1]

Douglas argued that the Connecticut law violated "a right of privacy older than the Bill of Rights." Although the word privacy is nowhere mentioned in the Constitution, Douglas insisted it belonged within the "penumbra" of a number of constitutional provisions. He cited the right of association in the First Amendment and the privacy provisions of the Fourth Amendment, and in a concurring opinion Justice Goldberg cited the seldom used Ninth Amendment's rights "retained by the people" as the constitutional basis for striking down Connecticut's anti-contraception law.

If Douglas refrained from using the due process clause of the Fourteenth Amendment for fear as Pritchett notes, "that he would be exhuming substantive due process,"[2] the dissenters chided the Court for doing precisely that. In particular Justice Black objected to the Court's reliance upon substantive due

1. Pritchett op. cit., at 540–41. Pritchett refers to voting and travel rights that the Court has confirmed under the umbrella of "due process."

2. Ibid., at 541.

process or what he called an abstract "sense of fairness" and "natural justice." These formulas, Black said, "require judges to determine what is or is not constitutional on the basis of their own appraisal of what laws are unwise or unnecessary." This power, black argued, belongs to the legislature, not the judicial branch of government. "I like my privacy as well as the next one," Black wrote, but "I am . . . compelled to admit that government has a right to invade it unless prohibited by some specific constitutional provision."[3] Justice Stewart also disagreed with the Court's position. Although he called the Connecticut statute "an uncommonly silly law," Stewart nevertheless challenged the majority's grounds for declaring it unconstitutional. Stewart could find nothing in the First, Third, Fourth, or Fifth Amendments to invalidate the Connecticut law. And to say (as Justice Goldberg did in his concurring opinion) that the Ninth Amendment was related to *Griswold,* Stewart said, "is to turn somersaults with history."[4]

Appellant Griswold was the Executive Director of the Connecticut Planned Parenthood League. He and appellant Buxton, a medical doctor and a professor at Yale's School of Medicine, gave information, instruction, and medical advice to married couples as to what means they might use to prevent conception. They were found guilty of violating Connecticut law. The Supreme Court reversed the conviction and ruled that the state statute violated the Fourth Amendment.

Mr. Justice Douglas delivered the opinion of the Court, saying in part:

> The association of people is not mentioned in the Constitution nor in the Bill of Rights. The right to educate a child in a school of the parents' choice — whether public or private or parochial — is also not mentioned. Nor is the right to study any particular subject or any foreign language. Yet the First Amendment has been construed to include certain of those rights. . . .
>
> . . . Various guarantees create zones of privacy. The right of association contained in the penumbra of the First Amendment is one, as we have seen. The Third Amendment in its prohibition against the quartering of soldiers "in any house" in time of peace without the consent of the owner is another facet of that privacy. The Fourth Amendment explicitly affirms the "right of the people to be secure in their persons, houses, papers, and effects, against unreasonable searches and seizures." The Fifth Amendment in its Self-Incrimination Clause enables the citizen to create a zone of privacy which government may not force him to surrender to his detriment. The Ninth Amendment provides: "The enumeration in the Constitution, of certain rights, shall not be construed to deny or disparage others retained by the people."
>
> The Fourth and Fifth Amendments were described in *Boyd* v. *United States,* 116 U.S. 616, 630, as protection against all governmental invasions "of the sanctity of a man's home and the privacies of life." . . .
>
> The present case, then, concerns a relationship lying within the zone of privacy created by several fundamental constitutional guarantees. And it concerns a law which, in forbidding the *use* of contraceptives rather than regulating their manufacture or sale, seeks to achieve its goals by means having a maximum destructive impact upon that relationship. Such a law cannot stand in light of the familiar principle, so often applied by this Court, that a "governmental purpose to control or prevent activities constitutionally subject to state regulation may not be achieved by means which sweep unnecessarily broadly and thereby invade the area of protected freedoms." . . . Would we allow the police to search the sacred

3. 381 U.S. at 510–12.

4. Ibid., at 528–29.

precincts of marital bedrooms for telltale signs of the use of contraceptives? The very idea is repulsive to the notions of privacy surrounding the marriage relationship.

We deal with a right of privacy older than the Bill of Rights — older than our political parties, older than our school system. Marriage is a coming together for better or for worse, hopefully enduring, and intimate to the degree of being sacred. It is an association that promotes a way of life, not causes; a harmony in living, not political faiths; a bilateral loyalty, not commercial or social projects. Yet it is an association for as noble a purpose as any involved in our prior decisions.

Eisenstadt v. Baird, 405 U.S. 438 (1972)

Seven years after *Griswold* had provided the constitutional framework for protecting the privacy of "married couples in their bedrooms," the Supreme Court reversed another state court's anti-contraceptive decision. Involved here was a Massachusetts statute making it a felony for anyone, except a registered physician or a registered pharmacist acting with a prescription from a physician, to give away a "drug, medicine, instrument or article for the prevention of conception." The appellant was convicted in a state superior court for exhibiting contraceptive articles and for giving a young woman a package of vaginal foam at the close of an address to Boston University students.

Speaking for a majority of six (Chief Justice Burger filed a dissent, Justices Powell and Rehnquist did not participate), Justice Brennan wrote that because the Massachusetts law made it illegal for single persons but not married couples to obtain contraceptive information and devices it violated the equal protection clause of the Fourteenth Amendment. Brennan also felt constrained to bring the Court's decision under the umbrella of the Fourth Amendment by asserting, "if the right of privacy means anything, it is the right of the *individual* [italics are Justice Brennan's], married or single, to be free from unwarranted governmental intrusion into matters so fundamentally affecting a person as the decision whether to bear or beget a child." Only Chief Justice Burger took issue with the Court's position. Eisenstadt's conviction "for dispensing medicinal material without a license," the Chief Justice wrote, "seems eminently correct to me and I would not disturb it . . ." Burger also noted that the Court's reasoning "seriously invade[s] the constitutional prerogatives of the States and regrettably harkens back to the heyday of substantive due process."[1]

Mr. Justice Brennan delivered the opinion of the Court, saying in part:

> The question for our determination in this case is whether there is some ground of difference that rationally explains the different treatment accorded married and unmarried persons under Massachusetts General Laws Ann., c. 272, §§21 and 21A. For the reasons that follow, we conclude that no such ground exists. . . .
>
> If under *Griswold* the distribution of contraceptives to married persons cannot be prohibited, a ban on distribution to unmarried persons would be equally impermissible. It is true that in *Griswold* the right of privacy in question inhered in the marital relationship. Yet the marital couple is not an independent entity

1. 405 U.S. at 438.

with a mind and heart of its own, but an association of two individuals each with a separate intellectual and emotional makeup. If the right of privacy means anything, it is the right of the *individual,* married or single, to be free from unwarranted governmental intrusion into matters so fundamentally affecting a person as the decision whether to bear or beget a child. . . .

On the other hand, if *Griswold* is no bar to a prohibition on the distribution of contraceptives, the State could not, consistently with the Equal Protection Clause, outlaw distribution to unmarried but not to married persons. In each case the evil, as perceived by the State, would be identical, and the underinclusion would be invidious.

Roe v. Wade, 410 U.S. 113 (1972)

Eisenstadt set the stage for the Court's abortion rulings of the following year. The key decision was *Roe* v. *Wade.* There the Supreme Court ruled unconstitutional a Texas statute that had forbidden abortions at any stage of pregnancy except if the mother's life was endangered.

In this historic decision (7–2) Justice Blackmun wrote for the majority of the Burger Court while Justices White and Rehnquist filed separate dissents. Blackmun quickly acknowledged the emotional nature of the abortion controversy by prefacing the majority opinion with the following words ending with Justice Holmes's famous phrase dissenting in *Lochner* v. *New York.* [1]

> We forthwith acknowledge our awareness of the sensitive and emotional nature of the abortion controversy, of the vigorous opposing views, even among physicians, and of the deep and seemingly absolute convictions that the subject inspires. One's philosophy, one's religious training, one's attitudes toward life and family and their values, and the moral standards one establishes and seeks to observe, are all likely to influence and to color one's thinking and conclusions about abortion.
>
> In addition, population growth, pollution, poverty, and racial overtones tend to complicate and not to simplify the problem.
>
> Our task, of course, is to resolve the issue by constitutional measurement, free of emotion and of predilection. We seek earnestly to do this, and, because we do, we have inquired into, and in this opinion place some emphasis upon, medical and medical-legal history and what that history reveals about man's attitudes toward the abortion procedure over the centuries. We bear in mind, too, Mr. Justice Holmes' admonition in his now-vindicated dissent in Lochner v. New York;
>
>> "[The Constitution] is made for people of fundamentally differing views, and the accident of our finding certain opinions natural and familiar or novel and even shocking ought not to conclude our judgment upon the question whether statutes embodying them conflict with the Constitution of the United States."

The facts showed that Jane Roe (a pseudonym), an unmarried pregnant woman, wished to have an abortion "performed by a competent, licensed physician under safe clinical conditions." Roe claimed that the Texas statute forbidding abortions abridged her right of "personal privacy" protected by

1. 198 U.S. 45 (1905).

the First, Fourth, Fifth, Ninth, and Fourteenth Amendments. The privacy thrust of Roe's argument was that Texas law "improperly invade[d] a right, said to be possessed by the pregnant woman to choose to terminate her pregnancy."

In the majority opinion Justice Blackmun reviewed the history of anti-abortion statutes in the United States, all of them "of relatively recent vintage" and noted that they derived not always from common law origin but from statutory changes effected in the latter half of the nineteenth century.

Blackmun also reviewed the evolution of anti-abortion statutes both in England and in the United States before getting to the heart of the majority's reasoning. Acknowledging that the constitution does not "explicitly mention any right of privacy," Justice Blackmun chronicled a long list of decisions in which the Court recognized that a right of personal privacy "or a guarantee of certain areas or zones of privacy, does exist under the Constitution."[1] Blackmun then went on to reach the astonishing historic conclusion "that the right of personal privacy includes the abortion decision."

Both Justice Stewart in a concurring opinion and Justice Rehnquist in dissent stressed their belief that the Court's decision in *Roe* was based upon "substantive due process," a judicial tradition dating back to *Lochner* v. *New York*,[2] wherein the Court passes judgment on the wisdom of laws enacted by state legislatures based upon what Black in *Griswold* called an "abstract sense of fairness" or "natural justice." Stewart maintained that the reasoning in *Eisenstadt* (above), "the right of the individual . . . to be free from unwarranted governmental intrusion into matters so fundamentally affecting a person as the decision whether to bear or beget a child, . . . that right necessarily includes the right of a woman to decide whether or not to terminate her pregnancy."

Yet not one of the Justices who expressed themselves in *Roe,* Blackmun, Stewart, or Rehnquist, paid much heed to the rights of the fetus that in established law also has substantial legal rights. It has long been acknowledged for example, that a fetus may inherit and may be a party to a damage or personal injury suit as a legal person. Blackmun's majority opinion does delve into the delicate matter of when a fetus becomes a separate person and notes that one reason for the state's interest in abortion matters is to "protect pre-natal life." "In assessing the State's interest," Blackmun wrote, "recognition may be given to the less rigid claim that as long as at least *potential* life is involved, the State may assert interests beyond the protection of the pregnant woman alone." Blackmun continued by noting that "it is with these interests (presumably the rights of the fetus) and the weight to be attached to them, that this case is concerned."

Mr. Justice Blackmun delivered the opinion of the Court, saying in part:

> This right of privacy, whether it be founded in the Fourteenth Amendment's concept of personal liberty and restrictions upon state action, as we feel it is, or, as the District Court determined, in the Ninth Amendment's reservation of rights to the people, is broad enough to encompass a woman's decision whether or not to terminate her pregnancy. The detriment that the State would impose upon the pregnant woman by denying this choice altogether is apparent. Specific

1. See 410 U.S. at 152 for Blackmun's references.
2. 198 U.S. 45 (1905).

and direct harm medically diagnosable even in early pregnancy may be involved. Maternity, or additional offspring, may force upon the woman a distressful life and future. Psychological harm may be imminent. Mental and physical health may be taxed by child care. There is also the distress, for all concerned, associated with the unwanted child, and there is the problem of bringing a child into a family already unable, psychologically and otherwise, to care for it. In other cases, as in this one, the additional difficulties and continuing stigma of unwed motherhood may be involved. All these are factors the woman and her responsible physician necessarily will consider in consultation.

On the basis of elements such as these, appellant and some *amici* argue that the woman's right is absolute and that she is entitled to terminate her pregnancy at whatever time, in whatever way, and for whatever reason she alone chooses. With this we do not agree. Appellant's arguments that Texas either has no valid interest at all in regulating the abortion decision, or no interest strong enough to support any limitation upon the woman's sole determination, are unpersuasive. The Court's decisions recognizing a right of privacy also acknowledge that some state regulation in areas protected by that right is appropriate. As noted above, a State may properly assert important interests in safeguarding health, in maintaining medical standards, and in protecting potential life. At some point in pregnancy, these respective interests become sufficiently compelling to sustain regulation of the factors that govern the abortion decision. The privacy right involved, therefore, cannot be said to be absolute. In fact, it is not clear to us that the claim asserted by some *amici* that one has an unlimited right to do with one's body as one pleases bears a close relationship to the right of privacy previously articulated in the Court's decisions. The Court has refused to recognize an unlimited right of this kind in the past. *Jacobson* v. *Massachusetts,* 197 U.S. 11 (1905) (vaccination); *Buck* v. *Bell,* 274 U.S. 200 (1927) (sterilization).

We, therefore, conclude that the right of personal privacy includes the abortion decision, but that this right is not unqualified and must be considered against important state interests in regulation.

We note that those federal and state courts that have recently considered abortion law challenges have reached the same conclusion. A majority, in addition to the District Court in the present case, have held state laws unconstitutional, at least in part, because of vagueness or because of overbreadth and abridgment of rights. . . .

Although the results are divided, most of these courts have agreed that the right of privacy, however based, is broad enough to cover the abortion decision; that the right, nonetheless, is not absolute and is subject to some limitations; and that at some point the state interests as to protection of health, medical standards, and prenatal life, become dominant. We agree with this approach. . . .

Texas urges that, apart from the Fourteenth Amendment, life begins at conception and is present throughout pregnancy, and that, therefore, the State has a compelling interest in protecting that life from and after conception. We need not resolve the difficult question of when life begins. When those trained in the respective disciplines of medicine, philosophy, and theology are unable to arrive at any consensus, the judiciary, at this point in the development of man's knowledge, is not in a position to speculate as to the answer.

It should be sufficient to note briefly the wide divergence of thinking on this most sensitive and difficult question. There has always been strong support for the view that life does not begin until live birth. This was the belief of the Stoics. It appears to be the predominant, though not the unanimous, attitude of the Jewish faith. It may be taken to represent also the position of a large segment of the Protestant community, insofar as that can be ascertained; organized groups that have taken a formal position on the abortion issue have generally regarded abortion as a matter for the conscience of the individual and her family. As we have noted, the common law found greater significance in quickening. Physicians and their scientific colleagues have regarded that event with less interest and have tended to focus either upon conception, upon live birth, or upon the interim point at which the fetus becomes "viable," that is, potentially able to live outside the mother's womb, albeit with artificial aid. Viability is usually placed at about seven months (28 weeks) but may occur earlier, even at 24 weeks. The Aristotelian theory of "mediate animation," that held sway throughout the Middle Ages and the Renaissance in Europe, continued to be official Roman Catholic dogma until the 19th century, despite opposition to this "ensoulment" theory from those in the Church who would recognize the existence of life from the moment of conception. The latter is now, of course, the official belief of the Catholic Church. As one brief *amicus* discloses, this is a view strongly held by many non-Catholics as well, and by many physicians. Substantial problems for precise definition of this view are posed, however, by new embryological data that purport to indicate that conception is a "process" over time, rather than an event, and by new medical techniques such as menstrual extraction, the "morning-after" pill, implantation of embryos, artificial insemination, and even artificial wombs.

In areas other than criminal abortion, the law has been reluctant to endorse any theory that life, as we recognize it, begins before live birth or to accord legal rights to the unborn except in narrowly defined situations and except when the rights are contingent upon live birth. For example, the traditional rule of tort law denied recovery for prenatal injuries even though the child was born alive. That rule has been changed in almost every jurisdiction. In most States, recovery is said to be permitted only if the fetus was viable, or at least quick, when the injuries were sustained, though few courts have squarely so held. In a recent development, generally opposed by the commentators, some States permit the parents of a stillborn child to maintain an action for wrongful death because of prenatal injuries. Such an action, however, would appear to be one to vindicate the parents' interest and is thus consistent with the view that the fetus, at most, represents only the potentiality of life. Similarly, unborn children have been recognized as acquiring rights or interests by way of inheritance or other devolution of property, and have been represented by guardians *ad litem*. Perfection of the interests involved, again, has generally been contingent upon live birth. In short, the unborn have never been recognized in the law as persons in the whole sense. . . .

In view of all this, we do not agree that, by adopting one theory of life, Texas may override the rights of the pregnant woman that are at stake. We repeat, however, that the State does have an important and legitimate interest in preserving and protecting the health of the pregnant woman, whether she be a resident of the State or a nonresident who seeks medical consultation and treatment there, and that it has still *another* important and legitimate interest in protecting the potentiality of human life. These interests are separate and distinct. Each grows in substantiality as the woman approaches term and, at a point during pregnancy, each becomes "compelling."

With respect to the State's important and legitimate interest in the health of the mother, the "compelling" point, in the light of present medical knowledge, is at approximately the end of the first trimester. This is so because of the now-established medical fact, referred to above at 149, that until the end of the first trimester mortality in abortion may be less than mortality in normal childbirth. It follows that, from and after this point, a

State may regulate the abortion procedure to the extent that the regulation reasonably relates to the preservation and protection of maternal health. Examples of permissible state regulation in this area are requirements as to the qualifications of the person who is to perform the abortion; as to the licensure of that person; as to the facility in which the procedure is to be performed, that is, whether it must be a hospital or may be a clinic or some other place of less-than-hospital status; as to the licensing of the facility; and the like.

This means, on the other hand, that, for the period of pregnancy prior to this "compelling" point, the attending physician, in consultation with his patient, is free to determine, without regulation by the State, that, in his medical judgment, the patient's pregnancy should be terminated. If that decision is reached, the judgment may be effectuated by an abortion free of interference by the State.

With respect to the State's important and legitimate interest in potential life, the "compelling" point is at viability. This is so because the fetus then presumably has the capability of meaningful life outside the mother's womb. State regulation protective of fetal life after viability thus has both logical and biological justifications. If the State is interested in protecting fetal life after viability, it may go so far as to proscribe abortion during that period, except when it is necessary to preserve the life or health of the mother.

Measured against these standards, Art. 1196 of the Texas Penal Code, in restricting legal abortions to those "procured" or attempted by medical advice for the purpose of saving the life of the mother," sweeps too broadly. The statute makes no distinction between abortions performed early in pregnancy and those performed later, and it limits to a single reason, "saving" the mother's life, the legal justification for the procedure. The statute, therefore, cannot survive the constitutional attack made upon it here.

Maher v. Roe, 53 L. Ed. 2d 484 (1977)

That *Roe* v. *Wade* has stirred up a hornets' nest of protest is self-evident. The National "Right to Life" (Pro-Life) movement has sprung up and grown rapidly. Hardly a day has gone by since January 1973 without some aspect of the abortion-anti-abortion controversy being at least page three news. Nor does it seem that the matter will abate. Dedication, emotional commitment, and considerable heat are characteristic of both sides in the dispute.

The Supreme Court itself added more fuel to the fire in 1977 when it ruled in two companion cases, *Beal* v. *Doe* and *Maher* v. *Roe* that states were *not* required to fund the cost of abortions for indigent women under medical programs. As *Roe* v. *Wade* had stirred the ire of anti-abortion forces, *Maher* called forth angry epithets at the Supreme Court by pro-abortion groups.

Maher dealt with the Medical Assistance Program (Medicaid) of Title XIX of the Social Security Act whereby participating states may provide federally funded medical assistance to needy persons. Connecticut law prescribed that Medicaid benefits for abortions would be granted upon written request and upon prior authorization from a designated official of the state's Department of Social Services. Two indigent women who were unable to obtain the required physician's certificate brought suit against the state, challenging Connecticut's regulation as a violation of Title XIX and further as a violation of their constitutional rights, including the Fourteenth Amendment's guarantees of due process and equal protection.

With Justice Powell writing for the majority of six (the dissenters were Justices Brennan, Marshall, and Blackmun) the Burger Court reversed a lower court ruling and decided that Connecticut's regulation did *not* violate the Constitution.

Justice Brennan, joined by the other two dissenters, disagreed. He argued that the Connecticut regulations "unjustifiably impinged upon a pregnant woman's due process privacy right to determine whether or not to carry her pregnancy to term." Brennan also chided the Court for forcing "indigent women to bear children they would otherwise not have."

In his dissent, Justice Blackmun (also joined by the other two dissenters) charged that the Supreme Court had allowed the states (in *Maher*) to do indirectly "that which [the Court] had ruled in its earlier decisions on abortion [*Roe v. Wade*] the states could not do directly."

Mr. Justice Powell delivered the opinion of the Court, saying in part:

> The Constitution imposes no obligation on the States to pay the pregnancy-related medical expenses of indigent women, or indeed to pay any of the medical expenses of indigents. But when a State decides to alleviate some of the hardships of poverty by providing medical care, the manner in which it dispenses benefits is subject to constitutional limitations. Appellees' claim is that Connecticut must accord equal treatment to both abortion and childbirth, and may not evidence a policy preference by funding only the medical expenses incident to childbirth. This challenge to the classifications established by the Connecticut regulation presents a question arising under the Equal Protection Clause of the Fourteenth Amendment. The basic framework of analysis of such a claim is well-settled:
>
> > "We must decide, first, whether [state legislation] operates to the disadvantage of some suspect class or impinges upon a fundamental right explicitly or implicitly protected by the Constitution, thereby requiring strict judicial scrutiny. . . . If not, the [legislative] scheme must still be examined to determine whether it rationally furthers some legitimate, articulated state purpose and therefore does not constitute an invidious discrimination...."
>
> Applying this analysis here, we think the District Court erred in holding that the Connecticut regulation violated the Equal Protection Clause of the Fourteenth Amendment.
>
> This case involves no discrimination against a suspect class. An indigent woman desiring an abortion does not come within the limited category of disadvantaged classes so recognized by our cases. Nor does the fact that the impact of the regulation falls upon those who cannot pay lead to a different conclusion. In a sense, every denial of welfare to an indigent creates a wealth classification as compared to nonindigents who are able to pay for the desired goods or services. But this Court has never held that financial need alone identifies a suspect class for purposes of equal protection analysis. See Rodriguez, supra, at 29, 36 L Ed 2d 16, 93 S Ct 1278; Dandridge v Williams, 397 US 471, 25 L Ed 2d 491, 90 S Ct 1153 (1970).[6] Accordingly, the central question in this case is whether the regulation "impinges upon a fundamental right explicitly or implicitly protected by the Constitution." The District Court read our decisions in Roe v Wade, supra, and the subsequent cases applying it, as establishing a fundamental right to abortion

and therefore concluded that nothing less than a compelling state interest would justify Connecticut's different treatment of abortion and childbirth. We think the District Court misconceived the nature and scope of the fundamental right recognized in Roe.

At issue in Roe was the constitutionality of a Texas law making it a crime to procure or attempt to procure an abortion, except on medical advice for the purpose of saving the life of the mother. Drawing on a group of disparate cases restricting governmental intrusion, physical coercion, and criminal prohibition of certain activities, we concluded that the Fourteenth Amendment's concept of personal liberty affords constitutional protection against state interference with certain aspects of an individual's personal "privacy," including a woman's decision to terminate her pregnancy.[7] 410 US, at 153, 35 L Ed 2d 147, 93 S Ct 705.

The Texas statute imposed severe criminal sanctions on the physicians and other medical personnel who performed abortions, thus drastically limiting the availability and safety of the desired service. As Mr. Justice Stewart observed, "it is difficult to imagine a more complete abridgement of a constitutional freedom. . . ." Id., at 170, 35 L Ed 2d 147, 93 S Ct 705 (Stewart, J., concurring). We held that only a compelling state interest would justify such a sweeping restriction on a constitutionally protected interest, and we found no such state interest during the first trimester. Even when judged against this demanding standard, however, the State's dual interests in the health of the pregnant woman and the potential life of the fetus were deemed sufficient to justify substantial regulation of abortions in the second and third trimesters. "These interests are separate and distinct. Each grows in substantiality as the woman approaches term and, at a point during pregnancy, each becomes 'compelling.'" Id., at 162–163, 35 L Ed 2d 147, 93 S Ct 705. In the second trimester, the State's interest in the health of the pregnant woman justifies state regulation reasonably related to that concern. Id., at 163, 35 L Ed 2d 147, 93 S Ct 705. At viability, usually in the third trimester, the State's interest in the potential life of the fetus justifies prohibition with criminal penalties, except where the life or health of the mother is threatened. Id., at 163–164, 35 L Ed 2d 147, 93 S Ct 705.

The Texas law in Roe was a stark example of impermissible interference with the pregnant woman's decision to terminate her pregnancy. In subsequent cases, we have invalidated other types of restrictions, different in form but similar in effect, on the woman's freedom of choice. Thus, in Planned Parenthood of Missouri v Danforth, 428 US 52, 70–71, n 11, 49 L Ed 2d 788, 96 S Ct 2831 (1976), we held that Missouri's requirement of spousal consent was unconstitutional because it "granted [the husband] the right to prevent unilaterally, and for whatever reason, the effectuation of his wife's and her physician's decision to terminate her pregnancy." Missouri had interposed an *"absolute obstacle* to a woman's decision that Roe held to be constitutionally protected from such interference." (Emphasis added.) Although a state-created obstacle need not be absolute to be impermissible, see Doe v Bolton, supra. Carey v Population Services International, — US —, 52 L Ed 2d 675, 97 S Ct — (1977), we have held that a requirement for a lawful abortion "is not unconstitutional unless it unduly burdens the right to seek an abortion." Bellotti v Baird, 428 US 132, 147, 49 L Ed 2d 844, 96 S Ct 2857 (1976). We recognized in Bellotti that "not all distinction between abortion and other procedures is forbidden" and that "[t]he constitutionality of such distinction will depend upon its degree and the justification for it." Id., at 149–150, 49 L Ed 2d 844, 96 S Ct 2857. We therefore declined to rule on the constitutionality of a Massachusetts statute regulating a minor's access to an abortion until the state courts had had an opportunity to determine whether the statute authorized a parental veto over the minor's decision or the less burdensome requirement of parental consultation.

These cases recognize a constitutionally protected interest "in making certain kinds of important decisions" free from governmental compulsion. Whalen v Roe, — US ——, 51 L Ed 2d 64, 97 S Ct 869, and nn 24 and 26 (1977). As Whalen makes clear, the right in Roe v Wade can be understood only by considering both the woman's interest and the nature of the State's interference with it. Roe did not declare an unqualified "constitutional right to an abortion," as the District Court seemed to think. Rather, the right protects the woman from unduly burdensome interference with her freedom to decide whether to terminate her pregnancy. It implies no limitation on the authority of a State to make a value judgment favoring childbirth over abortion, and to implement that judgment by the allocation of public funds.

The Connecticut regulation before us is different in kind from the laws invalidated in our previous abortion decisions. The Connecticut regulation places no obstacles — absolute or otherwise — in the pregnant woman's path to an abortion. An indigent woman who desires an abortion suffers no disadvantage as a consequence of Connecticut's decision to fund childbirth; she continues as before to be dependent on private sources for the service she desires. The State may have made childbirth a more attractive alternative, thereby influencing the woman's decision, but it has imposed no restriction on access to abortions that was not already there. The indigency that may make it difficult — and in some cases, perhaps, impossible — for some women to have abortions is neither created nor in any way affected by the Connecticut regulation. We conclude that the Connecticut regulation does not impinge upon the fundamental right recognized in Roe.

Our conclusion signals no retreat from Roe or the cases applying it. There is a basic difference between direct state interference with a protected activity and state encouragement of an alternative activity consonant with legislative policy. . . .

The question remains whether Connecticut's regulation can be sustained under the less demanding test of rationality that applies in the absence of a suspect classification or the impingement of a fundamental right. This test requires that the distinction drawn between childbirth and nontherapeutic abortion by the regulation be "rationally related" to a "constitutionally permissible" purpose. . . . We hold that the Connecticut funding scheme satisfies this standard.

Roe itself explicitly acknowledged the State's strong interest in protecting the potential life of the fetus. That interest exists throughout the pregnancy, "grow[ing] in substantiality as the woman approaches term." Roe, supra, at 162 — 163, 35 L Ed 2d 147, 93 S Ct 705. Because the pregnant woman carries a potential human being, she "cannot be isolated in her privacy. . . . [Her] privacy is no longer sole and any right of privacy she possesses must be measured accordingly." Id., at 159, 35 L Ed 2d 147, 93 S Ct 705. The State unquestionably has a "strong and legitimate interest in encouraging normal childbirth," Beal v Doe, ante, at   , 35 L Ed 2d 464, 97 S Ct   , an interest honored over the centuries. Nor can there be any question that the Connecticut regulation rationally furthers that interest. The medical costs associated with childbirth are substantial, and have increased significantly in recent years. As recognized by the District Court in this case, such costs are significantly greater than those normally associated with elective abortions during the first trimester. The subsidizing of costs incident to childbirth is a rational means of encouraging childbirth.

We certainly are not unsympathetic to the plight of an indigent woman who desires an abortion, but "the Constitution does not provide judicial remedies for every social and economic ill," Lindsey v Normet, 405 US, at 74, 31 L Ed 2d 36, 92 S Ct 862. Our cases uniformly have accorded the States a wider latitude in choosing among competing demands for limited public funds. In Dandridge v Williams, 397 US 471, 485, 25 L Ed 2d 491, 90 S Ct 1153 (1970), despite recognition that laws and regulations allocating welfare funds involve "the most basic economic needs of impoverished human beings," we held that classifications survive equal protection challenge when a "reasonable basis" for the classification is shown. As the preceding discussion makes clear, the state interest in encouraging normal childbirth exceeds this minimal level.

The decision whether to expend state funds for nontherapeutic abortion is fraught with judgments of policy and value over which opinions are sharply divided. Our conclusion that the Connecticut regulation is constitutional is not based on a weighing of its wisdom or social desirability, for this Court does not strike down state laws "because they may be unwise, improvident, or out of harmony with a particular school of thought." Williamson v Lee Optical Co. 348 US 483, 488, 99 L Ed 563, 75 S Ct 461 (1955), quoted in Dandridge v Williams, supra, at 484, 25 L Ed 2d 491, 90 S Ct 1153. Indeed, when an issue involves policy choices as sensitive as those implicated by public funding of nontherapeutic abortions, the appropriate forum for their resolution in a democracy is the legislature. We should not forget that "legislatures are ultimate guardians of the liberties and welfare of the people in quite as great a degree as the courts." Missouri, Kansas and Texas Ry. Co. v May, 194 US 267, 270, 48 L Ed 971, 24 S Ct 638 (1904) (Holmes, J.).

In conclusion, we emphasize that our decision today does not proscribe government funding of nontherapeutic abortions. It is open to Congress to require provision of medicaid benefits for such abortions as a condition of state participation in the medicaid program. Also, under Title XIX as construed in Beal v Doe, — US ——, 53 L Ed 2d 464, 97 S Ct ——, Connecticut is free — through normal democratic processes — to decide that such benefits should be provided. We hold only that the Constitution does not require a judicially imposed resolution of these difficult issues.

The District Court also invalidated Connecticut's requirements of prior written request by the pregnant woman and prior authorization by the Department of Social Services. Our analysis above rejects the basic premise that prompted invalidation of these procedural requirements. It is not unreasonable for a State to insist upon a prior showing of medical necessity to insure that its money is being spent only for authorized purposes. The simple answer to the argument that similar requirements are not imposed for other medical procedures is that such procedures do not involve the termination of a potential human life. In Planned Parenthood of Missouri v Danforth, supra, we held that the woman's written consent to an abortion was not an impermissible burden under Roe. We think that decision is controlling on the similar issue here.

The judgment of the District Court is reversed, and the case is remanded for further proceedings consistent with this opinion.

III

THE FIFTH
AMENDMENT

The Fifth Amendment to the Constitution contains five fundamental guarantees. Each was designed to ensure that citizens will be treated fairly in their involvement with government and the criminal justice procedure. The Amendment states that a grand jury indictment is necessary before a person can be brought to trial for a capital "or otherwise infamous" crime. It protects against double jeopardy (being tried twice for the same offense) and against self-incrimination. The due process clause, "nor [shall any person] be deprived of life, liberty or property, without due process of law" stands as a shield protecting citizens from possible abuses by government. These provisions are guarantees against capricious, arbitrary, or unfair practices. Finally the Amendment's "eminent domain" clause, "nor shall private property be taken for public use, without just compensation," protects property against improper or unfair confiscation by government.

1

SELF-INCRIMINATION

Brown v. Walker, 161 U.S. 519 (1896)

In recent years the Fifth Amendment's self-incrimination clause has brought about many of the Court's most significant judicial disputes. Most have involved the growing practice in criminal justice proceedings of granting immunity from prosecution in exchange for possibly self-incriminating evidence. The Supreme Court's first encounter with legislation granting immunity and the Fifth Amendment's protection against self-incrimination took place in 1896, in *Brown* v. *Walker.* There a divided Court (5 — 4) upheld an 1893 law passed by Congress that had granted immunity from prosecution to witnesses testifying before the Interstate Commerce Commission. Two dissenting opinions were written, one by Justice Shiras, joined by Justices Gray and White, and the other by Justice Field. Both dissenters argued that the Fifth Amendment's protection against self-incrimination could *not* be abrogated by Congress under any circumstances. Justice Shiras insisted "it is too obvious to require argument" that protection against self incrimination "should not be divested or impaired by an Act of Congress."[1] For his part, Justice Field cited what he called the "essential and inherent cruelty of compelling a man to expose his own guilt." A sense of "personal degradation in being compelled to incriminate one's self," Field wrote, "must create a feeling of abhorrence in the community . . . ."[2]

Despite these eloquent misgivings the rationale in *Brown* prevails to this day. For example, it was cited in 1956 as the authority for the Supreme Court to uphold the Immunity Act of 1954, which Congress passed as a response to the many uses (and some abuses) of the self-incrimination clause by witnesses during the Congressional anti-communist hearings of the 1940s and 1950s. That case was *Ullmann* v. *United States*[3] and only Justices Douglas and Black argued that *Brown* should be overruled.

In *Brown,* Justice Brown admitted for the majority that, interpreted literally, the self-incrimination clause must necessarily mean that any immunity

1. 161 U.S. at 610.

2. Ibid., at 637.

3. 350 U.S. 722 (1956).

statute is unconstitutional. Yet the Court sought to interpret the Fifth Amendment to strike a balance between the literalist view of the guarantee, no self-incrimination under any circumstances, and the public welfare that might, the Court reasoned, require an individual to besmirch his own name and reputation as "a penalty which it is reasonable he should be compelled to pay for the common good."

Mr. Justice Brown delivered the opinion of the Court, saying in part:

> The clause of the Constitution in question is obviously susceptible of two interpretations. If it be construed literally, as authorizing the witness to refuse to disclose any fact which might tend to incriminate, disgrace or expose him to unfavorable comments, then as he must necessarily to a large extent determine upon his own conscience and responsibility whether his answer to the proposed question will have that tendency, . . . the practical result would be, that no one could be compelled to testify to a material fact in a criminal case, unless he chose to do so, or unless it was entirely clear that the privilege was not set up in good faith. If, upon the other hand, the object of the provision be to secure the witness against a criminal prosecution, which might be aided directly or indirectly by his disclosure, then, if no such prosecution be possible — in other words, if his testimony operate as a complete pardon for the offence to which it relates — a statute absolutely securing to him such immunity from prosecution would satisfy the demands of the clause in question. . . .
>
> The maxim *nemo tenetur seipsum accusare* had its origin in a protest against the inquisitorial and manifestly unjust methods of interrogating accused persons, which has long obtained in the continental system, and, until the expulsion of the Stuarts from the British throne in 1688, and the erection of additional barriers for the protection of the people against the exercise of arbitrary power, was not uncommon even in England. While the admissions or confessions of the prisoner, when voluntarily and freely made, have always ranked high in the scale of incriminating evidence, if an accused person be asked to explain his apparent connection with a crime under investigation, the ease with which the questions put to him may assume an inquisitorial character, the temptation to press the witness unduly, to browbeat him if he be timid or reluctant, to push him into a corner, and to entrap him into fatal contradictions, which is so painfully evident in many of the earlier state trials, notably in those of Sir Nicholas Throckmorton, and Udal, the Puritan minister, made the system so odious as to give rise to a demand for its total abolition. The change in the English criminal procedure in that particular seems to be founded upon no statute and no judicial opinion, but upon a general and silent acquiescence of the courts in a popular demand. But, however adopted, it has become firmly embedded in English, as well as in American jurisprudence. So deeply did the iniquities of the ancient system impress themselves upon the minds of the American colonists that the States, with one accord, made a denial of the right to question an accused person a part of their fundamental law, so that a maxim, which in England was a mere rule of evidence, became clothed in this country with the impregnability of a constitutional enactment.
>
> Stringent as the general rule is, however, certain classes of cases have always been treated as not falling within the reason of the rule, and, therefore, constituting apparent exceptions. When examined, these cases will all be found to be based upon the idea that, if the testimony sought cannot possibly be used as a basis for, or in aid of, a criminal prosecution against the witness, the rule ceases to apply, its object being to protect the witness himself and no one else — much less that it shall be made use of as a pretext for securing immunity to others. . . .

It is entirely true that the statute does not purport, nor is it possible for any statute, to shield the witness from the personal disgrace or opprobrium attaching to the exposure of his crime; but, as we have already observed, the authorities are numerous and very nearly uniform to the effect that, if the proposed testimony is material to the issue on trial, the fact that the testimony may tend to degrade the witness in public estimation does not exempt him from the duty of disclosure. A person who commits a criminal act is bound to contemplate the consequences of exposure to his good name and reputation, and ought not to call upon the courts to protect that which he has himself esteemed to be of such little value. The safety and welfare of an entire community should not be put into the scale against the reputation of a self-confessed criminal, who ought not, either in justice or in good morals, to refuse to disclose that which may be of great public utility, in order that his neighbors may think well of him. The design of the constitutional privilege is not to aid the witness in vindicating his character, but to protect him against being compelled to furnish evidence to convict him of a criminal charge. If he secure legal immunity from prosecution, the possible impairment of his good name is a penalty which it is reasonable he should be compelled to pay for the common good. If it be once conceded that the fact that his testimony may tend to bring the witness into disrepute, though not to incriminate him, does not entitle him to the privilege of silence, it necessarily follows that if it also tends to incriminate, but at the same time operates as a pardon for the offence, the fact that the disgrace remains no more entitles him to immunity in this case than in the other. . . .

In the case under consideration, the grand jury was engaged in investigating certain alleged violations of the Interstate Commerce Act, among which was a charge against the Allegheny Valley Railway Company of transporting coal of the Union Coal Company from intermediate points to Buffalo, at less than the established rates between the terminal points, and a further charge of discriminating in favor of such coal company by rebates, drawbacks or commissions on its coal, by which it obtained transportation at less than the tariff rates. Brown, the witness, was the auditor of the road, whose duty it was to audit the accounts of the officers, and the money paid out by them. Having audited the accounts of the freight department during the time in question, he was asked whether he knew of any such discrimination in favor of the Union Coal Company, and declined to answer upon the ground that he would thereby incriminate himself.

As he had no apparent authority to make the forbidden contracts, to receive the money earned upon such contracts, or to allow or pay any rebates, drawbacks or commissions thereon, and was concerned only in auditing accounts, and passing vouchers for money paid by others, it is difficult to see how, under any construction of section 10 of the Interstate Commerce Act, he could be said to have wilfully done anything, or aided or abetted others in doing anything, or in omitting to do anything, in violation of the act — his duty being merely to see that others had done what they purported to have done, and that the vouchers rendered by them were genuine. But, however this may be, it is entirely clear that he was not the chief or even a substantial offender against the law, and that his privilege was claimed for the purpose of shielding the railway or its officers from answering a charge of having violated its provisions. To say that, notwithstanding his immunity from punishment, he would incur personal odium and disgrace from answering these questions, seems too much like an abuse of language to be worthy of serious consideration. But, even if this were true, under the authorities above cited, he would still be compelled to answer, if the facts sought to be elucidated were material to the issue.

If, as was justly observed in the opinion of the court below, witnesses standing in Brown's position were at liberty to set up an immunity from testifying, the enforcement of the Interstate Commerce law or other analogous acts, wherein it is for the interest of both parties to conceal their misdoings, would become impossible, since it is only from the mouths of those having knowledge of the inhibited contracts that the facts can be ascertained. While the constitutional provision in question is justly regarded as one of the most valuable prerogatives of the citizen, its object is fully accomplished by the statutory immunity, and we are, therefore, of opinion that the witness was compellable to answer, and that the judgment of the court below must be

Affirmed.

Twining v. New Jersey, 211 U.S. 78 (1908)

Because most criminal cases are tried in state courts the applicability of Fifth Amendment guarantees to the states was long a center of controversy in American jurisprudence. For many years, in fact until the *Malloy* case (below) in 1964, Supreme Court rulings had held that the Fifth Amendment's protection against self-incrimination applied in Federal courts but not in state courts. In recent years, however, as we have seen in First and Fourth Amendment cases (above), the major protections of the Bill of Rights have been applied (incorporated) to the states via the due process clause of the Fourteenth Amendment. Beginning with *Gitlow* in 1925, *Mapp* in 1961, and proceeding to *Gideon, Malloy, Escobedo, Miranda,* and *Benton* during the Warren Court years, First, Fourth, Fifth, and Sixth Amendment rights have been incorporated into the Fourteenth. Although not, as we shall see, without major objections.

The first significant case involving applicability of the self-incrimination guarantee in a state court was *Twining* v. *New Jersey*. There, with only Justice Harlan dissenting, the Supreme Court decided that exemption from compulsory self-incrimination was neither one of the fundamental rights nor one of the privileges and immunities guaranteed to citizens by the due process clause of the Fourteenth Amendment. Speaking for the Court, Justice Moody concluded, after a long, historical survey of self-incrimination, that exemption in state courts from compulsory self-incrimination is "not secured by any part of the Federal Constitution." *Twining* would stand until 1964 when the Warren Court specifically overruled it in *Malloy* v. *Hogan*.

Mr. Justice Moody delivered the opinion of the Court, saying in part:

Even if the historical meaning of due process of law and the decisions of this court did not exclude the privilege from it, it would be going far to rate it as an immutable principle of justice which is the inalienable possession of every citizen of a free government. Salutary as the principle may seem to the great majority, it cannot be ranked with the right to hearing before condemnation, the immunity from arbitrary power not acting by general laws, and the inviolability of private property. The wisdom of the exemption has never been universally assented to since the days of Bentham; many doubt it today, and it is best defended not as an unchangeable principle of universal justice but as a law proved by experience to be expedient. . . . It has no place in the jurisprudence of civilized and free countries outside the domain of the common law, and it is nowhere observed among our own people in the search for truth outside the administration of the law. It should, must and will be rigidly observed where it is secured by specific constitutional safeguards, but there is nothing in it which gives it a sanctity above and before constitutions themselves. Much might be said in favor of the view that the privilege was guaranteed against state impairment as a privilege and immunity of National citizenship, but, as has been shown, the decisions of this court have foreclosed that view. There seems to be no reason whatever, however, for straining the meaning of due process of law to include this privilege within it, because, perhaps, we may think it of great value. The States had guarded the privilege to the satisfaction of their own people up to the adoption of the Fourteenth Amendment. No reason is perceived why they cannot continue to do so. The power of their people ought not to be fettered, their sense of responsibility lessened, and their capacity for sober and restrained self-government weakened by forced construction of the Federal Constitution. If the people of New Jersey are not content with the law as declared in repeated decisions of their courts, the remedy is in their own hands. . . .

We have assumed only for the purpose of discussion that what was done in the case at bar was an infringement of the privilege against self-incrimination. We do not intend, however, to lend any countenance to the truth of that assumption. The courts of New Jersey, in adopting the rule of law which is complained of here, have deemed it consistent with the privilege itself and not a denial of it. The reasoning by which this view is supported will be found in the cases cited from New Jersey and Maine, and see *Reg.* v. *Rhodes* (1899), 1 Q. B. 77; *Ex parte Kops* (1894), A. C. 650. The authorities upon the question are in conflict. We do not pass upon the conflict, because, for the reasons given, we think that the exemption from compulsory self-incrimination in the courts of the States is not secured by any part of the Federal Constitution.

Adamson v. California, 322 U.S. 46 (1947)

Some thirty years after *Twining* the Supreme Court, now with its Roosevelt appointees and ostensibly a more liberal Court, continued to uphold the view that protection against self-incrimination that the Fifth Amendment guarantees in a federal court did *not* apply to the states through the due process clause of the Fourteenth Amendment. In *Adamson* the majority of six, led by Justice Reed, decided once again that protection against self-incrimination is *not* inherent in the right to a fair trial and is therefore *not* protected in a state court. Two dissents were written, one by Justice Black, the other by Justice Murphy joined by Justice Rutledge.

In both *Twining* and *Adamson* the Supreme Court upheld state statutes that allowed a court to draw unfavorable inferences from a defendant's failure to take the witness stand. Justice Murphy insisted that this practice was intolerable. The state statutes in question, Murphy said, compel a defendant to be a witness against himself in one of two ways: "If he does not take the stand his silence is used as the basis for drawing unfavorable inferences against him . . . thus he is compelled, through his silence to testify against himself. And silence can be as effective in this situation as oral statements. If he does take the stand thereby opening himself to cross-examination . . . he is necessarily compelled to testify against himself."[1]

1. 332 U.S. at 45.

Portions of Justice Black's long dissent in *Adamson* reviewing the relevant history of both the Bill of Rights and the Fourteenth Amendment are reproduced here. Seventeen years after *Adamson,* in *Malloy* v. *Hogan* (below), the Supreme Court would once again confront the question of immunity from self-incrimination in a state court. When it did so, it relied, as we shall see, in great part upon Black's dissent in *Adamson.*

The appellant in *Adamson* was convicted in a California court of first-degree murder. He did not testify at his trial. Provisions of California law permit the failure of a defendant to take the witness stand, to explain or deny evidence against him, to be commented upon by the judge and the prosecutor and to be considered by the judge and jury. Thus the central question: Is protection against self-incrimination a fundamental national privilege applicable in both federal and state courts (as Justices Black and Murphy argued in dissent)? Are all the guarantees of the Bill of Rights incorporated under the Fourteenth Amendment? If so, the California law plainly violated the Constitution. If not, then the Supreme Court must continue to uphold what seems to be a dual standard of justice: one applying to federal courts (no self-incrimination) and another applying to state courts (no *protection* against self-incrimination).

In *Adamson,* as it had in *Twining,* the Supreme Court maintained this peculiarly inconsistent double standard.

Mr. Justice Reed delivered the opinion of the Court, saying in part:

Appellant . . . contends that if the privilege against self-incrimination is not a right protected by the privileges and immunities clause of the Fourteenth Amendment against state action, this privilege, to its full scope under the Fifth Amendment, inheres in the right to a fair trial. A right to a fair trial is a right admittedly protected by the due process clause of the Fourteenth Amendment. Therefore, appellant argues, the due process clause of the Fourteenth Amendment protects his privilege against self-incrimination. The due process clause of the Fourteenth Amendment, however, does not draw all the rights of the federal Bill of Rights under its protection. That contention was made and rejected in *Palko* v. *Connecticut.* . . . It was rejected with citation of the cases excluding several of the rights, protected by the Bill of Rights, against infringement by the National Government. Nothing has been called to our attention that either the framers of the Fourteenth Amendment or the states that adopted intended its due process clause to draw within its scope the earlier amendments to the Constitution. *Palko* held that such provision of the Bill of Rights as were "implicit in the concept of ordered liberty," . . . became secure from state interference by the clause. But it held nothing more.

Specifically, the due process clause does not protect, by virtue of its mere existence, the accused's freedom from giving testimony by compulsion in state trials that is secured to him against federal interference by the Fifth Amendment. . . . For a state to require testimony from an accused is not necessarily a breach of a state's obligation to give a fair trial. Therefore, we must examine the effect of the California law applied in this trial to see whether the comment on failure to testify violates the protection against state action that the due process clause does grant to the accused. The due process clause forbids compulsion to testify by fear of hurt, torture or exhaustion. It forbids any other type of coercion that falls within the scope of due process. California follows Anglo-American legal tradition in excusing defendants in criminal prosecutions from compulsory testimony. . . . That is a matter of legal policy and not because of the requirements of due process under the Fourteenth Amendment. So our inquiry is directed, not at the broad question of the constitutionality of compulsory testimony from the accused under the due process clause, but to the constitutionality of the provision of the California law that permits comment upon his failure to testify. It is, of course, logically possible that while an accused might be required, under appropriate penalties, to submit himself as a witness without a violation of due process, comment by judge or jury on inferences to be drawn from his failure to testify, in jurisdictions where an accused's privilege against self-incrimination is protected, might deny due process. For example, a statute might declare that a permitted refusal to testify would compel an acceptance of the truth of the prosecution's evidence.

Generally, comment on the failure of an accused to testify is forbidden in American jurisdictions. This arises from state constitutional or statutory provisions similar in character to the federal provisions. . . . California, however, is one of a few states that permit limited comment upon a defendant's failure to testify. That permission is narrow. The California law is set out in note 3 and authorizes comment by court and counsel upon the "failure of the defendant to explain or to deny by his testimony any evidence or facts in the case against him." This does not involve any presumption, rebuttable or irrebuttable, either of guilt or of the truth of any fact, that is offered in evidence. . . . It allows inferences to be drawn from proven facts. Because of this clause, the court can direct the jury's attention to whatever evidence there may be that a defendant could deny and the prosecution can argue as to inferences that may be drawn from the accused's failure to testify. . . . There is here no lack of power in the trial court to adjudge and no denial of a hearing. California has prescribed a method for advising the jury in the search for truth. However sound may be the legislative conclusion that an accused should not be compelled in any criminal case to be a witness against himself, we see no reason why comment should not be made upon his silence. It seems quite natural that when a defendant has opportunity to deny or explain facts and determines not to do so, the prosecution should bring out the strength of the evidence by commenting upon defendant's failure to explain or deny it. The prosecution evidence may be of facts that may be beyond the knowledge of the accused. If so, his failure to testify would have little if any weight. But the facts may be such as are necessarily in the knowledge of the accused. In that case a failure to explain would point to an inability to explain. . . .

It is true that if comment were forbidden, an accused in this situation could remain silent and avoid evidence of former crimes and comment upon his failure to testify. We are of the view, however, that a state may control such a situation in accordance with its own ideas of the most efficient administration of criminal justice. The purpose of due process is not to protect an accused against a proper conviction but against an unfair conviction. When evidence is before a jury that threatens conviction, it does not seem unfair to require him to choose between leaving the adverse evidence unexplained and subjecting himself to impeachment through disclosure of former crimes. Indeed, this is a dilemma with which any defendant may be faced. If facts, adverse to the defendant, are proven by the prosecution, there may be no way to explain them favorably to the accused except by a witness who may be vulnerable to impeachment on cross-examination. The defendant must then decide whether or not to use such a witness. The fact that the witness may also be the defendant makes the choice more difficult but a denial of due process does not emerge from the circumstances.

There is no basis in the California law for appellant's objection on due process or other grounds that the statutory authorization to comment on the failure to explain or deny adverse testimony shifts the burden of proof or the duty to go forward with the evidence. Failure of the accused to testify is not an admission of the truth of the adverse evidence. Instructions told the jury that the burden of proof remained upon the state and the presumption of innocence with the accused. Comment on failure to deny proven facts does not in California tend to supply any missing element of proof of guilt. . . . It only directs attention to the strength of the evidence for the prosecution or to the weakness of that for the defense. The Supreme Court of California called attention to the fact that the prosecutor's argument approached the borderline in a statement that might have been construed as asserting "that the jury should infer guilt solely from defendant's silence." That court felt that it was improbable the jury was misled into such an understanding of their power. We shall not interfere with such a conclusion.

Mr. Justice Black dissented, saying in part:

The first ten amendments were proposed and adopted largely because of fear that Government might unduly interfere with prized individual liberties. The people wanted and demanded a Bill of Rights written into their Constitution. The amendments embodying the Bill of Rights were intended to curb all branches of the Federal Government in the fields touched by the amend-ments — Legislative, Executive, and Judicial. The Fifth, Sixth, and Eighth Amendments were pointedly aimed at confining exercise of power by courts and judges within precise boundaries, particularly in the procedure used for the trial of criminal cases. Past history provided strong reasons for the apprehensions which brought these procedural amendments into being and attest the wisdom of their adoption. For the fears of arbitrary court action sprang largely from the past use of courts in the imposition of criminal punishments to suppress speech, press, and religion. Hence the constitutional limitations of courts' powers were, in the view of the Founders, essential supplements to the First Amendment, which was itself designed to protect the widest scope for all people to believe and to express the most divergent political, religious, and other views.

But these limitations were not expressly imposed upon state court action. In 1833, *Barron* v. *Baltimore, supra,* was decided by this Court. It specifically held inapplicable to the states that provision of the Fifth Amendment which declares: "nor shall private property be taken for public use, without just compensation." In deciding the particular point raised, the Court there said that it could not hold that the first eight amendments applied to the states. This was the control-ling constitutional rule when the Fourteenth Amendment was proposed in 1866.

My study of the historical events that culminated in the Fourteenth Amend-ment, and the expressions of those who sponsored and favored, as well as those who opposed its submission and passage, persuades me that one of the chief objects that the provisions of the Amendment's first section, separately, and as a whole, were intended to accomplish was to make the Bill of Rights, applicable to the states. With full knowledge of the import of the *Barron* decision, the framers and backers of the Fourteenth Amendment proclaimed its purpose to be to overturn the constitutional rule that case had announced. This historical pur-pose has never received full consideration or exposition in any opinion of this Court interpreting the Amendment. . . .

Investigation of the cases relied upon in *Twining* v. *New Jersey* to support the conclusion there reached that neither the Fifth Amendment's prohibition of compelled testimony, nor any of the Bill of Rights, applies to the States, reveals an unexplained departure from this salutary practice. Neither the briefs nor opinions in any of these cases, except *Maxwell* v. *Dow,* 176 U.S. 581, make reference to the legislative and contemporary history for the purpose of demonstrating that those who conceived, shaped, and brought about the adoption of the Fourteenth Amendment intended it to nullify this Court's decision in *Barron* v. *Baltimore, supra,* and thereby to make the Bill of Rights applicable to the States. In *Maxwell* v. *Dow, supra,* the issue turned on whether the Bill of Rights guarantee of a jury trial was, by the Fourteenth Amendment, extended to trials in state courts. In that case counsel for appellant did cite from the speech of Senator Howard, Appendix, *infra,* p. 104, which so emphatically stated the understanding of the framers of the Amendment — the Committee on Reconstruction for which he spoke — that the Bill of Rights was to be made applicable to the states by the Amendment's first section. The Court's opinion in *Maxwell* v. *Dow, supra,* 601, acknowledged that counsel had "cited from the speech of one of the Senators," but indicated that it was not advised what other speeches were made in the Senate or in the House. The Court considered, moreover, that "What individual Senators or Representatives may have urged in debate, in regard to the meaning to be given to a proposed constitutional amendment, or bill or resolution, does not furnish a firm ground for its proper construction, nor is it important as explanatory of the grounds upon which the members voted in adopting it." . . .

In the *Twining* case itself, the Court was cited to a then recent book, Guthrie, Fourteenth Amendment to the Constitution (1898). A few pages of that work recited some of the legislative background of the Amendment, emphasizing the speech of Senator Howard. But Guthrie did not emphasize the speeches of Congressman Bingham, nor the part he played in the framing and adoption of the first section of the Fourteenth Amendment. Yet Congressman Bingham may, without extravagance, be called the Madison of the first section of the Fourteenth Amendment. In the *Twining* opinion, the Court explicitly declined to give weight to the historical demonstration that the first section of the Amendment was intended to apply to the states the several protections of the Bill of Rights. It held that that question was "no longer open" because of previous decisions of this Court which, however, had not appraised the historical evidence on that subject. . . . The Court admitted that its action had resulted in giving "much less effect to the Fourteenth Amendment than some of the public men active in framing it" had intended it to have. . . . With particular reference to the guarantee against compelled testimony, the Court stated that "Much might be said in favor of the view that the privilege was guaranteed against state impairment as a privilege and immunity of National citizenship, but, as has been shown, the decisions of this court have foreclosed that view.". . . Thus the Court declined, and again today declines, to appraise the relevant historical evidence of the intended scope of the first section of the Amendment. Instead it relied upon previous cases, none of which had analyzed the evidence showing that one purpose of those who framed, advocated, and adopted the Amendment had been to make the Bill of Rights applicable to the States. None of the cases relied upon by the Court today made such an analysis.

For this reason, I am attaching to this dissent an appendix which contains a résumé, by no means complete, of the Amendment's history. In my judgment that history conclusively demonstrates that the language of the first section of the Fourteenth Amendment, taken as a whole, was thought by those responsible for its submission to the people, and by those who opposed its submission, sufficiently explicit to guarantee that thereafter no state could deprive its citizens of the privileges and protections of the Bill of Rights. Whether this Court ever will, or whether it now should, in the light of past decisions, give full effect to what the Amendment was intended to accomplish is not necessarily essential to a decision here. However that may be, our prior decisions, including *Twining,* do not prevent our carrying out that purpose, at least to the extent of making applicable to the states, not a mere part, as the Court has, but the full protection of the Fifth Amendment's provision against compelling evidence from an ac- cused to convict him of crime. And I further contend that the "natural law" formula which the Court uses to reach its conclusion in this case should be abandoned as an incongruous excrescence on our Constitution. I believe that formula to be itself a violation of our Constitution, in that it subtly conveys to courts, at the expense of legislatures, ultimate power over public policies in fields where no specific provision of the Constitution limits legislative power. And my belief seems to be in accord with the views expressed by this Court, at least for the first two decades after the Fourteenth Amendment was adopted. . . .

Malloy v. Hogan, 378 U.S. 1 (1964)

Both *Twining* and *Adamson* were overruled in 1964 by the Supreme Court in still another 5–4 decision, *Malloy* v. *Hogan.* Speaking for the slim majority of the Warren Court, Justice Brennan addressed himself directly to the incon- gruity of the double standard in criminal justice procedures that had pre- vailed since *Twining,* immunity from self-incrimination in a federal court, no such immunity in a state court. Why should there be "different standards," Brennan asked, to determine the "validity of a claim of privilege depending on whether the claim was asserted in a state or federal court?" The majority clearly believed there should be no such differing standards. By so ruling, the Court incorporated the Fifth Amendment guarantee into the due process clause of the Fourteenth Amendment.

However not without two sharply worded dissenting opinions, one by Jus- tice Harlan, joined by Justice Clark, the other by Justice White joined by Justice Stewart. Harlan, who would be the Warren Court's leading spokesman against incorporation of the Bill of Rights, made the following point: "I accept and agree with the proposition that continuing re-examination of the con- stitutional conception of Fourteenth Amendment's 'due process' of law is required and that development of the community's sense of justice may in time lead to expansion of the protection which due process affords." Harlan went on to say that "principles of justice to which due process give expression . . . prohibit a State, as the Fifth Amendment prohibits the Federal govern- ment, from imprisoning a person *solely* because he refuses to give evidence which may incriminate him under the laws of the State. I do not understand, however, how this process of re-examination . . . can be short-circuited by the simple denial of incorporating into due process, without critical examination, the whole body of law which surrounds a specific prohibition directed against the Federal government." The consequence of this approach to due process, as it applies to the states, Harlan concluded, "inevitably disregard[s] all rele- vant differences which may exist between state and federal criminal law and its enforcement. The ultimate result is compelled uniformity, which is incon- sistent with the purpose of our federal system and which is achieved either by encroachment on the states' sovereign powers or by dilution in federal law enforcement of the specific protections found in the Bill of Rights."[1]

Justice White also objected to the court's decision overruling *Twining* and *Adamson*. White argued that a witness' claim of the immunity privilege is not final, "for the privilege qualifies a citizen's general duty of disclosure only when his answers would subject him to danger from the criminal law." Protection against self-incrimination, White insisted, "does not protect silence which is solely an expression of political protest, a desire not to inform, a fear of social obloquy or economic disadvantage or fear of prosecution for future crimes." White chided the Court for making the immunity privilege automatic "and without more, accepted." "I prefer," White said, "the rule permitting the judge rather than the witness to determine when an answer sought is incriminating."[2]

Evidence in *Hogan* showed that the petitioner was arrested during a gambling raid in 1959 by Hartford, Connecticut police officers. He pleaded guilty to a misdemeanor and was sentenced to one year in jail. The sentence was ordered suspended after 90 days. Some 16 months after his guilty plea, Hogan was ordered to testify before a Superior Court regarding alleged gambling and other criminal activity in the county. Hogan refused to answer questions, pleading protection against self-incrimination. Relying on *Twining* and *Adamson,* Connecticut's Supreme Court ruled that the Fifth Amendment guarantee against self-incrimination did not apply to the states.

A slim majority of the Supreme Court reversed this ruling. By so doing the Warren Court overturned both *Twining* and *Adamson* and established *one* self-incrimination standard applicable in both federal and state courts.

Mr. Justice Brennan delivered the opinion of the Court, saying in part:

> The Court has not hesitated to re-examine past decisions according the Fourteenth Amendment a less central role in the preservation of basic liberties than that which was contemplated by its Framers when they added the Amendment to our constitutional scheme. Thus, although the Court as late as 1922 said that "neither the Fourteenth Amendment nor any other provision of the Constitution of the United States imposes upon the States any restrictions about 'freedom of speech'. . . ." . . . three years later *Gitlow* v. *New York,* 268 U.S. 652, initiated a series of decisions which today hold immune from state invasion every First Amendment protection for the cherished rights of mind and spirit — the freedoms of speech, press, religion, assembly, association, and petition for redress of grievances.
>
> Similarly, *Palko* v. *Connecticut,* 302 U.S. 319, decided in 1937, suggested that the rights secured by the Fourth Amendment were not protected against state action, citing, 302 U.S., at 324, the statement of the Court in 1914 in *Weeks* v. *United States,* 232 U.S. 383, 398, that "the Fourth Amendment is not directed to individual misconduct of [state] officials." In 1961, however, the Court held that in the light of later decisions, it was taken as settled that ". . . the Fourth Amendment's right of privacy has been declared enforceable against the States through the Due Process Clause of the Fourteenth. . . ." . . . Again, although the Court held in 1942 that in a state prosecution for a noncapital offense, "appointment of counsel is not a fundamental right," . . . only last Term this decision was re-examined and it was held that provision of counsel in all criminal cases was "a fundamental right, essential to a fair trial," and thus was made obligatory on the States by the Fourteenth Amendment. . . .

1. 378 U.S. at 15–17.
2. Ibid., at 33.

We hold today that the Fifth Amendment's exception from compulsory self-incrimination is also protected by the Fourteenth Amendment against abridgment by the States. Decisions of the Court since *Twining* and *Adamson* have departed from the contrary view expressed in those cases. . . .

. . . The shift reflects recognition that the American system of criminal prosecution is accusatorial, not inquisitorial, and that the Fifth Amendment privilege is its essential mainstay. . . . Governments, state and federal, are thus constitutionally compelled to establish guilt by evidence independently and freely secured, and may not by coercion prove a charge against an accused out of his own mouth. Since the Fourteenth Amendment prohibits the States from inducing a person to confess through "sympathy falsely aroused," . . . or other like inducement far short of "compulsion by torture," . . . it follows *a fortiori* that it also forbids the States to resort to imprisonment, as here, to compel him to answer questions that might incriminate him. The Fourteenth Amendment secures against state invasion the same privilege that the Fifth Amendment guarantees against federal infringement — the right of a person to remain silent unless he chooses to speak in the unfettered exercise of his own will, and to suffer no penalty, as held in *Twining,* for such silence.

This conclusion is fortified by our recent decision in *Mapp* v. *Ohio,* 367 U.S. 643, overruling *Wolf* v. *Colorado,* 338 U.S. 25, which had held "that in a prosecution in a State court for a State crime the Fourteenth Amendment does not forbid the admission of evidence obtained by an unreasonable search and seizure," . . . . *Mapp* held that the Fifth Amendment privilege against self-incrimination implemented the Fourth Amendment in such cases, and that the two guarantees of personal security conjoined in the Fourteenth Amendment to make the exclusionary rule obligatory upon the States. We relied upon the great case of *Boyd* v. *United States,* 116 U.S. 616, decided in 1886, which, considering the Fourth and Fifth Amendments as running "almost into each other," . . . held that "Breaking into a house and opening boxes and drawers are circumstances of aggravation; but any forcible and compulsory extortion of a man's own testimony or of his private papers to be used as evidence to convict him of crime or to forfeit his goods, is within the condemnation of [those Amendments]. . . ." . . . We said in *Mapp:*

> "We find that, as to the Federal Government, the Fourth and Fifth Amendments and, as to the States, the freedom from unconscionable invasions of privacy and the freedom from convictions based upon coerced confessions do enjoy an 'intimate relation' in their perpetuation of 'principles of humanity and civil liberty [secured] . . . only after years of struggle,' *Bram* v. *United States,* 168 U.S. 532, 543–544. . . . The philosophy of each Amendment and of each freedom is complementary to, although not dependent upon, that of the other in its sphere of influence — the very least that together they assure in either sphere is that no man is to be convicted on unconstitutional evidence." . . .

In thus returning to the *Boyd* view that the privilege is one of the "principles of a free government," . . . *Mapp* necessarily repudiated the *Twining* concept of the privilege as a mere rule of evidence "best defended not as an unchangeable principle of universal justice but as a law proved by experience to be expedient." . . .

The State of Connecticut argues that the Connecticut courts properly applied the federal standards to the facts of this case. We disagree.

The investigation in the course of which petitioner was questioned began when the Superior Court in Hartford County appointed the Honorable Ernest

A. Inglis, formerly Chief Justice of Connecticut, to conduct an inquiry into whether there was reasonable cause to believe that crimes, including gambling, were being committed in Hartford County. Petitioner appeared on January 16 and 25, 1961, and in both instances he was asked substantially the same questions about the circumstances surrounding his arrest and conviction for pool selling in late 1959. The questions which petitioner refused to answer may be summarized as follows: (1) for whom did he work on September 11, 1959; (2) who selected and paid his counsel in connection with his arrest on that date and subsequent conviction; (3) who selected and paid his bondsman; (4) who paid his fine; (5) what was the name of the tenant of the apartment in which he was arrested; and (6) did he know John Bergoti. The Connecticut Supreme Court of Errors ruled that the answers to these questions could not tend to incriminate him because the defenses of double jeopardy and the running of the one-year statute of limitations on misdemeanors would defeat any prosecution growing out of his answers to the first five questions. As for the sixth question, the court held that petitioner's failure to explain how a revelation of his relationship with Bergoti would incriminate him vitiated his claim to the protection of the privilege afforded by state law.

The conclusions of the Court of Errors, tested by the federal standard, fail to take sufficient account of the setting in which the questions were asked. The interrogation was part of a wide-ranging inquiry into crime, including gambling, in Hartford. It was admitted on behalf of the State at oral argument — and indeed it is obvious from the questions themselves — that the State desired to elicit from the petitioner the identity of the person who ran the pool-selling operation in connection with which he had been arrested in 1959. It was apparent that petitioner might apprehend that if this person were still engaged in unlawful activity, disclosure of his name might furnish a link in a chain of evidence sufficient to connect the petitioner with a more recent crime for which he might still be prosecuted.

Analysis of the sixth question, concerning whether petitioner knew John Bergoti, yields a similar conclusion. In the context of the inquiry, it should have been apparent to the referee that Bergoti was suspected by the State to be involved in some way in the subject matter of the investigation. An affirmative answer to the question might well have either connected petitioner with a more recent crime, or at least have operated as a waiver of his privilege with reference to his relationship with a possible criminal. . . . We conclude, therefore, that as to each of the questions, it was "evident from the implications of the question, in the setting in which it [was] asked, that a responsive answer to the question or an explanation of why it [could not] be answered might be dangerous because injurious disclosure could result."

2

COERCION

Law enforcement practices that have compelled prisoners either by physical torture, psychological pressure or both into signing confessions have also run afoul of the Fifth Amendment's protection against self-incrimination. In recent years the Supreme Court has consistently reversed conviction in state courts where it found that a confession signed under some extreme form of physical or mental duress had been used as evidence to obtain a guilty verdict.

Brown v. Mississippi, 297 U.S. 278 (1936)

Brown v. *Mississippi* is the first significant case in point. There a unanimous Court, speaking through Chief Justice Hughes, reversed a murder conviction that rested solely upon confessions shown to have been extorted by police officers by torture and brutality. The Court ruled that such police tactics violated that sense of fairness and justice inherent in the due process clause of the Fourteenth Amendment. A Mississippi Court had decided that immunity from self-incrimination is not essential to due process to law.

Disagreeing with this judgment, the Supreme Court ruled that although a state is free to regulate the procedure of its courts in accordance with its own conceptions of policy, it may not offend "some principles of justice so rooted in the traditions and conscience of our people as to be ranked as fundamental." Chief Justice Hughes went on to say that "freedom of the State in establishing its policy is the freedom of constitutional government and is limited by the requirement of due process of law. Because a state may dispense with a jury trial, it does not follow that it may substitute trial by ordeal. The rack and torture chamber may not be substituted for the witness stand."

And from the record in *Brown* there was abundant, uncontroverted evidence that Mississippi police had indeed used "rack and torture chamber" tactics to coerce appellant into confessing. Brown was whipped repeatedly and hung from a tree several times. He suffered "intense pain and agony." Sheriff's deputies told Brown they would continue whipping him until he confessed. Brown finally broke down and signed a confession a Sheriff's deputy dictated. Chief Justice Hughes quoted from the record, which indicated that the facts were "not only disputed, they [were] admitted, and admitted to have been done by officers of the state . . . and all this was definitely well-known to everybody connected with the trial . . . including the state's prosecuting attorney and the trial judge presiding." A unanimous Supreme Court reversed Brown's conviction.

Mr. Chief Justice Hughes delivered the opinion of the Court, saying in part:

The State may not permit an accused to be hurried to conviction under mob domination — where the whole proceeding is but a mask — without supplying corrective process. . . . The State may not deny to the accused the aid of counsel. . . . Nor may a State, through the action of its officers, contrive a conviction through the pretense of a trial which in truth is "but used as a means of depriving a defendant of liberty through a deliberate deception of court and jury by the presentation of testimony known to be perjured." . . . And the trial equally is a mere pretense where the state authorities have contrived a conviction resting solely upon confessions obtained by violence. The due process clause requires "that state action, whether through one agency or another, shall be consistent with the fundamental principles of liberty and justice which lie at the base of all our civil and political institutions.". . . It would be difficult to conceive of methods more revolting to the sense of justice than those taken to procure the confessions of these petitioners, and the use of the confessions thus obtained as the basis for conviction and sentence was a clear denial of due process. . . .

In the instant case, the trial court was fully advised by the undisputed evidence of the way in which the confessions had been procured. The trial court knew that there was no other evidence upon which conviction and sentence could be based. Yet it proceeded to permit conviction and to pronounce sentence. The conviction and sentence were void for want of the essential elements of due process, and the proceeding thus vitiated could be challenged in any appropriate manner. . . . It was challenged before the Supreme Court of the State by the express invocation of the Fourteenth Amendment. That court entertained the challenge, considered the federal question thus presented, but declined to enforce petitioners' constitutional right. The court thus denied a federal right fully established and specially set up and claimed and the judgment must be

Reversed.

Chambers v. Florida, 309 U.S. 227 (1940)

Four years after *Brown*, in a similar ruling, a unanimous Supreme Court once again reversed a murder conviction in a state court which, the Court found, had been based upon confessions obtained by "repeated inquisitions of prisoners without friends or counsellors present, and under circumstances calculated to inspire terror." The case was *Chambers v. Florida*. Justice Black spoke for his unanimous colleagues and ruled that Florida had denied appellant his right to a fair trial under the Fourteenth Amendment's due process clause.

The record in *Chambers* indicated a "most dastardly and atrocious crime," the robbery and murder of an elderly man in Pompano, Florida. Within twenty-four hours after the crime, from twenty-five to forty black men (including the petitioner, Chambers) had been arrested and jailed without warrants. Chambers and the others were questioned for hours, singly, alone in a room with up to ten men including the County Sheriff and deputies. There was (disputed) evidence that Chambers had been beaten. After one week of constantly denying all guilt, petitioner broke down and confessed. His conviction rested upon his confession and testimony of three other confessors who had also broken down under similar circumstances. Once again the Supreme

Court reversed a state court's conviction on grounds that a coerced confession had been unconstitutionally extorted and improperly used at the trial in violation of due process of law.

Mr. Justice Black delivered the opinion of the Court, saying in part:

The scope and operation of the Fourteenth Amendment have been fruitful sources of controversy in our constitutional history. However, in view of its historical setting and the wrongs which called it into being, the due process provision of the Fourteenth Amendment — just as that in the Fifth — has led few to doubt that it was intended to guarantee procedural standards adequate and appropriate, then and thereafter, to protect, at all times, people charged with or suspected of crime by those holding positions of power and authority. Tyrannical governments had immemorially utilized dictatorial criminal procedure and punishment to make scapegoats of the weak, or of helpless political, religious, or racial minorities and those who differed, who would not conform and who resisted tyranny. The instruments of such governments were, in the main, two. Conduct, innocent when engaged in, was subsequently made by fiat criminally punishable without legislation. And a liberty loving people won the principle that criminal punishments could not be inflicted save for that which proper legislative action had already by "the law of the land" forbidden when done. But even more was needed. From the popular hatred and abhorrence of illegal confinement, torture and extortion of confessions of violations of the "law of the land" evolved the fundamental idea that no man's life, liberty or property be forfeited as criminal punishment for violation of that law until there had been a charge fairly made and fairly tried in a public tribunal free of prejudice, passion, excitement, and tyrannical power. Thus, as assurance against ancient evils, our country, in order to preserve "the blessings of liberty," wrote into its basic law the requirement, among others, that the forfeiture of the lives, liberties or property of people accused of crime can only follow if procedural safeguards of due process have been obeyed.

The determination to preserve an accused's right to procedural due process sprang in large part from knowledge of the historical truth that the rights and liberties of people accused of crime could not be safely entrusted to secret inquisitorial processes. The testimony of centuries, in governments of varying kinds over populations of different races and beliefs, stood as proof that physical and mental torture and coercion had brought about the tragically unjust sacrifices of some who were the noblest and most useful of their generations. The rack, the thumbscrew, the wheel, solitary confinement, protracted questioning and cross questioning, and other ingenious forms of entrapment of the helpless or unpopular had left their wake of mutilated bodies and shattered minds along the way to the cross, the guillotine, the stake and the hangman's noose. And they who have suffered most from secret and dictatorial proceedings have almost always been the poor, the ignorant, the numerically weak, the friendless, and the powerless.

This requirement — of conforming to fundamental standards of procedure in criminal trials — was made operative against the States by the Fourteenth Amendment. Where one of several accused had limped into the trial court as a result of admitted physical mistreatment inflicted to obtain confessions upon which a jury had returned a verdict of guilty of murder, this Court recently declared, *Brown* v. *Mississippi*, that "It would be difficult to conceive of methods more revolting to the sense of justice than those taken to procure the confessions of these petitioners, and the use of the confessions thus obtained as the basis for conviction and sentence was a clear denial of due process."

Here, the record develops a sharp conflict upon the issue of physical violence and mistreatment, but shows, without conflict, the dragnet methods of arrest on suspicion without warrant, and the protracted questioning and cross questioning of these ignorant young colored tenant farmers by state officers and other white citizens, in a fourth floor jail room, where as prisoners they were without friends, advisers or counselors, and under circumstances calculated to break the strongest nerves and the stoutest resistance. Just as our decision in *Brown* v. *Mississippi* was based upon the fact that the confessions were the result of compulsion, so in the present case, the admitted practices were such as to justify the statement that "The undisputed facts showed that compulsion was applied." . . .

We are not impressed by the argument that law enforcement methods such as those under review are necessary to uphold our laws. The Constitution proscribes such lawless means irrespective of the end. And this argument flouts the basic principle that all people must stand on an equality before the bar of justice in every American court. Today, as in ages past, we are not without tragic proof that the exalted power of some governments to punish manufactured crime dictatorially is the handmaid of tyranny. Under our constitutional system, courts stand against any winds that blow as havens of refuge for those who might otherwise suffer because they are helpless, weak, outnumbered, or because they are non-conforming victims of prejudice and public excitement. Due process of law, preserved for all by our Constitution, commands that no such practice as that disclosed by this record shall send any accused to his death. No higher duty, no more solemn responsibility, rests upon this Court, than that of translating into living law and maintaining this constitutional shield deliberately planned and inscribed for the benefit of every human being subject to our Constitution — of whatever race, creed or persuasion.

Ashcraft v. Tennessee, 322 U.S. 143 (1943)

"Psychological coercion" was the issue in *Ashcraft* v. *Tennessee*. There the Roosevelt Court reversed a murder conviction obtained in a state court that had been based upon the appellant's confession after thirty-six hours of constant grilling by teams of police officers and investigators. Whereas in *Brown* and *Chambers* the Supreme Court had been unanimous, in *Ashcraft* the Court was split. Justice Black, who became the Court's leading spokesman for procedural fairness, wrote for the majority of six. Justice Jackson, joined by Justices Frankfurter and Roberts, wrote a long dissenting opinion. The majority ruled that because Ashcraft had been held incommunicado for thirty-six hours, interrogated without sleep, rest, or counsel, his subsequent confession was "inherently coerced" and could not be used as evidence against him. Accordingly, the Court reversed Ashcraft's conviction, ruling that state law enforcement officers had violated his rights under the Federal Constitution.

Justice Jackson took sharp exception to the majority position. "The Court," Jackson said, "bases its decision on the premise that custody and examination of a prisoner for thirty-six hours is 'inherently coercive'; of course it is." Jackson then noted that "arrest *itself* is inherently coercive, and so is detention." But, Jackson asked, "does the Constitution prohibit use of all confessions made after arrest because questioning, while one is deprived of freedom is 'inherently coercive.'" Admitting that the Court did not go that far in

Ashcraft, Jackson nevertheless accused it of "moving far and fast in that direction."[1]

As evidenced by *Ashcraft,* there certainly was no unanimity during the late 1940s among the Roosevelt appointees to the Court concerning the admissibility of coerced confessions. In addition to *Ashcraft* the issue arose in at least five other similar disputes. [2] In each, the Court overturned state court convictions where a coerced confession had formed the basis for the guilty verdict. But in each it was badly divided (5–4). Justices Black, Douglas, Murphy, Rutledge, and Chief Justice Stone usually made up the majority while Justices Frankfurter, Jackson, Reed, and Roberts usually were the dissenters.

In *Ashcraft* the record disclosed that Mrs. Zelma Ashcraft, wife of the petitioner, was found murdered in her automobile. The petitioner was charged with having hired a young man to murder his wife. Both were tried and found guilty. Ashcraft argued, in vain at the state court level, that the confession used to convict him had been extorted from him by law enforcement officials after hours of constant grilling and coercion. In its review of the record the Supreme Court found that Ashcraft was "a citizen of excellent reputation." Ten days questioning by local officers of the Ashcraft family maid and others revealed nothing damaging about him, his reputation or his character. When Ashcraft was arrested, he denied repeatedly under questioning that he had anything to do with his wife's murder. Then, after thirty-six hours of this "psychological coercion," Ashcraft confessed. He was later found guilty with the confession used as evidence against him. The Supreme Court reversed the conviction.

Mr. Justice Black delivered the opinion of the Court, saying in part:

> Our conclusion is that if Ashcraft made a confession it was not voluntary but compelled. . . .
> We think a situation such as that here shown by uncontradicted evidence is so inherently coercive that its very existence is irreconcilable with the possession of mental freedom by a lone suspect against whom its full coercive force is brought to bear. It is inconceivable that any court of justice in the land, conducted as our courts are, open to the public, would permit prosecutors serving in relays to keep a defendant witness under continuous cross-examination for thirty-six hours without rest or sleep in an effort to extract a "voluntary" confession. Nor can we, consistently with Constitutional due process of law, hold voluntary a confession where prosecutors do the same thing away from the restraining influences of a public trial in an open court room.
> The Constitution of the United States stands as a bar against the conviction of any individual in an American court by means of a coerced confession. There have been, and are now, certain foreign nations with governments dedicated to an opposite policy: governments which convict individuals with testimony obtained by police organizations possessed of an unrestrained power to seize persons suspected of crimes against the state, hold them in secret custody, and wring from them confessions by physical or mental torture. So long as the Constitution remains the basic law of our Republic, America will not have that kind of government. . . .

1. 322 U.S. at 161.

2. See for example: *Malinski* v. *New York* 324 U.S. 401 (1945); *Haley* v. *Ohio* 332 U.S. 596 (1948); *Watts* v. *Indiana* 338 U.S. 68 (1949); *Turner* v. *Pennsylvania* 338 U.S. 62 (1949); *Harris* v. *South* 338 U.S. 49 (1949).

3

WITHOUT UNNECESSARY DELAY

McNabb v. United States, 318 U.S. 332 (1943)

Two significant Supreme Court decisions, fourteen years apart, also involving the inadmissibility of coerced confessions, dealt with a unique provision of federal law. The statute in question specified that suspects thought to have violated federal law must be taken to a federal judge or a United States Commissioner "without unnecessary delay" for a hearing, a committment, or a release on bail *before* interrogation by federal officers could take place. The controlling decision concerning this provision was *McNabb* v. *United States* (1943), which, despite the expected and predictable outcry by law enforcement officials that the Court's ruling for the defendant had placed unnecessary restraints on police officers, was once again reaffirmed by the Court in *Mallory* v. *United States.* [1]

Evidence in both *McNabb* and *Mallory* led the Court to conclude that federal law enforcement officers had often interpreted the phrase "without unnecessary delay" as loosely as possible in order to extract confessions from suspects before their appearance before a federal official and before counsel for the suspect was present. [2] In *McNabb,* for example, the record indicated that officers of the federal government's Alcohol Tax unit in Chattanooga, Tennessee had interrogated five male members of the McNabb clan, all simple, under-educated "mountain people" singly for up to five or six hours concerning the murder of a federal revenue agent. Three of the five McNabb's confessed. They were subsequently convicted in a federal court on the basis of these confessions. With only Justice Reed in dissent, the Supreme Court reversed the convictions. Justice Frankfurter spoke for the majority of seven (Justice Rutledge did not participate).

Fourteen years later, in the *Mallory* decision, the Supreme Court invalidated a death sentence for rape on much the same grounds as the reversal in *McNabb;* the "without unnecessary delay" provisions of the law had been violated by police officers, this time in Washington, D.C. *Mallory* touched off an uproar in Congress. The crime had taken place almost literally in Con-

1. 354 U.S. 449 (1957).

2. Pritchett makes this point, op. cit., at 448.

gress's backyard. Eventually, in 1967, Congress modified federal law to circumvent the *McNabb-Mallory* rule. The modifications allowed police officers in the District of Columbia to detain and interrogate suspects for up to three hours before the required appearance. Yet *McNabb* and *Mallory* have some significance as examples of judicial concern for proper procedural safeguards lest constitutional guarantees be lost to the zealots of law and order.

Mr. Justice Frankfurter delivered the opinion of the Court, saying in part:

> The circumstances in which the statements admitted in evidence against the petitioners were secured reveal a plain disregard of the duty enjoined by Congress upon federal law officers. Freeman and Raymond McNabb were arrested in the middle of the night at their home. Instead of being brought before a United States commissioner or a judicial officer, as the law requires, in order to determine the sufficiency of the justification for their detention, they were put in a barren cell and kept there for fourteen hours. For two days they were subjected to unremitting questioning by numerous officers. Benjamin's confession was secured by detaining him unlawfully and questioning him continuously for five or six hours. The McNabbs had to submit to all this without the aid of friends or the benefit of counsel. The record leaves no room for doubt that the questioning of the petitioners took place while they were in the custody of the arresting officers and before any order of commitment was made. Plainly, a conviction resting on evidence secured through such a flagrant disregard of the procedure which Congress has commanded cannot be allowed to stand without making the courts themselves accomplices in willful disobedience of law. Congress has not explicitly forbidden the use of evidence so procured. But to permit such evidence to be made the basis of a conviction in the federal courts would stultify the policy which Congress has enacted into law.
>
> Unlike England, where the Judges of the King's Bench have prescribed rules for the interrogation of prisoners while in the custody of police officers, we have no specific provisions of law governing federal law enforcement officers in procuring evidence from persons held in custody. But the absence of specific restraints going beyond the legislation to which we have referred does not imply that the circumstances under which evidence was secured are irrelevant in ascertaining its admissibility. The mere fact that a confession was made while in the custody of the police does not render it inadmissible. . . . But where in the course of a criminal trial in the federal courts it appears that evidence has been obtained in such violation of legal rights as this case discloses, it is the duty of the trial court to entertain a motion for the exclusion of such evidence and to hold a hearing, as was done here, to determine whether such motion should be granted or denied. . . . The interruption of the trial for this purpose should be no longer than is required for a competent determination of the substantiality of the motion. As was observed in the *Nardone* case, *supra,* "The civilized conduct of criminal trials cannot be confined within mechanical rules. It necessarily demands the authority of limited direction entrusted to the judge presiding in federal trials, including a well-established range of judicial discretion, subject to appropriate review on appeal, in ruling upon preliminary questions of fact. Such a system as ours must, within the limits here indicated, rely on the learning, good sense, fairness and courage of federal trial judges."
>
> In holding that the petitioners' admissions were improperly received in evidence against them, and that having been based on this evidence their convictions cannot stand, we confine ourselves to our limited function as the court of ultimate review of the standards formulated and applied by federal courts in the

trial of criminal cases. We are not concerned with law enforcement practices except in so far as courts themselves become instruments of law enforcement. We hold only that a decent regard for the duty of courts as agencies of justice and custodians of liberty forbids that men should be convicted upon evidence secured under the circumstances revealed here. In so doing, we respect the policy which underlies Congressional legislation. The history of liberty has largely been the history of observance of procedural safeguards. And the effective administration of criminal justice hardly requires disregard of fair procedures imposed by law.

4

DOUBLE JEOPARDY

Palko v. Connecticut, 302 U.S. 319 (1937)

In addition to enforcing state compliance with the Fifth Amendment's guarantee against self-incrimination by eventually incorporating it under the Fourteenth, the Supreme Court had two occasions to decide if the Fifth Amendment's double jeopardy clause also applied to the states via the Fourteenth. In *Palko* v. *Connecticut* the Court ruled it did not. Thirty-two years later in *Benton* v. *Maryland* (1969) the Warren Court overruled *Palko* and answered yes.

In the process the Warren Court virtually completed the incorporation of virtually all the civil liberty guarantees of the Bill of Rights into the Fourteenth Amendment. The incorporation controversy had plagued the Supreme Court for some sixty years, dating back, as we have seen, to the *Twining* and *Gitlow* decisions of 1908 and 1925.

In *Palko,* writing for the majority, Justice Cardozo, certainly one of the Court's most respected legal scholars, agreed that First Amendment freedoms, he called them "the matrix . . . the indispensible condition . . . ," have been absorbed through *Gitlow* into the Fourteenth Amendment. First Amendment guarantees are on a "different plane of social and moral values," Cardozo said. Neither he nor the Court could agree, however, that the Fifth Amendment's double jeopardy clause belonged on that same high "plane of moral values."

The defendant in *Palko* had been convicted of second-degree murder in a Connecticut court and sentenced to life in prison. Finding there had been an error prejudicial to the state in the first trial, the Connecticut Supreme Court granted the state's request for a new trial. At the second trial Palko was convicted of first-degree murder and sentenced to death. Thus the question: Was Palko's second trial a case of double jeopardy prohibited by the Fifth Amendment and applicable to the states via the Fourteenth? With only Justice Butler dissenting, the Supreme Court's majority of eight refused to incorporate the Fifth Amendment's double jeopardy clause and accordingly allowed Palko's second conviction to stand.

Mr. Chief Justice Cardozo delivered the opinion of the Court, saying in part:

The argument for appellant is that whatever is forbidden by the Fifth Amendment is forbidden by the Fourteenth also. The Fifth Amendment, which is not directed to the states, but solely to the federal government, creates immunity from double jeopardy. No person shall be "subject for the same offense to be twice put in jeopardy of life or limb." The Fourteenth Amendment ordains, "nor shall any State deprive any person of life, liberty, or property, without due process of law." To retry a defendant, though under one indictment and only one, subjects him, it is said, to double jeopardy in violation of the Fifth Amendment, if the prosecution is one on behalf of the United States. From this the consequence is said to follow that there is a denial of life or liberty without due process of law, if the prosecution is one on behalf of the People of a State. Thirty-five years ago a like argument was made to this court in *Dreyer* v. *Illinois,* 187 U.S. 71, 85, and was passed without consideration of its merits as unnecessary to a decision. The question is now here. . . .

We have said that in appellant's view the Fourteenth Amendment is to be taken as embodying the prohibitions of the Fifth. His thesis is even broader. Whatever would be a violation of the original bill of rights (Amendments I to VIII) if done by the federal government is now equally unlawful by force of the Fourteenth Amendment if done by a state. There is no such general rule. . . . In these and other situations immunities that are valid as against the federal government by force of the specific pledges of particular amendments have been found to be implicit in the concept of ordered liberty, and thus, through the Fourteenth Amendment, become valid as against the states.

The line of division may seem to be wavering and broken if there is a hasty catalogue of the cases on the one side and the other. Reflection and analysis will induce a different view. There emerges the perception of a rationalizing principle which gives to discrete instances a proper order and coherence. The right to trial by jury and the immunity from prosecution except as the result of an indictment may have value and importance. Even so, they are not of the very essence of a scheme of ordered liberty. To abolish them is not to violate a "principle of justice so rooted in the traditions and conscience of our people as to be ranked as fundamental." . . . Few would be so narrow or provincial as to maintain that a fair and enlightened system of justice would be impossible without them. What is true of jury trials and indictments is true also, as the cases show, of the immunity from compulsory self-incrimination. . . . This too might be lost, and justice still be done. Indeed, today as in the past there are students of our penal system who look upon the immunity as a mischief rather than a benefit, and who would limit its scope, or destroy it altogether. No doubt there would remain the need to give protection against torture, physical or mental. . . . Justice, however, would not perish if the accused were subject to a duty to respond to orderly inquiry. The exclusion of these immunities and privileges from the privileges and immunities protected against the action of the states has not been arbitrary or casual. It has been dictated by a study and appreciation of the meaning, the essential implications, of liberty itself.

We reach a different plane of social and moral values when we pass to the privileges and immunities that have been taken over from the earlier articles of the federal bill of rights and brought within the Fourteenth Amendment by a process of absorption. These in their origin were effective against the federal government alone. If the Fourteenth Amendment has absorbed them, the process of absorption has had its source in the belief that neither liberty nor justice would exist if they were sacrificed. . . . This is true, for illustration, of freedom of thought, and speech. Of that freedom one may say that it is the matrix, the indispensable condition, of nearly every other form of freedom. With rare aberrations a pervasive recognition of that truth can be traced in our history, political and legal. So it has come about that the domain of liberty, withdrawn by the Fourteenth Amendment from encroachment by the states, has been enlarged by latter-day judgments to include liberty of the mind as well as liberty of action. The extension became, indeed, a logical imperative when once it was recognized, as long ago it was, that liberty is something more than exemption from physical restraint, and that even in the field of substantive rights and duties the legislative judgment, if oppressive and arbitrary, may be overridden by the courts. . . .

Our survey of the cases serves, we think, to justify the statement that the dividing line between them, if not unfaltering throughout its course, has been true for the most part to a unifying principle. On which side of the line the case made out by the appellant has appropriate location must be the next inquiry and the final one. Is that kind of double jeopardy to which the statute has subjected him a hardship so acute and shocking that our polity will not endure it? Does it violate those "fundamental principles of liberty and justice which lie at the base of all our civil and political institutions"? . . . The answer surely must be "no." What the answer would have to be if the state were permitted after a trial free from error to try the accused over again or to bring another case against him, we have no occasion to consider. We deal with the statute before us and no other. The state is not attempting to wear the accused out by a multitude of cases with accumulated trials. It asks no more than this, that the case against him shall go on until there shall be a trial free from the corrosion of substantial legal error. . . . This is not cruelty at all, nor even vexation in any immoderate degree. If the trial had been infected with error adverse to the accused, there might have been review at his instance, and as often as necessary to purge the vicious taint. A reciprocal privilege, subject at all times to the discretion of the presiding judge, . . . has now been granted to the state. There is here no seismic innovation. The edifice of justice stands, its symmetry, to many, greater than before.

. . . The conviction of appellant is not in derogation of any privileges or immunities that belong to him as a citizen of the United States.

Benton v. Maryland, 385 U.S. 784 (1969)

Largely through the efforts of Justice Black, the Roosevelt Court of the 1940s had sought, albeit unsuccessfully, to win incorporation of all Bill of Rights guarantees into the Fourteenth Amendment. First Amendment guarantees had been incorporated as far back as the 1925 *Gitlow* decision (above). In 1932 and 1935, in two notorious cases involving the famous "Scottsboro Boys" (*Powell* and *Norris,* below), the Court had refused to incorporate the Sixth Amendment's right to counsel and jury trial provisions. Instead the Court had relied upon what it called an inherent sense of fairness that it said is an integral part of Fourteenth Amendment's due process clause to overrule state court convictions.

We have already examined Justice Black's long historical analysis of incorporation in *Adamson* v. *California* (above) in which, dissenting, he was joined by liberal colleagues Justices Douglas, Murphy, and Rutledge. *Adamson* is perhaps the most significant attempt by Black to carry the Court with him on the incorporation issue. As we have seen, *Adamson* involved the Fifth Amendment's self-incrimination clause, which the narrow majority of five ruled was not incorporated into the Fourteenth Amendment. *Adamson* was overruled in 1964 by *Malloy v. Hogan* (above).

Five years later, as part of what Pritchett called "the incorporationist tide" of the 1960s, the Warren Court also overruled *Palko*. It therefore brought the Fifth Amendment's double jeopardy clause within the umbrella of the Fourteenth Amendment. The case was *Benton v. Maryland*. Justice Marshall spoke for the majority of seven while Justice Harlan joined by Justice Stewart dissented. At issue in *Benton* were two convictions in a Maryland court; one was for burglary but not larceny and the second conviction, following a new indictment and a new trial, occasioned because the jury in Benton's first trial had been selected under an invalid constitutional provision, was for both burglary *and* larceny. The petitioner objected to retrial on the larceny charge, arguing that retrial would violate the Fifth Amendment's double jeopardy clause made applicable to the states by the Fourteenth Amendment. Relying on *Palko*, a Maryland Court of Special Appeals rejected Benton's claim. The Warren Court reversed.

In his dissent, Justice Harlan sharply criticized the Court's departure from *Palko*. Harlan stated that the "selective incorporation doctrine" the Court adopted in *Benton* "finds no support in history or in reason." As he insisted in virtually all incorporation disputes, Harlan would have relied, as earlier courts had, on what he called the concept of fairness inherent in the due process clause of the Fourteenth Amendment to reach a decision. He chided the Court for once again using the incorporation route. "I have no hesitation in stating," Harlan said, "that it would be denial of due process at least for a State to retry one previously acquitted following an errorless trial." Quoting *Palko*, Harlan noted this is "indubitably a 'principle of justice so rooted in the traditions and conscience of our people as to be ranked as fundamental.'"[1] Harlan, long a disciple of precedent and stare decisis, included these words of admonition in his dissent: ". . . that this Court should have apparently become so impervious to the pervasive wisdom of the constitutional philosophy embodied in *Palko,* and that it should have felt itself able to attribute to the perceptive and timeless words of Mr. Justice Cardozo nothing more than a 'watering down' of constitutional rights, are indeed revealing symbols of the extent to which we are weighing anchors from the fundamentals of our constitutional system."[2]

Undismayed by Harlan's biting dissent the majority overruled *Palko*. The Court decided that the Fifth Amendment's double jeopardy provision is "a fundamental ideal in our constitutional heritage" and is therefore enforceable against the states through the Fourteenth Amendment.

Mr. Justice Marshall delivered the opinion of the Court, saying in part:

> After consideration of all the questions before us, we find no bar to our decision of the double jeopardy issue. On the merits, we hold that the Double Jeopardy Clause of the Fifth Amendment is applicable to the States through the Fourteenth Amendment, and we reverse petitioner's conviction for larceny. . . .

1. 395 U.S. at 809–10.
2. Ibid., at 809.

In 1937, this Court decided the landmark case of *Palko* v. *Connecticut,* 302 U.S. 319. Palko, although indicted for first-degree murder, had been convicted of murder in the second degree after a jury trial in a Connecticut state court. The State appealed and won a new trial. Palko argued that the Fourteenth Amendment incorporated, as against the States, the Fifth Amendment requirement that no person "be subject for the same offence to be twice put in jeopardy of life or limb." The Court disagreed. Federal double jeopardy standards were not applicable against the States. Only when a kind of jeopardy subjected a defendant to "a hardship so acute and shocking that our polity will not endure it," . . . did the Fourteenth Amendment apply. The order for a new trial was affirmed. In subsequent appeals from state courts, the Court continued to apply this lesser *Palko* standard. . . .

Recently, however, this Court has "increasingly looked to the specific guarantees of the [Bill of Rights] to determine whether a state criminal trial was conducted with due process of law." . . . In an increasing number of cases, the Court "has rejected the notion that the Fourteenth Amendment applies to the States only a 'watered-down, subjective version of the individual guarantees of the Bill of Rights. . . .'" . . . Only last Term we found that the right to trial by jury in criminal cases was "fundamental to the American scheme of justice," . . . and held that the Sixth Amendment right to a jury trial was applicable to the States through the Fourteenth Amendment. For the same reasons, we today find that the double jeopardy prohibition of the Fifth Amendment represents a fundamental ideal in our constitutional heritage, and that it should apply to the States through the Fourteenth Amendment. Insofar as it is inconsistent with this holding, *Palko* v. *Connecticut* is overruled.

Palko represented an approach to basic constitutional rights which this Court's recent decisions have rejected. It was cut of the same cloth as *Betts* v. *Brady,* 316 U.S. 455 (1942), the case which held that a criminal defendant's right to counsel was to be determined by deciding in each case whether the denial of that right was "shocking to the universal sense of justice." . . . It relied upon *Twining* v. *New Jersey,* 211 U.S. 78 (1908), which held that the right against compulsory self-incrimination was not an element of Fourteenth Amendment due process. *Betts* was overruled by *Gideon* v. *Wainwright,* 372 U.S. 335 (1963); *Twining,* by *Malloy* v. *Hogan,* 378 U.S. 1 (1964). Our recent cases have thoroughly rejected the *Palko* notion that basic constitutional rights can be denied by the States as long as the totality of the circumstances does not disclose a denial of "fundamental fairness." Once it is decided that a particular Bill of Rights guarantee is "fundamental to the American scheme of justice," . . . the same constitutional standards apply against both the State and Federal Governments. *Palko*'s roots had thus been cut away years ago. We today only recognize the inevitable.

IV

THE SIXTH
AMENDMENT

"In all criminal prosecutions the accused shall enjoy the right to a speedy and public trial, by an impartial jury . . . and to be informed of the nature and cause of the accusation; to be confronted with the witnesses against him; to have compulsory process for obtaining witnesses in his favor, and to have the Assistance of Counsel for his defense."

1

RIGHT TO COUNSEL

These are the Sixth Amendment guarantees. Perhaps the more significant and, in recent years certainly the most controversial, has been the right to legal counsel, particularly during pretrial periods. Beginning in 1932, Supreme Court rulings on right to counsel cases have run the gamut from absolutely yes in federal courts (*Johnson* v. *Zerbst*) to a qualified yes in a state court rape trial (*Powell* v. *Alabama*) to a qualified no in a state robbery trial (*Betts* v. *Brady*) and on to an unqualified yes concerning the constitutional necessity of legal counsel in all state criminal trials (*Gideon* v. *Wainwright*). Yet it is likely that the Warren Court's two decisions dealing with right to counsel during pretrial periods (*Escobedo* v. *Illinois* and *Miranda* v. *Arizona,* below) have occasioned the greatest degree of interest and controversy in both legal and law enforcement circles. We examine all these in what follows here.

Johnson v. Zerbst, 304 U.S. 455 (1938)

The Sixth Amendment guarantee concerning legal counsel in a federal court has, in the past, been subject to several differing interpretations. Is it a privilege (or a right) that an accused may or may not exercise? Is it mandatory in all criminal trials? Does it apply to the states through the Fourteenth Amendment? In 1790, Congress, through the Federal Crimes Act, made legal counsel mandatory in all capital cases. What about other types of cases? Until *Johnson* v. *Zerbst* the unwritten rule was that if an accused desired counsel in a non-capital case but, for whatever reason, was not able to obtain one, federal courts were *not* obliged to provide counsel for him. *Johnson* changed this. There, in a landmark 6–2 ruling in which newly appointed Justice Black wrote his first major opinion, the Supreme Court decided that a person charged with a crime (any crime) in a federal court is entitled by the Sixth Amendment to the assistance of defense counsel. The right may be waived, the Court concluded, but the waiver must be an intelligent one and must depend upon the "particular facts and circumstances, including background, experience and conduct" of the accused. It is the duty of a federal court, Justice Black noted, "to protect the right of the accused to counsel, and if he has no counsel, to determine whether he has intelligently and competently waived the right." In *Johnson*, Justices McReynolds and Butler dissented and Justice Cardozo did not participate.

The petitioner, an enlisted Marine, was arrested in Charleston, South Carolina for passing and possessing counterfeit twenty-dollar bills. Upon arraignment he pleaded not guilty, said that he had no lawyer, but stated he was ready for trial. He was then tried, convicted, and sentenced without assistance of counsel. The Supreme Court reversed the conviction.

Mr. Justice Black delivered the opinion of the Court, saying in part:

The Sixth Amendment guarantees that "In all criminal prosecutions, the accused shall enjoy the right . . . to have the Assistance of Counsel for his defence." This is one of the safeguards of the Sixth Amendment deemed necessary to insure fundamental human rights of life and liberty. Omitted from the Constitution as originally adopted, provisions of this and other Amendments were submitted by the first Congress convened under that Constitution as essential barriers against arbitrary or unjust deprivation of human rights. The Sixth Amendment stands as a constant admonition that if the constitutional safeguards it provides be lost, justice will not "still be done." It embodies a realistic recognition of the obvious truth that the average defendant does not have the professional legal skill to protect himself when brought before a tribunal with power to take his life or liberty, wherein the prosecution is presented by experienced and learned counsel. That which is simple, orderly and necessary to the lawyer, to the untrained layman may appear intricate, complex and mysterious. Consistently with the wise policy of the Sixth Amendment and other parts of our fundamental charter, this Court has pointed to " . . . the humane policy of the modern criminal law . . ." which now provides that a defendant ". . . if he be poor, . . . may have counsel furnished him by the state . . . not infrequently . . . more able than the attorney for the state."

The ". . . right to be heard would be, in many cases, of little avail if it did not comprehend the right to be heard by counsel. Even the intelligent and educated layman has small and sometimes no skill in the science of law. If charged with crime, he is incapable, generally, of determining for himself whether the indictment is good or bad. He is unfamiliar with the rules of evidence. Left without the aid of counsel he may be put on trial without a proper charge, and convicted upon incompetent evidence, or evidence irrelevant to the issue or otherwise inadmissible. He lacks both the skill and knowledge adequately to prepare his defence, even though he have a perfect one. He requires the guiding hand of counsel at every step in the proceedings against him." The Sixth Amendment withholds from federal courts, in all criminal proceedings, the power and authority to deprive an accused of his life or liberty unless he has or waives the assistance of counsel.

. . . There is insistence here that petitioner waived this constitutional right. The District Court did not so find. It has been pointed out that "courts indulge every reasonable presumption against waiver" of fundamental constitutional rights and that we "do not presume acquiescence in the loss of fundamental rights." A waiver is ordinarily an intentional relinquishment or abandonment of a known right or privilege. The determination of whether there has been an intelligent waiver of the right to counsel must depend, in each case, upon the particular facts and circumstances surrounding that case, including the background, experience, and conduct of the accused. . . .

The purpose of the constitutional guaranty of a right to counsel is to protect an accused from conviction resulting from his own ignorance of his legal and constitutional rights, and the guaranty would be nullified by a determination that an accused's ignorant failure to claim his rights removes the protection of the Constitution. . . .

Since the Sixth Amendment constitutionally entitles one charged with crime to the assistance of counsel, compliance with this constitutional mandate is an essential jurisdictional prerequisite to a federal court's authority to deprive an accused of his life or liberty. When this right is properly waived, the assistance of counsel is no longer a necessary element of the court's jurisdiction to proceed to conviction and sentence. If the accused, however, is not represented by counsel and has not competently and intelligently waived his constitutional right, the Sixth Amendment stands as a jurisdictional bar to a valid conviction and sentence depriving him of his life or his liberty. A court's jurisdiction at the beginning of trial may be lost "in the course of the proceedings" due to failure to complete the court — as the Sixth Amendment requires — by providing counsel for an accused who is unable to obtain counsel, who has not intelligently waived this constitutional guaranty, and whose life or liberty is at stake. If this requirement of the Sixth Amendment is not complied with, the court no longer has jurisdiction to proceed. The judgment of conviction pronounced by a court without jurisdiction is void, and one imprisoned thereunder may obtain release by *habeas corpus*. A judge of the United States — to whom a petition for *habeas corpus* is addressed — should be alert to examine "the facts for himself when if true as alleged they make the trial absolutely void."

It must be remembered, however, that a judgment can not be lightly set aside by collateral attack, even on *habeas corpus*. When collaterally attacked, the judgment of a court carries with it a presumption of regularity. Where a defendant, without counsel, acquiesces in a trial resulting in his conviction and later seeks release by the extraordinary remedy of *habeas corpus,* the burden of proof rests upon him to establish that he did not competently and intelligently waive his constitutional right to assistance of counsel. If in a *habeas corpus* hearing, he does meet this burden and convinces the court by a preponderance of evidence that he neither had counsel nor properly waived his constitutional right to counsel, it is the duty of the court to grant the writ.

In this case, petitioner was convicted without enjoying the assistance of counsel. Believing *habeas corpus* was not an available remedy, the District Court below made no findings as to waiver by petitioner. In this state of the record we deem it necessary to remand the cause. If — on remand — the District Court finds from all of the evidence that petitioner has sustained the burden of proof resting upon him and that he did not competently and intelligently waive his right to counsel, it will follow that the trial court did not have jurisdiction to proceed to judgment and conviction of petitioner, and he will therefore be entitled to have his petition granted. If petitioner fails to sustain this burden, he is not entitled to the writ.

Powell v. Alabama, 287 U.S. 45 (1932)

Among the more famous (or infamous) disputes in American jurisprudence is the first Scottsboro case, *Powell* v. *Alabama*. It involved an almost classic southern confrontation, a charge of rape by two young white women against seven young black men and a trial conducted in the highly charged atmosphere of a southern community virtually under martial law. As the

Supreme Court found from the record, it was "perfectly apparent that the proceedings, from beginning to end, took place in an atmosphere of tense, hostile and excited public sentiment." The defendants were constantly under military guard, who stood duty around the Scottsboro courthouse throughout the trial. All seven young men pleaded not guilty. They were tried in groups of two, two, and three. In the three separate trials, each completed in a single day, juries found all seven guilty and sentenced them to death. The record indicated that the seven, all of them described as young, "ignorant and illiterate," were not asked if they had counsel or the means to employ legal assistance or if they wished court-appointed counsel. Nor were they asked if they had friends or relatives who might help in securing counsel. All seven were transients from out of state who were riding on a freight train through Alabama when the crime was supposed to have been committed. As Chief Justice Anderson of the Alabama Supreme Court noted in his dissenting opinion, the seven "had little time or opportunity to get in touch with their families and friends who were scattered throughout two other states, and time has demonstrated that they could or would have been represented by able counsel had a better opportunity been given by a reasonable delay in the trial of the cases, judging from the number and activity of counsel that appeared immediately or shortly after their conviction." [1]

The record did show that as an "expansive gesture" the trial judge appointed "all the members of the [Scottsboro] bar" as counsel for the seven. The first of the three trials began with no defense counsel present. Soon after, an attorney from out of state appeared and indicated that he had been asked to come to Scottsboro. He said he would be willing to act in concert with a member of the local bar as counsel for the seven. Thereupon a local attorney came forward. This arrangement won the approval of the Alabama Supreme Court, which ruled in a 2–1 decision that it satisfied the state constitution.

With Justice Sutherland speaking for the majority of seven, Justice Butler joined by Justice McReynolds dissented, the Supreme Court ruled that in capital cases the right of an accused to have legal counsel, which includes the right to have sufficient time to meet with counsel and prepare a defense, "is one of the fundamental rights guaranteed by the due process clause of the Fourteenth Amendment." The 1932 Court was not yet prepared to incorporate this Sixth Amendment guarantee into the Fourteenth Amendment but instead relied on the traditional concept of inherent fairness that the Supreme Court has virtually always insisted must be an integral part of due process. When a defendant is unable to employ counsel and obviously cannot conduct his own defense, the Court ruled, it is the duty of the trial court, "whether requested or not," to assign counsel for him. And, the majority went on, "that duty is not discharged by an assignment at such a time and under such circumstances as to preclude the giving of effective aid in the preparation [of the defense]."

Because it found that none of these requirements of due process had been met, the Supreme Court reversed the conviction of the "Scottsboro boys."

Mr. Justice Sutherland delivered the opinion of the Court, saying in part:

> In the light of the facts outlined in the forepart of this opinion — the ignorance and illiteracy of the defendants, their youth, the circumstances of public

1. 224 Alabama at 554–55; 114 So. 201 (as reproduced in 287 U.S. at 52–53).

hostility, the imprisonment and the close surveillance of the defendants by the military forces, the fact that their friends and families were all in other states and communication with them necessarily difficult, and above all that they stood in deadly peril of their lives — we think the failure of the trial court to give them reasonable time and opportunity to secure counsel was a clear denial of due process.

But passing that, and assuming their inability, even if opportunity had been given, to employ counsel, as the trial court evidently did assume, we are of opinion that, under the circumstances just stated, the necessity of counsel was so vital and imperative that the failure of the trial court to make an effective appointment of counsel was likewise a denial of due process within the meaning of the Fourteenth Amendment. Whether this would be so in other criminal prosecutions, or under other circumstances, we need not determine. All that it is necessary now to decide, as we do decide, is that in a capital case, where the defendant is unable to employ counsel, and is incapable adequately of making his own defense because of ignorance, feeble mindedness, illiteracy, or the like, it is the duty of the court, whether requested or not, to assign counsel for him as a necessary requisite of due process of law; and that duty is not discharged by an assignment at such a time or under such circumstances as to preclude the giving of effective aid in the preparation and trial of the case. To hold otherwise would be to ignore the fundamental postulate, already adverted to, "that there are certain immutable principles of justice which inhere in the very idea of free government which no member of the Union may disregard." . . .

Let us suppose the extreme case of a prisoner charged with a capital offense, who is deaf and dumb, illiterate and feeble minded, unable to employ counsel, with the whole power of the state arrayed against him, prosecuted by counsel for the state without assignment of counsel for his defense, tried, convicted and sentenced to death. Such a result, which, if carried into execution, would be little short of judicial murder, it cannot be doubted would be a gross violation of the guarantee of due process of law; and we venture to think that no appellate court, state or federal, would hesitate so to decide. . . . The duty of the trial court to appoint counsel under such circumstances is clear, as it is clear under circumstances such as are disclosed by the record here; and its power to do so, even in the absence of a statute, can not be questioned. Attorneys are officers of the court, and are bound to render service when required by such an appointment. . . .

The United States by statute and every state in the Union by express provision of law, or by the determination of its courts, make it the duty of the trial judge, where the accused is unable to employ counsel, to appoint counsel for him. In most states the rule applies broadly to all criminal prosecutions, in others it is limited to the more serious crimes, and in a very limited number, to capital cases. A rule adopted with such unanimous accord reflects, if it does not establish, the inherent right to have counsel appointed, at least in cases like the present, and lends convincing support to the conclusion we have reached as to the fundamental nature of that right.

Betts v. Brady, 316 U.S. 450 (1942)

Did the *Powell* rule require appointment of counsel in *all* state criminal cases? Or was the "Scottsboro boys" case one of a kind because of the "unique circumstances" associated with it? From *Betts* v. *Brady* to *Gideon* v. *Wainwright* the Court used a case by case approach considering "special circumstances" in each before deciding whether absence of counsel in state court criminal trials rendered the judgments a violation of due process of law.

In *Betts,* for example, the Supreme Court, over a forceful protest by Justice Black, ruled that refusal by a state court to appoint counsel to represent an indigent defendant in a robbery trial, did *not* deny him due process of law in violation of the Fourteenth Amendment. Justice Roberts spoke for the majority of six and Justice Black, joined by liberal colleagues Justices Douglas and Murphy, dissented. The record showed that the petitioner, an unemployed farm hand, was indicted in a Maryland court on a robbery charge. He was too poor to hire an attorney. He so informed the Court and asked that counsel be appointed to defend him. His request was denied on grounds that in Carroll County it was not the court's practice to appoint counsel for indigent defendants except in murder or rape prosecutions. Put to trial without counsel, Betts conducted his own defense, was found guilty and was sentenced to eight years in jail. The Supreme Court affirmed the judgment of the Maryland Court. The majority opinion reviewed the status of right-to-counsel statutes in all the states and concluded: "This material demonstrates that, in the great majority of the states, it has been the considered judgment of the people, their representatives and their courts that appointment of counsel is not a fundamental right, essential to a fair trial. On the contrary, the matter has generally been deemed one of legislative policy . . ." [1]

Dissenting, Justice Black, who believed the Sixth Amendment guarantee of right to counsel *was* incorporated into the Fourteenth, took sharp issue with the Court's position. We reproduce here portions of both the majority opinion and Justice Black's dissent. Some twenty-one years after *Betts,* Black's dissent became the law of the land in *Gideon* v. *Wainwright.*

Mr. Justice Roberts delivered the opinion of the Court, saying in part:

> . . . This material demonstrates that, in the great majority of the States, it has been the considered judgment of the people, their representatives and their courts that appointment of counsel is not a fundamental right, essential to a fair trial. On the contrary, the matter has generally been deemed one of legislative policy. In the light of this evidence, we are unable to say that the concept of due process incorporated in the Fourteenth Amendment obligates the States, whatever may be their own views, to furnish counsel in every such case. Every court has power, if it deems proper, to appoint counsel where that course seems to be required in the interest of fairness.
>
> The practice of the courts of Maryland gives point to the principle that the States should not be straight-jacketed in this respect, by a construction of the Fourteenth Amendment. Judge Bond's opinion states, and counsel at the bar confirmed the fact, that in Maryland the usual practice is for the defendant to waive a trial by jury. This the petitioner did in the present case. Such trials, as Judge Bond remarks, are much more informal than jury trials and it is obvious that the judge can much better control the course of the trial and is in a better position to see impartial justice done than when the formalities of a jury trial are involved.
>
> In this case there was no question of the commission of a robbery. The State's case consisted of evidence identifying the petitioner as the perpetrator. The defense was an alibi. Petitioner called and examined witnesses to prove that he

1. 316 U.S. at 471.

was at another place at the time of the commission of the offense. The simple issue was the veracity of the testimony for the State and that for the defendant. As Judge Bond says, the accused was not helpless, but was a man forty-three years old, of ordinary intelligence, and ability to take care of his own interests on the trial of that narrow issue. He had once before been in a criminal court, pleaded guilty to larceny and served a sentence and was not wholly unfamiliar with criminal procedure. It is quite clear that in Maryland, if the situation had been otherwise and it had appeared that the petitioner was, for any reason, at a serious disadvantage by reason of the lack of counsel, a refusal to appoint would have resulted in the reversal of a judgment of conviction. Only recently the Court of Appeals has reversed a conviction because it was convinced on the whole record that an accused, tried without counsel, had been handicapped by the lack of representation.

To deduce from the due process clause a rule binding upon the States in this matter would be to impose upon them, as Judge Bond points out, a requirement without distinction between criminal charges of different magnitude or in respect of courts of varying jurisdiction. As he says: "Charges of small crimes tried before justices of the peace and capital charges tried in the higher courts would equally require the appointment of counsel. Presumably it would be argued that trials in the Traffic Court would require it." And, indeed, it was said by petitioner's counsel both below and in this court, that as the Fourteenth Amendment extends the protection of due process to property as well as to life and liberty, if we hold with the petitioner, logic would require the furnishing of counsel in civil cases involving property.

As we have said, the Fourteenth Amendment prohibits the conviction and incarceration of one whose trial is offensive to the common and fundamental ideas of fairness and right, and while want of counsel in a particular case may result in a conviction lacking in such fundamental fairness, we cannot say that the Amendment embodies an inexorable command that no trial for any offense, or in any court, can be fairly conducted and justice accorded a defendant who is not represented by counsel.

Mr. Justice Black, joined by Justices Douglas and Murphy, dissented, saying in part:

To hold that the petitioner had a constitutional right to counsel in this case does not require us to say that "no trial for any offense, or in any court, can be fairly conducted and justice accorded a defendant who is not represented by counsel." This case can be determined by a resolution of a narrower question: whether in view of the nature of the offense and the circumstances of his trial and conviction, this petitioner was denied the procedural protection which is his right under the Federal Constitution. I think he was. . . .

If this case had come to us from a federal court, it is clear we should have to reverse it, because the Sixth Amendment makes the right to counsel in criminal cases inviolable by the Federal Government. I believe that the Fourteenth Amendment made the Sixth applicable to the states. But this view, although often urged in dissents, has never been accepted by a majority of this Court and is not accepted today. A statement of the grounds supporting it is, therefore, unnecessary at this time. I believe, however, that, under the prevailing view of due process, as reflected in the opinion just announced, a view which gives this Court such vast supervisory powers that I am not prepared to accept it without grave doubts, the judgment below should be reversed. . . .

A practice cannot be reconciled with "common and fundamental ideas of fairness and right," which subjects innocent men to increased dangers of conviction merely because of their poverty. Whether a man is innocent cannot be determined from a trial in which, as here, denial of counsel has made it impossible to conclude, with any satisfactory degree of certainty, that the defendant's case was adequately presented. No one questions that due process requires a hearing before conviction and sentence for the serious crime of robbery. As the Supreme Court of Wisconsin said, in 1859, ". . . would it not be a little like mockery to secure to a pauper these solemn constitutional guaranties for a fair and full trial of the matters with which he was charged, and yet to say to him when on trial, that he must employ his own counsel, who could alone render these guaranties of any real permanent value to him. . . . Why this great solicitude to secure him a fair trial if he cannot have the benefit of counsel?" . . .

Denial to the poor of the request for counsel in proceedings based on charges of serious crime has long been regarded as shocking to the "universal sense of justice" throughout this country. In 1854, for example, the Supreme Court of Indiana said: "It is not to be thought of, in a civilized community, for a moment, that any citizen put in jeopardy of life or liberty, should be debarred of counsel because he was too poor to employ such aid. No Court could be respected, or respect itself, to sit and hear such a trial. The defence of the poor, in such cases, is a duty resting somewhere, which will be at once conceded as essential to the accused, to the Court, and to the public." . . . And most of the other States have shown their agreement by constitutional provisions, statutes, or established practice judicially approved, which assure that no man shall be deprived of counsel merely because of his poverty. Any other practice seems to me to defeat the promise of our democratic society to provide equal justice under the law.

Gideon v. Wainwright, 373 U.S. 335 (1963)

After *Betts* the Supreme Court heard a considerable number of other right-to-counsel cases. By and large it used the case by case "special circumstances" rationale of *Powell* developed over Black's objections in *Betts*. Its record is mixed. Pritchett's summary of the Court's work in this area suggests that in most cases the Court *did* rule that special circumstances demanded counsel, especially in trials involving capital offenses.[1] In others it decided that absence of counsel was not objectionable.[2] Generally, the Supreme Court upheld the necessity of defense counsel in cases where the trial judge's conduct was questionable, or where the defendant was young, illiterate, or undereducated, or in cases where the finer points of the law were too complicated for someone without formal legal training.[3]

Yet slowly but surely in the years between 1942 and 1963 the Supreme Court seemed to be edging closer to a fixed position concerning the necessity of counsel in all state criminal trials. The breakthrough case was *Gideon* v. *Wainwright,* certainly one of the Warren Court's more memorable and significant decisions. In *Gideon* the Court decided that the right of an indigent defendant in a criminal trial to have legal counsel in a state court *is* fundamentally essential to a fair trial. Conviction without assistance of counsel, the

1. See for example, Tomkins v. Missouri 323 U.S. 485 (1945).

2. See for example, Bute v. Illinois 333 U.S. 640 (1948).

3. Pritchett makes these points, op. cit., at 453.

Court ruled, violates the Fourteenth Amendment. Here Justice Black, the dissenter in *Betts,* and the Court's major advocate for incorporating Sixth Amendment guarantees into the Fourteenth, spoke for his unanimous colleagues.

The petitioner was charged in a Florida court with having broken into a poolroom. Appearing in court without funds and without an attorney he asked the Florida court to appoint counsel for him. He was denied on grounds that Florida law allowed court-appointed counsel only in capital cases. The record indicates that petitioner responded to the trial judge's denial by saying, "The United States Supreme Court says I am entitled to be represented by counsel." Put to trial before a jury, Gideon conducted his own defense, and from the record, apparently did reasonably well. He was found guilty, however, and sentenced to five years in prison. From prison Gideon then drafted a petition directly to the Supreme Court asking for a review. The Court agreed and appointed Abe Fortas, a prominent Washington attorney and himself later to be a Justice of the Supreme Court, to represent Gideon.

In reversing Gideon's conviction, as it was urged to do by legal representatives of some twenty-two states, the Supreme Court finally overruled *Betts* v. *Brady.* In the process the Sixth Amendment's right-to-counsel guarantee was incorporated into the Fourteenth.

Mr. Justice Black delivered the opinion of the Court, saying in part:

We think the Court in *Betts* was wrong, however, in concluding that the Sixth Amendment's guarantee of counsel is not one of these fundamental rights.
. . . The fact is that in deciding as it did — that "appointment of counsel is not a fundamental right, essential to a fair trial" — the Court in *Betts* v. *Brady* made an abrupt break with its own well-considered precedents. In returning to these old precedents, sounder we believe than the new, we but restore constitutional principles established to achieve a fair system of justice. Not only these precedents but also reason and reflection require us to recognize that in our adversary system of criminal justice, any person haled into court, who is too poor to hire a lawyer, cannot be assured a fair trial unless counsel is provided for him. This seems to us to be an obvious truth. Governments, both state and federal, quite properly spend vast sums of money to establish machinery to try defendants accused of crime. Lawyers to prosecute are everywhere deemed essential to protect the public's interest in an orderly society. Similarly, there are few defendants charged with crime, few indeed, who fail to hire the best lawyers they can get to prepare and present their defenses. That government hires lawyers to prosecute and defendants who have the money hire lawyers to defend are the strongest indications of the widespread belief that lawyers in criminal courts are necessities, not luxuries. The right of one charged with crime to counsel may not be deemed fundamental and essential to fair trials in some countries, but it is in ours. From the very beginning, our state and national constitutions and laws have laid great emphasis on procedural and substantive safeguards designed to assure fair trials before impartial tribunals in which every defendant stands equal before the law. This noble ideal cannot be realized if the poor man charged with crime has to face his accusers without a lawyer to assist him. A defendant's need for a lawyer is nowhere better stated than in the moving words of Mr. Justice Sutherland in *Powell* v. *Alabama:*

"The right to be heard would be, in many cases, of little avail if it did not comprehend the right to be heard by counsel. Even the intelligent and educated layman has small and sometimes no skill in the science of law. If charged with crime, he is incapable, generally, of determining for himself whether the indictment is good or bad. He is unfamiliar with the rules of evidence. Left without the aid of counsel he may be put on trial without a proper charge, and convicted upon incompetent evidence, or evidence irrelevant to the issue or otherwise inadmissible. He lacks both the skill and knowledge adequately to prepare his defense, even though he have a perfect one. He requires the guiding hand of counsel at every step in the proceedings against him. Without it, though he be not guilty, he faces the danger of conviction because he does not know how to establish his innocence." . . .

The Court in *Betts* v. *Brady* departed from the sound wisdom upon which the Court's holding in *Powell* v. *Alabama* rested. Florida, supported by two other States, has asked that *Betts* v. *Brady* be left intact. Twenty-two States, as friends of the court, argue that *Betts* was "an anachronism when handed down" and that it should now be overruled. We agree.

Escobedo v. Illinois, 378 U.S. 478 (1964)

It is likely that at least seven of the Warren Court's landmark decisions will stand the test of time as truly momentous. Two, *Escobedo* v. *Illinois* and *Miranda* v. *Arizona* must, it seems clear, make the list.[1] Both revolutionized pretrial criminal justice procedures in American jurisprudence. And both, as might be expected, raised (and continue to raise) loud and furious uproar in law enforcement circles. When critics of the Warren Court maintain that the Court consistently hamstrung law enforcement by bending over backwards to protect the rights of an accused, they inevitably point to *Escobedo* and *Miranda* as the major cases in point.

In the years immediately preceding *Escobedo*, the Court decided three right-to-counsel cases, two of which were subsequently overturned in *Escobedo*. The third was used as a basis for the Court's finding in *Escobedo*. *Crooker* v. *California*[2] and *Cicenia* v. *Lagay*[3] denied the right of suspects to consult with counsel during interrogation by police officers. A year later, however, in *Spano* v. *New York*[4] the Court ruled that counsel could not be denied to a defendant after an indictment had been handed down. Thus the Warren Court relied on *Spano* when it decided in *Escobedo* that there was no "meaningful distinction" between interrogation without counsel before or after an indictment. That was the central issue in *Escobedo*, the right of an accused to counsel in the pretrial, pre-indictment period. Justice Goldberg spoke for the Court's slim majority of five while Justice Harlan dissented, as did Justice Stewart and Justice White (joined by Justices Clark and Stewart). All three dissenters took serious exception to the Court's position.

1. *Brown* v. *Board of Education* (1954), *Mapp* v. *Ohio* (1961), *Baker* v. *Carr* (1962), *Gideon* v. *Wainwright* (1963), and *Reynolds* v. *Sims* (1964) are the other five.

2. 357 U.S. 433 (1958).

3. 357 U.S. 504 (1958).

4. 360 U.S. 315 (1959).

In his brief, one-paragraph opinion, Harlan called the Court's decision "most ill-conceived" and argued that "it seriously and unjustifiably fetters perfectly legitimate methods of criminal law enforcement."[5] White took much the same view. "I do not suggest for a moment," he said, "that law enforcement will be destroyed by the rule announced today. The need for peace and order is too insistent for that. But it will be crippled and its task made a great deal more difficult, all in my opinion, for unsound, unstated reasons which can find no home in any of the provisions of the Constitution."[6]

Danny Escobedo, a twenty-two year old Mexican-American, was arrested in Illinois on a charge of murdering his brother-in-law. An alleged accomplice told police officers that Escobedo had fired the fatal shots. The record showed that during the course of the interrogation, the petitioner repeatedly asked to speak to his attorney. Police told him that his lawyer "didn't want to see him." The record also showed that the petitioner's attorney had repeatedly asked to see his client, also to no avail.

In the majority opinion Justice Goldberg expressed the Court's clear concern for the rights of suspects. He noted the likelihood of police abuses during the pretrial interrogation period. The guiding hand of counsel is essential, Goldberg wrote, "to advise petitioner of his rights in this delicate situaiton." This is the stage "when legal aid and advice" is most critical to petitioner. "It would exalt form over substance," the majority concluded, "to make the right to counsel . . . depend on whether at the time of interrogation, the authorities had secured a formal indictment." Accordingly, the Warren Court overruled the Illinois Court's decision.

Mr. Justice Goldberg delivered the opinion of the Court, saying in part:

> It is argued that if the right to counsel is afforded prior to indictment, the number of confessions obtained by the police will diminish significantly, because most confessions are obtained during the period between arrest and indictment, and "any lawyer worth his salt will tell the suspect in no uncertain terms to make no statement to police under any circumstances." . . . This argument, of course, cuts two ways. The fact that many confessions are obtained during this period points up its critical nature as a "stage when legal aid and advice" are surely needed. . . .
>
> . . . The right to counsel would indeed be hollow if it began at a period when few confessions were obtained. There is necessarily a direct relationship between the importance of a stage to the police in their quest for a confession and the criticalness of that stage to the accused in his need for legal advice. Our Constitution, unlike some others, strikes the balance in favor of the right of the accused to be advised by his lawyer of his privilege against self-incrimination.
>
> We have also learned the companion lesson of history that no system of criminal justice can, or should, survive if it comes to depend for its continued effectiveness on the citizens' abdication through unawareness of their constitutional rights. No system worth preserving should have to *fear* that if an accused is permitted to consult with a lawyer, he will become aware of, and exercise, these rights. If the exercise of constitutional rights will thwart the effectiveness of a system of law enforcement, then there is something very wrong with that system.
>
> We hold, therefore, that where, as here, the investigation is no longer a general inquiry into an unsolved crime but has begun to focus on a particular suspect, the suspect has been taken into police custody, the police carry out a

5. 378 U.S. at 493.

6. Ibid., at 499.

process of interrogations that lends itself to eliciting incriminating statements, the suspect has requested and been denied an opportunity to consult with his lawyer, and the police have not effectively warned him of his absolute constitutional right to remain silent, the accused has been denied "the Assistance of Counsel" in violation of the Sixth Amendment to the Constitution as "made obligatory upon the States by the Fourteenth Amendment," . . . and that no statement elicited by the police during the interrogation may be used against him at a criminal trial. . . .

Nothing we have said today affects the powers of the police to investigate "an unsolved crime," . . . by gathering information from witnesses and by other "proper investigative efforts." . . . We hold only that when the process shifts from investigatory to accusatory — when its focus is on the accused and its purpose is to elicit a confession — our adversary system begins to operate, and, under the circumstances here, the accused must be permitted to consult with his lawyer.

Miranda v. Arizona, 384 U.S. 436 (1966)

Escobedo made several points clear, among them that a suspect must have counsel during interrogation in a police station even before an indictment. In expressing its strong support for this aspect of the adversary system, the Court ruled that the system must come into play as soon as law enforcement investigation becomes accusatory. Yet *Escobedo* left several questions undecided or unanswered. Was the ruling retroactive? The Warren Court itself answered no in *Johnson* v. *New Jersey.*[1] When was it necessary to inform a suspect of his rights? Was any questioning, for example in a police car en route to the station, permissible in the absence of counsel?

The Warren Court undertook to answer *these* questions (and more) in *Miranda* v. *Arizona,* which would further fan the fires of controversy begun two years earlier by *Escobedo.* As Pritchett notes, *Escobedo* (and later *Miranda*) "quickly became the focus of a nationwide debate on law enforcement and the whipping boy of all who blamed the increase in crime on the 'coddling of criminals'" by the Supreme Court (especially "Earl Warren's" Supreme Court).[2] *Miranda* is related to two important constitutional guarantees, the Fifth Amendment's protection against self-incrimination and the Sixth Amendment's right to counsel.

A narrow majority (5–4) of the Warren Court reversed Ernesto Miranda's conviction in an Arizona court on grounds that both his Fifth and Sixth Amendment rights had been violated. Three dissents were filed, by Justices Clark (who dissented only in part), by Justice Harlan joined by Justices Stewart and White, and by Justice White joined by Justices Harlan and Stewart. Harlan's dissent was particularly sharp. "Nothing in the letter or the spirit of the Constitution," Harlan wrote, ". . . squares with the heavy-handed and one-sided action that is so precipitously taken by the Court in the name of fulfilling its constitutional responsibilities." Harlan concluded by quoting the words of Justice Jackson.[3] "This Court," Jackson wrote, "is forever adding new stories to the temples of constitutional law, and the temples have a way of

1. 384 U.S. 719 (1966).

2. Pritchett, op. cit., at 455.

3. 384 U.S. at 525–26.

collapsing when one story too many is added."[4] In his dissent, Justice White accused the Court of making "new law and new public policy" and suggested "it is wholly legitimate to examine the mode of this or any other constitutional decision . . . and to inquire into the advisability of its end product in terms of the long-range interest of the country." Justice White's long analysis of the criminal procedure requirements of the Fifth and Sixth Amendments led him to conclude that the Court's ruling "is neither compelled nor even strongly suggested by the language of the [Constitution, and] is at odds with American and English legal history . . ." White's dissent also raised some of the unanswered questions inherent in the *Miranda* rule.

> Today's decision leaves open such questions as whether the accused was in custody, whether his statements were spontaneous or the product of interrogation, whether the accused has effectively waived his rights and whether nontestimonial evidence introduced at trial is the fruit of statements made during a prohibited interrogation. . . . For all these reasons if further restrictions on police interrogations are desirable at this time, a more flexible approach makes much more sense than the Court's constitutional straight-jacket which forecloses more discriminating treatment by legislative or rule-making pronouncements."[5]

The majority opinion announced what has since become known as the "*Miranda* rule," including the following points: (1) the person in custody must, prior to interrogation, be clearly informed that he has the right to remain silent; (2) he must be clearly informed that anything he says will be used against him in court; (3) he must be clearly informed that he has the right to counsel with a lawyer and to have the lawyer with him during interrogation; (4) if the accused is indigent, he must be told that a lawyer will be appointed to represent him; (5) if the accused indicates that he wishes to remain silent, the interrogation must cease; (6) if he states that he wants an attorney, the questioning must cease until an attorney is present; (7) when an interrogation is conducted without the presence of an attorney, a heavy burden rests on the government to demonstrate that the defendant knowingly and intelligently waived his right to counsel. In his long majority opinion the Chief Justice quoted extensively from the most recent, representative police manuals, which note the interrogation procedure and the psychological pressure tactics officers are encouraged to use. Warren did so in order to emphasize that the Court's essential purpose was to restore an element of fairness and balance to the interrogation process. This was necessary, he noted, because too often law enforcement officers have knowingly (or unknowingly) violated basic constitutional rights in their zeal to obtain confessions. In effect what the Warren Court told law enforcement officials in *Escobedo,* and certainly in *Miranda,* was simply that they could no longer ride roughshod over constitutional guarantees while pursuing law and order. Get your convictions, the Court seemed to be saying, but not by violating the basic constitutional rights of the suspects: an accused also has rights that must be protected.

Mr. Chief Justice Warren delivered the opinion of the Court, saying in part:

4. In a separate opinion, see *Douglas* v. *Jeannette,* 319 U.S. at 181 (1942).

5. Ibid., at 531 and 545.

Again we stress that the modern practice of in-custody interrogation is psychologically rather than physically oriented. As we have stated before, "Since *Chambers* v. *Florida,* 309 U.S. 227, this Court has recognized that coercion can be mental as well as physical, and that the blood of the accused is not the only hallmark of an unconstitutional inquisition." . . . Interrogation still takes place in privacy. Privacy results in secrecy and this in turn results in a gap in our knowledge as to what in fact goes on in the interrogation rooms. A valuable source of information about present police practices, however, may be found in various police manuals and texts which document procedures employed with success in the past, and which recommend various other effective tactics. These texts are used by law enforcement agencies themselves as guides. It should be noted that these texts professedly present the most enlightened and effective means presently used to obtain statements through custodial interrogation. By considering these texts and other data, it is possible to describe procedures observed and noted around the country.

The officers are told by the manuals that the "principal psychological factor contributing to a successful interrogation is *privacy* — being alone with the person under interrogation." The efficacy of this tactic has been explained as follows:

"If at all practicable, the interrogation should take place in the investigator's office or at least in a room of his own choice. The subject should be deprived of every psychological advantage. In his own home he may be confident, indignant, or recalcitrant. He is more keenly aware of his rights and more reluctant to tell of his indiscretions or criminal behavior within the walls of his home. Moreover his family and other friends are nearby, their presence lending moral support. In his own office, the investigator possesses all the advantages. The atmosphere suggests the invincibility of the forces of the law."

To highlight the isolation and unfamiliar surroundings, the manuals instruct the police to display an air of confidence in the suspect's guilt and from outward appearance to maintain only an interest in confirming certain details. The guilt of the subject is to be posited as a fact. The interrogator should direct his comments toward the reasons why the subject committed the act, rather than court failure by asking the subject whether he did it. Like other men, perhaps the subject has had a bad family life, had an unhappy childhood, had too much to drink, had an unrequited desire for women. The officers are instructed to minimize the moral seriousness of the offense, to cast blame on the victim or on society. These tactics are designed to put the subject in a psychological state where his story is but an elaboration of what the police purport to know already — that he is guilty. Explanations to the contrary are dismissed and discouraged.

The texts thus stress that the major qualities an interrogator should possess are patience and perseverance. One writer describes the efficacy of these characteristics in this manner:

"In the preceding paragraphs emphasis has been placed on kindness and stratagems. The investigator will, however, encounter many situations where the sheer weight of his personality will be the deciding factor. Where emotional appeals and tricks are employed to no avail, he must rely on an oppressive atmosphere of dogged persistence. He must interrogate steadily and without relent, leaving the subject no prospect of surcease. He must dominate his subject and overwhelm him with his inexorable will to obtain the truth. He should interrogate for a spell of several hours pausing only for the subject's necessities in acknowledgment of the need to avoid a charge of duress that can be technically substantiated. In a serious case, the interrogation may continue for days, with the required intervals for food and sleep, but with no respite from the atmosphere of domination. It is possible in this way to induce the subject to talk without resorting to duress or coercion. The method should be used only when the guilt of the subject appears highly probable."

The manuals suggest that the suspect be offered legal excuses for his actions in order to obtain an initial admission of guilt. Where there is a suspected revenge-killing, for example, the interrogator may say:

"Joe, you probably didn't go out looking for this fellow with the purpose of shooting him. My guess is, however, that you expected something from him and that's why you carried a gun — for your own protection. You knew him for what he was, no good. Then when you met him he probably started using foul, abusive language and he gave some indication that he was about to pull a gun on you, and that's when you had to act to save your own life. That's about it, isn't it, Joe?"

Having then obtained the admission of shooting, the interrogator is advised to refer to circumstantial evidence which negates the self-defense explanation. This should enable him to secure the entire story. One text notes that "Even if he fails to do so, the inconsistency between the subject's original denial of the shooting and his present admission of at least doing the shooting will serve to deprive him of a self-defense 'out' at the time of trial."

When the techniques described above prove unavailing, the texts recommend they be alternated with a show of some hostility. One ploy often used has been termed the "friendly-unfriendly" or the "Mutt and Jeff" act:

". . . In this technique, two agents are employed. Mutt, the relentless investigator, who knows the subject is guilty and is not going to waste any time. He's sent a dozen men away for this crime and he's going to send the subject away for the full term. Jeff, on the other hand, is obviously a kindhearted man. He has a family himself. He has a brother who was involved in a little scrape like this. He disapproves of Mutt and his tactics and will arrange to get him off the case if the subject will cooperate. He can't hold Mutt off for very long. The subject would be wise to make a quick decision. The technique is applied by having both investigators present while Mutt acts out his role. Jeff may stand by quietly and demur at some of Mutt's tactics. When Jeff makes his plea for cooperation, Mutt is not present in the room."

The interrogators sometimes are instructed to induce a confession out of trickery. The technique here is quite effective in crimes which require identification or which run in series. In the identification situation, the interrogator may take a break in his questioning to place the subject among a group of men in a line-up. "The witness or complainant (previously coached, if necessary) studies the line-up and confidently points out the subject as the guilty party." Then the questioning resumes "as though there were now no doubt about the guilt of the subject." A variation on this technique is called the "reverse line-up":

"The accused is placed in a line-up, but this time he is identified by several fictitious witnesses or victims who associated him with different offenses. It is expected that the subject will become desperate and confess to the offense under investigation in order to escape from the false accusations."

The manuals also contain instructions for police on how to handle the individual who refuses to discuss the matter entirely, or who asks for an attorney or relatives. The examiner is to concede him the right to remain silent. "This usually has a very undermining effect. First of all, he is disappointed in his expectation of an unfavorable reaction on the part of the interrogator. Secondly, a concession of this right to remain silent impresses the subject with the apparent fairness of his interrogator." After this psychological conditioning, however, the officer is told to point out the incriminating significance of the suspect's refusal to talk:

"Joe, you have a right to remain silent. That's your privilege and I'm the last person in the world who'll try to take it away from you. If that's the way you want to leave this, O.K. But let me ask you this. Suppose you were in my shoes and I were in yours and you called me in to ask me about this and I told you, 'I don't want to answer any of your questions.' You'd think I had something to hide, and you'd probably be right in thinking that. That's exactly what I'll have to think about you, and so will everybody else. So let's sit here and talk this whole thing over."

Few will persist in their initial refusal to talk, it is said, if this monologue is employed correctly.

In the event that the subject wishes to speak to a relative or an attorney, the following advice is tendered:

"[T]he interrogator should respond by suggesting that the subject first tell the truth to the interrogator himself rather than get anyone else involved in the matter. If the request is for an attorney, the interrogator may suggest that the subject save himself or his family the expense of any such professional service, particularly if he is innocent of the offense under investigation. The interrogator may also add, 'Joe, I'm only looking for the truth, and if you're telling the truth, that's it. You can handle this by yourself.'"

From these representative samples of interrogation techniques, the setting prescribed by the manuals and observed in practice becomes clear. In essence, it is this: To be alone with the subject is essential to prevent distraction and to deprive him of any outside support. The aura of confidence in his guilt undermines his will to resist. He merely confirms the preconceived story the police seek to have him describe. Patience and persistence, at times relentless questioning, are employed. To obtain a confession, the interrogator must "patiently maneuver himself or his quarry into a position from which the desired objective may be attained." When normal procedures fail to produce the needed result, the police may resort to deceptive stratagems such as giving false legal advice. It is important to keep the subject off balance, for example, by trading on his insecurity about himself or his surroundings. The police then persuade, trick, or cajole him out of exercising his constitutional rights.

Even without employing brutality, the "third degree" or the specific stratagems described above, the very fact of custodial interrogation exacts a heavy toll on individual liberty and trades on the weakness of individuals. . . .

Today, then, there can be no doubt that the Fifth Amendment privilege is available outside of criminal court proceedings and serves to protect persons in all settings in which their freedom of action is curtailed in any significant way from being compelled to incriminate themselves. We have concluded that without proper safeguards the process of in-custody interrogation of persons suspected or accused of crime contains inherently compelling pressures which work to undermine the individual's will to resist and to compel him to speak where he would not otherwise do so freely. In order to combat these pressures and to permit a full opportunity to exercise the privilege against self-incrimination, the accused must be adequately and effectively apprised of his rights and the exercise of those rights must be fully honored.

It is impossible for us to foresee the potential alternatives for protecting the privilege which might be devised by Congress or the States in the exercise of their creative rule-making capacities. Therefore we cannot say that the Constitution necessarily requires adherence to any particular solution for the inherent compulsions of the interrogation process as it is presently conducted. Our decision in no way creates a constitutional straitjacket which will handicap sound efforts at reform, nor is it intended to have this effect. We encourage Congress and the States to continue their laudable search for increasingly effective ways of protecting the rights of the individual while promoting efficient enforcement of our criminal laws. However, unless we are shown other procedures which are at least as effective in apprising accused persons of their right of silence and in assuring a continuous opportunity to exercise it, the following safeguards must be observed.

At the outset, if a person in custody is to be subjected to interrogation, he must first be informed in clear and unequivocal terms that he has the right to remain silent. For those unaware of the privilege, the warning is needed simply to make them aware of it — the threshold requirement for an intelligent decision as to its exercise. More important, such a warning is an absolute prerequisite in overcoming the inherent pressures of the interrogation atmosphere. It is not just the subnormal or woefully ignorant who succumb to an interrogator's imprecations, whether implied or expressly stated, that the interrogation will continue until a confession is obtained or that silence in the face of accusation is itself damning and will bode ill when presented to a jury. Further, the warning will show the individual that his interrogators are prepared to recognize his privilege should he choose to exercise it.

The Fifth Amendment privilege is so fundamental to our system of constitutional rule and the expedient of giving an adequate warning as to the availability of the privilege so simple, we will not pause to inquire in individual cases whether the defendant was aware of his rights without a warning being given. Assessments of the knowledge the defendant possessed, based on information as to his age, education, intelligence, or prior contact with authorities, can never be more than speculation; a warning is a clearcut fact. More important, whatever the background of the person interrogated, a warning at the time of the interrogation is indispensable to overcome its pressures and to insure that the individual knows he is free to exercise the privilege at that point in time.

The warning of the right to remain silent must be accompanied by the explanation that anything said can and will be used against the individual in court. This warning is needed in order to make him aware not only of the privilege, but also of the consequences of forgoing it. It is only through an awareness of these consequences that there can be any assurance of real understanding and intelligent exercise of the privilege. Moreover, this warning may serve to make the individual more acutely aware that he is faced with a phase of the adversary system — that he is not in the presence of persons acting solely in his interest.

The circumstances surrounding in-custody interrogation can operate very quickly to overbear the will of one merely made aware of his privilege by his interrogators. Therefore, the right to have counsel present at the interrogation is indispensable to the protection of the Fifth Amendment privilege under the system we delineate today. Our aim is to assure that the individual's right to choose between silence and speech remains unfettered throughout the interrogation process. A once-stated warning, delivered by those who will conduct the interrogation, cannot itself suffice to that end among those who most require knowledge of their rights. A mere warning given by the interrogators is not alone sufficient to accomplish that end. Prosecutors themselves claim that the admonishment of the right to remain silent without more "will benefit only the recidivist and the professional." . . . Even preliminary advice given to the accused by his own attorney can be swiftly overcome by the secret interrogation process. . . . Thus, the need for counsel to protect the Fifth Amendment privilege comprehends not merely a right to consult with counsel prior to questioning, but also to have counsel present during any questioning if the defendant so desires.

The presence of counsel at the interrogation may serve several significant subsidiary functions as well. If the accused decides to talk to his interrogators, the assistance of counsel can mitigate the dangers of untrustworthiness. With a lawyer present the likelihood that the police will practice coercion is reduced, and if coercion is nevertheless exercised the lawyer can testify to it in court. The presence of a lawyer can also help to guarantee that the accused gives a fully accurate statement to the police and that the statement is rightly reported by the prosecution at trial. . . .

An individual need not make a pre-interrogation request for a lawyer. While such request affirmatively secures his right to have one, his failure to ask for a lawyer does not constitute a waiver. No effective waiver of the right to counsel during interrogation can be recognized unless specifically made after the warnings we here delineate have been given. The accused who does not know his rights and therefore does not make a request may be the person who most needs counsel. . . .

Accordingly we hold that an individual held for interrogation must be clearly informed that he has the right to consult with a lawyer and to have the lawyer with him during interrogation under the system for protecting the privilege we delineate today. As with the warnings of the right to remain silent and that anything stated can be used in evidence against him, this warning is an absolute prerequisite to interrogation. No amount of circumstantial evidence that the person may have been aware of this right will suffice to stand in its stead. Only through such a warning is there ascertainable assurance that the accused was aware of this right.

If an individual indicates that he wishes the assistance of counsel before any interrogation occurs, the authorities cannot rationally ignore or deny his request on the basis that the individual does not have or cannot afford a retained attorney. The financial ability of the individual has no relationship to the scope of the rights involved here. The privilege against self-incrimination secured by the Constitution applies to all individuals. The need for counsel in order to protect the privilege exists for the indigent as well as the affluent. In fact, were we to limit these constitutional rights to those who can retain an attorney, our decisions today would be of little significance. The cases before us as well as the vast majority of confession cases with which we have dealt in the past involve those unable to retain counsel. While authorities are not required to relieve the accused of his poverty, they have the obligation not to take advantage of indigence in the administration of justice. Denial of counsel to the indigent at the time of interrogation while allowing an attorney to those who can afford one would be no more supportable by reason or logic than the similar situation at trial and on appeal struck down in *Gideon* v. *Wainwright,* 372 U.S. 335 (1963), and *Douglas* v. *California,* 372 U.S. 353 (1963).

In order fully to apprise a person interrogated of the extent of his rights under this system then, it is necessary to warn him not only that he has the right to consult with an attorney, but also that if he is indigent a lawyer will be appointed to represent him. Without this additional warning, the admonition of the right to consult with counsel would often be understood as meaning only that he can consult with a lawyer if he has one or has the funds to obtain one. The warning of a right to counsel would be hollow if not couched in terms that would convey to the indigent — the person most often subjected to interrogation — the knowledge that he too has a right to have counsel present. As with the warnings of the right to remain silent and of the general right to counsel, only by effective and express explanation to the indigent of this right can there be assurance that he was truly in a position to exercise it.

Once warnings have been given, the subsequent procedure is clear. If the individual indicates in any manner, at any time prior to or during questioning, that he wishes to remain silent, the interrogation must cease. At this point he has shown that he intends to exercise his Fifth Amendment privilege; any statement taken after the person invokes his privilege cannot be other than the product of compulsion, subtle or otherwise. Without the right to cut off questioning, the setting of in-custody interrogation operates on the individual to overcome free choice in producing a statement after the privilege has been once invoked. If the individual states that he wants an attorney, the interrogation must cease until an attorney is present. At that time, the individual must have an opportunity to confer with the attorney and to have him present during any subsequent questioning. If the individual cannot obtain an attorney and he indicates that he wants one before speaking to police, they must respect his decision to remain silent.

This does not mean, as some have suggested, that each police station must have a "station house lawyer" present at all times to advise prisoners. It does mean, however, that if police propose to interrogate a person they must make known to him that he is entitled to a lawyer and that if he cannot afford one, a lawyer will be provided for him prior to any interrogation. If authorities conclude that they will not provide counsel during a reasonable period of time in which investigation in the field is carried out, they may refrain from doing so without violating the person's Fifth Amendment privilege so long as they do not question him during that time.

If the interrogation continues without the presence of an attorney and a statement is taken, a heavy burden rests on the government to demonstrate that the defendant knowingly and intelligently waived his privilege against self-incrimination and his right to retained or appointed counsel. . . . This Court has always set high standards of proof for the waiver of constitutional rights, *Johnson v. Zerbst,* 304 U.S. 458 (1938), and we re-assert these standards as applied to in-custody interrogation. Since the State is responsible for establishing the isolated circumstances under which the interrogation takes place and has the only means of making available corroborated evidence of warnings given during incommunicado interrogation, the burden is rightly on its shoulders. . . .

Whatever the testimony of the authorities as to waiver of rights by an accused, the fact of lengthy interrogation or incommunicado incarceration before a statement is made is strong evidence that the accused did not validly waive his rights. In these circumstances the fact that the individual eventually made a statement is consistent with the conclusion that the compelling influence of the interrogation finally forced him to do so. It is inconsistent with any notion of a voluntary relinquishment of the privilege. Moreover, any evidence that the accused was threatened, tricked, or cajoled into a waiver will, of course, show that the defendant did not voluntarily waive his privilege. The requirement of warnings and waiver of rights is a fundamental with respect to the Fifth Amendment privilege and not simply a preliminary ritual to existing methods of interrogation.

The warnings required and the waiver necessary in accordance with our opinion today are, in the absence of a fully effective equivalent, prerequisites to the admissibility of any statement made by a defendant. No distinction can be drawn between statements which are direct confessions and statements which amount to "admissions" of part or all of an offense. The privilege against self-incrimination protects the individual from being compelled to incriminate himself in any manner; it does not distinguish degrees of incrimination. Similarly, for precisely the same reason, no distinction may be drawn between inculpatory statements and statements alleged to be merely "exculpatory." If a statement made were in fact truly exculpatory it would, of course, never be used by the prosecution. In fact, statements merely intended to be exculpatory by the defendant are often used to impeach his testimony at trial or to demonstrate untruths in the statement given under interrogation and thus to prove guilt by implication. These statements are incriminating in any meaningful sense of the word and may not be used without the full warnings and effective waiver required for any other statement. In *Escobedo* itself, the defendant fully intended his accusation of another as the slayer to be exculpatory as to himself.

The principles announced today deal with the protection which must be given to the privilege against self-incrimination when the individual is first subjected to police interrogation while in custody at the station or otherwise deprived of his freedom of action in any significant way. It is at this point that our adversary system of criminal proceedings commences, distinguishing itself at the outset from the inquisitorial system recognized in some countries. Under the system of warnings we delineate today or under any other system which may be devised and found effective, the safeguards to be erected about the privilege must come into play at this point.

Our decision is not intended to hamper the traditional function of police officers in investigating crime. . . . When an individual is in custody on probable cause, the police may, of course, seek out evidence in the field to be used at trial against him. Such investigation may include inquiry of persons not under restraint. General on-the-scene questioning as to facts surrounding a crime or other general questioning of citizens in the fact-finding process is not affected by our holding. It is an act of responsible citizenship for individuals to give whatever information they may have to aid in law enforcement. In such situations the compelling atmosphere inherent in the process of in-custody interrogation is not necessarily present.

In dealing with statements obtained through interrogation, we do not purport to find all confessions inadmissible. Confessions remain a proper element in law enforcement. Any statement given freely and voluntarily without any compelling influences is, of course, admissible in evidence. The fundamental import of the privilege while an individual is in custody is not whether he is allowed to talk to the police without the benefit of warnings and counsel, but whether he can be interrogated. There is no requirement that police stop a person who enters a police station and states that he wishes to confess to a crime, or a person who calls the police to offer a confession or any other statement he desires to make. Volunteered statements of any kind are not barred by the Fifth Amendment and their admissibility is not affected by our holding today.

To summarize, we hold that when an individual is taken into custody or otherwise deprived of his freedom by the authorities in any significant way and is subjected to questioning, the privilege against self-incrimination is jeopardized. Procedural safeguards must be employed to protect the privilege, and unless other fully effective means are adopted to notify the person of his right of silence and to assure that the exercise of the right will be scrupulously honored, the following measures are required. He must be warned prior to any questioning that he has the right to remain silent, that anything he says can be used against him in a court of law, that he has the right to the presence of an attorney, and that if he cannot afford an attorney one will be appointed for him prior to any questioning if he so desires. Opportunity to exercise these rights must be afforded to him throughout the interrogation. After such warnings have been given, and such opportunity afforded him, the individual may knowingly and intelligently waive these rights and agree to answer questions or make a statement. But unless and until such warnings and waiver are demonstrated by the prosecution at trial, no evidence obtained as a result of interrogation can be used against him.

On March 13, 1963, petitioner, Ernesto Miranda, was arrested at his home and taken in custody to a Phoenix police station. He was there identified by the complaining witness. The police then took him to "Interrogation Room No. 2" of the detective bureau. There he was questioned by two police officers. The officers admitted at trial that Miranda was not advised that he had a right to have an attorney present. Two hours later, the officers emerged from the interrogation room with a written confession signed by Miranda. At the top of the statement was a typed paragraph stating that the confession was made voluntarily, without threats or promises of immunity and "with full knowledge of my legal rights, understanding any statement I make may be used against me."

At his trial before a jury, the written confession was admitted into evidence over the objection of defense counsel, and the officers testified to the prior oral confession made by Miranda during the interrogation. Miranda was found guilty of kidnapping and rape. He was sentenced to 20 to 30 years' imprisonment on each count, the sentences to run concurrently. On appeal, the Supreme Court of Arizona held that Miranda's constitutional rights were not violated in obtaining the confession and affirmed the conviction. . . . In reaching its decision, the court emphasized heavily the fact that Miranda did not specifically request counsel.

We reverse. From the testimony of the officers and by the admission of respondent, it is clear that Miranda was not in any way apprised of his right to consult with an attorney and to have one present during the interrogation, nor was his right not to be compelled to incriminate himself effectively protected in any other manner. Without these warnings the statements were inadmissible. The mere fact that he signed a statement which contained a typed-in clause stating that he had "full knowledge" of his "legal rights" does not approach the knowing and intelligent waiver required to relinquish constitutional rights.

United States v. Wade, 388 U.S. 218 (1967)

Despite the long and vociferous public outcry, by law enforcement officials, political figures in and out of Congress, and many private citizens, that met the Warren Court's decisions in *Escobedo* and *Miranda,* the Court refused to hedge or backtrack in its defense of procedural fairness in criminal justice situations. Indeed, the Warren Court quickly moved to extend the *Miranda* guarantees.

In *Mempa* v. *Rhay,*[1] for example, the Court broadened right to counsel to a probationer during a combined probation revocation and sentencing hearing. A year later in *Mathis* v. *United States,*[2] the Warren Court ruled that a defendant being questioned in jail by Internal Revenue Agents was entitled to his *Miranda* rights and legal counsel as well.

United States v. *Wade* also significantly extended the Sixth Amendment's right to counsel guarantee, here to police lineup procedure used for identi-

1. 389 U.S. 128 (1967).   2. 391 U.S. 1 (1968).

fication purposes prior to trial. In *Wade* the defendant also argued that the police lineup violated his Fifth Amendment protection against self-incrimination. A majority of the Court, led by Justice Brennan, whose majority opinion rejected the defendant's Fifth Amendment plea, upheld his right to counsel during a police lineup. Brennan's view on the applicability of the Fifth Amendment guarantee caused the Court to fragment. Justice Black, for one, agreed with the Sixth Amendment conclusion but disagreed with the Court's ruling against the Fifth Amendment plea. Justice Douglas's view was similar. Justice Fortas, joined by Chief Justice Warren and Justice Douglas, argued that an accused "may not be compelled (in a police lineup) to speak the words uttered by the person who committed the crime." "I am confident," Fortas wrote, "that it could not be compelled in Court. It cannot be compelled in a lineup."[3] Fortas insisted this was self-incrimination and could not be sanctioned under the Fifth Amendment.

Justice White joined by Justices Harlan and Stewart took serious objection to the entire majority position on the Fifth as well as Sixth Amendment. "The premise for the Court's [lineup] rule," White wrote, "is not the general unreliability of eyewitness identification, nor the difficulties inherent in observation, recall, and recognition." White noted that the majority assumed "a narrower evil" as a basis for its decision: improper police suggestions that contribute to erroneous identifications. The Court apparently believes, White said, "that improper police procedures are so widespread that a broad prophylactic rule must be laid down requiring the presence of counsel at all pretrial identification, in order to detect recurring instances of police misconduct." White then remarked that he did not share the Court's "pervasive distrust of all official investigations," which, he added, is unsupported by any factual evidence. Until the Court has a reliable, comprehensive survey of current police practices on which to base "its new rule," White said, it "should avoid excluding relevant evidence from state criminal trials."[4]

The facts in *Wade* indicated that defendant, while in custody on a bank robbery charge, was taken by an FBI agent to a police lineup. He and several other prisoners wearing strips of tape across their faces were directed to speak the words used by the robber at the bank. The defendant's court-appointed lawyer was not notified nor was he present during the lineup. At the trial two bank employees identified the defendant as the robber. Wade argued that forcing him to participate in the lineup and repeat words used by the robber, all without his counsel present, violated his rights under both the Fifth and Sixth Amendments.

Justice Brennan spoke for the Court's majority, which was made up in peculiar fashion. Four members of the Court, Chief Justice Warren and Justices Black, Douglas, and Fortas, agreed with Brennan's argument concerning the necessity for legal counsel during police lineups. They, along with Clark, made up the majority of six on that issue. However, the same four justices would have also upheld *Wade*'s claim under the Fifth Amendment's self-incrimination clause which Brennan rejected.

Mr. Justice Brennan delivered the opinion of the Court, saying in part:

3. 388 U.S. at 260.

4. Ibid., at 251–52.

The fact that the lineup involved no violation of Wade's privilege against self-incrimination does not, however, dispose of his contention that the court-room identifications should have been excluded because the lineup was conducted without notice to and in the absence of his counsel. Our rejection of the right to counsel claim in *Schmerber* rested on our conclusion in that case that "[n]o issue of counsel's ability to assist petitioner in respect of any rights he did possess is presented."

In contrast, in this case it is urged that the assistance of counsel at the lineup was indispensable. . . .

. . . When the Bill of Rights was adopted, there were no organized police forces as we know them today. The accused confronted the prosecutor and the witnesses against him, and the evidence was marshalled, largely at the trial itself. In contrast, today's law enforcement machinery involves critical confrontations of the accused by the prosecution at pretrial proceedings where the results might well settle the accused's fate and reduce the trial itself to a mere formality. In recognition of these realities of modern criminal prosecution, our cases have construed the Sixth Amendment guarantee to apply to "critical" stages of the proceedings. . . .

. . . Finally in *Miranda* v. *Arizona*, 384 U.S. 436, the rules established for custodial interrogation included the right to the presence of counsel. The result was rested on our finding that this and the other rules were necessary to safeguard the privilege against self-incrimination from being jeopardized by such interrogation.

Of course, nothing decided or said in the opinions in the cited cases links the right to counsel only to protection of Fifth Amendment rights. Rather those decisions "no more than reflect a constitutional principle established as long ago as *Powell* v. *Alabama*. . . ." . . . It is central to that principle that in addition to counsel's presence at trial, the accused is guaranteed that he need not stand alone against the State at any stage of the prosecution, formal or informal, in court or out, where counsel's absence might derogate from the accused's right to a fair trial. The security of that right is as much the aim of the right to counsel as it is of the other guarantees of the Sixth Amendment — the right of the accused to a speedy and public trial by an impartial jury, his right to be informed of the nature and cause of the accusation, and his right to be confronted with the witnesses against him and to have compulsory process for obtaining witnesses in his favor. The presence of counsel at such critical confrontations, as at the trial itself, operates to assure that the accused's interests will be protected consistently with our adversary theory of criminal prosecution. . . .

In sum, the principle of *Powell* v. *Alabama* and succeeding cases requires that we scrutinize *any* pretrial confrontation of the accused to determine whether the presence of his counsel is necessary to preserve the defendant's basic right to a fair trial as affected by his right meaningfully to cross-examine the witnesses against him and to have effective assistance of counsel at the trial itself. It calls upon us to analyze whether potential substantial prejudice to defendant's rights inheres in the particular confrontation and the ability of counsel to help avoid that prejudice. . . .

. . . In our view counsel can hardly impede legitimate law enforcement; on the contrary, for the reasons expressed, law enforcement may be assisted by preventing the infiltration of taint in the prosecution's identification evidence. That result cannot help the guilty avoid conviction but can only help assure that the right man has been brought to justice.

Legislative or other regulations, such as those of local police departments, which eliminate the risks of abuse and unintentional suggestion at lineup proceedings and the impediments to meaningful confrontation at trial may also

remove the basis for regarding the stage as "critical." But neither Congress nor
the federal authorities have seen fit to provide a solution. What we hold today
"in no way creates a constitutional straitjacket which will handicap sound efforts
at reform, nor is it intended to have this effect." ...

... The lineup is most often used, as in the present case, to crystallize the
witnesses' identification of the defendant for future reference. We have already
noted that the lineup identification will have that effect. The State may then rest
upon the witnesses' unequivocal courtroom identification, and not mention the
pretrial identification as part of the State's case at trial. Counsel is then in the
predicament in which Wade's counsel found himself — realizing that possible
unfairness at the lineup may be the sole means of attack upon the unequivocal
courtroom identification, and having to probe in the dark in an attempt to
discover and reveal unfairness, while bolstering the government witness' courtroom identification by bringing out and dwelling upon his prior identification.
Since counsel's presence at the lineup would equip him to attack not only the
lineup identification but the courtroom identification as well, limiting the impact
of violation of the right to counsel to exclusion of evidence only of identification
at the lineup itself disregards a critical element of that right. ...

On the record now before us we cannot make the determination whether the
in-court identifications had an independent origin. This was not an issue at trial,
although there is some evidence relevant to a determination. That inquiry is
most properly made in the District Court. We therefore think the appropriate
procedure to be followed is to vacate the conviction pending a hearing to determine whether the in-court identifications had an independent source, or
whether, in any event, the introduction of the evidence was harmless error, ...
and for the District Court to reinstate the conviction or order a new trial, as may
be proper.

The judgment of the Court of Appeals is vacated and the case is remanded to
that court with direction to enter a new judgment vacating the conviction and
remanding the case to the District Court for further proceedings consistent with
this opinion.

Harris v. New York, 401 U.S. 222 (1971)

The record of the generally more conservative Burger Court on Sixth
Amendment right-to-counsel cases is decidedly mixed. In its early years it
seemed to go along with both *Escobedo* and *Miranda.* Soon, however, probably
under pressure of conservative public opinion, it began chipping away at the
guarantees asserted by the Warren Court. For example, in *Argersinger* v. *Ham-
lin*[1] the Burger Court extended *Gideon* and *Escobedo* to require legal counsel in
any type of misdemeanor offense if a jail sentence of any length was possible.
But in *Kirby* v. *Illinois*[2] and *United States* v. *Ash*[3] the Court limited *Wade* by ruling
that legal counsel was not required in a police lineup before indictment.

Yet, because it was *Miranda* that caused the greatest uproar among law
enforcement officials, the Miranda rule came under the most severe criticism
in Congressional "law and order" circles. Largely in response to *Miranda,* in
1968 Congress passed the Crime Control Act, which gave federal judges the
right to decide on the admissibility of evidence basing their judgment on the

1. 407 U.S. 25 (1972).
2. 406 U.S. 682 (1972).
3. 413 U.S. 300 (1973).

"totality of circumstances" as opposed to a strict application of the *Miranda* rule. The Crime Control Act applied only to federal courts.

Harris v. *New York* was the first major encounter. There, in a 5–4 decision, the Supreme Court ruled that a statement that is inadmissible in the prosecution's case, because the *Miranda* rule is not followed, is *admissible* by the prosecutor during cross-examination if the defendant takes the witness stand. Chief Justice Burger spoke for the majority. The dissenters were Justice Black, who wrote no opinion, and Justice Brennan joined by Justices Douglas and Marshall. Brennan argued that if absence of the *Miranda* warnings prohibited the prosecuting attorney from using defendant's statement in presenting the state's case against him, then the absence of *Miranda* warnings also kept the prosecutor from using such statements during cross-examination. Brennan chided the majority's ruling for, in effect, telling police "that they may freely interrogate an accused incommunicado and without counsel and know that although any statement they obtain in violation of *Miranda* cannot be used in the state's direct case, it may be introduced if the defendant has the temerity to testify in his own defense." Brennan accused the majority of going "far toward undoing much of the progress made in conforming police methods to the Constitution."[4]

In *Harris,* the petitioner was convicted of selling heroin to an undercover police officer. Without benefit of counsel and without having been read the *Miranda* warnings, the petitioner made possibly incriminating statements to the police immediately following his arrest. Thus the question, could such statements, barred because of *Miranda* from the state's direct case, be used by the prosecution during cross-examination? The Burger Court's majority of five answered yes.

Mr. Chief Justice Burger delivered the opinion of the Court, saying in part:

Some comments in the *Miranda* opinion can indeed be read as indicating a bar to use of an uncounseled statement for any purpose, but discussion of that issue was not at all necessary to the Court's holding and cannot be regarded as controlling. *Miranda* barred the prosecution from making its case with statements of an accused made while in custody prior to having or effectively waiving counsel. It does not follow from *Miranda* that evidence inadmissible against an accused in the prosecution's case in chief is barred for all purposes, provided of course that the trustworthiness of the evidence satisfies legal standards.

Every criminal defendant is privileged to testify in his own defense, or to refuse to do so. But that privilege cannot be construed to include the right to commit perjury. . . . Having voluntarily taken the stand, petitioner was under an obligation to speak truthfully and accurately, and the prosecution here did no more than utilize the traditional truth-testing devices of the adversary process. Had inconsistent statements been made by the accused to some third person, it could hardly be contended that the conflict could not be laid before the jury by way of cross-examination and impeachment.

The shield provided by *Miranda* cannot be perverted into a license to use perjury by way of a defense, free from the risk of confrontation with prior inconsistent utterances. We hold, therefore, that petitioner's credibility was appropriately impeached by use of his earlier conflicting statements.

4. 401 U.S. at 232.

Oregon v. Hass, 420 U.S. 714 (1975)

Chipping away at *Miranda* continued after *Harris*. In *Michigan* v. *Tucker*,[1] for example, the Burger Court permitted testimony by a witness who had been sought and found by a prosecutor as a result of statements made by the defendant which were *not* admissible under *Miranda*. A year later in *Michigan* v. *Mosley*[2] the Court upheld action of law enforcement officials who, after a two-hour wait, resumed interrogating a suspect who had previously been read his rights under *Miranda* to remain silent. And, to cite one case that seems to arrest this trend somewhat, in *Doyle* v. *Ohio*[3] the Court ruled that the *Miranda* right to remain silent during police interrogations could *not* be used to discredit a defendant's testimony if he later chose to testify at his trial.

Movement away from *Miranda*, which began in *Harris*, was also evident in *Oregon* v. *Hass*, a case that presented a variation of the circumstance the Court had encountered in *Harris*. This time the Burger Court split 6–2 with Justice Blackmun writing for the majority and Justices Brennan and Marshall in dissent. Justice Douglas, then ailing, did not participate. In *Hass*, the Court again ruled that inadmissible testimony could be used by a prosecutor during cross-examination. The record indicated that, after arrest, the suspect was given his full *Miranda* warnings. Later he told police he wished to telephone his attorney. He was told this could not be done until the suspect and the arresting officer had reached the police station. Before getting to the station the suspect gave the officer inculpatory information. Thus the question, could this information, inadmissible because it was given in the absence of counsel, be used against the suspect (Hass) after he had taken the witness stand at his trial and testified contrary to the inculpatory information?

Justice Brennan repeated views expressed in his *Harris* dissent, charging that the Court had now gone even farther to undermine *Miranda*. After the Court's ruling in *Hass*, Brennan said, if a suspect states that he wants an attorney, "police interrogation will doubtless be vigorously pressed to obtain statements before the attorney arrives."

Brennan noted that he was unwilling "to join this fundamental erosion of Fifth and Sixth Amendment rights."[4]

Mr. Justice Blackmun delivered the opinion of the Court, saying in part:

In *Harris*, the defendant was charged by the State in a two-count indictment with twice selling heroin to an undercover police officer. The prosecution introduced evidence of the two sales. Harris took the stand in his own defense. He denied the first sale and described the second as one of baking powder utilized as part of a scheme to defraud the purchaser. On cross-examination, Harris was asked whether he had made specified statements to the police immediately following his arrest; the statements partially contradicted Harris' testimony. In response, Harris testified that he could not remember the questions or answers recited by the prosecutor. The trial court instructed the jury that the statements attributed to Harris could be used only in passing on his credibility and not as evidence of guilt. The jury returned a verdict of guilty on the second count of the indictment.

1. 417 U.S. 433 (1974).   3. 96 S. Ct. 224 (1976).
2. 96 S. Ct. 321 (1975).   4. 420 U.S. at 725.

The prosecution had not sought to use the statements in its case in chief, for it conceded that they were inadmissible under *Miranda* because Harris had not been advised of his right to appointed counsel. THE CHIEF JUSTICE, speaking for the Court, observed, . . . "It does not follow from *Miranda* that evidence inadmissible against an accused in the prosecution's case in chief is barred for all purposes, provided of course that the trustworthiness of the evidence satisfies legal standards." Relying on *Walder* v. *United States,* 347 U.S. 62 (1954), a Fourth Amendment case, we ruled that there was no "difference in principle" between *Walder* and *Harris;* that the "impeachment process here undoubtedly provided valuable aid to the jury in assessing petitioner's credibility"; that the "benefits of this process should not be lost"; that, "[a]ssuming that the exclusionary rule has a deterrent effect on proscribed police conduct, sufficient deterrence flows when the evidence in question is made unavailable to the prosecution in its case in chief," . . . and that the "shield provided by *Miranda* cannot be perverted into a license to use perjury by way of a defense, free from the risk of confrontation with prior inconsistent utterances." . . . It was held, accordingly, that Harris' credibility was appropriately impeached by the use of his earlier conflicting statements.

We see no valid distinction to be made in the application of the principles of *Harris* to that case and to Hass' case. Hass' statements were made after the defendant knew Osterholme's opposing testimony had been ruled inadmissible for the prosecution's case in, chief.

As in *Harris,* it does not follow from *Miranda* that evidence inadmissible against Hass in the prosecution's case in chief is barred for all purposes, always provided that "the trustworthiness of the evidence satisfies legal standards." . . . Again, the impeaching material would provide valuable aid to the jury in assessing the defendant's credibility; again, "the benefits of this process should not be lost," . . . and, again, making the deterrent-effect assumption, there is sufficient deterrence when the evidence in question is made unavailable to the prosecution in its case in chief. If all this sufficed for the result in *Harris,* it supports and demands a like result in Hass' case. Here, too, the shield provided by *Miranda* is not to be perverted to a license to testify inconsistently, or even perjuriously, free from the risk of confrontation with prior inconsistent utterances.

2

FAIR TRIAL

Moore v. Dempsey, 261 U.S. 86 (1923)

Right to a speedy and public trial by an impartial jury is another Sixth Amendment guarantee. In its supervision of criminal justice procedure at the state level the Supreme Court has often been called upon to determine if state court trials and verdicts have been fair, particularly when evidence suggests that "outside pressures" played a role in influencing the outcome of the trial.

One such instance of "outside pressure" occurred in *Moore* v. *Dempsey*. There, with Justice Sutherland dissenting, the Supreme Court decided that a trial for murder in a state court in which the accused are hurried to conviction "under mob domination" without regard to their constitutional rights "is without due process of law and absolutely void."

The case arose in Arkansas and involved, among other things, a race riot atmosphere of killings, beatings, and intimidation attacks on black churches, during which five black men were subsequently convicted of murdering a white man. The defendants maintained their innocence throughout. Daily newspapers in the area published highly inflammatory, hateful, racist articles. Mobs marched to the jail for the purpose of a lynching and were prevented only by the presence of U.S. troops. Justice Holmes's majority opinion noted the following facts concerning the atmosphere in which the trial was conducted. Blacks were "systematically excluded" from possible jury duty. The court and the surrounding neighborhood were "thronged with an adverse crowd" that threatened the most "dangerous consequences to anyone interfering with the desired result." Counsel for defendants "did not venture" to ask for a delay or a change of venue or to challenge the jury candidates. Defense counsel had no opportunity for preliminary consultation with the accused. He called no witnesses. The trial lasted about forty-five minutes and within five minutes the jury returned a guilty verdict of murder in the first degree. Given these circumstances the Supreme Court concluded that "there never was chance" for acquittal; no jury could have voted for an acquittal and continued to live in Phillips County. No prisoner acquitted by the jury "could . . . have escaped the mob."

Moore gave the eloquent Justice Holmes a brief opportunity to express the

226

responsibility the Supreme Court must assume in guaranteeing a fair trial in a state court, particularly in these circumstances, and to emphasize the essential quality of fairness inherent in "due process of law."

Mr. Justice Holmes delivered the opinion of the Court, saying in part:

> In *Frank* v. *Mangum,* 237 U.S. 309, 335, it was recognized of course that if in fact a trial is dominated by a mob so that there is an actual interference with the course of justice, there is a departure from due process of law; and that "if the State, supplying no corrective process, carries into execution a judgment of death or imprisonment based upon a verdict thus produced by mob domination, the State deprives the accused of his life or liberty without due process of law." We assume in accordance with that case that the corrective process supplied by the State may be so adequate that interference by *habeas corpus* ought not to be allowed. It certainly is true that mere mistakes of law in the course of a trial are not to be corrected in that way. But if the case is that the whole proceeding is a mask — that counsel, jury and judge were swept to the fatal end by an irresistible wave of public passion, and that the State Courts failed to correct the wrong, neither perfection in the machinery for correction nor the possibility that the trial court and counsel saw no other way of avoiding an immediate outbreak of the mob can prevent this Court from securing to the petitioners their constitutional rights.

3

A SPEEDY AND PUBLIC TRIAL

As we have seen, incorporation of Bill of Rights guarantees into the Four-teenth Amendment proceeded rapidly during the Warren Court years. After decades of controversy it is now virtually settled that the rights protected against infringement by the federal government are similarly protected against state action. There are holdouts, however, who continue to oppose incorporation. Justice Harlan is perhaps the leading opponent. Harlan and the other anti-incorporationists would rely upon the due process clause of the Fourteenth Amendment to achieve the required essential element of fairness in criminal justice procedure. Harlan also insists that the states bear the pri-mary responsibility for operating the machinery of criminal justice within their borders. Due process requires, Harlan argues, that these procedures be fundamentally fair in all respects.[1] Harlan writes as an advocate of the philos-ophy of judicial federalism, which allows for continuance of a two-tier system of criminal justice. He would use the Fourteenth Amendment but not the Sixth to make certain that the states abide by the principles of fairness and justice in their criminal justice procedures. Adherents of incorporation, and certainly the Chief Justice and other leading members of the Warren Court era were its principal advocates, insist that fairness in criminal justice proce-dure demands identical guarantees of rights in both federal and state courts. This can only be achieved, advocates would argue, by incorporating all the Bill of Rights into the Fourteenth Amendment.

Klopfer v. North Carolina, 386 U.S. 213 (1967)

Using this reasoning the Sixth Amendment guarantee of a "speedy and public trial" was made applicable to the states by the Warren Court in *Klopfer* v. *North Carolina*. Although the constitutional provision "a speedy trial" is an elastic term, Congress has attempted to clarify the issue. In 1974 it passed the Speedy Trial Act, which specified that an arrested person must be charged within thirty days, arraigned within ten days and brought to trial within sixty days of arraignment. There are some exceptions in the law to the 100-day

1. See Harlan's dissent in Duncan v. Louisiana, 391 U.S. at 172.

period, but it does specify that charges might be dismissed against any defendant not brought to trial in a federal court within the period.

The specific "speedy trial" issue involved in *Klopfer,* which was decided before the federal statute went into effect, was whether a state may indefinitely postpone prosecution without stated justification over the objection of an accused who has since been discharged from custody. North Carolina had a unique provision in its criminal procedure called "nolle proseque." It allowed a prosecutor to declare "that he will not, at that time, prosecute the suit further." Yet "nolle proseque" does not take the accused completely off the hook. He may be brought to trial at any time usually at the discretion of the state's solicitor. For this reason the applicability of the Sixth Amendment's speedy trial provision to North Carolina "nolle proseque" was the central issue in *Klopfer.* In this instance the Warren Court was unanimous as it continued a policy of incorporating Bill of Rights guarantees into the Fourteenth Amendment. Strangely enough in *Klopfer* there was no protest from Justice Harlan.

Mr. Chief Justice Warren delivered the opinion of the Court, saying in part:

> The consequence of this extraordinary criminal procedure is made apparent by the case before the Court. A defendant indicted for a misdemeanor may be denied an opportunity to exonerate himself in the discretion of the solicitor and held subject to trial, over his objection, throughout the unlimited period in which the solicitor may restore the case to the calendar. During that period, there is no means by which he can obtain a dismissal or have the case restored to the calendar for trial. In spite of this result, both the Supreme Court and the Attorney General state as a fact, and rely upon it for affirmance in this case, that this procedure as applied to the petitioner placed no limitations upon him, and was in no way violative of his rights. With this we cannot agree.

> We hold here that the right to a speedy trial is as fundamental as any of the rights secured by the Sixth Amendment. That right has its roots at the very foundation of our English law heritage. Its first articulation in modern jurisprudence appears to have been made in Magna Carta (1215), wherein it was written, "We will sell to no man, we will not deny or defer to any man either justice or right"; but evidence of recognition of the right to speedy justice in even earlier times is found in the Assize of Clarendon (1166). By the late thirteenth century, justices, armed with commissions of gaol delivery and/or oyer and terminer were visiting the countryside three times a year. These justices, Sir Edward Coke wrote in Part II of his Institutes, "have not suffered the prisoner to be long detained, but at their next coming have given the prisoner full and speedy justice, . . . without detaining him long in prison." To Coke, prolonged detention without trial would have been contrary to the law and custom of England; but he also believed that the delay in trial, by itself, would be an improper denial of justice. In his explication of Chapter 29 of the Magna Carta, he wrote that the words "We will sell to no man, we will not deny or defer to any man either justice or right" had the following effect:

>> "And therefore, every subject of this realme, for injury done to him *in bonis, terris, vel persona,* by any other subject, be he ecclesiasticall, or temporall, free, or bond, man, or woman, old, or young, or be he outlawed, excommunicated, or any other without exception, may take his remedy by the course of the law, and have justice, and right for the injury done to him, freely without sale, fully without any deniall, and speedily without delay."

Coke's Institutes were read in the American Colonies by virtually every student of the law. Indeed, Thomas Jefferson wrote that at the time he studied law (1762-1767). *"Coke Lyttleton* was the universal elementary book of law students." And to John Rutledge of South Carolina, the Institutes seemed "to be almost the foundation of our law." To Coke, in turn, Magna Carta was one of the fundamental bases of English liberty. Thus, it is not surprising that when George Mason drafted the first of the colonial bills of rights, he set forth a principle of Magna Carta, using phraseology similar to that of Coke's explication: "[I]n all capital or criminal prosecutions," the Virginia Declaration of Rights of 1776 provided, "a man hath a right . . . to a speedy trial. . . ." That this right was considered fundamental at this early period in our history is evidenced by its guarantee in the constitutions of several of the States of the new nation, as well as by its prominent position in the Sixth Amendment. Today, each of the 50 States guarantees the right to a speedy trial to its citizens.

The history of the right to a speedy trial and its reception in this country clearly establish that it is one of the most basic rights preserved by our Constitution.

4

TRIAL BY JURY

Duncan v. Louisiana, 391 U.S. 145 (1968)

There occurred in *Duncan* v. *Louisiana* a classic encounter between the two opposing views of incorporation, in this instance whether the Sixth Amendment's guarantee of a jury trial is applicable to a state whose law grants jury trials only in cases where capital punishment or imprisonment at hard labor may be imposed. Involved in *Duncan* was a misdemeanor charge. In *Duncan* the Warren Court's principle antagonists were Justice Black for incorporation and Justice Harlan opposed.

Although the laws of every state require jury trials in "serious" criminal cases, and that was an issue in *Duncan* (what is a "serious" crime), until *Duncan* the Supreme Court had never ruled that a jury trial in a state court was a right guaranteed by the Federal Constitution. If, as we have noted several times, famous or great cases often make bad law, perhaps "minor" cases may sometimes make "good" law. And the "crime" in *Duncan* seemed minor enough. It arose from a brief and seemingly innocent encounter on a Louisiana road between three black youths and four white youths, all in their late teens. The record indicated that the appellant Duncan, one of the blacks, was about to drive off in his car with the two other blacks who were his cousins, when an encounter of sorts took place. A white youth later testified that before he left, Duncan "had slapped . . . one of the white boys on the elbow." Duncan's cousins testified that he had merely *touched* the white boy on the elbow. Duncan was arrested and ultimately convicted on a simple battery charge and sentenced to sixty days in prison and fined $150. Under Louisiana law simple battery is a misdemeanor punishable by a maximum of two years imprisonment and a $300 fine. On appeal, Duncan argued that his Sixth Amendment right to trial by jury had been abrogated by Louisiana's refusal to grant him such a trial.

In a 7–2 decision the Warren Court reversed Duncan's conviction. It ruled that the penalty authorized for a particular crime (here a maximum of 2 years in jail and a $300 fine) is "of major relevance in determining whether it is a serious one subject to the mandates of the Sixth Amendment." It found that a crime punishable by two years in prison is "serious." The Court declared, therefore, that the appellant was entitled to a jury trial. Justice White spoke for the majority. Yet perhaps the more important and interesting opinions were written by Justice Black concurring and Justice Harlan (with Justice Stewart) dissenting. There the classic pro and con arguments concerning incorporation of Bill of Rights guarantees into the Fourteenth Amendment were expressed. The two jousted clearly and succinctly. For this reason, we reproduce a small portion of the majority opinion and longer portions of the two others.

Mr. Justice White delivered the opinion of the Court, saying in part:

Because we believe that trial by jury in criminal cases is fundamental to the American scheme of justice, we hold that the Fourteenth Amendment guarantees a right of jury trial in all criminal cases which — were they to be tried in a federal court — would come within the Sixth Amendment's guarantee. Since we consider the appeal before us to be such a case, we hold that the Constitution was violated when appellant's demand for jury trial was refused.

Mr. Justice Black wrote a concurring opinion, saying in part:

All of these holdings making Bill of Rights' provisions applicable as such to the States mark, of course, a departure from the *Twining* doctrine holding that none of those provisions were enforceable as such against the States. The dissent in this case, however, makes a spirited and forceful defense of that now discredited doctrine. I do not believe that it is necessary for me to repeat the historical and logical reasons for my challenge to the *Twining* holding contained in my *Adamson* dissent and Appendix to it. What I wrote there in 1947 was the product of years of study and research. My appraisal of the legislative history followed 10 years of legislative experience as a Senator of the United States, not a bad way, I suspect, to learn the value of what is said in legislative debates, committee discussions, committee reports, and various other steps taken in the course of passage of bills, resolutions, and proposed constitutional amendments. My Brother HARLAN's objections to my *Adamson* dissent history, like that of most of the objectors, relies most heavily on a criticism written by Professor Charles Fairman and published in the Stanford Law Review. 2 Stan. L. Rev. 5 (1949). I have read and studied this article extensively, including the historical references, but am compelled to add that in my view it has completely failed to refute the inferences and arguments that I suggested in my *Adamson* dissent. Professor Fairman's "history" relies very heavily on what was *not* said in the state legislatures that passed on the Fourteenth Amendment. Instead of relying on this kind of negative pregnant, my legislative experience has convinced me that it is far wiser to rely on what *was* said, and most importantly, said by the men who actually sponsored the Amendment in the Congress. I know from my years in the United States Senate that it is to men like Congressman Bingham, who steered the Amendment through the House, and Senator Howard, who introduced it in the Senate, that members of Congress look when they seek the real meaning of what is being offered. And they vote for or against a bill based on what the sponsors of that bill and those who oppose it tell them it means. The historical appendix to my *Adamson* dissent leaves no doubt in my mind that both its sponsors and those who opposed it believed the Fourteenth Amendment made the first eight Amendments of the Constitution (the Bill of Rights) applicable to the States.

In addition to the adoption of Professor Fairman's "history," the dissent states that "the great words of the four clauses of the first section of the Fourteenth

Amendment would have been an exceedingly peculiar way to say that 'The rights heretofore guaranteed against federal intrusion by the first eight Amendments are henceforth guaranteed against state intrusion as well.'" . . . In response to this I can say only that the words "No State shall make or enforce any law which shall abridge the privileges or immunities of citizens of the United States" seem to me an eminently reasonable way of expressing the idea that henceforth the Bill of Rights shall apply to the States. What more precious "privilege" of American citizenship could there be than that privilege to claim the protections of our great Bill of Rights? I suggest that any reading of "privileges or immunities of citizens of the United States" which excludes the Bill of Rights' safeguards renders the words of this section of the Fourteenth Amendment meaningless. Senator Howard, who introduced the Fourteenth Amendment for passage in the Senate, certainly read the words this way. . . . From this I conclude, contrary to my Brother HARLAN, that if anything, it is "exceedingly peculiar" to read the Fourteenth Amendment differently from the way I do.

While I do not wish at this time to discuss at length my disagreement with Brother HARLAN's forthright and frank restatement of the now discredited *Twining* doctrine, I do want to point out what appears to me to be the basic difference between us. His view, as was indeed the view of *Twining,* is that "due process is an evolving concept" and therefore that it entails a "gradual process of judicial inclusion and exclusion" to ascertain those "immutable principles . . . of free government which no member of the Union may disregard." Thus the Due Process Clause is treated as prescribing no specific and clearly ascertainable constitutional command that judges must obey in interpreting the Constitution, but rather as leaving judges free to decide at any particular time whether a particular rule or judicial formulation embodies an "immutable principl[e] of free government" or is "implicit in the concept of ordered liberty," or whether certain conduct "shocks the judge's conscience" or runs counter to some other similar, undefined and undefinable standard. Thus due process, according to my Brother HARLAN, is to be a phrase with no permanent meaning, but one which is found to shift from time to time in accordance with judges' predilections and understandings of what is best for the country. If due process means this, the Fourteenth Amendment, in my opinion, might as well have been written that "no person shall be deprived of life, liberty or property except by laws that the judges of the United States Supreme Court shall find to be consistent with the immutable principles of free government." It is impossible for me to believe that such unconfined power is given to judges in our Constitution that is a written one in order to limit governmental power.

Another tenet of the *Twining* doctrine as restated by my Brother HARLAN is that "due process of law requires only fundamental fairness." But the "fundamental fairness" test is one on a par with that of shocking the conscience of the Court. Each of such tests depends entirely on the particular judge's idea of ethics and morals instead of requiring him to depend on the boundaries fixed by the written words of the Constitution. Nothing in the history of the phrase "due process of law" suggests that constitutional controls are to depend on any particular judge's sense of values. The origin of the Due Process Clause is Chapter 39 of Magna Carta which declares that "No free man shall be taken, outlawed, banished, or in any way destroyed, nor will We proceed against or prosecute him, except by the lawful judgment of his peers and by the *law of the land.*" (Emphasis added.) As early as 1354 the words "due process of law" were used in an English statute interpreting Magna Carta, and by the end of the 14th century "due process of law" and "law of the land" were interchangeable. Thus the origin of this clause was the attempt by those who wrote Magna Carta to do away with the so-called trials of that period where people were liable to sudden arrest and summary conviction in courts and by judicial commissions with no sure and definite procedural protections and under laws that might have been improvised to try their particular cases. Chapter 39 of Magna Carta was a guarantee that the government would take neither life, liberty, nor property without a trial in accord with the law of the land that already existed at the time the alleged offense was committed. This means that the Due Process Clause gives all Americans, whoever they are and wherever they happen to be, the right to be tried by independent and unprejudiced courts using established procedures and applying valid pre-existing laws. There is not one word of legal history that justifies making the term "due process of law" mean a guarantee of a trial free from laws and conduct which the courts deem at the time to be "arbitrary," "unreasonable," "unfair," or "contrary to civilized standards." The due process of law standard for a trial is one in accordance with the Bill of Rights and laws passed pursuant to constitutional power, guaranteeing to all alike a trial under the general law of the land.

Finally I want to add that I am not bothered by the argument that applying the Bill of Rights to the States, "according to the same standards that protect those personal rights against federal encroachment," interferes with our concept of federalism in that it may prevent States from trying novel social and economic experiments. I have never believed that under the guise of federalism the States should be able to experiment with the protections afforded our citizens through the Bill of Rights. As Justice Goldberg said so wisely in his concurring opinion in Pointer v. Texas, 380 U.S. 400:

> "to deny to the States the power to impair a fundamental constitutional right is not to increase federal power, but, rather, to limit the power of both federal and state governments in favor of safeguarding the fundamental rights and liberties of the individual. In my view this promotes rather than undermines the basic policy of avoiding excess concentration of power in government, federal or state, which underlies our concepts of federalism." . . .

It seems to me totally inconsistent to advocate, on the one hand, the power of this Court to strike down any state law or practice which it finds "unreasonable" or "unfair" and, on the other hand, urge that the States be given maximum power to develop their own laws and procedures. Yet the due process approach of my Brothers HARLAN and FORTAS (see other concurring opinion, *post,* p. 211) does just that since in effect it restricts the States to practices which a majority of this Court is willing to approve on a case-by-case basis. No one is more concerned than I that the States be allowed to use the full scope of their powers as their citizens see fit. And that is why I have continually fought against the expansion of this Court's authority over the States through the use of a broad, general interpretation of due process that permits judges to strike down state laws they do not like.

In closing I want to emphasize that I believe as strongly as ever that the Fourteenth Amendment was intended to make the Bill of Rights applicable to the States. I have been willing to support the selective incorporation doctrine, however, as an alternative, although perhaps less historically supportable than complete incorporation. The selective incorporation process, if used properly, does limit the Supreme Court in the Fourteenth Amendment field to specific Bill of Rights' protections only and keeps judges from roaming at will in their own notions of what policies outside the Bill of Rights are desirable and what are not. And, most importantly for me, the selective incorporation process has the virtue of having already worked to make most of the Bill of Rights' protections applicable to the States.

Mr. Justice Harlan, joined by Justice Stewart, dissented, saying in part:

Every American jurisdiction provides for trial by jury in criminal cases. The question before us is not whether jury trial is an ancient institution, which it is; nor whether it plays a significant role in the administration of criminal justice, which it does; nor whether it will endure, which it shall. The question in this case is whether the State of Louisiana, which provides trial by jury for all felonies, is prohibited by the Constitution from trying charges of simple battery to the court alone. In my view, the answer to that question, mandated alike by our constitutional history and by the longer history of trial by jury, is clearly "no."

The States have always borne primary responsibility for operating the machinery of criminal justice within their borders, and adapting it to their particular circumstances. In exercising this responsibility, each State is compelled to conform its procedures to the requirements of the Federal Constitution. The Due Process Clause of the Fourteenth Amendment requires that those procedures be fundamentally fair in all respects. It does not, in my view, impose or encourage nationwide uniformity for its own sake; it does not command adherence to forms that happen to be old; and it does not impose on the States the rules that may be in force in the federal courts except where such rules are also found to be essential to basic fairness.

The Court's approach to this case is an uneasy and illogical compromise among the views of various Justices on how the Due Process Clause should be interpreted. The Court does not say that those who framed the Fourteenth Amendment intended to make the Sixth Amendment applicable to the States. And the Court concedes that it finds nothing unfair about the procedure by which the present appellant was tried. Nevertheless, the Court reverses his conviction: it holds, for some reason not apparent to me, that the Due Process Clause incorporates the particular clause of the Sixth Amendment that requires trial by jury in federal criminal cases — including, as I read its opinion, the sometimes trivial accompanying baggage of judicial interpretation in federal contexts. I have raised my voice many times before against the Court's continuing undiscriminating insistence upon fastening on the States federal notions of criminal justice, and I must do so again in this instance. With all respect, the Court's approach and its reading of history are altogether topsy-turvy.

5

DISCRIMINATION IN JURY SELECTION

The century-old practice in the South of systematically and deliberately keeping black people off grand and trial juries has raised constitutional questions concerning the fairness of trials when the defendant is black and the jury, because of racial discrimination, is all white. Supreme Court review of jury selection practices in states where evidence of such discrimination exists is required by both the due process clause and the equal protection clause of the Fourteenth Amendment, and, under incorporation, by the Sixth Amendment's fair-trial guarantee as well.

The Supreme Court first confronted the issue in 1880. In *Virginia* v. *Rives*[1] it ruled that the absence of blacks on a jury during a murder trial did not pose constitutional problems. This ruling that black petitioners had no constitutional *right* to blacks on juries made it possible for southern states to exclude blacks based upon the customs and racial attitudes of the region.

Norris v. Alabama, 294 U.S. 580 (1935)

The system was left undisturbed until *Norris* v. *Alabama,* the second of the famous Scottsboro cases. As we have seen in *Powell* v. *Alabama* (above) the Supreme Court reversed the conviction of the "Scottsboro boys" because the absence of defense counsel during their trial violated their rights under the Constitution. After this reversal a second trial was then held in another Alabama County. The defendants were once again found guilty of rape. This second conviction was attacked on different grounds. The defendants argued they had been denied a fair trial because blacks were intentionally excluded from duty on the grand jury that returned the second indictment and from the trial jury that returned the second guilty verdict. In fact, in its review the Supreme Court found that no blacks had ever served on juries in the two counties, at least for as long as anyone in the area could remember. In *Norris,* a unanimous Supreme Court reversed the Alabama conviction and ruled that exclusion of black people from grand and trial juries denied a black defendant equal protection of the law guaranteed by the Fourteenth Amendment.

Mr. Chief Justice Hughes delivered the opinion of the Court, saying in part:

1. 100 U.S. 313 (1880).

There is no controversy as to the constitutional principle involved. That principle, long since declared, was not challenged, but was expressly recognized, by the Supreme Court of the State. Summing up precisely the effect of earlier decisions, this Court thus stated the principle in *Carter v. Texas,* 177 U.S. 442, 447, in relation to exclusion from service on grand juries: "Whenever by any action of a State, whether through its legislature, through its courts, or through its executive or administrative officers, all persons of the African race are excluded, solely because of their race or color, from serving as grand jurors in the criminal prosecution of a person of the African race, the equal protection of the laws is denied to him, contrary to the Fourteenth Amendment of the Constitution of the United States. . . . And although the state statute defining the qualifications of jurors may be fair on its face, the constitutional provision affords protection against action of the State through its administrative officers in effecting the prohibited discrimination. . . ."

The question is of the application of this established principle to the facts disclosed by the record. That the question is one of fact does not relieve us of the duty to determine whether in truth a federal right has been denied. When a federal right has been specially set up and claimed in a state court, it is our province to inquire not merely whether it was denied in express terms but also whether it was denied in substance and effect. If this requires an examination of evidence, that examination must be made. Otherwise, review by this Court would fail of its purpose in safeguarding constitutional rights. Thus, whenever a conclusion of law of a state court as to a federal right and findings of fact are so intermingled that the latter control the former, it is incumbent upon us to analyze the facts in order that the appropriate enforcement of the federal right may be assured. . . .

Defendant adduced evidence to support the charge of unconstitutional discrimination in the actual administration of the statute in Jackson County. The testimony, as the state court said, tended to show that "in a long number of years no negro had been called for jury service in that county." It appeared that no negro had served on any grand or petit jury in that county within the memory of witnesses who had lived there all their lives. Testimony to that effect was given by men whose ages ran from fifty to seventy-six years. Their testimony was uncontradicted. It was supported by the testimony of officials. The clerk of the jury commission and the clerk of the circuit court had never known of a negro serving on a grand jury in Jackson County. The court reporter, who had not missed a session in that county in twenty-four years, and two jury commissioners testified to the same effect. One of the latter, who was a member of the commission which made up the jury roll for the grand jury which found the indictment, testified that he had "never known of a single instance where any negro sat on any grand or petit jury in the entire history of that county."

That testimony in itself made out a *prima facie* case of the denial of the equal protection which the Constitution guarantees. . . . The case thus made was supplemented by direct testimony that specified negroes, thirty or more in number, were qualified for jury service. Among these were negroes who were members of school boards, or trustees, of colored schools, and property owners and householders. It also appeared that negroes from that county had been called for jury service in the federal court. Several of those who were thus described as qualified were witnesses. While there was testimony which cast doubt upon the qualifications of some of the negroes who had been named, and there was also general testimony by the editor of a local newspaper who gave his opinion as to the lack of "sound judgment" of the "good negroes" in Jackson County, we think that the definite testimony as to the actual qualifications of individual negroes, which was not met by any testimony equally direct, showed that there were negroes in Jackson County qualified for jury service.

The question arose whether names of negroes were in fact on the jury roll. The books containing the jury roll for Jackson County for the year 1930–31 were produced. They were produced from the custody of a member of the jury commission which, in 1931, had succeeded the commission which had made up the jury roll from which the grand jury in question had been drawn. On the pages of this roll appeared the names of six negroes. They were entered, respectively, at the end of the precinct lists which were alphabetically arranged. The genuineness of these entries was disputed. It appeared that after the jury roll in question had been made up, and after the new jury commission had taken office, one of the new commissioners directed the new clerk to draw lines after the names which had been placed on the roll by the preceding commission. These lines, on the pages under consideration, were red lines, and the clerk of the old commission testified that they were not put in by him. The entries made by the new clerk, for the new jury roll, were below these lines.

The names of the six negroes were in each instance written immediately above the red lines. An expert of long experience testified that these names were superimposed upon the red lines, that is, that they were written after the lines had been drawn. The expert was not cross-examined and no testimony was introduced to contradict him. In denying the motion to quash, the trial judge expressed the view that he would not "be authorized to presume that somebody had committed a crime" or to presume that the jury board" had been unfaithful to their duties and allowed the books to be tampered with." His conclusion was that names of negroes were on the jury roll.

We think that the evidence did not justify that conclusion. The Supreme Court of the State did not sustain it. That court observed that the charge that the names of negroes were fraudulently placed on the roll did not involve any member of the jury board, and that the charge "was, by implication at least, laid at the door of the clerk of the board." The court, reaching its decision irrespective of that question, treated that phase of the matter as "wholly immaterial" and hence passed it by "without any expression of opinion thereon."

The state court rested its decision upon the ground that even if it were assumed that there was no name of a negro on the jury roll, it was not established that race or color caused the omission. The court pointed out that the statute fixed a high standard of qualifications for jurors . . . and that the jury commission was vested with a wide discretion. The court adverted to the fact that more white citizens possessing age qualifications had been omitted from the jury roll than the entire negro population of the county, and regarded the testimony as being to the effect that "the matter of race, color, politics, religion or fraternal affiliations" had not been discussed by the commission and had not entered into their consideration, and that no one had been excluded because of race or color.

The testimony showed the practice of the jury commission. One of the commissioners who made up the jury roll in question, and the clerk of that commission, testified as to the manner of its preparation. The other two commissioners of that period did not testify. It was shown that the clerk, under the direction of the commissioners, made up a preliminary list which was based on the registration list of voters, the polling list and the tax list, and apparently also upon the telephone directory. The clerk testified that he made up a list of all male citizens between the ages of twenty-one and sixty-five years without regard to their status or qualifications. The commissioner testified that the designation "col." was placed after the names of those who were colored. In preparing the final jury roll, the preliminary list was checked off as to qualified jurors with the aid of men whom the commissioners called in for that purpose from the different precincts. And the commissioner testified that in the selections for the jury roll no one was "automatically or systematically" excluded, or excluded on account of race or color; that he "did not inquire as to color, that was not discussed."

But, in appraising the action of the commissioners, these statements cannot be divorced from other testimony. As we have seen, there was testimony, not overborne or discredited, that there were in fact negroes in the county qualified for jury service. That testimony was direct and specific. After eliminating those persons as to whom there was some evidence of lack of qualifications, a considerable number of others remained. The fact that the testimony as to these persons, fully identified, was not challenged by evidence appropriately direct, cannot be brushed aside. There is no ground for an assumption that the names of these negroes were not on the preliminary list. The inference to be drawn from the testimony is that they were on that preliminary list, and were designated on that list as the names of negroes, and that they were not placed on the jury roll. There was thus presented a test of the practice of the commissioners. Something more than mere general asseverations was required. Why were these names excluded from the jury roll? Was it because of the lack of statutory qualifications? Were the qualifications of negroes actually and properly considered?

The testimony of the commissioner on this crucial question puts the case in a strong light. That testimony leads to the conclusion that these or other negroes were not excluded on account of age, or lack of esteem in the community for integrity and judgment, or because of disease or want of any other qualification. The commissioner's answer to specific inquiry upon this point was that negroes were "never discussed." . . .

We are of the opinion that the evidence required a different result from that reached in the state court. We think that the evidence that for a generation or longer no negro had been called for service on any jury in Jackson County, that there were negroes qualified for jury service, that according to the practice of the jury commission their names would normally appear on the preliminary list of male citizens of the requisite age but that no names of negroes were placed on the jury roll, and the testimony with respect to the lack of appropriate consideration of the qualifications of negroes, established the discrimination which the Constitution forbids. The motion to quash the indictment upon that ground should have been granted. . . .

For this long-continued, unvarying, and wholesale exclusion of negroes from jury service we find no justification consistent with the constitutional mandate. We have carefully examined the testimony of the jury commissioners upon which the state court based its decision. One of these commissioners testified in person and the other two submitted brief affidavits. . . . The member of the jury board, who testified orally, said that a list was made up which included the names of all male citizens of suitable age; that black residents were not excluded from this general list; that in compiling the jury roll he did not consider race or color; that no one was excluded for that reason; and that he had placed on the jury roll the names of persons possessing the qualifications under the statute. The affidavits of the other members of the board contained general statements to the same effect.

We think that this evidence failed to rebut the strong *prima facie* case which defendant had made. That showing as to the long-continued exclusion of negroes from jury service, and as to the many negroes qualified for that service, could not be met by mere generalities. If, in the presence of such testimony as defendant adduced, the mere general assertions by officials of their performance of duty were to be accepted as an adequate justification for the complete exclusion of negroes from jury service, the constitutional provision — adopted with special reference to their protection — would be but a vain and illusory requirement. The general attitude of the jury commissioner is shown by the following extract from his testimony: "I do not know of any negro in Morgan County over twenty-one and under sixty-five who is generally reputed to be honest and intelligent and who is esteemed in the community for his integrity,

good character and sound judgment, who is not an habitual drunkard, who isn't
afflicted with a permanent disease or physical weakness which would render him
unfit to discharge the duties of a juror, and who can read English, and who has
never been convicted of a crime involving moral turpitude." In the light of the
testimony given by defendant's witnesses, we find it impossible to accept such a
sweeping characterization of the lack of qualifications of negroes in Morgan
County. It is so sweeping, and so contrary to the evidence as to the many qualified negroes, that it destroys the intended effect of the commissioner's testimony.

In *Neal* v. *Delaware, supra,* decided over fifty years ago, this Court observed
that it was a "violent presumption," in which the state court had there indulged,
that the uniform exclusion of negroes from juries, during a period of many
years, was solely because, in the judgment of the officers, charged with the
selection of grand and petit jurors, fairly exercised, "the black race in Delaware
were utterly disqualified by want of intelligence, experience, or moral integrity,
to sit on juries." Such a presumption at the present time would be no less violent
with respect to the exclusion of the negroes of Morgan County. And, upon the
proof contained in the record now before us, a conclusion that their continuous
and total exclusion from juries was because there were none possessing the
requisite qualifications, cannot be sustained.

We are concerned only with the federal question which we have discussed,
and in view of the denial of the federal right suitably asserted, the judgment
must be reversed and the cause remanded for further proceedings not inconsistent with this opinion.

Smith v. Texas, 311 U.S. 128 (1940)

Five years after *Norris,* a unanimous Supreme Court reached similar conclusions concerning the fairness of a trial where the evidence indicated that
once again blacks were intentionally kept from serving on juries by the customs of the region. In *Smith* v. *Texas* the Court emphasized an important
principle of fairness. In order to meet fair trial constitutional requirements,
the Court said, jury selection must be based upon the principle that juries
should represent a cross section of the community.

Smith involved the rape conviction of a black man in a Harris County court.
Evidence indicated that blacks never turned up on juries in Harris County
despite the fact they were more than 20 percent of the county's population. As
it had in *Norris,* the Supreme Court reversed the state court conviction and
decided that a black defendant was denied rights under the Fourteenth
Amendment when tried by an all-white jury selected as a result of deliberate
racial discrimination against black citizens.

Mr. Justice Black delivered the opinion of the Court, saying in part:

It is petitioner's contention that his conviction was based on an indictment
obtained in violation of the provision of the Fourteenth Amendment that "No
State shall . . . deny to any person within its jurisdiction the equal protection of
the laws." And the contention that equal protection was denied him rests on a
charge that negroes were, in 1938 and long prior thereto, intentionally and
systematically excluded from grand jury service solely on account of their race
and color. That a conviction based upon an indictment returned by a jury so

selected is a denial of equal protection is well settled, and is not challenged by the state. But both the trial court and the Texas Criminal Court of Appeals were of opinion that the evidence failed to support the charge of racial discrimination. For that reason the Appellate Court approved the trial court's action in denying petitioner's timely motion to quash the indictment. But the question decided rested upon a charge of denial of equal protection, a basic right protected by the Federal Constitution. And it is therefore our responsibility to appraise the evidence as it relates to this constitutional right.

It is part of the established tradition in the use of juries as instruments of public justice that the jury be a body truly representative of the community. For racial discrimination to result in the exclusion from jury service of otherwise qualified groups not only violates our Constitution and the laws enacted under it but is at war with our basic concepts of a democratic society and a representative government. We must consider this record in the light of these important principles. The fact that the written words of a state's laws hold out a promise that no such discrimination will be practiced is not enough. The Fourteenth Amendment requires that equal protection to all must be given — not merely promised. . . .

The state argues that the testimony of the commissioners themselves shows that there was no arbitrary or systematic exclusion. And it is true that two of the three commissioners who drew the September, 1938, panel testified to that effect. Both of them admitted that they did not select any negroes, although the subject was discussed, but both categorically denied that they intentionally, arbitrarily or systematically discriminated against negro jurors as such. One said that their failure to select negroes was because they did not know the names of any who were qualified and the other said that he was not personally acquainted with any member of the negro race. This is, at best, the testimony of two individuals who participated in drawing 1 out of the 32 jury panels discussed in the record. But even if their testimony were given the greatest possible effect, and their situation considered typical of that of the 94 commissioners who did not testify, we would still feel compelled to reverse the decision below. What the Fourteenth Amendment prohibits is racial discrimination in the selection of grand juries. Where jury commissioners limit those from whom grand juries are selected to their own personal acquaintance, discrimination can arise from commissioners who know no negroes as well as from commissioners who know but eliminate them. If there has been discrimination, whether accomplished ingeniously or ingenuously, the conviction cannot stand.

Taylor v. Louisiana, 419 U.S. 522 (1975)

After *Norris* and *Smith* several other cases came before the Supreme Court dealing with the issue of racial discrimination in jury selection. We mention but three: *Akins* v. *Texas*,[1] *Cassell* v. *Texas*,[2] and *Hernandez* v. *Texas*.[3] In *Akins* the Supreme Court found that jury commissioners had placed one (token) black on the county grand jury. The Court upheld the practice on grounds that the equal protection clause did not mean an exact racial quota system was necessary in jury selection. Five years later, however, in *Cassell*, the Court ruled a Texas grand jury unconstitutionally formed because for twenty-one years there had never been more than one black person on the county grand jury.

1. 325 U.S. 398 (1945).
2. 339 U.S. 282 (1950).
3. 347 U.S. 475 (1954).

And in *Hernandez* the issue of Mexican-American representation on juries came up for the first time. There the Supreme Court again reversed a state court conviction on grounds that deliberate discrimination in jury selection against people of Mexican origin had deprived the defendant Hernandez of a fair trial.

The Supreme Court has also had two opportunities to rule on still another form of jury selection discrimination, discrimination against women. According to English common law principles, which became part of American constitutional and legal practice, women were ineligible for jury duty. In *Strauder* v. *West Virginia*[4] for example, where the issue came up for the first time, the Supreme Court decided that a state could limit jury duty to males without violating the Constitution. Then in 1898, Utah became the first state to allow women on juries. Soon thereafter all the other states followed suit. Many, however, had qualifications in their laws. Florida, for example, allowed women to serve on juries only if they specifically asked the court clerk to be included on a jury list. The Supreme Court upheld this provision in *Hoyt* v. *Florida*[5] recognizing, the Court said, that a woman has "special responsibilities" at home and to her family which might limit her jury availability.

Fourteen years later in *Taylor* v. *Louisiana,* the Supreme Court finally acknowledged "the current judgment of the country," and ruled unconstitutional a Louisiana law similar to the one it had upheld in *Hoyt.* In *Taylor,* appellant, a male, was convicted and sentenced to death[6] for "aggravated kidnapping" by an all-male jury. Louisiana's constitutional and statutory law required that a woman should not be selected for jury duty without first having filed a written declaration indicating that wish. Appellant challenged the Louisiana jury selection system arguing that it deprived him of a federal constitutional right to "a fair trial by jury of a representative segment of the community . . . ," the cross section principle of *Smith* v. *Texas* (above).

Speaking for the majority of eight (only Justice Rehnquist dissented), Justice White noted that the background against which *Taylor* was decided included the 1968 case, *Duncan* v. *Louisiana*[7] (above). There, as we have seen, in another of its famous incorporation decisions, the Warren Court had ruled that the Sixth Amendment's guarantee of a jury trial is made binding on the states via the Fourteenth Amendment. In *Taylor,* therefore, as the majority saw it, the issue became whether the presence of a "fair cross section of the community" on lists from which juries are drawn (women made up 53 percent of the citizens eligible for jury duty) is essential to fulfillment of the Sixth Amendment guarantee of an impartial jury trial in criminal prosecutions. The Burger Court ruled it was.

Mr. Justice White delivered the opinion of the Court, saying in part:

> The Louisiana jury-selection system does not disqualify women from jury service, but in operation its conceded systematic impact is that only a very few women, grossly disproportionate to the number of eligible women in the com-

4. 100 U.S. 303 (1880).

5. 368 U.S. 57 (1961).

6. The death sentence was set aside by the Supreme Court of Louisiana in accord with the Supreme Court's ruling in *Furman* v. *Georgia* (1972), see below.

7. 391 U.S. 145 (1968).

munity, are called for jury service. In this case, no women were on the venire from which the petit jury was drawn. The issue we have, therefore, is whether a jury-selection system which operates to exclude from jury service an identifiable class of citizens constituting 53 percent of eligible jurors in the community comports with the Sixth and Fourteenth Amendments. . . .

The unmistakable import of this Court's opinions, at least since 1940, *Smith* v. *Texas, supra,* and not repudiated by intervening decisions, is that the selection of a petit jury from a representative cross section of the community is an essential component of the Sixth Amendment right to a jury trial. Recent federal legislation governing jury selection within the federal court system has a similar thrust. . . .

We accept the fair-cross-section requirement as fundamental to the jury trial guaranteed by the Sixth Amendment and are convinced that the requirement has solid foundation. The purpose of a jury is to guard against the exercise of arbitrary power — to make available the commonsense judgment of the community as a hedge against the overzealous or mistaken prosecutor and in preference to the professional or perhaps overconditioned or biased response of a judge. . . . This prophylactic vehicle is not provided if the jury pool is made up of only special segments of the populace or if large, distinctive groups are excluded from the pool. Community participation in the administration of the criminal law, moreover, is not only consistent with our democratic heritage but is also critical to public confidence in the fairness of the criminal justice system. Restricting jury service to only special groups or excluding identifiable segments playing major roles in the community cannot be squared with the constitutional concept of jury trial. . . .

We are also persuaded that the fair-cross-section requirement is violated by the systematic exclusion of women, who in the judicial district involved here amounted to 53 percent of the citizens eligible for jury service. This conclusion necessarily entails the judgment that women are sufficiently numerous and distinct from men and that if they are systematically eliminated from jury panels, the Sixth Amendment's fair-cross-section requirement cannot be satisfied. . . .

It should also be emphasized that in holding that petit juries must be drawn from a source fairly representative of the community we impose no requirement that petit juries actually chosen must mirror the community and reflect the various distinctive groups in the population. Defendants are not entitled to a jury of any particular composition, . . . but the jury wheels, pools of names, panels, or venires from which juries are drawn must not systematically exclude distinctive groups in the community and thereby fail to be reasonably representative thereof. . . .

6

WITNESSES

Pointer v. Texas, 380 U.S. 400 (1965)

The Sixth Amendment guarantee that in all criminal proceedings defendant must be "confronted with the witnesses against him," was incorporated into the Fourteenth Amendment by the Warren Court in *Pointer* v. *Texas*. There a unanimous Supreme Court ruled that the right to be confronted by witnesses and to cross-examine them is fundamental to a fair trial and is made obligatory on the states by the Fourteenth Amendment.

This had not always been the Court's position. In *West* v. *Louisiana*[1] for example, an earlier Court had ruled that the Sixth Amendment's right of confrontation did not apply to trials in state courts. As we have seen, however, in a series of significant rulings the Warren Court incorporated most Fifth and Sixth Amendment criminal justice procedure into the due process clause of the Fourteenth Amendment. In *Pointer,* the Sixth Amendment's right to confrontation by witnesses was similarly incorporated. The Warren Court's leading advocate of incorporation, Justice Black, spoke for the majority.

The petitioner (Pointer) was arrested on a robbery charge and brought before a state judge for a preliminary hearing (in Texas it is called the "examining trial"). The complaining witness testified but Pointer, who had no counsel, did not cross-examine him. By the time Pointer was brought to trial, the witness had moved to another state. Nevertheless, his testimony at the hearing was introduced at the trial. The petitioner objected on grounds that he was being denied his right to confront the witness. Pointer was found guilty and the conviction was upheld by the Texas Supreme Court. The Warren Court reversed the conviction, arguing that the same standards must prevail in a state trial as would in a federal court. And in a federal court, Black said, the petitioner's right to confront and cross-examine witnesses would have been unquestioned. While concurring in the Court's decision, Justices Harlan and Stewart continued their insistence that the Fourteenth Amendment's due process clause controlled such cases. Both disagreed, however, with what Harlan called "another step in the onward march of the long since discredited 'incorporation' doctrine. . . ." But incorporation, (despite Harlan) by no means "discredited," continued to prevail.

Mr. Justice Black delivered the opinion of the Court, saying in part:

1. 194 U.S. 258 (1903).

244

We hold today that the Sixth Amendment's right of an accused to confront the witnesses against him is likewise a fundamental right and is made obligatory on the States by the Fourteenth Amendment.

It cannot seriously be doubted at this late date that the right of cross-examination is included in the right of an accused in a criminal case to confront the witnesses against him. And probably no one, certainly no one experienced in the trial of lawsuits, would deny the value of cross-examination in exposing falsehood and bringing out the truth in the trial of a criminal case. . . . The fact that this right appears in the Sixth Amendment of our Bill of Rights reflects the belief of the Framers of those liberties and safeguards that confrontation was a fundamental right essential to a fair trial in a criminal prosecution. Moreover, the decisions of this Court and other courts throughout the years have constantly emphasized the necessity for cross-examination as a protection for defendants in criminal cases. This Court in *Kirby* v. *United States,* 174 U.S. 47, 55, 56, referred to the right of confrontation as "[o]ne of the fundamental guarantees of life and liberty," and "a right long deemed so essential for the due protection of life and liberty that it is guarded against legislative and judicial action by provisions in the Constitution of the United States and in the constitutions of most if not of all the States composing the Union." Mr. Justice Stone, writing for the Court in *Alford v. United States,* 282 U.S. 687, 692, declared that the right of cross-examination is "one of the safeguards essential to a fair trial." And in speaking of confrontation and cross-examination this Court said in *Greene* v. *McElroy,* 360 U.S. 474:

> "They have ancient roots. They find expression in the Sixth Amendment which provides that in all criminal cases the accused shall enjoy the right 'to be confronted with the witnesses against him.' This Court has been zealous to protect these rights from erosion."

There are few subjects, perhaps, upon which this Court and other courts have been more nearly unanimous than in their expressions of belief that the right of confrontation and cross-examination is an essential and fundamental requirement for the kind of fair trial which is this country's constitutional goal. Indeed, we have expressly declared that to deprive an accused of the right to cross-examine the witnesses against him is a denial of the Fourteenth Amendment's guarantee of due process of law. . . .

Under this Court's prior decisions, the Sixth Amendment's guarantee of confrontation and cross-examination was unquestionably denied petitioner in this case. As has been pointed out, a major reason underlying the constitutional confrontation rule is to give a defendant charged with crime an opportunity to cross-examine the witnesses against him. . . . Since we hold that the right of an accused to be confronted with the witnesses against him must be determined by the same standards whether the right is denied in a federal or state proceeding, it follows that use of the transcript to convict petitioner denied him a constitutional right, and that his conviction must be reversed.

Washington v. Texas, 388 U.S. 14 (1967)

Two years after *Pointer,* in another Sixth Amendment "witness" case, *Washington* v. *Texas,* the Warren Court ruled that a defendant's right to have compulsory process for obtaining witnesses in his favor also applies to the states through the Fourteenth Amendment. Once again the Court was unanimous and once again Justice Harlan wrote a concurring opinion insisting that the due process clause of the Fourteenth Amendment was the proper vehicle to decide cases of this nature. As he had in *Pointer* (above) Harlan chided the Court for its "incorporationist approach," which, he said, "strain[ed]" the intent of the Sixth Amendment.

In *Washington*, the petitioner, an eighteen-year-old youth, was convicted in Dallas County of murder and sentenced to fifty years in prison. Conflicting evidence suggested that the fatal shotgun blast might have been fired either by Washington or by a friend (Fuller) in a jealousy-inspired, jilted suitor situation. The petitioner took the witness stand at his trial and testified that Fuller had fired the shotgun. The record indicates that had he been called as a witness, Fuller, himself, would have testified that Washington "pulled at him and tried to persuade him to leave and that petitioner ran before Fuller fired the fatal shot."[1] For this reason it was undisputed that Fuller's testimony was vital to the defense. However, Fuller had been previously convicted of the same murder and was confined in the Dallas County jail during Washington's trial. Two Texas statutes provided that persons charged or convicted as coparticipants in the same crime could not testify for one another. Did these statutes, therefore, prevent the petitioner from receiving a fair trial by denying him the right to have compulsory process for obtaining witnesses in his favor as the Sixth Amendment demands? The Warren Court ruled they did and reversed Washington's conviction.

Mr. Chief Justice Warren delivered the opinion of the Court, saying in part:

> We have not previously been called upon to decide whether the right of an accused to have compulsory process for obtaining witnesses in his favor, guaranteed in federal trials by the Sixth Amendment, is so fundamental and essential to a fair trial that it is incorporated in the Due Process Clause of the Fourteenth Amendment. At one time, it was thought that the Sixth Amendment had no application to state criminal trials. That view no longer prevails, and in recent years we have increasingly looked to the specific guarantees of the Sixth Amendment to determine whether a state criminal trial was conducted with due process of law. We have held that due process requires that the accused have the assistance of counsel for his defense, that he be confronted with the witnesses against him, and that he have the right to a speedy and public trial.
>
> The right of an accused to have compulsory process for obtaining witnesses in his favor stands on no lesser footing than the other Sixth Amendment rights that we have previously held applicable to the States. ... The right to offer the testimony of witnesses, and to compel their attendance, if necessary, is in plain terms the right to present a defense, the right to present the defendant's version of the facts as well as the prosecution's to the jury so it may decide where the truth lies. Just as an accused has the right to confront the prosecution's witnesses for the purpose of challenging their testimony, he has the right to present his own witnesses to establish a defense. This right is a fundamental element of due process of law. ...
>
> The [Texas] rule disqualifying an alleged accomplice from testifying on behalf of the defendant cannot even be defended on the ground that it rationally sets apart a group of persons who are particularly likely to commit perjury. The absurdity of the rule is amply demonstrated by the exceptions that have been made to it. For example, the accused accomplice may be called by the prosecution to testify against the defendant. Common sense would suggest that he often has a greater interest in lying in favor of the prosecution rather than against it,

1. From the opinion of the Court, 388 U.S. at 16.

especially if he is still awaiting his own trial or sentencing. To think that criminals will lie to save their fellows but not to obtain favors from the prosecution for themselves is indeed to clothe the criminal class with more nobility than one might expect to find in the public at large. Moreover, under the Texas statutes the accused accomplice is no longer disqualified if he is acquitted at his own trial. Presumably, he would then be free to testify on behalf of his comrade, secure in the knowledge that he could incriminate himself as freely as he liked in his testimony, since he could not again be prosecuted for the same offense. The Texas law leaves him free to testify when he has a great incentive to perjury, and bars his testimony in situations where he had a lesser motive to lie.

We hold that the petitioner in this case was denied his right to have compulsory process for obtaining witnesses in his favor because the State arbitrarily denied him the right to put on the stand a witness who was physically and mentally capable of testifying to events that he had personally observed, and whose testimony would have been relevant and material to the defense. The Framers of the Constitution did not intend to commit the futile act of giving to a defendant the right to secure the attendance of witnesses whose testimony he had no right to use. The judgment of conviction must be reversed.

7

JURY SIZE AND UNANIMITY

After the Warren Court ruled in *Duncan* v. *Louisiana* (above) that a jury trial in a state court was a fundamental constitutional right, thus incorporating the Sixth Amendment guarantee into the Fourteenth, it was assumed that the rules governing the composition of federal juries would also apply to state juries, particularly with respect to jury size. In 1898, the Supreme Court had (supposedly) settled the question of federal jury size. The case was *Thompson* v. *Utah*.[1]

There the Court ruled that a federal jury must consist of twelve persons as it had, and does, under English common law. Origin of the number twelve is itself unclear. Coke's explanation seems as plausible as any. It rests, Coke wrote, on the belief that the "number of twelve is much respected in holy writ," as in twelve Apostles, twelve stones, twelve tribes of Israel, twelve patriarchs, and Solomon's twelve officers. For whatever reason, by the fourteenth century jury size under common law was fixed at twelve.[2] And so it was in American jurisprudence particularly after the 1898 *Thompson* decision.

Williams v. Florida, 399 U.S. 78 (1970)

In 1967 Florida began the process of change. It adopted a statute providing that, for all but capital crimes, the jury would consist of six persons. The number of twelve was retained for capital crimes. Florida's law led to *Williams* v. *Florida*, where, by a 6–2 margin, the Supreme Court decided, to the surprise of virtually everyone concerned, that the Sixth Amendment guarantee of trial by jury did *not* mandate *federal* jury size at twelve. It followed then that *state* juries also need not be set at twelve. Justice White wrote for the majority and called the number twelve "a historical accident" resting on "little more than mystical or superstitious insights into the significance" of that number. Justices Harlan and Marshall wrote separate dissents and Justice Blackmun did not participate. Marshall argued that the *Thompson* rule, "twelve persons neither more nor less" was sound constitutional doctrine. Harlan, as he was

1. 170 U.S. 343 (1898).

2. I. E. Coke. *Institute of the Laws of England*, 155a as quoted in 399 U.S. at 88. Coke's *Institutes* were widely read in the colonies by virtually every student of law.

wont to do, chided the majority for still another break with precedent. "Stare decisis . . . is a solid foundation for our legal system," Harlan wrote. If twelve jurors are not essential, Harlan asked, "why are six . . . can it be doubted that a unanimous jury of twelve provides a greater safeguard than a majority of six?"[3] Harlan also took still another opportunity to criticize the Court's incorporation approach in which "each time over my protest . . . almost all the criminal protections found within the first eight Amendments [were] made . . . jot for jot and case for case applicable to the states." The Court's decision in *Williams,* Harlan added, "demonstrate[s] a constitutional schizophrenia born of the need to cope with national diversity under the constraints of the incorporation doctrine."[4]

In *Williams,* the petitioner, before his trial for robbery, filed a motion to impanel a twelve-man jury instead of the six-man jury provided by Florida law in all but capital cases. Motion was denied in a Florida Court and the denial was affirmed by the Supreme Court.

Mr. Justice White delivered the opinion of the Court, saying in part:

> We do not pretend to be able to divine precisely what the word "jury" imported to the Framers, the First Congress, or the States in 1789. It may well be that the usual expectation was that the jury would consist of 12, and that hence, the most likely conclusion to be drawn is simply that little thought was actually given to the specific question we face today. But there is absolutely no indication in "the intent of the Framers" of an explicit decision to equate the constitutional and common-law characteristics of the jury. Nothing in this history suggests, then, that we do violence to the letter of the Constitution by turning to other than purely historical considerations to determine which features of the jury system, as it existed at common law, were preserved in the Constitution. The relevant inquiry, as we see it, must be the function that the particular feature performs and its relation to the purposes of the jury trial. Measured by this standard, the 12-man requirement cannot be regarded as an indispensable component of the Sixth Amendment.
>
> The purpose of the jury trial, as we noted in *Duncan,* is to prevent oppression by the Government. "Providing an accused with the right to be tried by a jury of his peers gave him an inestimable safeguard against the corrupt or overzealous prosecutor and against the compliant, biased, or eccentric judge." . . . Given this purpose, the essential feature of a jury obviously lies in the interposition between the accused and his accuser of the commonsense judgment of a group of laymen, and in the community participation and shared responsibility that results from that group's determination of guilt or innocence. The performance of this role is not a function of the particular number of the body that makes up the jury. To be sure, the number should probably be large enough to promote group deliberation, free from outside attempts at intimidation, and to provide a fair possibility for obtaining a representative cross section of the community. But we find little reason to think that these goals are in any meaningful sense less likely to be achieved when the jury numbers six, than when it numbers 12 — particularly if the requirement of unanimity is retained. And, certainly the reliability of the jury as a factfinder hardly seems likely to be a function of its size.
>
> It might be suggested that the 12-man jury gives a defendant a greater advantage since he has more "chances" of finding a juror who will insist on acquittal and thus prevent conviction. But the advantage might just as easily belong to the State, which also needs only one juror out of twelve insisting on guilt to prevent

3. 399 U.S. at 126.

4. Ibid., at 131, 137.

acquittal. What few experiments have occurred — usually in the civil area — indicate that there is no discernible difference between the results reached by the two different-sized juries. In short, neither currently available evidence nor theory suggests that the 12-man jury is necessarily more advantageous to the defendant than a jury composed of fewer members.

Similarly, while in theory the number of viewpoints represented on a randomly selected jury ought to increase as the size of the jury increases, in practice the difference between the 12-man and the six-man jury in terms of the cross-section of the community represented seems likely to be negligible. Even the 12-man jury cannot insure representation of every distinct voice in the community, particularly given the use of the peremptory challenge. As long as arbitrary exclusions of a particular class from the jury rolls are forbidden, . . . the concern that the cross-section will be significantly diminished if the jury is decreased in size from 12 to six seems an unrealistic one.

We conclude, in short, as we began: the fact that the jury at common law was composed of precisely 12 is a historical accident, unnecessary to effect the purposes of the jury system and wholly without significance "except to mystics." . . . To read the Sixth Amendment as forever codifying a feature so incidental to the real purpose of the Amendment is to ascribe a blind formalism to the Framers which would require considerably more evidence than we have been able to discover in the history and language of the Constitution or in the reasoning of our past decisions. We do not mean to intimate that legislatures can never have good reasons for concluding that the 12-man jury is preferable to the smaller jury, or that such conclusions — reflected in the provisions of most States and in our federal system — are in any sense unwise. Legislatures may well have their own views about the relative value of the larger and smaller juries, and may conclude that, wholly apart from the jury's primary function, it is desirable to spread the collective responsibility for the determination of guilt among the larger group. In capital cases, for example, it appears that no State provides for less than 12 jurors — a fact that suggests implicit recognition of the value of the larger body as a means of legitimating society's decision to impose the death penalty. Our holding does no more than leave these considerations to Congress and the States, unrestrained by an interpretation of the Sixth Amendment that would forever dictate the precise number that can constitute a jury. Consistent with this holding, we conclude that petitioner's Sixth Amendment rights, as applied to the States through the Fourteenth Amendment, were not violated by Florida's decision to provide a six-man rather than a 12-man jury. The judgment of the Florida District Court of Appeal is

Affirmed.

Apodaca v. Oregon, 406 U.S. 404 (1972)

As we have seen, English common law tradition fixing jury size at twelve can be traced back to the fourteenth century. Its long history in American jurisprudence dating back at least to *Thompson* in 1898 was broken in the 1970 *Williams* decision (above). In a similar case two years later, the Supreme Court once again broke with tradition. This time the issue was the unanimity rule that had also prevailed in English common law from the fourteenth century onward and that until 1972 was recognized, virtually unanimously, as an integral feature of American criminal procedure. *Patton* v. *United States*[1] is the

1. 281 U.S. 276 (1930).

latest case where the Supreme Court upheld that position. Although both *Maxwell* v. *Dow*[2] and *Jordan* v. *Massachusetts*[3] held that jury unanimity was not required in state courts, both cases were decided before *Duncan* ruled in 1968 that the Sixth Amendment jury trial guarantee applied to the states.

Apodaca v. *Oregon* arose after Oregon had passed a statute changing the unanimity requirement in criminal cases.[4] The petitioners were convicted in an Oregon court of assault with a deadly weapon by an 11–1 jury vote. Oregon law had a minimum requisite of a 10–2 jury vote to sustain a conviction. The petitioners claimed that conviction for a crime by a less than unanimous jury violated their right to trial by jury in criminal cases guaranteed by the Sixth Amendment and made applicable to the states in 1968 by *Duncan* v. *Louisiana.*

In *Apodaca* the Court was badly split. As he had in *Williams,* Justice White spoke for the majority of five. Four separate dissents were filed, by Justices Douglas, Brennan, Marshall, and Stewart. All four dissenters vigorously defended the unanimity rules as the fairest, most historically based, method of doing justice to an accused. Unanimity, Justice Stewart wrote, "provides the simple and effective method endorsed by centuries of experience and history to combat the injuries to the fair administration of justice that can be inflicted by community passion and prejudice." As Pritchett notes, in 1973, unanimous jury verdicts were still required in most state courts.[5] Louisiana, Oregon, and four other states (one of them, Montana, permitted conviction by an 8–4 vote) permit less than unanimous decisions but only for offenses less than a felony.[6]

Although he joined Chief Justice Burger and Justices White, Rehnquist, and Blackmun to make up the slim majority of five, Justice Powell agreed only with that portion of the *Apodaca* ruling dealing with relaxing the unanimity rule in *state* criminal trials. Powell insisted that the Sixth Amendment demanded a unanimous jury verdict in federal criminal cases. Thus by a narrow 5–4 margin the principle of unanimity on federal criminal juries was sustained at the same time as the Court was ruling, also 5–4, against its necessity in state courts. Court watchers may correctly assume that the issue is still an open one.

Mr. Justice White announced the judgment of the Court in an opinion in which the Chief Justice, Mr. Justice Blackmun, and Mr. Justice Rehnquist joined, saying in part:

> Our inquiry must focus upon the function served by the jury in contemporary society. . . . As we said in *Duncan,* the purpose of trial by jury is to prevent oppression by the Government by providing a "safeguard against the corrupt or overzealous prosecutor and against the compliant, biased, or eccentric judge." . . . "Given this purpose, the essential feature of a jury obviously lies in the

2. 176 U.S. 581 (1900).

3. 225 U.S. 167 (1912).

4. Louisiana had also changed its requirement. Johnson v. Louisiana, 406 U.S. 356 (1972) was decided on the same day as *Apodaca* and in identical fashion.

5. op. cit., at 467 (n.99).

6. Pritchett makes the following comment in this footnote: "in his concurring opinions in *Johnson* and *Apodaca,* Justice Blackmun said he would find it difficult to approve a seven to five conviction though it is difficult to see what the distinguishing principle is between the two majorities."

interposition between the accused and his accuser of the commonsense judgment of a group of laymen. . . ." . . . A requirement of unanimity, however, does
not materially contribute to the exercise of this commonsense judgment. As we
said in *Williams,* a jury will come to such a judgment as long as it consists of a
group of laymen representative of a cross section of the community who have
the duty and the opportunity to deliberate, free from outside attempts at intimidation, on the question of a defendant's guilt. In terms of this function we
perceive no difference between juries required to act unanimously and those
permitted to convict or acquit by votes of 10 to two or 11 to one. Requiring
unanimity would obviously produce hung juries in some situations where
nonunanimous juries will convict or acquit. But in either case, the interest of the
defendant in having the judgment of his peers interposed between himself and
the officers of the State who prosecute and judge him is equally well served.

Petitioners nevertheless argue that unanimity serves other purposes constitutionally essential to the continued operation of the jury system. Their principal
contention is that a Sixth Amendment "jury trial" made mandatory on the States
by virtue of the Due Process Clause of the Fourteenth Amendment, *Duncan* v.
Louisiana, supra, should be held to require a unanimous jury verdict in order to
give substance to the reasonable-doubt standard otherwise mandated by the Due
Process Clause. . . .

We are quite sure, however, that the Sixth Amendment itself has never been
held to require proof beyond a reasonable doubt in criminal cases. The
reasonable-doubt standard developed separately from both the jury trial and the
unanimous verdict. As the Court noted in the *Winship* case, the rule requiring
proof of crime beyond a reasonable doubt did not crystallize in this country until
after the Constitution was adopted. . . . And in that case, which held such a
burden of proof to be constitutionally required, the Court purported to draw no
support from the Sixth Amendment.

Petitioners' argument that the Sixth Amendment requires jury unanimity in
order to give effect to the reasonable-doubt standard thus founders on the fact
that the Sixth Amendment does not require proof beyond a reasonable doubt
at all. . . .

Petitioners also cite quite accurately a long line of decisions of this Court
upholding the principle that the Fourteenth Amendment requires jury panels to
reflect a cross section of the community. . . . They then contend that unanimity is
a necessary precondition for effective application of the cross-section requirement, because a rule permitting less than unanimous verdicts will make it possible for convictions to occur without the acquiescence of minority elements within
the community.

There are two flaws in this argument. One is petitioners' assumption that
every distinct voice in the community has a right to be represented on every jury
and a right to prevent conviction of a defendant in any case. All that the Constitution forbids, however, is systematic exclusion of identifiable segments of the
community from jury panels and from the juries ultimately drawn from those
panels; a defendant may not, for example, challenge the makeup of a jury
merely because no members of his race are on the jury, but must prove that his
race has been systematically excluded. . . .

. . . No group, in short, has the right to block convictions; it has only the right
to participate in the overall legal processes by which criminal guilt and innocence
are determined.

We also cannot accept petitioners' second assumption — that minority groups,
even when they are represented on a jury, will not adequately represent the
viewpoint of those groups simply because they may be outvoted in the final

result. They will be present during all deliberations, and their views will be heard. We cannot assume that the majority of the jury will refuse to weigh the evidence and reach a decision upon rational grounds, just as it must now do in order to obtain unanimous verdicts, or that a majority will deprive a man of his liberty on the basis of prejudice when a minority is presenting a reasonable argument in favor of acquittal. We simply find no proof for the notion that a majority will disregard its instructions and cast its votes for guilt or innocence based on prejudice rather than the evidence.

V

THE EIGHTH AMENDMENT

1

THE DEATH PENALTY

"Excessive bail shall not be required, nor excessive fines imposed, nor cruel and unusual punishments inflicted." This is the Eighth Amendment to the Constitution, a part of the Bill of Rights that until recently had not been significantly involved in constitutional disputes. Then in 1972 the Supreme Court dropped a proverbial bombshell, especially into law and order ranks, by declaring, in *Furman* and *Georgia*, that the death penalty was cruel and unusual punishment and violated the Eighth Amendment. *Furman* ranks along with *Roe* v. *Wade* (above), the abortion decision, and the busing cases for the emotional, moral, and politically explosive hue and cry it raised. We will treat *Furman* and the furor it occasioned later. Although the Court's ruling in *Furman* was completely unexpected, especially from a Court largely dominated by conservative Nixon appointees, there were a number of previous death penalty decisions that threw some light on the Supreme Court's thinking on this issue.

Witherspoon v. Illinois, 391 U.S. 510 (1968)

One such case was *Witherspoon* v. *Illinois*. Involved in *Witherspoon* was an Illinois statute that gave prosecutors discretion to eliminate from jury duty in murder trials persons who expressed conscientious scruples against capital punishment. In a 6–3 decision the Supreme Court ruled the Illinois statute "fell woefully short" of the impartial jury requirements of the Sixth and Fourteenth Amendments. Justice Stewart wrote for the majority while Justice Black joined by Justices Harlan and White dissented. Justice White also wrote a separate dissent. The Court ruled that just as a state may not by law form its juries to *ensure* convictions, it also may not determine whether a person should live or die by deliberately forming its juries to return a verdict of death. Stewart's majority opinion concludes with the following paragraph, with which, as we shall see, Black's dissent took particular exception. "Whatever else might be said of capital punishment, it is at least clear that its imposition by a hanging jury cannot be squared with the Constitution. The state of Illinois has stacked the deck against the petitioner. To execute this death sentence would deprive him of his life without due process of law."

Black took sharp exception to this conclusion. "With all due deference," Black wrote in dissent, "it seems to me that one might much more appropriately charge that this Court had today written the law in such a way that the states are being forced to try their murder cases with biased juries." Black went on to say that if the Court wished to declare capital punishment unconstitutional, "it should do so forthrightly, not by making it impossible for states to get juries that will enforce the death penalty."[1]

In *Witherspoon* the majority was not yet ready to rule the death penalty as such unconstitutional. It *was* willing, however, to say that a state could not systematically exclude from murder trial juries persons who were conscientiously opposed to the death penalty, as the Illinois statute in question had.

Mr. Justice Stewart delivered the opinion of the Court, saying in part:

> The petitioner contends that a State cannot confer upon a jury selected in this manner the power to determine guilt. He maintains that such a jury, unlike one chosen at random from a cross-section of the community, must necessarily be biased in favor of conviction, for the kind of juror who would be unperturbed by the prospect of sending a man to his death, he contends, is the kind of juror who would too readily ignore the presumption of the defendant's innocence, accept the prosecution's version of the facts, and return a verdict of guilt. To support this view, the petitioner refers to what he describes as "competent scientific evidence that death-qualified jurors are partial to the prosecution on the issue of guilt or innocence."
>
> The data adduced by the petitioner, however, are too tentative and fragmentary to establish that jurors not opposed to the death penalty tend to favor the prosecution in the determination of guilt. We simply cannot conclude, either on the basis of the record now before us or as a matter of judicial notice, that the exclusion of jurors opposed to capital punishment results in an unrepresentative jury on the issue of guilt or substantially increases the risk of conviction. In light of the presently available information, we are not prepared to announce a *per se* constitutional rule requiring the reversal of every conviction returned by a jury selected as this one was. . . .
>
> It does not follow, however, that the petitioner is entitled to no relief. For in this case the jury was entrusted with two distinct responsibilities: first, to determine whether the petitioner was innocent or guilty; and second, if guilty, to determine whether his sentence should be imprisonment or death. It has not been shown that this jury was biased with respect to the petitioner's guilt. But it is self-evident that, in its role as arbiter of the punishment to be imposed, this jury fell woefully short of that impartiality to which the petitioner was entitled under the Sixth and Fourteenth Amendments. . . .
>
> The only justification the State has offered for the jury-selection technique it employed here is that individuals who express serious reservations about capital punishment cannot be relied upon to vote for it even when the laws of the State and the instructions of the trial judge would make death the proper penalty. But in Illinois, as in other States, the jury is given broad discretion to decide whether or not death *is* "the proper penalty" in a given case, and a juror's general views about capital punishment play an inevitable role in any such decision.
>
> A man who opposes the death penalty, no less than one who favors it, can make the discretionary judgment entrusted to him by the State and can thus obey the oath he takes as a juror. But a jury from which all such men have been excluded cannot perform the task demanded of it. Guided by neither rule nor standard, "free to select or reject as it [sees] fit," a jury that must choose between

1. 391 U.S. at 532.

life imprisonment and capital punishment can do little more — and must do nothing less — than express the conscience of the community on the ultimate question of life or death. Yet, in a nation less than half of whose people believe in the death penalty, a jury composed exclusively of such people cannot speak for the community. Culled of all who harbor doubts about the wisdom of capital punishment — of all who would be reluctant to pronounce the extreme penalty — such a jury can speak only for a distinct and dwindling minority.

If the State had excluded only those prospective jurors who stated in advance of trial that they would not even consider returning a verdict of death, it could argue that the resulting jury was simply "neutral" with respect to penalty. But when it swept from the jury all who expressed conscientious or religious scruples against capital punishment and all who opposed it in principle, the State crossed the line of neutrality. In its quest for a jury capable of imposing the death penalty, the State produced a jury uncommonly willing to condemn a man to die.

It is, of course, settled that a State may not entrust the determination of whether a man is innocent or guilty to a tribunal "organized to convict." . . . It requires but a short step from that principle to hold, as we do today, that a State may not entrust the determination of whether a man should live or die to a tribunal organized to return a verdict of death. Specifically, we hold that a sentence of death cannot be carried out if the jury that imposed or recommended it was chosen by excluding veniremen for cause simply because they voiced general objections to the death penalty or expressed conscientious or religious scruples against its infliction. No defendant can constitutionally be put to death at the hands of a tribunal so selected.

McGautha v. California, 401 U.S. 183 (1971)

Two companion cases were decided on the same day as *Witherspoon,* May 3, 1971: *McGautha* v. *California* and *Crampton* v. *Ohio.* Both dealt with unique capital punishment issues. One, *McGautha,* concerned the practice in California of having a separate jury decide whether or not to impose the death penalty after the trial jury had found a defendant guilty of a crime in which death was one possible punishment. The petitioner in *McGautha,* having been convicted of armed robbery and murder, challenged California's procedure as "constitutionally intolerable" on grounds that absence of consistent and objective standards to guide the jury's discretion on the punishment issue violated the due process clause of the Fourteenth Amendment. In *Crampton,* the petitioner, also convicted of murder, challenged the constitutionality of Ohio's practice, allowing a *single* guilt and punishment proceeding, as a violation of due process. With Justice Harlan speaking for the majority of six the Supreme Court affirmed both state court decisions. Justices Douglas and Brennan dissented. Each was also joined by Justice Marshall.

Speaking for the Court, Harlan noted that, in light of history, experience and "the limitations of human knowledge in establishing definitive standards" it was impossible to conclude that "leaving to the untrammeled discretion of the jury the power to pronounce life or death in capital cases violates the Constitution." While acknowledging that California's two-jury system might be preferable to Ohio's single-jury method, the Court concluded that both California and Ohio resolved the issue of punishment in accord with the Constitution.

Douglas dissented only with respect to *Crampton.* He was convinced that by fair-trial standards "the resolution of the question of punishment requires rules and procedures different from those pertaining to guilt."[1] In his dissent Brennan chided the Court for not coming to grips with what he felt was the fundamental question involved. That question, Brennan insisted, "is whether the rule of law basic to our society . . . is fundamentally inconsistent with capital sentencing procedures that are purposely constructed to allow the maximum possible variation from one case to the next, and provide no mechanisms to prevent consciously maximized variations from reflecting merely random or arbitrary choice."[2] Brennan's argument that applying the death penalty without consistent standards leads to "random and arbitrary" choices, means, of course, that in practice only the poor, racial minority, undereducated male has been the victim of capital punishment. This view is widely held by opponents of the death penalty. It was expressed several times in the *Furman* decision (below). In *McGautha* and *Crampton,* however, the Court was not yet prepared to grapple with that more fundamental issue. It hedged and ruled that neither California's dual system, nor Ohio's single system of imposing the death penalty violated the Constitution.

Mr. Justice Harlan delivered the opinion of the Court, saying in part:

> Before we conclude this opinion, it is appropriate for us to make a broader observation than the issues raised by these cases strictly call for. It may well be, as the American Law Institute and the National Commission on Reform of Federal Criminal Laws have concluded, that bifurcated trials and criteria for jury sentencing discretion are superior means of dealing with capital cases if the death penalty is to be retained at all. But the Federal Constitution, which marks the limits of our authority in these cases, does not guarantee trial procedures that are the best of all worlds, or that accord with the most enlightened ideas of students of the infant science of criminology, or even those that measure up to the individual predilections of members of this Court. . . . The Constitution requires no more than that trials be fairly conducted and that guaranteed rights of defendants be scrupulously respected. From a constitutional standpoint we cannot conclude that it is impermissible for a State to consider that the compassionate purposes of jury sentencing in capital cases are better served by having the issues of guilt and punishment determined in a single trial than by focusing the jury's attention solely on punishment after the issue of guilt has been determined.
>
> Certainly the facts of these gruesome murders bespeak no miscarriage of justice. The ability of juries, unassisted by standards, to distinguish between those defendants for whom the death penalty is appropriate punishment and those for whom imprisonment is sufficient is indeed illustrated by the discriminating verdict of the jury in McGautha's case, finding Wilkinson the less culpable of the two defendants and sparing his life.
>
> The procedures which petitioners challenge are those by which most capital trials in this country are conducted, and by which all were conducted until a few years ago. We have determined that these procedures are consistent with the rights to which petitioners were constitutionally entitled, and that their trials were entirely fair. Having reached these conclusions we have performed our task of measuring the States' process by federal constitutional standards, and accordingly the judgment in each of these cases is
>
> *Affirmed.*

1. 402 U.S. at 245.

2. Ibid., at 248.

Furman v. Georgia, 408 U.S. 238 (1972)

Although both *Witherspoon* and *McGautha* were significant death penalty decisions, it would *not* be accurate to conclude that they paved the way for the Supreme Court's principle death penalty decision, *Furman* v. *Georgia,* a year later. *Furman* was a distinct surprise, for hardly any court-watchers would have predicted that the law and order Burger Court would strike down capital punishment, widely believed to be one of the chief weapons in the law and order arsenal. Controversy regarding the Burger Court's decision in *Furman* has been matched in recent years only by the great furor raised by that same Court's 1973 abortion rule, *Roe* v. *Wade* (above) and perhaps by its busing decisions, *Swann, Keyes,* and *Millikin* (below).

Since *Furman,* many states have passed and repassed death penalty bills designed to meet objections to capital punishment the Court raised in *Furman.* It was widely assumed in legal circles at the time that the Court had *not* closed the door irrevocably to the death penalty. Although the Court's brief per curiam opinion in *Furman* declared capital punishment cruel and unusual punishment in violation of the Eighth Amendment, the supposition was that the Court had objected to the often arbitrary and capricious application of the death penalty rather than to the penalty as such. Reacting to this widely held conclusion, some thirty-five states quickly moved to amend or rewrite their capital punishment statutes to conform to what they believed would pass the Court's constitutional muster. And not without some success.

For example, four years after *Furman,* in *Gregg* v. *Georgia,*[1] the Court ruled that capital punishment was *not* inherently cruel and unusual. Speaking for the majority of seven, Justice Stewart took note of what he called "society's endorsement of the death penalty for murder." As we noted Georgia and other states had rewritten their capital punishment statutes to conform to the procedural guidelines they hoped would meet the Court's approval. Many states did little more than hastily reword existing statutes to make the death penalty mandatory for specific crimes, thus striving for the specificity and objectivity missing in previous capital punishment laws. Three of these statutes, those of North Carolina, Louisiana, and Oklahoma, were stricken down by the Supreme Court in 1976 decisions.[2] In them, Justices Brennan and Marshall, the two dissenters in *Gregg,* joined Justices Stewart, Powell, and Stevens to make up the slim majority of five. The Court ruled these mandatory statutes unconstitutional because they treated "all persons convicted of a designated offense not as uniquely individual human beings, but as members of a faceless, undifferentiated mass to be subjected to the blind infliction of the penalty of death." Justice White led the dissenters (Blackmun, Rehnquist, and Chief Justice Burger) and was sharply critical of Justice Stewart's majority view. White argued that the majority "had usurped the proper functions of state legislatures [which had decided] that mandatory death sentence would deter crime."

White's dissent touched upon the principle argument made by proponents of capital punishment that the death penalty acts as a deterrent to crime, despite no hard, fast evidence to confirm this. In fact, there is a wealth of data

1. 428 U.S. 179 (1976).

2. Woodson v. North Carolina, 96 S.Ct. 2978 (1976); Roberts v. Louisiana, 96 S.Ct. 3001 (1976); Green v. Oklahoma, 96 S.Ct. 3216 (1976).

that seems to contradict it. For example, many psychologists, criminologists, and others who have studied the criminal mind are convinced that fear of the death penalty plays little or no role in deterring those who would commit a capital punishment crime.

In addition to the often capricious and arbitrary application of the death penalty which itself may violate the Fourteenth Amendment's equal protection clause (in the past only poor, uneducated, friendless minority males ever went to the gas chamber), its opponents also argue that it brutalizes society; that killing is wrong even if done by the state; that it *is* uncivilized retribution, revenge is hardly a noble motive; that it leaves no margin for possible trial or procedural errors that may turn up long after the execution; and that, constitutionally, it *is* cruel and unusual punishment barred by the Eighth Amendment. To suggest that emotions run high on the issue of capital punishment, is to state the obvious.

In the five years since it was decided, *Furman* remains the key capital punishment ruling. Much of what has taken place since in the Courts and in the various state legislatures revolves around *Furman*.

Although the Court's per curiam opinion was brief, each of the nine justices wrote separate, sometimes lengthy opinions noting their views on the subject, which also indicates the intensity of the debate and controversy. Justices Douglas, Stewart, White, Brennan, and Marshall made up the majority. The four Nixon appointees, Chief Justice Burger and Justices Blackmun, Powell, and Rehnquist were the dissenters. We reproduce here the Court's per curiam opinion and excerpts from the opinions of Justices Douglas, Brennan, and Powell which seem to represent best the opposing points of view on this highly volatile subject.

PER CURIAM.

Petitioner in No. 69–5003 was convicted of murder in Georgia and was sentenced to death pursuant to Ga. Code Ann. §26–1005 (Supp. 1971) (effective prior to July 1, 1969). 225 Ga. 253. 167 S.E. 2d 628 (1969). Petitioner in No. 69–5030 was convicted of rape in Georgia and was sentenced to death pursuant to Ga. Code Ann. §26–1302 (Supp. 1971) (effective prior to July 1, 1969). 225 Ga. 790, 171 S.E. 2d 501 (1969). Petitioner in No. 69–5031 was convicted of rape in Texas and was sentenced to death pursuant to Tex. Penal Code, Art. 1189 (1961). 447 S.W. 2d 932 (Ct. Crim. App. 1969). Certiorari was granted limited to the following question: "Does the imposition and carrying out of the death penalty in [these cases] constitute cruel and unusual punishment in violation of the Eighth and Fourteenth Amendments?" 403 U.S. 952 (1971). The Court holds that the imposition and carrying out of the death penalty in these cases constitute cruel and unusual punishment in violation of the Eighth and Fourteenth Amendments. The judgment in each case is therefore reversed insofar as it leaves undisturbed the death sentence imposed, and the cases are remanded for further proceedings.

Mr. Justice Douglas, concurring, said in part:

There is increasing recognition of the fact that the basic theme of equal protection is implicit in "cruel and unusual" punishments. "A penalty . . . should be considered 'unusually' imposed if it is administered arbitrarily or discriminatorily." The same authors add that "[t]he extreme rarity with which applicable death penalty provisions are put to use raises a strong inference of arbitrariness." The President's Commission on Law Enforcement and Administration of Justice recently concluded:

> "Finally there is evidence that the imposition of the death sentence and the exercise of dispensing power by the courts and the executive follow discriminatory patterns. The death sentence is disproportionately imposed and carried out on the poor, the Negro, and the members of unpopular groups." . . .

Warden Lewis E. Lawes of Sing Sing said:

> "Not only does capital punishment fail in its justification, but no punishment could be invented with so many inherent defects. It is an unequal punishment in the way it is applied to the rich and to the poor. The defendant of wealth and position never goes to the electric chair or to the gallows. Juries do not intentionally favour the rich, the law is theoretically impartial, but the defendant with ample means is able to have his case presented with every favourable aspect, while the poor defendant often has a lawyer assigned by the court. Sometimes such assignment is considered part of political patronage; usually the lawyer assigned has had no experience whatever in a capital case."

Former Attorney General Ramsey Clark has said, "It is the poor, the sick, the ignorant, the powerless and the hated who are executed." One searches our chronicles in vain for the execution of any member of the affluent strata of this society. The Leopolds and Loebs are given prison terms, not sentenced to death.

Mr. Justice Brennan, concurring, said in part:

Ours would indeed be a simple task were we required merely to measure a challenged punishment against those that history has long condemned. That narrow and unwarranted view of the Clause, however, was left behind with the 19th century. Our task today is more complex. We know "that the words of the [Clause] are not precise, and that their scope is not static." We know, therefore, that the Clause "must draw its meaning from the evolving standards of decency that mark the progress of a maturing society." . . . That knowledge, of course, is but the beginning of the inquiry. At bottom, then, the Cruel and Unusual Punishments Clause prohibits the infliction of uncivilized and inhuman punishments. The State, even as it punishes, must treat its members with respect for their intrinsic worth as human beings. A punishment is "cruel and unusual," therefore, if it does not comport with human dignity.

This formulation, of course, does not of itself yield principles for assessing the constitutional validity of particular punishments. Nevertheless, even though "[t]his Court has had little occasion to give precise content to the [Clause]," . . . there are principles recognized in our cases and inherent in the Clause sufficient to permit a judicial determination whether a challenged punishment comports with human dignity. . . .

Death is truly an awesome punishment. The calculated killing of a human being by the State involves, by its very nature, a denial of the executed person's humanity. The contrast with the plight of a person punished by imprisonment is evident. An individual in prison does not lose "the right to have rights." A prisoner retains, for example, the constitutional rights to the free exercise of religion, to be free of cruel and unusual punishments, and to treatment as a "person" for purposes of due process of law and the equal protection of the laws.

A prisoner remains a member of the human family. Moreover, he retains the right of access to the courts. His punishment is not irrevocable. Apart from the common charge, grounded upon the recognition of human fallibility, that the punishment of death must inevitably be inflicted upon innocent men, we know that death has been the lot of men whose convictions were unconstitutionally secured in view of later, retroactively applied, holdings of this Court. The punishment itself may have been unconstitutionally inflicted, . . . yet the finality of death precludes relief. An executed person has indeed "lost the right to have rights." . . . Even before the moratorium on executions began in 1967, executions totaled only 42 in 1961 and 47 in 1962, an average of less than one per week; the number dwindled to 21 in 1963, to 15 in 1964, and to seven in 1965; in 1966, there was one execution, and in 1967, there were two.

When a country of over 200 million people inflicts an unusually severe punishment no more than 50 times a year, the inference is strong that the punishment is not being regularly and fairly applied. To dispel it would indeed require a clear showing of nonarbitrary infliction.

Although there are no exact figures available, we know that thousands of murders and rapes are committed annually in States where death is an authorized punishment for those crimes. However the rate of infliction is characterized — as "freakishly" or "spectacularly" rare, or simply as rare — it would take the purest sophistry to deny that death is inflicted in only a minute fraction of these cases. How much rarer, after all, could the infliction of death be?

When the punishment of death is inflicted in a trivial number of the cases in which it is legally available, the conclusion is virtually inescapable that it is being inflicted arbitrarily. Indeed, it smacks of little more than a lottery system. The States claim, however, that this rarity is evidence not of arbitrariness, but of informed selectivity: Death is inflicted, they say, only in "extreme" cases. . . .

I cannot add to my Brother MARSHALL's comprehensive treatment of the English and American history of this punishment. I emphasize, however, one significant conclusion that emerges from that history. From the beginning of our Nation, the punishment of death has stirred acute public controversy. Although pragmatic arguments for and against the punishment have been frequently advanced, this longstanding and heated controversy cannot be explained solely as the result of differences over the practical wisdom of a particular government policy. At bottom, the battle has been waged on moral grounds. The country has debated whether a society for which the dignity of the individual is the supreme value can, without a fundamental inconsistency, follow the practice of deliberately putting some of its members to death. In the United States, as in other nations of the western world, "the struggle about this punishment has been one between ancient and deeply rooted beliefs in retribution, atonement or vengeance on the one hand, and, on the other, beliefs in the personal value and dignity of the common man that were born of the democratic movement of the eighteenth century, as well as beliefs in the scientific approach to an understanding of the motive forces of human conduct, which are the result of the growth of the sciences of behavior during the nineteenth and twentieth centuries." It is this essentially moral conflict that forms the backdrop for the past changes in and the present operation of our system of imposing death as a punishment for crime. . . . Our concern for decency and human dignity, moreover, has compelled changes in the circumstances surrounding the execution itself. No longer does our society countenance the spectacle of public executions, once thought desirable as a deterrent to criminal behavior by others. Today we reject public executions as debasing and brutalizing to us all.

Also significant is the drastic decrease in the crimes for which the punishment of death is actually inflicted. While esoteric capital crimes remain on the books, since 1930 murder and rape have accounted for nearly 99 percent of the total executions, and murder alone for about 87 percent. In addition, the crime of capital murder has itself been limited. As the Court noted in *McGautha* v. *California,* 402 U.S., at 198, there was in this country a "rebellion against the common-law rule imposing a mandatory death sentence on all convicted murderers." . . .

The States' primary claim is that death is a necessary punishment because it prevents the commission of capital crimes more effectively than any less severe punishment. The first part of this claim is that the infliction of death is necessary to stop the individuals executed from committing further crimes. The sufficient answer to this is that if a criminal convicted of a capital crime poses a danger to society, effective administration of the State's pardon and parole laws can delay or deny his release from prison, and techniques of isolation can eliminate or minimize the danger while he remains confined.

The more significant argument is that the threat of death prevents the commission of capital crimes because it deters potential criminals who would not be deterred by the threat of imprisonment. The argument is not based upon evidence that the threat of death is a superior deterrent. Indeed, as my Brother MARSHALL establishes, the available evidence uniformly indicates, although it does not conclusively prove, that the threat of death has no greater deterrent effect than the threat of imprisonment. The States argue, however, that they are entitled to rely upon common human experience, and that experience, they say, supports the conclusion that death must be a more effective deterrent than any less severe punishment. Because people fear death the most, the argument runs, the threat of death must be the greatest deterrent.

It is important to focus upon the precise import of this argument. It is not denied that many, and probably most, capital crimes cannot be deterred by the threat of punishment. Thus the argument can apply only to those who think rationally about the commission of capital crimes. Particularly is that true when the potential criminal, under this argument, must not only consider the risk of punishment, but also distinguish between two possible punishments. The concern, then, is with a particular type of potential criminal, the rational person who will commit a capital crime knowing that the punishment is long-term imprisonment, which may well be for the rest of his life, but will not commit the crime knowing that the punishment is death. On the face of it, the assumption that such persons exist is implausible. . . .

In sum, the punishment of death is inconsistent with all four principles: Death is an unusually severe and degrading punishment; there is a strong probability that it is inflicted arbitrarily; its rejection by contemporary society is virtually total; and there is no reason to believe that it serves any penal purpose more effectively than the less severe punishment of imprisonment. The function of these principles is to enable a court to determine whether a punishment comports with human dignity. Death, quite simply, does not.

Mr. Justice Powell, dissenting, said in part:

Whatever uncertainties may hereafter surface, several of the consequences of today's decision are unmistakably clear. The decision is plainly one of the greatest importance. The Court's judgment removes the death sentences previously imposed on some 600 persons awaiting punishment in state and federal prisons throughout the country. At least for the present, it also bars the States and the Federal Government from seeking sentences of death for defendants awaiting trial on charges for which capital punishment was heretofore a potential alternative. The happy event for these countable few constitutes, however, only the most visible consequence of this decision. Less measurable, but certainly of no less significance, is the shattering effect this collection of views has on the root principles of *stare decisis,* federalism, judicial restraint and — most importantly — separation of powers.

The Court rejects as not decisive the clearest evidence that the Framers of the Constitution and the authors of the Fourteenth Amendment believed that those documents posed no barrier to the death penalty. The Court also brushes aside an unbroken line of precedent reaffirming the heretofore virtually unquestioned constitutionality of capital punishment. Because of the pervasiveness of the constitutional ruling sought by petitioners, and accepted in varying degrees by five members of the Court, today's departure from established precedent invalidates a staggering number of state and federal laws. The capital punishment laws of no less than 39 States and the District of Columbia are nullified. In addition, numerous provisions of the Criminal Code of the United States and of the Uniform Code of Military Justice also are voided. The Court's judgment not only wipes out laws presently in existence, but denies to Congress and to the legislatures of the 50 States the power to adopt new policies contrary to the policy selected by the Court. Indeed, it is the view of two of my Brothers that the people of each State must be denied the prerogative to amend their constitutions to provide for capital punishment even selectively for the most heinous crime.

In terms of the constitutional role of this Court, the impact of the majority's ruling is all the greater because the decision encroaches upon an area squarely within the historic prerogative of the legislative branch — both state and federal — to protect the citizenry through the designation of penalties for prohibitable conduct. It is the very sort of judgment that the legislative branch is competent to make and for which the judiciary is ill-equipped. Throughout our history, Justices of this Court have emphasized the gravity of decisions invalidating legislative judgments, admonishing the nine men who sit on this bench of the duty of self-restraint, especially when called upon to apply the expansive due process and cruel and unusual punishment rubrics. I can recall no case in which, in the name of deciding constitutional questions, this Court has subordinated national and local democratic processes to such an extent. . . .

Petitioners seek to salvage their thesis by arguing that the infrequency and discriminatory nature of the actual resort to the ultimate penalty tend to diffuse public opposition. We are told that the penalty is imposed exclusively on uninfluential minorities — "the poor and powerless, personally ugly and socially unacceptable." It is urged that this pattern of application assures that large segments of the public will be either uninformed or unconcerned and will have no reason to measure the punishment against prevailing moral standards.

Implicitly, this argument concedes the unsoundness of petitioners' contention, examined above under Part IV, that objective evidence shows a present and widespread community rejection of the death penalty. It is now said, in effect, not that capital punishment presently offends our citizenry, but that the public *would* be offended *if* the penalty were enforced in a nondiscriminatory manner against a significant percentage of those charged with capital crimes, and *if* the public were thereby made aware of the moral issues surrounding capital punishment. Rather than merely registering the objective indicators on a judicial balance, we are asked ultimately to rest a far-reaching constitutional determination on a prediction regarding the subjective judgments of the mass of our people under hypothetical assumptions that may or may not be realistic.

Apart from the impermissibility of basing a constitutional judgment of this magnitude on such speculative assumptions, the argument suffers from other defects. If, as petitioners urge, we are to engage in speculation, it is not at all certain that the public would experience deep-felt revulsion if the States were to execute as many sentenced capital offenders this year as they executed in the mid-1930s. It seems more likely that public reaction, rather than being characterized by undifferentiated rejection, would depend upon the facts and circumstances surrounding each particular case.

Members of this Court know, from the petitions and appeals that come before us regularly, that brutish and revolting murders continue to occur with disquieting frequency. Indeed, murders are so commonplace in our society that only the most sensational receive significant and sustained publicity. It could hardly be suggested that in any of these highly publicized murder cases — the several senseless assassinations or the too numerous shocking multiple murders that have stained this country's recent history — the public has exhibited any signs of "revulsion" at the thought of executing the convicted murderers. The public outcry, as we all know, has been quite to the contrary. Furthermore, there is little reason to suspect that the public's reaction would differ significantly in response to other less publicized murders. It is certainly arguable that many such murders, because of their senselessness or barbarousness, would evoke a public demand for the death penalty rather than a public rejection of that alternative. Nor is there any rational basis for arguing that the public reaction to any of these crimes would be muted if the murderer were "rich and powerful." The demand for the ultimate sanction might well be greater, as a wealthy killer is hardly a sympathetic figure. While there might be specific cases in which capital punishment would be regarded as excessive and shocking to the conscience of the community, it can hardly be argued that the public's dissatisfaction with the penalty in particular cases would translate into a demand for absolute abolition.

In pursuing the foregoing speculation, I do not suggest that it is relevant to the appropriate disposition of these cases. The purpose of the digression is to indicate that judicial decisions cannot be founded on such speculations and assumptions, however appealing they may seem.

But the discrimination argument does not rest alone on a projection of the assumed effect on public opinion of more frequent executions. Much also is made of the undeniable fact that the death penalty has a greater impact on the lower economic strata of society, which include a relatively higher percentage of persons of minority racial and ethnic group backgrounds. The argument drawn from this fact is two-pronged. In part it is merely an extension of the speculative approach pursued by petitioners, *i.e.,* that public revulsion is suppressed in callous apathy because the penalty does not affect persons from the white middle class which constitutes the majority in this country. This aspect, however, adds little to the infrequency rationalization for public apathy which I have found unpersuasive.

As MR. JUSTICE MARSHALL's opinion today demonstrates, the argument does have a more troubling aspect. It is his contention that if the average citizen were aware of the disproportionate burden of capital punishment borne by the "poor, the ignorant, and the underprivileged," he would find the penalty "shocking to his conscience and sense of justice" and would not stand for its further use. . . . This argument, like the apathy rationale, calls for further speculation on the part of the Court. It also illuminates the quicksands upon which we are asked to base this decision. Indeed, the two contentions seem to require contradictory assumptions regarding the public's moral attitude toward capital punishment. The apathy argument is predicated on the assumption that the penalty is used against the less influential elements of society, that the public is fully aware of this, and that it tolerates use of capital punishment only because of a callous indifference to the offenders who are sentenced. MR. JUSTICE MARSHALL's argument, on the other hand, rests on the contrary assumption that the public does not know against whom the penalty is enforced and that if the public were educated to this fact it would find the punishment intolerable. . . . Neither assumption can claim to be an entirely accurate portrayal of public attitude; for some acceptance of capital punishment might be a consequence of hardened apathy based on the knowledge of infrequent and uneven application, while for others acceptance may grow only out of ignorance. More significantly, however, neither supposition acknowledges what, for me, is a more basic flaw.

Certainly the claim is justified that this criminal sanction falls more heavily on the relatively impoverished and underprivileged elements of society. The "have-nots" in every society always have been subject to greater pressure to commit crimes and to fewer constraints than their more affluent fellow citizens. This is, indeed, a tragic byproduct of social and economic deprivation, but it is not an argument of constitutional proportions under the Eighth or Fourteenth Amendment. The same discriminatory impact argument could be made with equal force and logic with respect to those sentenced to prison terms. The Due Process Clause admits of no distinction between the deprivation of "life" and the deprivation of "liberty." If discriminatory impact renders capital punishment cruel and unusual, it likewise renders invalid most of the prescribed penalties for crimes of violence. The root causes of the higher incidence of criminal penalties on "minorities and the poor" will not be cured by abolishing the system of penalties. Nor, indeed, could any society have a viable system of criminal justice if sanctions were abolished or ameliorated because most of those who commit crimes happen to be underprivileged. The basic problem results not from the penalties imposed for criminal conduct but from social and economic factors that have plagued humanity since the beginning of recorded history, frustrating all efforts to create in any country at any time the perfect society in which there are no "poor," no "minorities" and no "underprivileged." The causes underlying this problem are unrelated to the constitutional issue before the Court.

Finally, yet another theory for abolishing the death penalty — reflected in varying degrees in each of the concurring opinions today — is predicated on the discriminatory impact argument. Quite apart from measuring the public's acceptance or rejection of the death penalty under the "standards of decency" rationale, MR. JUSTICE DOUGLAS finds the punishment cruel and unusual because it is "arbitrarily" invoked. He finds that "the basic theme of equal protection is implicit" in the Eighth Amendment, and that the Amendment is violated when jury sentencing may be characterized as arbitrary or discriminatory. . . . While MR. JUSTICE STEWART does not purport to rely on notions of equal protection, he also rests primarily on what he views to be a history of arbitrariness. . . . Whatever may be the facts with respect to jury sentencing, this argument calls for a reconsideration of the "standards" aspects of the Court's decision in *McGautha v. California*, 402 U.S. 183 (1971). Although that is the unmistakable thrust of these opinions today, I see no reason to reassess the standards question considered so carefully in Mr. Justice Harlan's opinion for the Court last Term. Having so recently reaffirmed our historic dedication to entrusting the sentencing function to the jury's "untrammeled discretion" (*id.*, at 207), it is difficult to see how the Court can now hold the entire process constitutionally defective under the Eighth Amendment. For all of these reasons I find little merit in the various discrimination arguments, at least in the several lights in which they have been cast in these cases. . . .

I agree that discriminatory application of the death penalty in the past, admittedly indefensible, is no justification for holding today that capital punishment is invalid in all cases in which sentences were handed out to members of the class discriminated against. But *Maxwell* does point the way to a means of raising the equal protection challenge that is more consonant with precedent and the Constitution's mandates than the several courses pursued by today's concurring opinions.

A final comment on the racial discrimination problem seems appropriate. The possibility of racial bias in the trial and sentencing process has diminished in recent years. The segregation of our society in decades past, which contributed substantially to the severity of punishment for interracial crimes, is now no longer prevalent in this country. Likewise, the day is past when juries do not represent the minority group elements of the community. The assurance of fair trials for all citizens is greater today than at any previous time in our history. Because standards of criminal justice have "evolved" in a manner favorable to the accused, discriminatory imposition of capital punishment is far less likely today than in the past. . . .

While I reject each of these attempts to establish specific categories of cases in which the death penalty may be deemed excessive, I view them as groping toward what is for me the appropriate application of the Eighth Amendment. While in my view the disproportionality test may not be used either to strike down the death penalty for rape altogether or to install the Court as a tribunal for sentencing review, that test may find its application in the peculiar cir- cumstances of specific cases. Its utilization should be limited to the rare case in which the death penalty is rendered for a crime technically falling within the legislatively defined class but factually falling outside the likely legislative intent in creating the category. Specific rape cases (and specific homicides as well) can be imagined in which the conduct of the accused would render the ultimate penalty a grossly excessive punishment. Although this case-by-case approach may seem painfully slow and inadequate to those who wish the Court to assume an activist legislative role in reforming criminal punishments, it is the approach dictated both by our prior opinions and by a due recognition of the limitations of judicial power. This approach, rather than the majority's more pervasive and less refined judgment, marks for me the appropriate course under the Eighth Amendment.

I now return to the overriding question in these cases: whether this Court, acting in conformity with the Constitution, can justify its judgment to abolish capital punishment as heretofore known in this country. It is important to keep in focus the enormity of the step undertaken by the Court today. Not only does it invalidate hundreds of state and federal laws, it deprives those jurisdictions of the power to legislate with respect to capital punishment in the future, except in a manner consistent with the cloudily outlined views of those Justices who do not purport to undertake total abolition. Nothing short of an amendment to the United States Constitution can reverse the Court's judgments. Meanwhile, all flexibility is foreclosed. The normal democratic process, as well as the oppor- tunities for the several States to respond to the will of their people expressed through ballot referenda (as in Massachusetts, Illinois, and Colorado), is now shut off. . . .

With deference and respect for the views of the Justices who differ, it seems to me that all these studies — both in this country and elsewhere — suggest that, as a matter of policy and precedent, this is a classic case for the exercise of our oft-announced allegiance to judicial restraint. I know of no case in which greater gravity and delicacy have attached to the duty that this Court is called on to perform whenever legislation — state or federal — is challenged on constitutional grounds. It seems to me that the sweeping judicial action undertaken today reflects a basic lack of faith and confidence in the democratic process. . . .

Coker v. Georgia, 53 L. Ed. 2d 982 (1977)

As we noted, four years after *Furman* in *Gregg* v. *Georgia,* the Supreme Court ruled that the death penalty was *not* inherently cruel and unusual punishment and therefore it was *not* automatically a violation of the Eighth Amendment. In *Gregg* the Court attempted to lay down guidelines for state legislatures that wished to reimpose the death penalty. State statutes could not be capriciously administered, the Court ruled in *Gregg.* They could not discriminate against the underclasses of society and they could not impose mandatory death penalties for certain crimes because by doing so states were treating all persons convicted of a designated offense as a mass, as "faceless" individuals. The Court was saying that state statutes must not be arbitrary but must judge each crime and each criminal separately and distinctly.

The Burger Court reemphasized this view a year later in *Coker* v. *Georgia.* Justice White, who had led the dissenters in 1976, sharply criticizing the Court's striking down of death penalty statutes in North Carolina, Louisiana and Oklahoma, said (in *Coker*) that "a sentence of death is grossly disproportionate and excessive punishment for the crime of rape and is therefore forbidden by the Eighth Amendment. . . ." Justice White was joined by Justices Stewart, Blackmun, and Stevens. Justices Brennan, Marshall, and Powell concurred and therefore made up the majority of seven. However, Brennan and Marshall reiterated their often-stated views that the death penalty, as such, is "cruel and unusual punishment prohibited by the Eighth Amendment." Justice Powell concurred with the majority judgment but only because there was no indication that the crime had been committed with "excessive brutality." Powell also noted that the four had gone too far in holding that capital punishment always, regardless of circumstances, was a disproportionate penalty "for the crime of raping an adult woman."

Chief Justice Burger, joined by Justice Rehnquist, dissented sharply, criticizing that in striking down the death penalty the Court had "overstepped the bounds of proper constitutional adjudication by substituting its policy judgment for that of the [Georgia] state legislature."

Mr. Justice White announced the judgment of the Court, saying in part:

Petitioner was charged with escape, armed robbery, motor vehicle theft, kidnapping, and rape. Counsel was appointed to represent him. Having been found competent to stand trial, he was tried. The jury returned a verdict of guilty, rejecting his general plea of insanity. A sentencing hearing was then conducted in accordance with the procedures dealt with at length in Gregg v Georgia, 428 US 153, 49 L Ed 2d 859, 96 S Ct 2909 (1976), where this Court sustained the death penalty for murder when imposed pursuant to the statutory procedures. The jury was instructed that it could consider as aggravating circumstances whether the rape had been committed by a person with a prior record of conviction for a capital felony and whether the rape had been committed in the course of committing another capital felony, namely, the armed robbery of Allen Carver. The court also instructed, pursuant to statute, that even if aggravating circumstances were present, the death penalty need not be imposed if the jury found they were outweighed by mitigating circumstances, that is, circumstances not constituting justification or excuse for the offense in question, "but which, in fairness and mercy, may be considered as extenuating or reducing the degree" of moral culpability or punishment. App 300. The jury's verdict on the rape count was death by electrocution. Both aggravating circumstances on which the court instructed were found to be present by the jury. . . .

Furman v Georgia, 408 US 238, and the Court's decision last Term make unnecessary the recanvassing of certain critical aspects of the controversy about the constitutionality of capital punishment. It is now settled that the death penalty is not invariably cruel and unusual punishment within the meaning of the Eighth Amendment: it is not inherently barbaric or an unacceptable mode of punishment for crime; neither is it always disproportionate to the crime for which it is imposed. It is also established that imposing capital punishment, at least for murder, in accordance with the procedures provided under the Georgia statutes saves the sentence from the infirmities which led the court to invalidate the prior Georgia capital punishment statute in Furman v Georgia, supra.

In sustaining the imposition of the death penalty in Gregg, however, the Court firmly embraced the holdings and dicta from prior cases, to the effect that the Eighth Amendment bars not only those punishments that are "barbaric" but also those that are "excessive" in relation to the crime committed. Under Gregg, a punishment is "excessive" and unconstitutional if it (1) makes no measurable contribution to acceptable goals of punishment and hence is nothing more than the purposeless and needless imposition of pain and suffering; or (2) is grossly out of proportion to the severity of the crime. A punishment might fail the test on either ground. Furthermore, these Eighth Amendment judgments should not be, or appear to be, merely the subjective views of individual Justices; judgment should be informed by objective factors to the maximum possible extent. To this end, attention must be given to the public attitudes concerning a particular sentence — history and precedent, legislative attitudes, and the response of juries reflected in their sentencing decisions are to be consulted. In Gregg, after giving due regard to such sources, the Court's judgment was that the death penalty for deliberate murder was neither the purposeless imposition of severe punishment nor a punishment grossly disproportionate to the crime. But the Court reserved the question of the constitutionality of the death penalty when imposed for other crimes. 428 US, at 187 n 35, 49 L Ed 2d 859, 96 S Ct 2909. . . .

That question, with respect to rape of an adult woman, is now before us. We have concluded that a sentence of death is grossly disproportionate and excessive punishment for the crime of rape and is therefore forbidden by the Eighth Amendment as cruel and unusual punishment.

As advised by recent cases, we seek guidance in history and from the objective evidence of the country's present judgment concerning the acceptability of death as a penalty for rape of an adult woman. At no time in the last 50 years has a majority of the States authorized death as a punishment for rape. In 1925, 18 States, the District of Columbia, and the Federal Government authorized capital punishment for the rape of an adult female. By 1971 just prior to the decision in Furman v Georgia, that number had declined, but not substantially, to 16 States plus the Federal Government. Furman then invalidated most of the capital punishment statutes in this country, including the rape statutes, because, among other reasons, of the manner in which the death penalty was imposed and utilized under those laws. . . .

The current judgment with respect to the death penalty for rape is not wholly unanimous among state legislatures, but it obviously weighs very heavily on the side of rejecting capital punishment as a suitable penalty for raping an adult woman. . . .

It was also observed in Gregg that "[t]he jury . . . is a significant and reliable index of contemporary values because it is so directly involved," 428 US, at 181, and that it is thus important to look to the sentencing decisions that juries have made in the course of assessing whether capital punishmenbt is an appropriate penalty for the crime being tried. Of course, the jury's judgment is meaningful only where the jury has an appropriate measure of choice as to whether the death penalty is to be imposed. As far as execution for rape is concerned, this is now true only in Georgia and in Florida; and in the latter State, capital punishment is authorized only for the rape of children.

According to the factual submissions in this Court, out of all rape convictions in Georgia since 1973 — and that total number has not been tendered — 63 cases had been reviewed by the Georgia Supreme Court as of the time of oral argument; and of these, six involved a death sentence, one of which was set aside, leaving five convicted rapists now under sentence of death in the State of Georgia. Georgia juries have thus sentenced rapists to death six times since 1973. This obviously is not a negligible number; and the State argues that as a practical matter juries simply reserve the extreme sanction for extreme cases of rape and that recent experience surely does not prove that jurors consider the death penalty to be a disproportionate punishment for every conceivable instance of rape, no matter how aggravated. Nevertheless, it is true that in the vast majority of cases, at least nine out of 10, juries have not imposed the death sentence. . . .

These recent events evidencing the attitude of state legislatures and sentencing juries do not wholly determine this controversy, for the Constitution contemplates that in the end our own judgment will be brought to bear on the question of the acceptability of the death penalty under the Eighth Amendment. Nevertheless, the legislative rejection of capital punishment for rape strongly confirms our own judgment, which is that death is indeed a disproportionate penalty for the crime of raping an adult woman.

We do not discount the seriousness of rape as a crime. It is highly reprehensible, both in a moral sense and in its almost total contempt for the personal integrity and autonomy of the female victim and for the latter's privilege of choosing those with whom intimate relationships are to be established. Short of homicide, it is the "ultimate violation of self." It is also a violent crime because it normally involves force, or the threat of force or intimidation, to overcome the will and the capacity of the victim to resist. Rape is very often accompanied by physical injury to the female and can also inflict mental and psychological damage. Because it undermines the community's sense of security, there is public injury as well.

Rape is without doubt deserving of serious punishment; but in terms of moral depravity and of the injury to the person and to the public, it does not compare with murder, which does involve the unjustified taking of human life. Although it may be accompanied by another crime, rape by definition does not include the death or even the serious injury to another person. The murderer kills; the rapist, if no more than that, does not. Life is over for the victim of the murderers; for the rape victim, life may not be nearly so happy as it was, but it is not over and normally is not beyond repair. We have the abiding conviction that the death penalty, which "is unique in its severity and revocability," 428 US 187 is an excessive penalty for the rapist who, as such, does not take human life.

This does not end the matter; for under Georgia law, death may not be imposed for any capital offense, including rape, unless the jury or judge finds one of the statutory aggravating circumstances and then elects to impose that sentence. For the rapist to be executed in Georgia, it must therefore be found not only that he committed rape but also that one or more of the following aggravating circumstances were present: (1) that the rape was committed by a person with a prior record of conviction for a capital felony: (2) that the rape was committed while the offender was engaged in the commission of another capital felony, or aggravated battery; or (3) the rape "was outrageously or wantonly vile, horrible or inhuman in that it involved torture, depravity of mind, or aggravated batter to the victim." Here, the first two of these aggravating circumstances were alleged and found by the jury.

Neither of these circumstances, nor both of them together, change our conclusion that the death sentence imposed on Coker is a disproportionate punishment for rape. Coker had prior convictions for capital felonies — rape, murder and kidnapping — but these prior convictions do not change the fact that the instant crime being punished is a rape not involving the taking of life.

It is also true that the present rape occurred while Coker was committing armed robbery, a felony for which the Georgia statutes authorize the death penalty. But Coker was tried for the robbery offense as well as for rape and received a separate life sentence for this crime; the jury did not deem the robbery itself deserving of the death penalty, even though accompanied by the aggravating circumstance, which was stipulated, that Coker had been convicted of a prior capital crime.

We note finally that in Georgia a person commits murder when he unlawfully and with malice aforethought, either express or implied, causes the death of another human being. He also commits that crime when in the commission of a felony he causes the death of another human being, irrespective of malice. But even where the killing is deliberate, it is not punishable by death absent proof of aggravating circumstances. It is difficult to accept the notion, and we do not, that the rape, with or without aggravating circumstances, should be punished more heavily than the deliberate killer as long as the rapist does not himself take the life of his victim. The judgment of the Georgia Supreme Court upholding the death sentence is reversed and the case is remanded to that court for further proceedings not inconsistent with this opinion.

So ordered.

Lockett v. Ohio, 98 S.Ct. 2954 (1978)

On July 3, 1978 the Supreme Court decided two additional death penalty disputes, both dealing with Ohio's death penalty statute. Of the two, *Lockett* is the controlling decision.[1] Reviewing the facts in *Lockett* the Court found that Ohio's death penalty statute had been rewritten in 1972 in response to its ruling in *Furman v. Georgia*.

After *Furman*, the Ohio legislature, attempting to meet the specific requirements the Court seemed to indicate necessary to pass the constitutional test, adopted a bill that required the death penalty for murder if at least one of seven "aggravating circumstances" was found to exist and if none of three specific mitigating circumstances was found to exist.

The seven aggravating circumstances that made the death penalty mandatory under the new statute were: (1) in a case of assassination of the president of the United States, any person in line of succession to the presidency, or the governor or lieutenant governor of Ohio; (2) if the offense was committed for hire; (3) if the offense was committed for the purpose of escaping detection; (4) if the offense was committed while the person was in prison; (5) if the offender had previously been convicted of murder; (6) if the victim was a law enforcement officer known as such by the offender; and (7) if the offense was

---

1. A companion case, Bell v. Ohio 98 S.Ct. 2977 (1978) was decided the same day.

committed during a kidnapping, rape, aggravated arson, aggravated robbery or aggravated burglary.

Ohio's statute also specified that the death penalty could *not* be imposed for aggravated murder when "considering the nature and circumstances of the offense and the history, character and condition of the offender one or more of the following is established by a preponderance of the evidence: (1) the victim induced or facilitated [the offense]; (2) it is unlikely that the offense would have been committed, but for the fact that the offender was under duress, coercion or strong provocation; (3) the offense was primarily the product of the offender's psychosis or mental deficiency, though such condition is insufficient to establish the defense of insanity."[2] From the trial record, which was largely the state's evidence testimony of an accomplice, Sandra Lockett was found guilty of aggravated murder under the Ohio Statute and sentenced to death. Testimony indicated that Lockett drove the getaway car in a pawn shop robbery during which the shop owner was killed by a gunshot as he struggled with the robber, one Al Parker. Parker, the accomplice, later turned state's evidence against Lockett in return for a lesser charge.

Before the Supreme Court, Lockett's defense attorney argued that Ohio's death penalty statute was unconstitutional on grounds that it did not permit the trial judge to consider such mitigating circumstances as "her character, age, prior record, lack of specific intent to cause death and her relatively minor part in the crime."

Led by Chief Justice Burger, joined by Justices Stewart, White, Blackmun, Powell, Rehnquist, and Stevens, the Supreme Court upheld Lockett's conviction. The Court split however, on the application of the death penalty to Lockett under the Ohio statute in question. On that issue, part III of the Chief Justice's opinion, he was joined only by Justices Stewart, Powell, and Stevens. Justices White, Marshall, and Blackmun each wrote separate concurring opinions agreeing with the Chief Justice's argument concerning the invalidity of Ohio's death penalty statute. Thus seven Burger Court justices voted to strike down Ohio's law. Only Justice Rehnquist would have upheld it. Justice Brennan did not participate in the case.

Lockett gave the Court an opportunity to review its death penalty decisions from *Furman* v. *Georgia* forward. It has additional value for this reason.

Chief Justice Burger delivered the opinion of the Court, saying in part:

> . . . Lockett challenges the constitutionality of Ohio's death penalty statute on a number of grounds. We find it necessary to consider only her contention that her death sentence is invalid because the statute under which it was imposed did not permit the sentencing judge to consider, as mitigating factors, her character, prior record, age, lack of specific intent to cause death, and her relatively minor part in the crime. To address her contention from the proper perspective, it is helpful to review the developments in our recent cases where we have applied the Eighth and Fourteenth Amendments to death penalty statutes. We do not write on a "clean slate."
>
> Prior to *Furman* v. *Georgia*, 408 U.S. 238 (1972), every State that authorized capital punishment had abandoned mandatory death penalties, and instead permitted the jury unguided and unrestrained discretion regarding the imposi-

2. These excerpts from the Ohio Statute are found in an appendix to the Chief Justice's opinion in *Lockett*.

tion of the death penalty in a particular capital case. Mandatory death penalties had proven unsatisfactory, as the plurality noted in *Woodson* v. *North Carolina*, 428 U.S. 280, 293 (1976), in part because juries "with some regularity disregarded their oaths and refused to convict defendants where a death sentence was the automatic consequence of a guilty verdict."

This Court had never intimated prior to *Furman* that discretion in sentencing offended the Constitution. . . . As recently as *McGautha* v. *California*, 402 U.S. 183 (1971), the Court had specifically rejected the contention that discretion in imposing the death penalty violated the fundamental standards of fairness embodied in Fourteenth Amendment due process, *id.*, at 207–208, and had asserted that States were entitled to assume that "jurors confronted with the truly awesome responsibility of decreeing death for a fellow human [would] act with due regard for the consequences of their decision." *Id.*, at 208.

The constitutional status of discretionary sentencing in capital cases changed abruptly, however, as a result of the separate opinions supporting the judgment in *Furman*. The question in *Furman* was whether "the imposition and carrying out of the death penalty [in the cases before the Court] constituted cruel and unusual punishment in violation of the Eighth and Fourteenth Amendments." 408 U.S., at 239. Two Justices concluded that the Eighth Amendment prohibited the death penalty altogether and on that ground voted to reverse the judgments sustaining the death penalties. *Id.*, at 305–306 (BRENNAN, J., concurring); *id.*, at 370–371 (MARSHALL, J., concurring). Three Justices were unwilling to hold the death penalty *per se* unconstitutional under the Eighth and Fourteenth Amendments, but voted to reverse the judgments on other grounds. In separate opinions, the three concluded that discretionary sentencing, unguided by legislatively defined standards, violated the Eighth Amendment because it was "pregnant with discrimination," *id.*, at 257 (Douglas, J., concurring), because it permitted the death penalty to be "wantonly" and "freakishly" imposed, *id.*, at 310 (STEWART, J., concurring), and because it imposed the death penalty with "great infrequency" and afforded "no meaningful basis for distinguishing the few cases in which it [was] imposed from the many cases in which it [was] not," *id.*, at 313 (WHITE, J., concurring). Thus, what had been approved under the Due Process Clause of the Fourteenth Amendment in *McGautha* became impermissible under the Eighth and Fourteenth Amendments by virtue of the judgment in *Furman*. See, *Gregg* v. *Georgia*, 428 U.S. 153 195 n. 47 (1976) (opinion of STEWART, POWELL, STEVENS, JJ.).

Predictably, the variety of opinions supporting the judgment in *Furman* engendered confusion as to what was required in order to impose the death penalty in accord with the Eighth Amendment. Some States responded to what was thought to be the command of *Furman* by adopting mandatory death penalties for a limited category of specific crimes thus eliminating all discretion from the sentencing process in capital cases. Other States attempted to continue the practice of individually assessing the culpability of each individual defendant convicted of a capital offense and, at the same time, to comply with *Furman*, by providing standards to guide the sentencing decision.

Four years after *Furman*, we considered Eighth Amendment issues posed by five of the post-*Furman* death penalty statutes. Four Justices took the position that all five statutes complied with the Constitution; two Justices took the position that none of them complied. Hence, the disposition of each case varied according to the votes of a plurality of three Justices who delivered a joint opinion in each of the five cases upholding the constitutionality of the statutes of Georgia, Florida, and Texas, and holding those of North Carolina and Louisiana unconstitutional.

The plurality reasoned that to comply with *Furman*, sentencing procedures should not create "a substantial risk that the death penalty [will] be inflicted in an arbitrary and capricious manner." *Gregg* v. *Georgia, supra,* at 188. In the view of the plurality, however, *Furman* did not require that all sentencing discretion be eliminated, but only that it be "directed and limited," *id.,* at 189, so that the death penalty would be imposed in a more consistent and rational manner and so that there would be a "meaningful basis for distinguishing the . . . cases in which it is imposed from . . . the cases in which it is not." The plurality also concluded, in the course of invalidating North Carolina's mandatory death penalty statute, that the sentencing process must permit consideration of the "character and record of the individual offender and the circumstances of the particular offense as a constitutionally indispensable part of the process of inflicting the penalty of death," *Woodson* v. *North Carolina, supra,* at 304, in order to ensure the reliability, under Eighth Amendment standards, of the determination that "death is the appropriate punishment in a specific case." *Id.,* at 305; see *Roberts (Harry)* v. *Louisiana,* 431 U.S. 637 (1977); *Jurek* v. *Texas,* 428 U.S. 262, 271–272 (1976).

In the last decade, many of the States have been obliged to revise their death penalty statutes in response to the various opinions supporting the judgments in *Furman, supra,* and *Gregg, supra,* and its companion cases. The signals from this Court have not, however, always been easy to decipher. The States now deserve the clearest guidance that the Court can provide; we have an obligation to reconcile previously differing views in order to provide that guidance.

With that obligation in mind we turn to Lockett's attack on the Ohio statute. Essentially she contends that the Eighth and Fourteenth Amendments require that the sentencer be given a full opportunity to consider mitigating circumstances in capital cases and that the Ohio statute does not comply with that requirement. She relies, in large part, on the plurality opinions in *Woodson, supra,* at 303–305, *Roberts, supra,* at 333–334, and *Jurek, supra,* at 271–272, but she goes beyond them.

We begin by recognizing that the concept of individualized sentencing in criminal cases generally, although not constitutionally required, has long been accepted in this country. See *Williams* v. *New York,* 337 U.S., at 247–248; *Pennsylvania ex rel. Sullivan* v. *Ashe,* 302 U.S., at 55. Consistent with that concept, sentencing judges traditionally have taken a wide range of factors into account. That States have authority to make aiders and abettors equally responsible, as a matter of law, with principals, or to enact felony murder statutes is beyond constitutional challenge. But the definition of crimes generally has not been thought automatically to dictate what should be the proper penalty. See *Pennsylvania ex rel. Sullivan* v. *Ashe, supra,* at 55; *Williams* v. *New York, supra,* at 247–248; *Williams* v. *Oklahoma, supra,* at 585. And where sentencing discretion is granted, it generally has been agreed that the sentencing judge's "possession of the fullest information possible concerning the defendant's life and characteristics" is "[h]ighly relevant — *if not essential* — [to the] selection of an appropriate sentence. . . ." *Williams* v. *New York, supra,* at 247 (emphasis added).

The opinions of this Court going back many years in dealing with sentencing in capital cases have noted the strength of the basis for individualized sentencing. For example, Mr. Justice Black, writing for the Court in *Williams* v. *New York, supra,* at 247–248 — a capital case — observed that the

> "whole country has traveled far from the period in which the death sentence was an automatic and commonplace result of convictions — even for offenses today deemed trivial."

Ten years later, in *Williams* v. *Oklahoma,* 358 U.S., at 585, another capital case, the Court echoed Mr. Justice Black, stating that

> "[i]n discharging his duty of imposing a proper sentence, the sentencing

judge is authorized, *if not required,* to consider all of the mitigating and aggravating circumstances involved in the crime." (Emphasis added.)

... Most would agree that "the 19th century movement away from mandatory death sentences marked an enlightened introduction of flexibility into the sentencing process." *Furman v. Georgia, supra,* at 402 (BURGER, C. J., dissenting).

Although legislatures remain free to decide how much discretion in sentencing should be reposed in the judge or jury in noncapital cases, the plurality opinion in *Woodson,* after reviewing the historical repudiation of mandatory sentencing in capital cases, 428 U.S., at 289–298, concluded that:

> "in capital cases the fundamental respect for humanity underlying the Eighth Amendment . . . requires consideration of the character and record of the individual offender and the circumstances of the particular offense as a constitutionally indispensable part of the process of inflicting the penalty of death." *Id.,* at 304.

That declaration rested "on the predicate that the penalty of death is qualitatively different" from any other sentence. *Id.,* at 305. We are satisfied that this qualitative difference between death and other penalties calls for a greater degree of reliability when the death sentence is imposed. The mandatory death penalty statute in *Woodson* was held invalid because it permitted *no* consideration of "relevant facets of the character and record of the individual offender or the circumstances of the particular offense." *Id.,* at 304. The plurality did not attempt to indicate, however, which facets of an offender or his offense it deemed "relevant" in capital sentencing or what degree of consideration of "relevant facets" it would require.

We are now faced with those questions and we conclude that the Eighth and Fourteenth Amendments require that the sentencer, in all but the rarest kind of capital case, not be precluded from considering *as a mitigating factor,* any aspect of a defendant's character or record and any of the circumstances of the offense that the defendant proffers as a basis for a sentence less than death. We recognize that, in noncapital cases, the established practice of individualized sentences rests not on constitutional commands but public policy enacted into statutes. The considerations that account for the wide acceptance of individualization of sentences in noncapital cases surely cannot be thought less important in capital cases. Given that the imposition of death by public authority is so profoundly different from all other penalties, we cannot avoid the conclusion that an individualized decision is essential in capital cases. The need for treating each defendant in a capital case with that degree of respect due the uniqueness of the individual is far more important than in noncapital cases. A variety of flexible techniques — probation, parole, work furloughs, to name a few — and various post conviction remedies, may be available to modify an initial sentence of confinement in noncapital cases. The nonavailability of corrective or modifying mechanisms with respect to an executed capital sentence underscores the need for individualized consideration as a constitutional requirement in imposing the death sentence.

There is no perfect procedure for deciding in which cases governmental authority should be used to impose death. But a statute that prevents the sentencer in all capital cases from giving independent mitigating weight to aspects of the defendant's character and record and to circumstances of the offense proffered in mitigation creates the risk that the death penalty will be imposed in spite of factors which may call for a less severe penalty. When the choice is between life and death, that risk is unacceptable and incompatible with the commands of the Eighth and Fourteenth Amendments.

The Ohio death penalty statute does not permit the type of individualized consideration of mitigating factors we now hold to be required by the Eighth and Fourteenth Amendments in capital cases. Its constitutional infirmities can best be understood by comparing it with the statutes upheld in *Gregg, Proffitt,* and *Jurek.*

In upholding the Georgia statute in *Gregg,* JUSTICES STEWART, POWELL, and STEVENS noted that the statute permitted the jury "to consider any aggravating or mitigating circumstances," see *Gregg, supra,* at 206, and that the Georgia Supreme Court had approved "open and far ranging argument" in presentence hearings, *id.,* at 203. Although the Florida statute approved in *Proffitt* contained a list of mitigating factors, six members of this Court assumed, in approving the statute, that the range of mitigating factors listed in the statute was not exclusive. *Jurek* involved a Texas statute which made no explicit reference to mitigating factors. *Jurek, supra,* at 272. Rather the jury was required to answer three questions in the sentencing process, the second of which was "whether there is a probability that the defendant would commit criminal acts of violence that would constitute a continuing threat to society." Tex. Code Crim. Proc., Art. 37.071 (b) (Supp. 1975-1976); see *Jurek, supra,* at 269. The statute survived the petitioner's Eighth and Fourteenth Amendment attack because three Justices concluded that the Texas Court of Criminal Appeals had broadly interpreted the second question — despite its facial narrowness — so as to permit the sentencer to consider "whatever mitigating circumstances" the defendant might be able to show. *Id.,* at 272–273 (opinion of STEWART, POWELL, and STEVENS, JJ.), citing and quoting, *Jurek* v. *State,* 522 S.W. 2d, 934, 939-940 (Tex. Ct. Crim. App. 1976). None of the statutes we sustained in *Gregg* and the companion cases clearly operated at that time to prevent the sentencer from considering any aspect of the defendant's character and record or any circumstances of his offense as an independently mitigating factor.

In this regard the statute now before us is significantly different. Once a defendant is found guilty of aggravated murder with at least one of seven specified aggravating circumstances, the death penalty must be imposed unless, considering "the nature and circumstances of the offense and the history, character, and conditions of the offender," the sentencing judge determines that at least one of the following mitigating circumstances is established by a preponderance of the evidence:

"(1) The victim of the offense induced or facilitated it.

"(2) It is unlikely that the offense would have been committed but for the fact that the offender was under duress, coercion, or strong provocation.

"(3) The offense was primarily the product of the offender's psychosis or mental deficiency, though such condition is insufficient to establish the defense of insanity."

The Ohio Supreme Court has concluded that there is no constitutional distinction between the statute approved in *Proffitt, supra,* and Ohio's statute, see *State* v. *Bayless,* 48 Ohio St. 2d 73, 86–87 (1976), because the mitigating circumstances in Ohio's statute are "liberally construed in favor of the accused," and because the sentencing judge or judges may consider factors such as the age and criminal record of the defendant in determining whether any of the mitigating circumstances is established. But even under the Ohio court's construction of the statute, only the three factors specified in the statute can be considered in mitigation of the defendant's sentence. We see, therefore, that once it is determined that the victim did not induce or facilitate the offense, that the defendant did not act under duress or coercion, and that the offense was not primarily the product of the defendant's mental deficiency, the Ohio statute mandates the sentence of death. The absence of direct proof that the defendant intended to cause the death of the victim is relevant for mitigating purposes only if it is determined that it sheds some light on one of the three statutory mitigating factors. Similarly, consideration of a defendant's comparatively minor role in the offense, or age, would generally not be permitted, as such, to affect the sentencing decision.

The limited range of mitigating circumstances which may be considered by the sentencer under the Ohio statute is incompatible with the Eighth and Fourteenth Amendments. To meet constitutional requirements, a death penalty statute must not preclude consideration of relevant mitigating factors.

Accordingly, the judgment under review is reversed to the extent that it sustains the imposition of the death penalty; the case is remanded for further proceedings.

VI

EQUAL PROTECTION
OF
THE LAWS

One of the three "Civil War" amendments to the Constitution, the Fourteenth, ratified in 1868, has been by far the most significant in moving American institutions toward the chimerical goal of "equal justice under law." Although number Thirteen, which put Lincoln's Emancipation Proclamation of January 1, 1863 into the Constitution and abolished slavery, and number Fifteen, which (supposedly) guaranteed newly freed black citizens the right to vote, were and are important milestones in the long struggle for equal justice, the Fourteenth Amendment has been in the constitutional forefront of that struggle, particularly in recent years.

Its most important provisions prohibit the states from depriving any person of life, liberty, or property without due process of law (as the Fifth Amendment prohibits the federal government from doing) and from denying any person the equal protection of the law. These two clauses, due process, involving the concept of fairness; and equal protection, involving the guarantee of equal treatment, have been involved in what perhaps have been the most far-reaching constitutional disputes of modern times. In recent times, for example, they have been used by the Supreme Court in several key decisions to intervene when states have infringed upon civil and human rights protected against federal encroachment by the Bill of Rights. Since 1925 (see *Gitlow,* above) the due process clause of the Fourteenth Amendment has been incorporated to prohibit states from denying citizens the freedoms guaranteed under the Federal Constitution. The Supreme Court's early incorporation decisions dealt with First Amendment freedoms. As we have seen, later, during the Warren Court years, rights enumerated in the Fourth and Eighth Amendments were also incorporated into the Fourteenth.

With respect to the modern-day civil rights movement, it has been the equal protection clause that has been the most effective constitutional tool to help bring about equal justice for black people and for the inner-city poor. For example, "equal protection" has been used by the Supreme Court to abolish and restrain racial segregation in universities, in public schools, and in the use of public facilities. In 1962 and 1964 it was invoked to effectuate fair apportionment of congressional as well as state legislative districts ("one person, one vote"), thus giving urban inner-city dwellers fairer political representation. And the Court has also used equal protection to help remove a number of other social and legal injustices from among the burdens of less fortunate members of American society.

As Pritchett notes in his scholarly study of the Constitution, Congressman John Bingham of Ohio is the "father of the Fourteenth Amendment."[1] Bingham in the House and Senators Wilson and Trumbull, the authors of the significant Civil Rights Act of 1866, were responsible for guiding the Fourteenth Amendment through Congress. It is clear from the debates in the House and Senate that Congress had the rights of the newly freed black people in mind when it drafted the Fourteenth Amendment. It should also be clear from even a cursory reading of the Supreme Court's record on this matter that it has only been since the mid 1940s that the Court has used the Amendment to do what Bingham and the others intended a century ago.

In what follows here we look at the Court's work in the areas of public transportation, public accommodations, housing, and education. Involved here are the Court's famous "separate but equal" dictum of the 1896 *Plessy* case, which was overturned in *Brown v. Board of Education,* as well as the more recent busing controversies in Charlotte, Denver, and Detroit which the *Brown* decision would open. Also following here are the landmark public accommodation cases that arose from the Civil Rights Act of 1964 and two housing cases, one involving the constitutionality of restrictive covenants in real estate contracts, and the other in which the Court used the "open housing" provision of the century-old 1866 Civil Rights Act to grant a racially mixed couple the right to purchase a home in a St. Louis, Missouri suburb.

1. Pritchett, at 295–96.

1

TRANSPORTATION

Before the Supreme Court, in *Plessy v. Ferguson,* refused to use the equal protection clause of the Fourteenth Amendment as a barrier against racial segregation in public transportation, it and Congress's commerce power had formed the principal constitutional bulwarks for equal treatment of blacks on the nation's railroads. Separate facilities and accommodations for the newly freed blacks on all public transportation quickly became the general rule in the southern states during the years immediately following the Civil War. Then in the Civil Rights Act of 1875, a reconstruction-minded Congress attempted to remedy the situation. Eight years later, however, the Supreme Court decided that the Fourteenth Amendment's equal protection clause could only be used against state legislation.[1] In addition, it refused to apply the 1875 federal law to the states via the Fourteenth Amendment. From this decision it would reasonably seem to follow that the Court *would* use the equal protection clause to strike down state racial segregation statutes. *Plessy* shattered that hope.

During the post-Civil War period the federal commerce power was also a possible shield against racial segregation in public transportation. Ironically, however, on two late-nineteenth century occasions the Supreme Court used the commerce power to *thwart* attempts by states to rid interstate commerce of racially segregated facilities. In *Hall* v. *DeCuir,*[2] for example, the Supreme Court used the commerce power to strike down an 1869 Louisiana statute that had prohibited racial discrimination in interstate commerce. The Louisiana law had been passed during the reconstruction era, when, as southerners insist, "carpetbaggers" controlled the legislature, as a way of ensuring travel rights for black people. Declaring the state law void, the Court ruled in *DeCuir* that prescribing uniform regulations for interstate commerce was a *congressional* function and not an area in which states could legislate. Twelve years later in *Louisville, New Orleans and Texas R. Co.* v. *Mississippi,*[3] for the first time, the Supreme Court had to deal with a reverse statutory situation. At issue here was an 1888 Mississippi statute requiring railways carrying passengers in

1. Civil Rights cases 109 U.S. 3 (1883).
2. 95 U.S. 485 (1878).
3. 133 U.S. 587 (1890).

the state to provide "equal but separate" accommodations for both races. As Pritchett has noted, "it seemed obvious that the Supreme Court which in *DeCuir* had declared a state statute *prohibiting* segregation an unconstitutional burden on interstate commerce would have to make a similar holding against a state statute *requiring* discrimination."[4] It would seem so, but the Supreme Court fudged. Instead of doing the obvious it accepted Mississippi's argument that its statute applied solely to intrastate commerce and therefore did not touch upon the interstate commerce Congress alone can regulate.

After this equivocation the Supreme Court soon took another major step away from equal treatment for blacks in public transportation. In *Plessy* v. *Ferguson* the Court laid down a constitutional standard establishing the supposed compatability of racial segregation and equal treatment under the law. The standard, "separate but equal" was to endure for some fifty-eight years.

Plessy v. Ferguson, 163 U.S. 537 (1896)

In 1890 the state of Louisiana passed a statute requiring railroads carrying passengers in their coaches in Louisiana to provide equal but separate accommodations for white and black passengers. The statute allowed railroads to comply either by providing two or more passenger coaches for each train (one or more for each race) or by dividing the coaches by partition so as to insure separate accommodations for each race. The statute specified that no person could occupy seats in coaches other than those assigned by race and it imposed fines or imprisonment upon anyone who insisted upon using a coach or compartment other than the one assigned.

Plessy, a resident of Louisiana of mixed racial parentage (the state's official classification of him was seven-eighths white and one-eighth black), boarded an East Louisiana Railway all-white coach bound from New Orleans to Covington. The date was June 7, 1892. He was ordered to move to the all-black coach by the train's conductor. He refused. Thereupon Plessy was forcibly removed from the train and jailed for violating the 1890 statute. Brought to trial, Plessy charged that the Louisiana statute violated his rights under the equal protection clause of the Fourteenth Amendment.

Similar to the Mississippi Act of 1888, Louisiana's statute was but one of the so-called "black codes" enacted in most states of the old confederacy to undo the guarantees of the three Civil War Amendments. Most were passed after the close of the reconstruction era following the inauguration of President Rutherford B. Hayes in 1877. "Black codes" reestablished systems of racial segregation under which blacks and whites were required to be separate when they used public or semipublic facilities. Thus, Louisiana's statute established separate railroad dining cars, restrooms, and other accommodations for each race.

In *Plessy* the Court had to decide whether Louisiana's 1890 "black code" violated the Fourteenth Amendment's equal protection clause. In a historic 7–1 decision the Court ruled it did not. By so doing the Court's new dictum, "separate but equal," became part of American Constitutional law. "Separate but equal" would later be used to segregate the races in the South's public school system.

4. Op. cit., at 490.

As Cushman has mentioned, there is an interesting footnote to the *Plessy* case. Justice Brown, a northerner (Michigan) and a Yale graduate, spoke for the majority while Justice Harlan, a southerner from Kentucky, was the lone dissenter.[5] Justice Harlan's dissent, quoted here at some length, is an eloquent statement for equal justice. It formed much of the constitutional rationale when the Supreme Court overturned *Plessy* in the *Brown* decision some fifty-eight years later.

Mr. Justice Brown delivered the opinion of the Court, saying in part:

> So far, then, as a conflict with the Fourteenth Amendment is concerned, the case reduces itself to the question whether the statute of Louisiana is a reasonable regulation, and with respect to this there must necessarily be a large discretion on the part of the legislature. In determining the question of reasonableness it is at liberty to act with reference to the established usages, customs and traditions of the people, and with a view to the promotion of their comfort, and the preservation of the public peace and good order. Gauged by this standard, we cannot say that a law which authorizes or even requires the separation of the two races in public conveyances is unreasonable, or more obnoxious to the Fourteenth Amendment than the acts of Congress requiring separate schools for colored children in the District of Columbia, the constitutionality of which does not seem to have been questioned, or the corresponding acts of state legislatures.
>
> We consider the underlying fallacy of the plaintiff's argument to consist in the assumption that the enforced separation of the two races stamps the colored race with a badge of inferiority. If this be so, it is not by reason of anything found in the act, but solely because the colored race chooses to put that construction upon it. The argument necessarily assumes that if, as has been more than once the case, and is not unlikely to be so again, the colored race should become the dominant power in the state legislature, and should enact a law in precisely similar terms, it would thereby relegate the white race to an inferior position. We imagine that the white race, at least, would not acquiesce in this assumption. The argument also assumes that social prejudices may be overcome by legislation, and that equal rights cannot be secured to the negro except by an enforced commingling of the two races. We cannot accept this proposition. If the two races are to meet upon terms of social equality, it must be the result of natural affinities, a mutual appreciation of each other's merits and a voluntary consent of individuals. As was said by the Court of Appeals of New York in *People* v. *Gallagher*, 93 N. Y. 438, 448, "this end can neither be accomplished nor promoted by laws which conflict with the general sentiment of the community upon whom they are designed to operate. When the government, therefore, has secured to each of its citizens equal rights before the law and equal opportunities for improvement and progress, it has accomplished the end for which it was organized and performed all of the functions respecting social advantages with which it is endowed." Legislation is powerless to eradicate racial instincts or to abolish distinctions based upon physical differences, and the attempt to do so can only result in accentuating the difficulties of the present situation. If the civil and political rights of both races be equal one cannot be inferior to the other civilly or politically. If one race be inferior to the other socially, the Constitution of the United States cannot put them upon the same plane.
>
> It is true that the question of the proportion of colored blood necessary to constitute a colored person, as distinguished from a white person, is one upon which there is a difference of opinion in the different States, some holding that any visible admixture of black blood stamps the person as belonging to the colored race, . . . others that it depends upon the preponderance of blood, . . .

5. Op. cit., at 409.

and still others that the predominance of white blood must only be in the proportion of three fourths. . . . But these are questions to be determined under the laws of each State and are not properly put in issue in this case. Under the allegations of his petition it may undoubtedly become a question of importance whether, under the laws of Louisiana, the petitioner belongs to the white or colored race.

The judgment of the court below is, therefore,

Affirmed.

Mr. Justice Harlan dissented, saying in part:

In respect of civil rights, common to all citizens, the Constitution of the United States does not, I think, permit any public authority to know the race of those entitled to be protected in the enjoyment of such rights. Every true man has pride of race, and under appropriate circumstances when the rights of others, his equals before the law, are not to be affected, it is his privilege to express such pride and to take such action based upon it as to him seems proper. But I deny that any legislative body or judicial tribunal may have regard to the race of citizens when the civil rights of those citizens are involved. Indeed, such legislation, as that here in question, is inconsistent not only with that equality of rights which pertains to citizenship, National and State, but with the personal liberty enjoyed by every one within the United States. . . .

It was said in argument that the statute of Louisiana does not discriminate against either race, but prescribes a rule applicable alike to white and colored citizens. But this argument does not meet the difficulty. Every one knows that the statute in question had its origin in the purpose, not so much to exclude white persons from railroad cars occupied by blacks, as to exclude colored people from coaches occupied by or assigned to white persons. Railroad corporations of Louisiana did not make discrimination among whites in the matter of accommodation for travellers. The thing to accomplish was, under the guise of giving equal accommodation for whites and blacks, to compel the latter to keep to themselves while travelling in railroad passenger coaches. No one would be so wanting in candor as to assert the contrary. The fundamental objection, therefore, to the statute is that it interferes with the personal freedom of citizens. "Personal liberty," it has been well said, "consists in the power of locomotion, of changing situation, or removing one's person to whatsoever places one's own inclination may direct, without imprisonment or restraint, unless by due course of law." . . . If a white man and a black man choose to occupy the same public conveyance on a public highway, it is their right to do so, and no government, proceeding alone on grounds of race, can prevent it without infringing the personal liberty of each. . . . The destinies of the two races, in this country, are indissolubly linked together, and the interests of both require that the common government of all shall not permit the seeds of race hate to be planted under the sanction of law. What can more certainly arouse race hate, what more certainly create and perpetuate a feeling of distrust between these races, than state enactments, which, in fact, proceed on the ground that colored citizens are so inferior and degraded that they cannot be allowed to sit in public coaches occupied by white citizens? That, as all will admit, is the real meaning of such legislation as was enacted in Louisiana.

The sure guarantee of the peace and security of each race is the clear, distinct, unconditional recognition by our governments, National and State, of every right that inheres in civil freedom, and of the equality before the law of all citizens of the United States without regard to race. State enactments, regulating the enjoyment of civil rights, upon the basis of race, and cunningly devised to defeat legitimate results of the war, under the pretence of recognizing equality of rights, can have no other result than to render permanent peace impossible, and to keep alive a conflict of races, the continuance of which must do harm to all concerned. This question is not met by the suggestion that social equality cannot exist between the white and black races in this country. That argument, if it can be properly regarded as one, is scarcely worthy of consideration; for social equality no more exists between two races when travelling in a passenger coach or a public highway than when members of the same races sit by each other in a street car or in the jury box, or stand or sit with each other in a political assembly, or when they use in common the streets of a city or town, or when they are in the same room for the purpose of having their names placed on the registry of voters, or when they approach the ballot-box in order to exercise the high privilege of voting. . . .

If evils will result from the commingling of the two races upon public highways established for the benefit of all, they will be infinitely less than those that will surely come from state legislation regulating the enjoyment of civil rights upon the basis of race. We boast of the freedom enjoyed by our people above all other peoples. But it is difficult to reconcile that boast with a state of the law which, practically, puts the brand of servitude and degradation upon a large class of our fellow-citizens, our equals before the law. The thin disguise of "equal" accommodations for passengers in railroad coaches will not mislead any one, nor atone for the wrong this day done.

The result of the whole matter is, that while this court has frequently adjudged, and at the present term has recognized the doctrine, that a State cannot, consistently with the Constitution of the United States, prevent white and black citizens, having the required qualifications for jury service, from sitting in the same jury box, it is now solemnly held that a State may prohibit white and black citizens from sitting in the same passenger coach on a public highway, or may require that they be separated by a "partition," when in the same passenger coach. May it now be reasonably expected that astute men of the dominant race, who affect to be disturbed at the possibility that the integrity of the white race may be corrupted, or that its supremacy will be imperilled, by contact on public highways with black people, will endeavor to procure statutes requiring white and black jurors to be separated in the jury box by a "partition," and that, upon retiring from the court room to consult as to their verdict, such partition, if it be a moveable one, shall be taken to their consultation room, and set up in such way as to prevent black jurors from coming too close to their brother jurors of the white race. If the "partition" used in the court room happens to be stationary, provision could be made for screens with openings through which jurors of the two races could confer as to their verdict without coming into personal contact with each other. I cannot see but that, according to the principles this day announced, such state legislation, although conceived in hostility to, and enacted for the purpose of humiliating citizens of the United States of a particular race, would be held to be consistent with the Constitution. . . .

I am of opinion that the statute of Louisiana is inconsistent with the personal liberty of citizens, white and black, in that State, and hostile to both the spirit and letter of the Constitution of the United States. If laws of like character should be enacted in the several States of the Union, the effect would be in the highest degree mischievous. Slavery, as an institution tolerated by law would, it is true, have disappeared from our country, but there would remain a power in the States, by sinister legislation, to interfere with the full enjoyment of the blessings of freedom; to regulate civil rights, common to all citizens, upon the basis of race; and to place in a condition of legal inferiority a large body of American citizens, now constituting a part of the political community called the People of the United States, for whom, and by whom through representatives, our government is administered. Such a system is inconsistent with the guarantee given by the Constitution to each State of a republican form of government, and may be stricken down by Congressional action, or by the courts in the discharge of their solemn duty to maintain the supreme law of the land, anything in the constitution or laws of any State to the contrary notwithstanding.

For the reasons stated, I am constrained to withhold my assent from the opinion and judgment of the majority.

McCabe v. Atchison Topeka and Santa Fe Railway Co., 235 U.S. 151 (1914)

Eighteen years after *Plessy*, the Supreme Court backed off a bit from its position that racial segregation and equal protection of the law were "compatible." Without budging from "separate but equal" it nevertheless moved to put more emphasis on equality than separation. The Court now said it would insist that states make a careful effort to achieve equality under segregation.

The case in point was *McCabe* v. *Atchison Topeka and Santa Fe Railway Co.* In *McCabe* the Court ruled that an Oklahoma law did *not* accord "equal protection" to black people when it allowed railroads to have sleeping, dining, and chair cars exclusively for white passengers without providing equal facilities for black passengers.

With Justice Hughes writing for his unanimous colleagues the Supreme Court ruled that the Oklahoma Separate Coach law violated the equal protection rights of black passengers. The Court dismissed the argument made by the railroad that because there was only a limited demand for the special railroad cars by black passengers, the railroad was not obliged to provide the facilities.

Mr. Justice Hughes delivered the opinion of the Court, saying in part:

It is not questioned that the meaning of this clause is that the carriers may provide sleeping cars, dining cars and chair cars exclusively for white persons and provide no similar accommodations for negroes. The reasoning is that there may not be enough persons of African descent seeking these accommodations to warrant the outlay in providing them. Thus, the Attorney General of the State, in the brief filed by him in support of the law, urges that "the plaintiffs must show that their own travel is in such quantity and of such kind as to actually afford the roads the same profits, not per man, but per car, as does the white traffic, or, sufficient profit to justify the furnishing of the facility, and that in such case they are not supplied with separate cars containing the same. This they have not attempted. What vexes the plaintiffs is the limited market value they offer for such accommodations. Defendants are not by law compelled to furnish chair cars, diners nor sleepers, except when the market offered reasonably demands the facility." And in the brief of counsel for the appellees, it is stated that the members of the legislature "were undoubtedly familiar with the character and extent of travel of persons of African descent in the State of Oklahoma and were of the opinion that there was no substantial demand for Pullman car and dining car service for persons of the African race in the intrastate travel" in that State.

This argument with respect to volume of traffic seems to us to be without merit. It makes the constitutional right depend upon the number of persons who may be discriminated against, whereas the essence of the constitutional right is that it is a personal one. Whether or not particular facilities shall be provided may doubtless be conditioned upon there being a reasonable demand therefor, but, if facilities are provided, substantial equality of treatment of persons traveling under like conditions cannot be refused. It is the individual who is entitled to the equal protection of the laws, and if he is denied by a common carrier, acting in the matter under the authority of a state law, a facility or convenience in the course of his journey which under substantially the same circumstances is furnished to another traveler, he may properly complain that his constitutional privilege has been invaded.

There is, however, an insuperable obstacle to the granting of the relief sought by this bill. It was filed, as we have seen, by five persons against five railroad corporations to restrain them from complying with the state statute. The suit had been brought before the law went into effect and this amended bill was filed very shortly after. It contains some general allegations as to discriminations in the supply of facilities and as to the hardships which will ensue. It states that there will be 'a multiplicity of suits,' there being at least 'fifty thousand persons of the negro race in the State of Oklahoma' who will be injured and deprived of their civil rights. But we are dealing here with the case of the complainants, and nothing is shown to entitle them to an injunction. It is an elementary principle that, in order to justify the granting of this extraordinary relief, the complainant's need of it, and the absence of an adequate remedy at law, must clearly appear. The complainant cannot succeed because someone else may be hurt. Nor does it make any difference that other persons who may be injured are persons of the same race or occupation. It is the fact, clearly established, of injury to the complainant — not to others — which justifies judicial intervention.

Morgan v. Virginia, 328 U.S. 373 (1946)

It was not until the 1940s, under the leadership of the newly appointed, generally liberal Roosevelt appointees, that the Supreme Court moved affirmatively against segregation in public transportation. At first it did so cautiously, more often than not using the "safer" commerce power rather than the equal protection clause. The Court took its first careful step in *Mitchell* v. *United States*,[1] a 1941 dispute in which a black Illinois Congressman had been denied pullman railroad accommodations in Arkansas. Although the Court did not confront the issue of segregation in public transportation head on, it did insist that accommodations must be "substantially equal" in order to meet the constitutional standard. In effect, the *Mitchell* ruling went but an inch or two farther than *McCabe* had gone twenty-seven years earlier.

Having gotten its feet wet in this manner, the Roosevelt Court then moved on to take two more steps to rid public transportation of racial segregation. Despite misgivings expressed by Justice Douglas, the Court again used, in Pritchett's alliterative expression, "the cold-blooded and clumsy constitutional concept of commerce to do the job." In his concurring opinion in *Bob Lo*, Douglas chided the Court for not having based its rulings upon the equal protection clause.

1. 313 U.S. 80 (1941).

The two cases were *Morgan* v. *Virginia* and *Bob Lo Excursion Co.* v. *Michigan*.[2] In *Bob Lo* the Court upheld a lower court conviction under the Michigan Civil Rights Act of a Detroit amusement park for refusing to transport a young black girl on its boat to an island on the Canadian side of the Detroit river. The majority had no difficulty overlooking the fact that the "commerce" here was technically "foreign" and therefore outside the purview of Michigan's law.

Morgan was the key case, however. It marked the first time that the Supreme Court actually struck down racial segregation in public transportation, albeit using the "clumsy, cold-blooded" commerce power. Ultimately the Court did what Douglas had suggested in *Bob Lo*. Ten years after *Morgan*, in *Gayle* v. *Browder*[3] it affirmed a lower court ruling that an Alabama statute that required racial segregation on intrastate buses violated both the equal protection clause and due process clause of the Fourteenth Amendment.

Morgan arose when a black woman who was travelling by interstate bus from Virginia to Baltimore refused to move to the back of the bus so that a white passenger could use the seat. (Shades of Rosa Parks and the Montgomery bus boycott that sparked the civil rights movement of the late nineteen fifties.)

Speaking for a 7–1 Court, Justice Burton dissented, Justice Reed noted that a state statute cannot "unlawfully burden interstate commerce" in this manner. Thus in 1946, some seventy-eight years after ratification of the Fourteenth Amendment, racial segregation in public interstate transportation became a thing of the past.

Mr. Justice Reed delivered the opinion of the Court, saying in part:

> Because the Constitution puts the ultimate power to regulate commerce in Congress, rather than the states, the degree of state legislation's interference with that commerce may be weighed by federal courts to determine whether the burden makes the statute unconstitutional. The courts could not invalidate federal legislation for the same reason because Congress, within the limits of the Fifth Amendment, has authority to burden commerce if that seems to it a desirable means of accomplishing a permitted end.
>
> This statute is attacked on the ground that it imposes undue burdens on interstate commerce. It is said by the Court of Appeals to have been passed in the exercise of the state's police power to avoid friction between the races. But this Court pointed out years ago "that a State cannot avoid the operation of this rule by simply invoking the convenient apologetics of the police power." Burdens upon commerce are those actions of a state which directly "impair the usefulness of its facilities for such traffic." That impairment, we think, may arise from other causes than costs or long delays. A burden may arise from a state statute which requires interstate passengers to order their movements on the vehicle in accordance with local rather than national requirements. . . .
>
> In weighing the factors that enter into our conclusion as to whether this statute so burdens interstate commerce or so infringes the requirements of national uniformity as to be invalid, we are mindful of the fact that conditions vary between northern or western states such as Maine or Montana, with practically no colored population; industrial states such as Illinois, Ohio, New Jersey and Pennsylvania with a small, although appreciable, percentage of colored citizens; and the states of the deep south with percentages of from twenty-five to nearly fifty percent colored, all with varying densities of the white and colored races in certain localities. Local efforts to promote amicable relations in difficult areas by

2. 333 U.S. 28 (1948).

3. 352 U.S. 903 (1956).

legislative segregation in interstate transportation emerge from the latter racial distribution. As no state law can reach beyond its own border nor bar transportation of passengers across its boundaries, diverse seating requirements for the races in interstate journeys result. As there is no federal act dealing with the separation of races in interstate transportation, we must decide the validity of this Virginia statute on the challenge that it interferes with commerce, as a matter of balance between the exercise of the local police power and the need for national uniformity in the regulations for interstate travel. It seems clear to us that seating arrangements for the different races in interstate motor travel require a single, uniform rule to promote and protect national travel. Consequently, we hold the Virginia statute in controversy invalid.

Henderson v. United States, 339 U.S. 816 (1950)

Four years later, *Henderson* v. *United States* added an interesting footnote to the *Morgan* ruling. In question here was a Southern Railway Company rule which allotted ten tables in its dining cars to white passengers, and two tables (nearest the kitchen), exclusively for blacks. The railway also placed a curtain or a partition separating the white tables from the two black tables. The facts in *Henderson* indicated that on May 17, 1942 the petitioner, a black passenger, was en route from Washington, D.C., where he was employed by the Federal government, to Birmingham, Alabama. When he went to the dining car, the two "black" tables were partially occupied by white passengers (railway rules allowed this if no black passengers were present) but one seat was unoccupied. Henderson was refused service until the white passengers sitting at the "black" tables had completed their meal. This was another railway rule. Thereupon Henderson filed a complaint with the Interstate Commerce Commission, which subsequently refused to find that the railway practice violated the 1887 Interstate Commerce Act. However, a three-judge United States District Court ruled that it did. Shortly thereafter, the Southern Railway "adjusted" its rules and provided ten tables exclusively for white passengers and one table exclusively for black passengers with a curtain between them. The Supreme Court then had to decide whether the railway's "new rules" were an "unconstitutional burden on interstate commerce." It ruled unanimously that they were.

Mr. Justice Burton delivered the opinion of the Court, saying in part:

The decision of this case is largely controlled by that in the *Mitchell* case. There a Negro passenger holding a first-class ticket was denied a Pullman seat, although such a seat was unoccupied and would have been available to him if he had been white. The railroad rules had allotted a limited amount of Pullman space, consisting of compartments and drawing rooms, to Negro passengers and, because that space was occupied, the complainant was excluded from the Pullman car and required to ride in a second-class coach. This Court held that the passenger thereby had been subjected to an unreasonable disadvantage in violation of §3 (1).

The similarity between that case and this is inescapable. The appellant here was denied a seat in the dining car although at least one seat was vacant and would have been available to him, under the existing rules, if he had been white. The issue before us, as in the *Mitchell* case, is whether the railroad's current rules and practices cause passengers to be subjected to undue or unreasonable prejudice or disadvantage in violation of §3 (1). We find that they do.

The right to be free from unreasonable discriminations belongs, under §3 (1), to each particular person. Where a dining car is available to passengers holding tickets entitling them to use it, each such passenger is equally entitled to its facilities in accordance with reasonable regulations. The denial of dining service to any such passenger by the rules before us subjects him to a prohibited disadvantage. Under the rules, only four Negro passengers may be served at one time and then only at the table reserved for Negroes. Other Negroes who present themselves are compelled to await a vacancy at that table, although there may be many vacancies elsewhere in the diner. The railroad thus refuses to extend to those passengers the use of its existing and unoccupied facilities. The rules impose a like deprivation upon white passengers whenever more than 40 of them seek to be served at the same time and the table reserved for Negroes is vacant.

We need not multiply instances in which these rules sanction unreasonable discriminations. The curtains, partitions and signs emphasize the artificiality of a difference in treatment which serves only to call attention to a racial classification of passengers holding identical tickets and using the same public dining facility. . . .

That the regulations may impose on white passengers, in proportion to their numbers, disadvantages similar to those imposed on Negro passengers is not an answer to the requirements of §3 (1). Discriminations that operate to the disadvantage of two groups are not the less to be condemned because their impact is broader than if only one were affected.

2

EDUCATION

Plessy's "separate but equal" encouraged and fostered unequal treatment of black people in other areas besides public transportation. Nowhere was this more apparent than in the field of education. After decades of racially segregated education, by the mid-1940s schools provided for black children in the "separate but equal" southern states were decidedly inferior to those provided for white children.

Time and again, however, before the great decisions of the 1950s the Supreme Court refused to confront the problem of "unequal educational opportunities." As it had in transportation cases until the 1940s, the Court skirted deftly around the issue of equal education for blacks. Then its ideological orientation shifted both under the impact of the more liberal Roosevelt appointees and the changing political climate in the country following World War II. The chronicle begins in 1899.

Cumming v. Richmond County Board of Education, 175 U.S. 528 (1899)

Cumming v. *Richmond County Board of Education* was the first post-*Plessy* instance of "separate but equal" as applied by the Supreme Court to education. The case arose from a decision of a Georgia school board to discontinue the district's only existing black high school so that the building might be used for some 300 elementary school children. Black parents in the county then tried to restrain the school board from using their tax dollars to support the county's white high schools until "separate but equal" facilities were provided for the county's black high school students.

A unanimous Supreme Court, speaking through Justice Harlan, the lone *Plessy* dissenter, completely avoided the racial segregation issue involved. In so doing the Court refused to accept the plaintiffs' argument that by discontinuing the black high school and thus leaving black high school students with nowhere to go within the district, the county school board was violating the equal protection clause of the Fourteenth Amendment.

Justice Harlan stressed the Court's belief that an injunction that would close the white high schools until the county provided a black high school was not the proper legal remedy for the plaintiffs to use. Such a course of action, Harlan noted, would not help the three hundred black elementary school children. In the Court's "trade off," rationale, using the former black high school facilities for 300 elementary school children and thus leaving sixty black high school students without a school was perfectly acceptable public policy. Obviously, the 1899 Court did not consider its own *Plessy* option, then only three years old, that is: ordering Richmond County, Georgia to provide "separate but equal" high school facilities for the county's black high school children *before* using the one black high school for the black elementary school children.

Mr. Justice Harlan delivered the opinion of the Court, saying in part:

Without, therefore, going into an analysis of the different clauses of the Fourteenth Amendment of the Constitution of the United States, we content ourselves by saying that, in our opinion, the action of the Board did not violate any of the provisions of that amendment. It does not abridge the privileges or immunities of citizens of the United States, nor does it deprive any person of life, liberty or property without due process of law, nor does it deny to any person within the State the equal protection of its laws.

The constitution of Georgia provides: "There shall be a thorough system of common schools for the education of children in the elementary branches of an English education only, as nearly uniform as practicable, the expenses of which shall be provided for by taxation or otherwise. The schools shall be free to all children of the State, but separate schools shall be provided for the white and colored races." . . .

It was said at the argument that the vice in the common school system of Georgia was the requirement that the white and colored children of the State be educated in separate schools. But we need not consider that question in this case. No such issue was made in the pleadings. Indeed, the plaintiffs distinctly state that they have no objection to the tax in question so far as levied for the support of primary, intermediate and grammar schools, in the management of which the rule as to the separation of races is enforced. We must dispose of the case as it is presented by the record.

The plaintiffs in error complain that the Board of Education used the funds in its hands to assist in maintaining a high school for white children without providing a similar school for colored children. The substantial relief asked is an injunction that would either impair the efficiency of the high school provided for white children or compel the Board to close it. But if that were done, the result would only be to take from white children educational privileges enjoyed by them, without giving to colored children additional opportunities for the education furnished in high schools. The colored school children of the county would not be advanced in the matter of their education by a decree compelling the defendant Board to cease giving support to a high school for white children. The Board had before it the question whether it should maintain, under its control, a high school for about sixty colored children or withhold the benefits of education in primary schools from three hundred children of the same race. It was impossible, the Board believed, to give educational facilities to the three hundred colored children who were unprovided for, if it maintained a separate school for the sixty children who wished to have a high school education. Its decision was in the interest of the greater number of colored children, leaving the smaller number to obtain a high school education in existing private institutions at an expense not beyond that incurred in the high school discontinued by the Board.

We are not permitted by the evidence in the record to regard that decision as having been made with any desire or purpose on the part of the Board to discriminate against any of the colored school children of the county on account of their race. But if it be assumed that the Board erred in supposing that its duty was to provide educational facilities for the three hundred colored children who were without an opportunity in primary schools to learn the alphabet and to read and write, rather than to maintain a school for the benefit of the sixty colored children who wished to attend a high school, that was not an error which a court of equity should attempt to remedy by an injunction that would compel the Board to withhold all assistance from the high school maintained for white children. If, in some appropriate proceeding instituted directly for that purpose, the plaintiffs had sought to compel the Board of Education, out of the funds in its hands or under its control, to establish and maintain a high school for colored children, and if it appeared that the Board's refusal to maintain such a school was in fact an abuse of its discretion and in hostility to the colored population because of their race, different questions might have arisen in the state court.

The state court did not deem the action of the Board of Education in suspending temporarily and for economic reasons the high school for colored children a sufficient reason why the defendant should be restrained by injunction from maintaining an existing high school for white children. It rejected the suggestion that the Board proceeded in bad faith or had abused the discretion with which it was invested by the statute under which it proceeded or had acted in hostility to the colored race. Under the circumstances disclosed, we cannot say that this action of the state court was, within the meaning of the Fourteenth Amendment, a denial by the State to the plaintiffs and to those associated with them of the equal protection of the laws or of any privileges belonging to them as citizens of the United States. We may add that while all admit that the benefits and burdens of public taxation must be shared by citizens without discrimination against any class on account of their race, the education of the people in schools maintained by state taxation is a matter belonging to the respective States, and any interference on the part of Federal authority with the management of such schools cannot be justified except in the case of a clear and unmistakable disregard of rights secured by the supreme law of the land. We have here no such case to be determined; and as this view disposes of the only question which this court has jurisdiction to review and decide, the judgment is

Affirmed.

Berea College v. Kentucky, 211 U.S. 45 (1908)

Nine years after *Cumming*, in *Berea College* v. *Kentucky,* the Supreme Court found another "ingenious" method to avoid coming to grips with the issue of racial segregation in education. In *Berea* it used a narrow, tortured interpretation of the state's "corporate law," and upheld a Kentucky statute that required racial segregation in all educational institutions, private as well as public.

The record indicated that on October 8, 1904 the grand jury of Madison County, Kentucky indicted Berea College for "unlawfully and willingly [permitting and receiving] both the white and negro races as pupils for instruction in said college, school and institution of learning." Berea College was subsequently found guilty in a state court of violating Kentucky's segregation statute. The Supreme Court sustained the guilty verdict 7–2, with Justices Harlan and Day in dissent. It decided that the only question was whether Kentucky could withhold privileges from one of its corporations (Berea College) "which it could not constitutionally withold from an individual." The Court decided it could. Justice Harlan's dissent argued that the Supreme Court should have addressed itself to the "broad [constitutional] question presented by the statute." In addition to the majority opinion, we also reproduce here a substantial portion of Harlan's important dissent.

Mr. Justice Brewer delivered the opinion of the Court, saying in part:

There is no dispute as to the facts. That the act does not violate the constitution of Kentucky is settled by the decision of its highest court, and the single question for our consideration is whether it conflicts with the Federal Constitution. The Court of Appeals discussed at some length the general power of the State in respect to the separation of the two races. . . .

Construing the statute, the Court of Appeals held that "if the same school taught the different races at different times, though at the same place or at different places at the same time it would not be unlawful." Now, an amendment to the original charter, which does not destroy the power of the college to furnish education to all persons, but which simply separates them by time or place of instruction, cannot be said to "defeat or substantially impair the object of the grant." The language of the statute is not in terms an amendment, yet its effect is an amendment, and it would be resting too much on mere form to hold that a statute which in effect works a change in the terms of the charter is not to be considered as an amendment, because not so designated. The act itself, being separable, is to be read as though it in one section prohibited any person, in another section any corporation, and in a third any association of persons to do the acts named. Reading the statute as containing a separate prohibition on all corporations, at least, all state corporations, it substantially declares that any authority given by previous charters to instruct the two races at the same time and in the same place is forbidden, and that prohibition being a departure from the terms of the original charter in this case may properly be adjudged an amendment.

Again, it is insisted that the Court of Appeals did not regard the legislation as making an amendment, because another prosecution instituted against the same corporation under the fourth section of the act, which makes it a misdemeanor to teach pupils of the two races in the same institution, even although one race is taught in one branch and another in another branch, provided the two branches are within twenty-five miles of each other, was held could not be sustained, the court saying: "This last section, we think, violates the limitations upon the police power: it is unreasonable and oppressive." But while so ruling it also held that this section could be ignored and that the remainder of the act was complete notwithstanding. Whether the reasoning of the court concerning the fourth section be satisfactory or not is immaterial, for no question of its validity is presented, and the Court of Appeals, while striking it down, sustained the balance of the act. We need concern ourselves only with the inquiry whether the first section can be upheld as coming within the power of a State over its own corporate creatures.

We are of opinion, for reasons stated, that it does come within that power, and on this ground the judgment of the Court of Appeals of Kentucky is

Affirmed.

Mr. Justice Harlan, joined by Justice Day, dissented, saying in part:

In my judgment the court should directly meet and decide the broad question presented by the statute. It should adjudge whether the statute, as a whole, is or is not unconstitutional, in that it makes it a crime against the State to maintain or operate a private institution of learning where white and black pupils are received, at the same time, for instruction. In the view which I have as to my duty I feel obliged to express my opinion as to the validity of the act as a whole. I am of opinion that in its essential parts the statute is an arbitrary invasion of the rights of liberty and property guaranteed by the Fourteenth Amendment against hostile state action and is, therefore, void.

The capacity to impart instruction to others is given by the Almighty for beneficent purposes and its use may not be forbidden or interfered with by Government — certainly not, unless such instruction is, in its nature, harmful to the public morals or imperils the public safety. The right to impart instruction, harmless in itself or beneficial to those who receive it, is a substantial right of property — especially, where the services are rendered for compensation. But even if such right be not strictly a property right, it is, beyond question, part of one's liberty as guaranteed against hostile state action by the Constitution of the United States. This court has more than once said that the liberty guaranteed by the Fourteenth Amendment embraces "the right of the citizen to be free in the enjoyment of all his faculties," and "to be free to use them in all lawful ways." . . . If pupils, of whatever race — certainly, if they be citizens — choose with the consent of their parents or voluntarily to sit together in a private institution of learning while receiving instruction which is not in its nature harmful or dangerous to the public, no government, whether Federal or state, can legally forbid their coming together, or being together temporarily, for such an innocent purpose. If the Commonwealth of Kentucky can make it a crime to teach white and colored children together at the same time, in a private institution of learning, it is difficult to perceive why it may not forbid the assembling of white and colored children in the same Sabbath-school, for the purpose of being instructed in the Word of God, although such teaching may be done under the authority of the church to which the school is attached as well as with the consent of the parents of the children. So, if the state court be right, white and colored children may even be forbidden to sit together in a house of worship or at a communion table in the same Christian church. In the cases supposed there would be the same association of white and colored persons as would occur when pupils of the two races sit together in a private institution of learning for the purpose of receiving instruction in purely secular matters. Will it be said that the cases supposed and the case here in hand are different in that no government, in this country, can lay unholy hands on the religious faith of the people? The answer to this suggestion is that in the eye of the law the right to enjoy one's religious belief, unmolested by any human power, is no more sacred nor more fully or distinctly recognized than is the right to impart and receive instruction not harmful to the public. The denial of either right would be an infringement of the liberty inherent in the freedom secured by the fundamental law. Again, if the views of the highest court of Kentucky be sound, that commonwealth may, without infringing the Constitution of the United States, forbid the association in the same private school of pupils of the Anglo-Saxon and Latin races respectively, or pupils of the Christian and Jewish faiths, respectively. Have we become so inoculated with prejudice of race that an American government, professedly based on the principles of freedom, and charged with the protection of all citizens alike, can make distinctions between such citizens in the matter of their voluntary meeting for innocent purposes simply because of their respective races? Further, if the lower court be right, then a State may make it a crime for white and colored persons to frequent the same market places at the same time, or appear in an assemblage of citizens convened to consider questions of a public or political nature in which all citizens, without regard to race, are equally interested. Many other illustrations might be given to show the mischievous, not to say cruel, character of the statute in question and how inconsistent such legislation is with the great principle of the equality of citizens before the law.

Of course what I have said has no reference to regulations prescribed for public schools, established at the pleasure of the State and maintained at the public expense. No such question is here presented and it need not be now discussed. My observations have reference to the case before the court and only to the provision of the statute making it a crime for any person to impart harmless instruction to white and colored pupils together, at the same time, in the same private institution of learning. That provision is in my opinion made an essential element in the policy of the statute, and if regard be had to the object and purpose of this legislation it cannot be treated as separable nor intended to be separated from the provisions relating to corporations. The whole statute should therefore be held void: otherwise, it will be taken as the law of Kentucky, to be enforced by its courts, that the teaching of white and black pupils, at the same time, even in a *private* institution, is a crime against that Commonwealth, punishable by fine and imprisonment.

In my opinion the judgment should be reversed upon the ground that the statute is in violation of the Constitution of the United States.

Missouri *ex rel* Gaines v. Canada, 305 U.S. 337 (1938)

In 1927, to use Pritchett's words, "having [twice, *Cumming* and *Berea*] successfully avoided the issue of racial segregation in education, the Court then felt [capable of ruling] as though established practice had foreclosed discussion of the question."[1] The case was *Gong Lum* v. *Rice.*[2] There a Chinese child was required by Mississippi law to attend a black school in accordance with the state constitution ordering separate schools for the "white and colored races."

Concerning the possible applicability of the Fourteenth Amendment's equal protection clause to *Gong Lum,* Chief Justice Taft wrote for the Court that it had long been established, apparently since *Cumming* and *Berea,* that issues such as racially segregated schools came "within the constitutional power of the state legislature to settle without intervention [by] the federal courts under the Federal constitution." Yet despite the fact that the Chief Justice cited some fifteen lower court decisions on the issue of racial segregation in education, as Pritchett says, the Supreme Court "could not hide the fact that there had been no Supreme Court ruling directly on the issue . . . and that there had never been 'full argument and consideration' by that body."[3]

Then in 1938, the Supreme Court made its first cautious move. The case was *Missouri* ex rel *Gaines* v. *Canada.* There, as it had done in its early transportation cases, the Court sought to effectuate change in the application of "separate but equal" by placing more emphasis on equality than on separation.

1. Op. cit., at 492.
2. 275 U.S. 78 (1927).
3. Op. cit., at 492.

The facts indicated that because there was no law school for black students in the state, Missouri adopted a policy of paying the out-of-state tuition charges for black Missouri residents to attend law schools in neighboring states. In lieu of creating its own "separate but equal" law school for black students, which the *Plessy* rationale would seem to insist upon, the state in effect shifted its responsibility to provide equal legal education for its citizens to several other states.

Speaking for a 7–2 Court (Justices McReynolds and Butler dissented), Chief Justice Hughes wrote that by not furnishing legal education opportunities for black students, Missouri was guilty of discrimination "repugnant to the Fourteenth Amendment." Carefully keeping within the "confines" of *Plessy*'s "separate but equal" rule, the Court nevertheless broke new ground by emphasizing the demands of equality rather than separation under both the equal protection clause and its own *Plessy* ruling. And in light of previous education decisions this *was* a significant step forward.

Mr. Chief Justice Hughes delivered the opinion of the Court, saying in part:

> In answering petitioner's contention that this discrimination constituted a denial of his constitutional right, the state court has fully recognized the obligation of the State to provide negroes with advantages for higher education substantially equal to the advantages afforded to white students. The State has sought to fulfill that obligation by furnishing equal facilities in separate schools, a method the validity of which has been sustained by our decisions. . . . Respondents' counsel have appropriately emphasized the special solicitude of the State for the higher education of negroes as shown in the establishment of Lincoln University, a state institution well conducted on a plane with the University of Missouri so far as the offered courses are concerned. It is said that Missouri is a pioneer in that field and is the only State in the Union which has established a separate university for negroes on the same basis as the state university for white students. But, commendable as is that action, the fact remains that instruction in law for negroes is not now afforded by the State, either at Lincoln University or elsewhere within the State, and that the State excludes negroes from the advantages of the law school it has established at the University of Missouri.
>
> It is manifest that this discrimination, if not relieved by the provisions we shall presently discuss, would constitute a denial of equal protection. . . . The basic consideration is not as to what sort of opportunities other States provide, or whether they are as good as those in Missouri, but as to what opportunities Missouri itself furnishes to white students and denies to negroes solely upon the ground of color. The admissibility of laws separating the races in the enjoyment of privileges afforded by the State rests wholly upon the equality of the privileges which the laws give to the separated groups within the State. The question here is not of a duty of the State to supply legal training, or of the quality of the training which it does supply, but of its duty when it provides such training to furnish it to the residents of the State upon the basis of an equality of right. By the operation of the laws of Missouri a privilege has been created for white law students which is denied to negroes by reason of their race. The white resident is afforded legal education within the State; the negro resident having the same qualifications is refused it there and must go outside the State to obtain it. That is a denial of the equality of legal right to the enjoyment of the privilege which the State has set up, and the provision for the payment of tuition fees in another State does not remove the discrimination.

The equal protection of the laws is "a pledge of the protection of equal laws."
... Manifestly, the obligation of the State to give the protection of equal laws can
be performed only where its laws operate, that is, within its own jurisdiction. It is
there that the equality of legal right must be maintained. That obligation is
imposed by the Constitution upon the States severally as governmental
entities, — each responsible for its own laws establishing the rights and duties of
persons within its borders. It is an obligation the burden of which cannot be cast
by one State upon another, and no State can be excused from performance by
what another State may do or fail to do. That separate responsibility of each
State within its own sphere is of the essence of statehood maintained under our
dual system. It seems to be implicit in respondents' argument that if other States
did not provide courses for legal education, it would nevertheless be the constitutional duty of Missouri when it supplied such courses for white students to make
equivalent provision for negroes. But that plain duty would exist because it
rested upon the State independently of the action of other States. We find it
impossible to conclude that what otherwise would be an unconstitutional discrimination, with respect to the legal right to the enjoyment of opportunities
within the State, can be justified by requiring resort to opportunities elsewhere.
That resort may mitigate the inconvenience of the discrimination but cannot
serve to validate it. ...

Here, petitioner's right was a personal one. It was as an individual that he was
entitled to the equal protection of the laws, and the State was bound to furnish
him within its borders facilities for legal education substantially equal to those
which the State there afforded for persons of the white race, whether or not
other negroes sought the same opportunity.

Sweatt v. Painter, 339 U.S. 629 (1949)

After the *Gaines* decision, Missouri and several other southern states established separate law schools for black students. Once again by every measurable educational standard these schools were clearly inferior to those provided
for white students. The question soon became how long the Supreme Court
would allow the states to violate its "separate but equal" rule with respect to
professional higher education. The answer came in two decisions handed
down during the Court's 1949 term, *McLaurin* v. *Oklahoma State Regents*[1] and
Sweatt v. *Painter.*

McLaurin, a black student, sought admission to the State University in
Oklahoma as a Ph.D. candidate in education. He was admitted but, in accordance with state law, McLaurin was given a "specially segregated" educational
program. Oklahoma characterized the "special segregation" in classrooms,
library, and cafeteria facilities as "merely nominal." A unanimous Supreme
Court disagreed. Speaking for the Court, Chief Justice Vinson wrote that
because Oklahoma's segregation rules impaired McLaurin's ability to study
and "learn his profession" they violated the equal protection clause of the
Fourteenth Amendment.

After *McLaurin* came *Sweatt* v. *Painter.* Sweatt was denied admission to the
University of Texas Law School solely because he was black. Texas law specifically forbade admission of black students to the state's law school. Sweatt was
offered, but refused, admission to a newly established law school exclusively
for black students. He argued that the Texas offer violated the equal protec-

1. 339 U.S. 637 (1949).

tion clause because the black law school could in no way be "equal" to the one Texas provided for white students. In its ruling for Sweatt the Supreme Court found that the evidence clearly supported its claim of unequal treatment. At the time, the University of Texas Law School for white students had sixteen full-time and three part-time professors. The new black law school had five full-time professors. The Texas Law School had 850 students, the black school, 23. The Texas Law School had a library of 65,000 volumes, a law review, moot court facilities, scholarship funds, many distinguished alumni, tradition, and prestige in the state. The black law school had a library of 16,500 volumes and none of the other attributes. For these reasons the Supreme Court ruled that the legal education Texas offered Sweatt was not "substantially equal" to that given white law students within the state. Texas was therefore violating the equal protection clause of the Fourteenth Amendment. This too was a giant step in the right direction.

Writing for a unanimous Court, Chief Justice Vinson said in part:

> Whether the University of Texas Law School is compared with the original or the new law school for Negroes, we cannot find substantial equality in the educational opportunities offered white and Negro law students by the State. In terms of number of the faculty, variety of courses and opportunity for specialization, size of the review and similar activities, the University of Texas Law School is superior. What is more important, the University of Texas Law School possesses to a far greater degree those qualities which are incapable of objective measurement but which make for greatness in a law school. Such qualities, to name but a few, include reputation of the faculty, experience of the administration, position and influence of the alumni, standing in the community, traditions and prestige. It is difficult to believe that one who had a free choice between these law schools would consider the question close.
>
> Moreover, although the law is a highly learned profession, we are well aware that it is an intensely practical one. The law school, the proving ground for legal learning and practice, cannot be effective in isolation from the individuals and institutions with which the law interacts. Few students and no one who has practiced law would choose to study in an academic vacuum, removed from the interplay of ideas and the exchange of views with which the law is concerned. The law school to which Texas is willing to admit petitioner excludes from its student body members of the racial groups which number 85 percent of the population of the State and include most of the lawyers, witnesses, jurors, judges and other officials with whom petitioner will inevitably be dealing when he becomes a member of the Texas Bar. With such a substantial and significant segment of society excluded, we cannot conclude that the education offered petitioner is substantially equal to that which he would receive if admitted to the University of Texas Law School.

Brown v. Board of Education, 347 U.S. 483 (1954)

Finally, in 1954, the Supreme Court met the constitutional question of "separate but equal" schools head on. As we have seen, in its previous education decisions (excepting *McLaurin* and *Sweatt*) the Court had been content to make certain that equal educational facilities were in fact being provided by the states for both black and white students. By so doing it had accepted racially segregated education as compatible with the Constitution.

In *Brown* v. *Board of Education,* however, the Supreme Court grappled with the more fundamental issue. Are the words "separate" and "equal" constitutionally compatible or are they mutually exclusive? Is it possible to treat people separately and equally at the same time? If they are mutually exclusive, how so? And ultimately, just what is the relationship between "separate but equal" and the equal protection clause of the Fourteenth Amendment? In a truly monumental decision, one of a handful in the Court's entire history which merit that accolade, *Brown* specifically overruled *Plessy* v. *Ferguson.* In the process it abolished segregated public schools and set the stage for the subsequent legal and constitutional disputes that have plagued public education to the present day.

Brown, with *Mapp* v. *Ohio* (1961), *Baker* v. *Carr* (1962), *Gideon* v. *Wainwright* (1963), *Reynolds* v. *Sims* (1964), *Escobedo* v. *Illinois* (1964), and *Miranda* v. *Arizona* (1966), ranks among the most significant and far-reaching Court decisions of this century. Certainly it is a lasting monument to the Warren Court's contribution to American life and jurisprudence.

Mr. Chief Justice Warren delivered the opinion of the unanimous Court, saying in part:

The doctrine of "separate but equal" did not make its appearance in this Court until 1896 in the case of *Plessy* v. *Ferguson, supra,* involving not education but transportation. American courts have since labored with the doctrine for over half a century. In this Court, there have been six cases involving the "separate but equal" doctrine in the field of public education. In *Cumming* v. *County Board of Education,* 175 U.S. 528, and *Gong Lum* v. *Rice,* 275 U.S. 78, the validity of the doctrine itself was not challenged. In more recent cases, all on the graduate school level, inequality was found in that specific benefits enjoyed by white students were denied to Negro students of the same educational qualifications. . . . In none of these cases was it necessary to re-examine the doctrine to grant relief to the Negro plaintiff. And in *Sweatt* v. *Painter, supra,* the Court expressly reserved decision on the question whether *Plessy* v. *Ferguson* should be held inapplicable to public education.

In the instant cases, that question is directly presented. Here, unlike *Sweatt* v. *Painter,* there are findings below that the Negro and white schools involved have been equalized, or are being equalized, with respect to buildings, curricula, qualifications and salaries of teachers, and other "tangible" factors. Our decision, therefore, cannot turn on merely a comparison of these tangible factors in the Negro and white schools involved in each of the cases. We must look instead to the effect of segregation itself on public education.

In approaching this problem, we cannot turn the clock back to 1868 when the Amendment was adopted, or even to 1896 when *Plessy* v. *Ferguson* was written. We must consider public education in the light of its full development and its present place in American life throughout the Nation. Only in this way can it be determined if segregation in public schools deprives these plaintiffs of the equal protection of the laws.

Today, education is perhaps the most important function of state and local governments. Compulsory school attendance laws and the great expenditures for education both demonstrate our recognition of the importance of education to our democratic society. It is required in the performance of our most basic public responsibilities, even service in the armed forces. It is the very foundation of good citizenship. Today it is a principal instrument in awakening the child to cultural values, in preparing him for later professional training, and in helping him to adjust normally to his environment. In these days, it is doubtful that any child may reasonably be expected to succeed in life if he is denied the opportunity of an education. Such an opportunity, where the state has undertaken to provide it, is a right which must be made available to all on equal terms.

We come then to the question presented: Does segregation of children in public schools solely on the basis of race, even though the physical facilities and other "tangible" factors may be equal, deprive the children of the minority group of equal educational opportunities? We believe that it does.

In *Sweatt* v. *Painter, supra,* in finding that a segregated law school for Negroes could not provide them equal educational opportunities, this Court relied in large part on "those qualities which are incapable of objective measurement but which make for greatness in a law school." In *McLaurin* v. *Oklahoma State Regents, supra,* the Court, in requiring that a Negro admitted to a white graduate school be treated like all other students, again resorted to intangible considerations: ". . . his ability to study, to engage in discussions and exchange views with other students, and, in general, to learn his profession." Such considerations apply with added force to children in grade and high schools. To separate them from others of similar age and qualifications solely because of their race generates a feeling of inferiority as to their status in the community that may affect their hearts and minds in a way unlikely ever to be undone. The effect of this separation on their educational opportunities was well stated by a finding in the Kansas case by a court which nevertheless felt compelled to rule against the Negro plaintiffs:

> "Segregation of white and colored children in public schools has a detrimental effect upon the colored children. The impact is greater when it has the sanction of the law; for the policy of separating the races is usually interpreted as denoting the inferiority of the negro group. A sense of inferiority affects the motivation of a child to learn. Segregation with the sanction of law, therefore, has a tendency to [retard] the educational and mental development of negro children and to deprive them of some of the benefits they would receive in a racial[ly] integrated school system."

Whatever may have been the extent of psychological knowledge at the time of *Plessy* v. *Ferguson,* this finding is amply supported by modern authority. Any language in *Plessy* v. *Ferguson* contrary to this finding is rejected.

We conclude that in the field of public education the doctrine of "separate but equal" has no place. Separate educational facilities are inherently unequal. Therefore, we hold that the plaintiffs and others similarly situated for whom the actions have been brought are, by reason of the segregation complained of, deprived of the equal protection of the laws guaranteed by the Fourteenth Amendment.

Griffin v. County Board of Prince Edward County, 377 U.S. 218 (1964)

Whether *Brown* was to be interpreted to mean that desegregation was mandatory or (more simply) that de jure racial discrimination in education had to be abolished was yet to be determined. The Supreme Court began confronting this issue ten years after *Brown* in *Griffin* v. *County School Board of Prince Edward County* (Virginia).

There the Court found that the Prince Edward County School Board had sought to circumvent its responsibilities under the *Brown* rule by closing all its public schools and providing direct tuition grants to parents for their children to attend private all-white or all-black schools. The county argued that it had no obligation under the Federal Constitution to provide a public school system, segregated or not, for its citizens. At the time there were several accredited private white schools in the district. There were none for black children. Prince Edward County's "scheme" to avoid desegregating its schools by abolishing the public school system was part of a "massive resistance" movement to the *Brown* decision that segregationist groups devised in Virginia and other southern states during the late 1950s.

However, the Warren Court would have none of it. It ruled that Prince Edward County's decision to close its public schools had a "clearly unconstitutional object." The Court found that closing Prince Edward County public schools while at the same time giving tuition grants and tax concessions to children so that the white children could attend racially segregated private schools violated the equal protection rights of the black children involved. Because there were no comparable private schools for black students and the black parents involved rejected offers to establish private black schools (they preferred to continue the legal battle for desegregated public schools), the private all-white schools, the Court ruled, were being operated "for constitutionally impermissible reasons of race."

While joining in the Court's opinion and thus maintaining the Court's consistent unanimity on school desegregation cases, Justices Clark and Harlan felt compelled to disagree with the Court's holding that federal courts have the constitutional power to order Prince Edward County to reopen its public schools, which is precisely what the Warren Court did.

Mr. Justice Black delivered the opinion of the Court, saying in part:

> Efforts to desegregate Prince Edward County's schools met with resistance. In 1956 Section 141 of the Virginia Constitution was amended to authorize the General Assembly and local governing bodies to appropriate funds to assist students to go to public or to nonsectarian private schools, in addition to those owned by the State or by the locality. The General Assembly met in special session and enacted legislation to close any public schools where white and colored children were enrolled together, to cut off state funds to such schools, to pay tuition grants to children in nonsectarian private schools, and to extend state retirement benefits to teachers in newly created private schools. The legislation closing mixed schools and cutting off state funds was later invalidated by the Supreme Court of Appeals of Virginia, which held that these laws violated the Virginia Constitution. . . . In April 1959 the General Assembly abandoned "massive resistance" to desegregation and turned instead to what was called a "freedom of choice" program. The Assembly repealed the rest of the 1956 legislation, as well as a tuition grant law of January 1959, and enacted a new tuition grant program. At the same time the Assembly repealed Virginia's compulsory attendance laws and instead made school attendance a matter of local option.
>
> In June 1959, the United States Court of Appeals for the Fourth Circuit directed the Federal District Court (1) to enjoin discriminatory practices in Prince Edward County schools, (2) to require the County School Board to take "immediate steps" toward admitting students without regard to race to the white high school "in the school term beginning September 1959," and (3) to require

the Board to make plans for admissions to elementary schools without regard to race. ,... Having as early as 1956 resolved that they would not operate public schools "wherein white and colored children are taught together," the Supervisors of Prince Edward County refused to levy any school taxes for the 1959-1960 school year, explaining that they were "confronted with a court decree which requires the admission of white and colored children to all the schools of the county without regard to race or color." As a result, the county's public schools did not reopen in the fall of 1959 and have remained closed ever since, although the public schools of every other county in Virginia have continued to operate under laws governing the State's public school system and to draw funds provided by the State for that purpose. A private group, the Prince Edward School Foundation, was formed to operate private schools for white children in Prince Edward County and, having built its own school plant, has been in operation ever since the closing of the public schools. An offer to set up private schools for colored children in the county was rejected, the Negroes of Prince Edward preferring to continue the legal battle for desegregated public schools, and colored children were without formal education from 1959 to 1963, when federal, state, and county authorities cooperated to have classes conducted for Negroes and whites in school buildings owned by the county. During the 1959-1960 school year the Foundation's schools for white children were supported entirely by private contributions, but in 1960 the General Assembly adopted a new tuition grant program making every child, regardless of race, eligible for tuition grants of $125 or $150 to attend a nonsectarian private school or a public school outside his locality, and also authorizing localities to provide their own grants. The Prince Edward Board of Supervisors then passed an ordinance providing tuition grants of $100, so that each child attending the Prince Edward School Foundation's schools received a total of $225 if in elementary school or $250 if in high school. In the 1960-1961 session the major source of financial support for the Foundation was in the indirect form of these state and county tuition grants, paid to children attending Foundation schools. At the same time, the County Board of Supervisors passed an ordinance allowing property tax credits up to 25 percent for contributions to any "nonprofit, nonsectarian private school" in the county. ...

[W]e agree with the District Court that, under the circumstances here, closing the Prince Edward County schools while public schools in all the other counties of Virginia were being maintained denied the petitioners and the class of Negro students they represent the equal protection of the laws guaranteed by the Fourteenth Amendment. ...

Virginia law, as here applied, unquestionably treats the school children of Prince Edward differently from the way it treats the school children of all other Virginia counties. Prince Edward children must go to a private school or none at all; all other Virginia children can go to public schools. Closing Prince Edward's schools bears more heavily on Negro children in Prince Edward County since white children there have accredited private schools which they can attend, while colored children until very recently have had no available private schools, and even the school they now attend is a temporary expedient. Apart from this expedient, the result is that Prince Edward County school children, if they go to school in their own county, must go to racially segregated schools which, although designated as private, are beneficiaries of county and state support. ... The time for mere "deliberate speed" has run out, and that phrase can no longer justify denying these Prince Edward County school children their constitutional rights to an education equal to that afforded by the public schools in the other parts of Virginia.

The judgment of the Court of Appeals is reversed, the judgment of the District Court is affirmed, and the cause is remanded to the District Court with directions to enter a decree which will guarantee that these petitioners will get the kind of education that is given in the State's public schools. And, if it becomes necessary to add new parties to accomplish this end, the District Court is free to do so.

Alexander v. Holmes County Board of Education, 396 U.S. 19 (1969)

In the controlling 1954 *Brown* ruling the Supreme Court had ordered school districts to put an end to racially segregated public schools "with all deliberate speed." Ten years later in the *Griffin* case (above), as we have seen, Justice Black noted that time for "deliberate speed" had run out. He went on to warn "massive resisters" in the South that they could no longer justify continued denial of constitutional rights to black children by using "all deliberate speed" to mean more and more stalling for more and more time.

In *Alexander* v. *Holmes County [Mississippi] Board of Education*, the Warren court went one step further. It angrily chastised "massive resistance" to the law of land and warned that the *Brown* standard "all deliberate speed" was "no longer constitutionally permissible." Its patience exhausted, the Court demanded instead that school districts "terminate dual school systems at once and . . . operate now and hereafter only unitary schools."

In a brief, unsigned, per curiam opinion the Court said in part:

> The question presented is one of paramount importance, involving as it does the denial of fundamental rights to many thousands of school children, who are presently attending Mississippi schools under segregated conditions contrary to the applicable decisions of this Court. Against this background the Court of Appeals should have denied all motions for additional time because continued operation of segregated schools under a standard of allowing "all deliberate speed" for desegregation is no longer constitutionally permissible. Under explicit holdings of this Court the obligation of every school district is to terminate dual school systems at once and to operate now and hereafter only unitary schools.

Keyes v. School District No. 1 Denver, 413 U.S. 189 (1973)

From *Brown* to *Swann*, a period of seventeen years, all Supreme Court decisions concerning school segregation issues had been unanimous. In 1972, however, with the impact of the four Nixon appointees making itself felt for the first time, the pattern began shifting. The change would become dramatically evident two years later in *Milliken* v. *Bradley*, the Detroit busing case. It was the decision in *Wright* v. *Council of City of Emporia* (Virginia),[1] however, which first presaged the Court's ultimate split in school desegregation cases. In *Wright* the Court's majority, now down to five, refused to allow Emporia,

1. 407 U.S. 451 (1972).

Virginia, which had fewer blacks in its school system than the surrounding county, to withdraw from the county system and establish a separate school district. Realignment of school districts in this fashion where there has been a history of state enforced racial segregation in the schools, the Court ruled, would inhibit the progress of desegregation that had begun in 1954 with *Brown.*

The four Nixon appointees, Burger, Blackmun, Powell, and Rehnquist, all in dissent, argued that the City of Emporia had a right to provide for the education of its own students and could therefore withdraw from the county system if it chose to do so.

A somewhat similar case came before the court a year later, in *School Board of Richmond (Virginia)* v. *State Board of Education.*[2] This time the Court split 4–4 (Justice Powell, a Virginian, did not participate and Justice Stewart joined the Nixon three). *Richmond* let stand a Court of Appeals decision that had overturned a district court ruling and therefore ordered the Richmond school system (70 percent black) to merge with two surrounding counties (90 percent white).

Griffin, Alexander, Wright, and *Richmond* all concerned southern cities where de jure segregation had long existed.

Beginning in 1973, the Court began dealing with the problem of de facto racial segregation in northern cities, Denver, Detroit, and Boston. The decision in *Keyes* v. *School District No. 1 Denver* edged cautiously toward the problem then backed off. Instead of meeting the de facto situation head on the Court hedged and decided that although Denver presented a somewhat less than classical de jure situation it was not a de facto case. The petitioners originally sought to desegregate schools in the Park Hill area of Denver. Later they expanded their suit to include the rest of the Denver school district. A district court denied the petitioners expansion of their suit holding that although there was evidence of deliberate racial segregation in Park Hill, that fact alone did *not* prove that the rest of Denver's schools were similarly and deliberately segregated. In effect the district court had required the petitioners to prove that de jure segregation existed in each area or subdivision of the Denver school district they sought to desegregate.

The Supreme Court reversed this lower court ruling and decided that where proof exists that school authorities have intentionally (de jure) segregated a substantial portion of a school district (Park Hill), this fact alone indicates that further inquiry is warranted to determine if a district-wide de jure "dual system" of public schools exists as the petitioners claim. The Supreme Court ordered the district court to undertake such an inquiry.

Keyes divided the Court in a peculiar fashion. Justice Brennan wrote for the majority, consisting of Douglas, Stewart, Marshall, and Blackmun. Strangely, Chief Justice Burger, while not joining the majority, or specifically agreeing with its viewpoint, concurred in the result. Justice Powell concurred in part and dissented in part. Justice Rehnquist filed a separate dissent and Justice White, a native of Colorado, took no part in the decision.

Powell's long, detailed opinion urged the Court to abandon once and for all time the "de jure, de facto distinction" that leaves to the petitioners the "tortuous effort" of identifying "segregative acts" or "segregative intent." "I would

2. 412 U.S. 92 (1973).

hold," Powell wrote, "that where segregated public schools exist" within a
school district to a substantial degree, "there is prima facie evidence" that the
local school boards "are sufficiently responsible to warrant imposing upon
them a nationally applicable burden to demonstrate they nonetheless are
operating a genuinely integrated school system."[3]

Justice Rehnquist, on the other hand, chided the majority for even suggesting that Denver might have sanctioned de jure segregation. He noted that
neither the state of Colorado nor the city of Denver had ever had a statute or
ordinance establishing segregated schools by law. This was proof enough for
Rehnquist that de jure segregation did not exist. He thought it unnecessary
for the Court to require "further factual determination" under what he called
the majority's "vague and unprecise mandate." The majority, however, was
not quite willing to abandon the de jure, de facto distinction, as Powell urged
it to do. It maintained instead that there was enough evidence of partial de
jure segregation in *Keyes* to establish need for further investigation.

Mr. Justice Brennan delivered the opinion of the Court, saying in part:

>   Before turning to the primary question we decide today, a word must be said
> about the District Court's method of defining a "segregated" school. Denver is a
> tri-ethnic, as distinguished from a bi-racial, community. The overall racial and
> ethnic composition of the Denver public schools is 66 percent Anglo, 14 percent
> Negro, and 20 percent Hispano. The District Court, in assessing the question of
> *de jure* segregation in the core city schools, preliminarily resolved that Negroes
> and Hispanos should not be placed in the same category to establish the segre-
> gated character of a school. . . . Later, in determining the schools that were likely
> to produce an inferior educational opportunity, the court concluded that a
> school would be considered inferior only if it had "a concentration of either
> Negro or Hispano students in the general area of 70 to 75 percent." . . . We
> intimate no opinion whether the District Court's 70 percent-to-75 percent re-
> quirement was correct. The District Court used those figures to signify educa-
> tionally inferior schools, and there is no suggestion in the record that those same
> figures were or would be used to define a "segregated" school in the *de jure*
> context. What is or is not a segregated school will necessarily depend on the facts
> of each particular case. In addition to the racial and ethnic composition of a
> school's student body, other factors, such as the racial and ethnic composition of
> faculty and staff and the community and administration attitudes toward the
> school, must be taken into consideration. The District Court has recognized
> these specific factors as elements of the definition of a "segregated" school, . . .
> and we may therefore infer that the court will consider them again on remand.
>   We conclude, however, that the District Court erred in separating Negroes
> and Hispanos for purposes of defining a "segregated" school. . . .
>   In our view the only other question that requires our decision at this time is
> . . . whether the District Court and the Court of Appeals applied an incorrect
> legal standard in addressing petitioners' contention that respondent School
> Board engaged in an unconstitutional policy of deliberate segregation in the core
> city schools. Our conclusion is that those courts did not apply the correct stan-
> dard in addressing that contention.
>   Petitioners apparently concede for the purposes of this case that in the case of
> a school system like Denver's, where no statutory dual system has ever existed,
> plaintiffs must prove not only that segregated schooling exists but also that it was
> brought about or maintained by intentional state action. Petitioners proved that

3. 413 U.S. at 224 (1973).

for almost a decade after 1960 respondent School Board had engaged in an unconstitutional policy of deliberate racial segregation in the Park Hill schools. Indeed, the District Court found that "[b]etween 1960 and 1969 the Board's policies with respect to these northeast Denver schools show an undeviating purpose to isolate Negro students" in segregated schools "while preserving the Anglo character of [other] schools." . . .

This is not a case, however, where a statutory dual system has ever existed. Nevertheless, where plaintiffs prove that the school authorities have carried out a systematic program of segregation affecting a substantial portion of the students, schools, teachers, and facilities within the school system, it is only common sense to conclude that there exists a predicate for a finding of the existence of a dual school system. Several considerations support this conclusion. First, it is obvious that a practice of concentrating Negroes in certain schools by structuring attendance zones or designating "feeder" schools on the basis of race has the reciprocal effect of keeping other nearby schools predominantly white. Similarly, the practice of building a school — such as the Barrett Elementary School in this case — to a certain size and in a certain location, "with conscious knowledge that it would be a segregated school," . . . has a substantial reciprocal effect on the racial composition of other nearby schools. So also, the use of mobile classrooms, the drafting of student transfer policies, the transportation of students, and the assignment of faculty and staff, on racially identifiable bases, have the clear effect on earmarking schools according to their racial composition, and this, in turn, together with the elements of student assignment and school construction, may have a profound reciprocal effect on the racial composition of residential neighborhoods within a metropolitan area, thereby causing further racial concentration within the schools. . . .

In short, common sense dictates the conclusion that racially inspired school board actions have an impact beyond the particular schools that are the subjects of those actions. This is not to say, of course, that there can never be a case in which the geographical structure of, or the natural boundaries within, a school district may have the effect of dividing the district into separate, identifiable and unrelated units. Such a determination is essentially a question of fact to be resolved by the trial court in the first instance, but such cases must be rare. In the absence of such a determination, proof of state-imposed segregation in a substantial portion of the district will suffice to support a finding by the trial court of the existence of a dual system. Of course, where that finding is made, as in cases involving statutory dual systems, the school authorities have an affirmative duty "to effectuate a transition to a racially nondiscriminatory school system." . . .

On remand, therefore, the District Court should decide in the first instance whether respondent School Board's deliberate racial segregation policy with respect to the Park Hill schools constitutes the entire Denver school system a dual school system. . . .

. . . Indeed, to say that a system has a "history of segregation" is merely to say that a pattern of intentional segregation has been established in the past. Thus, be it a statutory dual system or an allegedly unitary system where a meaningful portion of the system is found to be intentionally segregated, the existence of subsequent or other segregated schooling within the same system justifies a rule imposing on the school authorities the burden of proving that this segregated schooling is not also the result of intentionally segregative acts.

3

BUSING

After *Brown* v. *Board of Education*, the most significant Court decision in the long, checkered effort to wipe out the vestiges of racially segregated schools was *Swann* v. *Charlotte-Mecklenburg Board of Education*, the first in a series of controversial "busing" cases.

Swann v. Charlotte-Mecklenburg Board of Education, 402 U.S. 1 (1971)

In 1968, the petitioner, Swann, asked a district court in North Carolina to implement the rule of the *Green* case in Charlotte. In *Green* v. *County School Board*[1] the Supreme Court had ruled that school boards must "come forward with a plan that promises realistically to work . . . now . . . until it is clear that state-imposed segregation has been completely removed." The Warren Court went on to say in *Green* that school boards had a "positive duty" to plan for a prompt conversion to racially desegregated schools. The goal, the Court concluded, was complete integration, a "unitary nonracial system of public education."

In April 1969, in accordance with Swann's petition and in line with *Green,* a district court ordered the Charlotte School Board to provide a plan for faculty and student desegregation. Subsequently the district court found the board's plan unsatisfactory and appointed an expert of its own, Dr. John Finger, to submit a desegregation plan for the Charlotte-Mecklenburg School District. In February 1970, Dr. Finger submitted his proposal and the district court approved the Charlotte School Board's plan by incorporating Finger's suggested modifications. In 1969 the Charlotte-Mecklenburg school system had more than 84,000 students in 107 schools. Approximately 29 percent (24,000) of the students were black and about 14,000 of them attended 21 schools that were virtually (99 percent) all black.

1. 391 U.S. 430 (1968).

In reaching its unanimous decision confirming the lower court findings, the Supreme Court ruled that in a school system where "one race" schools existed it must be presumed that these racially segregated schools resulted from present or past deliberate discrimination policies by local school boards. Then the Court dropped two successive bombshells. It indicated that "the neighborhood school" might have to be at least partially abandoned in order to achieve racial desegregation. Then, by recognizing that "desegregation plans cannot be limited to the walk to a neighborhood school," the Supreme Court for the first time accepted the need for busing to achieve integration. This becomes the long-term significance of the *Swann* case. Busing controversies that have raged continuously in city after city, North as well as South, since 1971, are all related to the Supreme Court's ruling in *Swann*.

Chief Justice Burger wrote a long and detailed opinion for the unanimous Court. He carefully reviewed the facts of the case, the school board's attempts to comply with the district court's order, the Finger modifications, and finally the district court's decision incorporating the Finger recommendations into the final desegregation plans for the Charlotte-Mecklenburg School District. The Supreme Court's ruling, which upheld the findings of the district court and which for the first time suggested the possibility of cross-town busing as a solution to racially desegregated neighborhood schools, is reproduced at considerable length here because of the complexity and the significance of the issues involved.

Mr. Chief Justice Burger delivered the opinion of the Court, saying in part:

> As finally submitted, the school board plan closed seven schools and reassigned their pupils. It restructured school attendance zones to achieve greater racial balance but maintained existing grade structures and rejected techniques such as pairing and clustering as part of a desegregation effort. The plan created a single athletic league, eliminated the previously racial basis of the school bus system, provided racially mixed faculties and administrative staffs, and modified its free-transfer plan into an optional majority-to-minority transfer system.
>
> The board plan proposed substantial assignment of Negroes to nine of the system's 10 high schools, producing 17 percent to 36 percent Negro population in each. The projected Negro attendance at the 10th school, Independence, was 2 percent. The proposed attendance zones for the high schools were typically shaped like wedges of a pie, extending outward from the center of the city to the suburban and rural areas of the county in order to afford residents of the center city area access to outlying schools.
>
> As for junior high schools, the board plan rezoned the 21 school areas so that in 20 the Negro attendance would range from 0 percent to 38 percent. The other school, located in the heart of the Negro residential area, was left with an enrollment of 90 percent Negro.
>
> The board plan with respect to elementary schools relied entirely upon gerrymandering of geographic zones. More than half of the Negro elementary pupils were left in nine schools that were 86 percent to 100 percent Negro; approximately half of the white elementary pupils were assigned to schools 86 percent to 100 percent white.
>
> *The Finger Plan.* The plan submitted by the court-appointed expert, Dr. Finger, adopted the school board zoning plan for senior high schools with one modification: it required that an additional 300 Negro students be transported from the Negro residential area of the city to the nearly all-white Independence High School.

The Finger plan for the junior high schools employed much of the rezoning plan of the board, combined with the creation of nine "satellite" zones. Under the satellite plan, inner-city Negro students were assigned by attendance zones to nine outlying predominately white junior high schools, thereby substantially desegregating every junior high school in the system.

The Finger plan departed from the board plan chiefly in its handling of the system's 76 elementary schools. Rather than relying solely upon geographic zoning, Dr. Finger proposed use of zoning, pairing, and grouping techniques, with the result that student bodies throughout the system would range from 9 percent to 38 percent Negro. . . . Under the Finger plan, nine inner-city Negro schools were grouped in this manner with 24 suburban white schools.

On February 5, 1970, the District Court adopted the board plan, as modified by Dr. Finger, for the junior and senior high schools. The Court rejected the board elementary school plan and adopted the Finger plan as presented. . . .

Nearly 17 years ago this Court held, in explicit terms, that state-imposed segregation by race in public schools denies equal protection of the laws. At no time has the Court deviated in the slightest degree from that holding or its constitutional underpinnings. None of the parties before us challenges the Court's decision of May 17, 1954, that

> "in the field of public education the doctrine of 'separate but equal' has no place. Separate educational facilities are inherently unequal. Therefore, we hold that the plaintiffs and others similarly situated . . . are, by reason of the segregation complained of, deprived of the equal protection of the laws guaranteed by the Fourteenth Amendment. . . ."

Over the 16 years since *Brown II,* many difficulties were encountered in implementation of the basic constitutional requirement that the State not discriminate between public school children on the basis of their race. Nothing in our national experience prior to 1955 prepared anyone for dealing with changes and adjustments of the magnitude and complexity encountered since then. Deliberate resistance of some to the Court's mandates has impeded the good-faith efforts of others to bring school systems into compliance. The detail and nature of these dilatory tactics have been noted frequently by this Court and other courts. . . .

The problems encountered by the district courts and courts of appeals make plain that we should now try to amplify guidelines, however incomplete and imperfect, for the assistance of school authorities and courts. The failure of local authorities to meet their constitutional obligations aggravated the massive problem of converting from the state-enforced discrimination of racially separate school systems. This process has been rendered more difficult by changes since 1954 in the structure and patterns of communities, the growth of student population, movement of families, and other changes, some of which had marked impact on school planning, sometimes neutralizing or negating remedial action before it was fully implemented. Rural areas accustomed for half a century to the consolidated school systems implemented by bus transportation could make adjustments more readily than metropolitan areas with dense and shifting population, numerous schools, congested and complex traffic patterns.

The objective today remains to eliminate from the public schools all vestiges of state-imposed segregation. Segregation was the evil struck down by *Brown I* as contrary to the equal protection guarantees of the Constitution. That was the violation sought to be corrected by the remedial measures of *Brown II.* That was the basis for the holding in *Green* that school authorities are "clearly charged with the affirmative duty to take whatever steps might be necessary to convert to a unitary system in which racial discrimination would be eliminated root and branch." . . .

If school authorities fail in their affirmative obligations under these holdings, judicial authority may be invoked. Once a right and a violation have been shown, the scope of a district court's equitable powers to remedy past wrongs is broad, for breadth and flexibility are inherent in equitable remedies. . . .

We turn now to the problem of defining with more particularity the responsibilities of school authorities in desegregating a state-enforced dual school system in light of the Equal Protection Clause. Although the several related cases before us are primarily concerned with problems of student assignment, it may be helpful to begin with a brief discussion of other aspects of the process.

In *Green,* we pointed out that existing policy and practice with regard to faculty, staff, transportation, extra-curricular activities, and facilities were among the most important indicia of a segregated system. . . . Independent of student assignment, where it is possible to identify a "white school" or a "Negro school" simply by reference to the racial composition of teachers and staff, the quality of school buildings and equipment, or the organization of sports activities, a *prima facie* case of violation of substantive constitutional rights under the Equal Protection Clause is shown.

When a system has been dual in these respects, the first remedial responsibility of school authorities is to eliminate invidious racial distinctions. With respect to such matters as transportation, supporting personnel, and extracurricular activities, no more than this may be necessary. Similar corrective action must be taken with regard to the maintenance of buildings and the distribution of equipment. In these areas, normal administrative practice should produce schools of like quality, facilities, and staffs. Something more must be said, however, as to faculty assignment and new school construction.

In the companion *Davis* case, . . . the Mobile school board has argued that the Constitution requires that teachers be assigned on a "color blind" basis. It also argues that the Constitution prohibits district courts from using their equity power to order assignment of teachers to achieve a particular degree of faculty desegregation. We reject that contention.

In *United States* v. *Montgomery County Board of Education,* 395 U.S. 225 (1969), the District Court set as a goal a plan of faculty assignment in each school with a ratio of white to Negro faculty members substantially the same throughout the system. This order was predicated on the District Court finding that:

> "The evidence does not reflect any real administrative problems involved in immediately desegregating the substitute teachers, the student teachers, the night school faculties, and in the evolvement of a really legally adequate program for the substantial desegregation of the faculties of all schools in the system commencing with the school year 1968-69."

The District Court in *Montgomery* then proceeded to set an initial ratio for the whole system of at least two Negro teachers out of each 12 in any given school. The Court of Appeals modified the order by eliminating what it regarded as "fixed mathematical" ratios of faculty and substituted an initial requirement of *"substantially* or *approximately"* a five-to-one ratio. With respect to the future, the Court of Appeals held that the numerical ratio should be eliminated and that compliance should not be tested solely by the achievement of specified proportions. . . .

The construction of new schools and the closing of old ones are two of the most important functions of local school authorities and also two of the most complex. They must decide questions of location and capacity in light of population growth, finances, land values, site availability, through an almost endless list of factors to be considered. The result of this will be a decision which, when combined with one technique or another of student assignment, will determine the racial composition of the student body in each school in the system. Over the long run, the consequences of the choices will be far reaching. People gravitate toward school facilities, just as schools are located in response to the needs of people. The location of schools may thus influence the patterns of residential development of a metropolitan area and have important impact on composition of inner-city neighborhoods.

In the past, choices in this respect have been used as a potent weapon for creating or maintaining a state-segregated school system. In addition to the classic pattern of building schools specifically intended for Negro or white students, school authorities have sometimes, since *Brown*, closed schools which appeared likely to become racially mixed through changes in neighborhood residential patterns. This was sometimes accompanied by building new schools in the areas of white suburban expansion farthest from Negro population centers. . . .

The central issue in this case is that of student assignment, and there are essentially four problem areas:

(1) to what extent racial balance or racial quotas may be used as an implement in a remedial order to correct a previously segregated system;

(2) whether every all-Negro and all-white school must be eliminated as an indispensable part of a remedial process of desegregation;

(3) what the limits are, if any, on the rearrangement of school districts and attendance zones, as a remedial measure; and

(4) what the limits are, if any, on the use of transportation facilities to correct state-enforced racial school segregation.

The constant theme and thrust of every holding from *Brown I* to date is that state-enforced separation of races in public schools is discrimination that violates the Equal Protection Clause. The remedy commanded was to dismantle dual school systems.

We are concerned in these cases with the elimination of the discrimination inherent in the dual school systems, not with myriad factors of human existence which can cause discrimination in a multitude of ways on racial, religious, or ethnic grounds. The target of the cases from *Brown I* to the present was the dual school system. The elimination of racial discrimination in public schools is a large task and one that should not be retarded by efforts to achieve broader purposes lying beyond the jurisdiction of school authorities. One vehicle can carry only a limited amount of baggage. It would not serve the important objective of *Brown I* to seek to use school desegregation cases for purposes beyond their scope, although desegregation of schools ultimately will have impact on other forms of discrimination. We do not reach in this case the question whether a showing that school segregation is a consequence of other types of state action, without any discriminatory action by the school authorities, is a constitutional violation requiring remedial action by a school desegregation decree. This case does not present that question and we therefore do not decide it.

Our objective in dealing with the issues presented by these cases is to see that school authorities exclude no pupil of a racial minority from any school, directly or indirectly, on account of race; it does not and cannot embrace all the problems of racial prejudice, even when those problems contribute to disproportionate racial concentrations in some schools. . . .

As the voluminous record in this case shows, the predicate for the District Court's use of the 71 percent-29 percent ratio was twofold: first, its express finding, approved by the Court of Appeals and not challenged here, that a dual school system had been maintained by the school authorities at least until 1969; second, its finding, also approved by the Court of Appeals, that the school board had totally defaulted in its acknowledged duty to come forward with an acceptable plan of its own, notwithstanding the patient efforts of the District Judge who, on at least three occasions, urged the board to submit plans. As the statement of facts shows, these findings are abundantly supported by the record. It was because of this total failure of the school board that the District Court was obliged to turn to other qualified sources, and Dr. Finger was designated to assist the District Court to do what the board should have done.

We see therefore that the use made of mathematical ratios was no more than a starting point in the process of shaping a remedy, rather than an inflexible requirement. From that starting point the District Court proceeded to frame a decree that was within its discretionary powers, as an equitable remedy for the particular circumstances. As we said in *Green,* a school authority's remedial plan or a district court's remedial decree is to be judged by its effectiveness. Awareness of the racial composition of the whole school system is likely to be a useful starting point in shaping a remedy to correct past constitutional violations. In sum, the very limited use made of mathematical ratios was within the equitable remedial discretion of the District Court.

The record in this case reveals the familiar phenomenon that in metropolitan areas minority groups are often found concentrated in one part of the city. In some circumstances certain schools may remain all or largely of one race until new schools can be provided or neighborhood patterns change. Schools all or predominately of one race in a district of mixed population will require close scrutiny to determine that school assignments are not part of state-enforced segregation.

In light of the above, it should be clear that the existence of some small number of one-race, or virtually one-race, schools within a district is not in and of itself the mark of a system that still practices segregation by law. The district judge or school authorities should make every effort to achieve the greatest possible degree of actual desegregation and will thus necessarily be concerned with the elimination of one-race schools. No *per se* rule can adequately embrace all the difficulties of reconciling the competing interests involved; but in a system with a history of segregation the need for remedial criteria of sufficient specificity to assure a school authority's compliance with its constitutional duty warrants a presumption against schools that are substantially disproportionate in their racial composition. Where the school authority's proposed plan for conversion from a dual to a unitary system contemplates the continued existence of some schools that are all or predominately of one race, they have the burden of showing that such school assignments are genuinely nondiscriminatory. The court should scrutinize such schools, and the burden upon the school authorities will be to satisfy the court that their racial composition is not the result of present or past discriminatory action on their part.

An optional majority-to-minority transfer provision has long been recognized as a useful part of every desegregation plan. Provision for optional transfer of those in the majority racial group of a particular school to other schools where they will be in the minority is an indispensable remedy for those students willing to transfer to other schools in order to lessen the impact on them of the state-imposed stigma of segregation. In order to be effective, such a transfer arrangement must grant the transferring student free transportation and space must be made available in the school to which he desires to move. . . .

The maps submitted in these cases graphically demonstrate that one of the principal tools employed by school planners and by courts to break up the dual school system has been a frank — and sometimes drastic — gerrymandering of school districts and attendance zones. An additional step was pairing, "clustering," or "grouping" of schools with attendance assignments made deliberately to accomplish the transfer of Negro students out of formerly segregated Negro schools and transfer of white students to formerly all-Negro schools. More often than not, these zones are neither compact nor contiguous; indeed they may be on opposite ends of the city. As an interim corrective measure, this cannot be said to be beyond the broad remedial powers of a court.

Absent a constitutional violation there would be no basis for judicially ordering assignment of students on a racial basis. All things being equal, with no history of discrimination, it might well be desirable to assign pupils to schools nearest their homes. But all things are not equal in a system that has been deliberately constructed and maintained to enforce racial segregation. The remedy for such segregation may be administratively awkward, inconvenient, and even bizarre in some situations and may impose burdens on some; but all awkwardness and inconvenience cannot be avoided in the interim period when remedial adjustments are being made to eliminate the dual school systems.

No fixed or even substantially fixed guidelines can be established as to how far a court can go, but it must be recognized that there are limits. The objective is to dismantle the dual school system. "Racially neutral" assignment plans proposed by school authorities to a district court may be inadequate; such plans may fail to counteract the continuing effects of past school segregation resulting from discriminatory location of school sites or distortion of school size in order to achieve or maintain an artificial racial separation. When school authorities present a district court with a "loaded game board," affirmative action in the form of remedial altering of attendance zones is proper to achieve truly nondiscriminatory assignments. In short, an assignment plan is not acceptable simply because it appears to be neutral.

In this area, we must of necessity rely to a large extent, as this Court has for more than 16 years, on the informed judgment of the district courts in the first instance and on courts of appeals.

We hold that the pairing and grouping of noncontiguous school zones is a permissible tool and such action is to be considered in light of the objectives sought. Judicial steps in shaping such zones going beyond combinations of contiguous areas should be examined in light of what is said in subdivisions (1), (2), and (3) of this opinion concerning the objectives to be sought. Maps do not tell the whole story since noncontiguous school zones may be more accessible to each other in terms of the critical travel time, because of traffic patterns and good highways, than schools geographically closer together. Conditions in different localities will vary so widely that no rigid rules can be laid down to govern all situations.

The scope of permissible transportation of students as an implement of a remedial decree has never been defined by this Court and by the very nature of the problem it cannot be defined with precision. No rigid guidelines as to student transportation can be given for application to the infinite variety of problems presented in thousands of situations. Bus transportation has been an integral part of the public education system for years, and was perhaps the single most important factor in the transition from the one-room schoolhouse to the consolidated school. Eighteen million of the Nation's public school children, approximately 39 percent, were transported to their schools by bus in 1969-1970 in all parts of the country.

The importance of bus transportation as a normal and accepted tool of educational policy is readily discernible in this and the companion case. . . . The order to maintain the separation of the races with a minimum departure from the formal principles of "neighborhood zoning." Such a policy does more than simply influence the short-run composition of the student body of a new school. It may well promote segregated residential patterns which, when combined with "neighborhood zoning," further lock the school system into the mold of separation of the races. Upon a proper showing a district court may consider this in fashioning a remedy.

In ascertaining the existence of legally imposed school segregation, the existence of a pattern of school construction and abandonment is thus a factor of great weight. In devising remedies where legally imposed segregation has been established, it is the responsibility of local authorities and district courts to see to it that future school construction and abandonment are not used and do not serve to perpetuate or re-establish the dual system. . . .

Thus the remedial techniques used in the District Court's order were within that court's power to provide equitable relief; implementation of the decree is well within the capacity of the school authority.

The decree provided that the buses used to implement the plan would operate on direct routes. Students would be picked up at schools near their homes and transported to the schools they were to attend. The trips for elementary school pupils average about seven miles and the District Court found that they would take "not over 35 minutes at the most." This system compares favorably with the transportation plan previously operated in Charlotte under which each day 23,600 students on all grade levels were transported an average of 15 miles one way for an average trip requiring over an hour. In these circumstances, we find no basis for holding that the local school authorities may not be required to employ bus transportation as one tool of school desegregation. Desegregation plans cannot be limited to the walk-in school. . . .

Milliken v. Bradley, 418 U.S. 717 (1974)

As we have noted, the unanimity that had prevailed on the Supreme Court in school desegregation cases from *Brown* through *Swann* began to break down in the 1972 *Emporia, Virginia* dispute, with the advent of the four Nixon appointees. The breach accellerated in *Keyes* and *Richmond*. The unanimity came completely apart in the 1974 busing case *Milliken* v. *Bradley*. The issue in *Milliken*, as it had been in *Richmond*, was busing across school district lines to integrate all-black core-city (Detroit) schools with the virtually all-white suburban schools that ring the inner city. *Swann* concerned *intra* not inter school district busing.

In *Milliken*, the petitioner brought suit in a district court arguing that the Detroit Board of Education had deliberately "created and perpetuated" racially segregated schools. The district court agreed with the petitioner. Because the court found that the Detroit board was a "subordinating entity" of the state of Michigan, it ordered the Detroit board to submit a "city-only" desegregation plan and the state to submit a three-county desegregation plan encompassing the eighty-five school districts of the greater Detroit metropolitan area. Upon receipt of the dual plans, the district court decided to consider and implement the state's metropolitan plan because the Detroit-only plans "were inadequate to accomplish desegregation." The district court then appointed a separate panel of experts to submit plans to desegregate Detroit's inner-city schools that would include busing students to 53 of the 85 suburban school districts. The court also ordered the Detroit board to acquire 295 new school buses for massive inter-school district transportation. A federal court of appeals affirmed the district court's ruling but a badly split Supreme Court overturned both lower courts.

Speaking for himself, Justices Powell, Blackmun, and Rehnquist (the three other Nixon appointees), and Justice Stewart, Chief Justice Burger wrote that a federal court may *not* impose a multidistrict area-wide remedy for single-district de jure school segregation violations. The slim majority concluded, in effect, that where "there is no finding that the other included school districts have failed to operate unitary school systems," federal courts cannot resolve the problem of inner-city segregated schools by shifting the burden to the all-white suburbs. Chief Justice Burger went on to conclude that while school boundary lines may be altered where circumstances indicate there have been constitutional violations calling for interdistrict relief, "school district lines may not be casually ignored or treated as a mere administrative convenience."

In other words, what the Court said in *Milliken* is that "metropolitan" school districts cannot be created to deal with the problem of racially segregated schools in an inner city surrounded by largely white suburbs, with their separate school districts and their all-white schools. Substantial local control of public education, the Chief Justice said, "is a deeply rooted tradition" in American life.

The majority's ruling brought forth the two long and angry dissents. Justice White joined by Justices Douglas, Brennan, and Marshall wrote one, and Justice Marshall joined by his three colleagues wrote the other. Both White and Marshall bitterly criticized what they considered the majority's retreat from the "noble objectives," of Supreme Court rulings in school desegregation cases from *Brown* to *Swann*. Marshall's words are reproduced at some length because they are as significant and may in the future be as prophetic as Harlan's long dissent in *Plessy* so many years ago.

Mr. Chief Justice Burger delivered the opinion of the Court, saying in part:

> Here the District Court's approach to what constituted "actual desegregation" raises the fundamental question, not presented in *Swann,* as to the circumstances in which a federal court may order desegregation relief that embraces more than a single school district. The court's analytical starting point was its conclusion that school district lines are no more than arbitrary lines on a map drawn "for political convenience." Boundary lines may be bridged where there has been a constitutional violation calling for interdistrict relief, but the notion that school district lines may be casually ignored or treated as a mere administrative convenience is contrary to the history of public education in our country. No single tradition in public education is more deeply rooted than local control over the operation of schools; local autonomy has long been thought essential both to the maintenance of community concern and support for public schools and to quality of the educational process. . . . Thus, in *San Antonio School District* v. *Rodriguez,* 411 U.S. 1, 50 (1973), we observed that local control over the educational process affords citizens an opportunity to participate in decisionmaking, permits the structuring of school programs to fit local needs, and encourages "experimentation, innovation, and a healthy competition for educational excellence."
>
> The Michigan educational structure involved in this case, in common with most States, provides for a large measure of local control, and a review of the scope and character of these local powers indicates the extent to which the interdistrict remedy approved by the two courts could disrupt and alter the structure of public education in Michigan. The metropolitan remedy would require, in effect, consolidation of 54 independent school districts historically administered as separate units into a vast new super school district. . . . Entirely apart from the logistical and other serious problems attending large-scale transportation of students, the consolidation would give rise to an array of other

problems in financing and operating this new school system. Some of the more obvious questions would be: What would be the status and authority of the present popularly elected school boards? Would the children of Detroit be within the jurisdiction and operating control of a school board elected by the parents and residents of other districts? What board or boards would levy taxes for school operations in these 54 districts constituting the consolidated metropolitan area? What provisions could be made for assuring substantial equality in tax levies among the 54 districts, if this were deemed requisite? What provisions would be made for financing? Would the validity of long-term bonds be jeopardized unless approved by all of the component districts as well as the State? What body would determine that portion of the curricula now left to the discretion of local school boards? Who would establish attendance zones, purchase school equipment, locate and construct new schools, and indeed attend to all the myriad day-to-day decisions that are necessary to school operations affecting potentially more than three-quarters of a million pupils? . . .

It may be suggested that all of these vital operational problems are yet to be resolved by the District Court, and that this is the purpose of the Court of Appeals' proposed remand. But it is obvious from the scope of the interdistrict remedy itself that absent a complete restructuring of the laws of Michigan relating to school districts the District Court will become first, a *de facto* "legislative authority" to resolve these complex questions, and then the "school superintendent" for the entire area. This is a task which few, if any, judges are qualified to perform and one which would deprive the people of control of schools through their elected representatives.

Of course, no state law is above the Constitution. School district lines and the present laws with respect to local control, are not sacrosanct and if they conflict with the Fourteenth Amendment federal courts have a duty to prescribe appropriate remedies. . . .

[O]ur prior holdings have been confined to violations and remedies within a single school district. We therefore turn to address, for the first time, the validity of a remedy mandating cross-district or interdistrict consolidation to remedy a condition of segregation found to exist in only one district.

The controlling principle consistently expounded in our holdings is that the scope of the remedy is determined by the nature and extent of the constitutional violation. . . . Before the boundaries of separate and autonomous school districts may be set aside by consolidating the separate units for remedial purposes or by imposing a cross-district remedy, it must first be shown that there has been a constitutional violation within one district that produces a significant segregative effect in another district. Specifically, it must be shown that racially discriminatory acts of the state or local school districts, or of a single school district have been a substantial cause of interdistrict segregation. Thus an interdistrict remedy might be in order where the racially discriminatory acts of one or more school districts caused racial segregation in an adjacent district, or where district lines have been deliberately drawn on the basis of race. In such circumstances an interdistrict remedy would be appropriate to eliminate the interdistrict segregation directly caused by the constitutional violation. Conversely, without an interdistrict violation and interdistrict effect, there is no constitutional wrong calling for an interdistrict remedy.

The record before us, voluminous as it is, contains evidence of *de jure* segregated conditions only in the Detroit schools; indeed, that was the theory on which the litigation was initially based and on which the District Court took evidence. . . . With no showing of significant violation by the 53 outlying school districts and no evidence of any interdistrict violation or effect, the court went beyond the original theory of the case as framed by the pleadings and mandated a metropolitan area remedy. To approve the remedy ordered by the court would impose on the outlying districts, not shown to have committed any constitutional violation, a wholly impermissible remedy based on a standard not hinted at in *Brown I* and *II* or any holding of this Court. . . .

The constitutional right of the Negro respondents residing in Detroit is to attend a unitary school system in that district. Unless petitioners drew the district lines in a discriminatory fashion, or arranged for white students residing in the Detroit District to attend schools in Oakland and Macomb Counties, they were under no constitutional duty to make provisions for Negro students to do so. The view of the dissenters, that the existence of a dual system in *Detroit* can be made the basis for a decree requiring cross-district transportation of pupils, cannot be supported on the grounds that it represents merely the devising of a suitably flexible remedy for the violation of rights already established by our prior decisions. It can be supported only by drastic expansion of the constitutional right itself, an expansion without any support in either constitutional principle or precedent. . . .

We conclude that the relief ordered by the District Court and affirmed by the Court of Appeals was based upon an erroneous standard and was unsupported by record evidence that acts of the outlying districts effected the discrimination found to exist in the schools of Detroit. Accordingly, the judgment of the Court of Appeals is reversed and the case is remanded for further proceedings consistent with this opinion leading to prompt formulation of a decree directed to eliminating the segregation found to exist in Detroit city schools, a remedy which has been delayed since 1970.

Mr. Justice Marshall, joined by Justices Douglas, Brennan, and White, dissented, saying in part:

In *Brown* v. *Brown of Education*, 347 U.S. 483 (1954), this Court held that segregation of children in public schools on the basis of race deprives minority group children of equal educational opportunities and therefore denies them the equal protection of the laws under the Fourteenth Amendment. This Court recognized then that remedying decades of segregation in public education would not be an easy task. Subsequent events, unfortunately, have seen that prediction bear bitter fruit. But however imbedded old ways, however ingrained old prejudices, this Court has not been diverted from its appointed task of making "a living truth" of our constitutional ideal of equal justice under law. . . .

After 20 years of small, often difficult steps toward that great end, the Court today takes a giant step backwards. Notwithstanding a record showing widespread and pervasive racial segregation in the educational system provided by the State of Michigan for children in Detroit, this Court holds that the District Court was powerless to require the State to remedy its constitutional violation in any meaningful fashion. Ironically purporting to base its result on the principle that the scope of the remedy in a desegregation case should be determined by the nature and the extent of the constitutional violation, the Court's answer is to provide no remedy at all for the violation proved in this case, thereby guaranteeing that Negro children in Detroit will receive the same separate and inherently unequal education in the future as they have been unconstitutionally afforded in the past.

I cannot subscribe to this emasculation of our constitutional guarantee of equal protection of the laws and must respectfully dissent. Our precedents, in my view, firmly establish that where, as here, state-imposed segregation has been demonstrated, it becomes the duty of the State to eliminate root and branch all vestiges of racial discrimination and to achieve the greatest possible degree of actual desegregation. I agree with both the District Court and the Court of Appeals that, under the facts of this case, this duty cannot be fulfilled unless the State of Michigan involves outlying metropolitan area school districts in its desegregation remedy. Furthermore, I perceive no basis either in law or in the practicalities of the situation justifying the State's interposition of school district boundaries as absolute barriers to the implementation of an effective desegregation remedy. Under established and frequently used Michigan procedures, school district lines are both flexible and permeable for a wide variety of purposes, and there is no reason why they must now stand in the way of meaningful desegregation relief.

The rights at issue in this case are too fundamental to be abridged on grounds as superficial as those relied on by the majority today. We deal here with the right of all of our children, whatever their race, to an equal start in life and to an equal opportunity to reach their full potential as citizens. Those children who have been denied that right in the past deserve better than to see fences thrown up to deny them that right in the future. Our Nation, I fear, will be ill served by the Court's refusal to remedy separate and unequal education, for unless our children begin to learn together, there is little hope that our people will ever learn to live together.

The great irony of the Court's opinion and, in my view, its most serious analytical flaw may be gleaned from its concluding sentence, in which the Court remands for "prompt formulation of a decree directed to eliminating the segregation found to exist in Detroit city schools, a remedy which has been delayed since 1970." . . . The majority, however, seems to have forgotten the District Court's explicit finding that a Detroit-only decree, the only remedy permitted under today's decision, "would not accomplish desegregation."

Nowhere in the Court's opinion does the majority confront, let alone respond to, the District Court's conclusion that a remedy limited to the city of Detroit would not effectively desegregate the Detroit city schools. I, for one, find the District Court's conclusion well supported by the record and its analysis compelled by our prior cases. Before turning to these questions, however, it is best to begin by laying to rest some mischaracterizations in the Court's opinion with respect to the basis for the District Court's decision to impose a metropolitan remedy.

The Court maintains that while the initial focus of this lawsuit was the condition of segregation within the Detroit city schools, the District Court abruptly shifted focus in mid-course and altered its theory of the case. This new theory, in the majority's words, was "equating racial imbalance with a constitutional violation calling for a remedy." . . . As the following review of the District Court's handling of the case demonstrates, however, the majority's characterization is totally inaccurate. Nowhere did the District Court indicate that racial imbalance between school districts in the Detroit metropolitan area or within the Detroit School District constituted a constitutional violation calling for interdistrict relief. The focus of this case was from the beginning, and has remained, the segregated system of education in the Detroit city schools and the steps necessary to cure that condition which offends the Fourteenth Amendment.

The District Court's consideration of this case began with its finding, which the majority accepts, that the State of Michigan, through its instrumentality, the Detroit Board of Education, engaged in widespread purposeful acts of racial segregation in the Detroit School District. Without belaboring the details, it is sufficient to note that the various techniques used in Detroit were typical of methods employed to segregate students by race in areas where no statutory dual system of education has existed. . . . Exacerbating the effects of extensive residential segregation between Negroes and whites, the school board consciously drew attendance zones along lines which maximized the segregation of the races in schools as well. Optional attendance zones were created for neighborhoods undergoing racial transition so as to allow whites in these areas to escape integration. Negro students in areas with overcrowded schools were transported past or away from closer white schools with available space to more distant Negro schools. Grade structures and feeder-school patterns were created and maintained in a manner which had the foreseeable and actual effect of keeping Negro and white pupils in separate schools. Schools were also constructed in locations and in sizes which ensured that they would open with predominantly one-race student bodies. In sum, the evidence adduced below showed that Negro children had been intentionally confined to an expanding core of virtually all-Negro schools immediately surrounded by a receding band of all-white schools.

Contrary to the suggestions in the Court's opinion, the basis for affording a desegregation remedy in this case was not some perceived racial imbalance either between schools within a single school district or between independent school districts. What we confront here is "a systematic program of segregation affecting a substantial portion of the students, schools . . . and facilities within the school system. . . . The constitutional violation found here was not some *de facto* racial imbalance, but rather the purposeful, intentional, massive, *de jure* segregation of the Detroit city schools, which under our decision in *Keyes*, forms "a predicate for a finding of the existence of a dual school system." . . . and justifies "all-out desegregation." . . .

Having found a *de jure* segregated public school system in operation in the city of Detroit, the District Court turned next to consider which officials and agencies should be assigned the affirmative obligation to cure the constitutional violation. The court concluded that responsibility for the segregation in the Detroit city schools rested not only with the Detroit Board of Education, but belonged to the State of Michigan itself and the state defendants in this case — that is, the Governor of Michigan, the Attorney General, the State Board of Education, and the State Superintendent of Public Instruction. While the validity of this conclusion will merit more extensive analysis below, suffice it for now to say that it was based on three considerations. First, the evidence at trial showed that the State itself had taken actions contributing to the segregation within the Detroit schools. Second, since the Detroit Board of Education was an agency of the State of Michigan, its acts of racial discrimination were acts of the State for purposes of the Fourteenth Amendment. Finally, the District Court found that under Michigan law and practice, the system of education was in fact a *state* school system, characterized by relatively little local control and a large degree of centralized state regulation, with respect to both educational policy and the structure and operation of school districts.

Having concluded, then, that the school system in the city of Detroit was a *de jure* segregated system and that the State of Michigan had the affirmative duty to remedy that condition of segregation, the District Court then turned to the difficult task of devising an effective remedy. It bears repeating that the District Court's focus at this stage of the litigation remained what it had been at the beginning — the condition of segregation within the Detroit city schools. As the District Court stated: "From the initial ruling [on segregation] to this day, the basis of the proceedings has been and remains the violation: de jure school segregation. . . . The task before this court, therefore, is now, and . . . has always been, how to desegregate the Detroit public schools."

The District Court first considered three desegregation plans limited to the geographical boundaries of the city of Detroit. All were rejected as ineffective to desegregate the Detroit city schools. Specifically, the District Court determined that the racial composition of the Detroit student body is such that implementation of any Detroit-only plan "would clearly make the entire Detroit public school system racially identifiable as Black" and would "leave many of its schools 75 to 90 per cent Black." The District Court also found that a Detroit-only plan "would change a school system which is now Black and White to one that would be perceived as Black, thereby increasing the flight of Whites from the city and the system, thereby increasing the Black student population." Based on these findings, the District Court reasoned that "relief of segregation in the public schools of the City of Detroit cannot be accomplished within the corporate geographical limits of the city" because a Detroit-only decree "would accentuate the racial identifiability of the district as a Black school system, and would not accomplish desegregation." The District Court therefore concluded that it "must look beyond the limits of the Detroit school district for a solution to the problem of segregation in the Detroit public schools. . . ."

In seeking to define the appropriate scope of that expanded desegregation area, however, the District Court continued to maintain as its sole focus the condition shown to violate the Constitution in this case — the segregation of the Detroit school system. As it stated, the primary question "remains the determination of the area necessary and practicable effectively to eliminate 'root and branch' the effects of state-imposed and supported segregation and to desegregate the Detroit public schools."

There is simply no foundation in the record, then, for the majority's accusation that the only basis for the District Court's order was some desire to achieve a racial balance in the Detroit metropolitan area. . . .

The Court also misstates the basis for the District Court's order by suggesting that since the only segregation proved at trial was within the Detroit school system, any relief which extended beyond the jurisdiction of the Detroit Board of Education would be inappropriate because it would impose a remedy on outlying districts "not shown to have committed any constitutional violation." . . . The essential foundation of interdistrict relief in this case was not to correct conditions within outlying districts which themselves engaged in purposeful segregation. Instead, interdistrict relief was seen as a necessary part of any meaningful effort by the State of Michigan to remedy the state-caused segregation within the city of Detroit.

Rather than consider the propriety of interdistrict relief on this basis, however, the Court has conjured up a largely fictional account of what the District Court was attempting to accomplish. With all due respect, the Court, in my view, does a great disservice to the District Judge who labored long and hard with this complex litigation by accusing him of changing horses in midstream and shifting the focus of this case from the pursuit of a remedy for the condition of segregation within the Detroit school system to some unprincipled attempt to impose his own philosophy of racial balance on the entire Detroit metropolitan area. . . . The focus of this case has always been the segregated system of education in the city of Detroit. The District Court determined that interdistrict relief was necessary and appropriate only because it found that the condition of segregation within the Detroit school system could not be cured with a Detroit-only remedy. It is on this theory that the interdistrict relief must stand or fall. Unlike the Court, I perceive my task to be to review the District Court's order for what it is, rather than to criticize it for what it manifestly is not. . . .

The State had also stood in the way of past efforts to desegregate the Detroit city schools. In 1970, for example, the Detroit School Board had begun implementation of its own desegregation plan for its high schools, despite considerable public and official resistance. The State Legislature intervened by enacting Act 48 of the Public Acts of 1970, specifically prohibiting implementation of the desegregation plan and thereby continuing the growing segregation of the Detroit school system. Adequate desegregation of the Detroit system was also hampered by discriminatory restrictions placed by the State on the use of transportation within Detroit. While state aid for transportation was provided by statute for suburban districts, many of which were highly urbanized, aid for intracity transportation was excepted. One of the effects of this restriction was to encourage the construction of small walk-in neighborhood schools in Detroit, thereby lending aid to the intentional policy of creating a school system which reflected, to the greatest extent feasible, extensive residential segregation. Indeed, that one of the purposes of the transportation restriction was to impede desegregation was evidenced when the Michigan Legislature amended the State Transportation Aid Act to cover intracity transportation but expressly prohibited the allocation of funds for cross-busing of students within a school district to achieve racial balance. . . .

Also significant was the State's involvement during the 1950's in the transportation of Negro high school students from the Carver School District past a closer white high school in the Oak Park District to a more distant Negro high school in the Detroit system. Certainly the District Court's finding that the State Board of Education had knowledge of this action and had given its tacit or express approval was not clearly erroneous. Given the comprehensive statutory powers of the State Board of Education over contractual arrangements between school districts in the enrollment of students on a nonresident tuition basis, including certification of the number of pupils involved in the transfer and the amount of tuition charged, over the review of transportation routes and distances, and over the disbursement of transportation funds, the State Board inevitably knew and understood the significance of this discriminatory act.

Aside from the acts of purposeful segregation committed by the State Legislature and the State Board of Education, the District Court also concluded that the State was responsible for the many intentional acts of segregation committed by the Detroit Board of Education, an agency of the State. The majority is only willing to accept this finding *arguendo*. . . .I have no doubt, however, as to its validity under the Fourteenth Amendment.

"The command of the Fourteenth Amendment," it should be recalled, "is that no 'State' shall deny to any person within its jurisdiction the equal protection of the laws." . . .

In sum, several factors in this case coalesce to support the District Court's ruling that it was the State of Michigan itself, not simply the Detroit Board of Education, which bore the obligation of curing the condition of segregation within the Detroit city schools. The actions of the State itself directly contributed to Detroit's segregation. Under the Fourteenth Amendment, the State is ultimately responsible for the actions of its local agencies. And, finally, given the structure of Michigan's educational system, Detroit's segregation cannot be viewed as the problem of an independent and separate entity. Michigan operates a single statewide system of education, a substantial part of which was shown to be segregated in this case. . . .

After examining three plans limited to the city of Detroit, the District Court correctly concluded that none would eliminate root and branch the vestiges of unconstitutional segregation. The plans' effectiveness, of course, had to be evaluated in the context of the District Court's findings as to the extent of segregation in the Detroit city schools. As indicated earlier, the most essential finding was that Negro children in Detroit had been confined by intentional acts of segregation to a growing core of Negro schools surrounded by a receding ring of white schools. . . .

Under a Detroit-only decree, Detroit's schools will clearly remain racially identifiable in comparison with neighboring schools in the metropolitan community. Schools with 65 percent and more Negro students will stand in sharp and obvious contrast to schools in neighboring districts with less than 2 percent Negro enrollment. Negro students will continue to perceive their schools as segregated educational facilities and this perception will only be increased when whites react to a Detroit-only decree by fleeing to the suburbs to avoid integration. School district lines, however innocently drawn, will surely be perceived as fences to separate the races when, under a Detroit-only decree, white parents withdraw their children from the Detroit city schools and move to the suburbs in order to continue them in all-white schools. The message of this action will not escape the Negro children in the city of Detroit. . . . It will be of scant significance to Negro children who have for years been confined by *de jure* acts of segregation to a growing core of all-Negro schools surrounded by a ring of all-white schools that the new dividing line between the races is the school district boundary.

Nor can it be said that the State is free from any responsibility for the disparity between the racial makeup of Detroit and its surrounding suburbs. The State's creation, through *de jure* acts of segregation, of a growing core of all-Negro schools inevitably acted as a magnet to attract Negroes to the areas served by such schools and to deter them from settling either in other areas of the city or in the suburbs. By the same token, the growing core of all-Negro schools inevitably helped drive whites to other areas of the city or to the suburbs. As we recognized in *Swann:*

"People gravitate toward school facilities, just as schools are located in response to the needs of people. The location of schools may thus influence the patterns of residential development of a metropolitan area and have important impact on composition of inner-city neighborhoods. . . . [Action taken] to maintain the separation of the races with a minimum departure from the formal principles of 'neighborhood zoning' . . . does more than simply influence the short-run composition of the student body. . . . It may well promote segregated residential patterns which, when combined with 'neighborhood zoning,' further lock the school system into the mold of separation of the races. Upon a proper showing a district court may consider this in fashioning a remedy."

. . . The rippling effects on residential patterns caused by purposeful acts of segregation do not automatically subside at the school district border. With rare exceptions, these effects naturally spread through all the residential neighborhoods within a metropolitan area.

The State must also bear part of the blame for the white flight to the suburbs which would be forthcoming from a Detroit-only decree and would render such a remedy ineffective. Having created a system where whites and Negroes were intentionally kept apart so that they could not become accustomed to learning together, the State is responsible for the fact that many whites will react to the dismantling of that segregated system by attempting to flee to the suburbs. Indeed, by limiting the District Court to a Detroit-only remedy and allowing that flight to the suburbs to succeed, the Court today allows the State to profit from its own wrong and to perpetuate for years to come the separation of the races it achieved in the past by purposeful state action.

The majority asserts, however, that involvement of outlying districts would do violence to the accepted principle that "the nature of the violation determines the scope of the remedy." . . . Not only is the majority's attempt to find in this single phrase the answer to the complex and difficult questions presented in this case hopelessly simplistic, but more important, the Court reads these words in a manner which perverts their obvious meaning. The nature of a violation determines the scope of the remedy simply because the function of any remedy is to cure the violation to which it is addressed. In school segregation cases, as in other equitable causes, a remedy which effectively cures the violation is what is required. . . . No more is necessary, but we can tolerate no less. To read this principle as barring a district court from imposing the only effective remedy for past segregation and remitting the court to a patently ineffective alternative is, in my view, to turn a simple commonsense rule into a cruel and meaningless paradox. Ironically, by ruling out an interdistrict remedy, the only relief which promises to cure segregation in the Detroit public schools, the majority flouts the very principle on which it purports to rely.

Nor should it be of any significance that the suburban school districts were not shown to have themselves taken any direct action to promote segregation of the races. Given the State's broad powers over local school districts, it was well within the State's powers to require those districts surrounding the Detroit school district to participate in a metropolitan remedy. The State's duty should be no different here than in cases where it is shown that certain of a State's voting districts are malapportioned in violation of the Fourteenth Amendment. . . . Overrepresented electoral districts are required to participate in reapportionment although their only "participation" in the violation was to do nothing about it. Similarly, electoral districts which themselves meet representation standards must frequently be redrawn as part of a remedy for other over- and under-inclusive districts. No finding of fault on the part of each electoral district and no finding of a discriminatory effect on each district is a prerequisite to its involvement in the constitutionally required remedy. By the same logic, no finding of fault on the part of the suburban school districts in this case and no finding of a discriminatory effect on each district should be a prerequisite to their involvement in the constitutionally required remedy.

It is the State, after all, which bears the responsibility under *Brown* of affording a nondiscriminatory system of education. The State, of course, is ordinarily free to choose any decentralized framework for education it wishes, so long as it fulfills that Fourteenth Amendment obligation. But the State should no more be allowed to hide behind its delegation and compartmentalization of school districts to avoid its constitutional obligations to its children than it could hide behind its political subdivisions to avoid its obligations to its voters. . . .

One final set of problems remains to be considered. We recognized in *Brown II,* and have re-emphasized ever since, that in fashioning relief in desegregation cases, "the courts will be guided by equitable principles. Traditionally, equity has been characterized by a practical flexibility in shaping its remedies, and by a facility for adjusting and reconciling public and private needs." . . .

[T]he majority ignores long-established Michigan procedures under which school districts may enter into contractual agreements to educate their pupils in other districts using state or local funds to finance nonresident education. Such agreements could form an easily administrable framework for interdistrict relief short of outright consolidation of the school districts. The District Court found that interdistrict procedures like these were frequently used to provide special educational services for handicapped children, and extensive statutory provision is also made for their use in vocational education. Surely if school districts are willing to engage in interdistrict programs to help those unfortunate children crippled by physical or mental handicaps, school districts can be required to participate in an interdistrict program to help those children in the city of Detroit whose educations and very futures have been crippled by purposeful state segregation. . . .

First of all, the metropolitan plan would not involve the busing of substantially more students than already ride buses. The District Court found that, statewide, 35 percent–40 percent of all students already arrive at school on a bus. In those school districts in the tri-county Detroit metropolitan area eligible for state reimbursement of transportation costs, 42 percent–52 percent of all students rode buses to school. In the tri-county areas as a whole, approximately 300,000 pupils arrived at school on some type of bus, with about 60,000 of these apparently using regular public transit. In comparison, the desegregation plan, according to its present rough outline, would involve the transportation of 310,000 students, about 40 percent of the population within the desegregation area.

With respect to distance and amount of time traveled, 17 of the outlying school districts involved in the plan are contiguous to the Detroit district. The rest are all within 8 miles of the Detroit city limits. The trial court, in defining the desegregation area, placed a ceiling of 40 minutes one way on the amount of travel time, and many students will obviously travel for far shorter periods. As to distance, the average statewide bus trip is 8½ miles one way, and in some parts of the tri-county area, students already travel for one and a quarter hours or more each way. In sum, with regard to both the number of students transported and the time and distances involved, the outlined desegregation plan "compares favorably with the transportation plan previously operated. . . ." . . .

As far as economics are concerned, a metropolitan remedy would actually be more sensible than a Detroit-only remedy. Because of prior transportation aid restrictions, . . . Detroit largely relied on public transport, at student expense, for those students who lived too far away to walk to school. Since no inventory of school buses existed, a Detroit-only plan was estimated to require the purchase of 900 buses to effectuate the necessary transportation. The tri-county area, in contrast, already has an inventory of 1,800 buses, many of which are now under-utilized. Since increased utilization of the existing inventory can take up much of the increase in transportation involved in the interdistrict remedy, the District Court found that only 350 additional buses would probably be needed, almost two-thirds fewer than a Detroit-only remedy. Other features of an interdistrict remedy bespeak its practicality, such as the possibility of pairing up Negro schools near Detroit's boundary with nearby white schools on the other side of the present school district line.

Some disruption, of course, is the inevitable product of any desegregation decree, whether it operates within one district or on an interdistrict basis. As we said in *Swann*, however:

"Absent a constitutional violation there would be no basis for judicially ordering assignment of students on a racial basis. All things being equal, with no history of discrimination, it might well be desirable to assign pupils to schools nearest their homes. But all things are not equal in a system that has been deliberately constructed and maintained to enforce racial segregation. The remedy for such segregation may be administratively awkward, inconvenient, and even bizarre in some situations and may impose burdens on some; but all awkwardness and inconvenience cannot be avoided. . . ." . . .

Desegregation is not and was never expected to be an easy task. Racial attitudes ingrained in our Nation's childhood and adolescence are not quickly thrown aside in its middle years. But just as the inconvenience of some cannot be allowed to stand in the way of the rights of others, so public opposition, no matter how strident, cannot be permitted to divert this Court from the enforcement of the constitutional principles at issue in this case. Today's holding, I fear, is more a reflection of a perceived public mood that we have gone far enough in enforcing the Constitution's guarantee of equal justice than it is the product of neutral principles of law. In the short run, it may seem to be the easier course to allow our great metropolitan areas to be divided up each into two cities — one white, the other black — but it is a course, I predict, our people will ultimately regret. I dissent.

Regents of the University of California v. Bakke, 98 S. Ct. 2733 (1978)

Not since *Brown* v. *Board of Education* in 1954 had a civil liberties dispute stirred as much controversy, political as well as legal and constitutional. Court watchers had been waiting for months for the decision. The nation had taken sides and was torn by the many-sided implications of the dispute. Surely *Bakke* would be a momentous landmark.

On the one hand blacks, Chicanos, and their supporters were zealous to preserve the long-sought affirmative action programs of the 1960s, which had opened job opportunities and university doors until then largely closed to them. They were suspicious and fearful that a Supreme Court dominated by President Nixon's conservative appointees would attempt to turn back the clock and begin unraveling the very real progress minority groups had made since *Brown* and the Civil Rights Movement of the 1960s. There already had been substantial evidence that the Burger Court was beginning to chip away at the Warren Court's achievements in civil rights matters. The hesitant backtracking busing decisions of the early 1970s were, in fact, a part of its record. As *Bakke* approached, these decisions gave civil rights activists serious cause for concern. And so, throughout the waiting period during the spring of 1978, the apprehension was real.

On the other hand large segments of middle-class white America looked upon *Bakke* as the Court's opportunity to redress a balance that, they argued, the 1960s had tipped too heavily in favor of the nation's minority groups. There was widespread sentiment that "we" had gone too far, that the problem could now be characterized as "reverse discrimination," a situation wherein blacks, Chicanos, and others were actually given preferential treatment in job and educational considerations, often at the expense of what appeared to be better qualified white applicants. This then is the essence of the *Bakke* case; had Allan Bakke been denied admission to the University of California's Medical School at Davis so that the University could admit a "less qualified" minority applicant under its "special admission program?" Allan Bakke argued that the University's special admission program operated to exclude him on the basis of his race and it was, therefore, a violation of the Equal Protection Clause of the Fourteenth Amendment, the California Constitution, and Title VI of the 1964 Civil Rights Act. Title VI states that no person shall on grounds of race be excluded from participating in any program receiving federal funds. Thus for Bakke and his supporters the issue was clear-cut; they called it "reverse discrimination." However, it seems equally clear from the record of the legislation that the principal thrust of Title VI was to open doors hitherto closed because of racial discrimination to blacks and other minorities.

In *Regents* v. *Bakke,* the Burger Court was badly fragmented. Justice Stevens, joined by Chief Justice Burger and Justices Stewart and Rehnquist, took the view that the University of California, which admittedly was receiving federal financial assistance, had illegally and unconstitutionally excluded Bakke from its Medical School because of his race and had therefore clearly violated Title VI. "A different result," Stevens wrote, "cannot be justified unless that language (of Title VI) misstates that actual intent of the Congress . . . or the statute is not enforceable in a private action. Neither conclusion is warranted." For Justice Stevens and his colleagues, the answer was simple; race could *not* be used as an admission criteria.

Justice Brennan, joined by Justices White, Marshall, and Blackmun, differed dramatically with Stevens's view. "The difficulty of the issue," Brennan noted, "whether the government may use race-conscious programs to redress the continuing effects of past discrimination — and the mature consideration which each of our brethren has brought to it have resulted in many opinions, no single one speaking for the Court." Brennan went on: "But this should not and must not mask the central meaning of today's opinions: Government may take race into account when it acts not to demean or insult any racial group, but to remedy disadvantages cast on minorities by past racial prejudice, at least when appropriate findings have been made by judicial, legislative, or administrative bodies with competence to act in this area. . . ."

Thus with the Stevens four insisting that race could *not* be used as an admission criteria and with the Brennan four arguing that in order to redress past racial discrimination, race *could* be a factor in a university's admission program, Justice Powell became the Court's central figure. His long detailed opinion took the traditional, hallowed "middle ground." Powell concluded that Davis's special admission program was in fact a quota system that illegally and unconstitutionally discriminated against Allan Bakke. The Stevens four joined this part of Powell's opinion. However Powell went on to conclude that under "some circumstances . . . the goal of achieving a diverse student body is sufficiently compelling to justify consideration of race in admissions decisions . . ." The Brennan four concurred with this part of the Powell opinion. Thus with Powell as the critically significant "middle" man the Court in effect "straddled" the issues and perhaps diffused the explosive mixture presented in *Bakke.* Its "no quota systems" rule satisfied those made angry by what they called affirmative action's "reverse discrimination." And Powell's view (supported by the Brennan four) that race *might* be used as an admissions criteria to redress past racial discrimination at least partially satisfied blacks, Chicanos, and others who were deeply concerned that the advances since *Brown* and the 1960s would be scuttled and that they therefore would be back to square one in the struggle for equal opportunities.

In *Bakke* the Supreme Court found that the Medical School of the University of California at Davis had two separate admissions programs for its entering class of 100 students. Under the regular procedure candidates whose undergraduate grade point averages were below 2.5 on a scale of 4.0 were automatically rejected. Of those with above a 2.5 about one in six were given an interview and rated on a scale of 1 to 100 by each member of the admissions committee. An applicant's rating was based upon college sciences grades, the Medical College Admissions Test (MCAT) scores, letters of recommendation, extracurricular activities, and other biographical data. All this resulted in a "benchmark score."

Davis also had a separate committee to administer the special admissions program. Candidates were asked on the application form whether they wished to be considered "economically and/or educationally disadvantaged" or whether they were members of a minority group. Special candidates were not required to have a 2.5 grade point average and they were not ranked against candidates in the general admissions programs. During the years when Allan Bakke applied to Davis, about 20 percent of the special applicants were interviewed and given "benchmark scores." The top choices were then passed to the general admissions committee, which could reject the special candidates for failure to meet specific course requirements or "other deficiencies." The special committee continued to pass on candidates until the allotted sixteen special admissions places were filled.

Allan Bakke applied at Davis in both 1973 and 1974. Despite high scores, grade point average, and benchmark, he was twice rejected. After his second rejection, Bakke sued the University of California, arguing that the special admissions program discriminated against him on the basis of his race because less qualified minority students with lower scores *had* been admitted.

A trial court in California found that Davis's special admissions program operated as a racial quota system because minority applicants were rated only against one another and because a specific sixteen places in the class of a hundred were reserved for them. It ruled for Bakke. The California Supreme Court applying what it termed a necessarily "strict scrutiny standard" in racial classification disputes also ruled for Bakke on grounds that the University's special admissions program violated the equal protection clause of the Fourteenth Amendment.

Thus the stage was set for the Supreme Court's historic confrontation. That a badly divided Court fudged and hedged, attempting a compromise of sorts that would neither totally please or displease any of the adherents, is apparent from Justice Powell's long, tortuous, middle-ground opinion.

Mr. Justice Powell announced the judgment of the Court, saying in part:

> At the outset we face the question whether a right of action for private parties exists under Title VI. Respondent argues that there is a private right of action, invoking the test set forth in *Cort v. Ash,* 422 U.S. 66, 78 (1975). He contends that the statute creates a federal right in his favor, that legislative history reveals an intent to permit private actions, that such actions would further the remedial purposes of the statute, and that enforcement of federal rights under the Civil Rights Act generally is not relegated to the States. In addition, he cites several lower court decisions which have recognized or assumed the existence of a private right of action. Petitioner denies the existence of a private right of action, arguing that the sole function of §601, see n. 11, *supra,* was to establish a predicate for administrative action under §602, 42 U.S.C. §2000d–1. In its view, administrative curtailment of federal funds under that section was the only sanction to be imposed upon recipients that violated §601. Petitioner also points out that Title VI contains no explicit grant of a private right of action, in contrast to Titles II, III, IV, and VII, of the same statute, 42 U.S.C. §§2000a–3 (a), 2000b–2, 2000c–8, and 2000e–5 (f).
>
> We find it unnecessary to resolve this question in the instant case. The question of respondent's right to bring an action under Title VI was neither argued

nor decided in either of the courts below, and this Court has been hesitant to review questions not addressed below. ... We therefore do not address this difficult issue. Similarly, we need not pass upon petitioner's claim that private plaintiffs under Title VI must exhaust administrative remedies. We assume only for the purposes of this case that respondent has a right of action under Title VI. See *Lau* v. *Nichols,* 414 U.S. 563, 571 n. 2 (1974) (STEWART, J., concurring in the result).

The language of §601, like that of the Equal Protection Clause, is majestic in its sweep:

> "No person in the United States shall, on the ground of race, color, or national origin, be excluded from participation in, be denied the benefits of, or be subjected to discrimination under any program or activity receiving Federal financial assistance."

The concept of "discrimination," like the phrase "equal protection of the laws," is susceptible to varying interpretations, for as Mr. Justice Holmes declared, "[a] word is not a crystal, transparent and unchanged, it is the skin of a living thought and may vary greatly in color and content according to the circumstances and the time in which it is used." *Towne* v. *Eisner,* 245 U.S. 418, 425 (1918). We must, therefore, seek whatever aid is available in determining the precise meaning of the statute before us. ... Examination of the voluminous legislative history of Title VI reveals a congressional intent to halt federal funding of entities that violate a prohibition of racial discrimination similar to that of the Constitution. Although isolated statements of various legislators, taken out of context, can be marshalled in support of the proposition that §601 enacted a purely colorblind scheme, without regard to the reach of the Equal Protection Clause, these comments must be read against the background of both the problem that Congress was addressing and the broader view of the statute that emerges from a full examination of the legislative debates.

The problem confronting Congress was discrimination against Negro citizens at the hands of recipients of federal moneys. Indeed, the color-blindness pronouncements cited in the margin at n. 19, generally occur in the midst of extended remarks dealing with the evils of segregation in federally funded programs. Over and over again, proponents of the bill detailed the plight of Negroes seeking equal treatment in such programs. There simply was no reason for Congress to consider the validity of hypothetical preferences that might be accorded minority citizens; the legislators were dealing with the real and pressing problem of how to guarantee those citizens equal treatment.

In addressing that problem, supporters of Title VI repeatedly declared that the bill enacted constitutional principles. For example, Representative Celler, the Chairman of the House Judiciary Committee and floor manager of the legislation in the House, emphasized this in introducing the bill:

> "The bill would offer assurance that hospitals financed by Federal money would not deny adequate care to Negroes. It would prevent abuse of food distribution programs whereby Negroes have been known to be denied food surplus supplies when white persons were given such food. It would assure Negroes the benefits now accorded only white students in programs of higher education financed by Federal funds. It would, in short, *assure the existing right to equal treatment* in the enjoyment of Federal funds. It would not destroy any rights of private property or freedom of association." 110 Cong. Rec. 1519 (1964) (emphasis added).

Other sponsors shared Representative Celler's view that Title VI embodied constitutional principles.

In the Senate, Senator Humphrey declared that the purpose of Title VI was "to insure that Federal funds are spent in accordance with the Constitution and the moral sense of the Nation." *Id.*, at 6544. Senator Ribicoff agreed that Title VI embraced the constitutional standard: "Basically, there is a constitutional restriction against discrimination in the use of federal funds; and title VI simply spells out the procedure to be used in enforcing that restriction." *Id.*, at 13333. Other Senators expressed similar views.

Further evidence of the incorporation of a constitutional standard into Title VI appears in the repeated refusals of the legislation's supporters precisely to define the term "discrimination." Opponents sharply criticized this failure, but proponents of the bill merely replied that the meaning of "discrimination" would be made clear by reference to the Constitution or other existing law. For example, Senator Humphrey noted the relevance of the Constitution:

> "As I have said, the bill has a simple purpose. That purpose is to give fellow citizens — Negroes — the same rights and opportunities that white people take for granted. This is no more than what was preached by the prophets, and by Christ Himself. It is no more than what our Constitution guarantees." *Id.*, at 6553.

In view of the clear legislative intent, Title VI must be held to proscribe only those racial classifications that would violate the Equal Protection Clause or the Fifth Amendment.

Petitioner does not deny that decisions based on race or ethnic origin by faculties and administrations of state universities are reviewable under the Fourteenth Amendment. . . . For his part, respondent does not argue that all racial or ethnic classifications are *per se* invalid. . . . The parties do disagree as to the level of judicial scrutiny to be applied to the special admissions program. Petitioner argues that the court below erred in applying strict scrutiny, as this inexact term has been applied in our cases. That level of review, petitioner asserts, should be reserved for classifications that disadvantage "discrete and insular minorities." . . . Respondent, on the other hand, contends that the California court correctly rejected the notion that the degree of judicial scrutiny accorded a particular racial or ethnic classification hinges upon membership in a discrete and insular minority and duly recognized that the "rights established [by the Fourteenth Amendment] are personal rights." *Shelley* v. *Kraemer*, 334 U.S. 1, 22 (1948).

En route to this crucial battle over the scope of judicial review, the parties fight a sharp preliminary action over the proper characterization of the special admissions program. Petitioner prefers to view it as establishing a "goal" of minority representation in the medical school. Respondent, echoing the courts below, labels it a racial quota.

This semantic distinction is beside the point: the special admissions program is undeniably a classification based on race and ethnic background. To the extent that there existed a pool of at least minimally qualified minority applicants to fill the 16 special admissions seats, white applicants could compete only for 84 seats in the entering class, rather than the 100 open to minority applicants. Whether this limitation is described as a quota or a goal, it is a line drawn on the basis of race and ethnic status.

The guarantees of the Fourteenth Amendment extend to persons. Its language is explicit: "No state shall . . . deny to any person within its jurisdiction the equal protection of the laws." It is settled beyond question that the "rights created by the first section of the Fourteenth Amendment are, by its terms, guaranteed to the individual. They are personal rights.". . . The guarantee of equal protection cannot mean one thing when applied to one individual and something else when applied to a person of another color. If both are not accorded the same protection, then it is not equal.

Nevertheless, petitioner argues that the court below erred in applying strict scrutiny to the special admissions programs because white males, such as respondent, are not a "discrete and insular minority" requiring extraordinary protection from the majoritarian political process. This rationale, however, has never been invoked in our decisions as a prerequisite to subjecting racial or ethnic distinctions to strict scrutiny. Nor has this Court held that discreteness and insularity constitute necessary preconditions to a holding that a particular classification is invidious. . . . These characteristics may be relevant in deciding whether or not to add new types of classifications to the list of "suspect" categories or whether a particular classification survives close examination. . . . Racial and ethnic classifications, however, are subject to stringent examination without regard to these additional characteristics. We declared as much in the first cases explicitly to recognize racial distinctions as suspect:

> "Distinctions between citizens solely because of their ancestry are by their very nature odious to a free people whose institutions are founded upon the doctrine of equality." *Hirabayashi*, 320 U.S., at 100.
> ". . . [A]ll legal restrictions which curtail the rights of a single racial group are immediately suspect. That is not to say that all such restrictions are unconstitutional. It is to say that courts must subject them to the most rigid scrutiny." *Korematsu*, 323 U.S., at 216.

The Court has never questioned the validity of those pronouncements. Racial and ethnic distinctions of any sort are inherently suspect and thus call for the most exacting judicial examination.

This perception of racial and ethnic distinctions is rooted in our Nation's constitutional and demographic history. The Court's initial view of the Fourteenth Amendment was that its "one pervading purpose" was "the freedom of the slave race, the security and firm establishment of that freedom, and the protection of the newly-made freeman and citizen from the oppressions of those who had formerly exercised dominion over him." *Slaughter-House Cases*, 16 Wall. 36, 71 (1873). The Equal Protection Clause, however, was "[v]irtually strangled in its infancy by post-civil-war judicial reactionism." It was relegated to decades of relative desuetude while the Due Process Clause of the Fourteenth Amendment, after a short germinal period, flourished as a cornerstone in the Court's defense of property and liberty of contract. See, *e.g.*, *Mugler* v. *Kansas*, 123 U.S. 623, 661 (1887); *Allgeyer* v. *Louisiana*, 165 U.S. 578 (1897); *Lochner* v. *New York*, 198 U.S. 45 (1905). In that cause, the Fourteenth Amendment's "one pervading purpose" was displaced. See, *e.g.*, *Plessy* v. *Ferguson*, 163 U.S. 537 (1896). It was only as the era of substantive due process came to a close, see, *e.g.*, *Nebbia* v. *New York*, 291 U.S. 502 (1934); *West Coast Hotel* v. *Parrish*, 300 U.S. 379 (1937), that the Equal Protection Clause began to attain a genuine measure of vitality. . . .

By that time it was no longer possible to peg the guarantees of the Fourteenth Amendment to the struggle for equality of one racial minority. During the dormancy of the Equal Protection Clause, the United States had become a nation of minorities. Each had to struggle — and to some extent struggles still — to overcome the prejudices not of a monolithic majority, but of a "majority" composed of various minority groups of whom it was said — perhaps unfairly in many cases — that a shared characteristic was a willingness to disadvantage other groups. As the Nation filled with the stock of many lands, the reach of the Clause was gradually extended to all ethnic groups seeking protection from official discrimination. See *Strauder* v. *West Virginia*, 100 U.S. 303, 308 (1880). (Celtic Irishmen) (dictum); *Yick Wo* v. *Hopkins*, 118 U.S. 356 (1886) (Chinese); *Truax* v. *Raich*, 239 U.S. 33,41 (1915) (Austrian resident aliens); *Korematsu, supra* (Japanese); *Hernandez* v. *Texas*, 347 U.S. 475 (1954) (Mexican-Americans). The guarantees of equal protection, said the Court in *Yick Wo,* "are universal in their application, to all persons within the territorial jurisdiction, without regard to any differences of race, of color, or of nationality; and the equal protection of the laws is a pledge of the protection of equal laws." 118 U.S., at 369.

Although many of the Framers of the Fourteenth Amendment conceived of its primary function as bridging the vast distance between members of the Negro race and the white "majority," *Slaughter-House Cases, supra,* the Amendment itself was framed in universal terms, without reference to color, ethnic origin, or condition of prior servitude. As this Court recently remarked in interpreting the 1866 Civil Rights Act to extend to claims of racial discrimination against white persons, "the 39th Congress was intent upon establishing in federal law a broader principle than would have been necessary to meet the particular and immediate plight of the newly freed Negro slaves." *McDonald* v. *Santa Fe Trail Transp. Co.,* 427 U.S. 273, 296 (1976). And that legislation was specifically broadened in 1870 to ensure that "all persons," not merely "citizens," would enjoy equal rights under the law. See *Runyon* v. *McCrary,* 427 U.S. 160, 192-202 (1976) (WHITE, J., dissenting). Indeed, it is not unlikely that among the Framers were many who would have applauded a reading of the Equal Protection Clause which states a principle of universal application and is responsive to the racial, ethnic and cultural diversity of the Nation. . . .

Over the past 30 years, this Court has embarked upon the crucial mission of interpreting the Equal Protection Clause with the view of assuring to all persons "the protection of equal laws," *Yick Wo, supra,* at 369, in a Nation confronting a legacy of slavery and racial discrimination. . . . Because the landmark decisions in this area arose in response to the continued exclusion of Negroes from the mainstream of American society, they could be characterized as involving discrimination by the "majority" white race against the Negro minority. But they need not be read as depending upon that characterization for their results. It suffices to say that "[o]ver the years, this Court consistently repudiated '[d]istinctions between citizens solely because of their ancestry' as being 'odious to a free people whose institutions are founded upon the doctrine of equality.'" . . .

Petitioner urges us to adopt for the first time a more restrictive view of the Equal Protection Clause and hold that discrimination against members of the white "majority" cannot be suspect if its purpose can be characterized as "benign." The clock of our liberties, however, cannot be turned back to 1868. . . . It is far too late to argue that the guarantee of equal protection to *all* persons permits the recognition of special wards entitled to a degree of protection greater than that accorded others. "The Fourteenth Amendment is not directly solely against discrimination due to a 'two-class theory' — that is, based upon differences between 'white' and Negro." *Hernandez, supra,* at 478.

Once the artificial line of a "two-class theory" of the Fourteenth Amendment is put aside, the difficulties entailed in varying the level of judicial review according to a perceived "preferred" status of a particular racial or ethnic minority are intractable. The concepts of "majority" and "minority" necessarily reflect temporary arrangements and political judgments. As observed above, the white "majority" itself is composed of various minority groups, most of which can lay claim to a history of prior discrimination at the hands of the state and private individuals. Not all of these groups can receive preferential treatment and corresponding judicial tolerance of distinctions drawn in terms of race and nationality, for then the only "majority" left would be a new minority of White Anglo-Saxon Protestants. There is no principled basis for deciding which groups would merit "heightened judicial solicitude" and which would not. Courts would be asked to evaluate the extent of the prejudice and consequent harm suffered by various minority groups. Those whose societal injury is thought to exceed some arbitrary level of tolerability then would be entitled to preferential classifications at the expense of individuals belonging to other groups. Those classifications would be free from exacting judicial scrutiny. As these preferences began to have their desired effect, and the consequences of past discrimination were undone, new judicial rankings would be necessary. The kind of variable sociological and political analysis necessary to produce such rankings simply does not lie within the judicial competence — even if they otherwise were politically feasible and socially desirable.

Moreover, there are serious problems of justice connected with the idea of preference itself. First, it may not always be clear that a so-called preference is in fact benign. Courts may be asked to validate burdens imposed upon individual members of particular groups in order to advance the group's general interest. See *United Jewish Organizations* v. *Carey,* 430 U.S. 144, 172-173 (BRENNAN, J., concurring in part). Nothing in the Constitution supports the notion that individuals may be asked to suffer otherwise impermissible burdens in order to enhance the societal standing of their ethnic groups. Second, preferential programs may only reinforce common stereotypes holding that certain groups are unable to achieve success without special protection based on a factor having no relationship to individual worth. . . . Third, there is a measure of inequity in forcing innocent persons in respondent's position to bear the burdens of redressing grievances not of their making.

By hitching the meaning of the Equal Protection Clause to these transitory considerations, we would be holding, as a constitutional principle, that judicial scrutiny of classifications touching on racial and ethnic background may vary with the ebb and flow of political forces. Disparate constitutional tolerance of such classifications well may serve to exacerbate racial and ethnic antagonisms rather than alleviate them. . . . Also, the mutability of a constitutional principle, based upon shifting political and social judgments, undermines the chances for consistent application of the Constitution from one generation to the next, a critical feature of its coherent interpretation. *Pollock* v. *Farmers Loan & Trust Co.,* 157 U.S. 429, 650-651 (1895) (White, J., dissenting). In expounding the Constitution, the Court's role is to discern "principles sufficiently absolute to give them roots throughout the community and continuity over significant periods of time, and to lift them above the level of the pragmatic political judgments of a particular time and place." . . .

If it is the individual who is entitled to judicial protection against classifications based upon his racial or ethnic background because such distinctions impinge upon personal rights, rather than the individual only because of his membership in a particular group, then constitutional standards may be applied consistently. Political judgments regarding the necessity for the particular classification may be weighed in the constitutional balance, *Korematsu* v. *United States,* 323 U.S. 214 (1944), but the standard of justification will remain constant. This is as it should be, since those political judgments are the product of rough compromise struck by contending groups within the democratic process. When they touch upon an individual's race or ethnic background, he is entitled to a judicial determination that the burden he is asked to bear on that basis is precisely tailored to serve a compelling governmental interest. The Constitution guarantees that right to every person regardless of his background. . . .

Petitioner also cites *Lau* v. *Nichols,* 414 U.S. 563 (1974), in support of the proposition that discrimination favoring racial or ethnic minorities has received judicial approval without the exacting inquiry ordinarily accorded "suspect" classifications. In *Lau,* we held that the failure of the San Francisco school system to provide remedial English instruction for some 1,800 students of oriental ancestry who spoke no English amounted to a violation of Title VI of the Civil Rights Act of 1964, 42 U.S.C. §2000d, and the regulations promulgated thereunder.

Those regulations required remedial instruction where inability to understand English excluded children of foreign ancestry from participation in educational programs. *Id.*, at 568. Because we found that the students in *Lau* were denied "a meaningful opportunity to participate in the educational program," *ibid.*, we remanded for the fashioning of a remedial order.

Lau provides little support for petitioner's argument. The decision rested solely on the statute, which had been construed by the responsible administrative agency to reach educational practices "which have the effect of subjecting individuals to discrimination," *id.*, at 568. We stated: "Under these state-imposed standards there is no equality of treatment merely by providing students with the same facilities, textbooks, teachers and curriculum; for students who do not understand English are effectively foreclosed from any meaningful education." *Id.*, at 566. Moreover, the "preference" approved did not result in the denial of the relevant benefit — "meaningful participation in the educational program" — to anyone else. No other student was deprived by that preference of the ability to participate in San Francisco's school system, and the applicable regulations required similar assistance for all students who suffered similar linguistic deficiencies. *Id.*, at 570-571 (STEWART, J., concurring).

In a similar vein, petitioner contends that our recent decision in *United Jewish Organizations* v. *Carey,* 430 U.S. 144 (1977), indicates a willingness to approve racial classifications designed to benefit certain minorities, without denominating the classifications as "suspect." The State of New York had redrawn its reapportionment plan to meet objections of the Department of Justice under §5 of the Voting Rights Act of 1965, 42 U.S.C. §1973c. Specifically, voting districts were redrawn to enhance the electoral power of certain "nonwhite" voters found to have been the victims of unlawful "dilution" under the original reapportionment plan. *United Jewish Organizations*, like *Lau*, properly is viewed as a case in which the remedy for an administrative finding of discrimination encompassed measures to improve the previously disadvantaged group's ability to participate, without excluding individuals belonging to any other group from enjoyment of the relevant opportunity — meaningful participation in the electoral process.

In this case, unlike *Lau* and *United Jewish Organizations*, there has been no determination by the legislature or a responsible administrative agency that the University engaged in a discriminatory practice requiring remedial efforts. Moreover, the operation of petitioner's special admissions program is quite different from the remedial measures approved in those cases. It prefers the designated minority groups at the expense of other individuals who are totally foreclosed from competition for the 16 special admissions seats in every medical school class. Because of that foreclosure, some individuals are excluded from enjoyment of a state-provided benefit — admission to the medical school — they otherwise would receive. When a classification denies an individual opportunities or benefits enjoyed by others solely because of his race or ethnic background, it must be regarded as suspect. . . .

We have held that in "order to justify the use of a suspect classification, a State must show that its purpose or interest is both constitutionally permissible and substantial, and that its use of the classification is 'necessary . . . to the accomplishment' of its purpose or the safeguarding of its interest." . . . The special admissions program purports to serve the purposes of: (i) "reducing the historic deficit of traditionally disfavored minorities in medical schools and the medical profession," Brief for Petitioner 32; (ii) countering the effects of societal discrimination; (iii) increasing the number of physicians who will practice in communities currently underserved; and (iv) obtaining the educational benefits that flow from an ethnically diverse student body. It is necessary to decide which, if any, of these purposes is substantial enough to support the use of a suspect classification.

If petitioner's purpose is to assure within its student body some specified percentage of a particular group merely because of its race or ethnic origin, such a preferential purpose must be rejected not as insubstantial but as facially invalid. Preferring members of any one group for no reason other than race or ethnic origin is discrimination for its own sake. This the Constitution forbids. . . .

The State certainly has a legitimate and substantial interest in ameliorating, or eliminating where feasible, the disabling effects of identified discrimination. The line of school desegregation cases, commencing with *Brown,* attests to the importance of this state goal and the commitment of the judiciary to affirm all lawful means towards its attainment. In the school cases, the States were required by court order to redress the wrongs worked by specific instances of racial discrimination. That goal was far more focused than the remedying of the effects of "societal discrimination," an amorphous concept of injury that may be ageless in its reach into the past.

We have never approved a classification that aids persons perceived as members of relatively victimized groups at the expense of other innocent individuals in the absence of judicial, legislative, or administrative findings of constitutional or statutory violations. . . . After such findings have been made, the governmental interest in preferring members of the injured groups at the expense of others is substantial, since the legal rights of the victims must be vindicated. In such a case, the extent of the injury and the consequent remedy will have been judicially, legislatively, or administratively defined. Also, the remedial action usually remains subject to continuing oversight to assure that it will work the least harm possible to other innocent persons competing for the benefit. Without such findings of constitutional or statutory violations, it cannot be said that the government has any greater interest in helping one individual than in refraining from harming another. Thus, the government has no compelling justification for inflicting such harm.

Petitioner does not purport to have made, and is in no position to make, such findings. Its broad mission is education, not the formulation of any legislative policy or the adjudication of particular claims of illegality. For reasons similar to those stated in Part III of this opinion, isolated segments of our vast governmental structures are not competent to make those decisions, at least in the absence of legislative mandates and legislatively determined criteria. . . . Before relying upon these sorts of findings in establishing a racial classification, a governmental body must have the authority and capability to establish, in the record, that the classification is responsive to identified discrimination. . . . Lacking this capability, petitioner has not carried its burden of justification on this issue.

Hence, the purpose of helping certain groups whom the faculty of the Davis Medical School perceived as victims of "societal discrimination" does not justify a classification that imposes disadvantages upon persons like respondent, who bear no responsibility for whatever harm the beneficiaries of the special admissions program are thought to have suffered. To hold otherwise would be to convert a remedy heretofore reserved for violations of legal rights into a privilege that all institutions throughout the Nation could grant at their pleasure to whatever groups are perceived as victims of societal discrimination. That is a step we have never approved. Cf. *Pasadena City Board of Education v. Spangler,* 427 U.S. 424 (1976).

Petitioner identifies, as another purpose of its program, improving the delivery of health care services to communities currently underserved. It may be assumed that in some situations a State's interest in facilitating the health care of its citizens is sufficiently compelling to support the use of a suspect classification. But there is virtually no evidence in the record indicating that petitioner's special admissions program is either needed or geared to promote that goal. The court below addressed this failure of proof:

"The University concedes it cannot assure that minority doctors who entered under the program, all of whom express an 'interest' in participating in a disadvantaged community, will actually do so. It may be correct to assume that some of them will carry out this intention, and that it is more likely they will practice in minority communities than the average white doctor. . . . Nevertheless, there are more precise and reliable ways to identify applicants who are genuinely interested in the medical problems of minorities than by race. An applicant of whatever race who has demonstrated his concern for disadvantaged minorities in the past and who declares that practice in such a community is his primary professional goal would be more likely to contribute to alleviation of the medical shortage than one who is chosen entirely on the basis of race and disadvantage. In short, there is [sic] no empirical data to demonstrate that any one race is more selflessly socially oriented or by contrast that another is more selfishly acquisitive." 18 Cal. 3d, at 56, 553 P. 2d, at 1167.

Petitioner simply has not carried its burden of demonstrating that it must prefer members of particular ethnic groups over all other individuals in order to promote better health care delivery to deprived citizens. Indeed, petitioner has not shown that its preferential classification is likely to have any significant effect on the problem.

The fourth goal asserted by petitioner is the attainment of a diverse student body. This clearly is a constitutionally permissible goal for an institution of higher education. Academic freedom, though not a specifically enumerated constitutional right, long has been viewed as a special concern of the First Amendment. The freedom of a university to make its own judgments as to education includes the selection of its student body. Mr. Justice Frankfurter summarized the "four essential freedoms" that comprise academic freedom:

"'. . . . It is the business of a university to provide that atmosphere which is most conducive to speculation, experiment and creation. It is an atmosphere in which there prevail "the four essential freedoms" of a university — to determine for itself on academic grounds who may teach, what may be taught, how it shall be taught, and who may be admitted to study.'" *Sweezy* v. *New Hampshire*, 354 U.S. 234, 263 (1957) (Frankfurter, J., concurring).

Our national commitment to the safeguarding of these freedoms within university communities was emphasized in *Keyishian* v. *Board of Regents*, 385 U.S. 589, 603 (1967):

"Our Nation is deeply committed to safeguarding academic freedom which is of transcendent value to all of us and not merely to the teachers concerned. That freedom is therefore a special concern of the First Amendment. . . . The Nation's future depends upon leaders trained through wide exposure to that robust exchange of ideas which discovers truth 'out of a multitude of tongues, rather than through any kind of authoritative selection. . . .'"

The atmosphere of "speculation, experiment and creation" — so essential to the quality of higher education — is widely believed to be promoted by a diverse student body. As the Court noted in *Keyishian*, it is not too much to say that the "nation's future depends upon leaders trained through wide exposure" to the ideas and mores of students as diverse as this Nation of many peoples.

Thus, in arguing that its universities must be accorded the right to select those students who will contribute the most to the "robust exchange of ideas," petitioner invokes a countervailing constitutional interest, that of the First Amendment. In this light, petitioner must be viewed as seeking to achieve a goal that is of paramount importance in the fulfillment of its mission.

It may be argued that there is greater force to these views at the undergraduate level than in a medical school where the training is centered primarily on professional competency. But even at the graduate level, our tradition and experience lend support to the view that the contribution of diversity is substantial. In *Sweatt* v. *Painter*, 339 U.S. 629, 634 (1950), the Court made a similar point with specific reference to legal education:

> "The law school, the proving ground for legal learning and practice, cannot be effective in isolation from the individuals and institutions with which the law interacts. Few students and no one who has practiced law would choose to study in an academic vacuum, removed from the interplay of ideas and the exchange of views with which the law is concerned."

Physicians serve a heterogenous population. An otherwise qualified medical student with a particular background — whether it be ethnic, geographic, culturally advantaged or disadvantaged — may bring to a professional school of medicine experiences, outlooks and ideas that enrich the training of its student body and better equip its graduates to render with understanding their vital service to humanity.

Ethnic diversity, however, is only one element in a range of factors a university properly may consider in attaining the goal of a heterogeneous student body. Although a university must have wide discretion in making the sensitive judgments as to who should be admitted, constitutional limitations protecting individual rights may not be disregarded. Respondent urges — and the courts below have held — that petitioner's dual admissions program is a racial classification that impermissibly infringes his rights under the Fourteenth Amendment. As the interest of diversity is compelling in the context of a university's admissions program, the question remains whether the program's racial classification is necessary to promote this interest. *In re Griffiths*, 413 U.S. 717, at 721-722 (1973).

It may be assumed that the reservation of a specified number of seats in each class for individuals from the preferred ethnic groups would contribute to the attainment of considerable ethnic diversity in the student body. But petitioner's argument that this is the only effective means of serving the interest of diversity is seriously flawed. In a most fundamental sense the argument misconceives the nature of the state interest that would justify consideration of race or ethnic background. It is not an interest in simple ethnic diversity, in which a specified percentage of the student body is in effect guaranteed to be members of selected ethnic groups, with the remaining percentage an undifferentiated aggregation of students. The diversity that furthers a compelling state interest encompasses a far broader array of qualifications and characteristics of which racial or ethnic origin is but a single though important element. Petitioner's special admissions program, focused *solely* on ethnic diversity, would hinder rather than further attainment of genuine diversity.

Nor would the state interest in genuine diversity be served by expanding petitioner's two-track system into a multitrack program with a prescribed number of seats set aside for each identifiable category of applicants. Indeed, it is inconceivable that a university would thus pursue the logic of petitioner's two-track program to the illogical end of insulating each category of applicants with certain desired qualifications from competition with all other applicants.

In summary, it is evident that the Davis special admission program involves the use of an explicit racial classification never before countenanced by this

Court. It tells applicants who are not Negro, Asian, or "Chicano" that they are totally excluded from a specific percentage of the seats in an entering class. No matter how strong their qualifications, quantitative and extracurricular, including their own potential for contribution to educational diversity, they are never afforded the chance to compete with applicants from the preferred groups for the special admission seats. At the same time, the preferred applicants have the opportunity to compete for every seat in the class.

The fatal flaw in petitioner's preferential program is its disregard of individual rights as guaranteed by the Fourteenth Amendment. *Shelley* v. *Kraemer,* 334 U.S. 1, 22 (1948). Such rights are not absolute. But when a State's distribution of benefits or imposition of burdens hinges on the color of a person's skin or ancestry, that individual is entitled to a demonstration that the challenged classification is necessary to promote a substantial state interest. Petitioner has failed to carry this burden. For this reason, that portion of the California court's judgment holding petitioner's special admissions program invalid under the Fourteenth Amendment must be affirmed.

In enjoining petitioner from ever considering the race of any applicant, however, the courts below failed to recognize that the State has a substantial interest that legitimately may be served by a properly devised admissions program involving the competitive consideration of race and ethnic origin. For this reason, so much of the California court's judgment as enjoins petitioner from any consideration of the race of any applicant must be reversed.

With respect to respondent's entitlement to an injunction directing his admission to the Medical School, petitioner has conceded that it could not carry its burden of proving that, but for the existence of its unlawful special admissions program, respondent still would not have been admitted. Hence, respondent is entitled to the injunction, and that portion of the judgment must be affirmed.

4

PUBLIC ACCOMMODATIONS

In the historic 1964 Civil Rights Act, Congress moved to ban racial discrimination in public accommodations on a nationwide basis. It did so, at long last, in response to the vast and sustained public outcry for change occasioned in great measure by the black civil rights movement beginning in the late 1950s. What culminated in 1964 had its roots in the Montgomery, Alabama bus boycott and the sit-ins in restaurants, libraries, beaches, and other public places that had punctuated an almost decade-long demand by black people and their supporters for equal treatment. Congress used the equal protection clause of the Fourteenth Amendment and the commerce power as the constitutional foundations to bring about an end to racial segregation in public accommodations.

Two key cases, *Heart of Atlanta Motel* v. *United States* and *Katzenbach* v. *McClung* sustained the constitutionality of the 1964 statute. In both, the Supreme Court ruled that the power Congress has to regulate interstate commerce was sufficient by itself to support the statute.

Heart of Atlanta Motel v. United States, 379 U.S. 241 (1964)

Congress applied the 1964 statute to three types of businesses. One group included inns, hotels, and motels; another restaurants and cafeterias; and the last theaters and motion picture houses, if these businesses "affected commerce." In the *Atlanta* case, the appellant owned a large motel that had restricted its clientele to white people only. Evidence indicated some three fourths of its customers were transient interstate travellers. For this reason the case turned on whether the Congressional commerce power was broad enough to cover banning racial discrimination in such business establishments. A unanimous Supreme Court ruled that it was.

Mr. Justice Clark delivered the opinion of the Court, saying in part:

We shall not burden this opinion with further details since the voluminous testimony presents overwhelming evidence that discrimination by hotels and motels impedes interstate travel.

The power of Congress to deal with these obstructions depends on the meaning of the Commerce Clause. Its meaning was first enunciated 140 years ago by the great Chief Justice John Marshall in *Gibbons* v. *Ogden,* 9 Wheat. 1 (1824), in these words:

> "The subject to be regulated is commerce; and . . . to ascertain the extent of the power, it becomes necessary to settle the meaning of the word. The counsel for the appellee would limit it to traffic, to buying and selling, or the interchange of commodities . . . but it is something more: it is intercourse . . . between nations, and parts of nations, in all its branches, and is regulated by prescribing rules for carrying on that intercourse." . . .

It is said that the operation of the motel here is of a purely local character. But, assuming this to be true, "[i]f it is interstate commerce that feels the pinch, it does not matter how local the operation which applies the squeeze." . . . As Chief Justice Stone put it in *United States* v. *Darby, supra:*

> "The power of Congress over interstate commerce is not confined to the regulation of commerce among the states. It extends to those activities intrastate which so affect interstate commerce or the exercise of the power of Congress over it as to make regulation of them appropriate means to the attainment of a legitimate end, the exercise of the granted power of Congress to regulate interstate commerce." . . .

Thus the power of Congress to promote interstate commerce also includes the power to regulate the local incidents thereof, including local activities in both the States of origin and destination, which might have a substantial and harmful effect upon that commerce. One need only examine the evidence which we have discussed above to see that Congress may — as it has — prohibit racial discrimination by motels serving travelers, however "local" their operations may appear.

Nor does the Act deprive appellant of liberty or property under the Fifth Amendment. The commerce power invoked here by the Congress is a specific and plenary one authorized by the Constitution itself. The only questions are: (1) whether Congress had a rational basis for finding that racial discrimination by motels affected commerce, and (2) if it had such a basis, whether the means it selected to eliminate that evil are reasonable and appropriate. If they are, appellant has no "right" to select its guests as it sees fit, free from governmental regulation.

There is nothing novel about such legislation. Thirty-two States now have it on their books either by statute or executive order and many cities provide such regulation. Some of these Acts go back fourscore years. It has been repeatedly held by this Court that such laws do not violate the Due Process Clause of the Fourteenth Amendment. Perhaps the first such holding was in the *Civil Rights Cases* themselves, where Mr. Justice Bradley for the Court inferentially found that innkeepers, "by the laws of all the States, so far as we are aware, are bound, to the extent of their facilities, to furnish proper accommodation to all unobjectionable persons who in good faith apply for them." . . .

We, therefore, conclude that the action of the Congress in the adoption of the Act as applied here to a motel which concededly serves interstate travelers is within the power granted it by the Commerce Clause of the Constitution, as interpreted by this Court for 140 years. It may be argued that Congress could have pursued other methods to eliminate the obstructions it found in interstate commerce caused by racial discrimination. But this is a matter of policy that rests entirely with the Congress not with the courts. How obstructions in commerce may be removed — what means are to be employed — is within the sound and exclusive discretion of the Congress. It is subject only to one caveat — that the means chosen by it must be reasonably adapted to the end permitted by the Constitution. We cannot say that its choice here was not so adapted. The Constitution requires no more.

Katzenbach v. McClung, 379 U.S. 297 (1964)

In a companion case to *Heart of Atlanta Motel, Katzenbach* v. *McClung,* decided on the same day, December 14, 1964, the Supreme Court was called upon to determine if the Congressional Commerce power, and therefore the Civil Rights Act of 1964, stretched to cover a small family-owned barbeque restaurant in Birmingham, Alabama. The restaurant in question catered only to white customers on a sit-down basis and had take-out services only for black customers. A three-judge District Court had ruled that "there was [no] demonstrable connection" between food purchased in interstate commerce and sold to local customers only. It decided, therefore, that Congress had exceeded its authority to regulate such business under its commerce power. The Warren Court reversed the lower court ruling. It concluded that Congress had "ample power" under the Commerce clause to extend coverage of the 1964 Civil Rights Act to abolish racial discrimination in restaurants that served food, a substantial portion of which moved in interstate commerce. As it had been in *Heart of Atlanta,* once again the Court was unanimous.

Mr. Justice Clark delivered the opinion of the Court, saying in part:

[T]here was an impressive array of testimony that discrimination in restaurants had a direct and highly restrictive effect upon interstate travel by Negroes. This resulted, it was said, because discriminatory practices prevent Negroes from buying prepared food served on the premises while on a trip, except in isolated and unkempt restaurants and under most unsatisfactory and often unpleasant conditions. This obviously discourages travel and obstructs interstate commerce for one can hardly travel without eating. Likewise, it was said, that discrimination deterred professional, as well as skilled, people from moving into areas where such practices occurred and thereby caused industry to be reluctant to establish there. . . .

We believe that this testimony afforded ample basis for the conclusion that established restaurants in such areas sold less interstate goods because of the discrimination, that interstate travel was obstructed directly by it, that business in general suffered and that many new businesses refrained from establishing there as a result of it. Hence the District Court was in error in concluding that there was no connection between discrimination and the movement of interstate commerce. The court's conclusion that such a connection is outside "common experience" flies in the face of stubborn fact. . . .

This Court has held time and again that this power extends to activities of retail establishments, including restaurants, which directly or indirectly burden or obstruct interstate commerce. We have detailed the cases in *Heart of Atlanta Motel,* and will not repeat them here. . . .

. . . Congress has determined for itself that refusals of service to Negroes have imposed burdens both upon the interstate flow of food and upon the movement of products generally. Of course, the mere fact that Congress has said when particular activity shall be deemed to affect commerce does not preclude further examination by this Court. But where we find that the legislators, in light of the facts and testimony before them, have a rational basis for finding a chosen regulatory scheme necessary to the protection of commerce, our investigation is at an end. The only remaining question — one answered in the affirmative by the court below — is whether the particular restaurant either serves or offers to serve interstate travelers or serves food a substantial portion of which has moved in interstate commerce. . . .

Confronted as we are with the facts laid before Congress, we must conclude that it had a rational basis for finding that racial discrimination in restaurants had a direct and adverse effect on the free flow of interstate commerce. Insofar as the sections of the Act here relevant are concerned, §§201 (b) (2) and (c), Congress prohibited discrimination only in those establishments having a close tie to interstate commerce, *i.e.,* those, like the McClungs', serving food that has come from out of the State. We think in so doing that Congress acted well within its power to protect and foster commerce in extending the coverage of Title II only to those restaurants offering to serve interstate travelers or serving food, a substantial portion of which has moved in interstate commerce.

The absence of direct evidence connecting discriminatory restaurant service with the flow of interstate food, a factor on which the appellees place much reliance, is not, given the evidence as to the effect of such practices on other aspects of commerce, a crucial matter.

The power of Congress in this field is broad and sweeping; where it keeps within its sphere and violates no express constitutional limitation it has been the rule of this Court, going back almost to the founding days of the Republic, not to interfere. The Civil Rights Act of 1964, as here applied, we find to be plainly appropriate in the resolution of what the Congress found to be a national commercial problem of the first magnitude. We find it in no violation of any express limitations of the Constitution and we therefore declare it valid.

5

HOUSING

The history of the Fourteenth Amendment's equal protection clause clearly indicates that among the rights included in "equal protection" was the right to buy or dispose of real property. After the turn of the century, attempts were made in a number of southern cities to thwart exercise of this right by black citizens by adopting municipal ordinances sanctioning racial segregation in housing.

One such ordinance, in Louisville, was the issue in *Buchanan* v. *Warley.*[1] There the Supreme Court ruled the local segregation ordinance unconstitutional on grounds that it violated the property rights of owners to sell or rent real estate to whomever they wished.

With municipal ordinances thus removed as bastions of racially segregated housing a second "protective" device soon began to spring up; the restrictive covenant, a clause in a real estate contract obliging property owners not to sell, rent or lease real property to blacks or other national or religious groups. Because restrictive covenants were considered "private action" and not "state action" at first they successfully passed the constitutional test.

Shelley v. Kraemer, 334 U.S. 1 (1948)

The first "covenant" ruling was *Corrigan* v. *Buckley.*[2] There the Supreme Court dismissed the case on grounds that it lacked jurisdiction to rule in what it concluded was essentially a "private" matter. Nevertheless, speaking for the Court, Justice Sanford took pains to note that private restrictive covenants did *not* violate either the Constitution or public policy.

There the matter stood until *Shelley* v. *Kraemer,* one of two significant housing discrimination cases. In *Shelley* the Supreme Court had to decide whether restrictive covenants were legally enforceable by state action. Although the Court did not specifically declare restrictive covenants unconstitutional as many liberal observers had hoped, it *did* rule that they *were* legally unenforceable. The Court's reasoning in *Shelley* v. *Kraemer* soon led to still another question; could someone who had signed a restrictive covenant and then breached its provisions be sued for damages by other signers of the covenant?

1. 245 U.S. 60 (1917)
2. 271 U.S. 323 (1926).

Five years after *Shelley,* the Supreme Court confronted this issue in *Barrows* v. *Jackson.*[3] There a California property owner who had broken the provisions of his restrictive covenant by selling his home to a black family was sued by neighbors in the housing subdivision who argued that their property values had been diminished once blacks moved into the neighborhood. In line with its reasoning in *Shelley,* the Supreme Court decided it could *not* permit California to order a property owner to pay damages for violating a covenant that states did not have the power to enforce and that, as *Shelley* ruled, federal courts could not enforce because restrictive covenants were contrary to public policy.

Thus, with respect to the use of restrictive covenants as a device to achieve racially segregated housing, *Shelley* v. *Kraemer* is the key decision. The Supreme Court decided that states did not have the judicial authority to enforce such "private agreements," which denied black citizens equal protection of the law. Restricted covenants, the Court said, were a violation of the Fourteenth Amendment.

Chief Justice Vinson delivered the opinion of a unanimous Court, saying in part:

> Whether the equal protection clause of the Fourteenth Amendment inhibits judicial enforcement by state courts of restrictive covenants based on race or color is a question which this Court has not heretofore been called upon to consider. Only two cases have been decided by this Court which in any way have involved the enforcement of such agreements. The first of these was the case of *Corrigan* v. *Buckley,* 271 U.S. 323 (1926). There, suit was brought in the courts of the District of Columbia to enjoin a threatened violation of certain restrictive covenants relating to lands situated in the city of Washington. Relief was granted, and the case was brought here on appeal. It is apparent that that case, which had originated in the federal courts and involved the enforcement of covenants on land located in the District of Columbia, could present no issues under the Fourteenth Amendment; for that Amendment by its terms applies only to the States. Nor was the question of the validity of court enforcement of the restrictive covenants under the Fifth Amendment properly before the Court, as the opinion of this Court specifically recognizes. The only constitutional issue which the appellants had raised in the lower courts, and hence the only constitutional issue before this Court on appeal, was the validity of the covenant agreements as such. This Court concluded that since the inhibitions of the constitutional provisions invoked apply only to governmental action, as contrasted to action of private individuals, there was no showing that the covenants, which were simply agreements between private property owners, were invalid. Accordingly, the appeal was dismissed for want of a substantial question. Nothing in the opinion of this Court, therefore, may properly be regarded as an adjudication on the merits of the constitutional issues presented by these cases, which raise the question of the validity, not of the private agreements as such, but of the judicial enforcement of those agreements. . . .
>
> It is well, at the outset, to scrutinize the terms of the restrictive agreements involved in these cases. In the Missouri case, the covenant declares that no part of the affected property shall be "occupied by any person not of the Caucasian race, it being intended hereby to restrict the use of said property . . . against the occupancy as owners or tenants of any portion of said property for resident or other purpose by people of the Negro or Mongolian Race." Not only does the

3. 346 U.S. 249 (1953).

restriction seek to proscribe use and occupancy of the affected properties by members of the excluded class, but as construed by the Missouri courts, the agreement requires that title of any person who uses his property in violation of the restriction shall be divested. The restriction of the covenant in the Michigan case seeks to bar occupancy by persons of the excluded class. It provides that "This property shall not be used or occupied by any person or persons except those of the Caucasian race."

It should be observed that these covenants do not seek to proscribe any particular use of the affected properties. Use of the properties for residential occupancy, as such, is not forbidden. The restrictions of these agreements, rather, are directed toward a designated class of persons and seek to determine who may and who may not own or make use of the properties for residential purposes. The excluded class is defined wholly in terms of race or color; "simply that and nothing more."

It cannot be doubted that among the civil rights intended to be protected from discriminatory state action by the Fourteenth Amendment are the rights to acquire, enjoy, own and dispose of property. Equality in the enjoyment of property rights was regarded by the framers of that Amendment as an essential pre-condition to the realization of other basic civil rights and liberties which the Amendment was intended to guarantee. Thus, §1978 of the Revised Statutes, derived from §1 of the Civil Rights Act of 1866 which was enacted by Congress while the Fourteenth Amendment was also under consideration, provides:

> "All citizens of the United States shall have the same right, in every State and Territory, as is enjoyed by white citizens thereof to inherit, purchase, lease, sell, hold, and convey real and personal property."

This Court has given specific recognition to the same principle. . . .

It is likewise clear that restrictions on the right of occupancy of the sort sought to be created by the private agreements in these cases could not be squared with the requirements of the Fourteenth Amendment if imposed by state statute or local ordinance. . . .

We have no doubt that there has been state action in these cases in the full and complete sense of the phrase. The undisputed facts disclose that petitioners were willing purchasers of properties upon which they desired to establish homes. The owners of the properties were willing sellers; and contracts of sale were accordingly consummated. It is clear that but for the active intervention of the state courts, supported by the full panoply of state power, petitioners would have been free to occupy the properties in question without restraint.

These are not cases, as has been suggested, in which the States have merely abstained from action, leaving private individuals free to impose such discriminations as they see fit. Rather, these are cases in which the States have made available to such individuals the full coercive power of government to deny to petitioners, on the grounds of race or color, the enjoyment of property rights in premises which petitioners are willing and financially able to acquire and which the grantors are willing to sell. The difference between judicial enforcement and nonenforcement of the restrictive covenants is the difference to petitioners between being denied rights of property available to other members of the community and being accorded full enjoyment of those rights on an equal footing.

The enforcement of the restrictive agreements by the state courts in these cases was directed pursuant to the common-law policy of the States as formulated by those courts in earlier decisions. In the Missouri case, enforcement of the covenant was directed in the first instance by the highest court of the State after the trial court had determined the agreement to be invalid for want of the requisite number of signatures. In the Michigan case, the order of enforcement by the trial court was affirmed by the highest state court. The judicial action in each case bears the clear and unmistakable imprimatur of the State. We have noted that previous decisions of this Court have established the proposition that judicial action is not immunized from the operation of the Fourteenth Amendment simply because it is taken pursuant to the state's common-law policy. Nor is the Amendment ineffective simply because the particular pattern of discrimination, which the State has enforced, was defined initially by the terms of a private agreement. State action, as that phrase is understood for the purposes of the Fourteenth Amendment, refers to exertions of state power in all forms. And when the effect of that action is to deny rights subject to the protection of the Fourteenth Amendment, it is the obligation of this Court to enforce the constitutional commands.

We hold that in granting judicial enforcement of the restrictive agreements in these cases, the States have denied petitioners the equal protection of the laws and that, therefore, the action of the state courts cannot stand.

Jones v. Alfred H. Mayer Co., 392 U.S. 409 (1968)

In 1968 Congress passed a civil rights law that for the first time included a sweeping "open housing" provision making illegal a wide variety of private racially discriminatory housing practices. This law, coupled with the Supreme Court's 1968 decision in *Jones* v. *Alfred H. Mayer Co.*, seemed to sound the death knell, at least for officially sanctioned de jure racial segregation in housing. De facto segregation remains a major problem.

Surprisingly, in *Jones* the Court did not use the 1968 statute as the basis for its decision. Instead it relied on provisions of the century-old Civil Rights Act of 1866. It did so over the objections of Justices Harlan and White who, dissenting, insisted the Court should have used the fair housing provisions of the 1968 statute rather than the older law. However, the majority interpreted the 1866 law liberally and decided that it applied to "every racially motivated refusal by property owners to rent or sell." It ruled that the 1866 statute gave black citizens identical rights as white citizens "to inherit, purchase, lease, sell, and convey real and personal property."

Justice Stewart, who spoke for the Court's majority of seven, also used a broad interpretation of the Thirteenth Amendment, which, he noted, not only outlawed slavery but "the badges and the incidents of slavery" as well. Among the "badges and incidents," Stewart concluded, was racial discrimination in access to housing. The Court decided, therefore, that the Thirteenth Amendment authorized Congress to do more than merely dissolve the legal bonds of slavery. It gave Congress the power to determine what "the badges and incidents of slavery" were and additional power to translate that determination into effective legislation. For this reason, the Court went on to say, in 1866 Congress had authority under the Thirteenth Amendment to guarantee and secure for black citizens "those fundamental rights which are the essence of civil freedom, namely, the right to inherit, purchase, lease, sell, and convey real property."

Mr. Justice Stewart delivered the majority opinion of the Court, saying in part:

At the outset, it is important to make clear precisely what this case does *not* involve. Whatever else it may be, 42 U.S.C. §1982 [of 1866] is not a comprehensive open housing law. In sharp contrast to the Fair Housing Title (Title VIII) of the Civil Rights Act of 1968, . . . the statute in this case deals only with racial discrimination and does not address itself to discrimination on grounds of religion or national origin. It does not deal specifically with discrimination in the provision of services or facilities in connection with the sale or rental of a dwelling. It does not prohibit advertising or other representations that indicate discriminatory preferences. It does not refer explicitly to discrimination in financing arrangements or in the provision of brokerage services. It does not empower a federal administrative agency to assist aggrieved parties. It makes no provision for intervention by the Attorney General. And, although it can be enforced by injunction, it contains no provision expressly authorizing a federal court to order the payment of damages.

Thus, although §1982 contains none of the exemptions that Congress included in the Civil Rights Act of 1968, it would be a serious mistake to suppose that §1982 in any way diminishes the significance of the law recently enacted by Congress. . . .

We begin with the language of the statute itself. In plain and unambiguous terms, §1982 grants to all citizens, without regard to race or color, "the same right" to purchase and lease property "as is enjoyed by white citizens." . . .

On its face, therefore, §1982 appears to prohibit *all* discrimination against Negroes in the sale or rental of property — discrimination by private owners as well as discrimination by public authorities. Indeed, even the respondents seem to concede that, if §1982 "means what it says" — to use the words of the respondents' brief — then it must encompass every racially motivated refusal to sell or rent and cannot be confined to officially sanctioned segregation in housing. Stressing what they consider to be the revolutionary implications of so literal a reading of §1982, the respondents argue that Congress cannot possibly have intended any such result. Our examination of the relevant history, however, persuades us that Congress meant exactly what it said. . . . Hence the structure of the 1866 Act, as well as its language, points to the conclusion urged by the petitioners in this case — that §1 was meant to prohibit *all* racially motivated deprivations of the rights enumerated in the statute, although only those deprivations perpetrated "under color of law" were to be criminally punishable under §2.

In attempting to demonstrate the contrary, the respondents rely heavily upon the fact that the Congress which approved the 1866 statute wished to eradicate the recently enacted Black Codes — laws which had saddled Negroes with "onerous disabilities and burdens, and curtailed their rights . . . to such an extent that their freedom was of little value. . . ." . . . The respondents suggest that the only evil Congress sought to eliminate was that of racially discriminatory laws in the former Confederate States. But the Civil Rights Act was drafted to apply throughout the country, and its language was far broader than would have been necessary to strike down discriminatory statutes.

That broad language, we are asked to believe, was a mere slip of the legislative pen. We disagree. For the same Congress that wanted to do away with the Black Codes *also* had before it an imposing body of evidence pointing to the mistreatment of Negroes by private individuals and unofficial groups, mistreatment unrelated to any hostile state legislation. "Accounts in newspapers North and South, Freedmen's Bureau and other official documents, private reports and correspondence were all adduced" to show that "private outrage and atrocity" were "daily inflicted on freedmen. . . ." The congressional debates are replete with references to private injustices against Negroes — references to white employers who refused to pay their Negro workers, white planters who agreed among themselves not to hire freed slaves without the permission of their former masters, white citizens who assaulted Negroes or who combined to drive them out of their communities. . . .

The remaining question is whether Congress has power under the Constitution to do what §1982 purports to do: to prohibit all racial discrimination, private and public, in the sale and rental of property. Our starting point is the Thirteenth Amendment, for it was pursuant to that constitutional provision that Congress originally enacted what is now §1982. . . .

Those who opposed passage of the Civil Rights Act of 1866 argued in effect that the Thirteenth Amendment merely authorized Congress to dissolve the legal bond by which the Negro slave was held to his master. Yet many had earlier opposed the Thirteenth Amendment on the very ground that it would give Congress virtually unlimited power to enact laws for the protection of Negroes in every State. And the majority leaders in Congress — who were, after all, the authors of the Thirteenth Amendment — had no doubt that its Enabling Clause contemplated the sort of positive legislation that was embodied in the 1866 Civil Rights Act. Their chief spokesman, Senator Trumbull of Illinois, the Chairman of the Judiciary Committee, had brought the Thirteenth Amendment to the floor of the Senate in 1864. In defending the constitutionality of the 1866 Act, he argued that, if the narrower construction of the Enabling Clause were correct, then

> "the trumpet of freedom that we have been blowing throughout the land has given an 'uncertain sound,' and the promised freedom is a delusion. Such was not the intention of Congress, which proposed the constitutional amendment, nor is such the fair meaning of the amendment itself. . . . I have no doubt that under this provision . . . we may destroy all these discriminations in civil rights against the black man; and if we cannot, our constitutional amendment amounts to nothing. It was for that purpose that the second clause of that amendment was adopted, which says that Congress shall have authority, by appropriate legislation, to carry into effect the article prohibiting slavery. Who is to decide what that appropriate legislation is to be? The Congress of the United States; and it is for Congress to adopt such appropriate legislation as it may think proper, so that it be a means to accomplish the end."

Surely Senator Trumbull was right. Surely Congress has the power under the Thirteenth Amendment rationally to determine what are the badges and the incidents of slavery, and the authority to translate that determination into effective legislation. Nor can we say that the determination Congress has made is an irrational one. For this Court recognized long ago that, whatever else they may have encompassed, the badges and incidents of slavery — its "burdens and disabilities" — included restraints upon "those fundamental rights which are the essence of civil freedom, namely, the same right . . . to inherit, purchase, lease, sell and convey property, as is enjoyed by white citizens."

6

VOTING RIGHTS

In addition to poll taxes, unfairly administered literacy tests, and grandfather clauses, another legal or extralegal device used successfully in the past by several southern states to disenfranchise black voters was the so-called "all-white" primary. Because of the near monopoly enjoyed by the Democratic party in the South, the party's primary election was often the critical portion of the elective process, where, in the absence of effective Republican opposition in the November general election, the ultimate victor was chosen. For this reason the southern "all-white" primary denied black voters any meaningful participation in the political process. Those who made the effort could vote in the "no contest" general elections but not in the Democratic primaries where the real choices were made.

United States v. Classic, 313 U.S. 299 (1941)

An early Supreme Court decision, dealing with primary elections, was quickly interpreted in several southern states to encourage further discrimination against the voting rights of black people. In *Newberry v. United States*[1] the Court ruled, in a case involving the Corrupt Practices Act of 1910, that a primary election was *not* part of the election process that fell under the Congressional power to regulate. Southern states interpreted *Newberry* to conclude that primaries were outside the regulatory scope of the Federal Constitution. Accordingly, they began devising a set of rules and regulations to exclude blacks from voting in them. In 1923, for example, Texas simply banned blacks from voting in the Democratic primary by statute. When in *Nixon v. Herndon*[2] the Supreme Court declared the practice a violation of equal protection, Texas took another step and allowed the executive committee of the state party to determine who could vote in its primaries. The purpose was the same; to preserve the all-white Democratic primary. Again the Supreme

1. 256 U.S. 232 (1921).
2. 273 U.S. 536 (1927).

Court struck down this Texas innovation, this time in *Nixon v. Condon*,[3] as a violation of equal protection. Texas went one step further. Acting independently of the state legislature, the Texas Democratic party made membership in the party, and therefore eligibility to vote in the party primary, open to white persons only.

In a decision especially difficult to comprehend the 1935 Supreme Court ruled unanimously, in *Grovey v. Townsend*[4] that this action by the Texas Democratic Party did *not* violate equal protection under the Fourteenth Amendment because, in its judgment, what was involved in *Grovey* was "private" not "state" action. In effect the Supreme Court was saying that political parties, in particular the Democratic party in the South, were "private clubs" free to restrict their memberships as they saw fit without constitutional limitations. The Court also seemed to be saying, foolishly, that primary elections were not part of the election process protected by the Constitution. There the matter stood until *United States v. Classic*. In *Classic* the Supreme Court acknowledged for the first time that "the primary . . . is an integral part" of the election procedure.

Although *Classic* did not specifically overturn *Grovey v. Townsend*, and, therefore, did little to effect the all-white primary, it was an important step away from the "private club" concept held by segments of the Democratic party in the South. It is significant for this reason.

Mr. Justice Stone delivered the opinion of the Court, saying in part:

> The primary in Louisiana is an integral part of the procedure for the popular choice of Congressman. The right of qualified voters to vote at the Congressional primary in Louisiana and to have their ballots counted is thus the right to participate in that choice.
>
> We come then to the question whether that right is one secured by the Constitution. Section 2 of Article I commands that Congressmen shall be chosen by the people of the several states by electors, the qualifications of which it prescribes. The right of the people to choose, whatever its appropriate constitutional limitations, where in other respects it is defined, and the mode of its exercise is prescribed by state action in conformity to the Constitution, is a right established and guaranteed by the Constitution and hence is one secured by it to those citizens and inhabitants of the state entitled to exercise the right. . . .
>
> That the free choice by the people of representatives in Congress, subject only to the restrictions to be found in §§2 and 4 of Article I and elsewhere in the Constitution, was one of the great purposes of our constitutional scheme of government cannot be doubted. We cannot regard it as any the less the constitutional purpose, or its words as any the less guarantying the integrity of that choice, when a state, exercising its privilege in the absence of Congressional action, changes the mode of choice from a single step, a general election, to two, of which the first is the choice at a primary of those candidates from whom, as a second step, the representative in Congress is to be chosen at the election.
>
> Nor can we say that that choice which the Constitution protects is restricted to the second step because §4 of Article I, as a means of securing a free choice of representatives by the people, has authorized Congress to regulate the manner of elections, without making any mention of primary elections. For we think that the authority of Congress, given by §4, includes the authority to regulate primary elections when, as in this case, they are a step in the exercise by the people of their choice of representatives in Congress.

3. 286 U.S. 73 (1932).

4. 295 U.S. 45 (1935).

Smith v. Allwright, 321 U.S. 649 (1944)

Three years after *Classic,* the Supreme Court finally came to grips with the all-white primary. It concluded that the claim by Texas that its Democratic party was a private club not subject to regulation was an untenable travesty and a violation of the Constitution. This time the Roosevelt Court *did* specifically overrule *Grovey* v. *Townsend.* It decided that excluding black people from voting in the primary of the Texas Democratic party was, in effect, "state action" in violation of their rights under the Fifteenth Amendment. Only Justice Roberts did not go along with the majority view. He chided the Court for overruling *Grovey* and for breeding "fresh doubt and confusion in the public mind as to the stability of our institutions."

Mr. Justice Reed delivered the opinion of the Court, saying in part:

Texas is free to conduct her elections and limit her electorate as she may deem wise, save only as her action may be affected by the prohibitions of the United States Constitution or in conflict with powers delegated to and exercised by the National Government. The Fourteenth Amendment forbids a State from making or enforcing any law which abridges the privileges or immunities of citizens of the United States and the Fifteenth Amendment specifically interdicts any denial or abridgement by a State of the right of citizens to vote on account of color. Respondents appeared in the District Court and the Circuit Court of Appeals and defended on the ground that the Democratic party of Texas is a voluntary organization with members banded together for the purpose of selecting individuals of the group representing the common political beliefs as candidates in the general election. As such a voluntary organization, it was claimed, the Democratic party is free to select its own membership and limit to whites participation in the party primary. Such action, the answer asserted, does not violate the Fourteenth, Fifteenth or Seventeenth Amendment as officers of government cannot be chosen at primaries and the Amendments are applicable only to general elections where governmental officers are actually elected. Primaries, it is said, are political party affairs, handled by party, not governmental, officers. No appearance for respondents is made in this Court. Arguments presented here by the Attorney General of Texas and the Chairman of the State Democratic Executive Committee of Texas, as amici curiae, urged substantially the same grounds as those advanced by the respondents.

The right of a Negro to vote in the Texas primary has been considered heretofore by this Court. The first case was *Nixon* v. *Herndon,* 273 U.S. 536. At that time, 1924, the Texas statute . . . declared "in no event shall a Negro be eligible to participate in a Democratic Party primary election in the State of Texas." Nixon was refused the right to vote in a Democratic primary and brought a suit for damages against the election officers. . . . It was urged to this Court that the denial of the franchise to Nixon violated his Constitutional rights under the Fourteenth and Fifteenth Amendments. Without consideration of the Fifteenth, this Court held that the action of Texas in denying the ballot to Negroes by statute was in violation of the equal protection clause of the Fourteenth Amendment and reversed the dismissal of the suit.

The legislature of Texas reenacted the article but gave the State Executive Committee of a party the power to prescribe the qualifications of its members for voting or other participation. This article remains in the statutes. The State Executive Committee of the Democratic party adopted a resolution that white Democrats and none other might participate in the primaries of that party.

Nixon was refused again the privilege of voting in a primary and again brought suit for damages by virtue of §31, Title 8, U.S.C. This Court again reversed the dismissal of the suit for the reason that the Committee action was deemed to be state action and invalid as discriminatory under the Fourteenth Amendment. The test was said to be whether the Committee operated as representative of the State in the discharge of the State's authority. . . . The question of the inherent power of a political party in Texas "without restraint by any law to determine its own membership" was left open.

In *Grovey v. Townsend,* 295 U.S. 45, this Court had before it another suit for damages for the refusal in a primary of a county clerk, a Texas officer with only public functions to perform, to furnish petitioner, a Negro, an absentee ballot. The refusal was solely on the ground of race. This case differed from *Nixon v. Condon, supra,* in that a state convention of the Democratic party had passed the resolution of May 24, 1932, hereinbefore quoted. It was decided that the determination by the state convention of the membership of the Democratic party made a significant change from a determination by the Executive Committee. The former was party action, voluntary in character. The latter, as had been held in the *Condon* case, was action by authority of the State. The managers of the primary election were therefore declared not to be state officials in such sense that their action was state action. A state convention of a party was said not to be an organ of the State. This Court went on to announce that to deny a vote in a primary was a mere refusal of party membership with which "the State need have no concern," . . . while for a State to deny a vote in a general election on the ground of race or color violated the Constitution. Consequently, there was found no ground for holding that the county clerk's refusal of a ballot because of racial ineligibility for party membership denied the petitioner any right under the Fourteenth or Fifteenth Amendment.

Since *Grovey v. Townsend* and prior to the present suit, no case from Texas involving primary elections has been before this Court. We did decide, however, *United States v. Classic,* 313 U.S. 299. We there held that §4 of Article I of the Constitution authorized Congress to regulate primary as well as general elections, . . . "where the primary is by law made an integral part of the election machinery." . . . Consequently, in the *Classic* case, we upheld the applicability to frauds in a Louisiana primary of §§19 and 20 of the Criminal Code. Thereby corrupt acts of election officers were subjected to Congressional sanctions because that body had power to protect rights of federal suffrage secured by the Constitution in primary as in general elections. . . . This decision depended, too, on the determination that under the Louisiana statutes the primary was a part of the procedure for choice of federal officials. By this decision the doubt as to whether or not such primaries were a part of "elections" subject to federal control, which had remained unanswered since *Newberry v. United States,* 256 U.S. 232, was erased. The *Nixon Cases* were decided under the equal protection clause of the Fourteenth Amendment without a determination of the status of the primary as a part of the electoral process. The exclusion of Negroes from the primaries by action of the State was held invalid under that Amendment. The fusing by the *Classic* case of the primary and general elections into a single instrumentality for choice of officers has a definite bearing on the permissibility under the Constitution of excluding Negroes from primaries. This is not to say that the *Classic* case cuts directly into the rationale of *Grovey v. Townsend.* This latter case was not mentioned in the opinion. *Classic* bears upon *Grovey v. Townsend* not because exclusion of Negroes from primaries is any more or less state action by reason of the unitary character of the electoral process but because the recognition of the place of the primary in the electoral scheme makes clear that state delegation to a party of the power to fix the qualifications of primary elections is delegation of a state function that may make the party's action the action of the State. When *Grovey v. Townsend* was written, the Court looked upon the denial of a vote in a primary as a mere refusal by a party of party membership. . . . As the Louisiana statutes for holding primaries are similar to those of Texas, our ruling in *Classic* as to the unitary character of the electoral process calls for a reexamination as to whether or not the exclusion of Negroes from a Texas party primary was state action.

The statutes of Texas relating to primaries and the resolution of the Democratic party of Texas extending the privileges of membership to white citizens only are the same in substance and effect today as they were when *Grovey v. Townsend* was decided by a unanimous Court. The question as to whether the exclusionary action of the party was the action of the State persists as the determinative factor. In again entering upon consideration of the inference to be drawn as to state action from a substantially similar factual situation, it should be noted that *Grovey v. Townsend* upheld exclusion of Negroes from primaries through the denial of party membership by a party convention. A few years before, this Court refused approval of exclusion by the State Executive Committee of the party. A different result was reached on the theory that the Committee action was state authorized and the Convention action was unfettered by statutory control. Such a variation in the result from so slight a change in form influences us to consider anew the legal validity of the distinction which has resulted in barring Negroes from participating in the nominations of candidates of the Democratic party in Texas. Other precedents of this Court forbid the abridgement of the right to vote. . . .

It may now be taken as a postulate that the right to vote in such a primary for the nomination of candidates without discrimination by the State, like the right to vote in a general election, is a right secured by the Constitution. . . . By the terms of the Fifteenth Amendment that right may not be abridged by any State on account of race. Under our Constitution the great privilege of the ballot may not be denied a man by the State because of his color.

7

REAPPORTIONMENT

Are the states free to reapportion their legislative and congressional districts without federal controls? What is the relationship, if any, between the apportionment powers of the states and the equal protection clause of the Fourteenth Amendment? Are such matters "political questions" upon which the Supreme Court does not, or should not, have a voice? During the twenty-year period from the mid-forties to the mid-sixties the Supreme Court grappled with these questions on several occasions, with mixed results. Then in 1962 and 1964 came the Warren Court's great breakthrough on reapportionment issues, *Baker* v. *Carr* (below), *Reynolds* v. *Sims* (below), and *Wesberry* v. *Sanders*,[1] a breakthrough that has had as dramatic an impact upon American political institutions, at least potentially, as virtually any Supreme Court decision of recent times.

Colegrove v. Green, 328 U.S. 549 (1946)

The Supreme Court's record on reapportionment issues begins in the 1946 decision, *Colgrove* v. *Green*, a judgment that stood until it was specifically overturned sixteen years later in *Baker* v. *Carr. Colegrove* was a suit brought by a group of Illinois citizens seeking relief from unequal apportionment of congressional districts in the state. Also involved in *Colegrove* was the typical urban versus rural; city versus downstate; conservative versus liberal syndrome that has dominated politics in many eastern and midwestern states, Illinois included, since industrialization and urbanization altered the face of American life and politics during the last years of the nineteenth century.

At the time *Colegrove* arose, the state legislature in Illinois had failed to reapportion the state's congressional or state legislature districts since the 1900 census. As a result of almost fifty years of population growth and changes, the state's major urban areas were grossly underrepresented. For example, one congressional district in Chicago had more than 914 thousand people while another rural, downstate district had a population of only about 112 thousand, more than an 8 to 1 population discrepancy. Because the Illinois legisla-

---

1. 376 U.S. 1 (1964).

ture was dominated by downstate, rural, agricultural interests it was unwilling to give the Chicago metropolitan area its fair share of Congressional seats based upon its population. Accordingly, because of these apportionment inequities the Supreme Court was asked to prohibit Illinois from conducting the 1946 Congressional elections. A badly split Roosevelt Court (4–3), with Justice Frankfurter writing for the majority (plurality), refused to grant the injunction the petitioners were seeking. As Frankfurter noted, what was involved in *Colegrove* was a "political" issue outside the Court's jurisdiction to decide. Justice Frankfurter wrote for himself, Justice Reed, and Justice Burton. Justice Rutledge wrote a concurring opinion that, although it varied from Frankfurter's approach to the question, was similar enough in principle to make up the curiously formed majority of four. Justice Jackson, who was in Nuremberg at the time, did not participate and the late Chief Justice Stone had not yet been replaced by Fred Vinson.

Justice Black led Justices Douglas and Murphy in dissent. Black argued that, by failing to reapportion since 1901, the state was denying appellants equal protection of the laws in violation of the Fourteenth Amendment. "No one would deny," Black wrote, that the equal protection clause "would prohibit a state from giving some citizens half a vote and others a full vote."[2] The Fourteenth Amendment forbids such discrimination, Black concluded. There was no doubt in the mind of the three dissenters that the voting power of Chicago's citizens had, in fact, been diluted or "debased" by one half, one third, one fourth or more, in comparison to some downstate Illinois citizens. And there was no doubt in Justice Black's mind that the Supreme Court had the power to correct such inequities. But Justice Frankfurter for the plurality of three (or four counting Justice Rutledge) thought otherwise.

Mr. Justice Frankfurter announced the judgment of the Court, saying in part:

> We are of opinion that the appellants ask of this Court what is beyond its competence to grant. This is one of those demands on judicial power which cannot be met by verbal fencing about "jurisdiction." It must be resolved by considerations on the basis of which this Court, from time to time, has refused to intervene in controversies. It has refused to do so because due regard for the effective working of our Government revealed this issue to be of a peculiarly political nature and therefore not meet for judicial determination.
>
> This is not an action to recover for damage because of the discriminatory exclusion of a plaintiff from rights enjoyed by other citizens. The basis for the suit is not a private wrong, but a wrong suffered by Illinois as a polity. . . . In effect this is an appeal to the federal courts to reconstruct the electoral process of Illinois in order that it may be adequately represented in the councils of the Nation. Because the Illinois legislature has failed to revise its Congressional Representative districts in order to reflect great changes, during more than a generation, in the distribution of its population, we are asked to do this, as it were, for Illinois.
>
> Of course no court can affirmatively re-map the Illinois districts so as to bring them more in conformity with the standards of fairness for a representative system. At best we could only declare the existing electoral system invalid. The result would be to leave Illinois undistricted and to bring into operation, if the Illinois legislature chose not to act, the choice of members for the House of

2. 328 U.S. at 569 (1946).

Representatives on a state-wide ticket. The last stage may be worse than the first. The upshot of judicial action may defeat the vital political principle which led Congress, more than a hundred years ago, to require districting. This requirement, in the language of Chancellor Kent, "was recommended by the wisdom and justice of giving, as far as possible, to the local subdivisions of the people of each state, a due influence in the choice of representatives, so as not to leave the aggregate minority of the people in a state, though approaching perhaps to a majority, to be wholly overpowered by the combined action of the numerical majority, without any voice whatever in the national councils." . . . Nothing is clearer than that this controversy concerns matters that bring courts into immediate and active relations with party contests. From the determination of such issues this Court has traditionally held aloof. It is hostile to a democratic system to involve the judiciary in the politics of the people. And it is not less pernicious if such judicial intervention in an essentially political contest be dressed up in the abstract phrases of the law.

The appellants urge with great zeal that the conditions of which they complain are grave evils and offend public morality. The Constitution of the United States gives ample power to provide against these evils. But due regard for the Constitution as a viable system precludes judicial correction. Authority for dealing with such problems resides elsewhere. Article I, §4 of the Constitution provides that "The Times, Places and Manner of holding elections for . . . Representatives, shall be prescribed in each State by the Legislature thereof; but the Congress may at any time by Law make or alter such Regulations, . . ." The short of it is that the Constitution has conferred upon Congress exclusive authority to secure fair representation by the States in the popular House and left to that House determination whether States have fulfilled their responsibility. If Congress failed in exercising its powers, whereby standards of fairness are offended, the remedy ultimately lies with the people. Whether Congress faithfully discharges its duty or not, the subject has been committed to the exclusive control of Congress. An aspect of government from which the judiciary, in view of what is involved, has been excluded by the clear intention of the Constitution cannot be entered by the federal courts because Congress may have been in default in exacting from States obedience to its mandate. . . .

To sustain this action would cut very deep into the very being of Congress. Courts ought not to enter this political thicket. The remedy for unfairness in districting is to secure State legislatures that will apportion properly, or to invoke the ample powers of Congress. The Constitution has many commands that are not enforceable by courts because they clearly fall outside the conditions and purposes that circumscribe judicial action. . . . The Constitution has left the performance of many duties in our governmental scheme to depend on the fidelity of the executive and legislative action and, ultimately, on the vigilance of the people in exercising their political rights.

Baker v. Carr, 369 U.S. 186 (1962)

The Supreme Court maintained the position expressed by Justice Frankfurter in *Colegrove* that legislative reapportionment was a "political thicket" into which federal courts should not venture until 1960. Then, in *Gomillion* v. *Lightfoot*,[1] although the Court passed no judgment on the alleged racial discrimination involved, it did take a cautious step toward rejecting the *Colegrove* rule. It edged closer to acknowledging that apportionment issues

1. 364 U.S. 339 (1960).

were subject to judicial review. The Court used the voting rights guarantee of the Fifteenth Amendment rather than the equal protection clause as the basis for its decision. Involved in *Gomillion* was a 1957 Alabama statute that redrew the boundaries of the city of Tuskegee, home of the famous Tuskegee Institute. Boundaries were redrawn by the statute with the specific intent of denying almost four hundred black voters the right to vote in municipal elections. They were simply gerrymandered outside the new city limits. Lower courts dismissed the suit, citing the *Colegrove* decision as controlling.

However, in an opinion by Justice Frankfurter, the author of *Colegrove,* the Supreme Court (8–1) agreed that black citizens of Tuskegee must have access to judicial review to determine if their Fifteenth Amendment voting rights had been violated by the Alabama statute. For Justice Frankfurter the more narrowly drawn Fifteenth Amendment could be invoked in such cases but not the broader equal protection clause of the Fourteenth. Speaking in dissent, Justice Whitaker argued that because the statute did in fact, discriminate against black people, relief should be granted under the equal protection and due process clauses of the Fourteenth Amendment and not under the voting right guarantee of the Fifteenth.

Limited as it was, *Gomillion* nevertheless set the stage for *Baker* v. *Carr,* another monumental Warren Court decision. *Baker* helped redress the imbalance in rural-urban voting power. It also reestablished the often ignored principle that elected officials "represent people not acres or trees." The Court's conclusion in *Baker* v. *Carr,* and in other subsequent reapportionment cases, that federal courts *may* scrutinize state legislative apportionment schemes and rule on their "fairness" has done much to tilt what often had been rural domination of state and national politics toward more equitable representation of urban, metropolitan areas where most people now live.

The appellants were citizens of Tennessee, a state that, despite population growth of almost 75 percent, had not been reapportioned since 1901. Accordingly, the appellants argued that the state's failure to reapportion "debased their vote" and thereby denied them equal protection of the laws guaranteed by the Fourteenth Amendment. In a truly historic decision the Supreme Court, 6–2, specifically overruled *Colegrove* v. *Green* and stated that federal courts *do* have jurisdiction in reapportionment matters and that appellants had "standing" to present what constitutionally was a "justiciable controversy." As might be expected, Justice Brennan's majority opinion brought forth a long dissent by Justice Frankfurter who, joined by Justice Harlan, argued as he had in *Colegrove* that the Supreme Court was without jurisdiction in such essentially "political matters" as legislative reapportionment. Justice Frankfurter deplored the Court's use of the equal protection clause to "coerce states into allocating "proper electoral weight among the voting populations of their various geographical subdivisions."

Finally, however, in *Baker* v. *Carr,* a majority of the Warren Court discarded this narrow, restricted view of equal protection and ruled that the Fourteenth Amendment *was* violated when a state apportioned, or failed to apportion, its legislative district so as to give preference and added weight to the votes of one group of its citizens over others. In addition to relevant portions of the majority opinion we also include portions of Justice Frankfurter's dissent.

Mr. Justice Brennan delivered the opinion of the Court, saying in part:

In light of the District Court's treatment of the case, we hold today only (1) that the court possessed jurisdiction of the subject matter; (2) that a justiciable cause of action is stated upon which appellants would be entitled to appropriate relief; and (3) because appellees raise the issue before this Court, that the appellants have standing to challenge the Tennessee apportionment statutes. Beyond noting that we have no cause at this stage to doubt the District Court will be able to fashion relief if violations of constitutional rights are found, it is improper now to consider what remedy would be most appropriate if appellants prevail at the trial.

The District Court was uncertain whether our cases withholding federal judicial relief rested upon a lack of federal jurisdiction or upon the inappropriateness of the subject matter for judicial consideration — what we have designated "nonjusticiability." The distinction between the two grounds is significant. In the instance of nonjusticiability, consideration of the cause is not wholly and immediately foreclosed; rather, the Court's inquiry necessarily proceeds to the point of deciding whether the duty asserted can be judicially identified and its breach judicially determined, and whether protection for the right asserted can be judicially molded. In the instance of lack of jurisdiction the cause either does not "arise under" the Federal Constitution, laws or treaties (or fall within one of the other enumerated categories of Art. III, §2), or is not a "case or controversy" within the meaning of that section; or the cause is not one described by any jurisdictional statute. Our conclusion . . . that this cause presents no nonjusticiable "political question" settles the only possible doubt that it is a case or controversy. Under the present heading of "Jurisdiction of the Subject Matter" we hold only that the matter set forth in the complaint does arise under the Constitution. . . .

We hold that the appellants do have standing to maintain this suit. Our decisions plainly support this conclusion. Many of the cases have assumed rather than articulated the premise in deciding the merits of similar claims. And *Colegrove* v. *Green, supra,* squarely held that voters who allege facts showing disadvantage to themselves as individuals have standing to sue. A number of cases decided after *Colegrove* recognized the standing of the voters there involved to bring those actions.

These appellants seek relief in order to protect or vindicate an interest of their own, and of those similarly situated. Their constitutional claim is, in substance, that the 1901 statute constitutes arbitrary and capricious state action, offensive to the Fourteenth Amendment in its irrational disregard of the standard of apportionment prescribed by the State's Constitution or of any standard, effecting a gross disproportion of representation to voting population. The injury which appellants assert is that this classification disfavors the voters in the counties in which they reside, placing them in a position of constitutionally unjustifiable inequality *vis-à-vis* voters in irrationally favored counties. A citizen's right to a vote free of arbitrary impairment by state action has been judicially recognized as a right secured by the Constitution, when such impairment resulted from dilution by a false tally, . . . or by a refusal to count votes from arbitrarily selected precincts, [or] by a stuffing of the ballot box. . . .

In holding that the subject matter of this suit was not justiciable, the District Court relied on *Colegrove* v. *Green, supra,* and subsequent *per curiam* cases. The court stated: "From a review of these decisions there can be no doubt that the federal rule . . . is that the federal courts . . . will not intervene in cases of this type to compel legislative reapportionment." . . . We understand the District Court to have read the cited cases as compelling the conclusion that since the appellants sought to have a legislative apportionment held unconstitutional, their suit presented a "political question" and was therefore nonjusticiable. We hold that this challenge to an apportionment presents no nonjusticiable "political question." The cited cases do not hold the contrary.

Of course the mere fact that the suit seeks protection of a political right does not mean it presents a political question. Such an objection "is little more than a play upon words." . . . Rather, it is argued that apportionment cases, whatever the actual wording of the complaint, can involve no federal constitutional right except one resting on the guaranty of a republican form of government, and that complaints based on that clause have been held to present political questions which are nonjusticiable.

We hold that the claim pleaded here neither rests upon nor implicates the Guaranty Clause and that its justiciability is therefore not foreclosed by our decisions of cases involving that clause. The District Court misinterpreted *Colegrove* v. *Green* and other decisions of this Court on which it relied. Appellants' claim that they are being denied equal protection is justiciable, and if "discrimination is sufficiently shown, the right to relief under the equal protection clause is not diminished by the fact that the discrimination relates to political rights."

We conclude that the complaint's allegations of a denial of equal protection present a justiciable constitutional cause of action upon which appellants are entitled to a trial and a decision. The right asserted is within the reach of judicial protection under the Fourteenth Amendment.

The judgment of the District Court is reversed and the cause is remanded for further proceedings consistent with this opinion.

MR. JUSTICE FRANKFURTER, whom MR. JUSTICE HARLAN joins, dissenting.

The Court today reverses a uniform course of decision established by a dozen cases, including one by which the very claim now sustained was unanimously rejected only five years ago. The impressive body of rulings thus cast aside reflected the equally uniform course of our political history regarding the relationship between population and legislative representation — a wholly different matter from denial of the franchise to individuals because of race, color, religion or sex. Such a massive repudiation of the experience of our whole past in asserting destructively novel judicial power demands a detailed analysis of the role of this Court in our constitutional scheme. Disregard of inherent limits in the effective exercise of the Court's "judicial Power" not only presages the futility of judicial intervention in the essentially political conflict of forces by which the relation between population and representation has time out of mind been and now is determined. It may well impair the Court's position as the ultimate organ of "the supreme Law of the Land" in that vast range of legal problems, often strongly entangled in popular feeling, on which this Court must pronounce. The Court's authority — possessed of neither the purse nor the sword — ultimately rests on sustained public confidence in its moral sanction. Such feeling must be nourished by the Court's complete detachment, in fact and in appearance, from political entanglements and by abstention from injecting itself into the clash of political forces in political settlements.

A hypothetical claim resting on abstract assumptions is now for the first time made the basis for affording illusory relief for a particular evil even though it foreshadows deeper and more pervasive difficulties in consequence. The claim is hypothetical and the assumptions are abstract because the Court does not vouchsafe the lower courts — state and federal — guidelines for formulating specific, definite, wholly unprecedented remedies for the inevitable litigations that to-day's umbrageous disposition is bound to stimulate in connection with politically motivated reapportionments in so many States. In such a setting, to promulgate jurisdiction in the abstract is meaningless. It is as devoid of reality as "a brooding omnipresence in the sky," for it conveys no intimation what relief, if any, a

District Court is capable of affording that would not invite legislatures to play
ducks and drakes with the judiciary. For this Court to direct the District Court to
enforce a claim to which the Court has over the years consistently found itself
required to deny legal enforcement and at the same time to find it necessary to
withhold any guidance to the lower court how to enforce this turnabout, new
legal claim, manifests an odd — indeed an esoteric — conception of judicial
propriety. . . .

   . . . Even assuming the indispensable intellectual disinterestedness on the part
of judges in such matters, they do not have accepted legal standards or criteria or
even reliable analogies to draw upon for making judicial judgments. To charge
courts with the task of accommodating the incommensurable factors of policy
that underlie these mathematical puzzles is to attribute, however flatteringly,
omnicompetence to judges. The Framers of the Constitution persistently rejected a proposal that embodied this assumption and Thomas Jefferson never
entertained it. . . .

   We were soothingly told at the bar of this Court that we need not worry about
the kind of remedy a court could effectively fashion once the abstract constitutional right to have courts pass on a state-wide system of electoral districting is
recognized as a matter of judicial rhetoric, because legislatures would heed the
Court's admonition. This is not only a euphoric hope. It implies a sorry confession of judicial impotence in place of a frank acknowledgment that there is not
under our Constitution a judicial remedy for every political mischief, for every
undesirable exercise of legislative power. The Framers carefully and with deliberate forethought refused so to enthrone the judiciary. In this situation, as in
others of like nature, appeal for relief does not belong here. Appeal must be to
an informed, civically militant electorate. In a democratic society like ours, relief
must come through an aroused popular conscience that sears the conscience of
the people's representatives. In any event there is nothing judicially more unseemly nor more self-defeating than for this Court to make *in terrorem* pronouncements, to indulge in merely empty rhetoric, sounding a word of promise
to the ear, sure to be disappointing to the hope.

Reynolds v. Sims, 377 U.S. 533 (1964)

   Having once established the principle in *Baker* v. *Carr* that legislative apportionment was a "justiciable issue," the Supreme Court soon set about developing the standards, the constitutional principles, and the remedies to apply in
the legislative mal-apportionment cases coming before it. In *Gray* v. *Sanders,*[1]
decided just one year after *Baker,* the Warren Court declared invalid the
Georgia county unit system of primary elections, which was designed to favor
rural as opposed to urban voters in the state. The Court had refused to
tamper with the Georgia system thirteen years earlier in *South* v. *Peters.*[2] But in
Gray, with only Justice Harlan dissenting, the Court struck down the Georgia
scheme, in Justice Douglas's words, because ". . . all who participate in [an]
election are to have an equal vote . . . this is required by the Equal Protection
Clause of the Fourteenth Amendment."

   Douglas's "one person, one vote" reasoning in *Gray* led to *Reynolds* v. *Sims,*
after *Baker* v. *Carr* the most important legislative apportionment decision of
the era. In *Reynolds,* voters from several Alabama counties brought suit against

   1. 372 U.S. 568 (1963).
   2. 339 U.S. 276 (1950).

election officials in the state charging that existing legislative apportionment provisions were an unconstitutional denial of equal protection. A federal district court found that neither of the two alternate apportionment plans the state legislature had adopted under pressure from this suit would cure gross inequities in the existing system. The court then ordered temporary reapportionment for the 1962 general election by culling the equalizing aspects of the two plans adopted by the legislature. State officials argued that a federal court lacked authority under the Constitution to reapportion a state legislature. The petitioners were also unhappy with the district court's reapportionment plan, charging that it had failed to reapportion *both* houses of the state legislature on the basis of population.

With only Justice Harlan in dissent, the Warren Court ruled, in *Reynolds* v. *Sims,* that the right of suffrage is denied when a citizen's vote is "diluted or debased" in state or federal elections. Writing for the majority, Chief Justice Warren noted that equal protection requires "substantially equal legislative representation" for all voters regardless of where they reside in the state. The seats in both houses of a bicameral legislature, the Chief Justice said, must be apportioned "substantially on a population basis . . . legislators represent people not trees or acres."

Justice Harlan, the lone dissenter with Frankfurter gone, argued that his reading of neither the Fourteenth Amendment nor its legislative history required every state to "structure its legislature so that all the members of each house represent substantially the same number of people." Rejecting the majority's "one person, one vote" thesis, Justice Harlan stated that the Fourteenth Amendment "does not impose this political tenet on the States or authorize this Court to do so."

The Court's majority of eight took a different view. It is reasonable to conclude, the Chief Justice wrote, "that a majority of the people of a state should elect a majority of that State's legislature." To rule otherwise, he said, "would . . . deny majority rights in a way that far surpasses any possible denial of minority rights that might otherwise be thought to result."

Within a short time after the Court's decision in *Reynolds* v. *Sims* most of the nation's state legislatures had been reapportioned on the basis of the "one person, one vote" rule laid down in *Reynolds.* Thus *Reynolds,* and *Wesberry* v. *Sanders,*[3] which did for the House of Representatives what had been done for the state legislatures, greatly democratized the political system in the United States. It also enhanced the voting power of city dwellers and helped bring about a semblance of rural-urban balance in American politics.

Chief Justice Warren delivered the opinion of the Court, saying in part:

> In *Wesberry* v. *Sanders,* 376 U.S. 1, decided earlier this Term, we held that attacks on the constitutionality of congressional districting plans enacted by state legislatures do not present nonjusticiable questions and should not be dismissed generally for "want of equity." We determined that the constitutional test for the validity of congressional districting schemes was one of substantial equality of population among the various districts established by a state legislature for the election of members of the Federal House of Representatives.
>
> In that case we decided that an apportionment of congressional seats which "contracts the value of some votes and expands that of others" is unconstitu-

3. 376 U.S. 1 (1964).

tional, since "the Federal Constitution intends that when qualified voters elect members of Congress each vote be given as much weight as any other vote. . . ." We concluded that the constitutional prescription for election of members of the House of Representatives "by the People," construed in its historical context, "means that as nearly as is practicable one man's vote in a congressional election is to be worth as much as another's." We further stated:

> "It would defeat the principle solemnly embodied in the Great Compromise — equal representation in the House for equal numbers of people — for us to hold that, within the States, legislatures may draw the lines of congressional districts in such a way as to give some voters a greater voice in choosing a Congressman than others."

We found further, in *Wesberry*, that "our Constitution's plain objective" was that "of making equal representation for equal numbers of people the fundamental goal. . . ." We concluded by stating:

> "No right is more precious in a free country than that of having a voice in the election of those who make the laws under which, as good citizens, we must live. Other rights, even the most basic, are illusory if the right to vote is undermined. Our Constitution leaves no room for classification of people in a way that unnecessarily abridges this right."

Gray and *Wesberry* are of course not dispositive of or directly controlling on our decision in these cases involving state legislative apportionment controversies. Admittedly, those decisions, in which we held that, in statewide and in congressional elections, one person's vote must be counted equally with those of all other voters in a State, were based on different constitutional considerations and were addressed to rather distinct problems. But neither are they wholly inapposite. *Gray*, though not determinative here since involving the weighting of votes in statewide elections, established the basic principle of equality among voters within a State, and held that voters cannot be classified, constitutionally, on the basis of where they live, at least with respect to voting in statewide elections. And our decision in *Wesberry* was of course grounded on that language of the Constitution which prescribes that members of the Federal House of Representatives are to be chosen "by the People," while attacks on state legislative apportionment schemes, such as that involved in the instant cases, are principally based on the Equal Protection Clause of the Fourteenth Amendment. Nevertheless, *Wesberry* clearly established that the fundamental principle of representative government in this country is one of equal representation for equal numbers of people, without regard to race, sex, economic status, or place of residence within a State. Our problem, then, is to ascertain, in the instant cases, whether there are any constitutionally cognizable principles which would justify departures from the basic standard of equality among voters in the apportionment of seats in state legislatures.

A predominant consideration in determining whether a State's legislative apportionment scheme constitutes an invidious discrimination violative of rights asserted under the Equal Protection Clause is that the rights allegedly impaired are individual and personal in nature. As stated by the Court in *United States* v. *Bathgate*, 246 U.S. 220, 227, "[t]he right to vote is personal. . . ." While the result of a court decision in a state legislative apportionment controversy may be to require the restructuring of the geographical distribution of seats in a state legislature, the judicial focus must be concentrated upon ascertaining whether there has been any discrimination against certain of the State's citizens which constitutes an impermissible impairment of their constitutionally protected right to vote. Like *Skinner* v. *Oklahoma*, 316 U.S. 535, such a case "touches a sensitive and important area of human rights," and "involves one of the basic civil rights of man," presenting questions of alleged "invidious discriminations . . . against groups or types of individuals in violation of the constitutional guaranty of just and equal laws." . . . Undoubtedly, the right of suffrage is a fundamental matter in a free and democratic society. Especially since the right to exercise the franchise in a free and unimpaired manner is preservative of other basic civil and political rights, any alleged infringement of the right of citizens to vote must be carefully and meticulously scrutinized. . . .

Legislators represent people, not trees or acres. Legislators are elected by voters, not farms or cities or economic interests. As long as ours is a representative form of government, and our legislatures are those instruments of government elected directly by and directly representative of the people, the right to elect legislators in a free and unimpaired fashion is a bedrock of our political system. It could hardly be gainsaid that a constitutional claim had been asserted by an allegation that certain otherwise qualified voters had been entirely prohibited from voting for members of their state legislature. And, if a State should provide that the votes of citizens in one part of the State should be given two times, or five times, or 10 times the weight of votes of citizens in another part of the State, it could hardly be contended that the right to vote of those residing in the disfavored areas had not been effectively diluted. It would appear extraordinary to suggest that a State could be constitutionally permitted to enact a law providing that certain of the State's voters could vote two, five, or 10 times for their legislative representatives, while voters living elsewhere could vote only once. And it is inconceivable that a state law to the effect that, in counting votes for legislators, the votes of citizens in one part of the State would be multiplied by two, five, or 10, while the votes of persons in another area would be counted only at face value, could be constitutionally sustainable. Of course, the effect of state legislative districting schemes which give the same number of representatives to unequal numbers of constituents is identical. Overweighting and overvaluation of the votes of those living here has the certain effect of dilution and undervaluation of the votes of those living there. The resulting discrimination against those individual voters living in disfavored areas is easily demonstrable mathematically. Their right to vote is simply not the same right to vote as that of those living in a favored part of the State. Two, five, or 10 of them must vote before the effect of their voting is equivalent to that of their favored neighbor. Weighting the votes of citizens differently, by any method or means, merely because of where they happen to reside, hardly seems justifiable. One must be ever aware that the Constitution forbids "sophisticated as well as simple-minded modes of discrimination." . . .

State legislatures are, historically, the fountainhead of representative government in this country. A number of them have their roots in colonial times, and substantially antedate the creation of our Nation and our Federal Government. In fact, the first formal stirrings of American political independence are to be found, in large part, in the views and actions of several of the colonial legislative bodies. With the birth of our National Government, and the adoption and ratification of the Federal Constitution, state legislatures retained a most important place in our Nation's governmental structure. But representative government is in essence self-government through the medium of elected representatives of the people, and each and every citizen has an inalienable right to full and effective participation in the political processes of his State's legislative bodies. Most citizens can achieve this participation only as qualified voters through the election of legislators to represent them. Full and effective participation by all citizens in state government requires, therefore, that each citizen have an equally effective voice in the election of members of his state legislature.

Modern and viable state government needs, and the Constitution demands, no less.

Logically, in a society ostensibly grounded on representative government, it would seem reasonable that a majority of the people of a State could elect a majority of that State's legislators. To conclude differently, and to sanction minority control of state legislative bodies, would appear to deny majority rights in a way that far surpasses any possible denial of minority rights that might otherwise be thought to result. Since legislatures are responsible for enacting laws by which all citizens are to be governed, they should be bodies which are collectively responsive to the popular will. And the concept of equal protection has been traditionally viewed as requiring the uniform treatment of persons standing in the same relation to the governmental action questioned or challenged. With respect to the allocation of legislative representation, all voters, as citizens of a State, stand in the same relation regardless of where they live. Any suggested criteria for the differentiation of citizens are insufficient to justify any discrimination, as to the weight of their votes, unless relevant to the permissible purposes of legislative apportionment. Since the achieving of fair and effective representation for all citizens is concededly the basic aim of legislative apportionment, we conclude that the Equal Protection Clause guarantees the opportunity for equal participation by all voters in the election of state legislators. Diluting the weight of votes because of place of residence impairs basic constitutional rights under the Fourteenth Amendment just as much as invidious discriminations based upon factors such as race. . . . Our constitutional system amply provides for the protection of minorities by means other than giving them majority control of state legislatures. And the democratic ideals of equality and majority rule, which have served this Nation so well in the past, are hardly of any less significance for the present and the future.

We are told that the matter of apportioning representation in a state legislature is a complex and many-faceted one. We are advised that States can rationally consider factors other than population in apportioning legislative representation. We are admonished not to restrict the power of the States to impose differing views as to political philosophy on their citizens. We are cautioned about the dangers of entering into political thickets and mathematical quagmires. Our answer is this: a denial of constitutionally protected rights demands judicial protection; our oath and our office require no less of us. As stated in *Gomillion* v. *Lightfoot, supra:*

> "When a State exercises power wholly within the domain of state interest, it is insulated from federal judicial review. But such insulation is not carried over when state power is used as an instrument for circumventing a federally protected right."

To the extent that a citizen's right to vote is debased, he is that much less a citizen. The fact that an individual lives here or there is not a legitimate reason for overweighting or diluting the efficacy of his vote. The complexions of societies and civilizations change, often with amazing rapidity. A nation once primarily rural in character becomes predominantly urban. Representation schemes once fair and equitable become archaic and outdated. But the basic principle of representative government remains, and must remain, unchanged — the weight of a citizen's vote cannot be made to depend on where he lives. Population is, of necessity, the starting point for consideration and the controlling criterion for judgment in legislative apportionment controversies. A citizen, a qualified voter, is no more nor no less so because he lives in the city or on the farm. This is the clear and strong command of our Constitution's Equal Protection Clause. This is an essential part of the concept of a government of laws and not men. This is at the heart of Lincoln's vision of "government of the people, by the people, [and] for the people." The Equal Protection Clause demands no less than substantially equal state legislative representation for all citizens, of all places as well as of all races. . . .

We hold that, as a basic constitutional standard, the Equal Protection Clause requires that the seats in both houses of a bicameral state legislature must be apportioned on a population basis. Simply stated, an individual's right to vote for state legislators is unconstitutionally impaired when its weight is in a substantial fashion diluted when compared with votes of citizens living in other parts of the State.

Since we find the so-called federal analogy inapposite to a consideration of the constitutional validity of state legislative apportionment schemes, we necessarily hold that the Equal Protection Clause requires both houses of a state legislature to be apportioned on a population basis. The right of a citizen to equal representation and to have his vote weighted equally with those of all other citizens in the election of members of one house of a bicameral state legislature would amount to little if States could effectively submerge the equal-population principle in the apportionment of seats in the other house. If such a scheme were permissible, an individual citizen's ability to exercise an effective voice in the only instrument of state government directly representative of the people might be almost as effectively thwarted as if neither house were apportioned on a population basis. Deadlock between the two bodies might result in compromise and concession on some issues. But in all too many cases the more probable result would be frustration of the majority will through minority veto in the house not apportioned on a population basis, stemming directly from the failure to accord adequate overall legislative representation to all of the State's citizens on a nondiscriminatory basis. In summary, we can perceive no constitutional difference, with respect to the geographical distribution of state legislative representation, between the two houses of a bicameral state legislature.

We do not believe that the concept of bicameralism is rendered anachronistic and meaningless when the predominant basis of representation in the two state legislative bodies is required to be the same — population. A prime reason for bicameralism, modernly considered, is to insure mature and deliberate consideration of, and to prevent precipitate action on, proposed legislative measures. Simply because the controlling criterion for apportioning representation is required to be the same in both houses does not mean that there will be no differences in the composition and complexion of the two bodies. Different constituencies can be represented in the two houses. One body could be composed of single-member districts while the other could have at least some multimember districts. The length of terms of the legislators in the separate bodies could differ. The numerical size of the two bodies could be made to differ, even significantly, and the geographical size of districts from which legislators are elected could also be made to differ. And apportionment in one house could be arranged so as to balance off minor inequities in the representation of certain areas in the other house. In summary, these and other factors could be, and are presently in many States, utilized to engender differing complexions and collective attitudes in the two bodies of a state legislature, although both are apportioned substantially on a population basis. . . .

By holding that as a federal constitutional requisite both houses of a state legislature must be apportioned on a population basis, we mean that the Equal Protection Clause requires that a State make an honest and good faith effort to construct districts, in both houses of its legislature, as nearly of equal population as is practicable. We realize that it is a practical impossibility to arrange legislative districts so that each one has an identical number of residents, or citizens, or voters. Mathematical exactness or precision is hardly a workable constitutional requirement.

In *Wesberry* v. *Sanders, supra,* the Court stated that congressional representation must be based on population as nearly as is practicable. In implementing the basic constitutional principle of representative government as enunciated by the Court in *Wesberry* — equality of population among districts — some distinctions may well be made between congressional and state legislative representation. Since, almost invariably, there is a significantly larger number of seats in state legislative bodies to be distributed within a State than congressional seats, it may be feasible to use political subdivision lines to a greater extent in establishing state legislative districts than in congressional districting while still affording adequate representation to all parts of the State. To do so would be constitutionally valid, so long as the resulting apportionment was one based substantially on population and the equal-population principle was not diluted in any significant way. Somewhat more flexibility may therefore be constitutionally permissible with respect to state legislative apportionment than in congressional districting. Lower courts can and assuredly will work out more concrete and specific standards for evaluating state legislative apportionment schemes in the context of actual litigation. For the present, we deem it expedient not to attempt to spell out any precise constitutional tests. What is marginally permissible in one State may be unsatisfactory in another, depending on the particular circumstances of the case. Developing a body of doctrine on a case-by-case basis appears to us to provide the most satisfactory means of arriving at detailed constitutional requirements in the area of state legislative apportionment. . . . Thus, we proceed to state here only a few rather general considerations which appear to us to be relevant.

A State may legitimately desire to maintain the integrity of various political subdivisions, insofar as possible, and provide for compact districts of contiguous territory in designing a legislative apportionment scheme. Valid considerations may underlie such aims. Indiscriminate districting, without any regard for political subdivision or natural or historical boundary lines, may be little more than an open invitation to partisan gerrymandering. Single-member districts may be the rule in one State, while another State might desire to achieve some flexibility by creating multimember or floterial districts. Whatever the means of accomplishment, the overriding objective must be substantial equality of population among the various districts, so that the vote of any citizen is approximately equal in weight to that of any other citizen in the State.

History indicates, however, that many States have deviated, to a greater or lesser degree, from the equal population principle in the apportionment of seats in at least one house of their legislatures. So long as the divergences from a strict population standard are based on legitimate considerations incident to the effectuation of a rational state policy, some deviations from the equal-population principle are constitutionally permissible with respect to the apportionment of seats in either or both of the two houses of a bicameral state legislature. But neither history alone, nor economic or other sorts of group interests, are permissible factors in attempting to justify disparities from population-based representation. Citizens, not history or economic interests, cast votes. Considerations of area alone provide an insufficient justification for deviations from the equal-population principle. Again, people, not land or trees or pastures, vote. Modern developments and improvements in transportation and communications make rather hollow, in the mid-1960's, most claims that deviations from population-based representation can validly be based solely on geographical considerations. Arguments for allowing such deviations in order to insure effective representation for sparsely settled areas and to prevent legislative districts from becoming so large that the availability of access of citizens to their representatives is impaired are today, for the most part, unconvincing.

A consideration that appears to be of more substance in justifying some deviations from population-based representation in state legislatures is that of insuring some voice to political subdivisions, as political subdivisions. Several factors make more than insubstantial claims that a State can rationally consider according political subdivisions some independent representation in at least one body of the state legislature, as long as the basic standard of equality of population among districts is maintained. Local governmental entities are frequently charged with various responsibilities incident to the operation of state government. In many States much of the legislature's activity involves the enactment of so-called local legislation, directed only to the concerns of particular political subdivisions. And a State may legitimately desire to construct districts along political subdivision lines to deter the possibilities of gerrymandering. However, permitting deviations from population-based representation does not mean that each local governmental unit or political subdivision can be given separate representation, regardless of population. Carried too far, a scheme of giving at least one seat in one house to each political subdivision (for example, to each county) could easily result, in many States, in a total subversion of the equal-population principle in that legislative body. This would be especially true in a State where the number of counties is large and many of them are sparsely populated, and the number of seats in the legislative body being apportioned does not significantly exceed the number of counties. Such a result, we conclude, would be constitutionally impermissible. And careful judicial scrutiny must of course be given, in evaluating state apportionment schemes, to the character as well as the degree of deviations from a strict population basis. But if, even as a result of a clearly rational state policy of according some legislative representation to political subdivisions, population is submerged as the controlling consideration in the apportionment of seats in the particular legislative body, then the right of all of the State's citizens to cast an effective and adequately weighted vote would be unconstitutionally impaired.

South Carolina v. Katzenbach, 383 U.S. 301 (1966)

As we have noted, poll taxes, outlandish grandfather clauses, unfairly administered literacy tests, and the all-white primary have been among the most widely used legal and extralegal devices in the southern states to deprive black people of their right to vote. All have since been eliminated either by decisions of the Supreme Court, by Acts of Congress or by constitutional amendment.

In *Guinn* v. *United States*[1] for example, the Supreme Court struck down an Oklahoma grandfather clause that imposed literacy test requirements for voters but exempted persons whose ancestors had been eligible to vote in 1866. The Court saw this as a deliberate attempt by the state to circumvent the right to vote guaranteed to black people by the Fifteenth Amendment.

Poll taxes posed a different set of problems, although there was little doubt that their original purpose was also to reduce the incidence of black voting. Yet, because poll taxes applied equally to all citizens, they were not, as were grandfather clauses, discriminatory on their face. For this reason the Su-

1. 338 U.S. 347 (1915).

preme Court, in *Breedlove* v. *Suttles,*[2] refused to rule that poll taxes were a denial of equal protection or that they violated the Fifteenth Amendment. Slowly however, poll taxes began to disappear, probably because it became clear that they were also often depriving poor white people of their right to vote. By 1960, poll tax statutes were in force in only five states, Alabama, Arkansas, Mississippi, Texas, and Virginia. Congress had attempted to abolish poll taxes several times during the 1940s but each time the attempt was thwarted by a southern filibuster in the Senate. Then, in 1962, the Senate finally passed a constitutional amendment abolishing poll taxes in federal elections. With the ratification in 1964 of the twenty-fourth Amendment, poll taxes were eliminated from the federal scene. They remained a factor, however, in four states; Arkansas had abolished its poll tax after the ratification of the twenty-fourth Amendment.

The Supreme Court ruled on the constitutionality of the remaining state poll taxes in *Harper* v. *Virginia State Board of Elections.*[3] Overruling *Breedlove,* the Court called poll taxes unconstitutional "invidious discrimination" and a violation of the equal protection clause.

Literacy tests were also not discriminatory on their face, as they too at least in theory applied to all citizens across the board. For this reason, as late as 1959, in *Lassiter* v. *Northampton County Board of Elections,*[4] even the consistently liberal Justice Douglas would indicate for the Court that a state could insist "that only those who are literate should exercise the franchise." Yet the record indicates clearly that in many southern states literacy tests were used in conjunction with an "understanding the Constitution" component, for the sole purpose of excluding blacks from voting. Given wide discretionary power by state statutes, southern registers often used the "understanding the Constitution" device against black people by asking difficult, technical questions and then refusing to register them for even the smallest, often most trivial errors. It was not until passage of the 1965 Voting Rights Act that this situation was remedied. This monumental legislation took several giant steps to eradicate racial discrimination in voting. It stated unequivocally that "no voting qualifications" could be imposed "to deny or abridge" the voting rights of citizens because of their race. In the Act, Congress devised an innovative formula to determine when it could prohibit the various anti-voting schemes that had been devised in the south and which accounted for the greatest concentration of "legal discrimination." Congress decided that literacy or "understanding the Constitution" tests could be outlawed in those states, or in those voting districts, where less than 50 percent of the voting age population were, in fact, registered to vote in November 1964 or where less than 50 percent of the voting age population had actually voted in the 1964 presidential election. Congress went one step further and sent federal examiners into the delinquent states to insure prompt registration of qualified black voters. There seems little doubt, as its Congressional opponents charged, that the Act did in fact abridge the power of the less-than-50 percent states to police their own voting qualifications which hitherto had been their prerogative under the Constitution. Nevertheless Congress took the step holding that states could *not*

2. 300 U.S. 277 (1937).

3. 383 U.S. 663 (1966).

4. 360 U.S. 45 (1958).

violate voting rights protected by the Fourteenth and Fifteenth Amendments in the process of exercising a traditional states' right to control voter qualifications.

With Chief Justice Warren writing for the majority of eight, the Warren Court upheld the constitutionality of the 1965 Voting Rights Act in *South Carolina* v. *Katzenbach*. The Court ruled that the Act was a valid application of Congress's power to effectuate the Fifteenth Amendment's guarantee of voting rights to black people.

Justice Black noted that although he agreed with "substantially all" of the majority opinion, which sustained the power of Congress under Section 2 of the Fifteenth Amendment to suspend state literacy tests and to authorize appointment of federal examiners to register qualified black voters, he felt constrained to write an opinion dissenting in part with one aspect of the majority's conclusion. Black felt that Section 5 of the Voting Rights Act was unconstitutional because it gave the district court authority to approve or reject state laws or constitutional amendments, a power originally restricted to the Supreme Court.

In the majority opinion, Chief Justice Warren noted that case-by-case litigation against voting discrimination under the Civil Rights Acts of 1959, 1960, and 1964 had not been successful in appreciably increasing black registration figures. He concluded therefore that Congress was free to use whatever means were appropriate to carry out the objectives of the Fifteenth Amendment. For the Warren Court the 1965 Voting Rights Act was one such valid method.

Mr. Chief Justice Warren delivered the opinion of the Court, saying in part:

> The Voting Rights Act was designed by Congress to banish the blight of racial discrimination in voting, which has infected the electoral process in parts of our country for nearly a century. The Act creates stringent new remedies for voting discrimination where it persists on a pervasive scale, and in addition the statute strengthens existing remedies for pockets of voting discrimination elsewhere in the country. Congress assumed the power to prescribe these remedies from §2 of the Fifteenth Amendment, which authorizes the National Legislature to effectuate by "appropriate" measures the constitutional prohibition against racial discrimination in voting. We hold that the sections of the Act which are properly before us are an appropriate means for carrying out Congress' constitutional responsibilities and are consonant with all other provisions of the Constitution. We therefore deny South Carolina's request that enforcement of these sections of the Act be enjoined.
>
> The constitutional propriety of the Voting Rights Act of 1965 must be judged with reference to the historical experience which it reflects. Before enacting the measure, Congress explored with great care the problem of racial discrimination in voting. . . .
>
> Two points emerge vividly from the voluminous legislative history of the Act contained in the committee hearings and floor debates. First: Congress felt itself confronted by an insidious and pervasive evil which had been perpetuated in certain parts of our country through unremitting and ingenious defiance of the Constitution. Second: Congress concluded that the unsuccessful remedies which it had prescribed in the past would have to be replaced by sterner and more elaborate measures in order to satisfy the clear commands of the Fifteenth Amendment. . . .

The Fifteenth Amendment to the Constitution was ratified in 1870. Promptly thereafter Congress passed the Enforcement Act of 1870, which made it a crime for public officers and private persons to obstruct exercise of the right to vote. The statute was amended in the following year to provide for detailed federal supervision of the electoral process, from registration to the certification of returns. As the years passed and fervor for racial equality waned, enforcement of the laws became spotty and ineffective, and most of their provisions were repealed in 1894. The remnants have had little significance in the recently renewed battle against voting discrimination.

Meanwhile, beginning in 1890, the States of Alabama, Georgia, Louisiana, Mississippi, North Carolina, South Carolina, and Virginia enacted tests still in use which were specifically designed to prevent Negroes from voting. Typically, they made the ability to read and write a registration qualification and also required completion of a registration form. These laws were based on the fact that as of 1890 in each of the named States, more than two-thirds of the adult Negroes were illiterate while less than one-quarter of the adult whites were unable to read or write. At the same time, alternate tests were prescribed in all of the named States to assure that white illiterates would not be deprived of the franchise. These included grandfather clauses, property qualifications, "good character" tests, and the requirement that registrants "understand" or "interpret" certain matter. . . .

According to the evidence in recent Justice Department voting suits, the latter strategem is now the principal method used to bar Negroes from the polls. Discriminatory administration of voting qualifications has been found in all eight Alabama cases, in all nine Louisiana cases, and in all nine Mississippi cases which have gone to final judgment. Moreover, in almost all of these cases, the courts have held that the discrimination was pursuant to a widespread "pattern or practice." White applicants for registration have often been excused altogether from the literacy and understanding tests or have been given easy versions, have received extensive help from voting officials, and have been registered despite serious errors in their answers. Negroes, on the other hand, have typically been required to pass difficult versions of all the tests, without any outside assistance and without the slightest error. The good-morals requirement is so vague and subjective that it has constituted an open invitation to abuse at the hands of voting officials. Negroes obliged to obtain vouchers from registered voters have found it virtually impossible to comply in areas where almost no Negroes are on the rolls.

In recent years, Congress has repeatedly tried to cope with the problem by facilitating case-by-case litigation against voting discrimination. The Civil Rights Act of 1957 authorized the Attorney General to seek injunctions against public and private interference with the right to vote on racial grounds. Perfecting amendments in the Civil Rights Act of 1960 permitted the joinder of States as parties defendant, gave the Attorney General access to local voting records, and authorized courts to register voters in areas of systematic discrimination. Title I of the Civil Rights Act of 1964 expedited the hearing of voting cases before three-judge courts and outlawed some of the tactics used to disqualify Negroes from voting in federal elections.

Despite the earnest efforts of the Justice Department and of many federal judges, these new laws have done little to cure the problem of voting discrimination. According to estimates by the Attorney General during hearings on the Act, registration of voting-age Negroes in Alabama rose only from 14.2% to 19.4% between 1958 and 1964; in Louisiana it barely inched ahead from 31.7% to 31.8% between 1956 and 1965; and in Mississippi it increased only from 4.4% to 6.4% between 1954 and 1964. In each instance, registration of voting-age whites ran roughly 50 percentage points or more ahead of Negro registration.

The previous legislation has proved ineffective for a number of reasons. Voting suits are unusually onerous to prepare, sometimes requiring as many as 6,000 manhours spent combing through registration records in preparation for trial. Litigation has been exceedingly slow, in part because of the ample opportunities for delay afforded voting officials and others involved in the proceedings. Even when favorable decisions have finally been obtained, some of the States affected have merely switched to discriminatory devices not covered by the federal decrees or have enacted difficult new tests designed to prolong the existing disparity between white and Negro registration. Alternatively, certain local officials have defied and evaded court orders or have simply closed their registration offices to freeze the voting rolls. The provision of the 1960 law authorizing registration by federal officers has had little impact on local maladministration because of its procedural complexities. . . .

The Voting Rights Act of 1965 reflects Congress' firm intention to rid the country of racial discrimination in voting. The heart of the Act is a complex scheme of stringent remedies aimed at areas where voting discrimination has been most flagrant. Section 4 (a)-(d) lays down a formula defining the States and political subdivisions to which these new remedies apply. The first of the remedies, contained in §4 (a), is the suspension of literacy tests and similar voting qualifications for a period of five years from the last occurrence of substantial voting discrimination. Section 5 prescribes a second remedy, the suspension of all new voting regulations pending review by federal authorities to determine whether their use would perpetuate voting discrimination. The third remedy, covered in §§6 (b), 7, 9, and 13 (a), is the assignment of federal examiners on certification by the Attorney General to list qualified applicants who are thereafter entitled to vote in all elections.

Other provisions of the Act prescribe subsidiary cures for persistent voting discrimination. Section 8 authorizes the appointment of federal poll-watchers in places to which federal examiners have already been assigned. Section 10(d) excuses those made eligible to vote in sections of the country covered by §4 (b) of the Act from paying accumulated past poll taxes for state and local elections. Section 12(e) provides for balloting by persons denied access to the polls in areas where federal examiners have been appointed.

The remaining remedial portions of the Act are aimed at voting discrimination in any area of the country where it may occur. Section 2 broadly prohibits the use of voting rules to abridge exercise of the franchise on racial grounds. Sections 3,6 (a), and 13(b) strengthen existing procedures for attacking voting discrimination by means of litigation. Section 4 (e) excuses citizens educated in American schools conducted in a foreign language from passing English-language literacy tests. Section 10(a)-(c) facilitates constitutional litigation challenging the imposition of all poll taxes for state and local elections. Sections 11 and 12 (a)-(d) authorize civil and criminal sanctions against interference with the exercise of rights guaranteed by the Act. . . .

These provisions of the Voting Rights Act of 1965 are challenged on the fundamental ground that they exceed the powers of Congress and encroach on an area reserved to the States by the Constitution. South Carolina and certain of the *amici curiae* also attack specific sections of the Act for more particular reasons. They argue that the coverage formula prescribed in §4 (a)– (d) violates the principle of the equality of States, denies due process by employing an invalid presumption and by barring judicial review of administrative findings, constitutes a forbidden bill of attainder, and impairs the separation of powers by adjudicating guilt through legislation. They claim that the review of new voting rules required in §5 infringes Article III by directing the District Court to issue advisory opinions. They contend that the assignment of federal examiners authorized in §6 (b) abridges due process by precluding judicial review of administrative findings and impairs the separation of powers by giving the Attorney General judicial functions, also that the challenge procedure prescribed in §9 denies due process on account of its speed. Finally, South Carolina and certain of the *amici curiae* maintain that §§4(a) and 5, buttressed by §14(b) of the Act, abridge due process by limiting litigation to a distant forum.

Some of these contentions may be dismissed at the outset. The word "person" in the context of the Due Process Clause of the Fifth Amendment cannot, by any reasonable mode of interpretation, be expanded to encompass the States of the Union, and to our knowledge this has never been done by any court. ... The objections to the Act which are raised under these provisions may therefore be considered only as additional aspects of the basic question presented by the case: Has Congress exercised its powers under the Fifteenth Amendment in an appropriate manner with relation to the States?

The ground rules for resolving this question are clear. The language and purpose of the Fifteenth Amendment, the prior decisions construing its several provisions, and the general doctrines of constitutional interpretation, all point to one fundamental principle. As against the reserved powers of the States, Congress may use any rational means to effectuate the constitutional prohibition of racial discrimination in voting. ...

Congress exercised its authority under the Fifteenth Amendment in an inventive manner when it enacted the Voting Rights Act of 1965. First: The measure prescribes remedies for voting discrimination which go into effect without any need for prior adjudication. This was clearly a legitimate response to the problem, for which there is ample precedent under other constitutional provisions. ... Congress had found that case-by-case litigation was inadequate to combat widespread and persistent discrimination in voting, because of the inordinate amount of time and energy required to overcome the obstructionist tactics invariably encountered in these lawsuits. After enduring nearly a century of systematic resistance to the Fifteenth Amendment, Congress might well decide to shift the advantage of time and inertia from the perpetrators of the evil to its victims. The question remains, of course, whether the specific remedies prescribed in the Act were an appropriate means of combatting the evil, and to this question we shall presently address ourselves.

We now consider the related question of whether the specific States and political subdivisions within §4(b) of the Act were an appropriate target for the new remedies. South Carolina contends that the coverage formula is awkwardly designed in a number of respects and that it disregards various local conditions which have nothing to do with racial discrimination. These arguments, however, are largely beside the point. Congress began work with reliable evidence of actual voting discrimination in a great majority of the States and political subdivisions affected by the new remedies of the Act. The formula eventually evolved to describe these areas was relevant to the problem of voting discrimination, and Congress was therefore entitled to infer a significant danger of the evil in the few remaining States and political subdivisions covered by §4(b) of the Act. No more was required to justify the application to these areas of Congress' express powers under the Fifteenth Amendment. ...

To be specific, the new remedies of the Act are imposed on three States — Alabama, Louisiana, and Mississippi — in which federal courts have repeatedly found substantial voting discrimination. Section 4(b) of the Act also embraces two other States — Georgia and South Carolina — plus large portions of a third State — North Carolina — for which there was more fragmentary evidence of recent voting discrimination mainly adduced by the Justice Department and the

Civil Rights Commission. All of these areas were appropriately subjected to the new remedies. In identifying past evils, Congress obviously may avail itself of information from any probative source. . . .

The areas listed above, for which there was evidence of actual voting discrimination, share two characteristics incorporated by Congress into the coverage formula: the use of tests and devices for voter registration, and a voting rate in the 1964 presidential election at least 12 points below the national average. Tests and devices are relevant to voting discrimination because of their long history as a tool for perpetrating the evil; a low voting rate is pertinent for the obvious reason that widespread disenfranchisement must inevitably affect the number of actual voters. Accordingly, the coverage formula is rational in both practice and theory. It was therefore permissible to impose the new remedies on the few remaining States and political subdivisions covered by the formula, at least in the absence of proof that they have been free of substantial voting discrimination in recent years. Congress is clearly not bound by the rules relating to statutory presumptions in criminal cases when it prescribes civil remedies against other organs of government under §2 of the Fifteenth Amendment.

It is irrelevant that the coverage formula excludes certain localities which do not employ voting tests and devices but for which there is evidence of voting discrimination by other means. Congress had learned that widespread and persistent discrimination in voting during recent years has typically entailed the misuse of tests and devices, and this was the evil for which the new remedies were specifically designed. At the same time, through §§3, 6(a), and 13(b) of the Act, Congress strengthened existing remedies for voting discrimination in other areas of the country. Legislation need not deal with all phases of a problem in the same way, so long as the distinctions drawn have some basis in practical experience. . . . There are no States or political subdivisions exempted from coverage under §4(b) in which the record reveals recent racial discrimination involving tests and devices. This fact confirms the rationality of the formula.

APPENDIX

THE CONSTITUTION
OF THE UNITED STATES

THE PREAMBLE

We the People of the United States, in Order to form a more perfect Union, establish Justice, insure domestic Tranquility, provide for the common defence, promote the general Welfare, and secure the Blessings of Liberty to ourselves and our Posterity, do ordain and establish this Constitution for the United States of America.

ARTICLE I — THE LEGISLATIVE ARTICLE

Legislative power

Section 1. All Legislative Powers herein granted shall be vested in a Congress of the United States, which shall consist of a Senate and House of Representatives.

House of representatives: composition; qualification; apportionment; impeachment power

Section 2. The House of Representatives shall be composed of Members chosen every second Year by the People of the several States, and the Electors in each State shall have the Qualifications requisite for Electors of the most numerous Branch of the State Legislature.

No Person shall be a Representative who shall not have attained to the Age of twenty five Years, and been seven Years a Citizen of the United States, and who shall not, when elected, be an Inhabitant of that State in which he shall be chosen.

Representatives and direct Taxes shall be apportioned among the several States which may be included within this Union, according to their respective Numbers, which shall be de-termined by adding to the whole Number of free Persons, including those bound to Service for a Term of Years, and excluding Indians not taxed, three fifths of all other Persons. The actual Enumeration shall be made within three Years after the first Meeting of the Congress of the United States, and within every subsequent Term of ten Years, in such Manner as they shall by Law direct. The Number of Representatives shall not exceed one for every thirty Thousand, but each State shall have at Least one Representative; and until such enumeration shall be made, the State of New Hampshire shall be entitled to chuse three, Massachusetts eight, Rhode-Island and Providence Plantations one, Connecticut five, New-York six, New Jersey four, Pennsylvania eight, Delaware one, Maryland six, Virginia ten, North Carolina five, South Carolina five, and Georgia three.

When vacancies happen in the Representation from any State, the Executive Authority thereof shall issue Writs of Election to fill such Vacancies.

The House of Representatives shall chuse their speaker and other Officers; and shall have the sole Power of Impeachment.

Senate composition; qualifications; impeachment trials

Section 3. The Senate of the United States shall be composed of two Senators from each State, chosen by the Legislature thereof, for six Years; and each Senator shall have one Vote.

Immediately after they shall be assembled in Consequence of the first Election, they shall be divided as equally as may be into three Classes. The Seats of the Senators of the first Class shall be vacated at the Expiration of the second Year, of the second Class at the Expiration of the fourth Year, and of the third Class at the

Expiration of the sixth Year, so that one third may be chosen every second Year; and if Vacancies happen by Resignation, or otherwise, during the Recess of the Legislature of any State, the Executive thereof may make temporary Appointments until the next Meeting of the Legislature, which shall then fill such Vacancies.

No Person shall be a Senator who shall not have attained to the Age of thirty Years, and been nine Years a Citizen of the United States, and who shall not, when elected, be an Inhabitant of that State for which he shall be chosen.

The Vice President of the United States shall be President of the Senate, but shall have no Vote, unless they be equally divided.

The Senate shall chuse their other Officers, and also a President pro tempore, in the Absence of the Vice President, or when he shall exercise the Office of the President of the United States.

The Senate shall have the sole Power to try all Impeachments. When sitting for that Purpose, they shall be on Oath or Affirmation. When the President of the United States is tried, the Chief Justice shall preside: And no Person shall be convicted without the Concurrence of two thirds of the Members present.

Judgment in Cases of Impeachment shall not extend further than to removal from Office, and disqualification to hold and enjoy any Office of honor, Trust or Profit under the United States: but the Party convicted shall nevertheless be liable and subject to Indictment, Trial, Judgement and Punishment, according to law.

Congressional elections: time; place; manner

Section 4. The Times, Places and Manner of holding Elections for Senators and Representatives, shall be prescribed in each State by the legislature thereof; but the Congress may at any time by Law make or alter such Regulations, except as to the Places of chusing Senators.

The Congress shall assemble at least once in every Year, and such Meeting shall be on the first Monday in December, unless they shall by Law appoint a different Day.

Powers and duties of the houses

Section 5. Each House shall be the Judge of the Elections, Returns and Qualifications of its own Members, and a Majority of each shall constitute a Quorum to do Business; but a smaller Number may adjourn from day to day,

and may be authorized to compel the Attendance of absent Members, in such Manner, and under such Penalties as each House may provide.

Each House may determine the Rules of its Proceedings, punish its Members for disorderly Behaviour, and, with the Concurrence of two thirds, expel a Member.

Each House shall keep a Journal of its Proceedings, and from time to time publish the same, excepting such Parts as may in their Judgment require Secrecy; and the Yeas and Nays of the Members of either House on any question shall, at the Desire of one fifth of those Present, be entered on the Journal.

Neither House, during the Session of Congress, shall, without the Consent of the other, adjourn for more than three days, nor to any other Place than that in which the two Houses shall be sitting.

Rights of members

Section 6. The Senators and Representatives shall receive a Compensation for their Services, to be ascertained by Law, and paid out of the Treasury of the United States. They shall in all Cases, except Treason, Felony and Breach of the Peace, be privileged from Arrest during their Attendance at the Session of their respective Houses, and in going to and returning from the same; and for any Speech or Debate in either House, they shall not be questioned in any other Place.

No Senator or Representative shall, during the Time for which he was elected, be appointed to any civil Office under the Authority of the United States, which shall have been created, or the Emoluments whereof shall have been encreased during such time; and no Person holding any Office under the United States, shall be a Member of either House during his Continuance in Office.

Legislative powers: bills and resolutions

Section 7. All Bills for raising Revenue shall originate in the House of Representatives; but the Senate may propose or concur with Amendments as on other Bills.

Every Bill which shall have passed the House of Representatives and the Senate, shall, before it become a Law, be presented to the President of the United States. If he approve he shall sign it, but if not he shall return it with his Objections to that House in which it shall have originated, who shall enter the Objections at large on their Journal, and proceed to reconsider it. If after such Reconsideration two thirds of that House shall agree to pass the

Bill, it shall be sent, together with the Objections, to the other House, by which it shall likewise be reconsidered, and if approved by two thirds of the House, it shall become a Law. But in all such Cases the Votes of both Houses shall be determined by Yeas and Nays, and the Names of the Persons voting for and against the Bill shall be entered on the Journal of each House respectively. If any Bill shall not be returned by the President within ten Days (Sunday excepted) after it shall have been presented to him, the Same shall be a Law, in like Manner as if he had signed it, unless the Congress by their Adjournment prevent its Return, in which Case it shall not be a Law.

Every Order, Resolution, or Vote to which the Concurrence of the Senate and House of Representatives may be necessary (except on a Question of Adjournment) shall be presented to the President of the United States; and before the Same shall take Effect, shall be approved by him, or being disapproved by him, shall be repassed by two thirds of the Senate and House of Representatives, according to the Rules and Limitations prescribed in the Case of a Bill.

Powers of congress

Section 8. The Congress shall have Power To lay and collect Taxes, Duties, Imposts and Excises, to pay the Debts and provide for the common Defence and general Welfare of the United States; but all Duties, Imposts and Excises shall be uniform throughout the United States;

To borrow Money on the credit of the United States;

To regulate Commerce with foreign Nations, and among the several States, and with the Indian Tribes;

To establish an uniform Rule of Naturalization, and uniform Laws on the subject of Bankruptcies throughout the United States;

To coin Money, regulate the Value thereof, and of foreign Coin, and fix the Standard of Weights and Measures;

To provide for the Punishment of counterfeiting the Securities and current Coin of the United States;

To establish Post Offices and post Roads;

To promote the Progress of Science and useful Arts, by securing for limited Times to Authors and Inventors the exclusive Right to their respective Writings and Discoveries;

To constitute Tribunals inferior to the Supreme Court;

To define and punish Piracies and Felonies committed on the high Seas, and Offences against the Law of Nations;

To declare War, grant Letters of Marque and Reprisal, and make Rules concerning Captures on Land and Water;

To raise and support Armies, but no Appropriation of Money to that Use shall be for a longer Term than two Years;

To provide and maintain a Navy;

To make Rules for the Government and Regulation of the land and naval Forces;

To provide for calling forth the Militia to execute the Laws of the Union, suppress Insurrections and repel Invasions;

To provide for organizing, arming, and disciplining, the Militia, and for governing such Part of them as may be employed in the Service of the United States, reserving to the States respectively, the Appointment of the Officers, and the Authority of training the Militia according to the discipline prescribed by Congress;

To exercise exclusive Legislation in all Cases whatsoever, over such District (not exceeding ten Miles square) as may, by Cession of particular States, and the Acceptance of Congress, become the Seat of the Government of the United States, and to exercise like Authority over all Places purchased by the Consent of the Legislature of the State in which the Same shall be for the Erection of Forts, Magazines, Arsenals, dock-Yards, and other needful Buildings;-And

To make all Laws which shall be necessary and proper for carrying into Execution the foregoing Powers, and all other Powers vested by this Constitution in the Government of the United States, or in any Department or Officer thereof.

Powers denied to congress

Section 9. The Migration or Importation of such Persons as any of the States now existing shall think proper to admit, shall not be prohibited by the Congress prior to the Year one thousand eight hundred and eight, but a Tax or duty may be imposed on such Importation, not exceeding ten dollars for each Person.

The Privilege of the Writ of Habeas Corpus shall not be suspended, unless when in Cases of Rebellion or Invasion the public Safety may require it.

No Bill of Attainder or ex post facto Law shall be passed.

No Capitation, or other direct, Tax shall be laid, unless in Proportion to the Census or Enumeration herein before directed to be taken.

No Tax or Duty shall be laid on Articles exported from any State.

No Preference shall be given by any Regulation of Commerce or Revenue to the Ports of one State over those of another: nor shall Vessels bound to, or from, one State be obliged to enter, clear, or pay Duties in another.

No Money shall be drawn from the Treasury, but in Consequence of Appropriations made by Law; and a regular Statement and Account of the Receipts and Expenditures of all public Money shall be published from time to time.

No Title of Nobility shall be granted by the United States: And no Person holding any Office of Profit or Trust under them, shall, without the Consent of the Congress, accept of any present, Emolument, Office, or Title, of any kind whatever, from any King, Prince, or foreign States.

Powers denied to the states

Section 10. No State shall enter into any Treaty, Alliance, or Confederation; grant Letters of Marque and Reprisal; coin Money; emit Bills of Credit; make any Thing but gold and silver Coin a Tender in Payment of Debts; pass any Bill of Attainder, ex post facto Law, or Law impairing the Obligation of Contracts, or grant any Title of Nobility.

No State shall, without the Consent of the Congress, lay any Imposts or Duties on Imports or Exports, except what may be absolutely necessary for executing its inspection Laws: and the net Product of all Duties and Imposts, laid by any State on Imports or Exports, shall be for the Use of the Treasury of the United States; and all such Laws shall be subject to the Revision and Controul of the Congress.

No State shall, without the Consent of Congress, lay any Duty of Tonnage, keep Troops, or Ships of War in time of Peace, enter into any Agreement or Compact with another State, or with a foreign Power, or engage in War, unless actually invaded, or in such imminent Danger as will not admit of delay.

ARTICLE II — THE EXECUTIVE ARTICLE

Nature and scope of presidential power

Section 1. The executive Power shall be vested in a President of the United States of America. He shall hold his Office during the Term of four Years, and, together with the Vice President, chosen for the same term, be elected, as follows.

Each State shall appoint, in such Manner as the Legislature thereof may direct, a Number of Electors, Equal to the whole Number of Senators and Representatives to which the State may be entitled in the Congress: but no Senator or Representative, or Person holding an Office of Trust or Profit under the United States, shall be appointed an Elector.

The Electors shall meet in their respective States, and vote by Ballot for two Persons, of whom one at least shall not be an Inhabitant of the same State with themselves. And they shall make a List of all the Persons voted for, and the Number of Votes for each; which List they shall sign and certify, and transmit sealed to the Seat of the Government of the United States, directed to the President of the Senate. The President of the Senate shall, in the Presence of the Senate and House of Representatives, open all the Certificates, and the Votes shall then be counted. The Person having the greatest Number of Votes shall be the President, if such Number be a Majority of the whole Number of Electors appointed; and if there be more than one who have such Majority, and have an equal Number of Votes, then the House of Representatives shall immediately chuse by Ballot one of them for President: and if no Person have a Majority, then from the five highest on the List the said House shall in like Manner chuse the President. But in chusing the President, the Votes shall be taken by States, the Representation from each State having one Vote; A quorum for this Purpose shall consist of a Member or Members from two thirds of the States, and a Majority of all the States shall be necessary to a Choice. In every Case, after the Choice of the President, the Person having the greatest Number of Votes of the Electors shall be the Vice President. But if there should remain two or more who have equal Votes, the Senate shall chuse from them by Ballot the Vice President.

The Congress may determine the Time of chusing the Electors and the Day on which they shall give their Votes; which Day shall be the same throughout the United States.

No Person except a natural born Citizen, or a Citizen of the United States, at the time of the Adoption of this Constitution, shall be eligible to the Office of President; neither shall any Person be eligible to that Office who shall not have attained to the Age of thirty five Years, and been fourteen Years a Resident within the United States.

In Case of the Removal of the President from Office, or of his Death, Resignation, or Inability to discharge the Powers and Duties of the said Office, the Same shall devolve on the Vice President, and the Congress may by Law provide for the Case of Removal, Death, Resignation or Inability, both of the President and

Vice President, declaring what Officer shall then act as President, and such Officer shall act accordingly, until the Disability be removed, or a President shall be elected.

The President shall, at stated Times, receive for his Services a Compensation, which shall neither be encreased nor diminished during the Period for which he shall have been elected, and he shall not receive within that Period any other Emolument from the United States, or any of them.

Before he enter on the Execution of his Office, he shall take the following Oath or Affirmation:-"I do solemnly swear (or affirm) that I will faithfully execute the Office of President of the United States, and will to the best of my Ability, preserve, protect and defend the Constitution of the United States."

Powers and duties of the president

Section 2. The President shall be Commander in Chief of the Army and Navy of the United States, and of the Militia of the several States, when called into the actual Service of the United States; he may require the Opinion, in writing, of the principal Officer in each of the executive Departments, upon any Subject relating to the Duties of their Respective Offices, and he shall have power to grant Reprieves and Pardons for Offences against the United States, except in Cases of Impeachment.

He shall have Power, by and with the Advice and Consent of the Senate, to make Treaties, provided two thirds of the Senators present concur; and he shall nominate, and by and with the Advice and Consent of the Senate, shall appoint Ambassadors, other public Ministers and Consuls, Judges of the supreme Court, and all other Officers of the United States, whose Appointments are not herein otherwise provided for, and which shall be established by Law; but the Congress may by Law vest the Appointment of such inferior Officers, as they think proper, in the President alone, in the Courts of Law, or in the Heads of Departments.

The President shall have Power to fill up all Vacancies that may happen during the Recess of the Senate, by granting Commissions which shall expire at the End of their next Session.

Section 3. He shall from time to time give to the Congress Information of the State of the Union, and recommend to their Consideration such Measures as he shall judge necessary and expedient; he may, on extraordinary Occasions, convene both Houses, or either of them, and in Case of Disagreement between them, with Respect to the Time of Adjournment, he

may adjourn them to such Time as he shall think proper; he shall take Care that the Laws be faithfully executed, and shall Commission all the Officers of the United States.

Impeachment

Section 4. The President, Vice President and all civil Officers of the United States, shall be removed from Office on Impeachment for, and Conviction of, Treason, Bribery, or other High Crimes and Misdemeanors.

ARTICLE III – THE JUDICIAL ARTICLE

Judicial power, courts, judges

Section 1. The judicial Power of the United States, shall be vested in one supreme Court, and in such inferior Courts as the Congress may from time to time ordain and establish. The Judges, both of the supreme and inferior Courts, shall hold their Offices during good Behaviour, and shall, at stated Times, receive for their Services, a Compensation, which shall not be diminished during their Continuance in Office.

Jurisdiction

Section 2. The judicial Power shall extend to all Cases, in Law and Equity, arising under this Constitution, the Laws of the United States, and Treaties made, or which shall be made, under their Authority;-to all Cases affecting Ambassadors, other public Ministers and Consuls;-to all Cases of admiralty and maritime Jurisdiction;-to Controversies to which the United States shall be a Party;-to Controversies between two or more States; between a State and Citizens of another State; between Citizens of different States;-between Citizens of the same State claiming Lands under Grants of different States, and between a State or the Citizens thereof, and foreign States, Citizens or Subjects.

In all Cases affecting Ambassadors, other public Ministers and Consuls, and those in which a State shall be Party, the supreme Court shall have original Jurisdiction. In all the other Cases before mentioned, the supreme Court shall have appellate Jurisdiction, both as to Law and Fact, with such Exceptions, and under such Regulations as the Congress shall make.

The Trial of all Crimes, except in Cases of Impeachment, shall be by Jury; and such Trial shall be held in the State where the said Crimes shall have been committed; but when not committed within any State, the Trial shall be at such Place or Places as the Congress may by Law have directed.

Treason

Section 3. Treason against the United States, shall consist only in levying War against them, or in adhering to their Enemies, giving them Aid and Comfort. No Person shall be convicted of Treason unless on the Testimony of two Witnesses to the same overt Act, or on Confession in open Court.

The Congress shall have Power to declare the Punishment of Treason, but no Attainder of Treason shall work Corruption of Blood, or Forfeiture except during the Life of the Person attainted.

ARTICLE IV — INTERSTATE RELATIONS

Full faith and credit clause

Section 1. Full Faith and Credit shall be given in each State to the public Acts, Records, and judicial Proceedings of every other State. And the Congress may by general Laws prescribe the Manner in which such Acts, Records and Proceedings shall be proved, and the Effect thereof.

Privileges and immunities; interstate rendition

Section 2. The Citizens of each State shall be entitled to all Privileges and Immunities of Citizens in the several States.

A Person charged in any State with Treason, Felony, or other Crime, who shall flee from Justice, and be found in another State, shall on Demand of the executive Authority of the State from which he fled, be delivered up, to be removed to the State having Jurisdiction of the Crime.

No Person held to Service or Labour in one State, under the Laws thereof, escaping into another, shall, in Consequence of any Law or Regulation therein, be discharged from such Service or Labour, but shall be delivered up on Claim of the Party to whom such Service or Labour may be due.

Admission of states

Section 3. New States may be admitted by the Congress into this Union; but no new State shall be formed or erected within the Jurisdiction of any other State; nor any State be formed by the Junction of two or more States, or Parts of States, without the Consent of the Legislatures of the States concerned as well as of the Congress.

The Congress shall have Power to dispose of and make all needful Rules and Regulations respecting the Territory or other Property belonging to the United States; and nothing in this Constitution shall be so construed as to Prejudice any Claims of the United States, or of any particular State.

Republican form of government

Section 4. The United States shall guarantee to every State in this Union a Republican Form of Government, and shall protect each of them against Invasion; and on Application of the Legislature, or of the Executive (when the Legislature cannot be convened) against domestic Violence.

ARTICLE V — THE AMENDING POWER

The Congress, whenever two thirds of both Houses shall deem it necessary, shall propose Amendments to this Constitution, or, on the Application of the Legislatures of two thirds of the several States, shall call a Convention for proposing Amendments, which, in either Case, shall be valid to all Intents and Purposes, as Part of this Constitution, when ratified by the Legislatures of three fourths of the several States, or by Conventions in three fourths thereof as the one or the other Mode of Ratification may be proposed by the Congress; Provided that no Amendment which may be made prior to the Year One thousand eight hundred and eight shall in any Manner affect the first and fourth Clauses in the Ninth Section of the first Article; and that no State, without its Consent, shall be deprived of its equal Suffrage in the Senate.

ARTICLE VI — THE SUPREMACY ARTICLE

All Debts contracted and Engagements entered into, before the Adoption of this Constitution, shall be as valid against the United States under this Constitution, as under the Confederation.

This Constitution, and the Laws of the United States which shall be made in Pursuance thereof; and all Treaties made, or which shall be made, under the Authority of the United States, shall be the supreme Law of the Land; and the Judges in every State shall be bound thereby, any Thing in the Constitution or Laws of any State to the Contrary notwithstanding.

The Senators and Representatives before mentioned, and the Members of the several State Legislatures, and all executive and judicial Officers, both of the United States and of the several States, shall be bound by Oath or Affirmation, to support this Constitution; but no religious Test shall ever be required as a Qualification to any Office or public Trust under the United States.

ARTICLE VII — RATIFICATION

The Ratification of the Conventions of nine States, shall be sufficient for the Establishment of this Constitution between the States so ratifying the Same.

Done in Convention by the Unanimous Consent of the States present the Seventeenth Day of September in the Year of our Lord one thousand seven hundred and Eighty seven and of the Independence of the United States of America the Twelfth. In witness whereof We have hereunto subscribed our Names.

THE BILL OF RIGHTS

[The first 10 Amendments were ratified December 15, 1791, and form what is known as the Bill of Rights]

Amendent 1 — Religion, Speech, Assembly, and Politics

Congress shall make no law respecting an establishment of religion, or prohibiting the free exercise thereof; or abridging the freedom of speech, or of the press; or the right of the people peaceably to assemble, and to petition the Government for a redress of grievances.

Amendment 2 — Militia and the Right to Bear Arms

A well regulated Militia, being necessary to the security of a free State, the right of the people to keep and bear Arms, shall not be infringed.

Amendment 3 — Quartering of Soldiers

No Soldier shall, in time of peace be quartered in any house, without the consent of the Owner, nor in time of war, but in a manner to be prescribed by law.

Amendment 4 — Searches and Seizures

The right of the people to be secure in their persons, houses, papers, and effects, against unreasonable searches and seizures, shall not be violated, and no Warrants shall issue, but upon probable cause, supported by Oath or affirmation, and particularly describing the place to be searched and the persons or things to be seized.

Amendment 5 — Grand Juries, Self-Incrimination, Double Jeopardy, Due Process, and Eminent Domain

No person shall be held to answer for a capital, or otherwise infamous crime, unless on a presentment or indictment of a Grand Jury, except in cases arising in the land or naval forces, or in the Militia, when in actual service in time of War or public danger, nor shall any person be subject for the same offence to be twice put in jeopardy of life or limb; nor shall be compelled in any criminal case to be a witness against himself, nor be deprived of life, liberty, or property, without due process of law; nor shall private property be taken for public use, without just compensation.

Amendment 6 — Criminal Court Procedures

In all criminal prosecutions, the accused shall enjoy the right to a speedy and public trial, by an impartial jury of the State and district wherein the crime shall have been committed, which district shall have been previously ascertained by law, and to be informed of the nature and cause of the accusation; to be confronted with the witnesses against him; to have compulsory process for obtaining witnesses in his favor, and to have the Assistance of Counsel for his defence.

Amendment 7 — Trial by Jury in Common Law Cases

In Suits at common law, where the value in controversy shall exceed twenty dollars, the right of trial by jury shall be preserved, and no fact tried by a jury, shall be otherwise reexamined in any Court of the United States, than according to the rules of the common law.

Amendment 8 — Bail, Cruel and Unusual Punishment

Excessive bail shall not be required, nor excessive fines imposed, nor cruel and unusual punishments inflicted.

Amendment 9 — Rights Retained by the People

The enumeration in the Constitution, of certain rights, shall not be construed to deny or disparage others retained by the people.

Amendment 10 — Reserved Powers of the States

The powers not delegated to the United States by the Constitution, nor prohibited by it to the States, are reserved to the States respectively, or to the people.

PRE-CIVIL WAR AMENDMENTS

Amendment 11 — Suits Against the States

[Ratified February 7, 1795]

The Judicial power of the United States shall not be construed to extend to any suit in law or equity, commenced or prosecuted against one of the United States by Citizens of another State, or by Citizens or Subjects of any Foreign State.

Amendment 12 — Election of the President

[Ratified July 27, 1804]

The Electors shall meet in their respective states and vote by ballot for President and Vice-President, one of whom, at least, shall not be an inhabitant of the same state with themselves; they shall name in their ballots the person voted for as President, and in distinct ballots the person voted for as Vice-President, and they shall make distinct lists of all persons voted for as President, and of all persons voted for as Vice-President, and of the number of votes for each, which lists they shall sign and certify, and transmit sealed to the seat of the government of the United States, directed to the President of the Senate;-The President of the Senate shall, in the presence of the Senate and House of Representatives, open all the certificates and the votes shall then be counted;-The person having the greatest number of votes for President, shall be the President, if such number be a majority of the whole number of Electors appointed; and if no person have such majority, then from the persons having the highest numbers not exceeding three on the list of those voted for as President, the House of Representatives shall choose immediately, by ballot, the President. But in choosing the President, the votes shall be taken by states, the representation from

each state having one vote; a quorum for this purpose shall consist of a member or members from two-thirds of the states, and a majority of all the states shall be necessary to a choice. And if the House of Representatives shall not choose a President whenever the right of the choice shall devolve upon them, before the fourth day of March next following, then the Vice-President shall act as President, as in the case of the death or other constitutional disability of the President.-The person having the greatest number of votes as Vice-President, shall be the Vice-President, if such number be a majority of the whole number of Electors appointed, and if no person have a majority, then from the two highest numbers on the list, the Senate shall choose the Vice-President; a quorum for the purpose shall consist of two-thirds of the whole number of Senators, and a majority of the whole number shall be necessary to a choice. But no person constitutionally ineligible to the office of President shall be eligible to that of Vice-President of the United States.

CIVIL WAR AMENDMENTS

Amendment 13 — Prohibition of Slavery

[Ratified December 6, 1865]

Section 1. Neither slavery nor involuntary servitude, except as a punishment for crime whereof the party shall have been duly convicted, shall exist within the United States, or any place subject to their jurisdiction.

Section 2. Congress shall have power to enforce this article by appropriate legislation.

Amendment 14 — Citizenship, Due Process, and Equal Protection of the Laws

[Ratified July 9, 1868]

Section 1. All persons born or naturalized in the United States, and subject to the jurisdiction thereof, are citizens of the United States and of the State wherein they reside. No State shall make or enforce any law which shall abridge the privileges or immunities of citizens of the United States; nor shall any State deprive any person of life, liberty, or property, without due process of law; nor deny to any person within its jurisdiction the equal protection of the laws.

Section 2. Representatives shall be apportioned among the several States according to their respective numbers, counting the whole number of persons in each State, excluding Indians not taxed. But when the right to vote at any election for the choice of electors for President and Vice President of the United States, Representatives in Congress, the Executive and Judicial Officers of a State, or the members of the Legislature thereof, is denied to any of the male inhabitants of such State, being twenty-one years of age, and citizens of the United States, or in any way abridged, except for participation in rebellion, or other crime, the basis of representation therein shall be reduced in the proportion which the number of such male citizens shall bear to the whole number of male citizens twenty-one years of age in such State.

Section 3. No person shall be a Senator or Representative in Congress, or elector of President and Vice President, or hold any office, civil or military, under the United States, or under any State, who having previously taken an oath, as a member of Congress, or as an officer of the United States, or as a member of any State legislature, or as an executive or judicial officer of any State, to support the Constitution of the United States, shall have engaged in insurrection or rebellion against the same, or given aid or comfort to the enemies thereof. But Congress may by a vote of two-thirds of each House, remove such disability.

Section 4. The validity of the public debt of the United States, authorized by law, including debts incurred for payment of pensions and bounties for services in suppressing insurrection or rebellion, shall not be questioned. But neither the United States nor any State shall assume or pay any debt or obligation incurred in aid of insurrection or rebellion against the United States, or any claim for the loss or emancipation of any slave; but all such debts, obligations and claims shall be held illegal and void.

Section 5. The Congress shall have power to enforce, by appropriate legislation, the provisions of this article.

Amendment 15 — The Right to Vote

[Ratified February 3, 1870]

Section 1. The right of citizens of the United States to vote shall not be denied or abridged by the United States or by any State on account of race, color, or previous condition of servitude.

Section 2. The Congress shall have power to enforce this article by appropriate legislation.

TWENTIETH-CENTURY AMENDMENTS

Amendment 16 — Income Taxes

[Ratified February 3, 1913]

The Congress shall have power to lay and collect taxes on incomes, from whatever source derived, without apportionment among the several States, and without regard to any census or enumeration.

Amendment 17 — Direct Election of Senators

[Ratified April 8, 1913]

The Senate of the United States shall be composed of two Senators from each State, elected by the people thereof for six years; and each Senator shall have one vote. The electors in each State shall have the qualifications requisite for electors of the most numerous branch of the State legislatures.

When vacancies happen in the representation of any State in the Senate, the executive authority of such State shall issue writs of election to fill such vacancies: *Provided,* That the legislature of any State may empower the executive thereof to make temporary appointments until the people fill the vacancies by election as the legislature may direct.

This Amendment shall not be so construed as to affect the election or term of any Senator chosen before it becomes valid as part of the Constitution.

Amendment 18 — Prohibition

[Ratified January 16, 1919]

Section 1. After one year from the ratification of this article the manufacture, sale, or transportation of intoxicating liquors within, the importation thereof into, or the exportation thereof from the United States and all territory subject to the jurisdiction thereof for beverage purposes is hereby prohibited.

Section 2. The Congress and the several States shall have concurrent power to enforce this article by appropriate legislation.

Section 3. This article shall be inoperative unless it shall have been ratified as an amendment to the Constitution by the legislatures of the several States, as provided in the Constitution, within seven years from the date of the submission hereof to the States by the Congress.

Amendment 19 — For Women's Suffrage

[Ratified August 18, 1920]

The right of citizens of the United States to vote shall not be denied or abridged by the United States or by any State on account of sex. Congress shall have power to enforce this article by appropriate legislation.

Amendment 20 — The Lame Duck Amendment

[Ratified January 23, 1933]

Section 1. The terms of the President and Vice President shall end at noon on the 20th day of January, and the terms of Senators and Representatives at noon on the 3d of January, of the years in which such terms would have ended if this article had not been ratified; and the terms of their successors shall then begin.

Section 2. The Congress shall assemble at least once in every year, and such meeting shall begin at noon on the 3d day of January, unless they shall by law appoint a different day.

Section 3. If, at the time fixed for the beginning of the term of the President, the President elect shall have died, the Vice President elect shall become President. If a President shall not have been chosen before the time fixed for the beginning of his term, or if the President elect shall have failed to qualify, then the Vice President elect shall act as President until a President shall have qualified; and the Congress may by law provide for the case wherein neither a President elect nor a Vice President elect shall have qualified, declaring who shall then act as President, or the manner in which one who is to act shall be selected, and such person shall act accordingly until a President or Vice President shall have qualified.

Section 4. The Congress may by law provide for the case of the death of any of the persons from whom the House of Representatives may choose a President whenever the right of choice shall have devolved upon them, and for the case of the death of any of the persons from whom the Senate may choose a Vice President whenever the right of choice shall have devolved upon them.

Section 5. Sections 1 and 2 shall take effect on the 15th day of October following the ratification of this article.

Section 6. This article shall be inoperative unless it shall have been ratified as an amendment to the Constitution by the legislatures of three-fourths of the several States within seven years from the date of its submission.

Amendment 21 — Repeal of Prohibition

[Ratified December 5, 1933]

Section 1. The eighteenth article of amendment to the Constitution of the United States is hereby repealed.

Section 2. The transportation or importation into any State, Territory, or possession of the United States for delivery or use therein of intoxicating liquors, in violation of the laws thereof, is hereby prohibited.

Section 3. This article shall be inoperative unless it shall have been ratified as an amendment to the Constitution by conventions in the several States, as provided in the Constitution, within seven years from the date of the submission hereof to the States by the Congress.

Amendment 22 — Number of Presidential Terms

[Ratified February 27, 1951]

Section 1. No person shall be elected to the office of the President more than twice, and no person who has held the office of President, or acted as President for more than two years of a term to which some other person was elected President shall be elected to the office of the President more than once. But this Article shall not apply to any person holding the office of President when this Article was proposed by the Congress, and shall not prevent any person who may be holding the office of President, or acting as President, during the term within which this Article becomes operative from holding the office of President or acting as President during the remainder of such term.

Section 2. This article shall be inoperative unless it shall have been ratified as an amendment to the Constitution by the legislatures of three-fourths of the several States within seven years from the date of its submission to the States by the Congress.

Amendment 23 — Presidential Electors for the District of Columbia

[Ratified March 29, 1961]

Section 1. The District constituting the seat of Government of the United States shall appoint in such manner as the Congress may direct:

A number of electors of President and Vice President equal to the whole number of Senators and Representatives in Congress to which the District would be entitled if it were a State, but in no event more than the least populous State; they shall be in addition to those appointed by the States, but they shall be considered, for the purposes of the election of President and Vice President, to be electors appointed by a State; and they shall meet in the District and perform such duties as provided by the twelfth article of amendment.

Section 2. The Congress shall have power to enforce this article by appropriate legislation.

Amendment 24 — The Anti-Poll Tax Amendment

[Ratified January 23, 1964]

Section 1. The right of citizens of the United States to vote in any primary or other election for President or Vice President, for electors for President or Vice President, or for Senator or Representative in Congress, shall not be denied or abridged by the United States or any State by reason of failure to pay any poll tax or other tax.

Section 2. The Congress shall have power to enforce this article by appropriate legislation.

Amendment 25 — Presidential Disability, Vice Presidential Vacancies

[Ratified February 10, 1967]

Section 1. In case of the removal of the President from office or of his death or resignation, the Vice President shall become President.

Section 2. Whenever there is a vacancy in the office of the Vice President, the President shall nominate a Vice President who shall take office upon confirmation by a majority vote of both Houses of Congress.

Section 3. Whenever the President transmits to the President pro tempore of the Senate and the Speaker of the House of Representatives his written declaration that he is unable to discharge the powers and duties of his office, and until he transmits to them a written declaration to the contrary, such powers and duties shall be discharged by the Vice President as Acting President.

Section 4. Whenever the Vice President and a majority of either the principal officers of the executive departments or of such other body as Congress may by law provide, transmit to the President pro tempore of the Senate and the Speaker of the House of Representatives their written declaration that the President is unable to discharge the powers and duties of his office, the Vice President shall immediately assume the powers and duties of the office as Acting President.

Thereafter, when the President transmits to the President pro tempore of the Senate and the Speaker of the House of Representatives his written declaration that no inability exists, he shall resume the powers and duties of his office unless the Vice President and a majority of either the principal officers of the executive department or of such other body as Congress may by law provide, transmit within four days to the President pro tempore of the Senate and the Speaker of the House of Representatives their written declaration that the President is unable to discharge the power and duties of his office. Thereupon Congress shall decide the issue, assembling within forty-eight hours for that purpose if not in session. If the Congress, within twenty-one days after receipt of the latter written declaration, or, if Congress is not in session, within twenty-one days after Congress is required to assemble, determines by two-thirds vote of both Houses that the President is unable to discharge the powers and duties of his office, the Vice President shall continue to discharge the same as Acting President; otherwise, the President shall resume the powers and duties of his office.

Amendment 26 — Eighteen-Year-Old Vote

[Ratified June 30, 1971]

Section 1. The right of citizens of the United States, who are eighteen years of age or older, to vote shall not be denied or abridged by the United States or by any State on account of age.

Section 2. The Congress shall have the power to enforce this article by appropriate legislation.

Proposed Amendment 27 — Equal Rights Amendment

[Proposed March 22, 1972]

Section 1. Equality of rights under the law shall not be denied or abridged by the United States or by any State on account of sex.

Section 2. The Congress shall have power to enforce, by appropriate legislation, the provisions of this article.

Section 3. This amendment shall take effect two years after date of ratification.

INDEX OF CASES

NAME AND SUBJECT INDEX